FURNITURE
AND CABINET
CONSTRUCTION

FURNITURE AND CABINET CONSTRUCTION

William P. Spence
L. Duane Griffiths

PRENTICE HALL, Englewood Cliffs, New Jersey 07632

Library of Congress Cataloging-in-Publication Data

Spence, William Perkins
    Furniture and cabinet construction/William P. Spence,
    L. Duane Griffiths.
    p. cm.
    Includes index.
    ISBN 0-13-345471-1
    1. Furniture making. 2. Cabinet-work. I. Griffiths, L. Duane.
II. Title.
TT194.S64 1989
684.1—dc19

Editorial/production supervision: Mary Carnis
Interior design: Meryl Poweski
Cover design: Meryl Poweski
Page layout: Robert J. Wullen
Manufacturing buyer: Robert Anderson

Cover photo of hinges courtesy of The Woodworkers' Store.
Cover photo of veneering courtesy of The Woodworkers' Store.
Cover photo of table courtesy of Hekman Furniture Company.
Cover photo of kitchen courtesy of American Woodmark Corporation.
Cover photo of table saw courtesy of Black & Decker (U.S.) Inc.

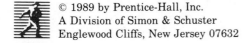 © 1989 by Prentice-Hall, Inc.
A Division of Simon & Schuster
Englewood Cliffs, New Jersey 07632

Printed in the United States of America
10 9 8 7 6 5 4 3 2 1

ISBN 0-13-345471-1

Prentice-Hall International (UK) Limited, *London*
Prentice-Hall of Australia Pty. Limited, *Sydney*
Prentice-Hall Canada Inc., *Toronto*
Prentice-Hall Hispanoamericana, S.A., *Mexico*
Prentice-Hall of India Private Limited, *New Delhi*
Prentice-Hall of Japan, Inc., *Tokyo*
Simon & Schuster Asia Pte. Ltd., *Singapore*
Editora Prentice-Hall do Brasil, Ltda., *Rio de Janeiro*

CONTENTS

Part IV
STATIONARY POWER TOOLS *339*

PREFACE

This book is a handbook for the professional wood-worker, the advanced home craftsman, or student. Detailed explanations plus liberal use of photographs and illustrations make it easy to understand even the more difficult constructions and machining techniques. A second color is used to highlight the important features on the illustrations. All of the figures emphasize the hands-on approach utilized throughout the book.

The text gives an introduction to materials used in furniture and cabinet construction. This includes hardwoods, reconstituted wood products, plastics, and related hardware.

Emphasis is placed on the design of furniture and cabinets. This includes classical as well as contemporary furniture.

One section gives detailed information about traditional or contemporary construction techniques such as the 32-millimeter system and the use of the lemon splines. The instructions are broken down much the way the units would be built by discussing each part separately. The chapters in this section include basic joinery, leg and rail construction, carcass construction, doors, drawers, shelves, and tabletops. An entire chapter is devoted to cabinet construction, showing the latest techniques and styles, including the European influence on cabinets.

The procedure for assemblying the units and using the proper bonding agent is covered in detail. Special features such as bending, laminating, veneering, inlaying, and applying plastic laminates are covered in separate chapters. These are given in detail and permit the reader to add these features to projects they design and build. This increases the variety of design solutions and enhances the finished product.

Another section covers the safe use of portable woodworking tools. These versatile tools can perform a wide range of machining tasks and the procedures are carefully detailed. Safe use of each power tool is stressed.

One of the major sections of the book is the safe and correct use of stationary power woodworking machines. In addition to the basic processes, advanced setups are explained and shown in carefully staged photographs. In addition, selected industrial production machinery is shown and explained. These power tools each have an entire chapter devoted to them. These include chapters covering the table saw, radial arm saw, bandsaw, and scroll saw. Wood removal is covered by chapters on using jointers, planers, and the wood lathe. Other tools covered in detail include the drill press, pin router, mortiser, tenoner, and a variety of sanders. A special chapter covering industrial production techniques concludes this section of the book. Safe operating procedures are stressed in each chapter.

No project is completed until it is properly finished and upholstered. A series of seven chapters covers the processes of preparing a product for the finishing, staining, filling, sealing, applying overtone treatments, and a protective coating.

The upholstery chapters include a description of the basic tools and materials and the more common methods and techniques for upholstering chairs and related furniture units.

As you examine this book you will quickly see that help was received from many companies representing all aspects of the furniture and cabinet industry. Their contributions are noted by each item developed with their assistance. Their part in making this book a reality is acknowledged and appreciated. Also, the help of the many students who so willingly assisted when help was needed is appreciated.

William P. Spence
L. Duane Griffiths

FURNITURE AND CABINET CONSTRUCTION

PART 1

Introduction

1

FINE FURNITURE: OUR HERITAGE

We are all affected by the furnishings in our home, school, place of employment, and social and recreational environments. The degree to which these are beautiful, comfortable, and useful produces a better mode of living and affects our attitudes toward life itself. An appreciation of good design and craftsmanship opens up a new world of enjoyment and cultural enrichment. An appreciation of furniture forms includes the general beauty of the contours of the units, pleasing proportions, grace and character of line divisions, and proper use of material. Good design includes embellishment that does not destroy the rhythm or structural character of the unit. Beauty is found in the many kinds of woods and fabrics used. In classical furniture, carving was an important means for introducing beauty into the furniture. It is most effective when it is subordinated to the general structural form. Finally, reproductions of classical furniture designs must adhere closely to the same specifications as the original. For example, it would be a serious error to reproduce a Hepplewhite chair in old English oak rather than using mahogany in carved pieces and beechwood where a piece was to be painted or gilded. Careful study and exact reproduction of the original classical design is essential to the production of a totally satisfactory and successful product.

THE EVOLUTION OF FURNITURE

The development of furniture follows the unfolding of history. It was influenced by the social, political, and religious life of the people. The development of tools and materials is reflected in furniture of different periods.

It is believed that the chest was one of the earliest forms of furniture. People could sit and sleep on the ground but needed a means of storage for valuables. Chests developed from crude boxes in which precious stones, bones, and metals were stored to the large, elaborately carved and painted units in the Italian Renaissance in the fifteenth and sixteenth centuries (Fig. 1-1). At some time in this development process backs and arms were placed on chests to form a means of sitting. Chests were given drawers to form our chest of drawers or made large enough to sleep on, forming a bed (Fig. 1-2).

As chairs developed from chests, some had high backs to protect the seated person from cold drafts. Others had bars between the legs so that people could keep their feet up off the typically cold or dirty floor. A type of footstool also developed as a seating device while some cultures sat on cushions on the floor (Fig. 1-3).

FIGURE 1-1
Italian carved oak chest of the fourteenth or early fifteenth century. The carvings reflect Gothic influence. (*Courtesy of Victoria and Albert Museum, Crown Copyright, London, England.*)

Through the centuries the cultures of Greece, Rome, France, China, Spain, Egypt, England, and Italy developed furniture suited to their situation. Wars led to one nation conquering another. This brought the influence of one culture in upon another. The contact by traders also extended the influence of these cultures upon each other. This influenced the furniture of that period.

Some believe that the furniture designed by the eighteenth century designers is the most beautiful in form ever developed. Others, while appreciating these classical designs, prefer the furniture designed to reflect the culture of the twentieth century. Although this is a personal matter, well-designed furniture of any period is worthy of understanding, study, and appreciation.

FIGURE 1-3
Early Jacobean chair from the early seventeenth century. Note the arms and extensive carving. The wood is oak. (*Courtesy of Victoria and Albert Museum, Crown Copyright, London, England.*)

FIGURE 1-2
Early Italian or Spanish chest of drawers (1660–1680). It is oak veneer with Brazilian rosewood and ebony. Note the use of drawers forming a chest. (*Courtesy of Victoria and Albert Museum, Crown Copyright, London, England.*)

REGENCY

FRENCH PROVINCIAL **CHIPPENDALE** **LOUIS XV** **TUDOR** **QUEEN ANNE**

CHINESE CHIPPENDALE **LOUIS XV** **SHERATON** **HEPPLEWHITE**

ADAM **DUNCAN PHYFE** **JACOBEAN** **COLONIAL**

FIGURE 1-4
Examples of chair leg design associated with some of the classical furniture periods. (*Courtesy of Hoover Universal.*)

DUNCAN PHYFE

ADAM

COLONIAL

QUEEN ANNE

VICTORIAN

SHERATON

HEPPLEWHITE

CHIPPENDALE

FIGURE 1-5
Examples of chairs from selected furniture periods. (*Courtesy of Hoover Universal.*)

It is impossible to discuss or show the total spectrum of furniture designs in our heritage. Those shown in this chapter have exerted considerable influence over the years and are considered classics of beauty, form, and function.

Identifying furniture as belonging to a particular period or style is sometimes difficult because the periods overlap and craftsmen copied features they liked from various styles. In general, certain characteristics are credited to a particular period or designer. The most descriptive furniture seems to be chairs. Characteristic leg designs of important periods are shown in Fig. 1-4, and selected classical chairs are shown in Fig. 1-5. These reflect the styling of that period.

Period furniture relied heavily on ornamentation as part of the design. Examples of typical designs and carvings are shown in Fig. 1-6. Artisans tended to use these general designs but varied them to suit their own ideas. Following are the major periods discussed in this chapter:

French Periods
Louis XIV, 1643–1715
Louis XV, 1715–1774
Louis XVI, 1774–1792
Empire, 1795–1830
French Provincial, 1610–1795

English Periods
William and Mary, 1688–1702
Queen Anne, 1702–1750
Chippendale, 1740–1780
Adam, 1762–1792
Hepplewhite, 1765–1800
Sheraton, 1775–1810
Regency, 1793–1830
Victorian, 1830–1890

Italian Provincial Period, 1700–1850

FIGURE 1-6
Examples of carvings and other forms of decoration. (*Courtesy of Hoover Universal.*)

American Periods
   Colonial (before the revolution)
   Federal or American Empire, 1789
   American Directoire, 1805–1820
   Duncan Phyfe, 1790–1830
   Shaker, 1776–1850
The Industrial Revolution 1830
   Victorian Period in America, 1840–1890
Since 1900

FRENCH PERIODS

Louis XIV, 1643–1715

Louis XIV of France was a patron of the arts and encouraged furniture designing. The furniture was of massive design with straight lines. Chairs were high backed, carved, and upholstered. Tables often had marble tops and carved understructure. Legs were heavy and braced with stretchers. Oak, walnut, and ebony were the woods commonly used. Decoration included painting, guilding, carving and metal mounts.

Louis XV, 1715–1774

Louis XV became king of France when he was a minor. He was brought up in a pleasure-loving court and his reign was gay and extravagant. Phillippe de Bourbon acted as the Regent (ruler) during the years that Louis XV was a minor and founded the main tendencies of the Louis XV furniture style.

The furniture was made smaller than was customary and more comfortable. The backs and legs of the chairs were lowered. The furniture was graceful and reflected a feminine character. Cabriole chair legs were used with slender ankles and scroll feet. There was carving at the tops of the legs, the front of the frame, and the center of the back frame.

Tables had marble or onyx tops and heavily carved skirts. The legs were of the cabriole type and heavily carved.

Tapestry with designs of flowers and pastoral scenes was used. Velvets, damasks, and silks were popular.

Woods used were oak, rosewood, mahogany, walnut, beech, ebony, holly, tulipwood, maple, and pear.

The furniture was guilded, painted, lacquered, veneered, or inlaid (Fig. 1-7).

Louis XVI, 1774–1792

This period brought a change in the contour and methods of decoration. It began a return to classical forms. Louis XVI furniture was of straight-line construction and was symmetrical. It was decorated with delicately carved ornament (Fig. 1-8). Chair legs were straight and tapered with carving or flutings that increased their slimness. They joined the seat with a square section having a carved flower. The seats and backs were rectangular or circular. Padded armrests were often used. Upholstery was usually tapestry, brocades, damask, velour, or taffeta in stripes or stripes and flowers. The furniture was gilded, painted, lacquered and inlaid. The most popular wood was mahogany, although ebony, tulipwood, rosewood, and fruitwood was used.

FIGURE 1-7
This dining room group features Louis XV styling. It uses walnut veneer panels and solid cherry lumber parts. (*Courtesy of Fine Hardwoods/American Walnut Association.*)

FIGURE 1-8
Louis XVI dining room group. It has an oval tabletop, reverse matched walnut veneers with ebony veneer bandings, and solid mahogany lumber parts. (*Courtesy of Fine Hardwoods/American Walnut Association.*)

Empire, 1795–1830

The Empire style, developed in France, was characterized by an attempt to reconstruct antique Roman and Greek furniture. The style has broad flat surfaces of straight lines and sharp edges. No attempt was made to soften these edges. Golden Greek palm leaves, wreaths of laurel, or figures of victory with outspread wings were used to decorate these surfaces.

A variety of Empire chairs were designed. The lines are simple and broad but not always straight. Some chairs have a rolled-over back. The front legs are joined with a curved rail. Arms are often curved and rest on top of perpendicular front legs. The rear legs are concave and tapered. The chair seat and back are both upholstered. Mahogany, rosewood, and ebony were the most often used woods (Fig. 1-9).

French Provincial 1610–1795

The furniture called French Provincial was made by local cabinetmakers for the peasants and middle-class people living in the provinces. It was the local cabinetmakers' version of the furniture style popular in Paris at the time. In general, it was of a simpler design and not finished as well as the originals. It was well constructed but had simplified ornamentation and basic shapes.

The early pieces were functional units such as bunk beds, stools, benches, commodes, and wardrobes. Later more stylish pieces, such as tables, desks, buffets, armoires, wardrobes, and clocks, were produced (Fig. 1-10). They were comfortable

FIGURE 1-9
Nineteenth century Empire side chair (1795–1830). Note the broad flat surfaces and straight lines. (*Courtesy of Cooper-Hewitt Museum, the Smithsonian Institution's National Museum of Design, New York.*)

and had a timeless quality which makes them popular as reproductions.

Certain developments occurred in various provinces. This included a ladderback chair, a ladderback settee, and straw-seated chairs, (Fig. 1-11). The chairs had flat curved arms resting on turned supports. Legs were either straight or cabriole. Armoires (linen cabinets) were popular, as were beds with high posts and canopies (Fig. 1-12). In one prov-

FIGURE 1-10
Reproduction of late French Provincial bedroom furniture (1610–1795). (*Courtesy of Drexel Heritage Furnishings Inc.*)

FIGURE 1-12
An armoire is used to hang clothing and often has drawers behind the swinging doors.

FIGURE 1-11
Contemporary ladderback chair with a caned seat. (*Courtesy of Danish Design Council.*)

ince the bed was built with solid wood-paneled sides which could be closed to protect against cold, damp drafts. Chests and buffets had curved fronts.

The woods used included walnut, beech, cherry, elm, and oak. Brass, copper, and steel hardware were commonly used. Decoration was mainly from adding moldings and geometric carvings.

ENGLISH PERIODS

William and Mary, 1688–1702

When Mary II ascended to the English throne, she had a Dutch husband and many new ideas, customs, and standards for furniture. She popularized the Dutch idea of comfort and brought Dutch designers to England. The designers brought with them craftsmen to make the furniture. The craftsmen introduced ideas of their own and used motifs borrowed from Spain, China, and India. A number of new furniture pieces were introduced such as the highboy (Fig. 1-13).

Upholstery was used extensively. Walnut was the most commonly used wood replacing English oak. Carving featured motifs of flowers, foliage, cupids, wreaths, scrolls, and serpentine designs. The main feature was the use of graceful lines and curves profiling the furniture. Legs often had an inverted cup near the top. All types of feet were used, including pear, club and hoof-shaped (Fig. 1-14).

FIGURE 1-14
Side chair dating about 1690 of the William and Mary period (1688–1702). This period was influenced by Dutch designers. (*Courtesy of Cooper-Hewitt Museum, the Smithsonian Institution's National Museum of Design, New York.*)

Chairs had high backs and stretchers set x-wise between the legs. Tables also had stretchers between the legs. The stretchers were flat and cut into curved forms. Upholstered settees or love seats resemble joined chairs.

Queen Anne, 1702–1750

This style developed during the reign of Queen Anne of England. Walnut was the chief wood in use, but mahogany began to be important. Woods used for inlaying include pine, lime, chestnut, pear, beech, elm, and yew.

The key design feature of this period is the cyma curve, which forms the cabriole leg on chairs, tables, settees, the backs of chairs, and the aprons of highboys and lowboys. This was a period of graceful curves (Fig. 1-15). The S and C scrolls of the earlier century continued to be used but were more controlled.

The cabriole legs had a club or a ball-and-claw foot. Early chairs had stretchers, but later chairs did not. The knees of legs were carved with lion's heads, satyr masks, or cockle shells. Backs were short and had a vase-shaped center splat (Fig. 1-16).

The Windsor chair was developed during the Queen Anne period. It was named for Windsor Castle but found its greatest popularity in America. Here the design evolved into a graceful and popular chair. They are sturdy, light, and comfortable (Fig. 1-17). Originally, these chairs were made by wheel-

FIGURE 1-13
Reproduction of a highboy. This piece of furniture was introduced during the period of William and Mary. (*Courtesy of Ethan Allen Inc.*)

FIGURE 1-15
Reproductions representative of the Queen Anne period (1702–1750). This style is very popular even today. (*Courtesy of Hekman Furniture Company.*)

FIGURE 1-16
Classic Queen Anne side chair made about 1725. It is walnut, carved, with some parts veneered, and has curved side uprights, a solid vase splat, and paw feet. (*Courtesy of Victoria and Albert Museum, Crown Copyright, London, England.*)

FIGURE 1-17
Reproduction of a Windsor chair first produced during the Queen Anne period. (*Courtesy of The Bartley Collection, Ltd.*)

wrights rather than cabinetmakers. This led to the use of bentwood frames which are supported by spindles and legs pegged into a saddle-type seat. There are many variations in shape, such as the comb, fan, hoop, and bow backs. Some have rockers and backs braced to a seat extension. Other pieces, as settees and tables, were later introduced using this styling and construction. The woods used were pine and birch for seats, hickory, ash, and birch for the bent parts, and oak, maple, and birch for the turned parts.

Chippendale, 1740–1780

The Chippendale period was one of the outstanding styles of the eighteenth century. The style was named for Thomas Chippendale, a designer of this period. However, it is believed that many of the designs he published were the work of those who worked for him.

Chippendale furniture designs are divided into three periods: French, Chinese, and Gothic. All types of furniture were designed. They were graceful and well proportioned. Early Chippendale pieces had cabriole legs, while later pieces had straight legs. They were of sturdy construction. Most of the decoration used was carving. Bold and delicate carvings of things in nature, such as paws, shells, acorns,

CHIPPENDALE CHARACTERISTICS

CHIPPENDALE WITH CHINESE INFLUENCE

FIGURE 1-18
Two original Chippendale chairs (1740–1780). The chair on the left is carved walnut and has a bulrush design back. The chair on the right is carved mahogany and the back is filled with latticework in "Chinese taste." (*Courtesy of Victoria and Albert Museum, Crown Copyright, London, England.*)

and roses, were used. Fretwork was used, as were gilding and lacquering. Almost all Chippendale furniture was made of mahogany (Fig. 1-18).

The Chippendale chair was produced in four distinct types: (1) the Dutch Chippendale, which used a pierced splat back similar to that in the Queen Anne period, cabriole legs, and claw and ball feet; (2) the French Chippendale, which had an elaborately decorated cabriole leg with a scroll foot; (3) the Chinese Chippendale, which had a square back with a fret design and straight legs decorated with a fret design; and (4) the Gothic Chippendale, which had straight-line construction. The back and legs were straight and had stretchers (Fig. 1-19).

Tables also had cabriole legs with claw and ball, club, scroll, or paw feet.

Upholstery material included damasks, silks, satins, brocades, horsehair, and morocco leather. The chairs could be carved, painted, gilded, veneered, or inlaid. Mahogany was the most commonly used wood.

Adam, 1762–1792

This style was named for Robert Adam, an architect who was inspired by the antiquities of Greece and Italy. He worked with his brothers, James and William. The furniture established a change from the Chippendale style to more classical designs borrowed from the Italian Renaissance and interpreted in a lighter style. The straight-line contour dominated. The furniture was light and graceful. Chairs

FIGURE 1-19
Reproduction of a Chippendale corner chair. Notice the straight legs and fretwork in the back. (*Courtesy of The Bartley Collection, Ltd.*)

FIGURE 1-20
Armchair of the Adam period (1762–1792). It is carved mahogany. The splat is lyre-shaped with metal strings. (*Courtesy of Victoria and Albert Museum, Crown Copyright, London, England.*)

FIGURE 1-21
Cabinet on stand designed by Robert Adam in 1771. It is rosewood with satinwood veneer. (*Courtesy of Victoria and Albert Museum, Crown Copyright, London, England.*)

had lyre, oval, and shield-shaped backs. The legs were round or square, tapered, and often fluted. They had small spade-type feet. The back legs were straight and curved backward. Armchairs often had a round upholstered seat (Fig. 1-20). Tables were rectangular, semicircular, or semioval. They had tapering fluted legs. Table tops were often marble. A cabinet on a stand is shown in Fig. 1-21.

Upholstery was generally plain fabrics of silk, satin, horsehair, damasks and leather. Satinwood was commonly used and was inlaid with ebony, hardwood, pear, amboyna, and holly. Ornamentation included carvings, veneering, overlays, and paintings. Classical designs include rams heads, medallions, honeysuckle, and the urn. Daintily carved moldings were used.

Hepplewhite, 1765–1800

The principles of design developed by Adam and others of his time were circulated through trade publications, showing the features of the new style. One of those working at this time was George Hepplewhite. He published a book in England in which the style of Adam was modified and written so that the cabinetmaker could understand it. The book contained 300 designs and was published two years after his death.

The practical character of the designs made them easy to produce. Hepplewhite used the curved line as a design feature. The backs of chairs were in the form of a shield, a pierced or fretted splat, an interlacing heart, an oval with wheel design, the three Prince of Wales feathers, or were hoop-backed with a central splat. The legs were square tapering to a spade foot. The seat was usually square (Fig. 1-22).

Hepplewhite tables took many shapes, including oval dining tables with drop leaves and console tables with semicircular or serpentine contour. Chests of drawers had serpentine fronts.

The major wood used was mahogany; however, satinwood, birch, sycamore, and rosewood were also used. The upholstery was horsehair, silk, satin, damask, velvet, or moiré. While painting was the major method of decoration, gilding, carving, veneering, and inlay were used.

Sheraton, 1775–1810

Thomas Sheraton published a trade catalog in England that was very comprehensive. It was so well accepted that the furniture produced in England be-

FIGURE 1-23
Commode of the Sheraton period (1775–1810). It is made of softwood with a bow front. It has pen-and-ink decoration on a black background. (*Courtesy of Victoria and Albert Museum, Crown Copyright, London, England.*)

tween 1790 and 1800 have been classified under his name. He proclaimed that Chippendale's designs were "antiquated."

Sheraton furniture has a severe simplicity due to an emphasis on straight lines and balanced ornamentation. The chairs had rectangular backs having a center panel with a vase or lyre ornament. The legs were round or square and were fluted or reeded. The backs of the chairs may have carving, inlay, hand-painted panels, or Wedgewood medallions. Seats of chairs were caned or upholstered. Armchairs had down-curved arms with turned vase-shaped supports.

A typical table was circular with a pillar and four claws. Card tables and console tables were circular or serpentine fronted with a plain or fluted tapered leg without a spade foot. The general lines of sideboards were straight with convex curves on the corners (Fig. 1-23).

Upholstery materials were silk, satin, horsehair, chintz, or damask.

Regency, 1793–1830

In England after the opening of the war with France in 1793, a revolution in taste in furniture began. It was a revival of the classical designs and imitation of the antique was of supreme importance. The

FIGURE 1-22
Armchair of the Hepplewhite period (1765–1800). It is carved mahogany with Prince of Wales feathers in the back. (*Courtesy of Victoria and Albert Museum, Crown Copyright, London, England.*)

FIGURE 1-24
Side chair of the Regency period (1793–1830). It is made of mahogany with round fluted front legs. (*Courtesy of Cooper-Hewitt Museum, the Smithsonian Institution's National Museum of Design, New York.*)

FIGURE 1-25
Table of the Regency period built in 1810. It is mahogany with the top cross banded with rosewood and inlaid with mother-of-pearl. (*Courtesy of Victoria and Albert Museum, Crown Copyright, London, England.*)

name "Regency style" was used because during this period (1811–1820), George, Prince of Wales, acted as Regent for the aged and mentally ailing king, George III. It was a period of prosperity and luxury when decoration of palaces set the styles.

The Regency style developed from the furniture of the late nineteenth century. It was a style of simplification and functionalism. Furniture pieces were scaled down to smaller and more intimate sizes. Regency chairs have both straight and concave backs. Legs were usually straight without stretchers, although some were slightly curved. They were sometimes fluted or carved. Flat, thin upholstery was used on the seat (Fig. 1-24).

Tables were elaborately inlaid, lacquered, and gilded. Larger tables had straight legs, while smaller tables were triangular and had three legs or pedestal (Fig. 1-25).

Mahogany was the most widely used wood, but rosewood and satinwood were also used. Much of the furniture was painted black, but white and ivory were also used.

Victorian, 1830–1890

A style of furniture developed during the reign of Queen Victoria developed in England and was widely copied in America. It was a period of sentimentality, primness, and stodgy respectability. It developed from the American and English Empire

designs. It was a large, heavy, often clumsy style. Fabrics and woods were sombre and deep shades. Horsehair was often used. Many consider it a period of bad design.

Black walnut and rosewoods were used. Carving, turning, and inlay of brass, wood, and mother-of-pearl were common. For examples, see Fig. 1-26.

FIGURE 1-26
Classic Victorian sofa with heavy carving and large upholstered surfaces. (*Courtesy of Cooper-Hewitt Museum, the Smithsonian Institution's National Museum of Design, New York.*)

ITALIAN PROVINCIAL PERIOD, 1700–1850

The style called Italian Provincial is used to describe the furniture produced by craftsmen in the Italian provinces of the eighteenth and nineteenth centuries. They were in the rural areas far from centers of culture and design. They copied the elaborate furniture being built in Rome, Milan, Venice, and Florence. As they did this they simplified the lines and removed much of the ornate decoration. The pieces produced in the various provinces differed a great deal from each other.

The early pieces were massive in size, while those built in later years were smaller because they were influenced by French styles of the eighteenth and nineteenth centuries. The Italian Provincial built today reflects those built in the later years. The designs in use today are basically rectangular with straight, square, tapered legs. Curves do appear in tables and chairs, but they are smooth and unbroken. Brass hardware is typical. Wood molding is used to outline doors and drawers. Woods used were walnut, olive, and fruitwoods. Some furniture was painted or enameled (Fig. 1-27).

the colonies were from England. Pattern books of English furniture were widely circulated in the colonies. The characteristics of the English styles are therefore the characteristics of the early American furniture.

Many changes in the English styles were made in the colonies according to the region in which it was made. The products were simpler in design because the colonists lacked the wealth needed to buy ornate, heavily carved furniture. The colonists worked to produce food and did not have time for the luxury of fine furniture for many years. The Pilgrims made strong plain furniture. The fine furniture that was made was largely in the larger cities where the wealthy businessmen lived. America's furniture styles are often divided into two historical groups, Colonial and Federal or American Empire.

Colonial

Colonial refers to styles existing before the revolution. This is through the Chippendale period in England. It usually took an English style 5 to 10 years to become popular in the colonies after it appeared in England. The William and Mary style was well

FIGURE 1-27
Reproduction of Italian Provincial tables placed with a contemporary overstuffed sofa and chair. (*Courtesy of Drexel Heritage Furnishings Inc.*)

AMERICAN PERIODS

The early settlers in America were primarily of English origin except for small numbers of Dutch in New York, Germans in southeastern Pennsylvania, and the Spanish in Florida. Most of the furniture built in America was therefore based on designs the colonists knew in England. Most of the craftsmen in

established by about 1695–1700. It introduced highboys and lowboys. This was followed by the Queen Anne style, which was fully established by 1720. It remained fashionable until about 1755–1760, when Chippendale furniture became popular. Philadelphia was the center of furniture manufacturing. Walnut was often used for fine furniture, but mahogany became the most fashionable wood in Amer-

FIGURE 1-28
Reproductions of early American furnishings. These were made from designs in Salem, Massachusetts, dating from about 1729. They are of antique pine. (*Courtesy of Ethan Allen Inc.*)

ica for at least 100 years. Native woods such as pine, hickory, gum, ash, oak, cherry, pear, and maple were used extensively for furniture. Chippendale furniture continued in popularity until about 1785, when the Hepplewhite fashion prevailed.

Federal or American Empire, 1789

The *Federal* or *American Empire* period includes those styles popular after the federal government was established in 1789. Hepplewhite furniture became fashionable about this time and remained in vogue until about 1800. This was followed by the Sheraton, American Directoire, and Duncan Phyfe. This period overlapped the Victorian period in America. There was always an overlapping of the styles and it is difficult to identify some of the furniture as clearly belonging to a specific style.

American designers of today have refined the furniture of the colonial days into a style that appeals to the modern citizen. The furniture is designed to go with modern features of a home, yet retain the original flavor of the design. Current furniture is made from maple, pine, and fruitwoods and generally has a natural or light finish (Fig. 1-28).

American Directoire, 1805–1820

This style became popular in America around 1805 and remained so for about 15 years. Its origin can be traced to French Directoire, which restored the purity of the antique Greek for chairs.

Duncan Phyfe, 1790–1830

Duncan Phyfe was a cabinetmaker whose name has been used to identify fine furniture made from 1800 to about 1820. The refined designs are based on the Sheraton, Adam, Hepplewhite, Directoire, and Empire styles. The designs possess elegance and simplicity which appeal to us even today. Some design features include fine lines of reeding, carved acanthus leaves on pillars and claw supports, carved eagles and hairy animal shanks on saber legs, and lyre standards and splats. Duncan Phyfe furniture is noted for fine proportion, excellent construction, and a careful combination of straight lines and curves. He used brass as terminals for legs and strings on lyres and glass and china for knobs. He used mahogany almost exclusively (Fig. 1-29).

Chairs have either straight or curved legs. One design uses x-crossed legs. His sofas have classic lines with arms similar to the front of a sleigh. Most tables have a single lyre or column pedestal and usually three curule feet.

FIGURE 1-29
Reproduction of Duncan Phyfe side and arm chairs, a Pembroke drop-leaf dining table, and a lowboy serving as a buffet. (*Courtesy of Ethan Allen Inc.*)

Shaker, 1776–1850

The *Shaker style* gets its name from an early American religious group, the Shakers. They appeared first in New York during the Revolutionary War and established villages over the eastern United States. Their lives were dominated by religion, and simplicity was important in all their activities. They preferred to make everything they needed rather than get items by trading.

The Shakers were good craftsmen, and their early furniture shows good workmanship. The furniture was functional in design and had excellent proportions. The legs were round or square and tapered to the foot. Desks and chests rested flat on the floor. No form of decoration was permitted. A light coat of varnish was used as a finish (Fig. 1-30).

Early chairs had slat back construction, while later ones used spindles. They developed pedestal tables, rockers, and tilting chairs. The favorite wood was pine, but maple, fruitwood, and other native woods were used.

the mechanical means to produce furniture in a factory developed, it was possible to make each piece exactly like the next. The artistic and creative talents of the craftsman were not needed. Since the industrial revolution developed early in England, it was one of the first countries to become concerned about the state of the arts and crafts. During this period many able designers worked to create new designs. Much of what was developed was a revolt against popular taste. One example is illustrated by the American Victorian period.

Victorian Period in America

This style was named for Queen Victoria of England, who reigned for 64 years. Victorian was the major style in the United States for many years (1840–1890).

The Victorian designers copied and mixed other styles. They used many rich and elaborate carvings appearing much like sculpture. Ornamental motifs from several styles were often placed to-

FIGURE 1-30
Reproductions of Shaker furniture. This furniture reflects economical solutions and stresses functional simplicity as a religious expression. (*Courtesy of Ethan Allen Inc.*)

THE INDUSTRIAL REVOLUTION, 1830

The Empire and Regency styles were the last consistent and recognizable styles before the impact of the industrial revolution. By 1830 almost all artistic industries were feeling the impact of the machine. Up to this time each piece of furniture was developed by the hands of a master craftsman. Although they made it following a particular style, a great deal of individual design was invested in each piece. When

gether, leaving little of the surface undecorated. With the new mass production, tool carvings could be duplicated much easier and cheaper than when they were hand carved. Other technical developments permitted cheaper woods to be painted to imitate mahogany, ebony, or marble. Glass was used to imitate semiprecious stones and panels were painted to imitate inlaid wood. There was a wide use of new materials. Beds were made of iron or brass. Chairs and tables were made of tubular material.

Papier-mache was used extensively. Wood was heated and bent to produce bentwood furniture.

One outstanding feature of the Victorian period was the use of broken lines. Straight lines of earlier styles were replaced by a series of scrolls and curves, giving much of the furniture a top-heavy look.

The chairs of the Victorian period had oval or horseshoe-shaped backs. They were solid and upholstered. Side rails were curved and had moldings. Arms were curved and low serving more as a brace than arm. The seats were low and the backs high (Fig. 1-31).

Occasional tables often had marble tops and a central pedestal. Sometimes the pedestal was made of several carved columns. Sofas had a sweeping curved back with carving on the top rail. The woods most commonly used were walnut and rosewood.

FIGURE 1-31
Victorian side chair made around 1840. It is made of laminated rosewood. (*Courtesy of Cooper-Hewitt Museum, the Smithsonian Institution's National Museum of Design, New York.*)

SINCE 1900

Developments during the years following 1900 are often referred to as the Modern movement. It refers to the trend to remove all ornamentation and use materials in an honest and straightforward manner. The structural form of the furniture was freed of the continual imitation of design concepts of the past.

Designers were becoming increasingly aware that society had changed. It was becoming an industrial society which was aware of the beauty of engineering. New materials were being developed, as

FIGURE 1-32
This chromium-plated steel chair with fabric webbing was developed in the Bauhaus style in 1956. (*Courtesy of Cooper-Hewitt Museum, the Smithsonian Institution's National Museum of Design, New York.*)

were ways to process existing materials. Designs were produced to meet the demands of mass production. The designers believed that furniture should be functional. The beauty of geometric forms was recognized.

Following are a few of the many furniture designs produced in the twentieth century.

One concept was chromium-plated steel furniture. The first tubular steel chair was designed by Marcel Breuer in 1925 in Germany. Another steel chromium-plated chair which is a classic was designed by Ludwig Mies van der Rohe in 1929. A chromium-plated steel chair developed in the Bauhaus in 1956 is shown in Fig. 1-32.

Molded wire mesh chairs were also developed in the late 1940s and early 1950s. Recently designed tables and chairs are shown in Fig. 1-33.

FIGURE 1-33
Molded wire mesh chairs with upholstered seats and backs. (*Courtesy of Knoll International, The Knoll Building, 655 Madison Ave., New York, NY 10021.*)

Tables and chairs with pedestal bases are another design concept. The chair arms, seat, and back are a single molded plastic shell. Sometimes the seat and back are upholstered (Fig. 1-34).

Designers worked with molded plywood chairs for many years. Practical molded plastic chairs with metal legs were developed in the 1940s. Some had

that the furniture is comfortable and functional. Two solutions are shown in Figs. 1-36 and 1-37.

There is a strong interest in casual furniture. It must be strong and usable indoors or outdoors. It must be lightweight so it can be easily moved. The designs reflect simple design solutions and comfort (see Figs. 1-38 and 1-39).

FIGURE 1-34
Molded plastic tables and chairs are another innovation in furniture design. (*Courtesy of Knoll International, The Knoll Building, 655 Madison Ave., New York, NY 10021.*)

upholstered backs and seats, while others were not upholstered. A chair designed by Charles Eames is shown in Fig. 1-35. Notice the molded plywood body, metal legs, and upholstered back, seat, and leg rest.

Swedish and Danish furniture has become widely accepted in this country. They emphasize simple, unpretentious solutions to furniture design situations. The design solutions are direct and emphasis is placed on the beauty of the wood. Much consideration is given to fitting the human form so

Comprehensive storage systems for home and office are another important product (Fig. 1-40). They permit the use of computers and typewriters and have shelf and drawer sections. These can be arranged on wall-mounted hanging strips to suit the current needs. Additional units can be added as needed.

Other influences are at work as contemporary furniture is designed and built. In addition to those from Italy, the Far East, and Scandinavia, designers

FIGURE 1-35
This molded plywood chair and footstool have upholstered seats, backs, and arms. The chair was designed by Charles Eames. (*Courtesy of Cooper-Hewitt Museum, the Smithsonian Institution's National Museum of Design, New York.*)

FIGURE 1-36
The handcrafted, sculptured look of this chair reflects the beauty and structure of Danish designs. (*Courtesy of Danish Design Council.*)

FIGURE 1-37
This chair exhibits straightforward design and beauty of materials. (*Courtesy of Danish Furniture Manufacturers' Association.*)

FIGURE 1-38
Casual furniture useful indoors or outdoors. (*Courtesy of Gold Medal, Inc.*)

FIGURE 1-39
This casual furniture uses large, sofa upholstered sections to provide maximum comfort. (*Courtesy of Gold Medal, Inc.*)

are gleaming concepts from our past, including the traditions of our forefathers in this country and their forefathers in Europe.

The important thing about our furniture today and tomorrow is that it be made of good-quality materials, reflect the best designs possible, and be of good-quality construction. Whether handcrafted or machine made, it must be of good quality. In the future designers will continue to look ahead to the social and political scene, use materials that are available, reflect the life-style of the people, yet look to the past as a resource to use as they express the world around them in their designs.

The current period of furniture development is commonly called Contemporary. New designs and applications of new materials are constantly being developed. These range from adaptations of previous styles or original creations. In general, the following characteristics appear in current furniture designs. The lines are clean, simple and restrained. Flat sur-

FIGURE 1-40
This comprehensive storage system provides shelves, drawer units, and a desk. Notice the molded plywood chair designed by Eames. It is a design classic. (*Courtesy of Herman Miller, Inc.*)

faces, straight lines, and curves are carefully combined. Function is an important feature and is reflected in the overall design. Comfort plus a pleasing appearance is part of the solution.

Ornamentation is avoided. The lines of the design, materials, and functional knobs and pulls provide the sense of beauty. Legs are smooth and not decorated. They may be of wood or metal and be square or round. Many are tapered to the foot. An attempt is made to produce units that are graceful and light in appearance.

All types of woods, plywoods, reconstituted wood products, and veneers are used. Extensive use of metal, glass, and plastic add to the appearance and durability of the furniture. A wide variety of colorful fabrics, plastics, and plastic and leather upholstery materials are available and form an important design feature.

STUDY QUESTIONS

Answer each of the following questions. If you are not sure of an answer, review the chapter.

1-1. How did the furniture of the Louis XV period change from that of Louis XIV?

1-2. What was the most popular wood used in Louis XVI furniture?

1-3. What characterized the design of the Empire-style furniture?

1-4. How did the French Provincial furniture develop?

1-5. From what countries did designers get ideas to influence a furniture style referred to as William and Mary?

1-6. What was the key design feature of Queen Anne furniture?

1-7. What are the three periods of Chippendale furniture?

1-8. How did Robert Adam change furniture design during his life?

1-9. What are the recognizable design features of furniture of the Hepplewhite period?

1-10. How did Sheraton furniture depart from the furniture of earlier periods?

1-11. What influence did furniture of the Regency period have on the size of furniture?

1-12. Why was furniture of the Victorian period considered poor design by many?

1-13. Where was the furniture identified as Italian Provincial developed?

1-14. What name is used to identify furniture produced in America before the revolution?

1-15. What furniture styles were popular in America during the American Empire period?

1-16. What styles did Duncan Phyfe refine to develop the furniture that carries his name?

1-17. Where does Shaker furniture get its name?

1-18. How did the industrial revolution influence furniture designs?

1-19. How have furniture designers in the last 50 years changed the furniture we use?

CLASS ACTIVITIES

Cut pictures from catalogs and magazines and make a notebook showing as many furniture styles as you can. Below each picture identify the style and list the specific features that make it fit that style.

2

FURNITURE AND CABINET DESIGN

A study of Chapter 1 reveals the work of furniture designers over several centuries. Many things influence the design, such as the materials readily available, technical developments, influences from other cultures, and the creative abilities of those in furniture design. Following are some general principles that are commonly accepted as basic to satisfactory design solutions.

DESIGNING FURNITURE AND CABINETS

The designing of wood products involves consideration of many factors. As these are studied, the proposed solutions are constantly changed until a final acceptable version is developed. The basic design considerations include the function of the product, its structural requirements, the materials to be used, its appearance, and the methods required to produce it.

Function

The product must serve the purpose for which it was designed. Cabinets in a kitchen must be sized to hold the dishes and appliances expected to be stored (Fig.

2-1). They must accommodate a dishwasher, range, or compactor. If these appliances cannot be installed, the cabinets are not functioning in the manner intended. Similarly, furniture as a chair or sofa is designed to permit a person to sit comfortably. Other furniture units serve other functions, such as eating, reading, or typing (Fig. 2-2).

Structure

The structure of a product depends on its intended use. The joints should be adequate for the loads to be applied. A small nightstand intended to hold a lamp and clock can have smaller structural members and possibly different joints than if it were to hold a television set.

If a piece of furniture is worth building, it is worth building well. Quality construction means using the best joints, properly sized members, and the correct bonding agents (Fig. 2-3). Furniture and cabinet building are described in great detail in later chapters.

Materials

An extensive variety of materials are used in furniture and cabinet construction. The designer must be

FIGURE 2-1
These cabinets are functional. They are serving the purpose for which they were designed. (*Courtesy of Connor Forest Products.*)

RABBET JOINT

DADO JOINTS

FIGURE 2-3
A product must be well designed structurally. These dado and rabbet joints are glued to the bulkheads to give the piece structural strength.

FIGURE 2-2
These chairs were designed to fit the human body and support it comfortably in a seated position. (*Courtesy of Gold Medal, Inc.*)

FIGURE 2-4
Notice the wide range of materials used in the furniture in this room. Can you identify some of the materials? (*Courtesy of Drexel Heritage Furnishings Inc.*)

familiar with the advantages and limitations of each. A real reproduction of a classical piece of furniture should use the same kinds of woods and fabrics that were in the original. These are discussed in Chapter 1. In situations where the units are exposed to unusually hard wear, plastic laminates could be used. Tops on tables to be used daily for family meals can be covered with a plastic laminate. It can have the grain and color of the real wood but will withstand moisture and resist impact damage. Plywood with the outer veneer a fine hardwood also provides a superior construction material. Although it is real wood, the panels resist warping and are easier to work with than large pieces formed by gluing together solid wood boards. Other materials often used are ceramics, plastics, glass, metal, cane, and textiles (Fig. 2-4).

FIGURE 2-5
This reproduction of a Brittany hall piece and mirror exhibit a combination of materials, shape, details, and hardware that produce a pleasing appearance. (*Courtesy of Drexel Heritage Furnishings Inc.*)

Appearance

The completed product must be pleasing to view. The combination of materials, overall shape, details, hardware, and colors must work together so that it is visually attractive and harmonious (Fig. 2-5).

Methods

As decisions are made concerning the appearance, materials, and structure, the designer must keep in mind the machining operations necessary to build the product. In some cases a simpler joint might be easier and less costly to make, yet be strong enough for the intended purpose. The product should be designed to be made using the equipment available in the factory or shop. This relates not only to joints but to features such as moldings, carvings, curved and laminated pieces, and panel construction.

DESIGN FACTORS

The basic elements of design are lines, planes, mass, texture, and color. These elements of design are basic to every two- and three-dimensional object. When combined they build the structure or form of the furniture or cabinet unit.

Lines

A *line* is a path formed by a point moving in space. It has only one dimension, length. The basic lines include straight, circles, circular arcs, and irregular curves (Fig. 2-6). A circular arc has a fixed radius. An irregular curve has no fixed radius. The preliminary sketching of a design idea is actually a series of lines describing the product. Lines produce a reaction from the viewer. A curved line that arcs out-

FIGURE 2-6
Lines are one of the basic elements of design.

ward produces a feeling of grace and charm. Those that curve inward create a feeling of emptiness (Fig. 2-7). Straight lines suggest strength and stability (Fig. 2-8). A vertical straight line suggests great strength, while a diagonal gives a feeling of movement. A diagonal used alone gives a feeling of falling. Therefore, it can be seen that lines can be used

FIGURE 2-7
Lines of various kinds produce reactions from the viewer. (*Courtesy of Knoll International, The Knoll Building, 655 Madison Ave., New York, NY 10021.*)

FIGURE 2-8
Straight lines suggest strength and stability. (*Courtesy of Herman Miller, Inc.*)

FIGURE 2-9
Planes are formed by joining lines of various kinds.

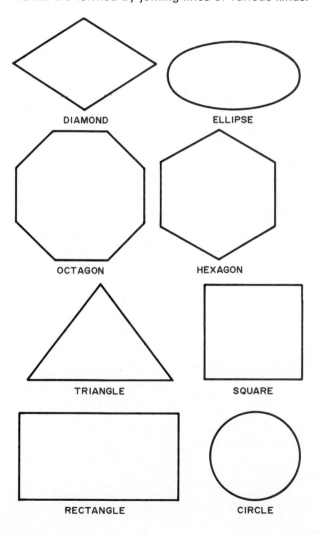

DIAMOND   ELLIPSE

OCTAGON   HEXAGON

TRIANGLE   SQUARE

RECTANGLE   CIRCLE

by the designer to convey feelings and determine basic shapes.

Planes

Planes are formed by the joining of lines. Typical two-dimensional shapes are the circle, square, rectangle, diamond, ellipse, hexagon, octagon, and triangle (Fig. 2-9). The plane created becomes an important design element. Notice your reaction to the circular tables in Fig. 2-10. The planes created are simple, basic shapes that dominate these tables.

FIGURE 2-10
The reaction to these round tables is a feeling of grace and charm. (*Courtesy of Knoll International, The Knoll Building, 655 Madison Ave., New York, NY 10021.*)

Mass

Mass is the three-dimensional form of an object. It is created by the joining of lines and planes. Generally, mass is the first element of design noted when looking at a product. Mass can be one of the basic geometric shapes or some variation of them (Fig. 2-11).

Texture

Texture refers to the way a surface feels when touched. It can be very smooth, as a glass table top, or rougher, as a woven cane chair seat. The degree of texture imparts a variety of visual responses to the surface as well as the sense of touch. A hard, smooth surface tends to produce cool reactions. A rougher, coarser surface produces warm reactions (Fig. 2-12).

Color

Color also produces a variety of reactions. Some colors, such as red, orange, and brown, produce a warm

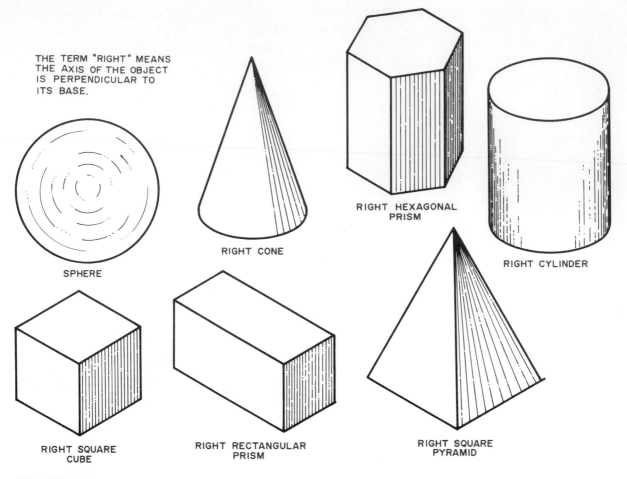

THE TERM "RIGHT" MEANS THE AXIS OF THE OBJECT IS PERPENDICULAR TO ITS BASE.

SPHERE

RIGHT CONE

RIGHT HEXAGONAL PRISM

RIGHT CYLINDER

RIGHT SQUARE CUBE

RIGHT RECTANGULAR PRISM

RIGHT SQUARE PYRAMID

FIGURE 2-11
Mass is the three-dimensional form of a product. These are the basic geometric shapes.

FIGURE 2-12
Notice your reaction to the texture of this caned chair seat. (*Courtesy of The Woodworkers' Store.*)

FIGURE 2-13
This kitchen makes effective use of color. (*Courtesy of General Electric Company.*)

reaction. Blues and greens produce cool reactions. The natural color of wood is warm. It can be changed by staining the wood. Color can be used to call attention to a feature of a design. For example, a cabinet may have a white case with yellow interiors. The colorful interiors become the point of focus while the case receives only secondary notice (Fig. 2-13).

Color properly used, is an important and sometimes difficult element of design to apply. There are three primary and three secondary colors (Fig. 2-14). All other colors are mixtures of these primary colors. The *primary colors* are red, yellow, and blue. The *secondary colors* are orange, green, and violet. The three secondary colors are made by mixing equal amounts of two primary colors. *Tertiary colors* are made by mixing a secondary color with a primary color.

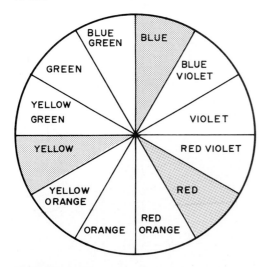

FIGURE 2-14
Color wheel. *Primary colors:* red, blue, yellow; *secondary colors:* orange, green, violet.

Colors opposite each other on the color wheel are called *complementary colors*. Colors near each other on the color wheel are called *analogous colors*. Generally, complementary colors are better for product design.

BASIC PRINCIPLES OF DESIGN

The basic principles of design are balance, proportion, rhythm, and unity.

Balance

A product is in *balance* when its elements viewed as a whole appear to be of equal significance. No one feature dominates another.

Balance can be either formal or informal. *Formal balance* occurs when the left and right sides of an object are the same size or shape (Fig. 2-15). *Informal balance* occurs when one-half of a product is different from the other, but because it is pleasing to the eye, it appears to be in balance (Fig. 2-16). Elements on one side tend to balance different elements on the other side.

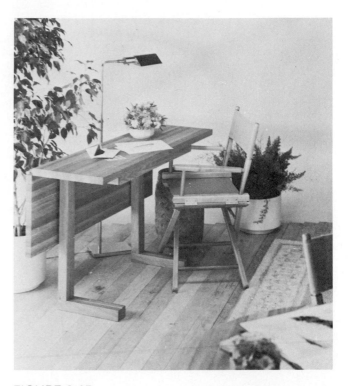

FIGURE 2-15
This desk and chair are examples of formal balance. (*Courtesy of Gold Medal, Inc.*)

FIGURE 2-16
This wall of cabinets exhibits informal balance. The side with the stove has the most cabinets and is the heaviest. However, it is balanced by the long sink counter and the refrigerator with cabinets above it. (*Courtesy of Connor Forest Products.*)

THE OPTICAL CENTER IS LOCATED SLIGHTLY ABOVE THE EXACT CENTER.

A MASS LOCATED ON THE EXACT CENTER APPEARS TO BE LOW.

A MASS LOCATED ON THE OPTICAL CENTER APPEARS TO BE STABLE.

FIGURE 2-17
The optical center is used to give the appearance of stability.

A geometric mass has an exact center point. When a smaller mass is located on the exact center point, it appears low and slightly out of balance. A geometric mass has a point located slightly above the actual center point called the *optical center*. It is located by estimation. When a smaller mass is centered on the optical center, it appears to be stable (Fig. 2-17).

When a larger unit has two smaller masses imposed on it of equal size, they appear in balance if placed the same distance from the optical centerline (Fig. 2-18). If the two masses are unequal in size, the larger is placed nearer the optical centerline to get the illusion of balance (Fig. 2-19).

Proportion

The size relationship of one part to another and of the parts to the whole is called *proportion*. Designers

FIGURE 2-18
Equal size masses appear balanced if they are kept the same distance from the optical point.

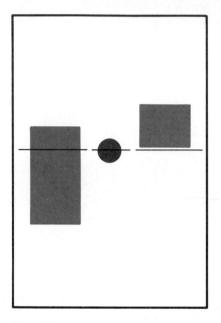

FIGURE 2-19
When two masses are of unequal size, place the larger nearer the optical center.

have found that a rectangular form is often more pleasing to view than a square.

Pleasing rectangular proportions can be found by using dynamic symmetry. *Dynamic symmetry* means dividing areas so that each part is in agreement with the others, as well as with the whole.

To use dynamic symmetry one dimension must be known. This dimension is used to form a square. The square is the basis for forming rectangles that are in perfect harmony. The side of the square could be the width of a coffee table. A pleasing length can then be found using dynamic symmetry.

The design process is shown in Fig. 2-20. The square *ABCD* is based on the desired width of the rectangle. Using corner *A* as a point, rotate the diagonal of the square to the bottom edge, point *F*. Rectangle *ABEF* has been formed. Other harmonious rectangles can be formed. Using the diagonal of the rectangle just formed, *AE,* swing point *E* to the bot-

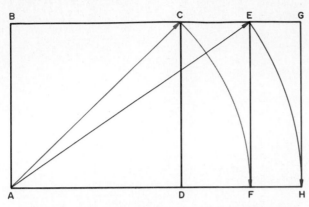

A,B,E,F IS THE RECTANGLE OFF OF SQUARE A,B,C,D.

A,B,G,H IS THE RECTANGLE OFF OF RECTANGLE
A,B,E,F.

FIGURE 2-20
Steps for finding harmonius rectangles when the width
is known.

tom edge at H. This forms another harmonious rectangle. This process can be repeated over and over,
forming many rectangles.

Another means for developing rectangles having pleasing proportions is to multiply the short side
by *design factors*. These factors produce rectangles
of various proportions (Table 2-1). For example, if
the width of the coffee table is to be 400 mm and the
golden rectangle proportion is desired, multiply 400
by the factor 1.6. The length of the table is therefore
640 mm.

TABLE 2-1
Harmonious Rectangles

	Design factor	Proportions produced
Long rectangle	2.0	1 : 2
Printer's rectangle	1.7	2 : 3.5
Golden rectangle	1.6	3 : 5
Regular rectangle	1.5	4 : 6
Hypotenuse rectangle	1.4	5 : 7

If the long side of the table is known, a pleasing
length for the short side is found by *dividing* the
long side by the design factor. The proportion to be
used depends on the judgment of the designer.

A rectangle can be divided vertically and horizontally. If it is divided vertically, the design is
more pleasing when the parts are unequal. The
parts, however, should not be too different in size
(Fig. 2-21). If divided horizontally, the rectangle

FIGURE 2-21
Principles for vertical and horizontal division of rectangular masses.

EQUAL DIVISIONS
LOSE INTEREST

UNEQUAL DIVISIONS
RELIEVE BOREDOM

EXPECTED DIVISIONS
UNINTERESTING

SURPRISE DIVISIONS
CREATE INTEREST

EQUAL PROPORTIONS
ARE NOT INTERESTING

UNEQUAL PROPORTIONS
MORE INTERESTING

EQUAL DIVISIONS
LOSE INTEREST

LARGE LOWER MASS
GIVES STABILITY

FIGURE 2-22
The careful use of vertical and horizontal divisions creates an attractive series of wall units. (*Courtesy of Drexel Heritage Furnishings Inc.*)

may have equal parts. But such a design tends to be monotonous. If the parts are not equal, the largest is usually at the bottom. This provides stability (Fig. 2-22).

Rhythm

The orderly repetition of some element of the design is its *rhythm*. This element might be a shape, a line, or a color. The details of the desk in Fig. 2-23 are an example of rhythm. The drawers give a rhythm to the desk. Rhythm can give a feeling of movement.

Unity

A design has *unity* when the various elements seem to belong together. If a product has unity, one ele-

FIGURE 2-23
This desk has rhythm. The orderly repetition of the small upper drawers plus the repetition of the lower drawers produces the feeling of rhythm. (*Courtesy of Ethan Allen Inc.*)

FIGURE 2-24
This sofa table has unity. All the elements of the design join together in harmony to form a unified whole. (*Courtesy of Ethan Allen Inc.*)

ment will not seem to be in conflict with another. The table in Fig. 2-24 has unity. Its parts are joined to form a single unit. The table also has balance, proportion, and rhythm.

FURNITURE SIZES

An important consideration to the sizing of furniture and cabinets is the size of the human body. A chair, for example, should be wide enough and the seat high enough from the floor to permit comfortable use. Base and wall cabinets in a kitchen must be of a size such that the counter is a comfortable height for working and the shelves in the wall cabinets can easily be reached. Typical sizes of furniture are shown in Table 2-2.

TABLE 2-2
Typical Sizes of Selected Furniture Units

Unit	Length	Width or depth	Height
Bed			
Twin	75 in. (1905 mm)	39 in. (990 mm)	
Double	75 in. (1905 mm)	54 in. (1371 mm)	
Queen	80 in. (2032 mm)	60 in. (1524 mm)	
King	80 in. (2032 mm)	76 in. (1920 mm)	
Bookshelves	30–36 in. (762–914 mm)	9–12 in. (18–25 mm)	36–42 in. (914–1066 mm)
Card table	34–35 in. (863–889 mm)	34–35 in. (863–889 mm)	30 in. (762 mm)
Coffee table			
Rectangular	30–60 in. (914–1524 mm)	18–24 in. (457–610 mm)	15–18 in. (380–457 mm)
Round	36 in. dia. (914 mm)		15–18 in. (380–457 mm)
Desk	48–72 in. (1219–1828 mm)	24–38 in. (609–965 mm)	28–30 in. (711–762 mm)
Dining table			
Rectangular	50–110 in. (1270–2794 mm)	30–42 in. (762–3046 mm)	28–30 in. (710–762 mm)
Round	42-in dia. (1066 mm)		28–30 in. (710–762 mm)
Dining chair	17 in. (430 mm)	17 in. (430 mm)	30–32 in. (762–812 mm)
Dresser			
Three-drawer	36–40 in. (914–1016 mm)	16–20 in. (406–508 mm)	30 in. (762 mm)
Double	56–58 in. (1422–1473 mm)	16–20 in. (406–508 mm)	30 in. (762 mm)
End table			
Rectangular	20–24 in. (508–609 mm)	12–14 in. (304–355 mm)	18–20 in. (457–508 mm)
Square	36 in. (914 mm)	36 in. (914 mm)	15–17 in. (381–431 mm)
Round	36-in. dia. (914 mm)		15–17 in. (381–431 mm)
Highboy	36 in. (914 mm)	18 in. (457 mm)	60–84 in. (1524–2133 mm)
Hutch	36–42 in. (914–1067 mm)	18–20 in. (457–508 mm)	60–72 in. (1524–1828 mm)
Lamp table	26 in. (660 mm)	22 in. (558 mm)	19 in. (482 mm)
Lowboy	30 in. (762 mm)	18 in. (457 mm)	30 in. (762 mm)
Occasional chair	33 in. (838 mm)	35 in. (889 mm)	35 in. (889 mm)
Sofa	62–75 in. (1574–1905 mm)	30–35 in. (762–889 mm)	29–36 in. (736–914 mm)
Table, informal dining	48–60 in. (1219–1524 mm)	36 in. (914 mm)	29 in. (736 mm)

FIGURE 2-25
When sketching, hold the pencil in a comfortable manner. Keep your fingers about 1 in. or more from the point. Notice that graph paper is being used.

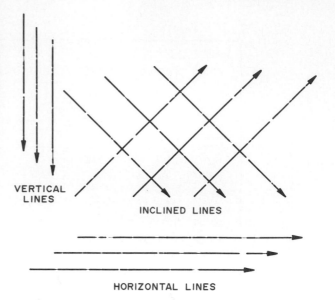

VERTICAL LINES

INCLINED LINES

HORIZONTAL LINES

FIGURE 2-26
A right-handed person will find it easiest to sketch lines in these directions. A left-handed person may find it easier to go in the opposite direction.

SKETCHING

Preliminary ideas can be developed quickly using sketching techniques. Sketches can be multiview or pictorial drawings.

Sketching techniques are rather simple. Use a soft lead pencil with a long point. Hold the pencil in a comfortable manner (Fig. 2-25). Lines are drawn in short strokes. The strokes do not have to touch. The lines should be kept reasonably straight but will not approach the quality of an instrument made drawing.

Right-handed people sketch horizontal lines easiest from left to right. They sketch vertical lines easiest from top to bottom. Slanting lines are best sketched as shown in Fig. 2-26.

Circles and arcs can be sketched by blocking in a square, drawing its diagonals and centerlines. Estimate the radius on the diagonals. Sketch the circle through the points (Fig. 2-27).

When sketching, turn the paper in any way to make it easier. Consider using graph paper. The printed lines help when sketching parallel lines, circles, and arcs.

Multiview drawings show views of the product by looking perpendicular to it from the various sides. Most products can be described by viewing them from the top, front, and one side (Fig. 2-28). The top view is always above the front view. In this position widths can project from one view to the other. The right-side view is to the right of the front view. Here the height projects between the views. Hidden features are shown with a dashed line. These same views are used when making carefully drawn scale or full-size furniture and cabinet drawings.

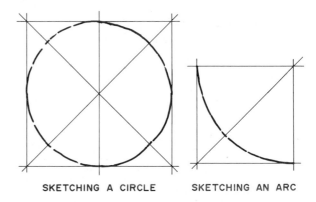

SKETCHING A CIRCLE   SKETCHING AN ARC

FIGURE 2-27
Sketch circles and arcs by blocking in a square and using it as a guide.

Two types of *pictorial drawings,* oblique and isometric are useful: An *oblique sketch* is made by drawing the front view in the same position as on a multiview drawing. Then sketch a box the size of the object with the depth on approximately a 45° angle. The depth is usually drawn one-half of true size. Then locate the features on the sides of the box and sketch them in place. Remember, lines parallel on the product will be parallel on the drawing. Circles in oblique are sketched by first making an oblique square and then drawing the circle inside (Fig. 2-29).

An *isometric sketch* is similar to the oblique except that the front view and side views are placed on approximately 30° angles. The depth is drawn the

FIGURE 2-28
Multiview drawing. The features project between the views.

actual size. Circles are drawn by first drawing an isometric square, then drawing the circle inside it. Graph paper with oblique and isometric grids is available. This makes the sketching much easier (Fig. 2-30).

DRAFTING PRACTICES IN THE WOOD PRODUCTS INDUSTRY

The wood products industry is divided into architectural woodwork, cabinets, fixture, and furniture production. *Architectural woodwork* includes such prod-ucts as doors and windows. *Cabinets* include such items as kitchen cabinets and bathroom vanities. *Fixtures* include such things as display shelving and merchandising display cabinets. *Furniture* includes household and office units, such as chairs, tables, and bedroom suites.

The basic drafting practices in these industries are the same as in other industries. The drafter should know how materials are processed and joined. Each company has drafting standards. The standards that follow are typical.

Full-size drawings are common. They are very large (Fig. 2-31). This drawing was reduced to fit in

1. DRAW THE FRONT VIEW.

DRAW LENGTH HALF OF TRUE SIZE

45°

2. BOX IN THE OVERALL SIZE OF THE PRODUCT.

3. LOCATE DETAILS

CIRCLES IN OBLIQUE

4. DARKEN VISIBLE LINES.

FIGURE 2-29
Oblique sketch. It is a quick way to make a pictorial view.

1. LAYOUT THE ISOMETRIC BOX THE OVERALL SIZE OF THE PRODUCT.

30°   30°

2. LAYOUT THE FRONT, SIDE AND TOP VIEWS.

3. DARKEN THE VISIBLE LINES

LAYOUT FOR ISOMETRIC CIRCLES

FIGURE 2-30
Isometric sketch. It produces a rather realistic pictorial view.

TOP VIEW

B-1 FRONT RAIL

B-6 TOP REAR RAIL

B-2 LOWER REAR RAIL

A-16 ARM RAIL

A-12 BACK LEG

CANVAS SLING

A-14 FRONT LEG

A-18 FOOT RAIL

FRONT VIEW IN SECTION

SIDE VIEW IN SECTION

FIGURE 2-31
This drawing was reproduced from a full-size furniture drawing. Each part is identified by a number. It shows the unit assembled. The outline of the upholstery is shown with a thin phantom line. Separate detail drawings are made of each part for use in production.

FIGURE 2-32
Typical production detail drawing. This is the front leg of the chair shown in
Figure 2-23.

FIGURE 2-33
Simple furniture drawing. Often, this will be drawn full size. Note that this is a
metric drawing.

FIGURE 2-34
Typical cabinet detail. These are often drawn full size. Sometimes construction
details are shown.

this book, but the original was full-size. This is a
production drawing. It shows the assembled unit
and identifies each part. It is a guide to assembling the complete unit after each part is mass produced.

Each part is drawn separately (Fig. 2-32). Detailed drawings, such as this, are completely dimensioned. Workers who produce the parts must make
them exactly as shown in the drawing. If they fail to
do so, the part will not fit and stall the assembly
operation.

A common type of drawing for simple furniture
is shown in Fig. 2-33. Here the front and side views
of a table are given. A top view would be needed if
the tabletop had an unusual shape. Because construction is simple, no sections are needed. An en-

larged detail of the leg is drawn. Patterns for curves
in the rails are laid out on a 10-mm grid. This drawing is a metric drawing. All dimensions are in millimeters.

Figure 2-34 shows a typical cabinet drawing.
Cabinet drawings generally are full size. To reduce
the size of the drawing, portions of the cabinets are
broken out. The dimensions show the actual size of
the finished unit.

Another type of furniture drawing is shown in
Fig. 2-35. The table is symmetrical (same on both
sides), so a partial front view is drawn. Because the
table has a drawer, sections are needed to show
drawer details.

The top view of the table is a special type of
drawing. The left half shows the wood top and the

FIGURE 2-35
This complex furniture drawing is actually several drawings in one. It shows
sections, elevations, and the top in place and removed.

BILL OF MATERIALS

NO. OF PIECES	PART NAME	MATERIAL	FINISHED SIZE			ROUGH SIZE		
			T	W	L	T	W	L

FIGURE 2-36
A bill of material provides information about each part of a product.

ROUTING SHEET

STOCK NO.	A-107		JOB NO.	26-173	TOLERANCE ± .10 ± $\frac{1}{64}$	
PCS IN ONE			ITEM NO.	10	SCALE: FULL SIZE	
PART	DRAWER GUIDE					
MAH		(OAK)		PLYWOOD		
CHERRY		BIRCH		PARTICAL BD		
WALNUT		S. MAPLE		HARDBOARD		

ROUGH SIZE	LENGTH	WIDTH	THICKNESS	NET SIZE	LENGTH	WIDTH	THICKNESS
	17	2	1		16½	1½	¾

ROUTING	CHECK OFF	
CUT	1	
FACE	3	
RIP	2	
STICK		
PLANE	4	
VENEER		
SIZE		
DADO	5	
SAND	6	

FIGURE 2-37
Typical routing sheet showing information needed by production to produce a single part.

direction of the grain. It also shows the rail and the drawers below the top as being visible even though they are really hidden. It really presents two visible views, one drawn over the other. The right half of the top view shows the tabletop removed. It also shows the details of the rail and the drawer.

STEPS IN DESIGNING FURNITURE AND CABINETS

1. In writing, clearly state the exact purpose the product is to serve.
2. List everything that relates to its use. This in-

STEPS IN DESIGNING FURNITURE AND CABINETS 41

cludes such things as size, weight, material, and color.

3. Now decide on the style. Will it be a traditional design or something contemporary?

4. Make some preliminary sketches or drawings. Reexamine decisions as to size and style. Refer to standards manuals and manufacturers' catalogs for the sizes of items to be a part of the product. Adjust until one or more possible solutions are developed.

5. It helps when designing complex products to build a scale model from cardboard. This gives a three-dimensional view.

6. Produce dimensioned working drawings. An assembly drawing will help to verify the sizes chosen for the individual parts.

7. Make final decisions on materials and hardware.

8. Prepare a bill of materials utilizing the drawings and material decisions (Fig. 2-36). The job is now ready for production. Some companies have the drafters prepare special routing drawings for each part (Fig. 2-37). These are used in the production of each part and follow the parts through the plant. It is easier for the worker to use a routing drawing than a full set of working drawings.

STUDY QUESTIONS

Answer each of the following questions. If you are not sure of an answer, review the chapter.

2-1. What factors must be considered as furniture is being designed?

2-2. How are function and structure related?

2-3. How does the design of a piece of furniture influence the manufacturing process?

2-4. What are the basic elements of design?

2-5. How does a circular arc differ from an irregular arc?

2-6. What is mass?

2-7. What shapes of planes are often used?

2-8. What is a person's reaction to a hard, smooth textured surface?

2-9. What are the primary and secondary colors?

2-10. What is meant by complementary colors?

2-11. What are the basic principles of design?

2-12. What is the difference between formal and informal balance?

2-13. What is dynamic symmetry?

2-14. How can you develop a rectangle that has pleasing proportions?

2-15. What two types of pictorial drawings are used to help visualize a product?

2-16. What type of drawings are made for use in the shop where the product is to be made?

2-17. What are the steps to follow to design a product?

IMPORTANT TECHNICAL TERMS

Following are technical terms that you should be able to use as part of your working vocabulary. Write a brief description of the meaning of each term.

Function
Structure
Mass
Texture
Primary colors

Secondary colors
Tertiary colors
Complementary colors
Analogous colors
Dynamic symmetry
Rhythm

Unity
Proportion
Balance
Oblique drawings
Multiview drawings
Isometric drawings

3

FURNITURE AND CABINET WOODS

It is the purpose of this chapter to present in brief form information about the solid woods used in the wood products industries.

THE STRUCTURE OF WOOD

A knowledge of the structure of wood is important to those who work with it. The cellular structure and

FIGURE 3-1
A tree begins with the sprouting of a small seed. (*Courtesy of St. Regis Paper Company.*)

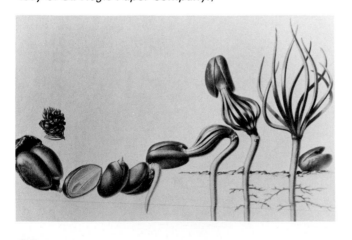

grain patterns determine to a large extent how it is machined, how parts are laid out on it, and how it is finished.

The life of a tree begins with the sprouting of a small seed (Fig. 3-1). As this small living plant develops, the characteristics associated with the wood in that species of tree are formed. A very small part of the tree is actually alive. The alive parts include the tips of the roots, the leaves, buds, flowers, seeds, and a thin layer of cells, called the cambium layer, which extends from the root tips to the buds (Fig. 3-2).

Each part of a tree has a specific function (Fig. 3-3). The *outer bark* provides the tree with a protective layer. Beneath it is the *inner bark* or phloem, through which food is passed to the rest of the tree. Next is the *cambium* layer, which produces new bark and new wood. The new wood produced, called the *sapwood*, serves as the pipeline to move water from the roots to the leaves. Beneath the sapwood is the *heartwood*, the central structural part of the tree. It is the mature wood which is dead. It has the color that is characteristic of the particular species of tree.

As a tree grows it adds new layers of wood in the spring and summer. The fast growth in the spring produces a light wood with large cells called

A large tree has hundreds of miles of roots to anchor it to the soil. But most of that length is dead, woody matter. At the very tips of the roots are living, growing cells that push a protective cap of dead cells through the soil. Just behind the tip are the roothairs, tiny, single-cell projections that absorb water and dissolved minerals from the soil, and start it on its way up to the leaves.

Extending from the tips of the roots to the ends of the branches is a single layer of living cells — the cambium layer. They are the only living cells in the trunk. In summer, when the tree grows, these cells divide continually — adding thickness but no height to the tree. The cells that form on the outside of the cambium layer become bark; those that form on the inside become wood.

The leaves — or needles, in coniferous trees — make sugar out of water passed up from the roots and carbon dioxide in the air. In doing this they utilize the energy of light, with the aid of chlorophyll. The sugar is passed back to the other living cells of the tree so that they can breathe — that is, combine the sugar with oxygen to create energy for the infinite processes of life which enable them to grow and develop.

The leaf buds on the twigs are alive, too. It is their growth that gives a tree height, and extends its branches. Cells at the base of the bud divide and elongate, building a new twig behind the developing leaf. This growth is coordinated with the growth in the cambium layer, so that as a tree grows in height, its trunk and its branches are all growing in thickness at the same time.

FIGURE 3-2
A tree has a living system extending from the roots to the leaves or needles. (*Courtesy of St. Regis Paper Company.*)

FIGURE 3-3
The tree trunk serves as the structural part of the tree as well as a pipeline to move water from the roots to the leaves. (*Courtesy of St. Regis Paper Company.*)

The outer bark is the protective outer layer. It develops from inside the tree.

The phloem is the outer layer of the cambium. It is the layer through which food is moved to all parts of the tree.

The xylem is the inner layer of the cambium. It produces new wood and new bark.

The sapwood moves water to the leaves.

The heartwood is the dead wood in the core of the tree. It gives the trunk strength.

Springwood is formed during a period of fast growth. It is lighter and has large cells so is softer.

Summerwood is formed because the growth is slower and smaller, darker cells are formed. It is very hard.

earlywood or spring wood. In the summer the rate of growth slows and the wood has smaller, darker cells. This band is called latewood or summer wood. A band of earlywood and latewood make up one growth ring. These rings can be seen when a tree is cut. The approximate age of a tree can be ascertained by counting the annual rings. One growth ring is usually added each year (Fig. 3-4).

SAWING LUMBER

Wood is cut to provide tangential, radial, and transverse surfaces. When a log is cut so that the annual rings are tangent with the face, it has a *tangential surface* and is called *plain or flat sawed*. This surface displays the highest figure in its grain pattern. When a board is cut so that the annual rings are at an angle of 45 to 90° to the face, it has a *radial surface* and is called *quarter sawed*. This is the most stable of all cuts of wood. The sides of the hard annual rings are exposed on the face of the board. When a log is cut on an angle of 35 to 45°, it is called *rift sawed*. It is a combination of plain sawed and quarter sawed (Fig. 3-5). The end grain of all three cuts expose the ends of the wood cells. This is called the *transverse surface.*

Softwoods are cut to get the most material from the log that is possible. The cuts are planed to get the various-size members that will produce the least waste. One example is shown in Fig. 3-6.

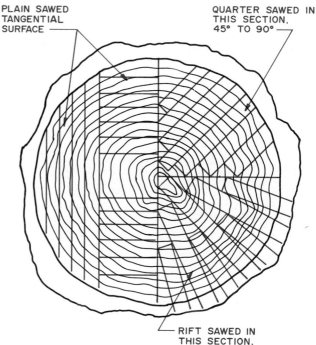

PLAIN SAWED TANGENTIAL SURFACE

QUARTER SAWED IN THIS SECTION. 45° TO 90°

RIFT SAWED IN THIS SECTION.

FIGURE 3-5
These are the ways boards are cut from the tree trunk.

HARDWOODS

Hardwoods come from *deciduous* trees (Fig. 3-7), which shed their broad leaves in the fall. They grow in the northern and southern parts of the United States. Hardwoods are used extensively in furniture and cabinet construction because of their strength

The bark is removed first.

When the log is squared the outer round slabs are cut off.

The outer part of the log has fewer knots. It is used for quality boards.

The inner part of the log has more knots. It is used for larger sizes.

FIGURE 3-6
Softwood is most generally used for construction, so the tree is cut to get the maximum number of standard-sized pieces from it. (*Courtesy of St. Regis Paper Company.*)

and great natural beauty. Most have a highly figured grain and resist dents and abrasion better than most softwoods.

Hardwood Grades

The grades of hardwood lumber are from highest to lowest, firsts, seconds, select, No. 1 common, No. 2 common, and No. 3A common, and No. 3B common.

Firsts and Seconds (FAS) is a combination of the best two grades which are combined for selling

purposes. The boards must be at least 6 in. (150 mm) wide and 8 ft (2440 mm) long. The poorest side yields 83% clear wood.

Select Grade must be at least 4 in. (200 mm) wide and 6 ft (1830 mm) long. The best side is as good as the FAS grade. The poorest side is permitted to have more defects.

No. 1 Common must be at least 4 in. (100 mm) wide and 2 ft long (610 mm) or 3 in. (75 mm) wide and 3 ft (915 mm) long. This is an excellent choice for furniture and cabinet work. It is lower in cost

HARDWOODS

SOFTWOODS

Hardwood is primarily decorative — or special wear & impact

Softwood primarily for structural use, with paneling grades

The Deciduous types which bear leaves that fall and that are replaced each season

The Coniferous types which bear needles that remain green the year round, sometimes called evergreen

FIGURE 3-7
The two classifications of trees are: deciduous and coniferous. (*Courtesy of Fine Hardwoods/ American Walnut Association.*)

than the higher grades and has at least 65% of the board clear.

Hardwoods are sold in random widths and lengths (RWL). Common thicknesses are listed in Table 3-1.

TABLE 3-1
Thicknesses of Hardwood Lumber

Nominal (rough) (in.)	Surfaced (S2S)	
	in.	Possible metric size (mm)
$\frac{3}{8}$	$\frac{3}{16}$	5
$\frac{1}{2}$	$\frac{5}{16}$	8
$\frac{5}{8}$	$\frac{7}{16}$	11
$\frac{3}{4}$	$\frac{9}{16}$	14
1	$1\frac{3}{16}$	21
$1\frac{1}{4}$	$1\frac{1}{16}$	27
$1\frac{1}{2}$	$1\frac{5}{16}$	33
$1\frac{3}{4}$	$1\frac{1}{2}$	38
2	$1\frac{3}{4}$	44
$2\frac{1}{2}$	$2\frac{1}{4}$	57
3	$2\frac{3}{4}$	70
$3\frac{1}{2}$	$3\frac{1}{4}$	82
4	$3\frac{3}{4}$	95

Source: National Hardwood Lumber Association.

SOFTWOODS

Softwoods come from coniferous or cone-bearing trees which retain their needle-shaped leaves all year. They grow mainly in the south and far western parts of the United States. Common softwoods include cedar, fir, pine, and redwood (Fig. 3-7).

Softwood Grades

Softwood lumber is divided into three size classifications: boards, dimension lumber, and timbers. Boards are used in furniture and cabinet construction.

The grades of softwood lumber from highest to lowest are select, common, factory, and molding.

Select grades are A, B, C, and D. Grades A and B are grouped together under a grade, B and Better. C Select is the second grade board and allows only a few tight pin knots. It is a top-quality paint board. D Select is the lowest select grade and can have obvious defects on the bad face.

Common grades run from No. 1 to No. 5. The higher the grade number, the more defects in the board. These are generally used for building construction work.

Factory grades are used to make doors and windows.

Molding boards are 1 in. (25 mm) and wider and 6 ft (1830 mm) or longer. They are used to manufacture molding.

Softwood lumber is sold in standardized sizes. The nominal size (size before planing) is used when ordering the material. When purchasing a board from a lumberyard you may order a 1 by 4. It will, however, measure $\frac{3}{4}$ by $3\frac{1}{2}$ in. (16 by 88 mm) because it has been planed to remove the saw marks. Standard widths and thicknesses for inch sizes with metric conversions are in Table 3-2.

IDENTIFYING HARDWOODS AND SOFTWOODS

There are several hundred different woods growing over the world. These vary considerably in their physical properties and color. Some are especially well suited for furniture and cabinet construction. Following are brief descriptions of the more popular woods used in the U.S. furniture and cabinet industry.

Selected Hardwoods

Red alder is light in weight compared to other hard woods. It has a fine texture and there is

TABLE 3-2
Standard Sizes of Softwood Lumber

	Thickness			Width	
Nominal (in.)	Dressed (in.)	Proposed dressed (mm)	Nominal (in.)	Dressed (in.)	Proposed dressed (mm)
1	$\frac{3}{4}$	16	2	$1\frac{1}{2}$	36
$1\frac{1}{4}$	$1\frac{1}{4}$	27	3	$2\frac{1}{2}$	62
$1\frac{1}{2}$	$1\frac{3}{8}$	40	4	$3\frac{1}{2}$	88
2	$1\frac{1}{2}$	36	5	$4\frac{1}{2}$	114
$2\frac{1}{2}$	2	50	6	$5\frac{1}{2}$	140
3	$2\frac{1}{2}$	62	8	$7\frac{1}{4}$	190
$3\frac{1}{2}$	3	76	10	$9\frac{1}{4}$	233
4	$3\frac{1}{2}$	88	12	$11\frac{1}{4}$	290

little contrast between the spring and summer wood. The heartwood is pale rose colored and the sapwood is lighter. It is easy to machine, stains easily, and is used to blend with more expensive woods.

Ash is heavy, hard, strong, and tough and is straight grained. It is open grained, machines well, and has excellent gluing properties. The sapwood is white and the heartwood is light tan. There are 18 species native to the United States. Of these, white ash is the best known. It can be stained or given a light or natural finish.

Basswood is one of the softest of the hardwoods. It is extremely soft, very light in weight, and pliable. It is used for furniture, picture frame moldings, toys, food containers, drawing boards, and foundry patterns. It is odorless and tasteless. It works easily with hand and power tools, glues well, and can be painted or stained. Basswood is light in color.

Yellow birch is a moderately heavy, hard, strong, close-grained cabinet wood. It has a variety of pleasing grain patterns. Sometimes it is difficult to machine but glues and stains easily. It is often stained with walnut or mahogany stain. Birch is widely used for furniture and cabinets. In color the sapwood is yellow-white and the heartwood is reddish brown.

Cherry is a moderately heavy, strong, close-grained wood that is moderately hard. It is easily worked and finishes well. For hundreds of years it has been a popular cabinet and furniture wood. It is becoming increasingly scarce. It has a rich, reddish heartwood and a figured grain. The sapwood varies from white to yellow-brown.

Cypress resists decay and insects. It is rather coarse in texture, nonporous, soft, light in weight, and stiff. The heartwood is used where the product is in contact with the elements, such as garden furniture, exterior house trim, and trellises. Cypress is pale brown to red in color.

Red gum is an important timber tree in the southern United States. It is one of the softer hardwoods and is strong. The wood is close grained and machines easily and finishes well. It is rated as only fair in stability. The heartwood is reddish brown and the sapwood an off-white. It is often used with more valuable woods such as walnut because it stains and finishes nicely. Much gum is used as outer veneer on plywood.

Honduras mahogany is imported from the tropical regions of Central and South America. It has been a popular cabinet wood for centuries. It has a moderate density and hardness that makes it easy to work. It turns and carves superbly. Mahogany is open grained and is beautifully figured. In color it ranges from a pale to medium reddish brown. It darkens with age.

African mahogany has much the same characteristics as those of genuine mahogany and is related botanically. The African mahogany has a more highly figured open grain and is not quite as good to work as genuine mahogany. It is a fine, first-rate cabinet wood.

Philippine mahogany is native to the Philippine Islands. It has a medium density and hardness and is easy to work. The pores are open and require a filler. There are several species making up the Philippine mahogany group. They range in color from dark red to light pink and are often sold with these color names. It is a fine cabinet wood and is also used to make trim, paneling, and molding.

Northern hard maple is a very hard, stiff, close-grained wood. It is odorless and tasteless and is therefore good for articles used with food. Accidental forms in the grain, called bird's-eye and curly maple, are prized for their unusual appearance. The heartwood is a very light tan and the sapwood is white. It is used in furniture and cabinet construction, woodware, and flooring.

Southern soft maple is really a moderately hard wood. It has medium density and strength. The machining and finishing properties are good and it is very stable. It is a close-grained wood, so does not require filling. The heartwood varies from pale tan to reddish gray. The sapwood is white. It is a very important wood in the manufacture of furniture.

Red oak is found over many parts of the United States. It is coarse textured, open grained, hard, and durable. It can be fairly hard to work. Red oak is used widely in the cabinet and furniture industries. Red oak is reddish brown.

White oak has a uniform strength, is close grained, and has good durability when exposed to weather. It is used in fine cabinet and furniture work and interior trim. It is somewhat difficult to work. White oak has a light brown color that can easily be bleached for furniture requiring a light natural finish.

Pecan/hickory are so closely related it is difficult to identify individual specimens. The wood is hard, heavy, elastic, and strong. The heartwood is light reddish brown and the sapwood is white. It machines well and steam bends nicely.

Yellow poplar is not actually related to the poplar species but to the magnolia family. It is a widely used hardwood because it is soft, straight grained, and easy to work. It can be stained to imitate walnut and mahogany. Because poplar is inexpensive it is frequently utilized for hidden structural parts in furniture and cabinets. The sapwood is light tan to white and the heartwood is yellow-tan.

Rosewood is imported from Asia, Central America, and Brazil. The wood is very hard and dense and has an open grain. When freshly cut it gives off a pleasant fragrance. The grain pattern is very irregular and beautiful. In color the heartwood is usually a deep reddish brown with black streaks. Since it is in limited supply it is usually used as veneer on plywood. It is used on the very best furniture manufactured.

Sycamore is our largest broadleaf tree. It has wood of medium density and is therefore a soft hardwood. It is close grained but has a coarse texture. The heartwood is pink to brownish pink and the sapwood is somewhat lighter.

Teak comes from Burma, India, Java, and Thailand. It is very dense and heavy and will not float. Teak can be worked fairly easily using carbide-tipped tools but will quickly dull ordinary tool-steel cutting devices. It has become one of the most prestigious imported hardwoods. It has a wide range of grain figures and is yellow-brown in color. Since it is expensive it is most often used as veneers on plywood.

North American walnut is one of the most prized American hardwoods. It has a wide range of beautifully figured grain patterns and a deep, rich, brown color. It is relatively hard, open grained, and easy to work. Walnut is durable, stable, easy to carve, and exceptionally nice to finish.

Willow is found in many species, but only the black willow produces trees of timber size. It is one of the softest of the hardwoods. It stains well and is often used to imitate walnut. The color of the heartwood varies from light gray to dark brown. The sapwood varies from white with a gray cast to light tan.

Zebrawood is found in Nigeria, West Africa, Gabon, and Cameroon. It is highly decorative, being light gold in color with narrow streaks of dark brown to black. It is hard and heavy and can be polished to high luster.

Samples of selected examples of these woods are shown in Fig. 3-8.

Selected Softwoods

Aromatic red cedar is not really a cedar but a juniper belonging to the cypress family. The lumber is narrow in width and knotty. The wood is light weight, soft, close grained, and is easily worked except around the knots. It is aromatic and is therefore in demand for cedar chests and clothes closet linings. It is normally left unfinished but can have transparent coatings, as varnish, to protect the natural color. The sapwood is white and the heartwood is reddish purple.

Western red cedar grows in a belt from southern Alaska to northern California. The wood is light in weight and very durable when exposed to the weather. It stains well and is easy to machine. The heartwood is reddish brown. It is used for shingles, windows, doors, tanks, and trim.

Ponderosa pine is used for reproduction of early American cabinets and furniture where small, sound knots are part of the classical appearance. Since it grows over a great part of the western United States, its characteristics differ. From some regions it can be a hardwood with a coarse texture. Grown in other places, it might be softer with a fine texture and grain. It is widely used for doors, windows, and millwork. Most of the time it is painted but can be stained or finished natural. In color it is usually a light tan with white sapwood.

Redwood is a softwood that resists decay and weathers extremely well. It is a softwood that is rather light in weight. It is easy to work and is generally left unfinished or stained. Outdoor furniture and decks are often made from redwood. It has a beautiful reddish color and pleasing grain figure.

KILN DRYING

Wood used in furniture and cabinet construction should have a moisture content of *6* to *8 percent* and must be kiln dried. *Kiln dried wood* is dried in large buildings called kilns, where moisture and temperatures are carefully controlled to reduce the moisture in the wood without causing it to check, split, or warp.

VENEERS

Veneer is a thin sheet of wood, usually about $\frac{1}{28}$ in. thick, which is glued to a base such as plywood or particleboard. It is an economical way of covering a large area with an expensive wood. This costs much less than using solid wood (Fig. 3-9, page 55).

Veneers are sold by the square foot. They are packed in a bundle called a *flitch*. The pieces of veneer in a flitch are stacked in the same order in which they were sliced from the log. The order is important when you want to match the grain on veneer strips used to make a wide panel.

Veneers of different grain patterns are produced by cutting them from different parts of the tree (Fig. 3-10, page 55). Veneer from the crotch contains swirls in the grain pattern. Stump wood produces a wavy grain pattern. Wartlike growths, called burls, have the most complex swirling pattern of all cuts. *Quarter-sliced veneers* are cut from the

Afrormosia   Aider   Apitong   Ash, brown

Ash, white   Balsa   Banak (virola)   Basswood, american

Beech, american   Birch   Butternut   Canalete

Cedar, aromatic red   Cedar, spanish   Cedar, western   Cherry

FIGURE 3-8
Selected wood samples. (*Courtesy of Frank Paxton Company.*)

Chestnut   Cocobolo   Cottonwood   Cypress

Damar Minyak   Ebony, black   Elm, american   Gum, unselected color

Hemlock, western   Imbuia   Koa   Korina®, Limba

Magnolia   Mahogany, african   Mahogany, genuine   Mahogany, philippine dark red

FIGURE 3-8 (*Continued*)

Mahogany	Mansonia	Maple, hard	Maple, soft
Oak, plain red	Oak, rift red	Oak, plain white	Obeche
Padauk	Pecan	Pine, parana	Pine, ponderosa
Pine, sugar white	Pine, yellow	Poplar	Pradu

FIGURE 3-8 (*Continued*)

Ramin

Redwood

Rosewood, brazilian

Rosewood, east indian

Sassafras

Satinwood, ceylon

Spruce, sitka

Sycamore, american

Teak

Tulipwood

Walnut, north american

Wenge

Willow

Zebrawood

Bird's-eye Figure

Burl Figure

FIGURE 3-8 (*Continued*)

FIGURE 3-9
Wood veneers are glued to less expensive woods.

nual growth ring. This produces figure characteristics similar to rotary- and plain-sliced veneer. A *rift-cut veneer* is produced in this way (Fig. 3-14).

Veneer Matching

When veneers are cut the grain patterns are matched in several ways. The most commonly used match is book matching. When *book matching*, every other sheet in a flitch is turned over just like the pages in a book. The back of one sheet meets the front of the next sheet. This produces a matching design along the joint (Fig. 3-15).

Slip matching places the sheets side by side repeating the figure (Fig. 3-15). This is often used with quarter-sliced veneers.

CROTCH

CROTCH FIGURE
(MAHOGANY)

BURL
AND
SWIRL

BURL FIGURE
(EUROPEAN)
(ASH)

HALF-ROUND,
SOFT-CUT
(WHITE)
(OAK)

PLAIN SLICED
GUMMY
CHERRY

SLICED
AND
QUARTERED

ROTARY
AND
HALF ROUND

FULL ROTARY
CHARACTER
MARKED
BIRCH

BUTT

BUTT FIGURE
(WALNUT)

QUARTER SLICED,
MOTTLED FIGURE
(MAHOGANY)

QUARTER
SLICED
(PIN KNOTTY)
(WALNUT)

FIGURE 3-10
The grain pattern of a veneer varies depending on the part of the tree from which it is cut. (*Courtesy of Fine Hardwoods/American Walnut Association.*)

bole (straight trunk). The trunk is first cut into quarters and the veneer cut from each quarter (Fig. 3-11). *Plain-sliced veneers* are also cut from the straight trunk. This trunk is sliced into veneers with large knives (Fig. 3-12). *Rotary-cut veneer* is produced by mounting a log in a veneer lathe and cutting a continuous sheet by feeding a knife into the log (Fig. 3-13). The log is literally unwound much like a roll of paper. *Semirotary slicing* sometimes called half-round slicing cuts across the an-

Random match involves placing sheets so that no repetitive pattern occurs. Sheets may be from several different logs (Fig. 3-16).

Vertical butt and horizontal book leaf match are used when the height of the sheets in a flitch are such that they do not produce the height needed (Fig. 3-16).

Three other matches are shown in Fig. 3-17. These include *diamond, reverse diamond,* and a *four-way center and butt.*

QUARTER SLICED

KNIFE ANGLE

FIGURE 3-11
Quarter-sliced veneers are cut from quartered sections of a log. (*Courtesy of Fine Hardwoods/American Walnut Association.*)

SEMI-ROTARY (HALF-ROUND)

KNIFE ANGLE

FIGURE 3-14
Semirotary-sliced veneers are made with half-round slicing cuts across the annual growth rings. (*Courtesy of Fine Hardwoods/American Walnut Association.*)

PLAIN SLICED

KNIFE ANGLE

FIGURE 3-12
Plain-sliced veneers are cut from the straight sections of the trunk. (*Courtesy of Fine Hardwoods/American Walnut Association.*)

Veneer Matching
BASIC MATCHING EFFECTS

BOOK MATCH   SLIP MATCH

FIGURE 3-15
Book-matched and slip-matched veneers. (*Courtesy of Fine Hardwoods/American Walnut Association.*)

ROTARY

KNIFE ANGLE

FIGURE 3-13
The log is "unpeeled" to form rotary-cut veneers. (*Courtesy of Fine Hardwoods/American Walnut Association.*)

Veneer Matching
BASIC MATCHING EFFECTS

RANDOM MATCH   VERTICAL BUTT AND HORIZONTAL BOOK LEAF MATCH

FIGURE 3-16
Veneer matching: random match and vertical butt and horizontal book lead match. (*Courtesy of Fine Hardwoods/American Walnut Association.*)

DIAMOND

REVERSE
DIAMOND

FOUR-WAY CENTER
AND BUTT

FIGURE 3-17
Veneer matching: diamond, reverse diamond, and four-way center butt. (*Courtesy of Fine Hardwoods/American Walnut Association.*)

"V"

HERRINGBONE

SUNBURST PATTERN

FIGURE 3-18
Veneer matching: vee, herringbone, and sunburst. (*Courtesy of Fine Hardwoods/American Walnut Association.*)

V and herringbone matches are popular. They are especially interesting on large surfaces. A special sunburst pattern is used on tabletops (Fig. 3-18).

ORDERING LUMBER

Solid lumber is sold by the board foot. A board foot is equal to a piece 1 in. thick by 1 ft square. It contains 144 in.³. Stock that is less than 1 in. thick is figured as 1-in. lumber. Board feet is figured on the size of the stock before it was surfaced (the nominal size). For example, a 2-in.-thick piece of hardwood when surfaced is 1¾ in. The board feet would be figured on the 2-in. thickness.

Large quantities of lumber are priced per 1000 board feet. The Roman numeral M stands for 1000 and is used to designate this quantity. For example, 1000 board feet at $1500 per M is worth $1500. Divide this by 1000 and the cost per board foot is found to be $1.50 per board foot.

Board feet when the length of the board is in inches can be found with either of the following formulas:

$$\frac{\text{thickness (in.)} \times \text{width (in.)} \times \text{length (in.)}}{144} = \text{bd.ft.}$$

The board feet when the length of the board is in feet can be found with the following formula:

$$\frac{\text{thickness (in.)} \times \text{width (in.)} \times \text{length (ft.)}}{12} = \text{bd.ft.}$$

STUDY QUESTIONS

Answer each of the following questions. If you are not sure of an answer, review the chapter.

3-1. What parts of a tree are actually alive?

3-2. What purpose does the inner bark serve?

3-3. What is the difference between sapwood and heartwood?

3-4. How are the annual rings formed?

3-5. What are the ways a tree can be cut to provide different surface appearances?

3-6. What kind of wood do we get from deciduous trees?

3-7. What are the grades of hardwoods?

3-8. In what sizes are hardwoods sold?

3-9. How can you identify a coniferous tree?

3-10. What grades of softwoods are used for building construction?

3-11. What factors do you consider when you attempt to identify the species of a board?

3-12. From what part of the world do we import Honduras mahogany?

3-13. What softwood is used when making reproductions of early American furniture?

3-14. What is the recommended moisture content for woods used for furniture and cabinet construction?

3-15. What is the thickness of a veneer?

3-16. In what quantities are veneers packed?

3-17. What are some of the ways veneers are matched as they are glued to the substrate?

3-18. What is the unit used to sell solid lumber?

3-19. How many board feet are in a piece 2 in. × 10 in. × 12 ft.?

IMPORTANT TECHNICAL TERMS

Following are technical terms that you should be able to use as part of your working vocabulary. Write a brief description of the meaning of each term.

Bark
Sapwood
Heartwood
Plain sawed

Quarter sawed
Rift sawed
Deciduous trees
Coniferous trees
Hardwoods
Softwoods
Kiln drying
Flitch
Board foot

4

PLYWOOD

Plywood is a manufactured panel widely used when building furniture and cabinets and in construction and industrial applications. It is a very strong product and does not split. Since it is made by joining alternating plies of veneer and in some cases solid wood layers, it resists warping better than solid wood. It is especially useful when large, flat surfaces are required, such as a tabletop or desktop or side panels (Fig. 4-1).

CONSTRUCTION OF PLYWOOD

Plywood is a panel made by gluing together layers of wood, with the grain in each ply perpendicular to the ply below it. A panel always has an odd number of plies; three, five, seven, or nine. Each ply may be a single thickness of veneer or two veneers glued together to form a thicker ply. In this case the grain in these two plies runs in the same direction.

The most common plywood constructions are with a veneer core, lumber core, particleboard core, and medium-density fiberboard core (Fig. 4-2). A *veneer-core* panel typically has three to nine veneer plies. It is the strongest of all panel cores. A *lumber-core panel* has many strips of lumber glued together,

FIGURE 4-1
Hardwood plywood is used extensively in furniture and cabinet construction. (*Courtesy of Fine Hardwoods/American Walnut Association.*)

forming the core and two veneer crossbands on each side. It is often used for cabinet doors where the edge will be exposed. *Particleboard and medium-density fiberboard-core* plywood have a single sheet of one of these as the core, with one veneer sheet glued on each side. These are discussed in detail in Chapter 5.

LUMBER CORE PLYWOOD

VENEER CORE PLYWOOD

PARTICLEBOARD,
COMPOSITE,
MEDIUM DENSITY
FIBERBOARD OR
HARDBOARD CORE

HARDWOOD PLYWOOD

The standards for hardwood plywood are reported in ANSI/HPMA HP 1983, American National Standard for Hardwood and Decorative Plywood. These standards are published by the Hardwood Plywood Manufacturers Association, P.O. Box 2789, Reston, VA 22090.

Grades of Veneers in Hardwood Plywood

Hardwood plywood is manufactured with six grades of veneers. These grades with their identifying symbols are listed in Table 4-1.

TABLE 4-1 Hardwood Veneer Grades	
Grade	Symbol
A grade	A
B grade	B
Sound grade	2
Industrial grade	3
Backing grade	4
Specialty grade	SP

A Grade (A) is the best. The face is made of hardwood veneers carefully matched as to color and grain. This grade is sometimes called *premium*.

B Grade (B) is suitable for a natural finish, but the face veneers are not as carefully matched as on the A grade. This grade is sometimes called *good*.

Sound grade (2) provides a face that is smooth. All defects have been repaired. It is used as a smooth base for a paint finish.

Industrial-grade (3) face veneers can have surface defects. This grade permits knotholes up to 1 in. (25 mm) in diameter, small open joints, and small areas of rough grain.

Backing grade (4) uses unselected veneers having knotholes up to 3 in. in diameter and certain types of splits. Any defect permitted does not affect the strength of the panel.

Specialty grade (SP) includes veneers having characteristics unlike any of those in the other grades. The characteristics are agreed upon between the manufacturer and the purchaser. For example, species such as wormy chestnut or bird's-eye maple are considered as Specialty Grade.

Veneer requirements for softwoods used in hardwood plywood panels are also specified in ANSI/HPMA HP 1983.

FIGURE 4-2
Common types of plywood construction.

Species Used in Hardwood Plywood

A wide range of species of wood are used in hardwood plywood. These are shown in Table 4-2. These species are divided into four categories, A, B, C, and D. The categories reflect the modulus of elasticity (stiffness) of each species. These data are used when

Detailed specifications for each type are in ASNI/HPMA HP 1983. Some of the major requirements are listed in Table 4-4.

Technical type hardwood plywood must withstand a three-cycle boil-shear test. Type I must withstand a two-cycle boil test. A boil test involves following standard procedures in which a sample is

---

TABLE 4-2
Categories of Commonly Used Decorative Species in Hardwood Plywood[a]

Category A	Category B	Category C	Category D
Ash, white	Ash, black	Alder, red	Aspen
Apitong	Avodire	Basswood, American	Cedar, eastern red
Beech, American	Birch, paper	Butternut	Cedar, western red
Birch, yellow, sweet	Cherry, black	Cativo	Fuma
Bubinga	Cypress	Chestnut, American	Willow, black
Hickory	Elm, rock	Cottonwood, black	
Kapur	Fir, Douglas	Cottonwood, eastern	
Keruing	Fir, white	Elm, American (gray,	
Oak (Oregon, red, or	Gum, sweet	red, or white)	
white)	Hemlock, western	Gum, black	
Paldao	Magnolia, cucumber	Hackberry	
Pecan	Sweetbay	Hemlock, eastern	
Rosewood	Maple, sugar (hard)	Lauan	
Sapele	Mahogany, African	Maple, red (soft)	
	Mahogany, Honduras	Maple, silver (soft)	
	Maple, black (hard)	Meranti, red	
	Pine, western white	Pine, ponderosa	
	Poplar, yellow	Pine, sugar	
	Spruce, red, Sitka	Pine, eastern white	
	Sycamore	Prima-vera	
	Tanoak	Redwood	
	Teak	Sassafras	
	Walnut, American	Spruce (black, Engelmann,	
		white)	
		Tupelo, water	

Source: Hardwood Plywood Manufacturers Association.
[a] Based on an evaluation of published modulus of elasticity (MOE) and specific gravity values.

---

establishing the maximum thickness of the veneer. The maximum veneer thickness is listed in Table 4-3.

The species for the *face* of a panel can be any hardwood species. If the face veneer is to be a decorative face, it could be any of the softwood species listed in Table 4-2. The species of the back and inner plies may be any hardwood or softwood species.

Types of Hardwood Plywood

The four types of hardwood plywood listed in decending order of water-resistance capability are:

Technical (exterior)

Type I (exterior)

Type II (interior)

Type III (interior)

boiled for 4 hours, dried, boiled again, and cooled in cold water. The technical type is tested for shear. Type I is examined to see if the veneers have separated. Any separation over 1 in. (25 mm) is a failure. Basically, this is a test of the glue bond. These panels can be designed to carry very large loads and are actually structural panels.

TABLE 4-3
Thicknesses for Hardwood
Plywood Veneer

Category	Maximum veneer thickness (in.)
A	$\frac{1}{12}$
B	$\frac{1}{8}$
C	$\frac{3}{16}$
D	$\frac{3}{16}$

TABLE 4-4
Specifications for Hardwood Plywood

	Technical (exterior)	Type I (exterior)	Type II (interior)	Type III (interior)
Glue bond	Waterproof	Waterproof	Water resistant	Water resistant
Veneer edge joints	No tape	No tape	Tape	Tape
Grade of lumber core	Not suitable	Specify	Specify	Specify
Particleboard or hardboard core	Not suitable	Specify	Specify	Specify

Type II panels must withstand a three-cycle soak test, and type III a two-cycle soak test. The soak test involves immersing samples in 75°F (24°C) water for 4 hours and drying them and resoaking. After the last cycle the sample is examined to see if the veneers have started to separate. A separation greater than 2 in. (50 mm) is a failure.

Construction of Hardwood Plywood

The construction of hardwood plywood is based on the type of core. Following are the standard constructions:

Hardwood veneer core: has an odd number of plies, such as 3-ply, 5-ply, and so on.

Softwood veneer core: has an odd number of plies, as 3-ply, 5-ply, and so on.

Hardwood lumber core: used in 3-ply, 5-ply, and 7-ply constructions.

Softwood lumber core: used in 3-ply, 5-ply, and 7-ply constructions.

Particleboard core: used in 3-ply and 5-ply constructions.

Medium-density fiberboard core: used in 3-ply construction.

Hardboard core: used in 3-ply construction.

Special cores: used in 3-ply construction. Special cores are those made of any other material than those listed above.

Sizes and Thicknesses of Hardwood Plywood

The thickness of the *veneers* varies with the intended use. These are specified in the standard. They range from $\frac{1}{12}$ to $\frac{1}{8}$ in. (2 to 3 mm). Face veneers on decorative plywood are usually $\frac{1}{80}$ in. (0.3 mm).

Hardwood plywood is made in *panels* 48 × 84 in., 48 × 96 in., and 48 × 120 in. The 48 × 96 in. is the most popular size and often is the only available size. Metric sizes have not been established, but the 48 × 96 in. panel will probably be 1200 × 2400 mm. Other sizes can be had by special order.

Standard thickness for veneer-core panels are $\frac{1}{4}$ in (6 mm), $\frac{3}{8}$ in. (9 mm), $\frac{1}{2}$ in. (12 mm), and $\frac{3}{4}$ in. (18 mm). Lumber-core and particleboard-core panels are generally only $\frac{3}{4}$ in. (18 mm) thick.

Product Identification

Hardwood plywood is manufactured to specifications provided by the Hardwood Plywood Manufacturers Association. The panel specifications are indicated with a grade stamp. It identifies the glue bond, the product standard under which it is manufactured, the structural description, the species of wood, the flame spread rating (the lower the number, the slower the flame spread or the more fire resistant), the mill number, and the veneer grade of the face (Fig. 4-3). The backstamp used on the back of prefinished hardwood plywood wall panels is shown in Fig. 4-4. It indicates the flame spread rating as well as formaldehyde emission requirements. The backstamp used on prefinished particleboard panels is shown in Fig. 4-5.

FIGURE 4-3
Grade stamp used on hardwood plywood sold to the furniture industry. (*Courtesy of Hardwood Plywood Manufacturers Association.*)

HARDWOOD PLYWOOD MANUFACTURERS ASSOCIATION		
FORMALDEHYDE EMISSION 0.2 PPM CONFORMS TO HUD REQUIREMENTS LAY UP 16 3.6MM THICK HP-SG-84	SIMULATED DECORATIVE FINISH ON PLYWOOD hpma ® MILL SPECIALTY GRADE	FLAME SPREAD 200 OR LESS ASTM E84 GLUE BOND TYPE II ANSI/HPMA HP 1983

FIGURE 4-4
Backstamp used on sheets of prefinished hardwood plywood wall panels. (*Courtesy of Hardwood Plywood Manufacturers Association.*)

HARDWOOD PLYWOOD MANUFACTURERS ASSOCIATION		
FORMALDEHYDE EMISSION 0.3 PPM CONFORMS TO HUD REQUIREMENTS	hpma ® MILL	FLAME SPREAD 200 OR LESS ASTM E84 SIMULATED DECORATIVE FINISH ON **PARTICLEBOARD**

FIGURE 4-5
Backstamp used on sheets of prefinished particleboard wall panels. (*Courtesy of Hardwood Plywood Manufacturers Association.*)

Industrial panels used by furniture manufacturers are shipped in large bundles. Rather than stamp each panel, a bundle grade stamp is used (Fig. 4-6). These panels will most likely be cut up into smaller sizes required for furniture and cabinet construction.

hpma ® FORMALDEHYDE EMISSION 0.3 PPM AT 0.13 LOADING STANDARDIZED TO 77°F FTM 2 - 1983
UNFINISHED INDUSTRIAL PANEL
TYPE II BOND ANSI/HPMA HP 1983 MILL NUMBER

FIGURE 4-6
The grade stamp used on bundles of hardwood plywood shipped to furniture and cabinet manufacturers. (*Courtesy of Hardwood Plywood Manufacturers Association.*)

MILL (NUMBER)

FLAME SPREAD 200 OR LESS ASTM E162

ON ALL EXPOSED CABINET SURFACES

FIGURE 4-7
This grade stamp is used on hardwood plywood used in the manufacture of kitchen cabinets. (*Courtesy of Hardwood Plywood Manufacturers Association.*)

Hardwood plywood used in kitchen cabinets for mobile homes and conventional houses must meet flame spread ratings set by ASTM E162. All exposed parts of the cabinets must have a flame spread rating of 200 or less (Fig. 4-7). Manufacturers are also meeting the HUD requirements for formaldehyde emissions in cabinets as well as wall panels. See the requirements shown in Fig. 4-6.

Molded Plywood

Molded, curved, or cut to size, hardwood plywood has taken a major place in furniture manufacturing. It is used in many areas, such as in chair backs, seats, legs, arms, stretches, body-shaped parts, and supports. The furniture manufacturer sends to the ply-

FIGURE 4-8
Bent and molded plywood is widely used in furniture construction. This chair and ottoman are made with molded plywood. The legs on the coffee table are also molded plywood. (*Courtesy of Hardwood Plywood Manufacturers Association.*)

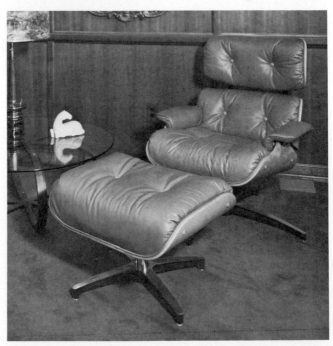

wood manufacturer a drawing of the shape desired and the grade and species of veneers wanted. The hardwood plywood manufacturer then uses molds to produce the desired parts. Bent plywood is used in place of bent solid wood frames in overstuffed furniture (Fig. 4-8). This produces a strong, light frame.

CONSTRUCTION AND INDUSTRIAL PLYWOOD

The requirements for the manufacture of plywood for construction and industrial uses are specified in U.S. Product Standard PS 1-83 for Construction and Industrial Plywood. The Office of Product Standards Policy of the National Bureau of Standards works with producers, distributors, consumers, and users (as American Plywood Association) to develop these voluntary product standards.

Although this type of plywood is used mainly for construction and industrial purposes, some types are used for hidden parts of furniture and cabinets.

Grades of Veneers in Construction and Industrial Plywood

The outer veneers are classified in five *appearance groups,* N, A, B, C, and D. N is the best and D is the lowest (Table 4-5). Panel grade designations for interior-type plywood are given in Table 4-6.

Species Used in Construction and Industrial Plywood

About 70 species of softwoods and hardwoods are used. They are divided into five groups depending on their strength and stiffness. Group 1 includes those species that are the strongest and stiffest, while Group 5 species have the lowest ratings (Table 4-7). The front and back plies can be from any of the five groups. When they are made of more than one piece,

TABLE 4-6
Panel Grade Designations for Interior-Type Grades

| Panel grade designation | Minimum veneer quality | | | Surface |
	Face	Back	Inner plies	
N-N	N	N	C	Sanded 2 sides
N-A	N	A	C	Sanded 2 sides
N-B	N	B	C	Sanded 2 sides
N-D	N	D	D	Sanded 2 sides
A-A	A	A	D	Sanded 2 sides
A-B	A	B	D	Sanded 2 sides
A-D	A	D	D	Sanded 2 sides
B-B	B	B	D	Sanded 2 sides
B-D	B	D	D	Sanded 2 sides

Source: American Plywood Association.

TABLE 4-5
Veneer Grades

N	Smooth surface ''natural finish'' veneer. Select, all heartwood or all sapwood. Free of open defects. Allows not more than 6 repairs, wood only, per 4 x 8 panel, made parallel to grain and well matched for grain and color.
A	Smooth, paintable. Not more than 18 neatly made repairs, boat, sled, or router type, and parallel to grain, permitted. May be used for natural finish in less demanding applications.
B	Solid surface. Shims, circular repair plugs and tight knots to 1 inch across grain permitted. Some minor splits permitted.
C Plugged	Improved C veneer with splits limited to 1/8-inch width and knotholes and borer holes limited to 1/4 x 1/2 inch. Admits some broken grain. Synthetic repairs permitted.
C	Tight knots to 1-1/2 inch. Knotholes to 1 inch across grain and some to 1-1/2 inch if total width of knots and knotholes is within specified limits. Synthetic or wood repairs. Discoloration and sanding defects that do not impair strength permitted. Limited splits allowed. Stitching permitted.
D	Knots and knotholes to 2-1/2 inch width across grain and 1/2 inch larger within specified limits. Limited splits are permitted. Stitching permitted. Limited to Interior (Exposure 1 or 2) panels.

Source: American Plywood Association.

TABLE 4-7
Classification of Species

Group 1	Group 2	Group 3	Group 4	Group 5
Apitong	Cedar, Port	Alder, Red	Aspen	Basswood
Beech,	Orford	Birch, Paper	Bigtooth	Poplar,
American	Cypress	Cedar, Alaska	Quaking	Balsam
Birch	Douglas	Fir,	Cativo	
Sweet	Fir 2[a]	Subalpine	Cedar	
Yellow	Fir	Hemlock,	Incense	
Douglas	Balsam	Eastern	Western	
Fir 1[a]	California	Maple,	Red	
Kapur	Red	Bigleaf	Cottonwood	
Keruing	Grand	Pine	Eastern	
Larch,	Noble	Jack	Black	
Western	Pacific	Lodgepole	(Western	
Maple, Sugar	Silver	Ponderosa	Poplar)	
Pine	White	Spruce	Pine	
Caribbean	Hemlock,	Redwood	Eastern	
Ocote	Western	Spruce	White	
Pine, South.	Lauan	Engelmann	Sugar	
Loblolly	Almon	White		
Longleaf	Bagtikan			
Shortleaf	Mayapis			
Slash	Red			
Tanoak	Tangile			
	White			
	Maple, Black			
	Mengkulang			
	Meranti,			
	Red[b]			
	Mersawa			
	Pine			
	Pond			
	Red			
	Virginia			
	Western			
	White			
	Spruce			
	Black			
	Red			
	Sitka			
	Sweetgum			
	Tamarack			
	Yellow-			
	Poplar			

(a) Douglas Fir from trees grown in the states of Washington, Oregon, California, Idaho, Montana, Wyoming, and the Canadian Provinces of Alberta and British Columbia shall be classed as Douglas Fir No. 1. Douglas Fir from trees grown in the states of Nevada, Utah, Colorado, Arizona and New Mexico shall be classed as Douglas Fir No. 2.

(b) Red Meranti shall be limited to species having a specific gravity of 0.41 or more based on green volume and oven dry weight.

Source: American Plywood Association.

each piece should be of the same species. Inner plies of Groups 1, 2, 3, or 4 panels may be of any species in Groups 1, 2, 3, or 4. Inner plies of Group 5 panels may be any species listed.

Types of Construction and Industrial Plywood

These plywoods are made in two types, interior and exterior. Following is a description of each.

Interior type bonded with interior glue. These panels are intended for interior applications.

Interior type bonded with intermediate glue. These panels are used where they will be pro-tected from the elements but may be exposed to high humidity or possible water leakage. This bonding is identified as Exposure 2.

Interior type bonded with exterior glue. These panels are used where they will be protected but where they may be exposed to the elements due to long construction delays or other severe conditions. This bonding is identified as Exposure 1.

Exterior type. These panels will retain their glue bond when repeatedly wetted and dried. This bonding is identified as Exposure 1.

Exposure 1 glues are used where exposure to moisture for long periods is severe. Exposure 2 glues are used where the panel will be protected when the construction is finished but will be exposed during construction.

There are. other construction and industrial panels that will not find much use in furniture and cabinet construction. Most notable of these are the Performance Rated Panels. These panels are manufactured to provide known load-carrying capacities. There are five performance-rated panels: plywood, composite, waferboard, oriented strand board, and structural particleboard (Fig. 4-9). *Plywood* panels are made from all-veneer cross laminations. *Composite* panels have a core of reconstituted wood with a face and back veneer ply. *Waferboard* is a panel made of large, waferlike flakes of wood randomly or directionally oriented. *Oriented strand board* is a panel of compressed strandlike particles arranged in layers (three to five) oriented at right angles to each other. *Structural particleboard* is a panel comprised of small particles arranged in layers by particle size but not oriented. Table 4-8 lists the panel construction specifications for interior-type plywood.

Sizes and Thicknesses of Construction and Industrial Plywood

Construction and industrial plywood is available in panel widths of 36, 48, and 60 in. (914, 1219, and

TABLE 4-8 Plywood Panel Specifications		
Thickness (in.)	Minimum number of plies	Minimum number of layers
Through $\frac{3}{8}$	3	3
Over $\frac{3}{8}$ through $\frac{1}{2}$	4	3
Over $\frac{1}{2}$ through $\frac{7}{8}$	5	5
Over $\frac{7}{8}$	6	5

1524 mm), and lengths from 60 to 144 in. (1524 to 3658 mm) in 12-in. (305-mm) increments. Other sizes are available on special order.

Standard thicknesses of sanded panels range from $\frac{1}{8}$ through $1\frac{1}{4}$ in. (3 through 31 mm) in $\frac{1}{8}$-in. (3-mm) increments. Unsanded panels range from $\frac{5}{16}$ to $1\frac{1}{4}$ in. (8 to 31 mm) in increments of $\frac{1}{8}$ in. (3 mm) for thicknesses over $\frac{3}{8}$ in. (10 mm).

Product Identification

The following trademarks for construction and industrial plywood are from the American Plywood Association. The *sanded grades* are most likely to be used in furniture and cabinet construction. The trademark for sanded grades includes the grade of

APA Performance-Rated
Panel Composition/Configurations

PLYWOOD
All-veneer panels consisting of an odd number of cross-laminated layers, each layer consisting of one or more plies. Many such panels meet all of the prescriptive or performance provisions of U.S. Product Standard PS 1-83/ANSI A199.1 for Construction and Industrial Plywood. Others may include panel constructions, grades and species not currently recognized in PS 1.

COMPOSITE (COMPLY®)
Panels of reconstituted wood cores bonded between veneer face and back plies.

WAFERBOARD
Panels of compressed wafer-like particles or flakes randomly or directionally oriented.

ORIENTED STRAND
BOARD
Panels of compressed strand-like particles arranged in layers (usually three to five) oriented at right angles to one another.

STRUCTURAL
PARTICLEBOARD
Panels comprised of small particles usually arranged in layers by particle size, but not usually oriented.

FIGURE 4-9
Five types of APA Performance-Rated panels. (*Courtesy of American Plywood Association.*)

veneer on the face and back, the species group number, the type of plywood, the number of the mill producing the plywood, and the product standard followed in making it. The *unsanded grades* are the Performance Rated Panels. Specialty panels include products such as exterior plywood siding. Examples of these trademarks are in Fig. 4-10.

SPECIALTY PLYWOODS

In addition to the plywood products manufactured under the specifications of PS 1-83 and ANSI/HPMA HP 1983, other special products are available.

Overlaid plywood is a high-grade panel of exterior-type plywood that has bonded to one or both

How to read the basic trademarks of the American Plywood Association

Product Standard PS 1-83 is a performance standard for clear understanding between buyer and seller. To identify plywood manufactured by association member mills under the requirements of Product Standard PS 1-83, four types of trademarks and one typical edge mark are used to illustrate the plywood's type, grade, group, class, and Span Rating. Here's how they look together with notations on what each element means.

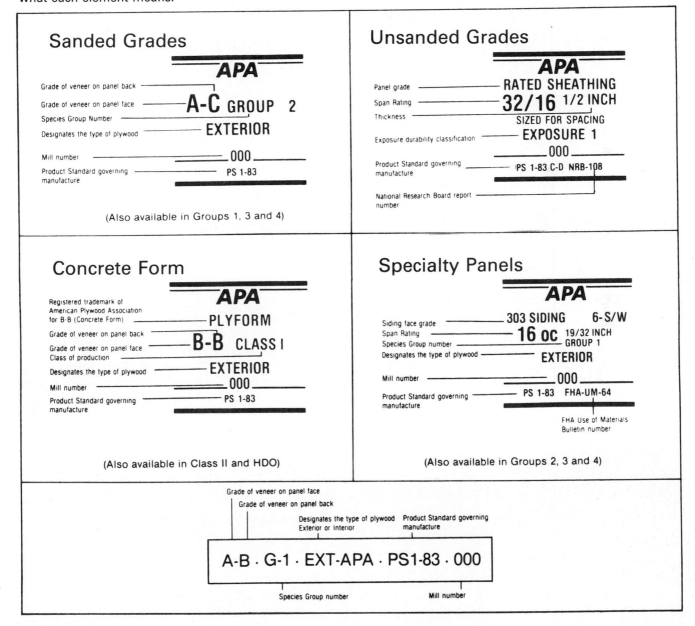

FIGURE 4-10
Basic trademarks of the American Plywood Association. (*Courtesy of American Plywood Association.*)

faces a resin-impregnated fiber sheet. It is available in high density and medium density. *High density* has a hard, smooth chemically resistant surface. It requires no additional finishing. It is available in several colors. It can be painted. *Medium density* has a smooth, opaque, nonglossy surface that hides the grain. It is used where a high-quality paint finish is desired.

Siding panels are used on the exterior of residential and commercial buildings. They are available in a variety of surface finishes, such as a grooved surface, rough-sawed surface, or with a striated design.

Paneling is a prefinished plywood product used on interior walls. Most panels are hardwoods, although some softwoods, such as knotty pine, are available. They are made in a variety of surface textures, such as V-groove, striated, and relief grain.

WORKING WITH PLYWOOD PANELS

Cutting

Plywood can be cut with any saw used to cut solid wood. It is important to prevent the veneer on the good face from chipping as it is cut. Always use a sharp, fine-toothed saw. To cut by hand, use a 10-point crosscut-type handsaw. Cut with the good face up. Support the panel below so that it does not sag.

When using a power circular saw, use a combination or hollow-ground blade, alternating-tip bevel carbide tipped blade, or specialized plywood blade. When using a table saw, keep the good face up. If there is splintering, it will be the bottom face. When cutting with a portable circular saw or radial arm saw, place the good face down. If splintering does occur, it can be reduced by applying masking tape on the face or scoring the face veneer with a sharp knife.

FIGURE 4-11
When drilling or boring through plywood back up the sheet with scrap stock.

Drilling or Boring Holes

Holes in plywood can be drilled or bored using the same tools as for solid wood. It is very important to bore through into a piece of scrap wood to keep the lower veneer from chipping (Fig. 4-11).

Planing

When necessary to plane the edges of plywood, work from each end toward the center. This prevents splitting that occurs if you plane off the ends. Because plywood is difficult to plane, cut the panel to exact size whenever possible.

ORDERING PLYWOOD

Plywood is normally available in sheets 4 ft × 8 ft. A sheet contains 32 ft². Plywood is priced per square foot. If it sells for 80 cents a square foot, a sheet would cost $25.60. The difference in thickness is taken care of by the price per square foot. For example, ¾-in.-thick material will cost more per foot than that ¼ in. thick.

STUDY QUESTIONS

Answer each of the following questions. If you are not sure of an answer, review the chapter.

4-1. How does plywood differ from solid wood?
4-2. What are the types of construction used for plywood?
4-3. What type of plywood construction is often used for cabinet doors?
4-4. Where can you find the standards for the manufacture of hardwood plywood?
4-5. What are grades of veneers used on hardwood plywood?

4-6. What are the maximum veneer thicknesses for the four categories used to identify hardwood veneers used in plywood?

4-7. What are the four types of hardwood plywood?

4-8. What is the boil test?

4-9. What is the soak test?

4-10. What are the standard panel sizes of hardwood plywood?

4-11. What are the standard thicknesses of veneer-core hardwood plywood?

4-12. What information is shown on the hardwood grade stamp?

4-13. What is the required flame spread rating for exposed surfaces of cabinets?

4-14. What furniture parts are made of molded plywood?

4-15. What is the standard that specifies the manufacturing requirements for construction plywood?

4-16. What are the appearance groups for the outer veneer on construction plywood?

4-17. What are the five groups into which wood species are divided for use in construction plywood?

4-18. What is the difference between the five groups?

4-19. What is the difference between sheets of construction plywood marked exposure 1 and exposure 2?

4-20. For what purposes are the sanded grades of plywood generally used?

4-21. What is an overlaid plywood?

4-22. When cutting plywood on a circular saw, which way does the good side face?

4-23. In what unit is plywood priced?

IMPORTANT TECHNICAL TERMS

Following are technical terms that you should be able to use as part of your working vocabulary. Write a brief description of the meaning of each term.

Core
HPMA
Boil test
Soak test
Flame spread
PS 1-83
Appearance groups
Species groups
Exposure 1
Exposure 2
Composite panels

5

RECONSTITUTED WOOD PANELS

There are a number of different types of reconstituted wood panels that find extensive use in furniture and cabinet construction. These panels include plywood, hardboard, medium-density fiberboard, particleboard, and waferboard. Plywood and related products are discussed in Chapter 4.

HARDBOARD

Hardboard is made from wood chips converted into fibers which are permanently bonded under heat and pressure into a panel. The wood fibers are bonded by their natural lignin and synthetic binders. Other materials are added to improve certain properties as stiffness, hardness, finishing properties, resistance to abrasion and moisture, and to increase strength and durability. Different hardboards have various fiber formulations that enable the product to be used for a wide variety of purposes.

Hardboard is made by chipping wood and wood residues into a chip about the size of your thumbnail. These are cooked under heat and pressure to soften and dissolve some of the natural resin in the wood. They are then reduced to fibers by building up pressure to a high level and then suddenly releasing it. This causes the chips to explode into fiber bun-

dles. These are then shredded into fibers by grinding and the additives needed are added.

The formation of the fibers into a mat can be wet or dry. In the *wet process* the watery pulp flows onto a screen and the water is drawn off through the screen. The mat is run through rollers removing more water. It is then loaded into a press.

In the *dry process* the fibers are rather dry before they are laid on a screen using air instead of water. These are loaded into a press.

The mats are placed in a press under heat of 380 to 550°F (193 to 288°C) and pressure of 500 to 1500 psi (3447 to 10 342 kPa). This welds the fibers back together, producing a product having characteristics unattainable in natural wood.

Hardboard is used for furniture and cabinet backs, drawer bottoms, dust panels, and other applications. It is also manufactured into products such as exterior siding, signs, wall paneling, and cabinet tops.

Hardboard is harder than most natural woods, and since it has no grain, it has nearly equal properties in all directions. It is not as stiff or as strong as natural wood along the grain, but is substantially stronger and stiffer than wood across the grain.

Standards for the manufacture of hardboard products include ANSI/AHA A135.4-1982, Basic

Hardboard; ANSI/AHA A135.5-1982, Prefinished Hardboard Paneling; and ANSI/AHA A135.6-1984, Hardboard Siding.

Hardboard is available in five classes, Tempered, Standard, Service-Tempered, Service, and Industrialite. Data on surface finish thickness and physical properties by class are in Table 5-1.

Class 1: Tempered. It is impregnated with siccative material, and stabilized by heat and spe-cial additives to impart substantially improved properties of stiffness, strength, hardness, and resistance to water and abrasion, as compared with the Standard Class.

Class 2: Standard. It is the form of the material as it comes from the press. It has high strength and water resistance.

Class 3: Service-Tempered. It is impregnated with siccative material, and stabilized by heat

TABLE 5-1
Classification of Hardboard by Surface Finish, Thickness, and Physical Properties

Class	Nominal thickness (in.)	Water resistance (max. av. per panel) Water absorption based on weight (%)	Thickness swelling (%)	Modulus of rupture (min. av. per panel) (psi)	Tensile strength (min. av. per panel, psi) Parallel to surface	Perpendicular to surface
1 Tempered	$\frac{1}{12}$	30	25			
	$\frac{1}{10}$					
	$\frac{1}{8}$	25	20			
	$\frac{3}{16}$			6000	3000	130
	$\frac{1}{4}$	20	15			
	$\frac{5}{16}$	15	10			
	$\frac{3}{8}$	10	9			
2 Standard	$\frac{1}{12}$	40	30			
	$\frac{1}{10}$					
	$\frac{1}{8}$	35	25			
	$\frac{3}{16}$			4500	2200	90
	$\frac{1}{4}$	25	20			
	$\frac{5}{16}$	20	15			
	$\frac{3}{8}$	15	10			
3 Service-tempered	$\frac{1}{8}$	35	30			
	$\frac{3}{16}$	30	30	4500	2000	75
	$\frac{1}{4}$	30	25			
	$\frac{3}{8}$	20	15			
4 Service	$\frac{1}{8}$	45	35			
	$\frac{3}{16}$	40	35			
	$\frac{1}{4}$	40	30			
	$\frac{3}{8}$	35	25			
	$\frac{7}{16}$	35	25			
	$\frac{1}{2}$	30	20			
	$\frac{5}{8}$	25	20	3000	1500	50
	$\frac{11}{16}$	25	20			
	$\frac{3}{4}$					
	$\frac{13}{16}$					
	$\frac{7}{8}$	20	15			
	1					
	$1\frac{1}{8}$					
5 Industrialite	$\frac{1}{4}$	50	30			
	$\frac{3}{8}$	40	25			
	$\frac{7}{16}$	40	25			
	$\frac{1}{2}$	35	25			
	$\frac{5}{8}$	30	20			
	$\frac{11}{16}$	30	20	2000	1000	25
	$\frac{3}{4}$					
	$\frac{13}{16}$					
	$\frac{7}{8}$	25	20			
	1					
	$1\frac{1}{8}$					

Source: American Hardboard Association.

and additives. Its properties are substantially better than Service Grade.

Class 4: Service. It is basically the same form as it comes from the press but has less strength than Standard Class.

Class 5: Industrialite. It is a medium-density hardboard that has moderate strength and lower unit weight than the other classes.

Standard thickness and manufacturing tolerances are shown in Table 5-2. Hardboard is available in thicknesses from $\frac{1}{12}$ to $1\frac{1}{8}$ in. It is available with one or two sides smooth. A panel with one side smooth will have a textured or screened back. This is utilized when the panel is glued to another surface. The most used panel size is 4 × 8 ft. (1219 × 2438 mm) though widths from 2 to 5 ft (610 to 1524 mm) and lengths from 4 to 16 ft. (1219 to 4877 mm) are available on special order.

Class	Number and color or stripes
Tempered	1 Red
Service Tempered	2 Red
Standard	1 Green
Service	2 Green
Industrialite	1 Blue

FIGURE 5-1
The classes of hardboard panels are indicated by colored stripes on the edges.

TABLE 5-2 Thickness Tolerances for Hardboard Panels	
Nominal thickness (in.)	Thickness tolerance (min.–max., in.)
$\frac{1}{12}$ (0.083)	0.070–0.090
$\frac{1}{10}$ (0.100)	0.091–0.110
$\frac{1}{8}$ (0.125)	0.115–0.155
$\frac{3}{16}$ (0.188)	0.165–0.205
$\frac{1}{4}$ (0.250)	0.210–0.265
$\frac{5}{16}$ (0.312)	0.290–0.335
$\frac{3}{8}$ (0.375)	0.350–0.400
$\frac{7}{16}$ (0.438)	0.410–0.460
$\frac{1}{2}$ (0.500)	0.475–0.525
$\frac{5}{8}$ (0.625)	0.600–0.650
$\frac{11}{16}$ (0.688)	0.660–0.710
$\frac{3}{4}$ (0.750)	0.725–0.775
$\frac{13}{16}$ (0.812)	0.785–0.835
$\frac{7}{8}$ (0.875)	0.850–0.900
1 (1.000)	0.975–1.025
$1\frac{1}{8}$ (1.125)	1.115–1.155

Source: American Hardboard Association.

Basic hardboard is identified by a colored vertical strip which indicates the class of the board (Fig. 5-1).

Working with Hardboard

Hardboard can be worked with standard woodworking tools. If much work is to be done, carbide-tipped cutting tools are recommended. Since there is no grain, the material can be worked in any direction without splitting. Cut edges can be smoothed by sanding or jointing. Faces of panels are very smooth and need no sanding. When drilling, bore from the best face and into a piece of scrap wood to reduce chipping out the back surface.

MEDIUM-DENSITY FIBERBOARD (MDF)

This material is manufactured under ANSI A208.2-1980, which was developed cooperatively by the American Hardboard Association and the National Particleboard Association. Medium-Density fiberboard has moderate strength and lower unit weight than other types of hardboard products.

It is widely used for interior paneling, doors, jambs, cabinets, moldings, interior stair treads, custom cabinet work, and shelves. It is frequently printed with a simulated wood grain for use in commercial furniture and cabinets. The recommended shelf spans for various thicknesses and loads are listed in Table 5-3. A shelf span is the distance between supports such as between bulkheads or partitions. To find the uniform load on the shelf, divide the probable load it will carry by the square footage of the shelf. Using this figure, read across the columns in the chart.

Medium-density fiberboard has smooth flat surfaces and tight edges that can be painted or finished without filling. It has excellent impact strength, is free from knots and voids, and has good screw-holding capacity. It can be worked with standard woodworking tools and does not splinter or chip.

TABLE 5-3
Maximum Shelf Spans for Medium-Density Hardboard or Fiberboard
(in inches for uniform loading)

LOAD	End supported Maximum span			Multiple supports Maximum span			Over hanging shelf Maximum overhang		
	1/2	5/8	3/4	1/2	5/8	3/4	1/2	5/8	3/4
50.0	15	19	23	20	25	30	7	9	10
45.0	16	19	23	21	26	32	7	9	11
40.0	16	20	24	22	27	33	7	9	11
35.0	17	21	25	23	28	34	8	10	12
30.0	18	22	27	24	30	38	8	10	12
25.0	19	23	28	25	32	38	9	11	13
20.0	20	25	30	27	34	40	9	12	14
17.5	21	26	31	28	35	42	10	12	14
15.0	22	27	33	30	37	44	10	13	15
12.5	23	29	34	31	39	48	11	13	18
10.0	25	31	37	33	41	49	11	14	17
7.5	27	33	39	38	45	53	12	15	18
5.0	30	37	43	40	49	58	14	17	20

(Column note: Thicknesses of MDF Shelf — Maximum Span in Inches)

Source: National Particleboard Association.

MDF can be nailed in place by driving nails through it. It will not hold nails. When fastening with screws, drill a shank hole through the panel. Thinner panels, as a cabinet back, can be joined to the cabinet with staples. Thicker types of fiberboard will hold screws such as for hinges. Drill a small pilot hole and use sheet metal screws.

MDF will take any of the commonly used finishes. Use the sealer or undercoat recommended by the manufacturer of the finish to be used.

PARTICLEBOARD AND WAFERBOARD

Particleboard is made from wood chips, water, and a synthetic resin binder. The resulting mixture is formed into thick mats which are placed in a heated press. The press applies approximately 1000 psi (6894.7 kPa) forming the panel. The panel is conditioned, sanded, and cut into standard sizes.

Particleboard is generally sold in panels 4 ft wide and 8 ft long and in thicknesses from $\frac{1}{8}$ to 2 in. The most commonly used thicknesses are $\frac{3}{8}, \frac{1}{2}, \frac{5}{8}$, and $\frac{3}{4}$ in. (10, 13, 16, and 19 mm). Panels are generally marked with a stamp giving the manufacturer's name, ANSI Standard 208.1, the grade, density in pounds per cubic foot, and the thickness in fractions of an inch. For example, ANSI 208.1, 1-H-1, 45, $\frac{5}{8}$ in. Type 2 panels are also marked "Exterior Bond."

Particleboard is available in two grades, 1 and 2. *Type 1, Interior* uses a urea-formaldehyde resin as the bonding agent, which is water resistant and for interior use. *Type 2, Exterior* uses a phenol-formaldehyde resin as the bonding agent, which is waterproof and for exterior use (Table 5-4).

Each grade is divided into density ranges. The grades containing the letter H are higher densities

TABLE 5-4
Grades of Particleboard

Type 1 interior	Type 2 exterior
1-H-1	2-H-1
1-H-2	2-H-2
1-H-3	2-H-3
1-M-1	2-M-1
1-M-2	2-M-2
1-M-3	2-M-3
1-L-1	2-M-W
	2-M-F

Source: National Particleboard Association.

(50 lb per cubic foot and over), M (indicates intermediate densities (37 to 50 lb per cubic foot), and L, lower densities (below 37 lb per cubic foot).

There are four types of particleboard. The *singlelayer* type is the most commonly used and is widely used in construction for underlayment on floors. The *threelayer* type has outer layers made of fines, which are fine wood particles. This produces a panel with a smooth surface suitable for printing. It is also used for doors and tops that are covered with plastic laminates. The *graded density* type is the most expensive and has the smoothest surface and highest density of all four types. It is used for the tops in expensive furniture. The fourth type is *extruded*. It is the least expensive and is commonly used for furniture backs.

Recommended uses for the interior grades, type 1, are shown in Table 5-5.

TABLE 5-5 Recommended Uses for Type 1 Particleboard	
Grade	Use
Shelving	1-M-1
	1-M-2
	1-M-3
Countertops	1-M-2
(with plastic	1-M-3
laminates)	
Kitchen cabinets	1-M-1
(sides, backs, shelves,	1-M-2
front panels)	
Door core	1-L-1
Moldings (vinyl covered)	1-M-3

Working with Particleboard

Particleboard can be worked with standard woodworking tools. If much work is done, carbide-tipped cutting tools are recommended.

Particleboard can be edge banded with solid wood. This can be glued to the particleboard with a butt joint, but it is stronger to use a joint as a tongue and groove or spline. Plastic laminates, veneers, and vinyls can be bonded to particleboard with contact cement (Fig. 5-2).

The nail-holding power of particleboard is less than solid wood. The use of annular threaded nails is recommended. The use of sheet metal screws with

FIGURE 5-2
This library table is constructed of particleboard covered with plastic laminate. (*Courtesy of Worden Company.*)

very small pilot holes is much stronger. There are special screws made just for use with particleboard (Fig. 5-3).

If particleboard is to be painted, enameled, or have a transparent finish, it is recommended that a filler and sealer be applied first.

Waferboard is an exterior grade of particleboard and is used for wall and roof sheathing, single-layer floors, siding, soffits, and other external applications. It is generally made from large thin wafers of aspen.

Particleboard and waferboard are manufactured to the standard ANSI A208.1-1979, Mat-Formed Wood Particleboard.

FIGURE 5-3
Special screw designed for use in particleboard.

A SPECIAL-PURPOSE SCREW DESIGNED FOR USE IN PARTICLE BOARD.

Answer each of the following questions. If you are not sure of an answer, review the chapter.

5-1. How is hardboard made?

5-2. What is the difference between the wet and dry processes for making hard-board?

5-3. How much heat and pressure are used to weld the fibers in hardboard to-gether?

5-4. What parts of furniture and cabinets are made from hardboard?

5-5. What are the five classes of hardboard?

5-6. What are some important uses for medium density fiberboard?

5-7. What are the four types of particleboard?

5-8. What is the least expensive type of particleboard?

5-9. Where is waferboard generally used?

5-10. What is the difference between type 1 and type 2 particleboard?

5-11. What information is in the grade stamp used on particleboard?

IMPORTANT TECHNICAL TERMS

Following are technical terms that you should be able to use as part of your working vocabulary. Write a brief description of the meaning of each term.

Hardboard
Wet process
Dry process
Medium-density fiberboard
Particleboard
Waferboard

6

HARDWARE AND OTHER PRODUCTS

The selection of the hardware for a product is important to its overall appearance and operation. Hardware should reflect the style of the furniture. For example, Colonial furniture should have hardware designed for that period. It should be of good quality, resist rust and tarnish, and be free of surface blemishes and other defects.

KNOBS AND DRAWER PULLS

Drawers and doors are opened with knobs and pulls (Fig. 6-1). Wood, metal, and porcelain *knobs* are held to the door or drawer front with a screw or bolt (Fig. 6-2). *Pulls* may be held with one or two bolts or screws. Some have a metal escutcheon behind the pull (Fig. 6-3).

HINGES

There are many types of hinges available for use on furniture and cabinets. Some are surface mounted and add to the decorative appearance (Fig. 6-4). Others are designed so that they are hidden or almost entirely hidden (Fig. 6-5). Some of the com-

FIGURE 6-1
A wide variety of drawer knobs are available. (*Courtesy of Amerock Corporation, an Anchor Hocking Company.*)

CRYSTAL

CHROME

WOOD

BRASS

PORCELAIN

FASTENED WITH A
WOOD SCREW THRU
THE KNOB.

THREADED FASTENER
IS PART OF THE KNOB.

FASTENED WITH
A WOOD SCREW
TYPE FASTENER.

FASTENED WITH
A BOLT.

FIGURE 6-2
Drawer knobs are mounted with screws or bolts.

FIGURE 6-4
These surface mounted hinges are part of the overall design of this cabinet. Note the decorative pulls on the door and drawer.

FIGURE 6-5
The hinges on this door are hidden. They are spring loaded and open when the door is pushed inward. No pulls or knobs are needed.

PITCHER
PULL

RING
PULL

PULL WITH ESCUTCHEON

FIGURE 6-3
Pulls are designed to blend with the style of furniture.

monly used hinges are shown in Fig. 6-6. Additional types of hinges and installation details are described in Chapter 13.

FIGURE 6-6
These are a few of the many types of hinges available. (*Courtesy of Amerock Corporation, an Anchor Hocking Company.*)

LOCKS, HASPS AND CATCHES

A variety of locks, catches and hasps are available (Figs. 6-7 and 6-8). They serve a functional as well as a decorative purpose. Those that are brass should be mounted with brass screws or escutcheon pins.

DRAWER AND SHELF HARDWARE

There are a variety of metal and plastic *drawer slides* available. It is a good idea to select the type you are going to use before starting a project so that the correct support and spacing is provided (Fig. 6-9). Additional information is given in Chapter 14. Shelves can be permanently installed in a cabinet or be made adjustable by using one of the several types

FIGURE 6-7
Most commonly used door catches. (*Courtesy of Amerock Corporation, an Anchor Hocking Company.*)

DRAWER LOCK

ORNAMENTAL HASP

FIGURE 6-8
Some furniture units use drawer locks or hasps for security.

FIGURE 6-9
Metal and plastic drawer slides provide stick-free, easy-sliding drawers. (*Courtesy of Amerock Corporation, an Anchor Hocking Company.*)

METAL CHANNELS ON EACH SIDE OF THE DRAWER RUN ON ROLLERS IN CHANNEL FASTENED TO SIDES OF THE CABINET.

A CENTER TRACK DRAWER GUIDE WITH THREE NYLON ROLLERS.

A CENTER TRACK DRAWER GUIDE WITH A NYLON ROLLER.

FIGURE 6-10
Adjustable shelves are held on metal clips set in perforated standards. (*Courtesy of Knape and Vogt Manufacturing Co.*)

TAPER PIN PRESSED IN HOLE AND GLUED.

CAST ZINC PIN

PLASTIC

CAST PLASTIC

RUBBER

NICKLE-PLATED STEEL

NICKLE-PLATED STEEL

TYPICAL FURNITURE GLIDES

FIGURE 6-11
Furniture glides are placed on the legs of furniture to protect the leg and the floor.

of *shelf hardware* available (Fig. 6-10). More information on shelf construction is presented in Chapter 15.

The bottoms of the legs of furniture are protected with some type of glide or caster. Glides are nailed into the bottom of the leg or set in holes bored in the end of the leg (Fig. 6-11). Casters of various types are available (Fig. 6-12). Base elevators are used to raise a cabinet or adjust it so that it is level (Fig. 6-13). Ferrules are tapered metal collars that fit over the ends of legs (Fig. 6-14).

DRAWER AND SHELF HARDWARE   **79**

FIGURE 6-12
Castors are used on heavier furniture units. (*Courtesy of H'a'fele America, 203 Feld Ave., High Point, NC 27261.*)

FIGURE 6-14
Ferrules are used to keep the ends of wood legs from splitting.

FIGURE 6-13
This base elevator allows a furniture unit to be leveled or adjusted to sit without rocking on an irregular floor. (*Courtesy of H'a'fele America, 203 Feld Ave., High Point, NC 27261.*)

FIGURE 6-15
Preformed fiber seat used on antique chairs. (*Courtesy of The Woodworkers' Store.*)

OTHER PRODUCTS

A variety of mass-produced wood products are available for furniture construction. Preformed fiber seats made of a special fiber and polymer are strong and tough. They are used on antique chairs (Fig. 6-15). Another material for chair seats is cane. There are many varieties and sizes of cane. It is available in prewoven sections or unwoven strands (Fig. 6-16).

Intricate reproductions of period hand-carved patterns are available in the form of mass-produced wood fiber carvings. These carvings are glued to the product or attached with brads. They will take stain and filler and can be matched to any project. An-

other product, carved pulls, are made from solid walnut, oak, or cherry (Fig. 6-17).

Inlays are popular on tables, vanities, fancy boxes, and other furniture units. There are a wide variety of inlays available in an assembled condition. They are $\frac{1}{20}$ in. thick.

Other inlay material is sold in strips (Fig. 6-18). They are installed by routing a groove the desired width and slightly shallower than the thickness of the inlay. Then the material in the groove is glued. Additional information is available in Chapter 21.

There are many other products available for use by the furniture manufacturer or craftsman. For

FIGURE 6-16
This chair has a handwoven cane seat.

FIGURE 6-17
There are many carvings and decorative overlays available for application to drawers and doors. (*Courtesy of The Woodworkers' Store.*)

FIGURE 6-18
Some of the inlay strips available. (*Courtesy of The Woodworkers' Store.*)

example, a wide variety of special moldings, both straight and curved, is available. Various wood turnings, such as table legs and spindles, are sold. Mechanisms for items such as salt-and-pepper grinders, coffee mills, music boxes, and clocks are in great variety. In addition, clock dials of various designs and periods are readily available (Fig. 6-19).

PLASTIC LAMINATES

Cabinets and tabletops are often covered with plastic laminates. A plastic laminate is made of five to seven layers of kraft paper treated with a phenolic resin. A printed layer of kraft paper is applied to the top, which gives the sheets its color and pattern. A translucent topcoat of melamine is applied over the top laminate to form a hard surface.

FIGURE 6-19
This clock face is one of many special products available for use when building wood products. (*Courtesy of The Woodworkers' Store.*)

Plastic laminates are available in a wide variety of patterns and colors. Solid colors, wood grains, and other patterns are available.

The grade of plastic laminates applies to the thickness of the material. Most countertops are made with *general grade,* which is $\frac{1}{16}$ in. (2 mm) thick. Walls and cabinet fronts and sides are usually covered with $\frac{1}{32}$-in. (1-mm)-thick plastic laminates. Additional information is available in Chapter 21.

UPHOLSTERY FABRICS

The finished fabric covering on upholstered furniture can be from a variety of materials. Common fibers in fabrics include cotton, rayon, silk, wool, and nylon. Some fabrics are a combination of several fibers. Plastic, artificial leather, and genuine leather are also used. Additional information is available in Chapters 48 to 50.

CABINET ACCESSORIES

Hardware manufacturers have available a wide array of accessories. These include items such as wood and plastic trays, wire racks for storage of lids, utensils and other items, lazy susans, trays, and units for storage of silverware. These accessories greatly improve the efficiency of the use of cabinet space (Fig. 6-20).

In Fig. 6-21 are shown accessories that increase the efficiency of storage space. The built-in wire baskets have overhanging edges at the top that slide in U-shaped channels fastened to the inside of the cabinet bulkhead. The steel baskets have been surface treated so that any type of material can be stored. The spice racks screw to the inside of cabinet doors, utilizing space that is usually wasted. The pull-out cupboard is equipped with a support frame onto which the wire storage components are fastened. These components include bread baskets, bottle baskets, laundry and cleaning agent baskets, lid racks, and similar storage units.

CONTOURED SHELF

WIRE LID RACK AND WOOD TRAYS

FULL ROUND SHELF

PIE-CUT SHELF

FIGURE 6-20
These shelving and tray units enable lost space in a cabinet to be effectively used. (*Courtesy of Amerock Corporation, an Anchor Hocking Company.*)

Side section

Slid in | Extended

Vertical adjustment | Front panel | Cupboard carcase

Top shelf

1100 to 1250

A

390 | 500

Shelf

Bottom

Dimensions in mm

PULL-OUT CUPBOARD UNIT

A

375 | 55

190

200 | 55

420

320 | 55

420

375 | 55

420

320

475

66

Dimensions in mm

SPICE RACKS

BUILT-IN WIRE BASKETS

FIGURE 6-21
These are a few of the accessories available that can be used to increase the storage capacity and efficiency of kitchen cabinets. (*Courtesy of H'a'fele America, 203 Feld Ave., High Point, NC 27261.*)

CABINET ACCESSORIES **83**

Answer each of the following questions. If you are not sure of an answer, review the chapter.

6-1. What factors do you consider when selecting hardware?

6-2. What are some of the commonly used hinges?

6-3. Why should you select the metal drawer slides to be used before starting to make the product?

6-4. What hardware is available for making shelves adjustable?

6-5. What is a furniture glide?

6-6. How do glides and casters differ?

6-7. What grade of plastic laminate is used on countertops?

6-8. What types of accessories for furniture and cabinets are available?

IMPORTANT TECHNICAL TERMS

Following are technical terms that you should be able to use as part of your working vocabulary. Write a brief description of the meaning of each term.

Knobs
Pulls
Hinges
Locks

Catches
Hasps
Drawer slides
Glides
Casters
Base elevators
Ferrules
Inlays
Plastic laminate

7

FASTENERS

Nails and screws are commonly used fastening devices. They are made in a variety of sizes and types. In addition to these, there are many other special-purpose fasteners. A knowledge of fasteners is important to the skilled craftsman and designer.

NAILS

The most commonly available nails are box, common, casing, and finishing (Fig. 7-1). Box and common nails are used in building construction and find limited use in furniture and cabinet construction. Casing nails are designed for the installation of interior trim in buildings. They are much like a finish-

FIGURE 7-2
The length of nails is given by their penny (d) size.

ing nail but are larger in diameter and have a cone-shaped head. The finishing nail is frequently used in furniture and cabinet construction. It is a slender nail with a small head. It is used where it will not be seen or where the head can be set below the surface of the wood and covered with a filler.

The length of nails is indicated by their *penny size* (Fig. 7-2). The small letter d is the symbol used for penny. For example, a 4d nail is a four-penny

FIGURE 7-1
Common kinds of nails.

COMMON

BOX

CASING

FINISH

BRAD

nail which is $1\frac{1}{2}$ in long. The penny and inch sizes of finishing nails are listed in Table 7-1.

A *wire brad* is another nail often used. It looks much like a finishing nail but is smaller. It is made in lengths of $\frac{1}{2}$ to $1\frac{1}{2}$ in. It is sold by length given in inches and by the diameter given by a gauge number.

TABLE 7-1
Finishing Nail Sizes

Penny size	Inch size	Approximate number of nails per pound
3d	$1\frac{1}{4}$	850
4d	$1\frac{1}{2}$	575
6d	2	300
8d	$2\frac{1}{2}$	192
10d	3	122

Joining with Nails

For most cabinet work, finishing nails are used. They are driven with a 13-oz curved claw hammer. Brads are driven with a 7-oz hammer. A typical application is nailing a cabinet back to the side (Fig. 7-3). For production work a pneumatic gun can rapidly drive these fasteners (Fig. 7-4).

Wood is joined by face nailing, slant nailing, and toenailing. Face nailing means driving the nail perpendicular to the wood. It does not have the holding power of slanted nailing (Fig. 7-5). When a butt joint is nailed, it can be straight nailed or toenailed

FIGURE 7-3
Finishing nails are commonly used in furniture and cabinet work. (*Courtesy of American Plywood Association.*)

FIGURE 7-4
Various types of nails and staples are power driven. (*Courtesy of Senco Fastening Systems.*)

HOLDING POWER IS INCREASED WHEN THE NAILS ARE SLANTED IN OPPOSITE DIRECTIONS.

FIGURE 7-5
Holding power is increased by slanting the nails.

A BUTT JOINT CAN BE TOENAILED

FIGURE 7-6
Butt joints can be joined by toenailing.

(Fig. 7-6). Finishing nails are either nailed flush with the surface or the head is set with a nail set. The head is covered with a filler (Fig. 7-7).

Generally, nails should be placed $\frac{3}{4}$ in. from the

SET THE FINISHING
NAIL. HIDE THE HEAD
WITH FILLER.

FIGURE 7-7
Nails can be hidden by setting the head and filling the hole.

edge of solid wood boards. If they are closer, a hole slightly smaller than the nail should be drilled. This will prevent splitting but may reduce the holding powers slightly (Fig. 7-8). You can usually nail a little closer to the edge of plywood than to solid wood. A major advantage of pneumatic fasteners is that they greatly reduce the tendency to split without diminishing the holding power.

FIGURE 7-8
When nailing close to the edge, drill a hole slightly smaller than the nail. (*Courtesy of American Plywood Association.*)

POWER STAPLING AND NAILING

There are many types of power stapling and nailing tools available. They are designed to use pressurized air to drive fasteners. These fasteners are available with a variety of heads and body sizes (Fig. 7-9).

FIGURE 7-9
Power-operated staplers and nailers: (A) staples for skid and case assembly; (B) brad tool for casegoods and subassembly; (C) coil nailers for casebacks and skids; (D) stapler for upholstery; (E) case clamp tool; (F) stapler for subassembly, casebacks, and drawer assembly. (*Courtesy of Bostitch, East Greenwich, RI 02818.*)

This varies from driving brads up to $1\frac{3}{4}$ in. long to small pin tacking machines. The machine in Fig. 7-10 works off a wire coil. It can be adjusted to cut a pin from $\frac{1}{4}$ to 1 in. in length, drive, and countersink it. The hole is so small that it is concealed during the normal finishing operation. One important use is applying decorative molding and panels to drawer fronts and doors.

Power nailing and stapling machines must be properly installed and maintained for maximum effectiveness and long life. The key to this is a properly set-up and maintained air system. A good air system must supply the correct *volume of clean air* at the necessary *pressure*. The air supply may also have to provide *lubrication* to the pneumatic tools.

Air Volume

The air supply system must provide an adequate volume of air *at the air tool*. Consult the manufacturer of the tool for recommended pressures. In most cases this should be 90 psi (63 275 kg/m²). Even

FIGURE 7-10
This power nailer drives small headless pin tacks cut from a wire coil. (*Courtesy of Bostitch, East Greenwich, RI 02818.*)

though the compressor may be of adequate size, restrictions in the air line might reduce the volume at the tool. Restrictions most commonly occur at the quick-disconnect fittings, in hose swivels, and at manifolds, where several air lines are taken off from the main air supply. These should be sized to maintain the needed airflow. The fittings attached to a tool must be of the free-flow type, so that when the air line is disconnected, the pressurized air will be discharged.

Air Filtering

Dirt and water in the air supply are major causes of wear in pneumatic equipment. Dirt, moisture, and oil from the tool exhaust cause objectionable stains on "clean" applications such as upholstery and assemblies which are to be finished. The air filters must be of the correct size and located so that they catch the contaminants before they enter the air lines to the tools. The filter must be cleaned regularly.

The major contaminants are *water, rust, dust, and oil*. Water vapor in the atmosphere condenses into liquid in the receiver tank and piping. These must be drained regularly. Rust and pipe scale are caused by moisture corroding the inside of iron pipe. This produces a creamy sludge that is highly abrasive and damaging to air tools. Filters should be mounted at the end of metal piping and only a flexible line run from the filter to the tool. Dust enters the system through the air compressor air intake. This must have a filter that is cleaned often. Oil is introduced from many compressors as an oil vapor

into the system. This should be filtered out along with the dirt and water.

Air Regulators

Most compressors will produce pressures that exceed the air tool's maximum operating pressure. Air pressure regulators are required to control the operating pressure. Using more air pressure than required for the tool will increase wear on the air tool and waste compressed air. Inadequate pressure will result in inconsistant tool performance and poor driving. Set the pressure as specified in the tool manual. Place the regulator as close to the tool as practical.

Lubrication

Most air tools require frequent but not excessive lubricating by adding small amounts of oil to the air line. This is done by using lubricators mounted downstream from the filters. The lubricators must have adequate flow for the application and be suitable for the cyclical flow of pneumatic fastener drivers. For clean applications, such as upholstery (Fig. 7-11) or work to be painted, be extremely careful to limit the oil added because it could get on the fabric or wood surface. Follow the manufacturer's recommendations.

FIGURE 7-11
Power staples are used in upholstery operations. (*Courtesy of Senco Fastening Systems.*)

Safety

When using air-powered staplers and nailers, wear safety glasses or a face shield (Fig. 7-12). The staples or nails leave the tool under a great deal of pressure, so do not point the tool at anyone. Keep your hands clear of the discharge mouth. Ideally, both hands should be kept on the air tool. Treat it much as you would a loaded gun. Be careful when you are holding a part in place that your hands are not in the direct line of the fastener. When making repairs, disconnect it from the air line.

FIGURE 7-12
Observe all safety regulations when using power staplers and nailers. (*Courtesy of Senco Fastening Systems.*)

Power Nails and Staples

There are a wide variety of nails and staples available for use in power-driven nailing and stapling tools. Some have large heads and resemble box nails. These are used for construction purposes where high holding power is needed. Others have screw threads on their bodies to increase holding power. For furniture and cabinetwork, the finishing nail and headless tack are more common. The headless tack is cut by the nailing tool from a wire coil and driven into place. The head is almost invisible. A variety of staples of various widths, length, and wire diameters are also available. They are used to secure wood parts, as cabinet backs, that will not be seen. They are used extensively for upholstery (Fig. 7-13).

WOOD SCREWS

Wood screws have greater holding power than nails and can easily be removed when necessary. They are used for many purposes, such as installing hinges, hasps, locks, and drawer slides. They are available in a variety of sizes, materials, slot types, head types, and finishes.

The most common head types are flat, round, and oval. Flat-head screws are set flush with the surface or in a counterbore and covered with a wood plug. Round heads are set above the surface and left exposed. Oval heads are most generally used with hinges and other hardware (Fig. 7-14).

The basic types of screw head recesses are slotted, Phillips, Pozidriv, clutch head, and Robertson type (Fig. 7-15). All but the slotted are easier to drive straight and generally drive faster. The head is stronger and the screwdriver is less likely to slip.

FIGURE 7-13
Examples of power-driven nails and staples: (A) finishing nail; (B) pin; (C) screw shank nail; (D) flat-head nail; (E) ring shank nail; (F) wire staples.

FIGURE 7-14
Common types of wood screws.

REGISTERED TRADEMARK
OF PHILLIPS SCREW CO.

FIGURE 7-15
Common types of wood screw heads.

TABLE 7-2 Typical Sizes of Wood Screws	
Length (in.)	Shank diameter (wire gauge number)
$\frac{1}{4}$	2, 4
$\frac{3}{8}$	2, 3, 4, 5, 6
$\frac{1}{2}$ and $\frac{5}{8}$	2, 3, 4, 5, 6, 7, 8
$\frac{3}{4}$, $\frac{7}{8}$, and 1	4, 5, 6, 7, 8, 9, 10, 11, 12
$1\frac{1}{4}$	4, 5, 6, 7, 8, 9, 10, 11, 12, 14, 16
$1\frac{1}{2}$	6, 7, 8, 9, 10, 11, 12, 14, 16
$1\frac{3}{4}$	6, 8, 9, 10, 12, 14, 16
2	8, 9, 10, 12, 14, 16
$2\frac{1}{4}$	10, 12, 14
$2\frac{1}{2}$	8, 9, 10, 12, 14, 16
3	10, 12, 14, 16

TABLE 7-3 Wood Screw Diameters (inches) by Gauge Number		
Wire gauge number	Decimal size	Fractional size
0	0.060	$\frac{1}{16}$
1	0.073	$\frac{5}{64}$
2	0.086	$\frac{3}{32}$
3	0.099	$\frac{7}{64}$
4	0.112	$\frac{1}{8}$
5	0.125	$\frac{1}{8}$
6	0.138	$\frac{9}{64}$
7	0.151	$\frac{5}{32}$
8	0.164	$\frac{11}{64}$
9	0.177	$\frac{3}{16}$
10	0.190	$\frac{13}{64}$
11	0.203	$\frac{13}{64}$
12	0.216	$\frac{7}{32}$
14	0.242	$\frac{1}{4}$
16	0.268	$\frac{9}{32}$
18	0.294	$\frac{19}{64}$
20	0.320	$\frac{21}{64}$

A SPECIAL-PURPOSE SCREW DESIGNED FOR FACE FRAMING CABINETS.

FIGURE 7-16
This screw is designed to join the faceframe to the carcass.

Wood screws are sold in lengths from $\frac{1}{4}$ to 6 in. The length of a wood screw is that part that enters the wood (see Fig. 7-14).

Wood screws are made in many diameters. The *shank diameters* are given in *gauge numbers*. The larger the number, the larger the diameter of the wire used to make the screw. The diameter is measured just below the head. The *root diameter* varies with the wire diameter. The root diameter is the largest diameter of the core at the threads (Fig. 7-14). Standard wood screw sizes are shown in Table 7-2; the diameter in inches for each gauge is listed in Table 7-3.

Several special-purpose screws for joining the face frame to the carcass and securing materials to particle board are used in furniture and cabinet construction. The *face framing* screw has a Phillips head and a special auger point. This point drills the screw directly into the wood. It is not necessary to drill holes prior to installing the screw (Fig. 7-16). It

has a dry lubricant on the surface that helps its installation. There are different screws for hard and soft woods. The *particleboard screw* is designed for fastening into particleboard. It has widely spaced threads that enable it to be securely set in particleboard (Fig. 7-17). Sheet metal screws have a similar

A SPECIAL-PURPOSE SCREW DESIGNED FOR USE IN PARTICLE BOARD.

FIGURE 7-17
Special screw for use in particleboard.

thread and are sometimes used for this same purpose. There are a variety of special screws used to install hinges and hardware that are usually supplied with them when they are purchased.

Installing Screws

To install a screw properly, a hole the same diameter as the shank must be drilled through the top piece. This is called the shank hole. In the bottom piece a hole must be drilled that is a little smaller

1. DRILL SHANK HOLE 2. DRILL PILOT HOLE 3. COUNTERSINK 4. INSTALL SCREW

FIGURE 7-18
Wood screws are installed by drilling shank and pilot holes.

FIGURE 7-19
Flat-head wood screws are set flush with the surface of the wood.

than the root diameter. It is called a pilot hole (Fig. 7-18). In softwood the pilot hole is about 60% of the root diameter. In hardwood it should be about 80%. Recommended hole sizes are shown in Table 7-4.

Flat-head screws can be set flush by countersinking the shank hole after it is drilled (Fig. 7-19). Typical countersinks are in Fig. 7-20. The diameter of the countersink can be checked by placing the head of the screw in the cone-shaped cavity. A Screw Mate can be used to drill the holes and the countersink (Fig. 7-21).

When the head of the screw is to be set below the surface and covered with a plug, a hole slightly larger than the diameter of the screw is bored to the

TABLE 7-4
Recommended Drill Sizes for Shank, Pilot, and Plug Holes

Screw gauge no.	Shank hole: hard and softwood	Pilot hole Softwood	Pilot hole Hardwood	Auger bit size for plug hole
0	$\frac{1}{16}$	$\frac{1}{64}$	$\frac{1}{32}$	—
1	$\frac{5}{64}$	$\frac{1}{32}$	$\frac{1}{32}$	—
2	$\frac{3}{32}$	$\frac{1}{32}$	$\frac{3}{64}$	3
3	$\frac{7}{64}$	$\frac{3}{64}$	$\frac{1}{16}$	4
4	$\frac{7}{64}$	$\frac{3}{64}$	$\frac{1}{16}$	4
5	$\frac{1}{8}$	$\frac{1}{16}$	$\frac{5}{64}$	4
6	$\frac{9}{64}$	$\frac{1}{16}$	$\frac{5}{64}$	5
7	$\frac{5}{32}$	$\frac{1}{16}$	$\frac{3}{32}$	5
8	$\frac{11}{64}$	$\frac{5}{64}$	$\frac{3}{32}$	6
9	$\frac{3}{16}$	$\frac{5}{64}$	$\frac{7}{64}$	6
10	$\frac{3}{16}$	$\frac{3}{32}$	$\frac{7}{64}$	6
11	$\frac{13}{64}$	$\frac{3}{32}$	$\frac{1}{8}$	7
12	$\frac{7}{32}$	$\frac{7}{64}$	$\frac{1}{8}$	7
14	$\frac{1}{4}$	$\frac{7}{64}$	$\frac{9}{64}$	8
16	$\frac{17}{64}$	$\frac{9}{64}$	$\frac{5}{32}$	9

USE IN A HAND OPERATED BRACE

STANLEY MADE IN USA No. 137

USED IN A POWER DRILL

FIGURE 7-20
Two types of countersinks. (*Courtesy of The Stanley Works.*)

DRILLS TO CORRECT DEPTH   1/4 × 10

COUNTERSINK

SHANK

CLEARANCE

PILOT HOLE

FIGURE 7-21
The Screw-Mate drills the pilot and shank holes and countersinks all in one operation. (*Courtesy of The Stanley Works.*)

FIGURE 7-22
How to counterbore and install a wood screw.

SPADE BIT

1. DRILL THE COUNTERBORE
2. THEN THE SHANK HOLE
3. THEN THE PILOT HOLE

A   B   C

Pic. A Drills accurate pilot hole and clearance hole. Scoring edges cut surface fibres, prevent splintering. Screw head compresses wood fibres exerting clamping force when driven flush.

Pic. B To counterbore, simply add more pressure. Chip remover cleans out screwhole as SCREW SINK™ counterbore is withdrawn.

Pic. C Use Stanley Plug Cutter to form perfectly mated plug; leave as "Button Tip" or sand smooth.

FIGURE 7-23
The Screw-Sink drills the pilot and shank holes and counterbores all in one operation. (*Courtesy of The Stanley Works.*)

desired depth. This is called a counterbore (Fig. 7-22). Then the shank and pilot holes are bored. Counterbores can be made with an auger bit, spade bit, Screw-Sink counterbore, or straight-shank twist drill (Fig. 7-23).

The wood plugs can be bought in a variety of sizes or can be cut from the same wood used in the product. These are cut with a plug cutter (Fig. 7-24). Plugs are usually cut ⅜ in. long. The plug is glued in the hole. Usually, the grain in the plug is lined up with the grain in the board. A contrast can be had by placing the grain perpendicular to the grain in the board using a lighter or darker wood.

When working with oak, use brass screws. The acid in the oak will react with steel screws and eventually may cause a blue-black stain.

When installing screws in hardwood, lubricate the threads of the screw with paraffin, wax, or soap. This eases its installation.

OTHER FASTENING DEVICES

Tee nuts are used for many purposes. One of the most common is the installation of legs. A hole is bored in the furniture base. The tee nut is hammered into the hole. Its prongs hold it in place and keep it from turning or a small brad is placed through the flange. A *hanger bolt* can be screwed into the leg and the end with machine threads is screwed into the tee nut (Fig. 7-25).

FIGURE 7-24
Plug cutter. (*Courtesy of The Stanley Works.*)

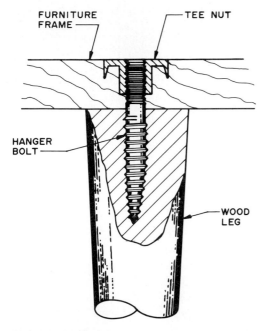

FIGURE 7-25
Legs can be joined to the carcass using tee nuts and hanger bolts.

FIGURE 7-26
Dowel screws can be used to join legs and other parts to a carcass.

FIGURE 7-27
Miters can be joined using corrugated fasteners.

A *dowel screw* has wood screw threads on both ends. It is often used to join short legs to the furniture frame (Fig. 7-26).

Edge and butt joints can be held together with corrugated fasteners, clamp nails, chevrons, or Skotch fasteners. These metal fasteners are used where strength and appearance is not a major factor (see Figs. 7-27 to 7-30).

WALL ANCHORS

Various types of cabinets and shelves are hung from the wall. There are a variety of anchors for hollow and masonry walls. Toggle bolts and hollow-wall anchors are used for hollow-wall installations. A *toggle bolt* has either a solid head that pivots flat along the bolt or a spring-loaded head (Fig. 7-31). They require that a hole be drilled in the wall large enough for the fastener to enter.

Hollow-wall fasteners are inserted in a hole drilled in the wall. When the screw is tightened, it

FIGURE 7-28
Clamp nails are driven into slots cut into the wood. They are slightly wedge shaped to pull the joint together.

FIGURE 7-29
Miters can be joined using chevron fasteners.

FIGURE 7-30
Skotch fasteners have several legs which are driven into the wood, pulling the joint together.

FINISH WALL
MATERIAL

1. BORE HOLE IN FINISH WALL. PUSH TOGGLE BOLT THROUGH HOLE.
2. TIGHTEN SCREW TO PULL BOLT TIGHT AGAINST OBJECT TO BE HELD TO WALL.

FIGURE 7-31
Toggle bolts are used to mount lightweight items on walls.

pulls the end toward the head. This squeezes the ribbed center section which expands and binds against the inside of the wall (Fig. 7-32).

Another type of anchor used for hollow walls or in solid masonry is the Poly-Set anchor. It is a polyethylene expansion anchor that forms a knot on the inside of a hollow wall when the screw is tightened. In solid masonry it expands and binds on the side of the drilled hole (Fig. 7-33). They are available for wall thicknesses of $\frac{3}{8}$, $\frac{1}{2}$, $\frac{5}{8}$, and $\frac{3}{4}$ in.

A Toggler screw anchor is used to join something to a surface having a cavity behind it (Fig. 7-34). It is available for use in surface thicknesses of $\frac{1}{8}$, $\frac{3}{8}$, and $\frac{5}{8}$ in. A sheet metal screw is driven into the anchor to hold the item to be hung to the wall.

A Pronto block anchor is used in the web or hollow sections of hollow masonry. A $\frac{3}{8}$-in.-diameter hole is bored and the anchor is driven into the hole. The wedge on the end expands the end, holding it in place. A $\frac{1}{4}$-in. 20 hex head machine screw is fastened into the anchor (Fig. 7-35).

A Wedge Anchor is to fasten items to solid concrete. A hole the proper size is drilled. Its depth must exceed the minimum embedment desired. Assemble the anchor with the nut and washer. Drive through the material to be fastened so that the washer is flush with the surface. Then tighten the nut three to five turns to expand the anchor (Fig. 7-36). Wedge Anchors are available in diameters of $\frac{1}{4}$, $\frac{5}{8}$, $\frac{3}{4}$, $\frac{7}{8}$, $1\frac{1}{8}$, and $1\frac{1}{4}$ in.

There are many types of mechanical fasteners used to assemble furniture. These are used in place of the traditional wood joints (Fig. 7-37). Additional information is presented in Chapter 17.

A HOLLOW-WALL FASTENER

1. BORE A HOLE IN THE WALL. INSERT HOLLOW WALL ANCHOR.

2. TIGHTEN SCREW TO BEND ANCHOR INSIDE OF WALL.

FIGURE 7-32
Hollow-wall fasteners penetrate the wall and bind against the inside surface.

FIGURE 7-33
This Poly-Set hollow-wall anchor is plastic and forms a knot as the screw is tightened. (*Courtesy of ITT, Phillips Drill Division.*)

FIGURE 7-34
Toggler screw anchors can be used in hollow walls or as anchors in solid wall materials. (*Courtesy of ITT, Phillips Drill Division.*)

FOLD

Drill hole using 5/16" drill. Fold legs of the Toggler Screw Anchor together.

INSERT

Insert the Toggler Screw Anchor into the hole and tap flush to wall.

"POP"

In hollow walls, "pop" the Toggler Screw Anchor open with red key provided. Then install item and tighten screw.

FIGURE 7-35
Pronto block anchors are driven into holes bored into solid masonry. (*Courtesy of ITT, Phillips Drill Division.*)

1 DRILL 2 DRIVE 3 TIGHTEN

FIGURE 7-36
Wedge anchors are made with a threaded shaft that extends out from wall. (*Courtesy of ITT, Phillips Drill Division.*)

FIGURE 7-37
Two types of multipiece mechanical fasteners used to assemble knock-down furniture and cabinets. (*Courtesy of H'a'fele America, 203 Feld Ave., High Point, NC 27261.*)

Shelf
Side
Housing
Connecting bolt

Dowel
Shelf
Side
Housing
Connecting bolt

Answer each of the following questions. If you are not sure of an answer, review the chapter.

7-1. What are the common types of nails?

7-2. What is the difference between a finishing nail and a casing nail?

7-3. How is the length of a nail given?

7-4. How are nails driven in a factory manufacturing furniture?

7-5. What is face nailing?

7-6. What tool is used to set the head of a finishing nail below the surface of the wood?

7-7. How close to the edge of solid boards can nails be driven?

7-8. What power machine is used to nail decorative moldings to doors?

7-9. What contaminates must be removed from the air lines leading to power staplers and nailers?

7-10. Where is the filter on the air lines on power staplers and power nailers?

7-11. How does water get into air lines?

7-12. How is the air pressure controlled on lines to power staplers and nailers?

7-13. What safety equipment should a person wear when using power staplers and nailers?

7-14. What advantages do screws have over nails?

7-15. What are the common wood screw head types?

7-16. What types of recesses are available in wood screws?

7-17. How is the size of a wood screw given?

7-18. What holes are drilled to permit proper installation of wood screws?

Following are technical terms that you should be able to use as part of your working vocabulary. Write a brief description of the meaning of each term.

Nails
Brads
Penny
Pins
Wood screws

Shank diameter
Root diameter
Faceframing screw
Particleboard screw
Pilot hole
Shank hole
Counterbore
Tee nuts
Hanger bolt
Dowel screw
Wall anchors

8

LAYOUT TOOLS AND TECHNIQUES

After a product is designed, the next step is to lay out the parts on the materials to be used. The product could be designed using *customary* or *metric units*. Production people in the wood industry must be familiar with both systems. Both systems measure the same quantities but use different units to establish the quantity (Table 8-1, page 98).

CUSTOMARY SYSTEM

The customary system of linear measurement is based on the *yard*, which is divided into three divisions called *feet*. A foot is divided into 12 smaller units called *inches* (Fig. 8-1). Inches are divided into common fractions or decimal fractions. A *common*

FIGURE 8-1
The customary system of measurement is based on the yard, which is subdivided into feet, inches, and fractions of an inch.

TABLE 8-1
Customary and Metric Units

Measurement	Customary units	Symbol	Metric units	Symbol
Length	yard	yd	meter	m
	foot	ft	decimeter	dm
	inch	in.	centimeter	cm
	mile	mi	millimeter	mm
			kilometer	km
Weight	ton	t	metric ton	t
	pound	lb	kilogram	kg
	ounce	oz	gram	g
Volume	gallon	gal	cubic meter	m³
	quart	qt	cubic decimeter	dm³
	pint	pt	cubic centimeter	cm³
	fluid ounce	oz	cubic millimeter	mm³
Area	square yard	yd²	square meter	m²
	square foot	ft²	square decimeter	dm²
	square inch	in²	square centimeter	cm²
			square millimeter	mm²
Temperature	degree Fahrenheit	°F	degree Celsius	°C
Speed, velocity	miles per hour	mph	meters per second	m/s

fraction is when the inch is divided into $\frac{1}{2}$, $\frac{1}{4}$, $\frac{1}{8}$, or $\frac{1}{16}$ of an inch (Fig. 8-1). A *decimal fraction* is when an inch is divided into .1 or .01 (one-tenth or one-hundredth) of an inch (Fig. 8-2). Much of the furniture and cabinets produced by industry is manufactured in decimal inches, which are more accurate and easier to use.

The units for weight are *pounds* and *ounces*. There are 16 ounces in a pound. Some materials, such as nails, are sold by the pound. Finishing materials are often sold by ounces.

TRUE SIZE

FIGURE 8-2
Decimal fractions of an inch.

Liquids are sold by volume measure. In the customary system this includes gallons, quarts (4 to a gallon), pints (2 to a quart), and fluid ounces (16 to a pint). Paint, varnish, and adhesives are sold by liquid measure.

METRIC SYSTEM

The metric system of linear measurement is based on a unit called a *meter* (m). A meter is a little longer than a yard. The meter is divided into 10 parts called *decimeters* (dm). A decimeter is divided into 10 parts called *centimeters* (cm). A centimeter is divided into 10 parts called *millimeters* (mm) (Fig. 8-3).

Metric units of measure are specified by adding a prefix to the base units, such as a meter (Table 8-2). The prefix *milli* means 1/000 of the base unit, so a millimeter is 1/1000 of a meter. The prefix *centi* means 1/100 of the base unit, and *deci* is 1/10 of a base unit. The prefix *kilo* means 1000, so a kilometer (km) is 1000 meters.

TABLE 8-2
Prefixes Used on Metric Base Units

Prefix	+ Base unit =	Metric unit of measurement	Means
milli (m)	meter (m)	millimeter (mm)	1/1000
	gram (g)	milligram (mg)	
centi (c)	meter (m)	centimeter (cm)	1/100
	gram (g)	centigram (cg)	
deci (d)	meter (m)	decimeter (dm)	1/10
	gram (g)	decigram (dg)	
kilo (k)	meter (m)	kilometer (km)	1000
	gram (g)	kilogram (kg)	

Since the metric system is based on the unit 10 it is possible to move from one prefix to another simply by moving the decimal point. For example, 5500 mm equals 550.0 cm, which equal 55.00 dm, which equal 5.500 m.

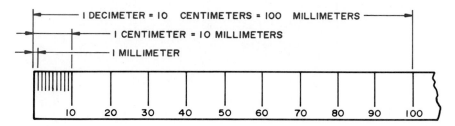

FIGURE 8-3
The metric system of measurement is based on the meter, which is subdivided into decimeters, centimeters, and millimeters.

Working drawings for wood products are dimensioned in *millimeters* (Fig. 8-4). The centimeter and decimeter are not widely used. The meter is used for larger distances, such as a land survey.

The units for *weight* are the *kilogram* (kg) and the gram (g) (1/1000 kilogram). The units for *volume* are derived by multiplying the length by width by height of rectangular objects. The volume is expressed in terms of cubic measure. For example, a cube 1 meter square is 1 cubic meter (m^3). A cubic millimeter is mm^3. The term liter is sometimes used to express a cubic decimeter (dm^3).

FIGURE 8-4
Typical metric working drawing of a cabinet door.

Metrics in Product Design

If a product is to be manufactured using metric units, it should be originally designed with these units. To take a product originally designed in inches and convert these to millimeters to produce a metric product is an improper procedure. This reduces the value of going to metric units and actually makes the manufacturing process more difficult because you end up with inconvenient measurements. For example, if you convert $3\frac{1}{4}$ in. to millimeters, you multiply it by 25.4 mm and get 82.550 mm. You have to convert $\frac{1}{4}$ in. to a decimal fraction before you multiply. Then the result 82.550 mm is extremely difficult to measure. A designer would probably make this part 80 mm, which is easy to measure. The 2.550 mm dropped is about $\frac{3}{32}$ in., which is not of importance for most parts of furniture or cabinets. When designing using metric units, consider keeping all measurements based on units of 5 or 10 mm (i.e., 30, 35, 40, etc.).

MEASURING TOOLS

There are a variety of measuring tools used to lay out parts for production. To achieve the desired results, the proper tool must be correctly used.

Rules

The bench rule, folding rule, and tape rule are most often used for linear measurements (Fig. 8-5). The *bench rule* is used for measuring short distances and is available in lengths of 1, 2, and 3 ft and 1 m. The *folding rule* is usually 6 ft and 1 and 2-m long. It is used for measuring longer distances. The *tape rule* is used for measuring very long distances. Those used

FIGURE 8-5
Rules used for linear layout. (*Courtesy of The Stanley Works.*)

in furniture and cabinet production are usually 8, 10 and 12 ft long and 2 and 3 m long. They are available in 25-, 50- and 100-ft and 15-, 20-, 25- and 30-m lengths.

Squares

The squares most often used are the try square, combination square, framing or steel square, and bevel square or T-bevel (Fig. 8-6). They are used to lay out 90° angles and check for squareness.

The *try square* is available with 6-, 8-, 10-, and 12-in. blades. The blade is rigidly fastened to the handle at a 90° angle. Some have a 45° angle, where the blade and handle join, enabling it to be used to lay out both 90° and 45° angles (Fig. 8-7). The try square must be handled carefully so that the 90° angle is not changed. When not being used, place in a holder on your tool rack. Do not pile tools on top of

FIGURE 8-6
Squares used for layout and checking stock for squareness and angles. (*Courtesy of The Stanley Works.*)

it or use it as a hammer. The *combination square* has a 12-in. adjustable blade. The length that the blade extends beyond the face of the head can be adjusted. This allows it to be used as a depth gauge. It has a locknut in the head that locks the blade and head together. It can also be used to lay out 45° angles. Some have a steel scriber in the bottom of the head. This is used to scratch a line along the edge of the blade when laying out on wood or metal.

The *steel square* is available with a 12-in. body

FIGURE 8-7
A try square is a basic layout tool.

and 8-in. tongue and a 24-in. body and 16-in. tongue. A carpenter's square has a 24-in. body and a 16-in. tongue. Some have rafter tables stamped into the body and tongue. Both are flat metal tools with the body and tongue meeting at right angles. Measurements in inches are marked on both parts. Since they do not have a thick handle like the try square, the tongue is dropped down along the edge of the board as it is used to lay out a 90° angle.

The *bevel square,* sometimes called a T-bevel, has a steel blade 4 to 8 in. long that pivots on a pin through the handle. The blade can be adjusted to any desired angle and is locked to the handle with a thumbscrew. It is used to lay out a series of identical angles and test bevels and chamfers for accuracy.

Marking Tools

The tools most commonly used to lay out on wood are a hard lead pencil with a sharp point, a utility knife, an awl, a compass, and trammel points (Fig. 8-8).

FIGURE 8-8
Commonly used layout tools.

When using the knife, use only the tip of the blade (Fig. 8-9). The centers of holes are located using an awl. The center is located by measurement and the wood is indented by pressing down on the awl with your hand (Fig. 8-10). This helps to accurately locate

FIGURE 8-9
A utility knife is used for accurate scribing of lines.

FIGURE 8-10
Centers are accurately marked with an awl.

the point of the bit to be used to bore a hole at this point.

Dividers have two steel legs ending in a point. The distance between these legs is adjustable (Fig. 8-11). Dividers are used to lay out equal distances and transfer measurements from one place to another. They can be used to scribe circles but a compass does a better job.

A *compass* has one steel leg and one leg that holds a pencil or pencil lead. The most accurate work is performed using a drafting compass (Fig. 8-12). Very large diameter circles are drawn using a woodworker's trammel points (Fig. 8-13). One leg is a steel pin and the other holds a pencil. Do not hammer an awl into the wood. An awl can also be used to scribe lines as described for a pencil or utility knife.

FIGURE 8-11
Wing-type divider used to lay out equal distances.

FIGURE 8-12
Small circles are drawn with a compass.

FIGURE 8-13
Large circles are drawn with trammel points.

STARTING THE LAYOUT

After selecting the stock to be used, the various parts of the product must be laid out. There are several things to consider. One is to avoid the defects in the stock. If knots are not acceptable, you must work

around them. Splits, surface checks, and insect damage must be avoided. Occasionally, the piece can be turned so that minor defects are on the back or are hidden on the inside of a furniture unit. The flatness of the stock must be considered. If it has cup, warp, or twist, the piece might have to be discarded or used for small pieces where these defects can be minimized (Fig. 8-14).

FIGURE 8-14
Stock in crook and cup can be salvaged by cutting into smaller or thinner pieces.

AMOUNT OF BOW

AMOUNT OF BOW WHEN CUT INTO SMALL LENGTHS.

MAXIMUM CLEAR AREA

AMOUNT OF CROOK

AMOUNT OF CROOK WHEN CUT INTO SMALL LENGTHS.

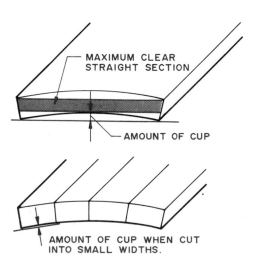

MAXIMUM CLEAR STRAIGHT SECTION

AMOUNT OF CUP

AMOUNT OF CUP WHEN CUT INTO SMALL WIDTHS.

FIGURE 8-15
Avoid defects when making the parts layout on the stock.

Make your layout from a good, straight edge. If necessary, straighten an edge on the jointer. Take all width measurements from this good edge. Length measurements are taken from a good square end or a square line scribed across the end of the stock. Allow extra material between parts for the saw kerf. A typical parts layout is in Fig. 8-15.

When making a layout of parts on stock, make it near the edge and end (Fig. 8-16). This leaves the rest of the stock for other parts. If a part is laid out near the center, much of the stock will become wasted.

Remember to watch the direction and color of the grain. Keep the grain running in the direction desired in the part. A part is stronger with the grain than across the grain (Fig. 8-17). Ideally, all exposed pieces should be close to the same color and general grain pattern.

FIGURE 8-16
Careful planning is necessary when laying out on stock, so that waste is minimized.

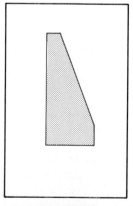

THIS LOCATION
LEAVES ONLY
SMALL PIECES
AND IS WASTEFUL.

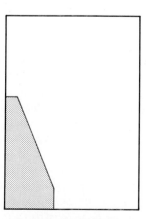

THIS LOCATION
LEAVES A LARGE
PIECE OF STOCK.

FIGURE 8-17
Consider the direction of the grain and how it affects the strength of each part.

Measuring Linear Distances

Thickness can be measured with a bench rule or try square (Fig. 8-18). *Width* is measured by placing a rule perpendicular to the good edge (Fig. 8-19) or with a try square (Fig. 8-20). Measurements with the bench rule or folding rule are more accurate if the tool is placed on edge. Width can also be measured and marked with a combination square. The blade is extended from the handle the desired width. The head is slid along the good edge and a pencil is held on the end of the blade (Fig. 8-21). A marking

FIGURE 8-18
Thickness can be checked with a try square.

FIGURE 8-21
Width can be marked using a combination square.

FIGURE 8-19
When measuring width, place the rule on edge and keep it perpendicular to the side of the stock.

FIGURE 8-22
A marking gauge is sometimes used to mark stock to width.

FIGURE 8-20
Width can be measured with a try square.

gauge is also used to lay out the width. Set the required distance between the pin and the head. Place the head against the edge of the stock. Roll it until the pin in the end of the beam touches the wood. Then push the gauge away from you (Fig. 8-22).

The length of short pieces can be measured with a bench rule or a folding rule. Longer pieces require a tape rule (Fig. 8-23). Keep the rule parallel with the edge and press it flat against the surface. The tape has a hook on one end that is placed over the good end of the stock.

Laying Out Angles

Angles can be laid out using a protractor. Place the center point on the vertex of the angle and read the degrees on the scale (Fig. 8-24). A T-bevel can also be used (Fig. 8-25) to take the angle from the protractor. It is then drawn on the wood as shown in Fig. 8-26.

FIGURE 8-23
Long lengths are measured with a tape rule.

FIGURE 8-24
Angles are measured with a protractor.

FIGURE 8-25
A T-bevel is used to lay out and transfer angles.

FIGURE 8-26
The T-bevel is placed flat on the stock as the angle is drawn.

FIGURE 8-27
Round corners are laid out by using the radius to locate the center.

Laying Out a Rounded Corner

First locate the center by measuring the radius from each corner. Then place the pin leg of the compass on this point and swing the arc (Fig. 8-27).

Laying Out Irregular Curves

An irregular curve is one that does not have a fixed radius. It is drawn using a tool called an irregular curve (Fig. 8-28). The line of the curve is indicated by a series of points. These are then connected by placing various sides of the irregular curve along the points until three or more fit the curve. Draw this part. Move the irregular curve until additional

FIGURE 8-28
Irregular curve.

FIGURE 8-29
Irregular curves are drawn by connecting points that are known to be on the curve.

points line up and draw the next section (Fig. 8-29). There are many shapes and sizes of irregular curves, and those working with them will have an entire set.

Enlarging and Reducing Patterns

If you have a drawing of an irregular part and you want to enlarge or reduce it, this can be done by drawing a grid over the drawing. The grid can be any convenient size such as $\frac{1}{2}$ in. If you want to en-

large it 100%, draw another grid with 1-in. squares. Mark where the lines cross the $\frac{1}{2}$-in. grid on the 1-in. grid. Then connect the points with an irregular curve (Fig. 8-30).

If you want to reduce this design 50%, draw another grid with $\frac{1}{4}$-in. squares and repeat the foregoing process.

Template Layouts

Duplicate parts can be laid out using a template. A template is a full-size pattern of the part cut out of cardboard, metal, or hardboard. It is placed on the stock and traced around with a pencil. If a part is symmetrical (same on each side of a centerline), only half a template need be made. It is traced and flipped over to draw the other half (Fig. 8-31).

GEOMETRIC CONSTRUCTIONS

Three basic forms, hexagons, octagons, and ellipses, are used frequently in furniture and cabinet construction. The steps for laying out these forms are in the following examples.

Laying Out a Hexagon

A hexagon has six equal sides and angles. The steps to lay out a hexagon are:

1. Draw a circle with a diameter equal to the distance from one corner of the hexagon to the other (Fig. 8-32).

FIGURE 8-30
Patterns can be enlarged or reduced using this grid method.

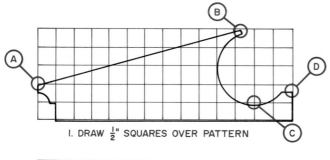

1. DRAW $\frac{1}{2}$" SQUARES OVER PATTERN

2. ENLARGE PATTERN BY DRAWING ON GRID WITH 1" SQUARES.

FIGURE 8-31
Templates can be used to lay out patterns on the stock.

Laying Out an Octagon

An octagon has eight equal sides and angles. The steps to lay out an octagon are:

1. Draw a square having sides equal to the desired width of the octagan from one flat side to the other (Fig. 8-33).
2. Locate the center of this square.
3. Set a compass the distance from one corner of the square to the center. Swing arcs from each corner through the center until they cross the sides of the square.
4. Connect these intersections to form the octagon.

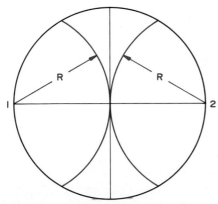

I. DRAW CIRCLE DIAMETER EQUAL TO HEXAGON CORNER TO CORNER DIAMETER. THEN SWING ARCS FROM I AND 2 USING THE RADIUS OF THE CIRCLE.

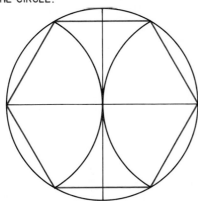

2. CONNECT THE POINTS ON THE CIRCLE LOCATED BY THE ARCS.

FIGURE 8-32
Steps to lay out a hexagon.

2. Locate the diameter through the center.
3. From each end of the diameter, swing arcs having a radius equal to the radius of the circle.
4. Connect to points where the arcs meet the circle.

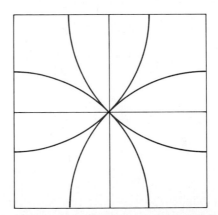

I. DRAW A SQUARE EQUAL TO THE OCTAGON ACROSS THE FLAT SIDES. SWING ARCS FROM EACH CORNER THROUGH THE CENTER UNTIL THEY TOUCH THE SQUARE.

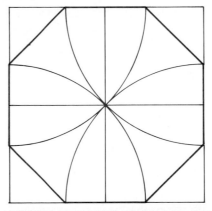

2. CONNECT THE POINTS LOCATED ON THE SQUARE.

FIGURE 8-33
Steps to lay out an octagon.

Laying Out an Ellipse

An ellipse is a plane surface formed by looking at a circle with a line of sight that is inclined to the circle. An ellipse has two axes, major and minor. The

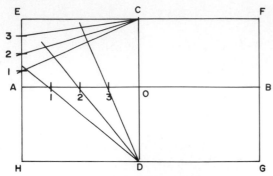

1. DIVIDE OA AND AE INTO AND EQUAL NUMBER OF PARTS. DRAW LINES FROM LIKE-NUMBERED POINTS TILL THEY INTERSECT.

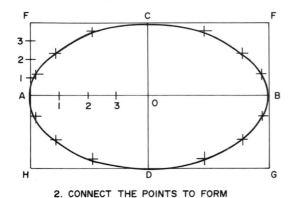

2. CONNECT THE POINTS TO FORM THE ELLIPSE.

FIGURE 8-34
Steps to lay out an ellipse.

major axis is the longest. The steps to lay out an ellipse are:

1. Draw the major axis, *AB,* and minor axis, *CD,* at right angles to each other (Fig. 8-34).
2. Draw a rectangle with its sides parallel with the axes.
3. Divide *OA* and *AE* into the same number of equal parts.
4. Draw lines through these points from *C* and *D* until the like-numbered lines cross. This locates a point on the ellipse.
5. Connect the points with an irregular curve to form the ellipse.

SOME LAYOUT TECHNIQUES

Following are some basic layout techniques that will be helpful.

Bisecting an Arc or Line

The steps are shown in Fig. 8-35.

1. Set a compass on a radius greater than half the length of the line or arc, *AB.*

FIGURE 8-35
How to bisect a line or arc.

2. Using *A* and *B* as centers, swing arcs that intersect above and below the line or arc at *C* and *D*.
3. Connect *C* and *D*. This line divides *AB* into two equal parts.

Dividing a Line into Equal Parts

Most wood is in odd widths. It can be divided into equal parts using a rule. For example, to divide a board into three equal parts, place the rule as shown in Fig. 8-36. The zero is on one edge and the 6 is on the other. Place a mark at the 2- and 4-in. locations. This divides the board into three equal parts.

To divide a line into equal parts, first draw a line below it on any angle and length (Fig. 8-37). Divide this into the desired number of parts. Connect the end of the line, *C,* with *B*. Draw lines parallel with *CB* through the other points on *AC*.

Bisecting an Angle

The steps are shown in Fig. 8-38.

1. Set a compass to any radius desired.

FIGURE 8-36
How to divide a board into equal parts.

FIGURE 8-37
Lines can be divided in any number of equal parts using this technique.

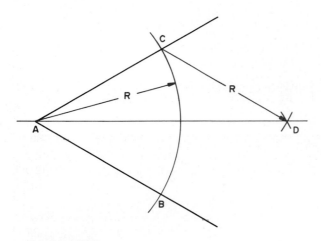

FIGURE 8-38
A compass can be used to bisect an angle.

FIGURE 8-39
It is more accurate to lay out duplicate parts together.

2. From vertex A swing arcs that cross the sides of the angle at B and C.
3. Swing arcs from B and C until they intersect at D.
4. Connect A and D to bisect the angle.

Duplicate Parts

If a product has several identical parts or several identical joints, it is more accurate if they are laid out together. Clamp the parts together. Be certain they are flush and square. Mark the locations needed on all at the same time (Fig. 8-39).

Transferring Equal Distances

Accuracy is important when transferring one measurement to several parts. This transfer is made more accurately if a dividers is used rather than a rule. To transfer a distance, set the dividers on the distance to be moved. Move the dividers to the new part and locate the points (Fig. 8-40).

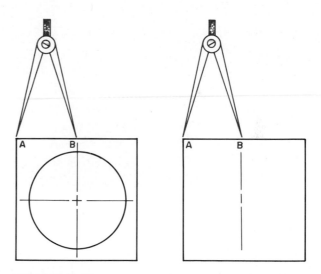

FIGURE 8-40
A divider is used to transfer a distance from one place to another.

The divider can also be used to check dimensions of actual parts or dimensions that are on drawings that are supposed to be the same size. Set the divider on the desired size and use it instead of a rule to check the others for size. This will be faster and more accurate than using a rule. Be careful you do not bump the divider and change its setting.

Answer each of the following questions. If you are not sure of an answer, review the chapter.

8-1. How many feet are there in a yard?

8-2. What is the difference between a common fraction and a decimal fraction?

8-3. How many millimeters are there in a meter?

8-4. A decimeter is what part of a meter?

8-5. What does the metric prefix *kilo* mean?

8-6. How many millimeters are there in 5.5 m?

8-7. What tool is used to measure distances over 6 ft?

8-8. What is the difference between a divider and a compass?

8-9. What do you do if you are laying out a pattern on stock that has an end split?

8-10. Why should you allow extra material for the saw kerf?

8-11. How do you enlarge a pattern?

8-12. What do you use to lay out duplicate parts?

IMPORTANT TECHNICAL TERMS

Following are technical terms that you should be able to use as part of your working vocabulary. Write a brief description of the meaning of each term.

Meter
Millimeter
Gram
Try square
Combination square
Compass
Dividers
T-bevel
Irregular curve
Hexagon
Octagon
Ellipse
Duplicate parts

9

GENERAL SAFETY

Safety is everybody's business. If we each develop a positive attitude toward the need for safe working procedures, accidents in woodworking situations would be greatly reduced. Most accidents do not just happen; they are caused by negligence on the part of the operator. Many things enter into the equation for safety. Major factors include our knowledge about proper use of tools, correct dress, a safe working environment, a "safety attitude," good-quality tools kept in good working condition, and stopping work when you begin to feel fatigue. Consideration of these and the other factors mentioned in this chapter will contribute to a safe and happy woodworking experience.

In the other chapters of this book, additional specific safety recommendations are made relating to the tools and materials used in each chapter.

OCCUPATIONAL SAFETY AND HEALTH ACT

This act, commonly known as OSHA, was passed by the Congress of the United States in 1971 to "assure as far as possible every working man and woman in the nation safe and healthful working conditions and to preserve our human resources."

This law establishes a wide range of standards relating to the safety of employees in American industry. Employers who fail to provide the proper working conditions are subject to investigation and possible penalities.

CLOTHING

Wear the required eye, ear, and respiratory protection (Fig. 9-1). Dust and chips will injure the eyes. Wear eye protection the entire time you are working with wood (Fig. 9-2). Prolonged exposure to loud and high-pitched sounds can damage hearing. Wear earplugs or earmuffs (Fig. 9-3). Dust, especially while sanding or working a lathe, clogs the nose and adversely affects the respiratory tract. Wear a respirator or at least a filter. Filters are available at any drugstore (Fig. 9-4). It is recommended that you equip your shop with dust collection equipment connected to each machine. These produce a vacuum and pull dust and chips from the machine into a storage container.

Be certain you do not wear loose clothing that can catch in moving machinery parts. It is best to wear shirts with short, tight-fitting sleeves. Do not wear ties, scarves, or other loose items. If you have

GLASSES WITH SIDE SHIELD

MOLDED EYE SHIELD

SAFETY GLASSES

FIGURE 9-1
Eye protection is required to keep the eyes free of wood chips and dust particles. (*Courtesy of American Optical Safety Products.*)

FIGURE 9-2
A full-face shield is effective for jobs where a considerable amount of chips are produced, as when using a wood lathe. (*Courtesy of American Optical Safety Products.*)

FIGURE 9-3
Ear protection is required for operations producing loud, high-pitched sounds. (*Courtesy of American Optical Safety Products.*)

long hair, wear a hair net or tie your hair above your shirt collar. Remove all jewelry, including rings, bracelets, necklaces, and earrings. (Fig. 9-5). In industrial situations heavy work shoes are required, and in some cases they must have steel toes. Wear shoes having soles that are least likely to get slippery. Do not wear shoes with open toes.

PHYSICAL CONDITIONS

1. Have a good, strong, steady workbench with a good vise firmly attached.
2. Keep the floor clean of scraps and sawdust. Sweep it often and keep scraps picked up.
3. Store all supplies and tools in proper cabinets. Wood must be neatly stored on racks, finishes in metal fire-resistant cabinets, and tools on racks made especially for them.
4. Provide adequate lighting. Every part of the work area should be fully illuminated.
5. All electrical outlets should be grounded, and better still, should have ground-fault interrupters. *Ground-fault interrupters* (GFIs), detect small electrical leaks that will not cause a circuit breaker to kick off but could cause a shock. When a leak is detected, the GFI breaks the circuit.

DISPOSABLE FILTER MASK

RESPIRATOR

FIGURE 9-4
Respiratory filters are needed to keep the nose and lungs free of wood dust particles. (*Courtesy of American Optical Safety Products.*)

FIGURE 9-5
This person is dressed for safe power tool operation.

HAND TOOL SAFETY RULES

1. Do not use dull or broken tools. They are more likely to require extra pressure or an unusual procedure which can cause them to slip.
2. Keep both hands behind the cutting edge at all times. It is almost impossible to cut yourself this way. Push cutting tools away from you. However, be certain that other people are also in the clear and will not be cut if the tool slips.
3. Clamp your stock to a bench or secure it in a vise before working on it. Loose stock causes accidents.

POWER TOOL SAFETY RULES

1. Never use a power tool unless you have been instructed in its use and you are certain that you understand the instructions completely. Often, you do not get a second chance.
2. Keep all saws and cutters sharp. Destroy heavily chipped or damaged saws and cutters. Make certain that they are properly sharpened and in balance.
3. Install all saws and cutters properly. Make certain that the teeth or bevels are facing in the proper direction as determined by the direction of rotation. If there is any doubt, consult your machine manual.
4. Keep a complete set of power tool manuals available.
5. Do not talk to or get anywhere near someone operating a power tool unless they have asked you to help with the job at hand.
6. After setting up a machine, remove all tools used and replace all guards before giving it a trial startup.
7. Make certain that you know where the switch is located and stay near it so you can shut off the machine if an emergency occurs.
8. Never work in a shop alone if you are planning to use power tools.
9. Make certain that all electrical wires, plugs, and connections are in perfect repair.
10. When using portable power tools, arrange the electrical cord so that it is clear of the work *before* you begin operation.
11. Do not use electrical tools if there are inflammable materials, gases, or vapors present.
12. Before replacing saws or cutters, cut off the electrical power at the fuse box or trip the circuit breaker. If the machine is plugged into a duplex outlet, unplug it.

FIGURE 9-6
Always get help when cutting long boards or large panels.

13. Never run a machine with the guards removed or broken. There are a few cuts that require guards to be removed. These are discussed later in the book.

14. If a piece of wood is badly warped, cupped, twisted, or has large knots or splits, be especially careful. These can cause binding and kickbacks. Consider making some of the preliminary cuts with a handsaw, thus reducing or removing some of the hazards.

15. When cutting long boards or large panels, get help (Fig. 9-6).

16. Do not start to cut with any machine until it is running at full speed.

17. Do not try to force a machine to cut faster than normal. Feed the stock so that the cut proceeds easily without excess pressure or binding. If the blade gets hot and burns the wood, seek the cause. The cut may be too deep, or the saw or cutters may be dull. Either is a hazard. Lighten up the cut and sharpen the tool.

18. Stop the machine and allow the cutter to come to a complete stop before making adjustments.

19. Buy portable power tools that have a threewire cord or have a double-insulated plastic housing (Fig. 9-7). If the tool has a three-prong plug, be certain to plug it into electrical circuits that have the third (ground) wire. They appear as shown in Fig. 9-8.

20. Make and use safety devices to help feed materials, such as featherboards and push sticks. These are covered later in the book (Fig. 9-9).

21. In shops where several people will be working at the same time, paint safety zones around the

GROUNDING PRONG

FIGURE 9-7
Portable power tools should have a three-prong plug or be of double-insulated construction.

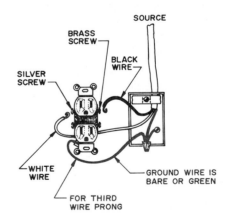

FIGURE 9-8
120-V duplex outlet that has a third (ground) wire.

machines. Only the operator should be in this zone (Fig. 9-10).

22. Plan your shop so that the operator is not standing next to a major aisle of traffic. This will prevent the passerby from distracting or bumping the operator. Arrange equipment so

FIGURE 9-9
The use of guards, push sticks, and other safety devices will greatly reduce the chance of an accident.

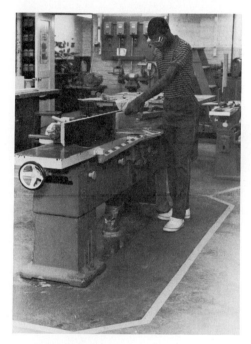

FIGURE 9-10
Safety zones painted on the floor give the operator safe operating space.

that if a kickback does occur, no one will be in the area behind the machine.

FINISHING SAFETY RULES

1. Wear eye protection. Finishing materials are liquid and caustic and can easily cause permanent eye damage.

2. When working with caustic materials such as paint remover, wear protective gloves. Inexpensive plastic throwaway gloves are available in any drugstore.

3. Know where the fire extinguishers are kept and the kinds of fires they are designed to extinguish. There are three classes of fires: A, B, and C. Type A refers to combustible materials such as wood or paper. Type B refers to materials such as paints, lacquers, oils, and gasoline. Type C is used on electrical fires. These are marked on the label of the extinguisher. Shown in Fig. 9-11 is a universal extinguisher, often referred to as an ABC because it can be used on all three types of fires.

4. Store dirty rags and paper in metal, fire-resistant containers. Remove them from the building as often as possible.

5. Store flammable finishing materials in metal fire-resistant cabinets. Ground these cabinets and large storage containers to prevent accidental sparking and ignition of materials.

6. Provide mechanical ventilation to remove fumes rapidly. Do everything possible to avoid breathing fumes, including some type of respirator. Keep all containers covered when not in use.

7. Cleanliness is important to safety. Immediately wipe up material spilled on the bench or floor.

8. Do not pour finishing materials down a sink or mix them together.

FIGURE 9-11
This fire extinguisher can be used on type A, B, and C fires.

Answer each of the following questions. If you are not sure of an answer, review the chapter.

9-1. Why was the Occupational Safety and Health Act passed by the Congress of the United States?

9-2. What are the types of eye-protective devices available?

9-3. Why are loose clothes not worn in the workplace?

9-4. How should long hair be contained?

9-5. What safety precautions should be taken regarding the workshop floor?

9-6. What is the purpose of a ground-fault interrupter?

9-7. Why do dull tools cause more accidents than are caused by sharp tools?

9-8. If you have some doubt about replacing the blade or cutters on a power tool, what should you do?

9-9. What is the first thing you do before replacing a saw blade or cutters on power tools?

9-10. How do you handle large plywood panels when you want to cut them?

9-11. What may be wrong if the blade of a power saw gets hot and burns?

9-12. What safety features do you look for when buying portable power tools?

9-13. List the safety precautions that must be taken in a wood-finishing area.

IMPORTANT TECHNICAL TERMS

Following are technical terms that you should be able to use as part of your working vocabulary. Write a brief description of the meaning of each term.

OSHA

Muffs
Respirator
GFI
Power tool manual
Ground wire
Safety zones
Fire extinguisher

PART 2

Furniture and Cabinet Construction

10

WOODWORKING JOINTS

Selecting which wood joints to use is part of a designer's work. There are many kinds of joints (Fig. 10-1). Each has advantages and disadvantages. As designers decide on joints, they consider the following factors.

Strength. Some joints are stronger than others. The joint selected must fit the job it is supposed to do. Joints must not separate during use.

Appearance. Sometimes, the joint should be hidden. A joint not visible is called a blind joint. Sometimes a joint is exposed so that it becomes part of the overall design.

Cost. A complicated joint is costly to cut. Is it worth the cost? Would metal fasteners give acceptable results for less money?

Difficulty. Select the simplest joint that will do the job.

Assembly. Ease of assembly influences the cost and time of production. Can the product be assembled easily and accurately?

Quality. A low-cost product often has joints that are not the best but that are the least costly. What is the quality of the product that you will be making?

Disassembly. Is the product one that will be taken apart for shipping? Knocked-down furniture has many joints that can be easily assembled. This feature makes it easy to move the product from a store to a home.

JOINT STRENGTH

The strength of a joint depends on a good fit. The contact area between mating pieces must be smooth and flat. This is necessary for maximum contact of glued surfaces.

The direction of the wood influences the strength of the joint. Wood is strongest in the with-the-grain direction. The strongest joints have edge or face grain as the contact surface. The end grain is weak and difficult to join by gluing or with mechanical fasteners.

CUTTING CONSIDERATIONS

The pieces to be joined are cut to their finished sizes before the joints are cut. All pieces having identical joint sizes are cut together. The power tools should be set so that the cuts are very accurately made. Use only sharp cutting tools.

FIGURE 10-1
Joints are an important part of the design solution. (*Courtesy of Worden Company.*)

FLAT BUTT JOINT JOINED WITH DOWEL PINS.

EDGE BUTT JOINT JOINED WITH DOWEL PINS.

FLAT BUTT JOINT FASTEN WITH NAILS, SCREWS, CORRUGATED FASTENERS OR CLAMP NAILS.

EDGE BUTT JOINT FASTEN WITH NAILS, SCREWS OR CLAMP NAILS.

GLUE BLOCK

FIGURE 10-2
End butt joints are the easiest to cut.

FIGURE 10-3
This butt joint is being secured with wood screws.

BUTT JOINTS

The butt joint is the easiest to cut, but assembly can be difficult. One of the butting surfaces is end grain, and glues are therefore ineffective (Fig. 10-2). Butt joints can be joined using screws, nails, wood dowels, corrugated fasteners, Skotch fasteners, or clamp nails (Figs. 10-3 to 10-7). Glue blocks help stiffen butt joints (Fig. 10-8). Butt joints used in knock-down furniture are discussed later in this chapter.

EDGE JOINTS

Edge joints can be assembled using glue. The joining edges must be square and straight so that the glue contacts both surfaces and does not have to fill a crack between the boards. Wood can be joined edge to edge using only glue. If additional strength is

FIGURE 10-4
Butt joints can be secured with corrugated fasteners when strength and appearance are not important.

FIGURE 10-6
Skotch fasteners provide a quick way to secure a butt joint.

FIGURE 10-5
The easiest way to secure a butt joint is with nails.

FIGURE 10-7
Butt joints can be securely joined with clamp nails.

desired, dowels or some form of machined spline, tongue and groove, rabbet, or other shape can be used (Fig. 10-9). If it is desired that the spline or tongue not show, it can be stopped several inches from the edge (Fig. 10-10). A well-made edge joint is stronger than the wood itself. Edge joints can also be joined using corrugated fasteners, Skotch fasteners, or clamp nails (Figs. 10-3 to 10-7).

DOWELS

Wood dowel pins are widely used in joint construction. Dowel pins range in diameter from $\frac{1}{8}$ to $\frac{1}{2}$ in. by $\frac{1}{16}$ths and from $\frac{1}{2}$ to 1 in. by $\frac{1}{8}$ths. They are available

FIGURE 10-8
Glue blocks can be used to strengthen joints.

I. NAIL THE BUTT
JOINT.

THEN GLUE THE GLUE
BLOCK IN PLACE.

120 CHAPTER 10 WOODWORKING JOINTS

FIGURE 10-9
Stock can be joined edge to edge with these joints.

PLAIN EDGE

DOWELED EDGE

TONGUE AND GROOVE EDGE

RABBET EDGE OR EDGE LAP

MILLED EDGE

SPLINE GRAIN DIRECTION

SPLINED EDGE

STOPPED TONGUE OR SPLINE

STOPPED GROOVE

FIGURE 10-10
A stopped tongue or spline can be used on edge joints when it is desired that it not show on the end.

cut to standard length. Some have straight or spiral grooves in the side to help carry excess glue and allow air to escape as the joint is clamped (Fig. 10-11). They are also beveled on each end.

For most work the diameter of the dowel to use should be half the thickness of the wood. For example, a $\frac{3}{8}$-in. dowel is used in wood $\frac{3}{4}$ in. thick. The spacing of dowels is a matter of judgment. Small

butt joints should have at least two dowels. On longer joints, as an edge joint, they should be 4 to 6 in. apart. The dowel should enter the wood at least two and one-half times its diameter. A $\frac{3}{8}$-in. dowel should enter each piece of wood $\frac{15}{16}$ in. or more. The dowel holes should be bored at least $\frac{1}{8}$ in. deeper than the length of the dowel. This provides a pocket for excess glue (Fig. 10-12).

Dowel holes can be drilled one at a time on a

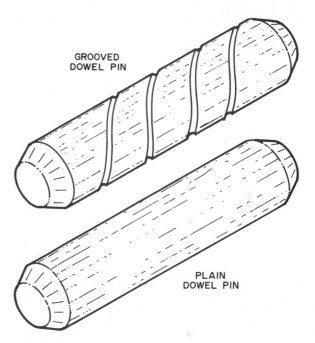

GROOVED DOWEL PIN

PLAIN DOWEL PIN

FIGURE 10-11
Dowel pins are chamfered on each end. Some have grooves to carry the glue.

FIGURE 10-12
This section through a dowel joint shows that the hole is deeper than the length of the dowel.

DOWEL HOLE 2"

$\frac{3}{4}$"

DOWEL 1$\frac{3}{4}$"

$\frac{1}{8}$" POCKET ON EACH END FOR GLUE.

FIGURE 10-13
Several dowel holes can be drilled at the same time with a multiple drill head on a drill press. (*Courtesy of Forest City Tool Company.*)

standard drill press, or several can be drilled with a multiple drill head (Fig. 10-13). Another dowel joint system, the 32-millimeter system, is discussed in detail in Chapter 17.

MITER JOINTS

A miter joint is much like the butt joint. The main difference is that the members are cut on a 45° angle. This joint has no end grain showing. It is a weak joint because both meeting surfaces are end grain. Plain miters can be fastened with some type of mechanical fastener. Those commonly used include nails, corrugated fasteners, clamp nails, Skotch nails, and wood and plastic dowels (Figs. 10-14 to 10-18).

Recommended joints for fastening flat miters are shown in Fig. 10-19, page 124. Notice the grain of the feather and spline runs perpendicular to the face of the miter. The half-lap miter can be joined by gluing because it has face grain exposed in the joint. Flat miters can be cut with a power miter saw or a radial arm saw (Fig. 10-20).

Recommended ways to join edge miters are shown in Fig. 10-21. In addition to using nails, dowels, or splines, various joints can be cut to increase the joining surface and lock the two pieces together.

FIGURE 10-14
The use of a miter vise helps when fastening a miter joint with nails.

FIGURE 10-15
Flat miters can be fastened with corrugated fasteners.

FIGURE 10-16
Clamp nails can be used to produce a strong flat miter joint.

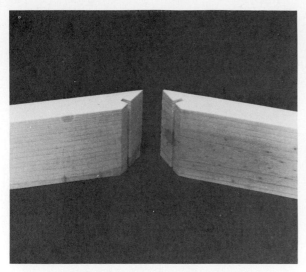

1. CUT GROOVES FOR THE CLAMP NAIL.

2. DRIVE CLAMP NAIL IN THE GROOVES.

FIGURE 10-17
Edge miters can be fastened with long clamp nails. The kerf is perpendicular to
the face of the miter.

FIGURE 10-18
Edge miters can be joined using plastic dowels that are
formed at a 90° angle.

The rabbet miter should be glued and nailed. The
lock miter does not require nailing. A glue block can
be used to strengthen and stiffen the joint.

Edge miters can be cut using a table or radial
arm saw (Fig. 10-22, page 125). Polygon miters are
those cut on an angle other than 45°. To find the
angle to cut the miter, divide 180° by the number of
sides and subtract the answer from 90° (Fig. 10-23).

A compound miter forms products that have a
tapered shape (Fig. 10-24). The angle may be 45°
or one of the angles for a polygon miter. The joint
is a combination of a miter and a bevel cut (Fig.

10-25, page 126). It is cut with a radial arm saw
(Fig. 10-26).

GROOVES AND DADOES

A dado is a rectangular slot cut across the grain of a
board. Use the *dado joint* for holding the ends of
shelves, cabinet sides and bottoms, and partitions or
dividers. It is a strong joint but must be cut so that
the members fit snugly. The edge of the dado provides a lip on which a shelf can rest. It also helps
align members as they are assembled (Fig. 10-27,
page 126).

There are many variations of the dado. Examples are shown in Fig. 10-28. The through dado is
exposed to view when assembled. If this is not desired, a blind, or stopped, dado can be used. The dado
can be used with a rabbet joint. The rabbet should be
one-half to two-thirds of the width of the board on
which it was cut. The dovetail dado is strong and is
cut with a router.

Dadoes on solid lumber are usually cut to a
depth of half the thickness of the board. Dadoes in $\frac{3}{4}$-
in. (19-mm) plywood should be only $\frac{1}{4}$ in. (6 mm)
deep. If the dado is cut deeper, too many plies of
veneer will be cut, thus weakening the board. They
are often cut with a radial arm saw (Fig. 10-29).

Join dadoes by gluing. For additional strength,
nail the glued joint or join it with screws. You usually do not need clamps when the joint is fastened
with glue plus nails or screws.

A groove is a rectangular slot cut with the
grain. A *groove joint* frequently is used to hold pan-

FIGURE 10-19
These are other ways of securing flat miter joints.

DOWELED MITER

PLAIN MITER JOINT

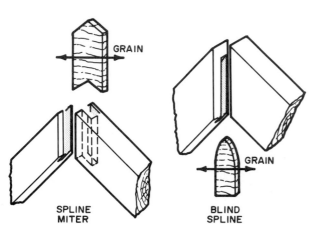

GRAIN

SPLINE MITER

GRAIN

BLIND SPLINE

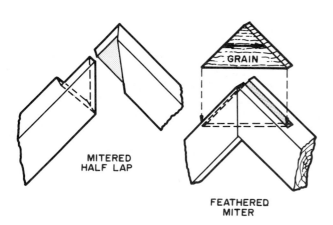

MITERED HALF LAP

GRAIN

FEATHERED MITER

LAMELLO PLATE

LAMELLO

MITER WITH LAMELLO JOINING TONGUES

FIGURE 10-20
A radial arm saw can be used to cut miters.

els. A drawer bottom usually is set in a groove. Grooves most often are cut to a depth of half the thickness of the board. Panels set in grooves, such as drawer bottoms, often are not glued. The assembled unit, the drawer, is thus permitted to expand and contract around the bottom of the unit. This prevents the wood from cracking or buckling. Grooves are often cut on a table saw or radial arm saw (Fig. 10-30, page 127).

RABBET JOINTS

A rabbet joint is used to form corners of cases and drawers and backs of cabinets. It is not a strong joint and must be glued and reinforced with nails or screws. It is stronger than a butt joint because it has a greater glue area. Commonly used rabbet joints are in Fig. 10-31.

The recess is usually cut about two-thirds of the thickness of the board. In a $\frac{3}{4}$-in. (19 mm) board this would be $\frac{1}{2}$ in. (13 mm). They are often cut on a table saw (Fig. 10-32).

LAP JOINTS

A lap joint is used when two pieces of wood meet or cross and their surfaces must be flush (Fig. 10-33). The half lap is used to join boards end to end. The end lap forms a corner. The middle lap forms a T.

MITER WITH SPLNE

PLAIN MITER

LOCK MITER

RABBETED MITER

DOWELS PERPENDICULAR TO MITER SURFACE

MITER WITH DOWELS

ANY MITER JOINT IS STIFFENED BY A GLUE BLOCK

NAILS

MITER WITH GLUE BLOCK

LAMELLO JOINING TONGUES IN AN EDGE MITER

FIGURE 10-21
These are ways that edge miters can be fastened.

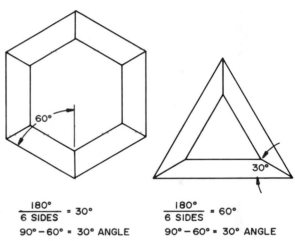

FIGURE 10-22
Edge miters can be cut with a table saw. (*Courtesy of Rockwell International.*)

$$\frac{180°}{6 \text{ SIDES}} = 30°$$

$$90° - 60° = 30° \text{ ANGLE}$$

$$\frac{180°}{6 \text{ SIDES}} = 60°$$

$$90° - 60° = 30° \text{ ANGLE}$$

FIGURE 10-23
How to find miter angles for any type of polygon.

FIGURE 10-24
The sides of this planter required that compound miters be cut.

FIGURE 10-25
A compound miter is a combination of a miter and a bevel cut.

FIGURE 10-26
This compound miter is being cut on a radial arm saw.

FIGURE 10-27
The construction of this library carrel required the use of several dados. (*Courtesy of Library Bureau.*)

Usually, each member is cut one-half its thickness. They are joined by gluing. Nails or screws may be added if needed. Lap joints are most often cut with a radial arm saw or a table saw.

END-TO-END JOINTS

Two commonly used joints that unite two boards end to end are *scarf* and *finger joints* (Fig. 10-34, page 128). The scarf joint is cut at a low angle to provide maximum gluing surface. Sometimes, it is strengthened by adding dowels.

The finger joint is widely used in the construction industry. The joint is cut with special, powered cutters. It is used to join short pieces of wood to form longer pieces. The joint is then glued. This joint is as strong as or even stronger than the original board.

MORTISE-AND-TENON JOINTS

A *mortise* is a rectangular opening cut into the wood. A *tenon* is a projecting part designed to fit into a

FIGURE 10-28
Variations of the dado and groove joints.

PLAIN DADO

STOPPED DADO – CURVED SHOULDER

SHOULDERED DADO

STOPPED DADO – SQUARE SHOULDER

FULL DOVETAIL DADO

HALF DOVETAIL DADO

GROOVE

FIGURE 10-29
A radial arm saw can be used to cut a dado.

FIGURE 10-30
Grooves can be cut with a radial arm saw.

FIGURE 10-31
End and edge rabbet joints are commonly used in furniture and cabinet construction.

RABBET CUT WITH THE GRAIN

RABBET CUT ACROSS GRAIN

MORTISE-AND-TENON JOINTS 127

FIGURE 10-32
This rabbet is being cut on a table saw.

mortise. Together they make a strong joint. For maximum strength they must be accurately cut to size.

The mortise-and-tenon joint is widely used to join cross members—for example, a rail to the leg of a chair or table. It is used in high-quality cabinet and frame construction. There are many adaptations of this joint. The common ones are shown in Fig. 10-35.

The blind mortise-and-tenon joint is completely hidden. The shoulders cut around the tenon and cover the edges of the mortise. The open mortise-and-tenon joint is easier to cut. It is useful when joining members at corners. The haunched mortise-and-tenon is designed for frames that have a panel.

FIGURE 10-33
Variations of the lap joint.

FIGURE 10-34
Scarf and finger joints are used to join stock end to end.

The haunch on top fits in the panel groove in the side rail. The stub joint has a short tenon that fits in a long groove. A plywood panel is held in the remaining portion of the groove. It does not have shoulders at top or bottom. The barefaced mortise-and-tenon places the tenon on one side of the rail. This is done when the rail is to be flush with the surface of the leg.

The tenon should be cut as large as possible without reducing the strength of the member containing the mortise. Generally, the thickness of the tenon is one-half the thickness of the piece on which it is cut. It is usually $\frac{1}{2}$ in. (13 mm) from the top of the rail and $\frac{1}{4}$ in. (6 mm) from the bottom of the rail. The length depends somewhat on the thickness of the piece to contain the mortise. Generally, the tenon length should be two and one-half times its thickness (Fig. 10-36, page 130).

The mortise should be no closer to the top of the part than $\frac{1}{2}$ in. (13 mm). It should be no closer to the face of the part than $\frac{5}{16}$ in. (8 mm) (Fig. 10-36). The joint will be stronger if these distances can be larger. Cut the mortise $\frac{1}{8}$ in. deeper than the length of the tenon. This forms a glue pocket. Cut the mortise

FIGURE 10-35

Variations of the mortise-and-tenon joint.

before you cut the tenon. It is easier to adjust the size of the tenon to fit the mortise.

Tenons are cut with a table saw, radial arm saw or tenoner (Fig. 10-37). Mortises are cut with a mortiser or router (Fig. 10-38).

BOX AND DOVETAIL JOINTS

The dovetail joint is used to join drawer sides and fronts and forms a decorative way to join corners of chests. It is a strong joint but must be carefully cut. Several variations are in Fig. 10-39. The half-blind dovetail provides a corner where the joint does not show on the front. It is widely used on good-quality furniture construction.

The box joint is used to join corners of boxes and chests. It is a strong joint and easy to cut. The through dovetail is similar but stronger than the box joint.

The sizes of pins on a box joint will vary depending upon the desire of the designer. Generally, they are the same thickness as the wood on which they are cut. This produces a square pin. When cutting a box joint, remember that one side starts with a notch and the other a pin (Fig. 10-40).

Dovetail joints are usually sized by the size and selection of templates and router cutters available. Generally, they are on an angle of 80°. When cutting them, start with a half pin on one side and a half notch on the other (Fig. 10-41). It is best if the joint stops with a half pin on the bottom end of the wood.

Dovetail joints are cut with a router and a dovetail attachment (Fig. 10-42). Box joints are usually cut with a table saw.

FIGURE 10-36
Recommended proportions for laying out mortises and tenons.

FIGURE 10-38
Mortises are cut with a mortiser.

FIGURE 10-37
This tenon is being cut on a table saw. The guard has been removed so that you can see the relationship between the dado cutters and the wood. (*Courtesy of Rockwell International.*)

FIGURE 10-39
Dovetail and box joints are strong and decorative.

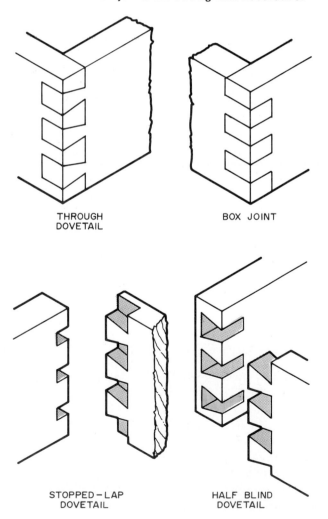

THROUGH DOVETAIL

BOX JOINT

STOPPED-LAP DOVETAIL

HALF BLIND DOVETAIL

FIGURE 10-40
When laying out a box joint, alternate the notches and pins starting at the top of the stock.

FIGURE 10-41
Start the dovetail with a half pin on the top of one side and a half notch on the other side.

FIGURE 10-42
Dovetails are cut with a router and a dovetail template.

THE LEMON SPLINE SYSTEM

The lemon spline system can be used to join butt and miter joints, and install knock-down furniture fittings and special hinges (Fig. 10-43). The joints are joined using an elliptical plate that is set into slots cut to fit the plate (Fig. 10-44). A plate joiner machine is used to cut the curved bottom slot in both pieces to be joined. The adhesive is placed in the slot followed by the insertion of the plate (Fig. 10-45). After the joint is closed, the pieces may be slid $\frac{1}{8}$ in. (3 mm) in either direction to assure perfect align-

FIGURE 10-43
Typical applications of Lamello plates. (*Courtesy of Colonial Saw.*)

FIGURE 10-44
The Lamello plate is glued in the slot cut by the Lamello machine. (*Courtesy of Colonial Saw.*)

FIGURE 10-45
Lamello saw being used to cut slots in a table leg. (*Courtesy of Colonial Saw.*)

FIGURE 10-46
The Lamello Lamex is a mechanical fastener used to assemble knock-down furniture. (*Courtesy of Colonial Saw.*)

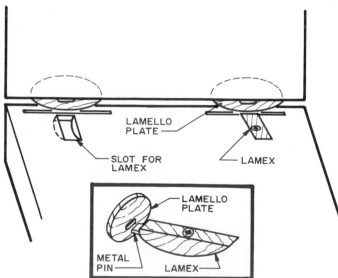

ment of the parts. The plate, which is manufactured in a compressed condition, expands when wetted by the adhesive. This ensures a tight-fitting strong joint.

The Lamello Lamex is a system for detachable wood joining. The Lamello plates have a slot in them. The Lamex is a wood mechanical fastener

FIGURE 10-47
These joints are used with mechanical carcass fasteners.

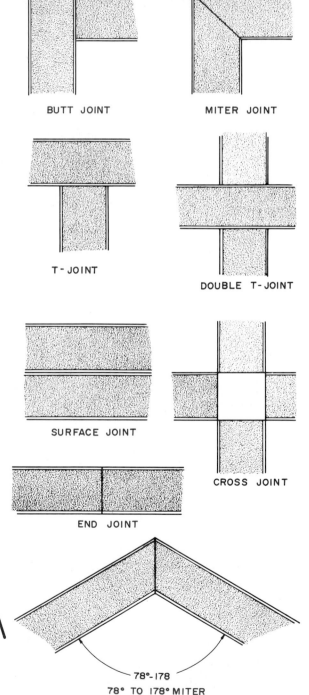

with a metal pin adjusted by a screw. The Lamello plate is glued as described earlier. The Lamex is glued in a curved bottom slot cut in the matching piece. A turn of the screw moves the metal pin into the slot joining the two wood members (Fig. 10-46).

MECHANICAL FASTENERS FOR JOINTS

A variety of mechanical fasteners that are finding extensive use in cabinet construction and furniture units use box-type carcass construction. The joints used include butt, miter, T-joint, end, cross, double T, and surface (Fig. 10-47). These can be joined by one of three types of fasteners, forming (1) rigid non-releasable joints, (2) rigid releasable joints, or (3) flexible releasable joints.

A rigid releasable joint can be secured using a special one-piece fastener (Fig. 10-48). Another type uses a fastener that goes through the one material to be joined and is secured in an insert set into the second piece (Fig. 10-49). Still another uses a cylinder head machine screw that is secured in a cross-nut in the second member (Fig. 10-50). Detailed information on these and other mechanical fasteners is provided in Chapter 17.

FIGURE 10-48
Butt joint secured with a one-piece fastener forming a rigid releasable joint. (*Courtesy of H'a'fele America, 203 Feld Ave., High Point, NC 27261.*)

FIGURE 10-49
This two-piece mechanical fastener uses a decorative countersunk head machine screw and a threaded insert. (*Courtesy of H'a'fele America, 203 Feld Ave., High Point, NC 27261.*)

FIGURE 10-50
This mechanical fastener uses a decorative cylinder head machine screw and a cross-nut. (*Courtesy of H'a'fele America, 203 Feld Ave., High Point, NC 27261.*)

STUDY QUESTIONS

Answer each of the following questions. If you are not sure of an answer, review the chapter.

10-1. What are the factors to consider when selecting a wood joint?

10-2. What ways are used to secure butt joints?

10-3. How can edge joints be strengthened?

10-4. What mechanical fasteners are used to secure miter joints?

10-5. What is the difference between a groove and a dado?

10-6. What are the types of lap joints?

10-7. How are boards joined end to end?

10-8. What is a good use for a mortise-and-tenon joint?

10-9. Describe a mortise and tenon.

10-10. What is a Lamello plate?

10-11. What power tools are used to cut a dovetail joint?

Following are technical terms that you should be able to use as part of your working vocabulary. Write a brief description of the meaning of each term.

Butt joint
Edge joint
Miter joint

Groove
Dado
Rabbet joint
Lap joint
Mortise-and-tenon joint
Box joint
Dovetail joint
Lamello plates

11

LEG AND RAIL CONSTRUCTION

Leg and rail construction is a commonly used method for building tables and chairs. It produces a strong furniture unit that can be made with standard machine tools (Fig. 11-1).

The vertical legs are joined by the horizontal rails. The rails distribute the load placed on the furniture unit to the legs and keep the legs from spreading apart. The legs transmit the load to the floor (Fig. 11-2). This provides the structural framework for the furniture unit.

Joints must be properly made so that maximum strength is achieved. Joint construction is covered in detail in Chapter 10.

TABLES

The size and design of tables varies widely. The types commonly found include dining tables, end tables, coffee tables, writing tables, workbenches, and many others. They may be square, rectangular, round, oval, or other shapes. Their height varies with their use. They may have drawers, doors, folding leaves, and shelves. Following are examples of leg and rail construction.

FIGURE 11-1
A strong furniture unit uses proper leg and rail construction. (*Courtesy of Hekman Furniture Company.*)

FIGURE 11-2
The load on tables is carried by the legs to the floor.

Rails

Rails on tables are usually located directly below the top. They are commonly joined to the legs with dowel or mortise-and-tenon joints (Fig. 11-3). Leg-rail joints are often reinforced with metal or wood corner blocks (Figs. 11-4 and 11-5). Rails can run on a diagonal between legs (Fig. 11-6). Another variation uses a single rail and stretcher to connect the pedestals on each end (Fig. 11-7). The *stretcher* is a horizontal structural member that keeps the legs from spreading apart.

There are several ways in which rails are generally arranged. The rail can be set flush with the face of the leg, recessed or overlapped (Fig. 11-8). The joints used must be adjusted for each type. If the rail is set flush and a mortise and tenon is to be used, the tenon must be cut on the back of the rail. This is called a *barefaced tenon*. If it overlaps the leg, a dowel joint or wood screws can be used. (See Chapter 10 for additional leg-to-rail joints.)

Rails can be straight, rounded, or elliptical and often meet the legs on an angle (Fig. 11-9). Rounded

FIGURE 11-3
Typical leg-to-rail connections.

rails can be joined with dowels as shown in Fig. 11-10. Most chairs are narrower in the back than in the front. This requires the side rails to be cut on an angle. If a mortise and tenon is to be used, the tenon must be cut on an angle. If a dowel is used, it is set on an angle to the end of the rail (Fig. 11-11).

Some forms of contemporary furniture use a sculptured joint. When making a rail-to-leg connection, form the curved section by cutting and shaping it on the leg. If the rail is shaped, the curved sections, being very weak, easily break off (Figs. 11-12 and 11-10).

FIGURE 11-4
Leg–rail joints are strengthened with wood and metal corner blocks.

FIGURE 11-5
This cabriole leg and rail connection is strengthened with a wood corner block. Notice that it uses two hanger bolts into the leg and eight screws into the rail. (*Courtesy of Thomasville Furniture Industries, Inc.*)

FIGURE 11-6
Rails can run diagonally between legs.

FIGURE 11-7
This table uses a single center rail between the pedestals at each end. Notice the use of a stretcher.

FIGURE 11-8
Rails can overlap, be set flush with, or recessed on the leg.

FIGURE 11-9
This table has curved rails, including a drawer with a curved front. (*Courtesy of Hekman Furniture Company.*)

DOWEL MEETS RAIL AT AN ANGLE.

TENON MEETS RAIL AT AN ANGLE.

TENON

DOWEL

STRAIGHT RAILS MEETING LEGS ON AN ANGLE.

DOWELS OR TENONS ARE SET PERPENDICULAR TO THE LEGS.

FIGURE 11-10
The rounded rails and stretchers on this chair are held with dowels. (*Courtesy of Danish Design Council.*)

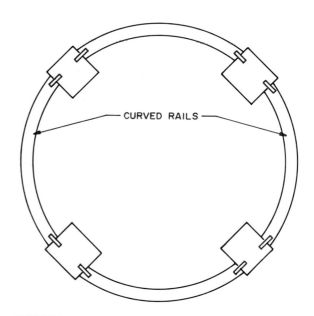

CURVED RAILS

FIGURE 11-11
When rails meet a leg on an angle, the dowel or tenon is perpendicular to the leg.

Rails can be flat, have a shaped bottom edge, or have molding applied (Fig. 11-13). The choice depends on the design of the furniture unit. On chairs the rail is usually located directly below the seat. Since chairs are often placed under very heavy loads, a strong leg-rail joint is of special importance. Corner blocks are often used to reinforce and stiffen the joint (Fig. 11-4).

Stretchers

On both tables and chairs, a lower rail, called a *stretcher,* is sometimes used. It strengthens and adds a decorative touch to the furniture unit (Fig. 11-14). Sometimes a table will have a lower shelf instead of stretchers (Fig. 11-15). The shelf can be installed by

FIGURE 11-12
Sculpture features are cut to take advantage of the strongest position of the grain.

FIGURE 11-13
Rails are formed in many ways.

FLAT RAIL

SHAPED LOWER EDGE

MOLDING ON BOTTOM

MOLDING ON FACE

MOLDING ON FACE

RAIL WITH SHAPED EDGE

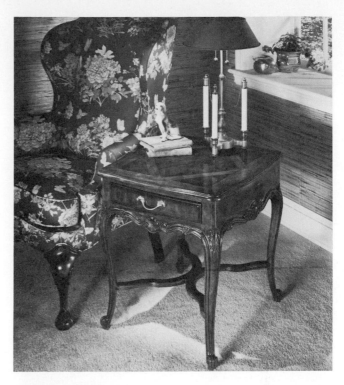

FIGURE 11-14
This table has stretchers connecting the cabriole legs. Notice the carving on the legs and the feet. The top has inlaid veneers. (*Courtesy of Drexel Heritage Furnishings Inc.*)

FIGURE 11-15
A lower shelf serves the same structural purpose as stretchers. (*Courtesy of Drexel Heritage Furnishings Inc.*)

fitting the shelf between the legs and joining them with a dowel. The leg could have a dado cut into it and the corner of the shelf cut to fit into the dado (Fig. 11-16).

Drawers

If a table has a drawer, the rail in which it fits can be in many forms. The drawer could either pierce the

FIGURE 11-16
Some of the ways a shelf can be secured to a leg.

SECTION

SECTION

FRONT VIEW

FRONT VIEW

JOIN SHELF TO SQUARE SECTION IN LEG.

SET THE SHELF IN A DADO CUT IN THE SQUARE SECTION IN THE LEG.

NOTCH THE LEG TO FIT THE SHELF.

SHELF CUT TO FIT CURVATURE OF LEG.

SECTION

SECTION

FRONT VIEW

FRONT VIEW

rail, have one small rail below it, use a dust panel, or have no rail at all (Fig. 11-17). Wood drawer guides can be used in small drawers. Large drawers work best if metal drawer guides are used. Information on drawer construction is given in Chapter 14.

CHAIRS

Most chairs use the basic structure of four legs and rails forming a rectangular frame for a seat. Usually, the back legs are longer and form the structural support for the back. A chair is often wider in the front than in the back. On some chairs the front legs extend above the seat to support arm rests which extend from the back to front legs (Fig. 11-18).

When designing a chair, the forces exerted on it must be considered. The major force is down on the rails and legs due to the weight of the person seated in the chair. The rails transmit the weight to the legs (Fig. 11-19). The legs receive the full load and transmit it to the floor. The weight on the end of each leg is equal to the total weight divided by the number of legs. The weight per square inch of bearing surface (end of the leg) is equal to the total weight divided by the area of the ends of all the legs added together. For example, if a 200-lb person sits in the chair in Fig. 11-19, each leg will carry 50 lb. If the end of each leg is 1 inch in diameter, its area would be 0.78 in^2. The weight per square inch on each leg would be $200 \div 3.12$ or 64.1 lb. By enlarging the leg diameter at the floor, it is possible to reduce the load per square inch on it. The downward force tends to force the legs to spread apart at the floor. The rail-to-leg joint must be strong enough to resist this force. Stretchers can be placed between the legs to help resist this action.

Legs are usually square, rectangular, or round and taper to the foot to improve appearance. The back legs can be straight or curved. The angle of the back to the seat is adjusted so that the chair is comfortable to use. Rails are shaped for strength and appearance.

Dowel or mortise and tenon joints are generally used to join the rails and legs (Fig. 11-20). Since there is a lot of weight on a chair, the joints must be properly made to achieve maximum strength. Wood or metal corner reinforcing is often used to strengthen the rail-to-leg connection. If a chair has armrests, they are connected to the front and back legs. Typical details are shown in Fig. 11-21. The chair in Fig. 11-22 was designed so that most of it could be assembled with wood screws and metal angles.

Chairs are designed to fit the human body (Fig. 11-23). The chair back must support the person in

FIGURE 11-17
Rails may be exposed, hidden, entirely eliminated, or replaced with a dust panel.

SINGLE LOWER RAIL

DOUBLE RAIL ON A
FLUSH DRAWER

HIDDEN RAILS

RAIL

DRAWER FRONT

RAIL

FULL WIDTH DRAWER FRONT

DRAWER FRONT

DRAWER PIERCED FRONT RAIL

UNIT WITH METAL DRAWER
SLIDES AND NO RAILS OR
DUST PANELS.

UNIT WITH DUST PANEL
AND NO RAILS.

FIGURE 11-18
The legs on this chair support the rails forming the seat as well as the sculptured back and arm rests. (*Courtesy of Danish Design Council.*)

FIGURE 11-19
A chair must be designed to carry a heavy load and resist the forces it produces which tend to pull the frame apart.

the chair at a comfortable angle. The angle of the seat is also important. If it is sloped too much, it is hard to get out of the chair. The height of the seat must allow a person to keep his or her feet on the floor. Research into human body sizes and normal positions is used to design chairs that fit the human body.

Most people prefer chairs that are made from small rails and rather small-diameter legs. This produces a light, graceful chair. However, it does leave minimal surfaces for producing joints. The mortise and tenon is the strongest joint. Since rails often meet the leg at an angle, a mortise and tenon is hard to cut. The dowel joint is often used because it is easier to make.

If tenons are used, they have to be mitered where they intersect in the leg (Fig. 11-24). If dowels are used, they should be at least $\frac{3}{8}$ in. in diameter. Each rail-to-leg joint should have at least two dowels. Use three dowels if the rail is wide enough. Consider staggering the dowels in each leg (Fig. 11-24). If this cannot be done, dowel and glue the legs and front rail together. When dry, bore the holes for the dowels for the side rails and assemble.

When rails meet a round leg, the ends of the rails must be cut to fit the curve of the leg. The leg could have a section cut flat, so the square end of the rail meets it. If the rail is round or tapered, it can enter a round leg in a round or tapered hole. Metal fasteners can also be used (Fig. 11-25).

Seat construction varies considerably. Generally, the front edge of the seat overlaps the rail. If it is an upholstered seat, it can drop inside the frame and rest on battens screwed to the inside of the frame. A cane seat has the caning set into grooves cut on top of the rail or in a separate frame. The frame is set on battens. Solid wood seats can have the legs set in tapered holes and glued in place (Fig. 11-26).

Details of upholstered furniture are shown in Chapters 48 to 50.

FIGURE 11-20
This chair is assembled using dowel joints and corner blocks.

DOWEL   SCREW WITH   DOWEL INTO
              WOOD PLUG   A TOP RAIL.
              OVER IT.

FIGURE 11-21
Typical armrest connections.

FIGURE 11-22
This chair utilizes simple joints, most of which are secured with wood screws and metal angles. (*Courtesy of Danish Design Council.*)

FIGURE 11-23
These chairs are designed to support the human body in a comfortable position. Notice that the legs on the chairs and table are laminated wood. (*Courtesy of Danish Design Council.*)

FIGURE 11-24
When tenons meet in a leg, miter them. When possible, stagger the dowels.

FIGURE 11-26
Seats can be positioned on the chair frame in many ways.

| ROUND TAPERED RAIL WITH TAPERED HOLE. | ROUND STRAIGHT RAIL WITH ROUND DOWEL. | ROUND STRAIGHT RAIL WITH SCREW TYPE FASTENER. | RECTANG- ULAR RAIL WITH CURVED END. | RECTANG- ULAR RAIL LEG FLATTENED. |

FIGURE 11-25
Some ways to join a rail to a round leg.

FIGURE 11-27
This eighteenth-century table has graceful cabriole legs. (*Courtesy of Drexel Heritage Furnishings Inc.*)

LEGS, POSTS, PEDESTALS, AND FEET

Legs are one of the basic parts of many furniture units. They are part of the structural framework for units using leg and rail construction. The design of legs is influenced by the style of furniture. The eighteenth-century mahogany table in Fig. 11-27 has gracefully curved cabriole legs. Some styles of furniture use straight legs that are square or round and have no taper (Fig. 11-28). Square tapered legs are typical of Oriental Chippendale furniture (Fig. 11-29). Tapered legs have also been popular on many styles of furniture.

Posts serve the same purpose as legs but are usually longer. The vertical supports on a bed are called posts (Fig. 11-30) The rear legs on chairs usually rise above the seat and support the back. They are also called posts.

Some tables have a pedestal stem and three or more feet. The pedestal can be square, round, or turned to any design desired. The feet are joined to the pedestal with dowels, dovetails, or mortises (Fig. 11-31).

FIGURE 11-28
Round and square legs with no taper are often used as shown on this Chippendale table. (*Courtesy of Drexel Heritage Furnishings Inc.*)

FIGURE 11-30
This poster bed features two tall posts. (*Courtesy of Drexel Heritage Furnishings Inc.*)

FIGURE 11-29
The base supporting this cabinet uses slender, square-tapered legs. (*Courtesy of Drexel Heritage Furnishings Inc.*)

FIGURE 11-31
This tabletop is supported by a large round pedestal having four feet.

Answer each of the following questions. If you are not sure of an answer, review the chapter.

11-1. What type of furniture is often built using leg and rail construction?

11-2. What joints are used to join legs and rails?

11-3. Why are stretchers used on tables and chairs?

11-4. Why are corner blocks used?

11-5. What is often used to replace the stretcher on a table?

11-6. How can you figure the weight to be carried by the bottom of each chair leg?

11-7. What angles must be carefully selected when designing a chair?

11-8. Where are posts used on furniture?

11-9. What is a pedestal?

IMPORTANT TECHNICAL TERMS

Following are technical terms that you should be able to use as part of your working vocabulary. Write a brief description of the meaning of each term.

Rail
Stretcher
Posts
Pedestal
Cabriole leg

12

CARCASS CONSTRUCTION FOR FURNITURE UNITS

Carcass construction involves building a wood box-like unit with one or more open sides. These open sides receive doors, drawers, or shelves. The carcass is made up of bulkheads, top, bottom, back, partitions, dust panels (also called web frames), face-frames, shelf supports, drawer guides, and various types of legs and bases (Fig. 12-1). The actual design of the carcass will vary depending on the end use of the product and the desired quality. Furniture such as dressers, desks, and bookcases use carcass construction, as do kitchen cabinets (Fig. 12-2).

BULKHEADS AND PARTITIONS

Bulkheads can be made from solid wood, plywood, particleboard, or be of panel construction. *Solid wood* bulkheads are made of narrow strips, 4 to 5 in. wide, glued together as shown in Fig. 12-3. *Plywood and particleboard bulkheads* are more stable than solid wood. Since they do not warp or expand and contract very much, they are widely used for end panels. Plywood bulkheads have a hardwood veneer as the outer ply. Particleboard bulkheads are usually covered with a plastic laminate or veneer.

Bulkheads of *panel construction* use solid wood rails and stiles and plywood panels or panels machined from solid wood (Fig. 12-4). The *rails* are the members parallel with the floor. *Stiles* are perpendicular to the floor. Panels are usually ¼-in. (6-mm) plywood: however, any material, such as solid wood, hardboard, glass, metal, or plastic, could be used (Fig. 12-5). Rails and stiles are joined with dowel, mortise-and-tenon, or stuck joints. The tenon is set in the groove cut for the panel. A recommended tenon length is ½ in. (12 mm). Panels with stuck joint construction require a matched set of shaper cutters to shape the edges and ends. This is discussed in further detail in Chapter 36.

Partitions are vertical dividers within a cabinet. Most often, they are made of plywood, but panel construction can be utilized (Fig. 12-6, page 150). They are used to strengthen long cabinets and carry shelves and drawers using side guides.

CONSTRUCTION OF THE CARCASS

The types of joints used in carcass construction depend on the quality of construction desired and the design of the carcass. Joints used in good-quality furniture are stronger but more difficult and costly

147

FIGURE 12-1
These parts make up the carcass.

to make. They tend to conceal the union between the two pieces. Following are examples that illustrate typical construction situations.

The carcass *corner joints* for flush-top construction can be butt, dovetail, rabbet, spline miter, offset miter, lock miter, and half-blind tongue and rabbet. The butt joint is the easiest to make and is glued and nailed or fastened with dowels. The rabbet joint has a shoulder and gives a stiffer joint (Fig. 12-7, page 150). A glue block can be used to stiffen the joints if necessary. A glue block is a wood strip that is glued and stapled or nailed to two pieces to stiffen them.

Another way to join corners is to use a vertical, solid wood corner piece. The actual design of the piece can vary. Several examples are shown in Fig. 12-8.

Interior partitions and fixed shelves can be installed with a rabbet and dado, dado, blind dado and tongue, dovetail, butt joint with dowels or nails, spline, or battens (Fig. 12-9). If the furniture is to have a faceframe or banded edges, the dado can be cut through the front edge. If the edge is to be exposed, a blind dado is used. It is usually stopped $\frac{1}{2}$ in. (13 mm) from the front edge.

If the design calls for the use of rails to connect the bulkheads, they can be joined as shown in Fig. 12-10, page 152. More information on joints is provided in Chapter 10.

BACKS

The back on a unit of lesser quality is cut slightly smaller ($\frac{1}{4}$ in. or 6 mm) than the overall size and is nailed or stapled to the back edges. In better-quality work the back edges of the bulkhead and top are rabbeted, or a groove is cut to receive the back.

FIGURE 12-2
This cherry chest uses carcass construction. (*Courtesy of Drexel Heritage Furnishings Inc.*)

TENON $\frac{1}{2}$"

PLYWOOD PANEL

STILE

RAIL

$\frac{1}{4}$" × $\frac{1}{2}$" GROOVE FOR PLYWOOD

FIGURE 12-3
Typical bulkhead construction.

PLYWOOD OR PARTICLEBOARD

GLUED UP SOLID WOOD BOARDS

PLYWOOD, HARDWOOD, VENEER

SOLID WOOD FRAME WITH INSET PANEL

FIGURE 12-4
Panel construction used for bulkheads.

FIGURE 12-5
Typical panel details.

STILE OR RAIL

STILE OR RAIL

PLYWOOD PANEL

SHAPED SOLID WOOD RAISED PANEL

TYPICAL PANEL DETAILS

INTERIOR PARTITION

FIGURE 12-6
Interior partitions are vertical dividers within a cabinet.

TOP

GLUE BLOCK

BULKHEAD

RABBET

TOP

BULKHEAD

HALF BLIND TONGUE AND RABBET

TOP

BULKHEAD

SPLINED MITER

TOP

BULKHEAD

THROUGH DOVETAIL

TOP

BULKHEAD

HALF BLIND DOVETAIL

TOP

BULKHEAD

BUTT JOINT WITH DOWELS

TOP

BULKHEAD

OFFSET MITER

TOP

BULKHEAD

LOCK MITER

FIGURE 12-7
Corner joints used for flush-top carcass construction.

FIGURE 12-8
Corner joints may be made using a solid wood vertical corner piece.

Since the dust panel and bottom butt the back of the cabinet, their depth is reduced the same amount as the depth of the rabbet or groove cut in the bulkhead for the back. Sometimes the rabbet is cut a little deeper ($\frac{1}{4}$ in. or 6 mm) than the thickness of the backing material. The lip produced can be trimmed to get the unit to fit tightly against the wall (Fig. 12-11, page 152). If a groove is used, a lip is also provided (Fig. 12-12). The backing material can be $\frac{1}{8}$ to $\frac{1}{4}$-in. (3- to 6-mm) plywood or hardboard. A back adds considerable strength to the unit. Without it, the unit would tend to rack.

DUST PANELS

Dust panels, sometimes called web frames, are placed under each drawer and sometimes under the top. They provide a surface on which the drawer sides can slide. Dust panels may be open or closed. A *closed panel* has a piece of plywood or hardboard in the center opening of the frame. This helps reduce the flow of dust into each drawer. *Open panels* have the wood frame but do not have the plywood or hardboard insert (Fig. 12-13). Long dust panels usually have a center support to provide extra stiffness. This is especially important when several heavy drawers are to slide on it. If wood-center-type drawer slides are used, they are cut to fit on top of the dust panel (Fig. 12-14). There is more information on drawers and slides in Chapter 14.

Dust panels may be hidden or exposed (Fig. 12-15). If they are hidden, the drawer fronts, doors, and face frames cover them. In this case they are made of a less expensive wood such as poplar. When the dust panel is exposed, the front rail is made of the same wood as the drawer fronts and doors or this is covered with a matching veneer (Fig. 12-16, page 154).

Dust panels are constructed using dowel, haunched mortise-and-tenon, or stub mortise-and-

FIGURE 12-9
Shelves and dividers can be joined to bulkheads and partitions in many ways.

TOP FASTENS TO RAIL

RAIL JOINS TO SIDE IN ONE OF THESE POSITIONS

RAIL HORIZONTAL   RAIL VERTICAL

HORIZONTAL   VERTICAL   TENON   DOWELS
DOVETAIL   DOVETAIL
             (SET RAIL BACK
             FROM EDGE OF
             BULKHEAD)

FIGURE 12-10
Ways to join rails to bulkheads and partitions.

FIGURE 12-11
The dust panel and cabinet bottom are cut narrower than the top when the back is recessed into the furniture unit.

LIP

SIDE OR TOP

A

A

BACK

SECTION A

CABINET BACK

BACK

BOTTOM

SECTION B

B

SIDE, TOP OR BOTTOM

A

A

BACK

SECTION 'A'

CABINET BACK

A

A

FIGURE 12-12
The back may be set in a groove.

tenon joints (Fig. 12-17). They are usually joined to the bulkhead or partition with a dado; however, corner blocks are sometimes used (Fig. 12-18).

If a finished top is to be placed over the carcass, the panel below this top can be an open dust panel. The top is joined to the dust panel with screws.

FACEFRAMES

Faceframes are solid wood pieces attached to the front of the furniture unit. They hold the doors and frame the drawer openings. They are usually the same species of wood as is used for the doors and drawer fronts. A faceframe is made up of rails, stiles, and mullions (Fig. 12-19). Rails are horizontal pieces running parallel with the floor. *Stiles* are vertical pieces on the outside edges of the unit. *Mullions* are vertical pieces between doors or drawers.

The corners of a faceframe are joined with dowels, mortise-and-tenon, or stub tenon joints in the same manner as dust panels. Faceframes are often glued to the face of the cabinet. In inexpensive construction they are nailed and the nails are set and hidden.

TOPS

Tops are usually made from the same material as the sides. If made from solid wood, the edges are

GROOVE FOR PANEL

HARDBOARD OR PLYWOOD PANEL

$\frac{1}{4}$" X $\frac{1}{2}$" GROOVE

$\frac{1}{4}$" X $\frac{1}{2}$" TENON

JOINT IS A STUB TENON IN A GROOVE. OTHER JOINTS CAN BE USED.

FRONT EDGE

FIGURE 12-13
This is a closed dust panel.

WOOD CENTER TYPE DRAWER SLIDES

CENTER SUPPORT

FIGURE 12-14
Wood center drawer slides are cut to fit into the dust panel.

FIGURE 12-15
Dust panels may be hidden or exposed.

FURNITURE TOP

FURNITURE TOP

DRAWER FRONT

DRAWER BOTTOM

OPEN DUST PANEL

DRAWER FRONT

CLOSED DUST PANEL

CLOSED DUST PANEL

EXPOSED DUST PANEL

HIDDEN DUST PANEL

FIGURE 12-16
The dust panels, bulkheads, and partitions in this dresser are exposed. (*Courtesy of Drexel Heritage Furnishings Inc.*)

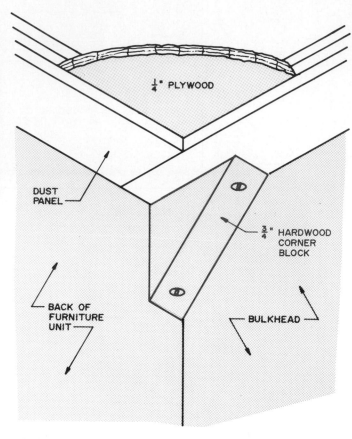

FIGURE 12-18
Corner blocks are sometimes used to join the dust panel to the bulkhead.

FIGURE 12-17
These joints are generally used to build dust panels.

STUB MORTISE AND TENON JOINT

DOWEL JOINT

HAUNCHED MORTISE AND TENON JOINT

often shaped with a decorative molding. Plywood and particleboard have unattractive edges that must be covered with a solid wood band, veneer, or plastic laminate. If the top overhangs the end panel, they can be joined as shown in Fig. 12-20. Flush tops are joined as shown in Fig. 12-7. More information on tops is given in Chapter 16.

DOORS

Doors may be lipped, flush, folding, overlay, horizontal sliding, and tambour. They may be paneled or plain style. Additional material on doors is presented in Chapter 13.

BASES

The base used for furniture units made with carcass construction depends on the design of the unit (Fig. 12-21, page 156). A recessed toe board can be used when the bulkhead meets the floor. A solid wood base can be recessed on the front and side. A plinth, a wood base on the outside of the unit base, is a

FIGURE 12-19
Parts of a faceframe.

FIGURE 12-20
When the top overhangs the bulkhead, it can be joined in these ways.

frequently used base. It is fastened to the bottom with cleats and screws. Glue blocks are also used (Fig. 12-22). A wide variety of legs are also used (Fig. 12-23). Additional information on legs is presented in Chapter 11.

A base that is commonly used on cabinets and large storage units has a recessed toe space. This is typically $3\frac{1}{2}$ in. (88 mm) high and $3\frac{1}{2}$ in. (88 mm) deep but can be varied to suit the design. The bottom shelf is set into a dado in the bulkhead. The top of this shelf is located so that the bottom of the faceframe is the design distance ($3\frac{1}{2}$ in.) from the floor. The open space below the faceframe is covered with a toe board. It is rabbeted to fit between the bulkheads and is glued to them (Fig. 12-24). If the cabinet is long, $\frac{3}{4}$-in.-thick wood members, called *sleepers,* are placed from the front to the back under the cabinet bottom perpendicular to the toe board (Fig. 12-25).

CORNICES

A *cornice* is a decorative molding at the top of an upper cabinet (Fig. 12-26). It may be applied over the top rail or extend above the top of the cabinet. Typical construction details are in Fig. 12-27.

TYPICAL CONSTRUCTION EXAMPLES

There are many ways to construct furniture carcasses. A variety of joints can be used as well as a number of design possibilities. The examples in

FIGURE 12-21
This eighteenth-century mahogany credenza was designed using a plinth-type base. (*Courtesy of Drexel Heritage Furnishings Inc.*)

RECESSED TOEBOARDS

RECESSED ON SIDE AND FRONT

PLINTH OUTSIDE CARCASS

LEG AND RAIL

INDIVIDUAL LEGS

PLINTH WITH SHAPED LEGS

FIGURE 12-23
Typical bases used on furniture units.

FIGURE 12-24
A toe board is recessed into the bulkhead.

FIGURE 12-22
The furniture unit may sit on top of a plinth.

FURNITURE UNIT SITS ON TOP OF PLINTH.

CORNER BLOCKS GLUED AND SCREWED IN PLACE.

SPLINE MITER OR DOWEL CORNER

A PLINTH

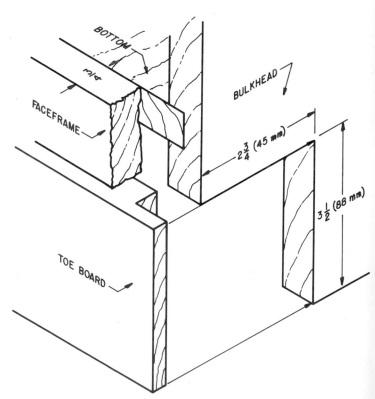

BOTTOM

FACEFRAME

BULKHEAD

$2\frac{3}{4}$ (45 mm)

$3\frac{1}{2}$ (88 mm)

TOE BOARD

FIGURE 12-25
Sleepers are used to reinforce the base on long furniture units.

FIGURE 12-26
This door chest has a large decorative molding at the top, forming a cornice. (*Courtesy of Drexel Heritage Furnishings Inc.*)

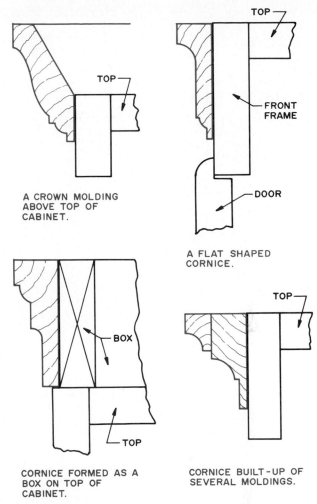

A CROWN MOLDING ABOVE TOP OF CABINET.

A FLAT SHAPED CORNICE.

CORNICE FORMED AS A BOX ON TOP OF CABINET.

CORNICE BUILT-UP OF SEVERAL MOLDINGS.

FIGURE 12-27
Typical cornice construction details.

Figs. 12-28 and 12-29 illustrate a number of frequently used construction solutions for good-quality furniture.

KNOCKED-DOWN FURNITURE

A lot of furniture on the market is sold in a disassembled condition. Special fasteners are used that permit the purchaser to assemble it using simple tools, such as an Allen wrench or screwdriver. Pozidriv screw heads are commonly used. These fasteners require only a butt joint, so manufacturing is simplified. The stereo cabinet shown in Fig. 12-30 is typical of this type of furniture. Hardware for this type of construction is described in Chapter 17.

FIGURE 12-28
This carcass construction has a flush top and a recessed plinth.

FIGURE 12-29
This carcass construction has an over-hanging top and a leg and rail base.

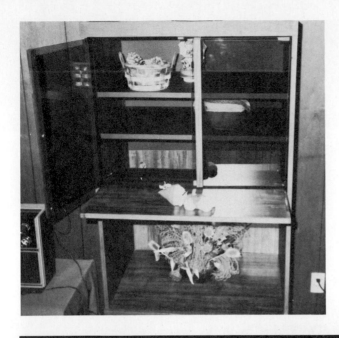

FIGURE 12-30
This TV-stereo cabinet was shipped knocked-down, and assembled with one-piece mechanical fasteners.

Answer each of the following questions. If you are not sure of an answer, review the chapter.

12-1. What are the names of the parts that make a carcass for a furniture unit?

12-2. What types of furniture are often made using carcass construction?

12-3. In what ways can bulkheads be constructed?

12-4. What is the difference between a rail and a stile?

12-5. How are rails and stiles joined to form the faceframe?

12-6. What purposes do partitions serve within the carcass?

12-7. Identify the carcass corner joints used with flush-top construction.

12-8. How is the cabinet back held in place?

12-9. What is the purpose for having dust panels?

12-10. What is the difference between an open and a closed dust panel?

12-11. What purpose is served by the faceframe?

12-12. What types of doors are used with carcass construction?

IMPORTANT TECHNICAL TERMS

Following are technical terms that you should be able to use as part of your working vocabulary. Write a brief description of the meaning of each term.

Carcass
Partition
Dust panel
Web frame

Bulkhead
Faceframe
Rail
Stile
Glue block
Mullions
Plinth
Toe board
Cornice

13

DOOR CONSTRUCTION

Doors serve functional purposes such as hiding the contents of a cabinet from view or protecting items from dust. They are also a part of the design and influence how people react to a furniture or cabinet unit. Doors are made in many different ways and from a variety of materials (Fig. 13-1).

FRAME-AND-PANEL DOORS

Frame-and-panel doors have solid wood frames with panels filling the space between. Small doors have top and bottom rails and stiles on the sides. Larger doors will have a middle rail and perhaps a mullion (Fig. 13-2).

Panels are usually flush or raised (Fig. 13-3). The flush panel may be set in a groove or rabbet in the stiles and rails. It can have molding and decorative overlays bonded to it (Fig. 13-4). Raised panels are thick panels having the edges machined to fit into a groove in the edges of the rails and stiles (Fig. 13-5).

Frame-and-panel doors can be built using a stub tenon, open mortise and tenon, dowel, or haunched mortise-and-tenon joint (Fig. 13-6). Good-quality factory manufactured cabinets use the stuck

FIGURE 13-1
The doors on this china cabinet form a major element in the design. The top doors have glass panels and the lower doors matched veneer panels. (*Courtesy of Drexel Heritage Furnishings Inc.*)

160

FIGURE 13-2
Parts of a paneled door.

FIGURE 13-3
Panels can be flush or raised.

PANEL RAISED ON
ONE SIDE.

STRAIGHT PANEL

BEVELED RAISED PANEL.

PANEL IN A RABBET.

FIGURE 13-4
Decorative overlays are often used.

FIGURE 13-5
The doors on this handsome armorie have raised panels.
(*Courtesy of Drexel Heritage Furnishings Inc.*)

FIGURE 13-6
These joints are used to build frame-and-panel doors.

STUB TENON

HAUNCHED MORTISE AND TENON.

OPEN MORTISE AND TENON.

DOWEL

FIGURE 13-7
The stuck joint is used when manufacturing doors for good-quality furniture.

COPED END ON RAIL

RAIL

STILE

GROOVE FOR PANEL

STICKING ON RAIL AND STILE

RAIL WITH COPED END

STILE

STICKING

GROOVE FOR PANEL

TENON FITS INTO GROOVE IN STILE USED FOR THE PANEL.

GROOVE FOR PANEL IN RAIL

COPED END OF RAIL

joint shown in Fig. 13-7. The edge of the stile and rail is shaped to receive a panel, and the outer edge is rounded. This is referred to as *sticking*. The ends of the rail are cut in the shape of the reverse of the sticking so that they match when the door is assembled. This shaped end is referred to as *coping*. Another method of molding an inside edge is with a router (Fig. 13-8).

FIGURE 13-8
It improves the appearance of frame-and-panel doors if the square edge is relieved by shaping it.

SOLID DOORS

Doors can be *solid wood*. If the wood is edge-glued lumber, it may be difficult to keep the door from warping. Cleats may be screwed to the inside of the door to help keep it flat.

Plywood is a good door material because it is stable. Veneer-core plywood shows the multiple plies along the edges unless it is banded. Hinges on these doors must screw into the face of the plywood. Screws do not hold well in the edge of the panel. Lumber-core plywood doors can have shaped or banded edges. Since the door has a solid lumber core, hinges can be screwed into the face or edge.

Particleboard doors are stable but require that a plastic laminate be glued to them to improve their appearance. Painted, stained, or natural finish particleboard can be used for storage cabinets where a high-quality grain is not necessary. Special screws are needed to secure hinges into particleboard.

Hardboard can be used for doors of all kinds. Wood or plastic laminates can be applied to the surface.

Many doors are *glass panels, plastic panels* that are translucent and opaque, and *metal grills* of various types. With special hinges or tracks, glass doors do not need a supporting frame.

TAMBOUR DOORS

Tambour doors are made of narrow wood strips fastened to heavy canvas, or flexible plastic hinges are used. The wood strips are cut to slide in a groove cut in the sides of the cabinet (Fig. 13-9). A canvas back is glued to the back of the tambour to hold the slats in place as the door is moved up or down. Plastic hinges are either set in a saw kerf or have a U-

FIGURE 13-9
Tambour doors can slide in a groove cut in the sides of the furniture unit.

HINGE SET IN KERF

U-TYPE SLIP-OVER HINGE.

FIGURE 13-10
Plastic hinges can be used to assemble a tambour door.

FIGURE 13-11
Horizontally sliding tambour doors can slide on plastic rails.

GROOVE FOR TOP TRACK

PLASTIC TRACK SET IN CURVED GROOVE.

shaped channel that slips over the wood strip (Fig. 13-10). Tambour doors can slide vertically as in Fig. 13-9 or horizontally as in Fig. 13-11. These can slide in a groove or on a plastic track that is set in a groove in the cabinet bottom.

SLIDING DOORS

Sliding doors are often used on bookshelves, wall cabinets, and other furniture units. The simplest and least expensive way to do this is to cut grooves in the unit bottom and the rail above the door, or nail wood strips to them and slide the doors in between the strips (Fig. 13-12). Cut the bottom groove about $\frac{1}{4}$ in. deep and the top groove $\frac{1}{2}$ in. deep. To insert the door, slide the top up into the top groove and lower the door into the bottom groove. The height of the door should be $\frac{3}{16}$ in. higher than the opening. Plastic and metal tracks are available for this purpose (Fig. 13-13). They provide a superior means for sliding the doors. The doors can be of any suitable material. They can be the same width as the groove or rabbetted on each end to fit the groove.

FIGURE 13-12
Horizontal sliding doors can run in grooves or channels.

LIFT DOOR TO REMOVE

WOOD STRIPS FORM SLIDING CHANNELS.

SLIDING DOORS IN GROOVES.

DOOR RABBETED TO FIT IN GROOVE.

DOORS SLIDING IN PLASTIC OR ALUMINUM TRACK.

DOORS SLIDE ON RAISED PLASTIC OR FIBER TRACK.

FIGURE 13-13
Aluminum, fiber, and plastic tracks are available for guiding sliding doors.

Allow a generous allowance between the width of the groove and the part of the door to slide in it.

STYLES OF DOORS

The most commonly used styles of doors are the lipped, reveal overlay, flush overlay, flush with faceframe, and flush without faceframe. These are described in great detail in Chapter 17.

The *lipped door* has the advantage of covering the crack around the door opening, reducing the need for the accuracy required with flush doors. A rabbet is cut on three or four sides, depending on the design of the frame. The edge can be square, rounded, or shaped (Fig. 13-14).

A lipped door is usually mounted with semi-concealed hinges. These are made for a $\frac{3}{8}$-in. lip.

FIGURE 13-14
Lipped doors cover the crack between the door and faceframe.

$\frac{3}{8}$" X $\frac{3}{8}$" RABBET

DOOR

LIPPED DOOR WITH FACE FRAME.

These hinges are made in various styles, such as modern or colonial. Before installing the hinges, place the door in the opening to be certain it fits. Mount the hinges on the door first. Place it on the cabinet, and check to be certain that it is square and centered in the opening. Then fasten the hinges to the faceframe with screws.

Flush doors fit inside the faceframe, or if it has no faceframe, the front edge of the carcass. They must be made carefully so that the crack around the edges is uniform (Fig. 13-15). These doors use butt, wraparound, invisible, and European-style hinges.

Flush overlay doors cover the side of the carcass and any bulkheads between doors. They give a clean, modern look. Knife and invisible hinges are commonly used (Fig. 13-16). These doors use wraparound, pivot, and European-style hinges.

DOOR

DOOR

DOOR FLUSH WITH FACE FRAME.

DOOR FLUSH WITHOUT FACE FRAME.

FIGURE 13-15
Flush doors may be with or without faceframe.

FIGURE 13-16
Flush overlay doors cover the end panels and bulkheads. Reveal overlay doors partially overlap the end panels and bulkheads.

DOOR

DOOR

FLUSH OVERLAY DOOR.

REVEAL OVERLAY DOOR.

Reveal overlay doors are sized so that they partially overlap the end panels and bulkheads. This provides a three-dimensional appearance and an interesting shadow line around each. The amount of overlap is usually $\frac{3}{8}$ in. on end panels, which reveals $\frac{3}{8}$ in. of the end of the panel. When two doors meet on a bulkhead, the overlap is about $\frac{3}{16}$ in. for each door (Fig. 13-16). These doors use wraparound, pivot, and European-style hinges.

HINGES

There are many types of hinges available for use on furniture and cabinets. Some are visible and decorative and become a part of the design. Others reflect the hinges used at a certain period of history. Still others are hidden or partially hidden. The parts of a hinge are shown in Fig. 13-17. The door wing or leaf is fastened to the door. The frame wing or leaf is fastened to the frame. *Butt hinges* are available ei-

FIGURE 13-17
Parts of a hinge.

ther swaged or unswaged. Swaging is a slight offset of the leaf hinge at the barrel. This permits the leaves to come closer together (Fig. 13-18). *Cabinet hinges* are available with loose or fast pins in light narrow and broad hinge types (Fig. 13-19). *Plain steel hinges* are available in broad, narrow, and back flap types. *Continuous hinges* are also available in

FIGURE 13-18
Hinges may be swaged or not swaged.

FIGURE 13-19
Cabinet hinges are available in broad and narrow types.

lengths from 30 to 72 in. They are available in steel, brass, aluminum, and stainless steel.

The *drop-leaf hinge* is a butt type. It has one leaf longer than the other, designed for use on a drop-leaf table. The *butler tray hinge* is used on tray tables with leaves that fold up. It has a friction element that can be adjusted to bind the pin in the knuckle so that its leaf will not easily fall but still can be moved (Fig. 13-20).

FIGURE 13-20
Other types of hinges used on furniture.

Installing Butt Hinges

Butt hinges are usually installed on the edge of the door and faceframe. This sets the door flush with the faceframe (Fig. 13-21). First place the door in the faceframe. Mark the location of the hinge on both. Using a try square, mark the hinge location on the edges of the frame and door. Then mark the depth of the gain. A gain is a rectangular notch cut to receive

1. LOCATE THE HINGE ON THE DOOR AND FRAME.

2. MARK THE GAIN.

3. CUT THE GAIN.

4. INSTALL THE HINGE.

FIGURE 13-21
How to install butt hinges.

the leaf of the hinge. The gain could be cut into the frame and door the thickness of one leaf. It could be cut into the frame the thickness of two leaves (Fig. 13-22). After cutting the gain, place the hinge in it to locate the screw holes. Drill the anchor holes and install the screws.

FIGURE 13-22
Hinges may be recessed into the door or faceframe.

DOOR

DOOR

DOOR

DOOR

BUTT HINGE SET INTO FRAME.

BUTT HINGE SET INTO FRAME AND DOOR.

Decorative Butt Hinges

Decorative butt hinges are used to enhance the appearance of the furniture or cabinet unit. They are mounted on the face of the frame and door (Fig. 13-23).

To install, locate and install the hinges on the door. Place the door inside the frame and put one screw in each hinge. If the door moves freely, install the other screws (Fig. 13-24).

FIGURE 13-23
Decorative surface-mounted hinges enhance the appearance of the furniture or cabinet unit. (*Courtesy of American Plywood Association.*)

HOLD DOOR WITH WOOD OR CARDBOARD STRIPS.

MEASURE

1. MOUNT THE HINGES ON THE DOOR.

2. MOUNT THE DOOR IN THE FACE FRAME.

FIGURE 13-24
How to install a door using surface-mounted hinges.

Mortiseless Hinges

Mortiseless hinges do not require a gain because the one leaf fits inside an opening in the other leaf (Fig. 13-25).

Pivot Hinges

Pivot hinges are used where it is desired to have the hinge less noticeable than with butt hinges. They are mounted to the stile or cabinet side and the back of the door (Fig. 13-26). Two types are available. One mounts on the vertical stile and the other on a horizontal rail. They are used on flush doors (Fig. 13-27).

FIGURE 13-25
Mortiseless hinge.

FRAME

DOOR

PIVOT HINGE FOR VERTICAL STILE.

FIGURE 13-26
The pivot hinge is designed to mount on the vertical stile. (*Courtesy of Stanley Hardware.*)

FIGURE 13-27
This flush door is mounted using pivot hinges. (*Courtesy of American Plywood Association.*)

Knife Hinges

A knife hinge is similar to the pivot hinge. It mounts on the horizontal frame and on top of the door. It is used on flush doors (Fig. 13-28).

Semiconcealed Hinges

Semiconcealed hinges are used for lipped doors and reveal overlay doors (Fig. 13-29). The lipped door hinge is formed to fit into the $\frac{3}{8}$-in. rabbet on the door edge. The reveal overlay door hinge has a straight leaf (Fig. 13-30).

FIGURE 13-28
The knife hinge mounts on the horizontal frame.

LIPPED DOOR FASTENED TO FACE OF FRAME.

REVEAL OVERLAY DOOR.

FIGURE 13-30
Two types of semiconcealed hinges.
(*Courtesy of Stanley Hardware.*)

FIGURE 13-29
The semiconcealed hinge fits in the lip and is screwed to the inside of the door. (*Courtesy of American Plywood Association.*)

Wrap-Around Hinges

Wrap-around hinges are used on flush, lipped, and reveal overlay doors. They are called wraparound because the leaves wrap around the frame and/or the door.

Typical wraparound hinges are shown in Fig. 13-31, page 170. The lipped door hinge wraps around the door and fastens to the edge of the frame. The flush door hinge fastens to the edge of the frame. The recessed hinge fastens to the inside face of the cabinet (Fig. 13-32). It can also be used without recessing the door.

Concealed or European Hinges

The trend toward European-style cabinets that do not have faceframes has led to an increased need for concealed hinges that are sometimes called European hinges. A number of designs are available.

The concealed hinge in Fig. 13-33 is designed for overlay and flush inset doors. The hinge has adjusting screws that permit lateral adjustment of the door after the hinge has been installed. The hinge requires a mortise hole in the door. A typical mortise is $1\frac{3}{8}$ in. in diameter and $\frac{1}{2}$ in. deep with a flat bottom. It can be bored with a multispur or Forstner bit. The hinge is fastened to the door with screws through the plate above the round part that fits into the mortise. It fastens to the cabinet bulkhead with a mounting base plate. The plate is screwed to the bulkhead. The arm of the hinge slides over the plate and is secured to it with setscrews. Installation locations for flush overlay and reveal overlay doors are shown in Fig. 13-33.

Various types of concealed hinges allow the door to open through a range of angles. These vary from 95 to 180° (Fig. 13-34). Some types of concealed hinges have a self-closing function.

Another type of concealed hinge is the invisible link-stop hinge. It is set in the edge of the door and cabinet frame in a mortise (Fig. 13-35). A no-mortise concealed-cylinder-type hinge is set into round holes

FULL WRAP-AROUND

LIPPED DOOR FASTENED
TO EDGE OF FRAME.
(PARTIAL WRAP-AROUND)

FLUSH DOOR HINGE

RECESSED FLUSH DOOR

FIGURE 13-31
These are typical of the wraparound hinges available. (*Courtesy of Stanley Hardware.*)

FIGURE 13-32
This wraparound hinge fits into a recess cut in the cabinet side panel. (*Courtesy of American Plywood Association.*)

BASEPLATE

100° OPENING
CONCEALED HINGE

BASEPLATE

DOOR
FLUSH INSET

$\frac{5}{8}$ "

DOOR   DOOR

OVERLAY REVEAL
CENTER MOUNT

$\frac{5}{16}$ "

DOOR

OVERLAY REVEAL
END MOUNT

DOOR

FLUSH OVERLAY
END MOUNT

DOOR   DOOR

FLUSH OVERLAY
CENTER MOUNT

FIGURE 13-33
This concealed hinge will mount flush and overlay doors. (*Courtesy of Stanley Hardware.*)

bored in the door and frame edges. The outside of the round body is heavily knurled, so it binds tightly when inserted in the hole. No screws are necessary (Fig. 13-36).

FIGURE 13-34
Concealed hinges are available that permit doors to swing through 180°. (*Courtesy of Grass America Inc.*)

FIGURE 13-36
The no-mortise concealed cylinder hinge is set into round holes bored into the door and frame.

FIGURE 13-37
This glass door hinge holds the glass with setscrews. (*Courtesy of The Woodworkers' Store.*)

FIGURE 13-35
An invisible link-stop concealed hinge is mortised into the edge of the door.

Glass Door Hinges

In Fig. 13-37 is shown a hinge for glass doors as found on stereo and television cabinets. The hinge mounts on the side of the cabinet and the glass door fits into a channel. It will hold glass up to 1¼ in. in thickness. A plastic spacer is inserted between the glass and the side of the channel. Screws in the channel press the plastic against the glass, holding it in place. This is designed for inset doors.

Plastic Hinges

Flat plastic hinges are available in coils up to 500 ft long. They are made from a tough extruded polypropylene. They are self-aligning and do not require mortising. They are attached with screws, nails, or staples. They are not recommended for outdoor use. Use with particleboard is especially helpful because they cover the edge grain (Fig. 13-38).

MAGNETIC CATCH

FIGURE 13-38
Plastic hinges are fastened to the surface of the door or frame.

CATCHES

Some of the new hinges available are *self-closing* and do not require a catch. Self-closing hinges have a built-in spring that assists with the closing of the door. It also holds the door shut. If a catch is needed, the magnetic catch is most useful. There are a variety of friction catches available. These must be carefully installed so that they line up when the door is closed. They are made with elongated holes for the screws, which permits some adjustment to be made after they are installed. Some commonly used catches are in Fig. 13-39.

PULLS AND KNOBS

The style of pull or knob used must be in keeping with the period of the furniture (Fig. 13-40). Sliding doors usually use recessed pulls so that the doors slide freely past each other. The pulls and knobs should be coordinated with those used on drawers (Fig. 13-41).

FRICTION CATCH

ROLLER CATCH

FIGURE 13-39
These are typical magnet and friction catches used to secure cabinet doors. (*Courtesy of The Stanley Works.*)

FIGURE 13-40
These pulls and knobs are styled for colonial period furniture. (*Courtesy of Amerock Corporation, an Anchor Hocking Company.*)

FIGURE 13-41
The knobs and pulls are designed so that they form a coordinated set. (*Courtesy of Amerock Corporation, an Anchor Hocking Company.*)

STUDY QUESTIONS

Answer each of the following questions. If you are not sure of an answer, review the chapter.

13-1. How does a frame-and-panel door differ in construction from a solid door?

13-2. What joints are used to build frame-and-panel doors?

13-3. What is the difference between sticking and coping?

13-4. What materials are used to make solid doors?

13-5. How is the cabinet prepared so that tambour doors can slide?

13-6. What types of tracks are used for sliding doors?

13-7. What are the different styles of cabinet doors?

13-8. What kinds of hinges are used on flush overlay doors?

13-9. What kinds of hinges are available for use on furniture and cabinet doors?

13-10. How do semiconcealed and concealed hinges differ?

13-11. What kinds of door catches are commonly used?

IMPORTANT TECHNICAL TERMS

Following are technical terms that you should be able to use as part of your working vocabulary. Write a brief description of the meaning of each term.

Frame-and-panel door
Sticking

Coping
Tambour door
Flush door
Flush overlay door
Reveal overlay door
Lipped door

14

DRAWER CONSTRUCTION

There are many ways to build and install drawers. The type chosen depends on the quality of the furniture unit being produced, the drawer size, the type of drawer guide to be used, the style of the cabinet, the load the drawer will be expected to carry, and the possible frequency of use (Fig. 14-1).

Good-quality drawers must be constructed so that they remain square even when loaded. They should slide out of the cabinet easily and not tip downward when pulled out to their full extent.

When choosing a drawer design, it is necessary to consider the type of drawer guide to be used and the requirements for the style of furniture. A drawer can be designed so that it can accommodate shop-made or commercial drawer guides. The type of commercial guide must be known before construction starts. Similarly, the type of drawer front required due to the furniture design must be known.

TYPES OF DRAWER FRONTS

There are four basic types of drawer fronts: flush with a faceframe, lipped, flush overlay and reveal overlay, and flush without a faceframe (Fig. 14-2). The front of the *flush drawer* is flush with the stiles

FIGURE 14-1
This Chippendale silver cabinet has drawers sized to store silver. The drawers are covered with doors. (*Courtesy of Drexel Heritage Furnishings Inc.*)

BULKHEAD

BULKHEAD

DRAWER SIDE

DRAWER FRONT

STILE

STILE

DRAWER FLUSH WITH FACEFRAME

LIPPED DRAWER

DRAWER FLUSH WITH NO FACEFRAME

FLUSH OVERLAY WITH NO FACEFRAME

BULKHEAD

REVEAL OVERLAY

FIGURE 14-2
Drawer fronts are made in four types.

FIGURE 14-3
This door chest has flush drawers and doors which have molding applied along the edge. The exposed dust panel is a significant part of the exterior design. (*Courtesy of Drexel Heritage Furnishings Inc.*)

FIGURE 14-4
These drawers are set flush with the edge of the case. (*Courtesy of Thomasville Furniture Industries, Inc.*)

FIGURE 14-5
This low chest has lipped drawer fronts with shaped edges. The dust panel is exposed. (*Courtesy of Drexel Heritage Furnishings Inc.*)

and rails of the faceframe (Fig. 14-3) or with the exposed edge of the case if a faceframe is not used (Fig. 14-4).

The *lipped drawer* has a rabbet cut on the edges. The lip overlaps the stiles and rails. This enables the drawer front to cover the space between the stiles and the sides of the drawer. While the lip can be any thickness desired, $\frac{3}{8}$ in. is frequently used (Fig. 14-5).

The *flush overlay drawer* front overlaps the sides completely, covering the front of the case. With this construction a faceframe is not needed (Fig. 14-6).

The *reveal overlay drawer* covers part of the stile and rail, or part of the side of the case if stiles and rails are not used. The edges of the drawer front can be left square, slightly rounded, or shaped.

DRAWER CONSTRUCTION

A drawer is made up of a front, bottom, back, and two sides. The requirements of the drawer and the

FIGURE 14-6
These cabinets are made with flush overlay drawers and doors. (*Courtesy of Kleweno of Kansas City.*)

quality of construction can vary and the actual design is influenced by these (Fig. 14-7).

Drawer Front

The front is the only part of a drawer that is exposed to view. The style of front and the material from which it is made must fit in with the style of the furniture or cabinet. The style of the drawer front will usually be the same as the adjacent doors. Most good-quality furniture units require drawer fronts made from wood that matches the outside of the carcass or cabinet in grain and color. These are usually $\frac{3}{4}$-in. solid wood, but thicker material could be used. The drawer front could be plywood with a proper wood veneer on the face and edges or solid-core plywood with a wood veneer on the exposed face. The drawer front can be covered with plastic laminate over plywood. If the edges are exposed or shaped, they can be painted to blend in with the basic color on the laminate. On some units, such as kitchen cabinets, the plastic laminate might be a color that is different from the basic cabinet producing a totally different appearance. Drawer fronts can be dec-

FIGURE 14-7
Typical drawer construction.

SIDE

BACK

BOTTOM SET IN
GROOVE IN FRONT,
SIDES AND BACK.

SIDE

FRONT

FIGURE 14-8
The drawer fronts on this lingerie chest are deeply recessed with a shaped, mitered frame over the front of a flat drawer front panel. (*Courtesy of Drexel Heritage Furnishings Inc.*)

FIGURE 14-9
This lipped drawer front has a ⅜ × ⅜ in. lip.

orated by adding molding on the surface or carving into them (Fig. 14-8).

The drawer front has a groove cut across it to hold the bottom. The ends are cut to suit the type of drawer (flush, lipped, reveal, flush overlay) and the joint to be used (Fig. 14-9).

FIGURE 14-10
Drawer sides have the top rounded.

FIGURE 14-11
Drawer sides have grooves for the bottom and back.

Drawer Sides and Back

Drawer sides are usually made from ½-in.-thick plywood or solid stock. If a side guide is to be used which requires that a groove be cut in the drawer side, use ⅝-in. (16-mm)-thick stock. Very small drawers can use ¼- to ⅜-in. (6- to 10-mm)-thick stock.

The wood used in the sides and back is usually less expensive than that in the drawer front. For lower-cost units, sycamore, poplar, and pine are used. For higher-quality units, maple, red oak, and mahogany are used.

To give a finished appearance, the *top edge* of the sides are rounded with a shaper or router to a ¼-in. radius (Fig. 14-10). In all but the lowest-quality units, the *sides of the drawer* are grooved to receive the bottom. The groove is usually cut ¼ in. deep (Fig. 14-11). The *back* may also be grooved (Fig. 14-12). Sometimes the back and sides sit on top of the bottom and are nailed or stapled to it (Fig. 14-13). This is frequently used with the newer European hardware where the side-mounted drawer slides over the bottom edge of the side.

GROOVE FOR BOTTOM
¼" D X ¼" W

FIGURE 14-12
The back of the drawer is grooved to receive the bottom.

DRAWER SIDE WITH TOP EDGE ROUNDED

DRAWER BACK

NAIL OR STAPLE BOTTOM TO BACK

BOTTOM

BOTTOM SET IN GROOVE IN BACK

LOWER COST CONSTRUCTION

GOOD QUALITY CONSTRUCTION

FIGURE 14-13
Drawer bottoms are stapled in place in low-quality drawer construction.

Drawer Bottom

The drawer bottom is usually made from ¼-in. hardboard or plywood. In small drawers ⅛-in. hardboard could be used. The bottom is set in grooves and *not glued*. As the drawer expands and contracts, it can slide over the edges of the bottom. Plywood and hardboard expand and contract very little and provide a stable base.

Remember to cut the bottom $\frac{1}{16}$ to $\frac{1}{8}$ in. (2 to 4 mm) shorter in length and width than the distance from the bottom of the grooves. This allows $\frac{1}{32}$ to $\frac{1}{16}$ in. (1 to 2 mm) of clearance on all sides of the bottom in the assembled drawer. The bottom, if fit properly, should help to square up the drawer when it is assembled.

JOINTS IN DRAWER CONSTRUCTION

The strongest and also the most difficult joints to use to join the drawer front and sides are shown in Fig.

14-14. The French dovetail and multifinger dovetail are cut with router cutters. The blind French dovetail is cut with a dovetail router bit using a router table. The milled shaper joint requires a special shaper cutter. The others can be cut on the table saw. All these joints are assembled by gluing.

Other joints, which are easier to cut but not quite as strong or decorative, are shown in Fig. 14-15. They can all be cut easily on a table saw. The dado and rabbet joints are assembled by gluing. The rabbet butt and dado joints are glued and nailed.

Cutting a Milled Shaper Joint

This joint is usually cut on a shaper using a milled glue joint cutter. To cut this joint on a shaper, a special stubbed spindle must be installed. This allows the spindle nut to be recessed flush with the top of the shaper table.

FIGURE 14-14
Strongest joints used in drawer construction.

GLUE
FRONT
FRENCH DOVETAIL

GLUE
SIDE
FRONT

MULTI-FINGER DOVETAIL

GLUE
SIDE
FRONT
SHAPED MILLED EDGE

GLUE
¼
¼
DOUBLE DADO

GLUE
⅛
⅛
LOCK SHOULDER

GLUE
FRONT
3/16
3/16
⅛
⅛
⅛
⅛
LOCK JOINT

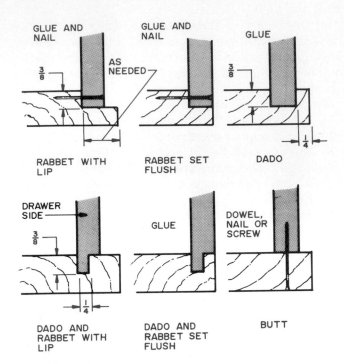

FIGURE 14-15
These drawer joints are easy to cut.

STEP 1:
CUTTING THE JOINT ON THE DRAWER SIDE.

STEP 2:
CUTTING THE JOINT ON THE DRAWER FACE.

FIGURE 14-16
Steps to cut a milled shaper joint.

The steps to cut a milled shaper joint are:

1. Adjust the spindle to cut the drawer sides as shown in Fig. 14-16, step 1. The distance *A* on the draw side must be cut exactly the same as *B* on the top of the cutter. Stand the drawer side on end and cut the joint on the inside face. For narrow drawer sides, use a tenoning jig to guide the material past the cutter.

2. Place the drawer front flat on the shaper table with the inside face down. Adjust the fence to give the desired depth of cut, and cut each end (Fig. 14-16, step 2). You will note that the drawer front extends over the top of the cutter.

Cutting a Locked Shoulder Joint

This joint is cut on a circular saw using a dado head. The following tells how to lay out and cut it on a drawer having $\frac{1}{2}$-in. sides and a $\frac{3}{4}$-in. front.

1. Use two $\frac{1}{8}$-in. dado cutters. Cut a dado in the side (Fig. 14-17, step 1). Cut the dado $\frac{1}{16}$-in. deeper than the length of the tongue to enter it.

2. Cut the $\frac{1}{4}$-in. (6-mm) dado in both ends of the drawer front (Fig. 14-17, step 2). Use a tenoning jig to guide the stock.

3. Set the dado head to cut slightly higher than $\frac{1}{4}$ in. Clamp a piece of stock to the fence. Butt the end of the drawer front against it with the inside face down. Position the fence so that the dado head cuts $\frac{5}{16}$ in. off the tongue on the in-

side face of the drawer front (Fig. 14-17, step 3). Use a miter gauge to guide the stock.

Assembling the Drawer

After cutting the drawer parts, assemble them without glue to make certain that they will go together. The joints should fit snugly but go together without forcing. Remember to assemble the sides around the

LOCKED SHOULDER JOINT

STEP 1: CUT THE DADO IN THE DRAWER SIDE.

STEP 2: CUT A DADO IN EACH END OF THE DRAWER FRONT.

STEP 3: POSITION THE FENCE SO THE DADO CUTTERS REMOVES ⅝ in. OF THE TONGUE ON THE INSIDE FACE.

FIGURE 14-17
Steps to cut a locked shoulder joint.

bottom, which is not glued. After the drawer is clamped and before the adhesive sets, check it for squareness. It is best to measure across the diagonals or from corner to opposite corner. If they are the same, the box is square. Place it on a flat surface while the adhesive is setting.

Drawer Supports and Guides

Good-quality furniture and some cabinets have dust panels. These provide support to the sides and back of the unit, and the drawer slides on top of them. The dust panel may be exposed or hidden by the drawer front (Fig. 14-18).

FIGURE 14-18
This small chest has flush drawer fronts and exposed dust panels. (*Courtesy of Hekman Furniture Company.*)

Furniture and cabinets may or may not have a face frame. This will influence the drawer guides selected as well as the size of the drawer. A variety of wood guides are shown in Fig. 14-19. The simplest guides are cleats that may be fastened to the bulkhead. Cleats are satisfactory for work that will not carry heavy loads. When several drawers are one above the other, the cleat could also serve as a kicker. A kicker is a strip that keeps the front end of the drawer from dropping as it is opened (Fig. 14-20). Cleats should be of hard wood and heavily waxed.

Another simple drawer slide is to cut a groove in the side of the drawer. The cleat slides in this groove. Cut the groove wide enough so that the cleat

FIGURE 14-19
Typical drawer guides.

CLEAT TO BULKHEAD

CLEAT TO BULKHEAD
CUT GROOVE IN SIDE
OF DRAWER.

CLEAT TO TOP

L-SHAPED GUIDE
TO BULKHEAD

CLEAT TO DUST
PANEL

CENTER DRAWER
GUIDE TO DUST
PANEL.

FIGURE 14-20
Cleats are the simplest form of a kicker.

slides freely in it (Fig. 14-21). A plastic drawer slide is available for drawers with side grooves. They could also serve as cleats. Because the plastic slides have rounded edges and ends, drawers slide easily, making plastic slides superior to wood slides (Fig. 14-22).

Another shop-made drawer guide is an L-shaped strip that is fastened to the sides of the unit. It could be a single piece of stock with a rabbet or

FIGURE 14-21
A cleat in a groove in the drawer sides is a simple slide system.

FIGURE 14-22
Slides from plastic cleats slide easily.

T-GUIDE WITH PLASTIC BACK GUIDE.

STANDARD WOOD CENTER
DRAWER GUIDE.

FIGURE 14-23
Typical wood center drawer guides.

FIGURE 14-24
A commercial center drawer guide using rollers fastened to the front stile. (*Courtesy of Knape and Vogt Manufacturing Co.*)

two pieces glued and nailed together. The actual size of the guide can vary. The method of securing it to the cabinet will vary with the design. The drawer face will have to be laid out to allow for the thickness of the vertical part of the guide. The L-shaped wood guide can also be used with a face frame.

The two common types of wood center guides are shown in Fig. 14-23. One type uses a wood runner fastened to the dust panel. It is rounded and tapered on the front end. A U-shaped channel is glued to the bottom of the drawer. Another type has a T-shaped hardwood runner fastened to the dust panel. A U-shaped runner is fastened to the bottom of the drawer. Screwed to the back of the drawer on the end of the runner is a plastic guide that fits into the T-shaped runner. This helps guide the drawer and serves as a kicker.

There are a variety of commercial drawer slides available. For commercially made residential furniture a metal center guide is generally used. The center rail of the one shown in Fig. 14-24 is screwed to the front rail and the back of the cabinet.

FIGURE 14-25
This heavy-duty drawer side slide is used on commercial furniture and drawers that might carry heavy loads. (*Courtesy of Knape and Vogt Manufacturing Co.*)

JOINTS IN DRAWER CONSTRUCTION **183**

It is often called a *monorail*. A metal guide that fits over the rail is screwed to the drawer back. This serves as a guide and a kicker. There are available plastic pads and rollers that can be mounted on the front rail for the sides of the drawer to slide upon. Although it is easy to mount, this slide has much side-to-side play and is somewhat noisy.

Furniture and cabinets which have drawers that could be expected to carry heavy loads will use side drawer slides. Office furniture is one type that generally uses these heavy-duty slides. A metal track is mounted on the sides of the cabinet. A metal rail is mounted on the sides of the drawer. The rail or track will have one or more rollers on which the drawer will move (Fig. 14-25). When designing pieces to use these units, be certain to get the design specifications telling the clearance needed for installing these guides.

STUDY QUESTIONS

Answer each of the following questions. If you are not sure of an answer, review the chapter.

14-1. What are the features of a good-quality drawer?
14-2. What are the types of drawer fronts in common use?
14-3. How does a flush drawer front differ from a lipped front?
14-4. What are the parts that make up a drawer?
14-5. What thickness of stock is usually used for a drawer front?
14-6. How thick are drawer sides usually constructed?
14-7. How does the wood in drawer sides differ from that used in drawer fronts?
14-8. From what materials are drawer bottoms made?
14-9. What joints are used to join the drawer front to the drawer sides?
14-10. Describe the various types of drawer guides and slides.

IMPORTANT TECHNICAL TERMS

Following are technical terms that you should be able to use as part of your working vocabulary. Write a brief description of the meaning of each term.

Flush drawer front
Lipped drawer front

Flush overlay drawer front
Reveal overlay drawer front
Milled shaper joint
Locked shoulder joint
Drawer slides
Kicker

15

SHELF CONSTRUCTION

As furniture and cabinets are designed, the efficient use of the interior space should receive considerable attention. A flexible arrangement of shelves and the use of special-purpose accessories enables the designer to make use of all the enclosed space. It enables the user to adjust the interior arrangement to suit a variety of storage problems.

DESIGN CONSIDERATIONS

The following things must be considered as shelves are designed:

1. *Depth.* The depth must be great enough to hold the intended objects. Book shelves are usually 8 to 10 in. deep. Shelves in deeper furniture units may be the same depth as the unit or in some cases less than this width. A series of shelves in a deep cabinet may be undesirable because items get pushed to the back and are not easily available. Kitchen wall cabinets are usually 12 in. (300 mm) deep on the outside, so the actual shelves will be closer to 11 in. (280 mm). Kitchen base cabinets are 24 in. (610 mm) deep on the outside. Shelves can range from 15 to 23 in. (380 to 585 mm) deep.

2. *Length.* The length of shelves is controlled by the size of the furniture or cabinet unit and the load it is expected to carry. A very wide cabinet with very long shelves presents some problems. First, the flexibility of arrangement is limited because when one shelf is moved, it changes a large part of the storage. If the long shelves were installed as two shorter shelves, greater flexibility is available. The long shelf tends to bend under a heavy load more readily than does a shorter shelf. If heavy loads are expected, the load-carrying capabilities of the shelf and the distance it must span need to be considered. Span data for hardboard and fiberboard shelves are given in Chapter 5.

3. *Spacing.* For greatest flexibility, shelving should use hardware that permits the spacing between shelves to be changed. If shelves are fixed, the spacing used must be chosen with care. In bookcases the lower shelf is spaced wider than those above it. The large books are placed here. This is normally 12 to 14 in. Spacing for regular-size books is usually $10\frac{1}{2}$ in. minimum. Again, consider the use of the unit. If it is to hold a television set, the space must be large enough to hold any of the portable television sets on the market. Examples of

fixed and adjustable-shelving are shown later in this chapter.

4. *Special accessories.* Hardware manufacturers have available a wide variety of special accessories for improving the efficiency of interior cabinet space. This includes items such as revolving shelves, wire and plastic storage racks, and shelves that slide in and out like a drawer (Fig. 15-1). Additional information on accessories for cabinets is given in Chapter 17.

5. *Material.* Shelving can be made from any material that will carry the loads and be pleasing in appearance. This usually includes solid wood, plywood, particleboard, hardboard, and fiberboard products. Glass shelves are used in china cabinets and display units.

FIXED SHELVING

Fixed shelves are attached using metal angles, shelf brackets, wood cleats, or dados. The metal angles and wood cleats are the easiest to use but are not attractive. The wood cleats can be glued and screwed to the sides. Metal shelf brackets are installed by screwing one leg to the cabinet or wall. The shelf is screwed to the other leg. They are available in several sizes with 6 × 8 in. and 10 × 12 in. being common (Fig. 15-2).

A stronger and more attractive way to install fixed shelves is with a plain or stop dado. The plain dado is the easiest to cut but is visible on the edge of the side. This can be covered with a molding glued to the edge or with a faceframe. The stop dado is more difficult to cut. The edge of the shelf must also be cut to fit into the dado (Fig. 15-3). When exposed joinery is to be used, other types of dados, such as a full dovetail or half dovetail dado, can be used.

ADJUSTABLE SHELVING

Most good-quality furniture and cabinets use adjustable shelving because of the advantages it offers. In

The pull-out unit is equipped with a support frame onto which all the mounting parts of the "Vario-pull" system can be mounted thanks to the row of hooks welded on one side. These parts – bread baskets, bottle baskets, laundry and cleaning agent baskets, shoe racks, lid racks and various other basket inserts are also available in a wider variation than illustrated here.

PULL-OUT STORAGE RACKS

SPICE RACK

These steel wire baskets can be used for various applications since they have been surface treated, suitable for any type of material to be stored. They are also extremely easy to clean.

All baskets have overhanging edges on the sides so that they smoothly run in the guide strips. This not only facilitates easy installation but also provides a clear arrangement of the baskets in the frame of the cabinet.

The baskets can be stacked, saving space, due to their tapered walls.

The guide strips are available in three widths in order to be able to adapt to various cabinet widths without having to double the unit.

WIRE BASKETS THAT SLIDE ON SIDE TRACKS

FIGURE 15-1
Special accessories increase the efficiency of the use of interior cabinet space. (*Courtesy of H'a'fele America, 203 Feld Ave., High Point, NC 27261*)

FIGURE 15-2
Ways to install fixed shelves.

FIGURE 15-3
Fixed shelves can be set in dadoes.

addition to improving the efficiency of the unit, it is easy to install.

The least expensive adjustable way is to use wood dowel pins or metal or plastic shelf pins set in holes bored into the sides (Fig. 15-4). The metal and plastic pins are supplied by several hardware manufacturers. If using wood dowel pins, chamfer each end to help start the pins in the hole. A pencil sharpener is a good tool to use to chamfer wood dowels. The holes should be $\frac{1}{2}$ in. deep. Use $\frac{3}{8}$-in.-diameter wood dowels. The spacing between holes is in the range 1 to 2 in. Set the holes in about $\frac{3}{4}$ in. from the front and back of the edges of the shelf so that it will not tilt. The bored holes should be a little deeper than the length of the pin to be inserted in it. Remember when locating the holes to allow for the door as well as the set back from the edge of the shelf (Fig. 15-5).

Metal shelf standards provide the strongest support for adjustable shelves (Fig. 15-6). The perforated metal strips are screwed or nailed to the sides of the cabinet. The shelves are laid on top of adjustable clips that snap into the slots on the standard.

FIGURE 15-4
Shelf pins are an inexpensive way to provide adjustable shelves.

FIGURE 15-5
When locating holes for shelf pins, remember to allow for doors and the cabinet back.

FIGURE 15-6
Metal shelf standards provide the best way to support adjustable shelves. (*Courtesy of Knape and Vogt Manufacturing Co.*)

The standards are $\frac{5}{8}$ in. wide and $\frac{3}{16}$ in. deep and can be surface mounted or set flush by cutting a groove. Mounting holes are every 6 in. Use $\frac{5}{8}$-in. flat-head wood screws or special standard nails to secure it to the bulkhead. Be certain to install each strip so that the mounting screws are exactly in line. Otherwise, the shelf will slope or wobble. Every strip must also start with the same number at the bottom of the standard. If the standard is turned upside down or the numbers are not in the same order, the clips cannot be mounted at the same level.

Another system uses a metal standard that mounts on the back of the cabinet or on a wall. The shelves are held by metal brackets that extend out from the standard and hold the shelves. They are available in light and heavy-duty sizes. The brackets are available for various width shelves (Fig. 15-7).

Another type of shelf support is made from high-impact polyvinyl chloride. It is set into a groove cut into the sides of the shelving unit. The support is installed by driving it into the groove. Place a wood block over the support and tap on it to force the support into the groove. It can be glued in the groove if additional strength is needed (Fig. 15-8).

FIGURE 15-7
These metal standards mount on the wall and use metal brackets to hold the shelves. (*Courtesy of Knape and Vogt Manufacturing Co.*)

FIGURE 15-8
Polyvinyl chloride shelf supports are driven into grooves.

A shop-made system for adjustable shelves involves cutting $\frac{3}{8}$-in.-deep dadoes across the sides of the unit. Space them as desired, but 2 in. is a good distance. Cut the dadoes $\frac{1}{8}$ in. wider than the thickness of the shelf. This will allow for expansion and the finish on each part. The parallel dadoes provide an interesting pattern in addition to supporting the shelf (Fig. 15-9).

MAKING THE SHELVES

The shelves are normally $\frac{3}{4}$-in. solid wood or plywood stock. This will carry almost any load that can be placed on shelves found in most cabinets. Reconstituted wood products such as particleboard, hardboard, and fiberboard can also be used as shelving. Since the shelves are not fastened to other parts of the cabinet, they are most susceptible to warping. Be certain the moisture content is in the 6 to 8% moisture range. Each shelf should be finished on all sides, edges, and ends to keep out moisture.

FIGURE 15-9
Adjustable shelves can be set in dadoes cut in the sides of the cabinet.

FIGURE 15-10
Shelves can be stiffened by adding wood strips on the edge.

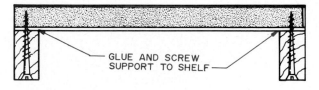

GLUE AND SCREW
SUPPORT TO SHELF

Adjustable shelves should be cut $\frac{1}{4}$ in. shorter than the clear area between the actual supporting brackets or clips.

If a shelf is to be very long, it can be stiffened by installing $\frac{3}{4} \times 1$ in. or wider solid wood strips to the front and back edges (Fig. 15-10).

FIGURE 15-11
This small cabinet unit is set into the shelving unit and is held by the clips that hold the shelves.

ADJUSTABLE SHELF STANDARDS

REMOVABLE BINS

REMOVABLE CABINET

ADJUSTABLE SHELVES

REMOVABLE DRAWER UNIT

FIGURE 15-12
This shelving unit has a variety of internal storage units.

$\frac{1}{4}$" HARDWOOD STRIP

$\frac{3}{4}$" NOSING

$\frac{3}{4}$" COVE MOLDING

WOOD OR PLASTIC VENEER

HARDWOOD BAND AND SHELF STIFFENER

PLASTIC OR ALUMINUM T-MOLDING

FIGURE 15-13
These are a few of the ways to band the edges of shelves.

Storage on shelves can be increased in efficiency by designing small cabinet units that will rest on the adjustable shelf clips (Fig. 15-11). These can give enclosed storage, provide small drawers, or be divided into horizontal or vertical compartments. Since they can be moved like a shelf, the flexibility of the storage unit is greatly increased. They can also be arranged to create interesting designs (Fig. 15-12).

SHELF EDGING

If the shelf is made from materials other than solid wood, it may be desirable to band the front edge to improve the appearance. Some of the frequently used methods are shown in Fig. 15-13. Additional information on banding these materials is given in Chapter 17.

STUDY QUESTIONS

Answer each of the following questions. If you are not sure of an answer, review the chapter.

15-1. What design considerations should be considered as the use of shelves is planned?

15-2. What is the standard size of kitchen cabinet wall and base units?

15-3. What problems arise if long shelves are used in a furniture unit?

15-4. What materials are used to make shelves?

15-5. How are fixed shelves joined to the sides of the cabinet?

15-6. How are adjustable shelves installed?

16

TABLE CONSTRUCTION

The type, size, and shape of tables is almost endless. Typically, these range from large dining tables that are expandable by adding leaves to small end tables and coffee tables. A wide range of tables for commercial use also exists. These can range from a large executive conference table to computer or computer printer tables (Fig. 16-1). When designing tables they must be strong enough to serve their purpose, have a finish that can stand up under the intended use and be pleasing in shape and color.

TABLETOP CONSTRUCTION

The type of construction used is influenced by the quality of the unit being produced and its style. Following are the basic types of tabletop construction.

Solid Wood Tops

Solid wood tops are not used extensively in the furniture industry because of the problems in producing them and caring for them when in use. They are made by gluing hardwood strips edge to edge. An edge dowel joint or a milled glue joint is recommended to aid in aligning the boards in the top. Since wide boards tend to warp more than narrow

FIGURE 16-1
This octagonal table provides a large work surface and the top is enhanced by the use of wormy oak veneers. (*Courtesy of Hekman Furniture Company.*)

boards, these strips should be approximately 4 in. wide. When they are edge glued the pieces are alternated so that the heart side is up on every other piece (Fig. 16-2). Be certain that the grain is running the same direction in every piece.

The large solid wood top expands and contracts more across the grain than with the grain. In an

FIGURE 16-2
When gluing solid wood tops, alternate the annual rings in each piece.

FIGURE 16-3
End boards are sometimes used to help keep solid wood tops flat. A small V-groove is used to conceal the crack that often develops.

attempt to control this, end boards are sometimes joined on each end of the top (Fig. 16-3). This helps to resist warping and covers the end grain. The end board can be joined to the top with a tongue-and-groove joint, but a dovetail is much better. If the top is not sealed with a finish on all sides, the expansion force is sometimes great enough to cause a crack to develop between the top and the end board. To hide this crack, the joint can be cut to form a shallow V-groove.

Another technique that strengthens tops glued up from solid stock and produces a thicker-appearing top is shown in Fig. 16-4. The boards are edge glued forming the top, but the rough top is made 3 in. (75 mm) wider and longer than the finished size. A 1½-in. (38-mm) piece is cut off each edge and end. These are rotated and glued to the bottom. In this way the grain matches and the top appears thicker.

1. GLUE STOCK EDGE TO EDGE 4 INCHES WIDER AND LONGER THAN FINISHED TOP.

2. CUT OFF 2 INCH STRIPS ON EACH EDGE.

3. ROTATE CUT STRIPS TO BOTTOM AND GLUE IN PLACE.

FIGURE 16-4
A top may be strengthened and given a thicker appearance by gluing wood strips to the bottom.

It is also advisable to fasten solid wood tops securely to a strong leg and rail frame. This helps keep it flat.

Plywood Tops

Plywood makes a good top because its laminated construction greatly reduces the amount of expansion and contraction and the chances that it will warp. Usually, ¾-in. plywood is adequate for most furniture tops.

Hardwood plywood is used for tabletops. *Hardwood plywood* has an outer veneer in various species of hardwoods and therefore presents a surface that is attractive, the proper color, and the species to match the legs and rails. It provides a very fine finished top. Since it is wood and will absorb moisture and stain when liquids, such as a cold drink, and hot items such as coffee or a dropped cigarette, are placed on it, a transparent but tough finish must be used. Additional information on finishes is provided in Part V. Veneer-core, particleboard-core, and lumber-core plywood can be used to make table tops.

The edges of plywood sheets are not attractive and require some treatment to cover them. Banding methods are covered later in this chapter.

Particleboard Tops

Particleboard is the most widely used material for tops for all types of commercial furniture. It is solid, stable, and strong. It can be covered with wood veneer or plastic laminates. Remember to use special wood screws designed for use with this material when fastening it to the legs and rails or fastening hardware to it. Information as applying veneers and laminates is given in Chapter 21.

BANDING PLYWOOD AND PARTICLEBOARD TOPS

There are many ways to cover the edges of plywood and particleboard (Fig. 16-5). The type used varies somewhat with the desired design and style of the furniture or cabinet. The banding can vary from a simple square edge to a wide frame enclosing a plywood, particleboard, marble, or other material forming a center panel. The banding material can be made wide enough so that the edges can be shaped with a router or shaper (Figs. 16-6 and 16-7).

EXPANDABLE TABLES

Two basic types of expandable tables are used. One is where the legs and rails remain stationary and the top slides out over them. The other is where the legs move apart as the top slides open (Fig. 16-8).

The slide shown in Fig. 16-9 is for a pedestal table. The slide is made in three parts that slide on each other. The center section is fastened to the pedestal. Each of the other two are fastened to opposite sides of the top. Each side slides out on the center rail. The table requires two slides (Fig. 16-10, page 196).

The slide shown in Fig. 16-11 is for a table that has the legs move out as the table is expanded. One

FIGURE 16-5
There are many ways to edge bond a top.

TONGUE ON EDGE	TONGUE ON PLYWOOD TOP

HARDWOOD STRIP	HARDWOOD STRIP

TRIANGULAR STRIP IN V-GROOVE	SOLID WOOD WITH EDGE SHAPED

COVE MOLDING	COVE MOLDING

PLASTIC OR ALUMINUM T-MOLDING

HARDWOOD SHELF STIFFENER

STOCK MOLDING ON BLOCKING PRODUCES A THICK EDGE

RABBETED SHELF STIFFENER

RABBET SHELF LEAVING TOP VENEER INTACT	APPLY PLASTIC LAMINATES OR WOOD VENEER

(NOTE: SOLID WOOD EDGES CAN BE SHAPED WITH A ROUTER OR SHAPER TO DESIRED DESIGN).

FIGURE 16-6
Interesting tops can be made by enclosing a material with a solid wood frame.

FIGURE 16-7
This marble insert is framed with a curved wood edge.

TABLE IN CLOSED POSITION

NEW LEAVES

TABLE EXPANDED WITH LEGS THAT DO NOT MOVE, ONLY THE TOP MOVES TO ACCEPT THE NEW LEAF.

TABLE EXPANDED WITH LEGS FASTENED TO TOP CAUSING THEM TO MOVE AS TOP IS EXPANDED.

FIGURE 16-8
Expandable tables may be designed so that the legs remain fixed or move.

FIGURE 16-9
Slide used on a pedestal table.

HARDWOOD SIDE SLIDE FASTENED TO ONE HALF THE TOP

CENTER SLIDE JOINED TO PEDESTAL

SLIDE FASTENED TO OTHER HALF OF TOP

HARDWOOD DOVETAIL KEYS

BOARD SCREWED TO PEDESTAL TO SUPPORT SLIDE

CENTER SLIDE $\frac{1}{8}$" WIDER THAN SIDE SLIDES

PEDESTAL IN SECTION

of the two slides is fastened to one half of the top. The other slide is fastened to the other half. They slide on a hardwood slide that fits into dovetails. A table requires two slides like this. Commercially made metal slides are also available (Fig. 16-12).

To help line up the open top and the leaves to be added, dowels are used. One side of the top has dowel pins and the other has dowel holes. Each extra leaf also has pins on one side and holes on the other (Fig. 16-13). The ends of dowels should be tapered. Wood and plastic dowel pins are available.

There are metal locks that are placed under the table to hold the top together when it is being used without leaves.

FIGURE 16-10
Typical slide arrangement on a pedestal table.

FIGURE 16-11
This slide permits the table legs to move apart as it is expanded.

FIGURE 16-12
Metal table top slide.

FIGURE 16-13
The extra leaves in expandable tabletops use dowels to hold them in place.

DROP-LEAF TABLES

There are several ways to design tabletops so that the end leaves can fold down (Fig. 16-14). The style of the furniture sometimes determines this because a particular type of joint was common. For example, in Colonial tables a square edge was common, while on traditional designs a *rule joint* was used. The common joints include the *square, 45°,* and *rule*.

The *square joint* is the easiest to use. The drop-leaf can be fastened to the top with simple butt table hinges or continuous hinges. When the leaf is in an up position, it is flush with the tabletop. When it is dropped, it sticks out beyond the top (Fig. 16-15).

FIGURE 16-14
This Pembroke table has dropped end leaves. (*Courtesy of Drexel Heritage Furnishings Inc.*)

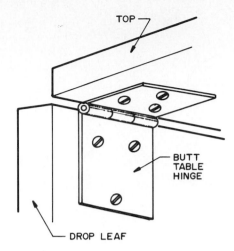

FIGURE 16-15
Dropped end leaves can be held with butt table hinges.

A special metal drop-leaf table hinge for square joints is available. It swings the dropped leaf below the top and does not have the gap that butt hinges leave. This hinge also serves as a leaf support and holds it in a horizontal position after the leaf is raised. The short leaf is mounted to the fixed table-top. This hinge will only work on ¾-in.-thick tops (Fig. 16-16). If it is desired to reduce the amount the

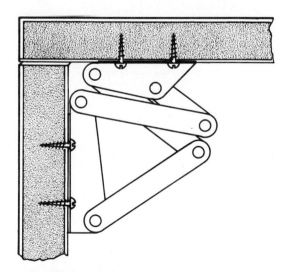

FIGURE 16-16
This hinge holds the end leaf in the horizontal position and swings it below the top when it is lowered.

leaf sticks out in the down position, a *45° joint* can be used (Fig. 16-17).

The *rule joint* is used most frequently because it presents a neatly shaped edge and very little of the dropped leaf extends beyond the table top (Fig. 16-18). This joint must be carefully laid out before it is cut with a shaper. Before cutting the actual top,

SECTION VIEW   FRONT VIEW

FIGURE 16-17
A 45° edge joint can be used to reduce the amount a leaf sticks out when a butt table hinge is used.

FIGURE 16-18
This dropped end leaf uses a rule joint.

make trial cuts on scrap of the same thickness. Mount a hinge to make certain that the joint will close when the leaf is raised. Be certain to use drop-leaf hinges. One leaf is longer than the other (Fig. 16-19). The hinge is swaged so that the leaves are offset and fit closely together.

A rule joint is cut by using a matched set of cutters on a shaper. This will produce a joint similar to that shown in Fig. 16-20. The assembled hinge, top, and drop leaf are shown in Fig. 16-21.

Supporting Drop-Leaves

There are many ways to support drop leaves. Some are used because they are part of the styling of a classical piece of furniture.

The easiest support to use is a metal table drop-leaf support. The short arm is fastened to the drop leaf. Notice that the parts screwed to the rail and leaf face toward the table. For it to work properly, it must be installed according to the dimen-

Length	Width open (inches)	Width of each leaf (inches)	
		Long	Short
1	$2\frac{5}{8}$	$1\frac{1}{2}$	$1\frac{1}{8}$
$1\frac{1}{8}$	$2\frac{3}{4}$	$1\frac{9}{16}$	$1\frac{3}{16}$
$1\frac{1}{4}$	$2\frac{7}{8}$	$1\frac{5}{8}$	$1\frac{1}{4}$
$1\frac{1}{2}$	$3\frac{3}{8}$	$1\frac{3}{4}$	$1\frac{3}{8}$

FIGURE 16-19
This type of drop-leaf hinge is used with a rule joint edge.

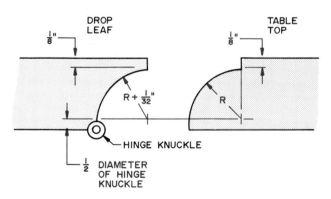

FIGURE 16-20
Steps to lay out a rule joint.

FIGURE 16-21
The knuckle in the drop-leaf hinge is lined up with the radius of the center used to lay out the rule joint.

	Distance A			
	$1''$	$1\frac{1}{2}''$	$2''$	$2\frac{1}{2}''$
	Distance B			
6" long	$3\frac{3}{16}''$	$2\frac{13}{16}''$	$2\frac{1}{2}''$	$2\frac{1}{8}''$
8" long	$3\frac{5}{16}''$	$2\frac{7}{8}''$	$2\frac{1}{2}''$	$2\frac{1}{8}''$
12" long	$4\frac{7}{8}''$	$4\frac{1}{2}''$	$4''$	$3\frac{7}{16}''$

FIGURE 16-22
This pivoted support holds a dropped leaf firmly in a horizontal position.

sions shown in Fig. 16-22. Small drop leaves can be held with one support. Large leaves should have two. If you plan to use these, design your tabletop so that the overhang places the center of the knuckle the proper distance from the rail. They are available in 6-, 8-, and 12-in. sizes.

Another type of table drop-leaf support is designed for tables without aprons (Fig. 16-23). The brackets for fastening to the top provide the support of the drop leaf. They are available in 6-, 8-, 10-, and 12-in. sizes. The two smaller sizes are used for normal-size drop leaves. The large sizes are for heavy-duty use.

Sliding supports are also used. One commercially available support has a metal channel through which a wood support slides. One slide is

FIGURE 16-23
This drop-leaf support is used on tables that do not have an apron.

enough for small leaves. On wide leaves, use two supports (Fig. 16-24). Shop-made wood supports are typical of those used on original pieces of traditional furniture. One type uses a three-piece slide with the center piece sliding on two fixed outside guides (Fig. 16-25).

The traditional butterfly drop-leaf table uses two wood wings which pivot on dowels set in each end. The wing swings out to support the leaf and folds in when it is dropped (Fig. 16-26).

A gate-leg table has its leaves supported by a rail and a stretcher that swing out from the table. This is called a fly rail. It is connected to the table rail. With this type of construction, the table can be quite narrow yet have large drop leaves which form a much larger table when extended (Fig. 16-27).

Still another method uses hinged wood brackets that fasten to the table rail and swing out under the drop-leaf. This will support short leaves (Fig. 16-28).

Two simple shop-made drop-leaf supports are the pivot rail and the swinging bracket using a finger joint for a hinge (Fig. 16-29). They are used on small leaves that will not carry heavy loads.

FIGURE 16-24
A simple metal frame can be used to hold horizontally moving wood slides.

FIGURE 16-25
Horizontal slides can be made with wood guides and wood slides.

FIGURE 16-26
A swinging wood wing is traditionally used to support drop leaves on butterfly tables.

199

FIGURE 16-27
Swinging legs and rails have been commonly used on many traditional tables.

FIGURE 16-28
Short swinging arms can be used to support small drop leaves.

HINGED BRACKETS

PIVOT RAIL

ROUND TONGUE

SWINGING RAIL

FIGURE 16-29
These are other ways to support small drop leaves.

JOINING TOPS TO BASES

There are many devices available for fastening tops to the bases of furniture and cabinets. If the top is solid wood, the fastening device should allow the expansion and contraction as shown in Fig. 16-30. The various metal tabletop fasteners available are the fastest and easiest to use. Place them about 12 to 15 in. apart. The wood fasteners can be made from any available scrap material. They are screwed but not glued in place (Fig. 16-31). Another method is to counterbore the rail and run the screw through it or bore *pocket holes* which permit the screw to run through the rail into the top (Fig. 16-32).

FIGURE 16-31
Other ways to secure a tabletop to the table frame.

CORNER IRON
BRACE

WOOD CLEAT

METAL ANGLE
IRON

FASTENER
RECESSED
INTO RAIL

STEEL TOP
FASTENER

FIGURE 16-30
These tabletop connectors permit the top to expand and
contract independently from the table frame.

RABBETED
WOOD BLOCK

MANUFACTURED
METAL FASTENER

SET SCREW IN
COUNTERBORE
THROUGH RAIL

SET SCREW
THROUGH
POCKET
HOLES

FIGURE 16-32
Tabletops can be secured to the
frame with screws.

Answer each of the following questions. If you are not sure of an answer, review the chapter.

16-1. What kinds of materials are used to make table tops?

16-2. Why are solid wood tops not widely used?

16-3. How are solid boards positioned for gluing?

16-4. What type of plywood is used for table tops?

16-5. How are the unattractive edges of plywood tops covered?

16-6. What are the two types of expandable tables?

16-7. What joints are used on the drop leaves of drop-leaf tables?

16-8. What type of hinges are used on drop-leaf tables?

16-9. How are drop leaves supported in the horizontal position?

16-10. How are table tops secured to the base of the table?

IMPORTANT TECHNICAL TERMS

Following are technical terms that you should be able to use as part of your working vocabulary. Write a brief description of the meaning of each term.

Expandable tables
Drop-leaf tables
Banding
Rule joint
Butterfly drop-leaf table
Gate-leg table

17

CUSTOM CABINETS AND MODULAR CASEWORK

Custom-made cabinets are those that are produced for a specific single order. They are sized to meet the specific desires of the owners and to fit into a specific space. Custom cabinet companies may employ one person or as many as 100 or more.

The shift has been to the development of large manufacturing companies producing hundreds of units a day that are made to standard sizes. These are often referred to as production or modular casework. This may be an integrated operation or an assembly operation.

The *integrated operation* is one where the wood parts are made, starting with the rough lumber and producing a finished part. These parts are then assembled and finished, producing the finished cabinet.

For the *assembly operation* parts are purchased either fully or partly machined. They do minor machining to complete the parts and then assemble and finish the cabinets. This type of operation eliminates the need for highly expensive production machines and skilled workers, which they would most likely not keep busy all the time because of the size of the production runs.

Both types of operations use hardboard, particleboard, medium-density fiberboard, plywood, hardware, finishing materials, and shipping materials.

STANDARD CABINET SIZES

The standard sizes of American modular cabinet units are shown in Fig. 17-1.

Modular cabinets are those built to standard sizes that have been agreed upon by a trade organization representing cabinet manufacturers such as the National Kitchen Cabinet Association. All cabinets built by members of this organization are certified by the NKCA and must meet the standards set forth in the American National Standards Institute Standard ANSl A161.1-1980. Their certification label is placed on cabinets that meet these standards (Fig. 17-2). Certified cabinets are also subject to flame spread ratings. These ratings are established by testing materials used in cabinet construction to determine the rate at which they will burn. The tests compare to the rate at which flame spreads on a material with the rate of untreated red oak. The classes of flame spread are listed in Table 17-1.

Certified cabinets must have a class C flame spread rating of 200 or less. This relates to combustible doors, exposed end panels, bottoms, and countertops. Cabinet faceframes, mullions, and toe strips are exempted. Those meeting this standard have a certifying seal placed on them (Fig. 17-3). Wood can be treated with chemicals to improve its flame spread rating.

FIGURE 17-1
Standard modular kitchen cabinet sizes.

TABLE 17-1
Classes of Flame Spread

Classification	Flame spread
Class I or A	0–25
Class II or B	26–75
Class III or C	76–200

Cabinets are divided into wall cabinets, base cabinets, vanity cabinets, and tall oven and utility cabinets. The main components making up these units are drawers, doors, front frames, shelves, unit sides, backs and bottoms, bases, tops, and hardware.

Doors are made from plywood, particleboard, medium-density fiberboard, and lumber. They may be flat or have designs routed in, molding overlays, or raised panels and inserts such as glass or woven reed or wood slats. Doors are discussed in Chapter 13.

Faceframes are usually $\frac{3}{4}$ in. thick finished. They are usually solid wood and make what is called a *bound cabinet*. Some cabinet styles do not use a faceframe. They are referred to as *unbound cabinets*.

Drawer fronts usually match the doors and faceframes. Sometimes doors and drawers are made of a material that sharply contrasts with the faceframe, such as white plastic laminate door and drawer fronts over a natural finished wood faceframe.

Cabinet sides are usually $\frac{3}{16}$- to $\frac{3}{4}$-in.-thick plywood, particleboard, or medium-density fiberboard. Exposed sides are finished to match the faceframe.

Shelves are $\frac{1}{2}$ to $\frac{3}{4}$ in. thick and made from plywood, lumber, particleboard, or medium-density fiberboard. All exposed surfaces are finished to protect against moisture. Sometimes the shelves are

FIGURE 17-2
Cabinets manufactured to ANSI A161.1-1980 requirements are certified by the National Kitchen Cabinet Association.

FIGURE 17-4
Standard cabinet heights and widths. (Courtesy of Architectural Woodwork Institute.)

A. 84"
B. 68", 59" FOR HANDICAPPED
C. 66", 57" FOR HANDICAPPED
D. 4"
E. 12", 16", 24"
F. 11" MUST HAVE 24" CABINET
G. 3"

TALL CABINETS

A. COUNTER ADJUSTABLE TO 28", 32" AND 36", VANITY 31"
B. 15" TO 20"
C. 18", 24", 30"
D. 10"
E. 29½" CLEARANCE FOR WHEEL CHAIR
F. 4"
G. 12"
H. 24" MAX, VANITY 22½"
I. 1½"
J. 22½" MAX.
K. 7"

**CABINETS DESIGNED
FOR THE HANDICAPPED**

A. STAND UP COUNTER 36"
   SIT DOWN COUNTER 30"
   VANITY 31"
   SEWING, TYPING 26"
B. 18"
C. 18", 24", 30", 36"
D. 4"
E. 1¼" TO 1½"
F. 4"
G. 12"
H. CABINET 24", VANITY 22½"
I. 21", 22½"
J. 3"
K. KNEE SPACE IF SEATED 24½"

STANDARD CABINETS

FIGURE 17-3
This seal certifies the cabinet has a flame spread rating of 200 or less. (Courtesy of National Kitchen Cabinet Association.)

dadoed into the sides of cabinets, while others are made adjustable. Shelves are discussed in Chapter 15.

The standard dimensions for cabinets are shown in Fig. 17-4. These represent the most comfortable height for the majority of people. Custom-built cabinets can be higher or lower, as desired by the owner. Special considerations for accommodating the handicapped are necessary.

Base Units

The base cabinet supports sinks, surface cooking units, and many small portable appliances. Below the top is considerable storage in the form of drawers, shelves, or special accessory storage units. Base cabinets at the sink or range may contain only a front and bottom. Special units are built to fit in the corner. The corner has a lot of dead space and requires special planning. Often a lazy susan unit is placed here. A lazy susan is a unit with round shelves that rotate.

The widths of modular cabinets are based on a 3-in. module and range from 9 to 48 in. Custom-built cabinets are made to fit the exact wallspace. Both types have a variety of drawer and door combinations. Base cabinets are usually 22½ to 24 in. deep from the back to the front of the faceframe, with the top being 24 to 25 in. deep. Bathroom vanities are 22½ in. deep. Standard kitchen cabinet base units are 34½ in. high without the top. Any counter to be used from a chair is 30 in. high. For people in a wheelchair the kitchen counter should be adjustable or replaceable to provide alternative heights of 28, 32, and 36 in. measured from the floor to the top of the counter. This includes the sink cabinets. The door handles should be placed as near the top of the door as possible. One 30-in. section of base cabinet should be clear below so that a wheelchair can move under it, allowing a person to work on the counter. Standards for planning for the handicapped can be found in ANSI A117.1-1980, Specifications for Making Buildings and Facilities Accessible to, and Usable by, Physically Handicapped People.

Wall Cabinets

Wall cabinets are securely mounted on the wall above the base cabinet. They are usually 12 in. deep from the back to the front of the face frame. They are made in standard widths from 9 to 48 in. A variety of heights are available, but 30 in. is the most common. A special corner unit is made for use when they have to turn a corner (Fig. 17-5).

To serve the handicapped, at least one shelf must be no more than 48 in. above the floor. Door pulls should be mounted as close to the bottom as possible.

Oven and Utility Cabinets

These are tall cabinets generally 84 in. high. Oven cabinets are designed to hold an oven separated from the surface cooking unit. They are 24, 27, and 33 in. wide and 24 to 25 in. deep. Space above and below the oven opening is used for shelves and serves as a pantry or for general storage purposes. Utility cabinets are usually 12, 16, or 24 in. deep and 18 or 24 in. wide.

Special Accessories

Cabinet manufacturers provide a wide array of special storage units to increase the efficiency of the space. These include drawers for holding silverware, wire racks for pots and pans, and units to hold canned goods, spices, and cleaning materials (Fig.

FIGURE 17-5
A special wall cabinet is used when they have to turn a corner.

17-6). Hardware and accessories used in cabinets certified by the National Kitchen Cabinet Association must meet the standards set forth in the American National Standards on cabinet hardware.

Kitchen Planning

A kitchen is planned around one activity: food storage, cooking, preparation, and cleanup. The food storage area includes the refrigerator-freezer and cabinets for storage of canned and dry foods. The cooking area includes the range and oven. If a separate oven is to be used, it need not be near the range because it does not require constant attention. The preparation and cleanup area includes a sink, disposal, compactor, and dishwasher.

The basic kitchen arrangements include the I-shape, L-shape, U-shape, and corridor (Fig. 17-7).

FIGURE 17-6
Many special accessories are used to improve the efficient use of cabinet space. (Courtesy of American Woodmark Corp.)

WALL CABINETS

BASE CABINETS

3'-0" MIN.

1'-0" MIN.

2'-0" MIN.

REF.

WORK TRIANGLE 22'-0" MAX.

U-SHAPED KITCHEN

REF.

L-SHAPED KITCHEN

OVEN CABINET

REF.

4'-0" MIN.

CORRIDOR KITCHEN

REF.

I-SHAPED KITCHEN

FIGURE 17-7
Basic types of kitchen arrangements.

ELEVATION - A

AN ISLAND CABINET

FIGURE 17-8
An island counter helps improve the efficiency of a kitchen. (Courtesy of Kleweno of Kansas City.)

ELEVATION-B

Sometimes an island counter is used. This can contain a sink or cooking unit or simply be extra counter space (Fig. 17-8).

To make a kitchen efficient, it is wise to plan it around a work triangle. A *work triangle* is formed by measuring the straight-line distances between the refrigerator, cooking unit, and sink (Fig. 7-7). This distance should not exceed 22 ft. When planning the counter space, allow 3 to 4 ft on each side of the sink. Allow 2 ft or more of counter space on each side of the cooking unit. Allow at least 1 ft of counter beside the refrigerator-freezer so that you have somewhere to place things.

Developing the Cabinet Layout

First make a drawing of the room, locating doors and windows that are involved in the walls to receive cabinets. Then locate the sink, refrigerator and range, or surface unit and oven. Locate other items that will affect the cabinets, such as a dishwasher or compactor. Then draw the base cabinets and wall cabinets. Measure existing kitchens carefully and record on the drawing. Indicate the size of the spaces to contain cabinets (Fig. 17-9).

NOTE: ALL DIMENSIONS INCHES. WALL CABINETS SHOWN WITH DASHED LINES.

FIGURE 17-9
The preliminary kitchen plan is developed to ascertain the sizes of the base and wall cabinet units. Elevations are drawn to help decide on door and drawer locations.

Then draw elevations of each wall to a scale of $\frac{3}{4}$ in = 1 ft 0 in. or 1 in. = 1 ft 0 in. This will let you decide on the location of drawers and doors. Dimension each section of cabinets. Using these sizes you can have the cabinets custom built or select units from a factory made modular cabinet system.

As you plan your kitchen, consider the various shapes available and study the established recommendations for the amount of cabinet space needed.

Installing Cabinets

The cabinets are delivered to the job safely stored in boxes or protective blankets. The finish carpenter installs them according to the kitchen plan on the working drawings of the house.

The base cabinets are installed first. Begin the installation in a corner. There are three ways to handle a corner. One is to butt the ends of two cabinets together, filling between them with a filler strip. However, the corner is thus completely wasted for storage (Fig. 17-10). A second way is to use a rectangular cabinet designed to fill the corner space. The cabinet on the other wall butts into it. While the

space provided is difficult to reach, it provides good storage (Fig. 17-11). A third way is to use a corner cabinet with a door on a 45° angle or a 90° door, butting the adjoining cabinets. This space is easier to reach and is the best solution (Fig. 17-12).

Preparatory Instructions

1. Make certain that the wall is free of obstructions. In remodeling it may be necessary to remove the old baseboard.
2. Locate the wall studs and mark clearly.
3. Using a level and a long straightedge, find the highest spot on the floor. From this spot mark a line on the wall the height of each unit, 34½ in. for base, 54 in. for wall cabinets, and 84 in. for tall cabinets.

Installing the Base Cabinets

1. Start with a corner unit. Shim it at the floor until it lines up with the 34½-in. mark on the wall (Fig. 17-13, page 212). If the wall is crooked, shim the cabinets at the wall so that

FIGURE 17-10
The butting of cabinets in a corner wastes considerable space.

CORNER OF ROOM
LEFT OPEN AND
IS WASTED SPACE.

FILLER STRIPS
AS NEEDED.

FIGURE 17-11
One base unit is built to fill the corner. The adjoining unit butts against it. A filler strip is used as needed. Note that these units use a faceframe.

Labels in figure:
- CABINET EXTENDED TO FILL CORNER
- CORNER BLOCK
- THIS CABINET BUTTS ONE ON OTHER WALL.
- FILLER STRIP SIZED AS NEEDED.

they line up straight (Fig. 17-14). Check to make sure that it is level along its length and width.

2. Drill ¼-in. holes through the rigid back at each stud.

3. Fasten to the wall using No. 10 sheet metal or wood screws with either washer heads or use a washer. The screws should go at least ¾ in. into the stud.

4. Place the next base unit next to the first. Clamp it to the first unit and drill ⅛-in. pilot holes 6 in. from the top and bottom through the first frame and ¾ in. into the second frame. Shim at the floor as necessary to keep level.

5. Drill a ¼-in. clearance hole over the pilot hole in the first frame.

6. Fasten the cabinets together with No. 10 sheet metal or wood screws with either a washer head or washer.

7. Now fasten the second unit to the wall as explained earlier.

Installing the Countertop

Position the counter top and join to the base with screws. Predrill the necessary holes and fasten

through the corner blocks or the front and back cleats (Fig. 17-15).

Installing Wall Cabinets

1. Make certain that the wall is free of bows or crooks. If it is not flat, shim it out so that the cabinets rest on shims, providing a straight wall (Fig. 17-16). If the unit turns a corner, make certain the corner is square. If it is not, shim it out as shown in Fig. 17.17.

2. Start the wall cabinets in a corner. Use blocking resting on the countertop to hold the cabinets in position. Be certain to pad the top so that it is not damaged (Fig. 17-18).

3. Fasten the first cabinet to the wall, being very certain it is level and plumb. Its position will affect all the other cabinets.

4. Fasten each of the other cabinets together and then to the wall as explained for base units.

CABINET CONSTRUCTION

The parts of cabinets can be identified by surface visibility. *Exposed surfaces* are those that are visible

CORNER UNIT WITH
90° DOOR

DOOR FOR
CORNER
BASE UNIT

FIGURE 17-12
The use of a corner cabinet makes the space in the
corner usable.

BASE CABINETS
BUTT CORNER
UNIT

CORNER UNIT WITH
45° DOOR

FIGURE 17-13
Start by installing the corner base unit. Shim it at the floor until it is level.

FIGURE 17-14
Shim the cabinet at the wall so that it is straight.

FIGURE 17-15
Fasten the top to the base through cleats or corner blocks.

FIGURE 17-16
Shim out the wall cabinets so they line up straight.

when doors and drawers are closed, behind glass doors, cabinet bottoms more than 42 in. (1066 mm) off the floor, and tops of cabinets lower than 78 in. (1980 mm) above the floor. They require good-quality materials because they will be seen. *Semiexposed surfaces* are surfaces that become visible when opaque doors are open or drawers are extended and cabinet bottoms more than 30 in. (762 mm) and less than 42 in. (1066 mm) above the floor. They should also be good-quality materials. *Concealed surfaces* include surfaces not visible after installation, such as bottoms of cabinets less than 30 in. (762 mm) above the floor, cabinet tops more than 78 in. (1980 mm) above the floor, and stretchers, blocking, and components concealed by drawers. These parts can be made from any species of wood that is adequate for the job. In some cases metal and plastic parts are used instead of wood.

CABINET
90°

WALL ANGLE
GREATER THAN 90°

SHIMMING A WALL WHEN
THE CORNER IS GREATER
THAN 90°

SHIM

CABINET
90°

WALL ANGLE LESS
THAN 90°

FIGURE 17-17
It may be necessary to shim cabinets around a corner that is not square.

SHIM AS NEEDED

FIRST INSTALL CABINET
WITH CORNER FILL
SECTION

THEN BUTT SECOND
CABINET TO IT

FILLER STRIP
AS NEEDED

SUPPORT WALL
CABINETS WITH
BLOCKING WHILE
INSTALLING THEM

PROTECT PLASTIC
LAMINATE ON TOP

54

$34\frac{1}{2}$

FIGURE 17-18
Start installing wall cabinets in a corner.

FIGURE 17-19
These bathroom cabinets have a faceframe and doors with raised panels. (Courtesy of American Woodmark Corp.)

FIGURE 17-20
Conventionally built cabinet with faceframes.

CONSTRUCTION WITH A FACEFRAME

Cabinets can be constructed in several ways. In this chapter you will be shown several different construction methods. One type that is widely used has an exposed faceframe (Fig. 17-19, page 213). The carcass of this type of cabinet is $\frac{3}{4}$-in. (18-mm) plywood or reconstituted wood panels. The faceframe, doors, and drawer fronts are solid wood.

Construction details and identification of the parts of this type of cabinet are shown in Fig. 17-20. *Exterior bulkheads* are those that are visible. *Interior bulkheads* are those that meet another cabinet or butt against a wall or appliance. *Partitions* are vertical interior dividers. The *faceframe* is a solid wood frame nailed or glued to the front edges of the carcass. Horizontal members of the faceframe are called *rails* and vertical members or *stiles*. *Mullions* are vertical members that run between doors or drawers. The *rigid back* is a brace used to strengthen the cabinet. The *cleats* are used to fasten the top to the base. Corner blocks such as those shown in Fig. 17-15 can be used instead of cleats.

The base unit is built by cutting the bottom, bulkheads, and partitions to size, cutting $\frac{1}{4}$ in. (6-mm)-deep dadoes for the bottom and shelves. A rabbet $\frac{1}{4} \times \frac{1}{2}$ in. is made in the back edge of the exterior bulkhead for the back. A typical set of bulkheads and a partition are shown in Fig. 17-21. The exterior bulkhead is the full width of the cabinet. The partition and interior bulkhead are $\frac{1}{2}$ in. (12 mm) narrower because the cabinet back is nailed directly on to them rather than having a rabbet as is the case with the exterior bulkhead. Although the base unit can be assembled without dadoes by using nailed butt joints, the dadoes produce a stronger cabinet. The exterior bulkheads are glued to the bottom and shelves. They may be nailed with finishing nails. If this is done, set the nailheads and fill the holes with a filler that matches the color of the finished cabinet. Premium-quality cabinets should be glued and clamped with no exposed nail holes. The interior bulkheads and partitions are nailed to the shelves and bottom with 6d finishing nails. Interior-bulkheads and partitions are nailed to the shelves and bottom. No glue is necessary.

Faceframe construction can be used with lipped, flush, and overlay doors and drawers (Fig. 17-22). The lip used is normally $\frac{3}{8} \times \frac{3}{8}$ in. (9×9 mm). Flush construction places the outer face of the doors and drawers flush with the outer surface of the faceframe (Fig. 17-23). *Overlay doors* may be of the flush overlay or reveal overlay types. The flush overlay door and draw front hide the faceframe completely. The reveal overlay design permits some of the faceframe to be seen.

FIGURE 17-21
Typical bulkheads and partitions.

IF ADJUSTABLE SHELVES
ARE TO BE USED SHELF
DADOES ARE OMITTED.

22"

DADOES FOR
SHELVES

DISTANCE A

DADO FOR
BOTTOM

CUT-OUT
FOR TOEBOARD

AN INTERIOR
BULKHEAD

22"

3/4" X 3" NOTCH FOR
RIGID BACK

DADOES FOR FIXED
SHELVES

DISTANCE A

PARTITION

22 1/2"

3/8"

1/2"

SHELF WIDTH

RABBET

1/4" DEEP DADOES

DADO FOR
BOTTOM

EXTERIOR
BULKHEAD

BULKHEAD

FACEFRAME

LIPPED
DOOR

LIPPED DOOR ON FACEFRAME

BULKHEAD

FACEFRAME

DOOR

OVERLAY ON FACEFRAME

BULKHEAD

FACEFRAME

DOOR

HINGE
MORTISE

REVEAL OVERLAY ON FACEFRAME

DOOR

FACEFRAME

FACEFRAME HINGE

FIGURE 17-22
Types of door and drawer construction used with faceframe construction.

CONSTRUCTION WITH A FACEFRAME   **215**

Conventional flush construction with face frame ■

With this style of construction, all door and drawer faces are flush with the face of the cabinet. This style is highly functional and allows the use of different thicknesses of door and drawer fronts. Conventional as well as concealed hinges are available for a variety of door thicknesses.

This is the most expensive of the four styles shown in this publication due to the increased care necessary in the fitting and aligning of the doors and drawers plus the cost of providing the face frame. This style does not lend itself to the economical use of plastic laminate covering.

Note: A, B, C, D, E designates appropriate hardware compatible to particular cabinet construction.
SEE FIG. 17-38.

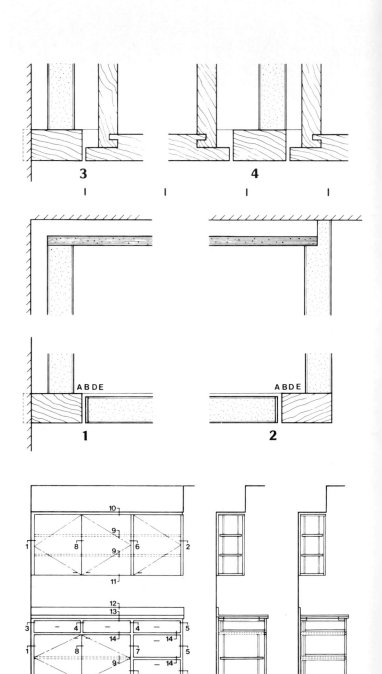

Elevation   Section at Doors   Section at Drawers

FIGURE 17-23
Conventional flush construction with a faceframe. (Courtesy of Architectural Woodwork Institute.)

5

6

ABDE

7

ABDE

12

8

9

← Sofit

10

11

13

14

15

1. MARK LOCATIONS OF PARTITIONS AND BULKHEADS.

LOCATION OF PARTITION

FRONT EDGE

BOTTOM

LOCATION OF INTERIOR BULKHEAD

3. JOIN THE INTERIOR AND EXTERIOR BULKHEAD TO THE CARCASS.

INTERIOR BULKHEAD

EXTERIOR BULKHEAD

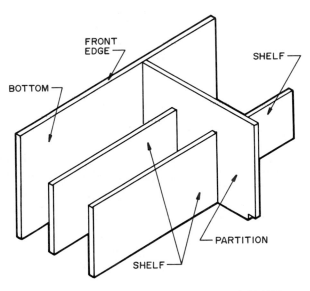

2. NAIL PARTITION TO BOTTOM. NAIL SHELVES TO PARTITION.

FRONT EDGE

SHELF

BOTTOM

PARTITION

SHELF

FIGURE 17-24
Steps to assemble a cabinet.

4. TURN CARCASS OVER AND NAIL RIGID BACK, CHECK FOR SQUARENESS AND NAIL $\frac{1}{4}$" BACK IN PLACE.

MEASURE DIAGONALS CHECK FOR SQUARENESS

BACK EDGE

NAIL RIGID BACK

BOTTOM

Assembling the Base Unit

Start by marking the location of partitions on the bottom. Then stand the bottom on its back edge. Nail the partition to the bottom with 6d finishing nails (Fig. 17-24). Then insert the shelves into the dadoes in the partition and nail. Next join the interior and exterior bulkheads to the bottom. Make cer-

tain that they are flush with the front edge of the cabinet bottom. Turn the unit over and nail the rigid back in place. Measure the diagonals to be certain that the unit is square as the rigid back is being nailed. Then place the back on the unit and nail or staple. Use 2d finishing nails or $\frac{3}{4}$-in. staples. Again make absolutely certain that the unit is square before nailing the back in place. Turn the unit over and nail the toe board in place. The unit is now ready for the faceframe.

Assembling the Faceframe

The faceframe is usually assembled using ⅜-in. (10-mm) dowels. After the faceframe members are cut to length, locate and bore the dowel holes. Assemble on a large flat surface such as a table or on the floor. Begin by putting glue in the dowel holes with a small brush. Join the inside pieces first and work toward the outer rails and stiles (Fig. 17-25). Then clamp using long bar clamps. Clamp just tight enough to close the joints. Check to make certain that the faceframe is square and flat on the clamps. If the clamps cause the faceframe to bow, clamp it to the table or the bar clamp with C-clamps so that it stays flat.

Attaching the Faceframe

The faceframe can be attached to the carcass with finishing nails. However, its appearance is improved if it is glued instead.

Place the carcass on its back on two sawhorses. Place the assembled faceframe on the carcass and check to see that it fits. If it fits properly, remove the faceframe and apply adhesive to the front edges of the carcass. Lay the faceframe in position and begin clamping it to the carcass with bar clamps. Begin at one end of the carcass and apply clamps toward the other end. Make certain that the faceframe is flat

against the edge of the carcass. Use as many clamps as necessary to assure good contact (Fig. 17-26).

If you decide to nail the faceframe instead of clamping, follow the steps just mentioned except that you nail it to the carcass with 6d finishing nails. Begin nailing at a lower corner and nail one end. Then work your way to the other end, nailing into the top and bottom rails and partitions (Fig. 17-27).

Cleaning Up after Assembly

After the adhesive has dried, the faceframe and exterior panels can be sanded and excess glue removed. Sanding can also reduce slight variations in the joint so that the faceframe is flat and doors and drawers fit tightly against them. Sanding must be done very carefully or more damage than good might occur. Since the grain of the stock in the faceframe meets at right angles, careless sanding can produce across-grain scratches. To minimize these, sand the horizontal members first, sanding lightly across the joint as shown in Fig. 17-28. Then sand the vertical rail, removing any scratches. Work lightly back and forth in each direction until the joint is flush. Then give the vertical member a final sanding, being very careful not to run over on the horizontal member.

Constructing a Wall Cabinet

The bathroom wall cabinet in Fig. 17-29 is typical of units having solid wood faceframes. The doors are

FIGURE 17-25
Assemble and clamp the faceframe.

HANDSCREWS USED
TO GLUE CLEAT TO
FACEFRAME.

SCRAP
STOCK

SCRAP
STOCK

FIGURE 17-26
Glue and clamp the faceframe to the carcass.

FIGURE 17-27
Suggested order for nailing a faceframe to the carcass.

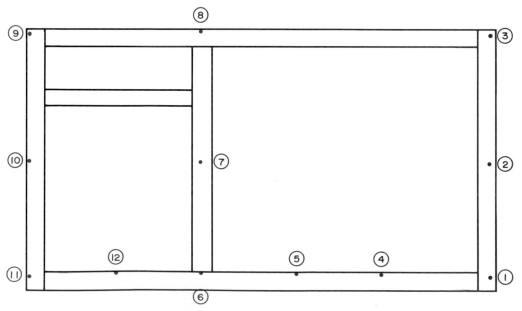

CHAPTER 17   CUSTOM CABINETS AND MODULAR CASEWORK

1. SAND THE RAIL LIGHTLY ACROSS THE JOINT.
2. THEN SAND THE STILE REMOVING THE SCRATCHES.
3. REPEAT UNTIL JOINT IS SMOOTH.
4. FINAL SANDING ON STILE BUT DO NOT OVERLAP RAIL.

FIGURE 17-28
Steps to sand faceframe joints so that the surfaces are flush.

FIGURE 17-29
The bathroom wall cabinet has a faceframe and lipped doors. (Courtesy of American Woodmark Corp.)

FIGURE 17-30
Typical construction details for wall cabinets with faceframes.

lipped and hung with semiconcealed hinges. Several designs for wall cabinets using faceframes are shown in Fig. 17-30. These designs can use lipped, flush, or overlay doors. The design of the wall cabinet generally is the same as used for the base cabinet.

Doors and Drawers

If it is desired to have a continuous grain, cut as many doors and drawer fronts as possible from a single sheet of plywood (Fig. 17-31). If drawer fronts are to be from solid wood, try to find stock long enough to enable you to cut all the drawer fronts from one board.

Cabinets with faceframes can have flush or overlay-type doors and drawers (Fig. 17-22) or lipped or overlay doors and drawers (Fig. 17-23). The lipped door uses a semiconcealed or wraparound hinge. The overlay door may use a faceframe hinge that is set into a 35-mm-diameter hole in the door. The flush style has all the doors and drawers flush with the front of the faceframe. This permits the use of drawer fronts and doors that are different thicknesses. Conventional as well as concealed hinges can be used. (See Chapter 13 for more information on hinges.)

The flush style is more expensive than most because of the extra care necessary to fit and align the doors and drawers into the openings in the faceframe. The crack between these must be uniform and parallel on all sides. The faceframe adds to the cost when compared to units without faceframes. This style does not lend itself to the economical use

WIDTH OF PLYWOOD 4'—0" MAXIMUM

FIGURE 17-31
To have a continuous grain pattern cut the doors and drawers from a single sheet of plywood.

of plastic laminate covering. Hardwood plywood and solid wood are commonly used.

Lipped drawer and door fronts are usually $\frac{3}{4}$ in. (18 mm) thick and have a $\frac{3}{8}$-in. (9-mm) lip. The lip should be planned so that it clears the faceframe at least $\frac{1}{8}$ in. (3 mm) on all sides.

The overlay door is set over the faceframe a distance recommended by the hinge manufacturer. This is generally about $1\frac{13}{32}$ in. (36 mm).

Lipped doors often are made with a solid wood frame to avoid the problem of seeing the edge grain of the plywood, particleboard ,or medium-density fiberboard that is often used (Fig. 17-32).

Drawers are usually hung using metal side-mounted slides or a single center-mounted slide. Detailed information on drawers and doors is given in Chapters 13 and 14.

FIGURE 17-32
This lavatory cabinet uses solid wood drawer fronts and doors. (Courtesy of American Woodmark Corp.)

Shelves

Shelves may be fixed or adjustable. Fixed shelves are strongest if set in a $\frac{1}{4}$-in. (6-mm) dado, but can be butted to a partition and nailed. If plywood or a reconstituted wood product is used, the front edge is often banded with solid wood, metal, or plastic. Details on shelf construction are given in Chapter 15.

Making a Split Stile

When a cabinet is too long to be made easily as a single unit, it can be made as two units and joined with a split stile. The details for this are shown in Fig. 17-33. When installing the wood screws, be certain to drill shank and pilot holes. Bolts can also be used. However, the nut must be counterbored. To join the cabinets, locate three screws or bolts vertically about $1\frac{1}{2}$ in. (38 mm) behind the faceframe and three more in the rear about $1\frac{1}{2}$ in. (38 mm) in from the cabinet back.

Prepare the faceframe so that it overlaps the adjoining interior bulkheads $\frac{1}{8}$ in. (3 mm). This will allow the faceframes to be tightly joined by the screws or bolts. It is easiest to join the cabinets if

FIGURE 17-33
A split stile is used when two cabinets are joined to form a single long unit.

C' BORE

MACHINE SCREW

INTERIOR BULKHEAD

$\frac{1}{4}$" BLOCKING

$\frac{1}{8}$ $\frac{1}{8}$

SPLIT FACEFRAME

they are lying on their backs on sawhorses. The cabinets can now be separated if they have to be moved to a distant location and rejoined at that point.

An increasing number of cabinets are being built without a faceframe. These types include flush construction without a faceframe flush overlay and reveal overlay.

CONSTRUCTION WITHOUT A FACEFRAME

This type of construction is often called European style. The cabinets have a sleeker look (Fig. 17-34). The end panels and bulkheads have their exposed edges banded. The cost is less because the faceframe, which is time consuming to build and install, is eliminated. The common types of cabinets using this construction are the flush, flush overlay, and reveal overlay.

FIGURE 17-34
These cabinets are built without faceframes. (Courtesy of Kleweno of Kansas City.)

Flush Construction

Details for flush construction without a faceframe are shown in Fig. 17-35. The overall design is the same as that described for cabinets with faceframes. The cabinet must be accurately built and the doors and drawer fronts carefully sized so that the space between them and the bulkheads and partitions is uniform on all sides. This style of cabinet does not lend itself to the economical use of plastic laminate covering.

Flush Overlay Construction

Flush overlay construction does not use the conventional faceframe (Fig. 17-36, pages 226, 227). It is built much like the conventional construction without a faceframe. It offers a clean, contemporary look because only the drawer fronts and doors are visible. This style lends itself to the economical use of plastic laminates. When hardwood plywood is used, the grain matching of the fronts can be achieved by cutting all the pieces from the same panel. Conventional or concealed hinges can be used (Fig. 17-36).

Reveal Overlay Construction

In this style the drawer fronts and doors are sized so that the edge of the end panels and bulkheads is revealed. This provides an interesting depth and shadow lines around each drawer and door. It can be built using hardwood plywood or plastic laminate construction. The reveal is usually $\frac{3}{8}$ in., although it could be a maximum of $\frac{1}{2}$ in. if desired. Conventional or concealed hinges can be used (Fig. 17-37, pages 228, 229).

HARDWARE

The chart in Fig. 17-38, page 230, will assist in the selection of hinges generally used for commercial construction.

32-MILLIMETER CARCASS SYSTEM

The European 32-mm system is finding increasing use in cabinet construction as a replacement for the more traditional dado and rabbet methods. It is a much faster way to prepare to join two parts of a cabinet together. The system involves drilling dowel holes spaced 32, 64, or 96 mm center to center along the butting edges of the carcass. These are drilled using a multiple drilling machine that makes it possible to drill simultaneously many holes uniformly spaced (Fig. 17-39, page 231). It also makes it easy to install the many special accessories and interior hardware used in cabinets. It eliminates the need for elaborate jigs and fixtures to hold the cabinet during the assembly operation.

This system requires the use of precision woodworking machinery which permits fast setups and accurate machining. Specially designed hardware

CONVENTIONAL flush CONSTRUCTION without face frame ■

The design features of this casework style are the same as conventional flush with face frame except that the face frame has been eliminated resulting in a cost savings. This style also does not lend itself to the economical use of plastic laminate covering.

Note: A, B, C, D, E designates appropriate hardware compatible to particular cabinet construction.
SEE FIG. 17-38.

Elevation   Section at Doors   Section at Drawers

FIGURE 17-35
Conventional flush construction without a faceframe. (Courtesy of Architectural Woodwork Institute.)

5

6

ABE ABE

7

ABE

12

8

9

10

Sofit

11

13

14

15

Flush overlay construction ■

Flush overlay construction offers a
very clean, contemporary look
since only the doors and drawer
fronts are visible in elevation.
When specified, grain matching
between doors and drawer fronts
can be achieved by having all
pieces cut from the same panel.
This style is increasingly popular
and lends itself well to the use of
plastic laminate for exposed surfaces. Conventional as well as
concealed hinges are available for
a variety of door thicknesses.

Note: A, B, C, D, E designates appropriate hardware
compatible to particular cabinet construction.
SEE FIG. 17-38.

FIGURE 17-36
Flush overlay construction. (Courtesy of Architectural Woodwork Institute.)

Optional Block for Pivot Hinge

C BE   BE C

C BE

5

6

7

12

8

9

13

Sofit

10

14

11

15

Reveal overlay construction ■

In this style, the separation between doors and drawer fronts is accented by the reveal. The style is equally suited to either wood or plastic laminate construction. Although the detail shown here incorporates a reveal at all horizontal and vertical joints, this can be varied by the designer. It should be noted that a reveal over 1/2 inch would require the addition of a face frame and, therefore, increases the cost. The addition of a face frame would also change the hinge requirements. With or without a face frame, this style allows the use of conventional or concealed hinges.

Note: A, B, C, D, E designates appropriate hardware compatible to particular cabinet construction.
SEE FIG. 17-38

FIGURE 17-37
Reveal overlay construction. (Courtesy of Architectural Woodwork Institute.)

5

6   ABE   ABE

7   ABE

12

8

9

Sofit

10

11

13

14

15

	A BUTT	B WRAP AROUND	C PIVOT	D INVISIBLE	E EUROPEAN STYLE
Hinge Type					
Applications	Conventional Flush Front with Face Frame	Conventional Flush Front Reveal Overlay Flush Overlay	Reveal Overlay Flush Overlay	Conventional Flush with Face Frame	Reveal Overlay Flush Overlay Conventional Flush without Face Frame
Strength	High	Very High	Moderate	Low	Moderate
Concealed when closed	No	No	Semi	Yes	Yes
Requires Mortising	Yes	Occasionally	Usually	Yes	Yes
Cost of Hinge	Low	Moderate	Low	High	High
Ease of Installation (cost)	Moderate	Easy	Moderate	Difficult	Very Easy
Can be easily adjusted after installation	No	No	No	No	Yes
Remarks	door requires hardwood edge			door requires hardwood edge	1. Specify degree of opening 2. No catch required

FIGURE 17-38
This chart can be used to evaluate the hinges commonly used in commercial and institutional cabinets. (Courtesy of Architectural Woodwork Institute, Architectural Caseworker General Detail and Specification Guide, Copyright 1984, AWI.)

used with this system enables cabinets to be produced much faster and at less cost than by using the traditional methods used with faceframe cabinets. It must be noted that all panels must be cut very accurately and all drilling and machining operations be carefully performed or doors and drawers will not align properly in the carcass.

Preliminary Machining

After the various parts of the carcass (top, sides, bottom) are accurately cut to size, the cut for the toeboard on the side panels is made. The back of the cabinet is set in grooves which are now cut in the side panels (Fig. 17-40). Edge banding is then per-

FIGURE 17-39
This multiple-spindle boring machine has one horizontal head with 21 spindles and two vertical heads with 15 spindles each. This permits it to drill a single line of 30 holes or parallel lines of holes, 15 in each line. (Courtesy of Altendorf America.)

FIGURE 17-40
Typical carcass layout using the 32-mm assembly system.

FIGURE 17-41
This edge bander automatically applies high-pressure laminates, veneers, melamines, solid wood, and PVC coil bands to the edges of stock. (Courtesy of Altendorf America.)

formed on panels where it is required. The edge bander applies PVC coil material as well as high-pressure laminate, veneer coil stock, melamines, and solid lumber bands up to $\frac{3}{4}$ in. (18 mm) thick. It has a hot melt glue system. It will straight or bevel end trim the banding on the top and bottom surfaces (Fig. 17-41).

Material Requirements

Particleboard and fiberboard are the most common materials used. A 45-lb density is recommended. They can be used for carcasses, doors, shelves, and frames. They accept plastic laminates and are easily edge banded. Some panel materials come precoated with melamine or an acrylic finish. This saves finishing or laminating the material. Hardboard can also be used but is limited to backs and drawer bottoms.

For kitchen cabinets $\frac{5}{8}$- or $\frac{3}{4}$-in.-(16- or 19-mm)-thick particleboard is recommended. The back can be 3-mm ($\frac{1}{8}$-in.) laminated hardboard or $\frac{3}{16}$- or $\frac{1}{4}$-in. (4- or 6-mm) hardboard. This construction requires a top rail for screwing the cabinet to the wall. If a $\frac{1}{2}$-in.-thick back panel is used, the top rail is not needed.

Drill Pattern Layout

After the panels have been cut and edge banded, they are ready for the hole drilling operation. These involve two factors: (1) holes used for dowels which assemble the cabinet, and (2) holes for hardware.

Two types of holes are used, dowel holes and line holes. *Dowel holes* are those used to join structural members such as a top or bottom to the bulkheads. *Line holes* are those used for installing hardware. They are generally 5 mm in diameter.

Dowel holes are 8 or 10 mm in diameter and spaced 32 or 64 mm on center as required to form the dowel joint. The distance from the end or edge of the panel depends on the thickness and location of each panel. A layout for a side panel is shown in Fig. 17-42. This layout has dowel holes for joining the top and bottom to the sides (A), line holes for securing fixed shelves (B), line holes for pins for adjustable shelves (C), and line holes for base plates of hinges for the doors (D).

Multigroove hardwood dowels are used. On long butting edges dowels should be 96 mm apart. On short pieces, such as a 100-mm top rail, at least two dowels should be used. The dowel hole should penetrate the side panel 9 mm and the end of the adjoining panel 25 mm. The dowel should be 4 to 6 mm shorter than the overall depth of the hole.

In Fig. 17-43 is shown a layout of a side panel for a unit with drawers. Metal side-mounted drawer slides are used. The metal track is fastened to the sides of the cabinet. A second track is fastened to the bottom of the drawer on each side. They run on nylon rollers (Fig. 17-44). The holes in the slide mounted on the cabinet are spaced 32 mm on center. Typical drawer construction and hardware is shown in Fig. 17-45. The layout in Fig. 17-43 shows the holes for the horizontal top stiles (A), the bottom panel (B), and the metal drawer tracks (C). A con-

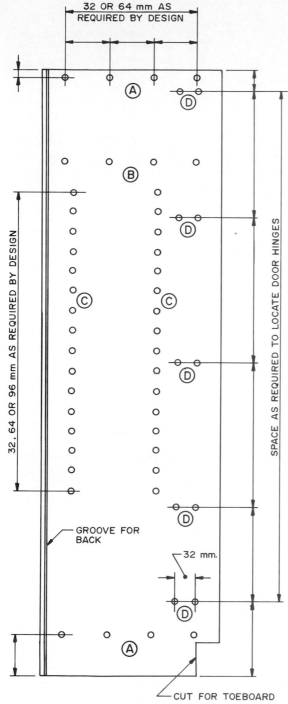

32 OR 64 mm AS
REQUIRED BY DESIGN

32, 64 OR 96 mm AS REQUIRED BY DESIGN

SPACE AS REQUIRED TO LOCATE DOOR HINGES

GROOVE FOR
BACK

32 mm.

CUT FOR TOEBOARD

(A) 8 mm DIAMETER DOWEL HOLES FOR WOOD DOWELS
FOR CARCASS CONSTRUCTION.

(B) 8 mm DIAMETER DOWEL HOLES FOR WOOD DOWELS
FOR FIXED SHELF.

(C) 5 mm DIAMETER LINE HOLES FOR PINS FOR
ADJUSTABLE SHELVES.

(D) 10 mm DIAMETER HOLES FOR INSERTION OF HINGE
BASEPLATES.

NOTE:

HOLES IN COLOR ARE DOWEL HOLES FOR CARCASS
ASSEMBLE.

HOLES IN BLACK ARE LINE HOLES FOR HARDWARE.

FIGURE 17-42
Layout for a bulkhead for a cabinet using the 32-mm
system. (Courtesy of Grass America, Inc.)

cealed hinge and base plate are shown in Fig. 17-46. Details for installing a hidden hinge are shown in Fig. 17-47. First mount the hinge on the door. Mount the base plate on the cabinet side. The base plate is mounted 32 to 37 mm from the edge of the door opening. Slide the hinge onto the base plate and tighten screw B to secure it to the hinge. Screw A adjusts the door horizontally, and C is the vertical adjustment.

The number of hinges to use depends on the size of the door. Recommendations are shown in Fig. 17-48. The holes drilled for hinge installation are 5 mm in diameter and spaced 32 mm on-center (Fig. 17-49).

Assembling the Cabinet

After all the holes are drilled, the cabinet is assembled using wood dowels and adhesive. The adhesive can be applied using a glue bottle or an automatic dowel-inserter machine. The case itself is assembled with a case clamp or hand clamps (Fig. 17-50, page 236). Unclamp as soon as the glue has reached the manufacturer's set time. Install hardware.

MECHANICALLY JOINED CASEWORK

Furniture and cabinets are increasingly being assembled using mechanical fasteners rather than the traditional joints such as dowels or mortise and tenon. A wide variety of fasteners are available. Some are designed for installation and assembly in the manufacturing plant. Others are designed so that the furniture can be shipped knocked down and assembled by the purchaser. Mechanical fasteners for the knock-down market are designed so that only the simplest tools are needed, such as a screwdriver or Allen wrench.

The joints commonly used for mechanically joined casework include the butt, miter, T and double-T, surface, cross, and end joints. These are explained in Chapter 10. These joints can be secured mechanically in two ways: (1) with rigid nonreleasable fasteners, or (2) with rigid releasable fasteners.

Rigid Nonreleasable Joints

Rigid nonreleasable joints include the traditional joints shown in Chapter 10, such as the mortise-and-tenon or dowel joints. Variations of these include the miter joint using a folding technique, a miter with a flow channel, and the use of H-nails. The folded miter is used in box construction where the box is

SUB-TOP

(B) 8 mm DIAMETER DOWEL HOLES FOR WOOD DOWELS FOR RAILS.

(B) 8 mm DIAMETER DOWEL HOLES FOR WOOD DOWELS FOR BOTTOM AND SUB-TOP.

(C) 5 mm DIAMETER LINE HOLES FOR INSTALLING METAL DRAWER SLIDES.

NOTE:
HOLES IN COLOR ARE DOWEL HOLES OR CARCASS ASSEMBLY.

HOLES IN BLACK ARE LINE HOLES FOR HARDWARE.

GROOVE FOR BACK PANEL

AS REQUIRED BY DRAWER DESIGN SIZE

AS DESIGNED

AS LOCATED ON METAL DRAWER SLIDE

BOTTOM

32, 64 OR 96 mm AS REQUIRED BY DESIGN

DRAWER FRONTS

TOEBOARD CUTOUT

FIGURE 17-43
Side panel with rail, drawer slide, and dowel holes for carcass assembly located. (Courtesy of Grass America, Inc.)

FRONT VIEW OF 6020 and 6040 DRAWER SLIDE

12.5 mm (½")

12.5 mm (½")

37 mm (1⁷⁄₁₆")

19 mm (¾") 16 mm (⅝")

Left Runner

Right Runner

FIGURE 17-44
Metal drawer slides used with the 32-mm system. (Courtesy of Grass America, Inc.)

FIGURE 17-45
These drawers slide easily on metal slides. (Courtesy of Grass America, Inc.)

FIGURE 17-46
Concealed hinge. The door can be adjusted by sliding the hinge on the baseplate. (Courtesy of Grass America, Inc.)

Door width up to 600 mm/2'

Door height
up to 2400 mm/8'
up to 2000 mm/7'
up to 1600 mm/5'
up to 900 mm/3'

5 Hinges
4 Hinges
3 Hinges
2 Hinges

RECOMMENDED USAGE:
Use the chart to determine number of hinges needed. A trial mounting is advisable due to the variability of quality of material and whether hinge cups are knocked-in or screwed on.

For stabilization, the distance between hinges should be as wide as possible.

For doors up to 24" wide, weighing
      up to 20 lbs. — 2 hinges
      20 - 40 lbs. — 3 hinges
      40 - 60 lbs. — 4 hinges

FIGURE 17-48
Recommendations for determining the number of concealed hinges to use on various door sizes. (Courtesy of Grass America, Inc.)

HINGE

BASEPLATE

MOUNTED ON CABINET

DOOR CAN BE ADJUSTED

FIGURE 17-47
Installing and adjusting a concealed hinge. (Courtesy of Grass America, Inc.)

FIGURE 17-49
Mounting dimensions for a concealed hinge. (Courtesy of Grass America, Inc.)

formed from a single sheet of stock coated with a polyvinyl chloride laminate (Fig. 17-51). The sides of the case are folded to form the box, with the laminate producing a finished corner. The case is then edge banded and end matched along the two long sides.

Another technique is to machine a special miter joint with a channel that receives a molten thermoplastic bonding agent (Fig. 17-52). The channel is filled with polyamide injected by a plastic injection molding machine at 300°F. The plastic penetrates the porous wood in the joint, sealing it and filling the gap between them. As the polyamide cools it shrinks, forcing the panels together to form a rigid nonreleasable joint.

5mm
32mm
32mm-37mm

FIGURE 17-50
This power-operated case clamp is used to assemble drawers and carcasses. (Courtesy of Altendorf America.)

THE MITER CUT

THE MITER CLOSED

FIGURE 17-51
This folded miter uses the PVC laminate to form the finished corner.

FIGURE 17-52
This special miter is joined by injecting polyamide in a machined channel.

THERMOPLASTIC
BONDING AGENT

FIGURE 17-53
H-nails can be used to join panels. (Courtesy of H'a'fele America, 203 Feld Ave., High Point, NC 27261.)

H-nails are used to form a drive-in joint that is rigid and nonreleasable (Fig. 17-53). The parts to be joined are stacked with the H-nails between them. They are pressed together, forcing the nails into the wood. There are no nails visible on the exterior of the panel. This type of fastener is stronger than conventional nails or screws. The panels do not require gluing.

Rigid, Releasable Joints

Mechanical fasteners for forming rigid, releasable joints enable a manufacturer to produce furniture and cabinet units that can be assembled without gluing in the factory or shipped in a knocked-down condition. This decreases shipping costs and damage to the units.

These fasteners are available in two types: (1) one-piece fastener, and (2) multipiece fasteners.

A one-piece fastener is shown in Fig. 17-54. The head section is countersunk so that it fits flush with the panel surface. Cover caps can be used to form a button over the head. The threads are designed so that the fastener can be used in wood or

FIGURE 17-54
A boring diagram for one-piece fasteners. (Courtesy of H'a'fele America, 203 Feld Ave., High Point, NC 27261.)

Boring diagram:

Pocket hole

Through hole for accommodation of the Confirmat shank

Pocket hole Ø	4 mm	5 mm	5.4 mm
Through hole Ø	5 mm	7 mm	7 mm

FIGURE 17-55
This multipiece fastener has an insert set into one panel and a screw runs through the joining panel. (Courtesy of H'a'fele America, 203 Feld Ave., High Point, NC 27261.)

FIGURE 17-56
This multipiece fastener is secured in the adjoining piece with a cross-nut. (Courtesy of H'a'fele America, 203 Feld Ave., High Point, NC 27261.)

FIGURE 17-57
This fastener uses a cam in the casing to lock the shelf to the bolt screwed in the side. (Courtesy of H'a'fele America, 203 Feld Ave., High Point, NC 27261.)

particleboard. They are used in low-stress areas such as lightweight partitions. They may be removed and reinstalled several times. However, if the application is known to require frequent disassembly, a multipiece fastener is recommended. A through hole is bored in the panel and a pocket hole is bored in the material to serve as the anchor. The sawlike screw threads cut internal threads in the pocket hole. The centering tip on the screw guides it through the pocket hole, assuring evenly cut threads in the wood or particleboard. Note that these are metric fasteners with pocket and through-hole diameters given in millimeters.

The following fasteners to be described are multipiece units. One of the simplest uses a decorative countersunk head machine screw which screws into an insert set in the mating part (Fig. 17-55). This fastener has the insert parallel to the axis of the screw. Another type uses a decorative cylinder head machine screw with a cross-nut bolt. Cross-nut bolts are usually steel but some are plastic (Fig. 17-56).

A widely used fastener for knock-down furniture uses an eccentric cam and a mating bolt (Fig. 17-57). Metal eccentric is enclosed in a plastic casing. The casing is set into a hole bored in the shelf or horizontal member. The bolt is available in many designs (Fig. 17-58). Some screw into inserts set into the inside of the bulkhead. Others run through the bulkhead. Various installations are shown in Fig. 17-59. The joint is fastened by inserting the head of the bolt into the casing, which has an eccentric cam. When the casing is rotated, the cam binds tightly against the head and the recessed body below it. The cam can be rotated with a Pozidriv or standard screwdriver or an Allen key (Fig. 17-60). These fasteners are metric and require metric drills to prepare the holes required for installation.

A mechanical shelf fastener is shown in Fig. 17-61. This connector permits rapid connection of shelves to the sides of the carcass. The mating surfaces of the parts are sloped to ensure that the shelf is held firmly. This connector has a high load-carrying capacity and is suitable for heavy wood shelves. It also provides lateral support, which sustains the sides of the carcass. The support is fastened to the bulkhead with special screws. The boss is set in a hole bored in the bottom of the shelf. Typical appli-

"minifix 15" mounting examples for single or double connections by:

FIGURE 17-58
Variations of the bolts used. (Courtesy of H'a'fele America, 203 Feld Ave., High Point, NC 27261.)

BA

BB

BC

Screwing the connecting bolts directly into a ∅ 5 mm hole

Screwing the connecting bolt with M 4 thread into a spreading dowel with M 4 internal thread

Screwing the connecting bolt with M 6 thread into dowels for pressing in or screwing in

BD

BE

Direct fitting of the connecting bolt with harpoon-type thread in a ∅ 5 mm hole

Connecting by inserting the end cap bolt from the outside

Screwing the connecting bolt into a sleeve with end screw in series of holes with ∅ 5 mm holes

BF

VH

Connecting by screwing connecting bolts into a threaded sleeve (or two threaded sockets)

Connecting by screwing in a double connecting bolt as a twin fitting with snap ring

FIGURE 17-59
Applications of the multipiece cam-operated fastener and the various bolt designs available. (Courtesy of H'a'fele America, 203 Feld Ave., High Point, NC 27261.)

BG

BH

The combined tightening element of the "minifix 15" casing is particularly easy to install: The marking notch must point precisely in the direction of the bolt when fitting the casing.

It can be screwed in either with a **Pozidriv blade, size 3** or with

a **flat blade, size 6 x 1.5** or with

an **Allan key, SW4**

FIGURE 17-60
The cam can be turned with any of these tools. (Courtesy of H'a'fele America, 203 Feld Ave., High Point, NC 27261.)

238

FIGURE 17-61
This shelf connector uses a boss set in a hole in the shelf. (Courtesy of H'a'fele America, 203 Feld Ave., High Point, NC 27261.)

cations are shown in Fig. 17-62. The support, boss, connecting screws, and boring diagram are shown in Fig. 17-63.

Another type of fastener used to join structural panels or shelves has a screw with a cone-shaped head that is installed in the bulkhead. The horizontal panel has a hole bored in the edge to receive an insert. The insert is fastened to the panel with a special screw. The cone head fits into a recess in the insert (Fig. 17-64).

There are mechanical fasteners designed to be used with the 32-millimeter joining system. This system is described in detail in this chapter. One fastener uses a connecting bolt that fits into the holes spaced 32 mm apart in the bulkhead. A housing with an eccentric cam fits into a hole bored in the bottom of the shelf. This system permits shelves to be easily moved when desired and accommodates hinges, catches, and other hardware (Fig. 17-65). Normally, the line of holes in the bulkhead is set in 37 mm from the edge and are 5 mm in diameter.

"rasant-tab" mounting examples

The support is screwed on with "Hospa" chip-board screws, countersunk head ⌀ 4 mm

The support is screwed on with VARIANTA special screws in series of holes with ⌀ 3 and 5 mm

⌀ 3 or 5 mm

⌀ 5 mm

Both supports are connected with VARIANTA threaded screws M 4 and sleeve in grid holes ⌀ 5 mm.

FIGURE 17-62
Installation details for the shelf connector. (Courtesy of H'a'fele America, 203 Feld Ave., High Point, NC 27261.)

FIGURE 17-63
The shelf connector parts and its boring diagram. (Courtesy of H'a'fele America, 203 Feld Ave., High Point, NC 27261.)

x = drilling depth

9,5

⌀ 20

x

Boring diagram

VA   VB   VD

FIGURE 17-64
This insert is used to join horizontal and vertical panels and shelves. (Courtesy of H'a'fele America, 203 Feld Ave., High Point, NC 27261.)

Another system designed for 32-millimeter construction uses brackets and bolts (Fig. 17-66). The brackets can be used to join surface and butt joints. The screws require 5-mm holes in particleboard. Typical applications are shown in Fig. 17-67.

Another application is the use of a multipiece fastener using a threaded sleeve that runs through a hole in the wood section (Fig. 17-68). This makes it possible to secure horizontal panels on both sides of the vertical bulkhead. This system is used in 32-millimeter construction.

Two other knock-down fittings are shown in Figs. 17-69 and 17-70. These secure the sides of the carcass to the top or bottom. The mating wedge-shaped fittings in Fig. 69 are fastened to the top and side. When the butt joint is put together, a metal cover is slid in grooves in the wedged parts, locking them together.

FIGURE 17-65
These shelf connectors are designed to be used with the 32-millimeter system. (Courtesy of H'a'fele America, 203 Feld Ave., High Point, NC 27261.)

FIGURE 17-67
Applications of the brackets being used in connection with the 32-millimeter system. (Courtesy of H'a'fele America, 203 Feld Ave., High Point, NC 27261.)

Application example

FIGURE 17-66
These brackets can be used in many ways to join panels. (Courtesy of H'a'fele America, 203 Feld Ave., High Point, NC 27261.)

FIGURE 17-68
This connector has a threaded sleeve that runs through a bulkhead permitting the joining of panels on both sides. (Courtesy of H'a'fele America, 203 Feld Ave., High Point, NC 27261.)

Top

Side

Cover for tightening

Side   Top

FIGURE 17-69
Knock-down fitting used to assemble the carcass. (Courtesy of H'a'fele America, 203 Feld Ave., High Point, NC 27261.)

FIGURE 17-70
Another knock-down carcass assembly fitting. (Courtesy of H'a'fele America, 203 Feld Ave., High Point, NC 27261.)

Answer each of the following questions. If you are not sure of an answer, review the chapter.

17-1. What is a modular cabinet?

17-2. What association develops standard kitchen cabinet sizes?

17-3. How can you be certain that kitchen cabinets meet national standards?

17-4. What are the flame spread classifications?

17-5. What classification should certified cabinets meet?

17-6. What is the difference between bound and unbound cabinets?

17-7. What is the basic module used when establishing cabinet widths?

17-8. What are the three major activities around which a kitchen is planned?

17-9. What are the basic kitchen arrangements?

17-10. What preparatory things are done before you begin to install cabinets?

17-11. When installing base cabinets, which part is installed first?

17-12. Where do you start to install wall cabinets?

17-13. How can the face frame be installed on the cabinet?

17-14. What is a split stile?

17-15. What is the 32-millimeter system?

17-16. What type of connector is used in the 32-millimeter system?

17-17. Why are rigid releasable joints finding increasing use in cabinet construction?

Following are technical terms that you should be able to use as part of your working vocabulary. Write a brief description of the meaning of each term.

Integrated operation
Assembly operation
ANSI
NKCA-certified cabinets
Flame spread

Bound cabinet
Unbound cabinet
Work triangle
Exposed surfaces
Semiexposed surfaces
Concealed surfaces
Rigid back
Split stile
32-millimeter construction
Rigid releasable joints

18

GLUING AND CLAMPING

The permanent fastening of wood parts is often accomplished with some type of bonding agent, such as a glue, adhesive, or cement. *Glues* are made from natural materials, whereas *adhesives* are made from synthetic materials. *Cements* are rubber-based bonding agents.

When these are used properly, a strong and almost invisible bond is produced. The selection of the correct bonding agent, properly applied and cured, is vital to furniture and cabinet construction. There are many kinds of glues, adhesives, and cements. It is important to select the right one for each job (Fig. 18-1).

JOINT PREPARATION

Before even considering applying an adhesive to a joint, it must be checked to make certain that it is properly made. The joint must fit closely because most adhesives do not fill in large gaps between mating surfaces. It must not fit too tight because space must be left for the adhesive. If the joint is too tight, the adhesive is stripped away or squeezed out as it is clamped. Mating edges, as found in long boards, must be straight to get the maximum strength and have the smallest visible glue joint.

FIGURE 18-1
There are many types of bonding agents to choose from. (Courtesy of The Woodworkers' Store.)

Before starting to glue, make certain that everything needed is at the workstation. This includes adhesives, clamps, a mallet, and scrap stock to protect the work from the clamps.

Make certain that the wood has the proper moisture content. Wood that is too dry or has too high a moisture content will not bond properly. Generally, a 7 to 10% moisture content is satisfactory.

BONDING ACTION

Some agents bond by *mechanical adhesion*. The bonding agent is spread on a wood surface and that

243

TABLE 18-1
Characteristics of Bonding Agents

Type	Form	Mixing procedure	Color of glue line	Chief application
Glues				
Casein	Powder	Mix with water	Cream	Laminated timbers, doors, assembly edge gluing
Liquid hide	Liquid	None	Off-white-brown	Assembly, edge gluing and laminating
Adhesives				
Thermoplastics				
Aliphatic resin (yellow glue)	Liquid	None	Cream	Assembly, edge and face gluing, laminating
Hot melts	Solid	Melt with applicator	Varies	Quick assembly
Polyvinyl (white glue)	Liquid	None	Yellowish or whitish transparent	Assembly gluing, laminating, edge gluing
Thermosets				
Epoxy	Liquid	Mix with liquid catalyst	Varies	Quick assembly
Resorcinol resin	Liquid	Mix with powdered catalyst	Dark red	Laminated timbers, sandwich panels, general bonding, boats, skis
Urea-formaldehyde	Powder	Mix with water	Tan	Lumber and hardwood plywood, assembly gluing
Contact Cement	Liquid	None	Yellow-tan, red	Plastic and similar laminating

surface is brought into contact with another surface. As pressure is applied, the bonding agent enters into pores of the wood and hardens.

Materials are also bonded by *specific adhesion*. Materials without pores, such as glass and plastic, are also bonded by specific adhesion. This bonding is caused by the attraction of unlike electrical charges. Every material has an electrical charge. The positive (+) and negative (−) charges in the bonding agent are attracted by the electrical charges on the surface of the wood or other material. They are thus molecularly attracted to each other, providing the strongest possible holding force between the adjoining surfaces. Specific adhesion occurs when edge or face grain is bonded. Porous end grain cannot be successfully joined by either mechanical or specific adhesion. End grain joints, such as a miter, must be reinforced with splines, which provide face grain for bonding. In most cases apply the bonding agent to only one of the surfaces to be joined. This provides more cohesive force than when the agent is applied to both surfaces. On cements, follow the manufacturer's directions.

TYPES OF ADHESIVES

Adhesives are made from synthetic materials. They are the most commonly used bonding agents. They are divided into two types, thermosets and thermoplastics. A summary of the characteristics of woodworking bonding agents is presented in Table 18-1.

Thermosets

Thermosets produce a chemical reaction when they are mixed and therefore are water and heat resistant. Following are the four major types of thermosets.

1. *Epoxy* is used to bond almost any kind of material. It is not used in furniture and cabinet construction because it is expensive. It produces a very strong joint and is often used when regluing wood joints on furniture being restored. Epoxy is packaged in two tubes one containing a resin and one a hardener. To use, these are mixed in equal amounts. A thin coat is applied to both surfaces. The surfaces are clamped to-

Service durability	Application temperature	Clamp time	Brand names
Water resistant	32°F	2 hours	
Interior use	70°F	2 hours	Franklin Liquid Hide Glue
Interior use	45°F	1 hour	Titebond, Elmer's Carpenter's Wood Glue
Interior use	Determined by electronic welder	None	Thermogrip, Jet-Melt
Interior use	60°F	1 hour	Elmer's Glue-All
Interior use	60°F	2 hours	Elmer's Epoxy, Scotch-Weld Epoxy
Waterproof	70°F	16 hours	Weldwood Resorcinal Waterproof Glue, Elmer's Waterproof Glue
Water resistant	70°F	16 hours at 70°F	Plastic Resin, Elmer's Plastic Resin
Water resistant	70°F	No clamp time	Elmer's Contact Cement, Franklin Contact Cement

gether for at least 2 hours. Epoxy reaches full strength in 12 to 24 hours. Excess material is removed with nail polish remover or denatured alcohol while the epoxy is still tacky (Fig. 18-2).

2. *Phenol-formaldehyde* is used in the production of exterior plywood. It is not used for furniture and cabinet construction.

3. *Resorcinol-formaldehydes* are used where a waterproof glue line is needed, such as when building a boat or surfboard. They are sold in two parts: a resin and a catalyst. After thorough mixing they are ready for use, which must be within 8 hours after mixing. The material is applied to both surfaces in a thin coat. Since it stains wood a dark brown, hiding the glue line is difficult. It is slow to gain strength and must be kept clamped for about 16 hours.

4. *Urea-formaldehyde* is sold in powder form and is mixed with water to form a pastelike mixture. It is moisture resistant but not waterproof. Since it has poor gap-filling qualities,

FIGURE 18-2
An epoxy is packaged in two containers, the resin and a hardener.

joints must be very accurately made. The recommended clamp time is 6 hours. It is widely used with radio-frequency glue-drying equipment and will cure in a few seconds.

Thermoplastics

Thermoplastics are the most widely used bonding agent for wood products. Although most are resistant to moisture, they should not be used on products that will be exposed to moist conditions. Following are the four major types.

1. *Hot melts* are sold in solid form. There are different types for bonding plastics, particleboard, softwoods, and hardwoods. Hot melts are applied by placing the solid material in an electric applicator (Fig. 18-3). This melts the adhesive stick and applies it to the surface through a nozzle. The surface to be bonded must be free of dust and oily films. The viscosity of the adhesive must be thin enough to wet thoroughly the surface to be bonded. The viscosity can be lowered by raising the temperature of the adhesive. Other factors affecting viscosity are the amount of adhesive used, the temperature and type of material to be bonded, and the air temperature (Fig. 18-4).

FIGURE 18-3
Hot melt adhesive applicator and samples of the adhesive, which is in stick form. (Courtesy of Adhesives, Coatings and Sealers Division/3M.)

FIGURE 18-4
The hot melt applicator melts the adhesive stick and applies it to the surface through a nozzle. (Courtesy of Adhesives, Coatings and Sealers Division/3M.)

The shorter the open time (time lapsed between applying adhesive and closing the joint), the better the bond. The firmer the pressure when the bond is closed, the stronger the bond. Firm hand pressure is usually adequate. Apply pressure from a few seconds with thin films to a few minutes with thicker films and larger areas.

Hot melts produce a wide glue line that may be objectionable if on a visible part. They are fast but not very strong. Their best use is in applying overlays to furniture exteriors (Fig. 18-5).

FIGURE 18-5
The decorative overlays on these doors can be bonded with hot melts. (Courtesy of Thomasville Furniture Industries, Inc.)

2. *Alpha-Cyanoacrylate* is used with metals, plastics, and other dense materials. It is not suited for use with porous materials such as wood. It is often called "superglue."

It dries very rapidly but does not reach full strength for 24 hours. Avoid getting it on your hands. If you do, it can be softened with fingernail polish or acetone.

3. *Polyvinyl adhesives* are often called white glues. They are the most widely used of the thermoplastic types. They are excellent for furniture and cabinet work. Although they are moisture resistant, they are not suitable for exterior use Polyvinyls are sold premixed ready to use. Since the mix is creamy, it is easy to apply. Set-up time is 30 minutes, but stock should be allowed to cure for 24 hours before working it.

Since polyvinyl adhesives cure by the loss of moisture, the wood to be bonded must have a moisture content of 6 to 12% to get the maximum strength. Polyvinyl adhesives soften under heat and solvents such as lacquer.

4. *Aliphatic resins* are a form of polyvinyl resin and are yellow in color. They are stronger and more heat resistant than other polyvinyls and are not affected by lacquer finishes. These features make them superior to the white polyvinyl adhesives, and the choice of those making good-quality furniture and cabinets.

GLUES

Glues are made from vegetable and animal products, such as hides and bones. Although still an effective material, they have been largely replaced by adhesives and cements. The most commonly used glues are animal, casein, blood albumin, vegetable, and fish glues.

1. *Casein glue* is made from dried milk curds. It is sold in powdered form and is prepared by mixing with water until it forms a thick, creamy mixture. It must stand 15 minutes after mixing before it is applied to wood, to allow a chemical reaction to occur in the casein.

    Casein glue is water resistant and can be used for exterior work that will not be directly subjected to the elements. It can be applied in cold temperatures and will harden as long as the temperature is above freezing. It takes longer to set up in colder temperatures.

2. *Animal glue* is available as a hot glue or a ready-mixed liquid. *Hot animal glue* is sold as a dry powder or as large flakes. It is mixed with water in an electric glue pot. Here it is heated until it dissolves, forming a liquid. It is applied to the wood surfaces while hot. The joint must be clamped before it begins to chill, or a weak joint will result. This type of glue is not widely used anymore.

    Liquid hide glue is a ready-mixed form of animal glue. It is applied directly from the container to the wood. It is especially good for filling gaps in joints as well as small cracks and chips. When it dries it develops a dark glue line. Therefore, it is especially useful with dark woods such as walnut and mahogany. It is not waterproof and should be used for interior purposes. It sets best if temperatures are above 70°F. If used below this temperature, the glue must be kept warm. Normally, clamps can be removed in 2 hours.

3. Blood albumin, vegetable, and fish glues are not used in the assembly of furniture and cabinets. Blood albumin and vegetable glues are used in some types of interior plywood. Fish glues are used on packing tapes and for sealing cartons.

CEMENTS

Cements are made from synthetic rubber, such as neoprene, nitrile, or polysulfide, suspended in a liquid. Some are flammable and others are nonflammable.

1. *Contact cement* is used to adhere plastic laminates, veneers, and other surface decorations. It is applied to both surfaces and allowed to dry. When these surfaces are brought together, they bond instantly. It is not possible to slide or shift the position of a part. No clamping is necessary. Contact cement can be cleaned off surfaces with lacquer thinner. Since contact cement is flammable, the area in which it is being used should be well ventilated.

2. *Mastic* is a thick form of contact cement that is sold in tubes and is applied with a caulking gun. It is used in building construction to join sheathing to studs and floor joists and paneling to walls.

HAND CLAMPING TOOLS

There are a number of hand-operated clamping tools available (Fig. 18-6). These are too slow and inaccurate for use in mass-production situations, where power-operated clamping devices of great speed and accuracy are used.

The *hand screw* is used to provide clamping pressure over a broad surface with two parallel jaws. To adjust it rapidly, it can be held in two hands and spun like a propeller (Fig. 18-7). Final adjustments are made by turning each handle to apply pressure. Be certain the jaws are kept parallel as pressure is applied (Fig. 18-8).

Clamp sizes are specified by number. The larger the number, the longer the jaws and the wider they will open. The most commonly used sizes are listed in Table 18-2.

C-clamps, sometimes called carriage clamps, have a strong C-shaped frame and a threaded shaft that applies pressure. Since the clamping parts are metal, scrap stock is placed between them and the wood (Fig. 18-9).

They are specified by the size of the opening and the depth of the C-shaped frame, called the throat size. There are many different styles available with a wide range of opening and throat sizes. The larger sizes most commonly used in woodworking shops are listed in Table 18-3.

Press frames are used to apply pressure to large surfaces. An example is the need to apply pressure to hold the veneer on a tabletop (Fig. 18-10).

FIGURE 18-6
Basic hand clamping tools used in furniture and cabinet construction. (Courtesy of Adjustable Clamp Co.)

CLAMP FIXTURES
to be mounted on black pipe

steel bar clamps
SLIDING HEAD TYPE
screw is in the "sliding" head

steel bar clamps
FIXED HEAD TYPE
screw is in the "fixed" head

steel bar clamps
HINGED TYPE

BAND CLAMPS

HANDSCREWS

CLAMP FIXTURES
to be mounted on wood bars

"C" clamps
VERY LIGHT SERVICE

"C" clamps
INDUSTRIAL SERVICE

"C" clamps
INDUSTRIAL SERVICE

PRESS SCREWS

SPRING CLAMPS

EDGE-CLAMP FIXTURES

MITER CLAMPS

PILING CLAMPS

FIGURE 18-7
Hand screws are adjusted by turning the handles. (Courtesy of Adjustable Clamp Co.)

INCORRECT
JAWS INCLINED

CORRECT
JAWS PARALLEL

FIGURE 18-8
When face clamping keep the jaws parallel. (Courtesy of Adjustable Clamp Co.)

C- CLAMP

May Be Applied With Right Angle Screw "Off Center"

May Be Applied With Right Angle Screw "Centered"

May Be Applied To Clamp Around "Returns"

3- WAY CLAMP

FIGURE 18-9
Typical carriage clamps. (Courtesy of Adjustable Clap Co.)

TABLE 18-2
Handscrew Clamp Sizes

No.	Jaw length (in.)	Jaw opening (in.)
5/0	4	2
4/0	5	$2\frac{1}{2}$
3/0	6	3
2/0	7	$3\frac{1}{2}$
0	8	$4\frac{1}{2}$
1	10	6
2	12	$8\frac{1}{2}$
3	14	10
4	16	12
5	18	14

TABLE 18-3
C-Clamp Sizes

Opening (in.)	Depth (in.)
2	$1\frac{3}{4}$
3	$2\frac{1}{4}$
4	$2\frac{1}{2}$ and $4\frac{1}{2}$
6	$3\frac{1}{8}$ and $6\frac{1}{2}$
8	$3\frac{3}{4}$ and $8\frac{1}{2}$
10	4
12	$4\frac{1}{4}$

FIGURE 18-10
Press frames are used to apply pressure over a large area. (Courtesy of Adjustable Clamp Co.)

FIGURE 18-11
Types of bar clamps. (Courtesy of Adjustable Clamp Co.)

They are suspended over a sturdy wood base on which is placed the material to be clamped. This is covered with a sheet of plywood or caul board and pressure is applied to the top of the plywood.

Bar clamps have a long metal bar with an adjustable foot on one end and a foot moved with a screw on the other (Fig. 18-11). They are used to clamp stock for edge-to-edge assembly as well as to clamp cabinet and furniture carcasses together. A variety of sizes is available. The short clamps are available with opening sizes of 6, 8, 12, 18, 24, and 30 in. The long clamps have opening sizes of 2, 3, 4, 5, 6, 7, and 8 ft. One type has a 5 in. throat opening. It is available in opening sizes of 6, 8, 12, 18, 24, 30, and 36 in. A common style of bar clamp is a *pipe clamp;* $\frac{1}{2}$- and $\frac{3}{4}$-in. black pipe is used to make up the clamps. Since the clamp mechanism is easily removed, different lengths of clamps can be made. Stock as narrow as 6 in. or as wide as 120 in. can be clamped with this style. Another type of bar clamp is a *piling clamp*. It has two sets of jaws facing in opposite directions. Each layer of wood is clamped from above as well as from below (Fig. 18-12). In this way each board is clamped twice—once below and once on top. This helps keep the stock from buckling during the clamping operation.

CLAMP FIXTURE MOUNTED ON PIPE

"Jorgensen"

BAR CLAMP

PILING CLAMP

Mounted clamp hangs free, out of the way, ready for use.

With work in place, the clamp swings into position.

The sliding-head zips against work. Head locks automatically without prior adjustment.

Final screw-pressure is applied by a turn of the screw.

When work is completed, pressure is released and clamp swings out of the way.

FIGURE 18-12
The piling clamp is used in production shops. (Courtesy of Adjustable Clamp Co.)

Spring clamps use a torsion spring to keep the plastic-covered jaws together. They are available with openings of 1, 2, 3, and 4 in. (Fig. 18-13).

Web clamps are made with a nylon band running through a metal clamping device. They are used to hold irregularly shaped objects (Fig. 18-14).

A *corner clamp* and a *miter frame clamp* are used to hold mitered corners as they are glued with splines or nailed together (Fig. 18-15). The corner clamp holds one corner at a time, while the miter frame clamp holds all four corners (Fig. 18-16). The miter frame clamp can be enlarged to hold any size frame by adding extension screws to each side. The miter vise will hold stock up to 4 in. wide.

FIGURE 18-13
Spring clamp. (Courtesy of Adjustable Clamp Co.)

FIGURE 18-14
Web clamps are used to hold irregular objects. (Courtesy of Adjustable Clamp Co.)

FIGURE 18-15
Corner clamp. (Courtesy of Adjustable Clamp Co.)

FIGURE 18-16
Miter frame clamp.

PRODUCTION ASSEMBLING DEVICES

A key to successful mass production of furniture and cabinets is rapid and accurate assembly. The following power actuated clamps are designed for this purpose. These are only a few of the many available but illustrate the range of machines in use.

FIGURE 18-17
This two-way clamping machine is shown holding a faceframe. (Courtesy of J. M. Lancaster, Inc.)

In Fig. 18-17 is shown a two-way frame clamping machine. It uses air cylinders to apply pressure simultaneously from the sides and ends. Hand cranks are used to move the long sides against the work. Then the pressure is applied by the air cylinders. Adjustments can be made to $\frac{1}{32}$ in. It is used to assemble such things as faceframes, mirrors, and paneled case ends and doors.

A drawer assembly clamp is used to hold cabinet drawers as they are glued and stapled together (Fig. 18-18). Glue is applied to the parts with a glue spreading machine before they are brought together on the assembly machine. An operator can assemble 80 to 100 drawers an hour. An attachment is available that is designed specifically to assemble drawers using a French dovetail to join the sides to the front.

The high-frequency assembly machine shown in Fig. 18-19 uses a 10-kW-output general-purpose

high-frequency generator to produce the radio waves needed to cure the glue in seconds. The electrodes are placed over the glue line about $\frac{1}{4}$ in. above their surface. The curing cycle must be varied to suit the conditions of the job. It is useful for all types of framework and cabinet doors as well as headboards and lumber rimming on table tops.

Another power clamp is designed for the rapid assembly of dining room chairs (Fig. 18-20). The

FIGURE 18-19
This high-frequency assembly machine cures the bonding agent in a few seconds. (Courtesy of J. M. Lancaster, Inc.)

FIGURE 18-20
This power clamp is designed for the assembly of chairs. (Courtesy of J. M. Lancaster, Inc.)

FIGURE 18-18
Drawer assembly clamp. Notice the hydraulic cylinder used to apply the pressure. (Courtesy of J. M. Lancaster, Inc.)

setup and pressure jaw behind the chair is positioned by screws. Side pressure jaws apply pressure on the front legs. The pressure is applied by the cylinders. This advance can be finely adjusted to produce the exact pressure needed to close the joint.

A case clamp is designed to assemble all types of case goods (Fig. 18-21). It is designed to assemble cases up to 36 in. high where two-way pressure is needed. The main jaw is set rapidly with fast-lead screws on each side of the base. The overhead units provide downward pressure and are also quickly set with hand screws. Pressure jaws are then inched forward using air-operated cylinders.

A very large machine that will clamp sofa, chairs, cabinets, and tables is shown in Fig. 18-22. The needed machine opening is quickly set. Various clamping units can be rearranged to apply pressure as needed, such as on stretchers between legs.

A clamp carrier used in furniture and cabinet production is shown in Fig. 18-23. It is used to edge glue and laminate wood parts ranging from very small furniture parts to beams 8 in. $\times$ 24 in. $\times$ 16 ft. The stock with glue applied is laid on each row of clamps. After the clamps are tightened, the panels are rotated down and away from the operator. They cure naturally as they pass under the machine. After one revolution the glued panels are removed and new stock is placed in the clamps.

A glue spreader is shown in Fig. 18-24. The stock moves from the right side to the left. It passes over a roller in the center that applies glue to the bottom side of the stock. The top rack is a multiwheel conveyor used to handle the stock after glue has been applied.

FIGURE 18-23
This clamp carrier will edge glue stock. (Courtesy of J. M. Lancaster, Inc.)

FIGURE 18-21
This hydraulic clamp is designed to assemble all types of casegoods. (Courtesy of J. M. Lancaster, Inc.)

FIGURE 18-22
This large clamping machine will assemble large pieces of furniture as sofas and tables. This picture shows it holding a sofa frame. (Courtesy of J. M. Lancaster, Inc.)

FIGURE 18-24
This power glue spreader applies glue to the bottom face of stock. (Courtesy of James L. Taylor Manufacturing Co.)

FIGURE 18-25
Two types of glue spreaders. (Courtesy of J. M. Lancaster, Inc.)

Two other glue spreaders are shown in Fig. 18-25. One is an edge-bond glue applicator and the other is used for applying glue to dovetail joints.

GLUING CONDITIONS

The surfaces to be joined must be clean, smooth, and free of defects. The joints should fit properly since most bonding agents cannot fill a gap in a poorly made joint. A joint could also be too tight, resulting in a starved glue joint.

The glue film should wet both surfaces to be joined. It must be a thin, uniform layer free of dust. Dense woods such as maple require a thicker glue mixture. In more porous, lighter woods a thinner mixture is better because it absorbs some of the moisture in the glue, increasing its thickness.

Be aware of the *pot life* of the glue being used. The pot life is the length of time glue retains all its properties. It is a good practice not to mix any more than you think you are going to use. Select glues that have an open assembly time long enough to permit you to assemble the unit. Complex units take more assembly time and require bonding agents with a longer open assembly time. *Open assembly time* is the period from when the glue is first applied until the boards are brought together. Fast-setting glues enable you to free your clamps rapidly for additional work.

Consider the moisture content of the wood. Since a high moisture content weakens glue joints, consider using kiln-dried wood for all projects.

The clamping pressure should be enough to close the joint and hold it until the bonding agent has set. As a general rule, 100 to 125 lb of pressure should be used. Thinner glues, such as polyvinyl resins, require light clamp pressures. Thick glues, such as plastic resin, require higher clamp pressures. Clamping times vary with the bonding agent. Use the times recommended by the manufacturer.

CLAMPING PROCEDURES

A joint attains its maximum strength when it is properly clamped and kept clamped during the entire recommended set time. The clamps must be placed to hold the joints together and keep the furniture or cabinet unit square. Following are some clamping recommendations.

Edge-to-Edge Clamping

1. Gather the tools needed for the job. Select bar clamps long enough to span the board to be assembled. Get blocks of scrap wood to use to protect the edges where the clamps will rest. A few hand screws or C-clamps will be needed to clamp the stock to the bar clamp to prevent buckling.

2. Place several bar clamps on a table and place the boards on top. Space the clamps not over 16 in. apart. Check to make certain that the boards are placed in the direction and order they were in when the edge joint was made. No board should be wider than 4 in., and the end grain should be reversed on each piece. They should have been marked on the face with chalk as shown in Fig. 18-26.

3. Assemble the boards *without adhesive*. This ensures that the joint will close properly before the adhesive is applied.

4. Loosen the clamps and separate the boards.

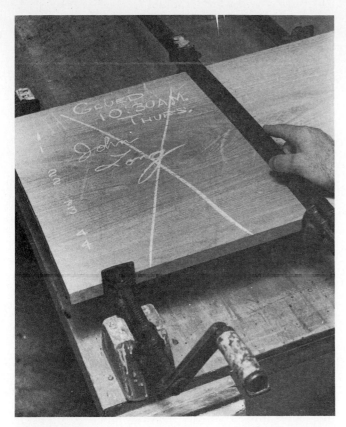

FIGURE 18-26
After clamping stock mark the date and time it was clamped.

FIGURE 18-27
This faceframe assembly requires the use of long bar clamps. (Courtesy of Adjustable Clamp Co.)

Apply the adhesive to one edge and in the dowel holes. Slide the dowels in the dowel holes. Place the boards on the lower bar clamps, put scrap blocks in place, and lightly tighten to close the joint.

5. Put bar clamps on the top of the boards in between those on the bottom. Put scrap blocks under each jaw and start to tighten the clamps from one end. As the clamps are tightened, work from one end to the other.

6. It is important that the boards stay flat on the bar clamps. If they buckle, use hand screws or C-clamps to clamp the boards to the bar clamp.

7. Store in a flat condition to avoid twisting the assembled unit. Leave the clamps on for the full recommended clamp time for the adhesive used. An assembly for a faceframe is in Fig. 18-27. Notice the use of bar clamps in both directions.

Case Assembly

1. Gather the tools needed for the job. This will normally include bar clamps, hand screws, C- clamps, scrap blocks, a framing square, and a measuring tape.

2. Make a trial assembly without the adhesive. The exact procedure will vary depending on the situation, but generally the corner joints will be assembled and bar clamps used to close the joints. Place the bar clamps 6 to 9 in. apart. Tighten each gradually rotating from one clamp to the other. If each is fully tightened before the others, the case may become warped. Check the squareness of the case by measuring the diagonals of each opening. If all joints close and the case is square, remove the clamps.

3. Apply the adhesive to the joints and reassemble the joints. Replace the bar joists and again tighten gradually in rotation until the joints are closed (Fig. 18-28).

FIGURE 18-28
When clamping a case, gradually tighten the clamps in rotation until the joints are closed.

FIGURE 18-29
Check the case for squareness.

FIGURE 18-30
Measure the diagonals to see if the case is square.

FIGURE 18-31
A bar clamp can be used to pull a case square.

4. Check the unit for squareness with a framing square (Fig. 18-29). Another check that can be used is to measure the diagonals. They should be exactly the same (Fig. 18-30). If the unit is out of square, place a bar clamp along the longest diagonal and tighten until the cabinet is square (Fig. 18-31).

ELECTRONIC GLUE CURING

Electronic glue curing is a way to speed up the initial set time of the adhesive. The joint is clamped in the normal manner. The controls on the electronic glue welder are set for the thickness of the wood and the type of adhesive. The electrodes connected to the welder are placed over the joint and radio energy is passed into it. The adhesive sets in just a few seconds.

The glue welders contain a generator that produces *high-frequency radio* energy (Fig. 18-32). The electrode is connected to it by a heavy cable. The welder works by generating a short-length high-frequency radio signal similar to that used by shortwave radios. This energy excites the adhesive molecules and heats the bonding agent to its polymerizing temperature, which is about 200°F (93°C). This cures the glue line in a few seconds. When this happens the clamps can be removed. The cabinet should be carefully set aside and allowed to cure for the recommended time specified by the adhesive manufacturer.

To operate the welder, it will have to be set for the adhesive used and the thickness of the stock. After the stock is clamped, place the electrodes across the glue line and pull the trigger. Keep it in

FIGURE 18-32
Electronic glue welder. (Courtesy of Workrite Products Company.)

place for the required time, usually 3 to 5 seconds. You will notice that the adhesive boils. Move the electrodes 3 in. down the glue line and pull the trigger again. Continue until the entire joint is cured.

A variety of electrodes are available. For edge joints straight electrodes are used (Fig. 18-33). Inverted electrodes are used on inside corners (Fig. 18-34). Outside electrodes are used on outside corners (Fig. 18-35). Roller electrodes are used on banding, moldings, and shelf edging. The most commonly used adhesive is urea-formaldehyde. Polyvinyls can be used but do not develop maximum strength.

There are several safety factors to consider. Do not pull the trigger on the electrode unless it is against the stock. Do not hold the stock being bonded in your hand. An electric shock could result. Do not touch the metal clamps while the welder is operating.

FIGURE 18-34
Inverted electrodes are used to cure inside joints.

FIGURE 18-33
Straight electrodes are used to cure edge joints.

FIGURE 18-35
Outside electrodes are used on outside corners.

STUDY QUESTIONS

Answer each of the following questions. If you are not sure of an answer, review the chapter.

18-1. How do glues and adhesives differ?

18-2. What is the difference between mechanical adhesion and specific adhesion?

18-3. What adhesives are water resistant?

18-4. Which adhesive is sold in powder form?

18-5. What are the major types of adhesives?

18-6. What type of adhesive is sold in solid stick form?

18-7. What is the correct technical name for "superglue"?

18-8. Which of the thermoplastic adhesives is most widely used for furniture and cabinet construction?

18-9. What are the major types of glues?

18-10. What glue is applied while hot?

18-11. What are good uses for contact cement?

18-12. List the various types of manually operated clamps that hold wood parts together during the curing processes.

18-13. What is the main use for a case clamp?

18-14. What conditions must exist to produce a good-quality glue joint?

IMPORTANT TECHNICAL TERMS

Following are technical terms that you should be able to use as part of your working vocabulary. Write a brief description of the meaning of each term.

Glues
Adhesives
Cements
Mechanical adhesion
Specific adhesion

Thermosets
Thermoplastics
Press frame
Bar clamp
Web clamp
Power-activated clamps
Pot life
Open assembly time
Electronic glue curing

19

BENDING
AND LAMINATING

As you examine the wood products on the market, you will notice that they make extensive use of curved parts. Wood is a good material for this purpose because it is easy to work and has the properties necessary for forming (Fig. 19-1). The common ways to produce curved parts is by cutting, softening the wood and bending it around a form, and gluing thin layers, producing a laminate that is bent around a form.

PRINCIPLES OF WOOD BENDING

When a wood member is bent to a desired curvature, it retains its cross-sectional shape. However, in the bent state the lengths of the faces are no longer equal as they were before bending occurred. This is because the fibers on the concave surface are in compression and therefore shortened, and in the convex surface they are stretched because they are in tension (Fig. 19-2).

Wood in its natural state has limited elastic properties. When it is bent it will return to its original condition if it is not bent beyond its limiting stress. When the limiting stress is exceeded, permanent deformation occurs. If the strain is great enough to cause the piece to break, it will fracture

FIGURE 19-1
This Windsor chair utilizes bent wood parts. (Courtesy of Cornucopia, Inc., Harvard, Mass.)

on the convex surface before the concave surface has been stressed to its fracture limit (Fig. 19-3).

Some species of wood become semiplastic when subjected to heat and moisture (as steam). This greatly increases their compressibility and they can be subject to considerable strain without fracturing.

259

FIGURE 19-2
Fibers in wood members under load are in compression and tension.

FIGURE 19-3
Tension causes fibers to break. Compression causes them to buckle.

This new semiplastic wood tends to retain its new bent shape if it is held in the bent position and dried. It becomes set in the curved shape produced by the bending.

Some woods are easier than others to bend. Most temperate-zone hardwoods react well to bending. Woods from tropical areas and most softwoods are not suitable for bending in solid form. While some are better than others, wood is not a perfectly uniform material, so all species will produce some broken parts.

CUTTING CURVED PARTS

Curved parts can be quickly cut using a bandsaw (Fig. 19-4). The part is strongest if the grain runs the long way of the part. This is satisfactory for parts with slight curvature. If the radius of the curve is small, the part will break rather easily (Fig. 19-5). The curved surface can be covered with a veneer to produce a piece with a high-quality appearance, while the curved parts can be of less expensive wood.

FIGURE 19-4
Pieces with large radius curves can be cut from solid stock.

FIGURE 19-5
Curved pieces with a large radius can be cut from solid stock.

Cross Kerfing

Large-radius curves can be made by cutting kerfs in the back of the area to be formed (Fig. 19-6). The cuts are made through to within $\frac{1}{16}$ in. of the front surface. Use as straight a grain piece as is available. To make such a curve, mark one end of the curve on the stock. Using a radial arm or table saw, make a saw cut to within $\frac{1}{16}$ in. of the face on this mark. Measure the radius of the curve to be formed on the stock. Hold one end of the stock to the table and raise the other until the kerf closes. Measure the distance it rises above the table at the mark locating the radius (Fig. 19-7). Lay out this distance on the inside of the stock in the area to be curved. This distance will vary depending on the number of degrees in the curve. Cut each kerf. Place adhesive in each kerf, bend it around a form, and clamp until dry. A strip of veneer is often bonded to the inside of the curve to help it retain its shape.

1. CUT A KERF AT ONE END OF THE CURVE, LAYOUT THE RADIUS OF THE CURVE.

2. LIFT THE WOOD UNTIL THE KERF CLOSES. MEASURE THE DISTANCE "A" AT THE OTHER END OF THE CURVE.

3. LAYOUT AND CUT EACH KERF. THE NUMBER OF KERFS DEPENDS ON THE NUMBER OF DEGREES IN CURVE.

FIGURE 19-6
Cross kerfing is one way to bend stock when large radius curves are acceptable.

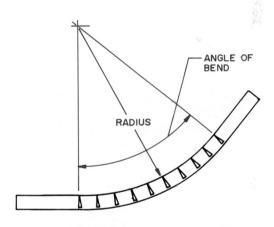

4. MAKE THE BEND. PUT GLUE IN KERFS BEFORE BENDING AND CLAMPING.

FIGURE 19-7
Steps to lay out and cut cross kerfing.

Parallel Kerfing

When a part requires a rather short bend in one end of a flat piece, such as skis, parallel kerfing can be used. A series of cuts are made in the end to be bent parallel with the surface of the stock (Fig. 19-8). This produces a series of thin layers of wood which are flexible. A thickness of $\frac{1}{28}$ in. is commonly used. The kerfs are filled with layers of veneer coated with adhesive. The piece is clamped in a mold until the adhesive sets. The kerfs are cut several inches deeper than the length of the curve. This enables the veneers to be clamped to the mold, preventing them from slipping as the wood is bent (Fig. 19-9). Addi-

tional information on molds for laminating bends is provided later in this chapter.

SOLID BENDING

Wood to be bent must be carefully selected. It should be free of defects, such as knots, surface checks, and pitch pockets. Straight-grained, clear material should be selected.

Selecting the Species

The properties of the wood and the intended use of the bent part need to be considered. Oak and beech

1. CUT THE KERFS PARALLEL WITH THE FACE OF THE STOCK.

2. PUT ADHESIVE ON BOTH SIDES OF THE VENEER AND INSERT IN THE KERFS.

FIGURE 19-8
Parallel kerfing involves cutting into the end of the stock.

FIGURE 19-9
Bent part using parallel kerfing with glued laminations.

TABLE 19-1
Safe[a] Radius of Bend, 1-in. Laminations

	Supported by a strap		Unsupported	
	in.	mm	in.	mm
Ash, American	4.5	110	13.0	330
Beech, European	1.5	38	13.0	330
Birch, Canadian	3.0	76	17.0	430
Cherry, European	2.0	51	17.0	430
Chestnut, horse	6.0	150	18.0	460
Douglas fir	18.0	460	33.0	840
Elm, Dutch	0.5	13	9.5	240
Hickory	1.8	46	15.0	380
Mahogany, African	33.0	840	36.0	910
Oak, red	1.0	38	11.5	320
Oak, white	0.5	13	13.0	330
Sycamore	1.5	38	14.5	370
Teak, Nigeria	18.0	460	35.0	890
Walnut, European	1.0	25	11.0	280

Source: Forest Products Laboratory, Forest Service, U.S. Department of Agriculture.
[a] Less than 5% of the parts will fracture.

are popular for furniture because they are in good supply and have good bending properties. Ash and hickory also have good bending qualities and are tough and have a high impact strength. The bending properties of a number of commonly used woods are listed in Table 19-1. These data refer to good-quality, air-dried, 1-in.-thick stock that was steamed at atmospheric pressure. It should be noted that supporting straps greatly influence the radius of curvature.

Moisture Content

Moisture content directly influences the bending properties of wood. Some species can be bent green shortly after they have been cut. Others will rupture if bent to a small curvature while green because hydraulic pressures are built up in the cells. The properties of wood dried to a moisture content of 25% are similar to the wood in green condition, but fracture is less likely. Also, the clamps and straps can be removed sooner because the wood dries and sets faster.

Wood can be bent satisfactorily below 25% moisture, but fracture is more likely to occur. Very dry material tends to buckle and wrinkle on the concave surface. If stock is too dry, it is soaked in cold water for 8 to 12 hours before bending.

Preparing the Wood Blanks

The wood blanks to be bent should all be cut to length with squared ends. If the operation requires extra material for clamping, make allowances for it. Since some longitudinal movement occurs during the steaming, it is best in cases where this poses a length problem to cut the blank to length after steaming but before bending. Better results are obtained if the blanks are machined smooth before bending, than bending them rough cut from the saw.

Softening Methods

Wood can be softened for bending by steaming. It is exposed to saturated steam at 212°F (100°C) at atmospheric pressure. The steaming chamber can be any container that will hold the wood, maintain the 212°F temperature, and retain the moisture from the steam. The vessel needs racks or shelves to hold the wood pieces apart so that steam can reach all sides. Some species of wood, such as oak, become stained when exposed to iron or steel and water, so supports must be of a material that prevents this, such as wood.

When the wood has been heated thoroughly at 212°F, it is ready to be bent. For most woods this takes 45 minutes per inch or 1.8 minutes per millimeter of thickness. Steaming beyond this point does not improve bending properties.

A steam retort can be made from large-diameter pipe that has one end welded closed. The other end could have a lid with holes in it. This will help retain the moisture in the vessel, yet keep the pressure from building up inside. A natural gas or propane burner can heat the water in the vessel (Fig. 19-10). Steam can be had by connecting to a building's hot water heating system or using an independent source, such as an auto engine steam cleaner.

Bending the Wood

The wood is bent by clamping it over a form and backing it up with a mating wood member or around a metal form such as an angle iron.

Wood bent by placing it between mating wood forms is shown in Fig. 19-11. The difficulty with this method is that it takes a long time for the wood to dry and achieve a permanent set.

The use of metal forms is preferred, but heavy

FIGURE 19-10
Simple steam chambers for preparing wood for bending.

A HORIZONTAL STEAM CHAMBER

A VERTICAL STEAM CHAMBER

FIGURE 19-11
Steamed wood can be bent between simple wood forms.

wood forms can be used for limited production. Some provision must be made to clamp the wood to the form. If many parts are to be made, it is worthwhile to weld an end grip. Clamps can be used if only a few pieces are needed (Fig. 19-12). Thicker pieces and smaller radii are less likely to fracture if they are supported by a metal backing strap as they are bent around a form (Fig. 19-13). Provision must be made to provide enough leverage to bend the part. This can be done by adding handles to the strap. The addition of a metal back plate is sometimes needed to provide the stiffness required to complete the bend (Figs. 19-14 and 19-15). Bending with a backing strap makes it possible to bend to a sharper radii.

The bent wood must be held firmly in the bent position until it sets. *Setting* refers to the reduction of the remaining stresses. This occurs when the moisture begins to leave the wood and it cools. The setting process can be accelerated by exposing the wood in the form to hot, dry air at 150°F (66°C). In industry, setting rooms are used that are much like

FIGURE 19-12
Metal angle irons make a strong, permanent form for bending wood.

1. CLAMP THE STRAP AND STOCK TO THE FORM. USING THE HANDLE BEGIN TO WRAP AROUND THE FORM.

2. THE BACK PLATE STIFFENS THE STRAP SO IT FLATTENS THE STOCK AGAINST THE FORM.

FIGURE 19-13
Metal straps help to clamp the steamed wood to the form.

FIGURE 19-14
Bend the steamed wood around the form.

FIGURE 19-15
Clamp to the form if necessary so that wood fits tightly to it.

FIGURE 19-16
After the formed wood has been bent, dried, and removed from the form, hold it in shape with a jig until it is completely dry.

the kilns used to dry lumber. Setting can be speeded up by removing the wood from the bending form after it has set for a period of hours. However, it must still be held to shape by some type of tie or cooling clamp (Fig. 19-16).

There is no definite length of time for set to occur. This will vary with the thickness, species of wood, the form used, and the air temperature. Generally, when the clamps used to hold the wood feel loose, it is an indication that the wood has set. After a piece has set and been removed from the form, it should be stored at normal room temperature for at least 2 or 3 days before it is machined.

Chemical Bending

Wood can also be plasticized by a number of chemicals. They are absorbed by the wood and cause it to swell, much like water and steam. Chemicals that plasticize wood include urea, dimethylol urea, low-molecular-weight phenol-formaldehyde resin, dimethylol sulfoxide, and liquid ammonia. Urea and dimethylol urea have found some commercial use. A free-bending process using liquid ammonia has been patented. Special care must be taken when using chemicals to protect the physical well-being of the workers.

LAMINATED BENDING

Very thin wood strips can be easily bent in their untreated condition. However, since there is nothing to hold them in the bent position, they tend to resume their original shape when the bending force is released. To keep the bent strips in position, something must be done to hold them permanently. This is done by a process called laminated bending. *Laminated bending* involves assembling thin wood strips next to each other with the grain in each piece in the same direction. The pieces are coated with adhesive and bent over forms to the desired shape. The ends of each lamination are not restrained. They are allowed to slide over the adjoining wood strip as they are clamped to the form. After the adhesive has set, the individual pieces are no longer free to slide. This restraint holds the bend permanently in position.

Using this process it is possible to fabricate small-radius bends in relatively thick pieces of stock (Fig. 19-17). It is recommended that the thickest laminations that will bend around the form without breaking be used. This can be determined by bending sample pieces. Low-quality stock having defects as knots or splits can be used on the inside laminations. The most economical production of parts is with the use of laminations produced by the sliced or rotary cut methods. Sawed laminations are more costly because of the loss of stock produced by the saw kerf. Short pieces can be end joined with a scarf joint and used to form longer pieces. The joints should be staggered in the laminated pieces. Generally, laminated bends are easier to form and hold the bent shape better than do the same parts made from solid wood. Usually, the parts produced by laminated bending cost more than solid bent wood does because of the need to produce the thin laminations and the cost of gluing, forming, and drying.

Selecting the Laminations

When selecting the species of wood to use, one factor besides the desired color and grain pattern is the

FIGURE 19-17
The legs on this table and chairs were formed with laminated bent wood. (Courtesy of Krueger.)

ability of the wood to be formed to the desired radii. See Table 19-2 for the radii for laminations $\frac{1}{8}$ in. (3.2 mm) thick or less. These relate to good-quality, straight-grained wood free of defects and bent in unheated forms. The laminations from woods grown in temperate zones can be bent to smaller radii than softwoods or those grown in tropical areas. For example, red oak has a ratio of 35, compared to African mahogany at 68.

When preparing the material to be laminated, each piece must be of uniform thickness. Tapered pieces would not permit the pressures applied to close the glue joint completely. This would produce a thick glue line and a weakened part. Pieces may have defects as knots or splits but must be free of decay. Decayed sections would not produce a solid, strong lamination.

The laminations must be dried to a moisture content suitable for the conditions under which it is to be used. In any case it should be below 20% to ensure proper bonding. Most furniture requires a moisture content of 6 to 8%.

The bending properties of thin laminations can be improved by increasing the moisture content and the temperature of the wood. Again the influence this will have on the adhesive bonding must be con-

TABLE 19-2 Limiting Radii of Curvature of Thin Laminations[a]			
	Radius		Approximate ratio: radius/lamination thickness
	in.	mm	
Ash, European	4.8	122	38
Beech, European	4.5	114	36
Cedar, western red	8.0	203	64
Cherry, European	5.9	150	47
Chestnut, horse	5.5	140	44
Douglas fir	7.8	198	62
Elm, Dutch	3.9	99	31
Hickory	5.8	147	46
Mahogany, African	8.5	216	68
Oak, red	4.4	112	35
Oak, white	5.4	137	43
Sycamore	4.0	102	32
Teak, Nigeria	6.5	165	52
Walnut, European	3.6	91	29

Source: Forest Products Laboratory, Forest Service, U.S. Department of Agriculture.

[a] Based on ⅛ in. (3.2 mm) thick at 12% moisture.

FIGURE 19-18
Bent, laminated wood members are glued and clamped between wood or metal forms.

FIGURE 19-19
Wood molds should have guide pins and a firm compressive material on the mating surfaces.

sidered. This can be offset by first bending the parts using steam or hot water as explained earlier. After they have set, the wood is dried until the moisture content is below 20%. Adhesive is then applied to bond the prebent laminations in a cold form as just described.

Adhesives

Any of the adhesives used in furniture and cabinet construction can be used. See Chapter 18 for detailed information.

Forming the Laminated Part

The simplest shapes can be formed by pressing the laminates between mating forms (Fig. 19-18). The forms could be wood or metal. Most industrial plants use metal molds. Wood molds can be used for short runs. The forms must be made to fit accurately, so a uniform pressure is applied. An irregular glue line and loss of strength will occur otherwise. Some prefer to line the form with a firm but compressive material, such as cork or rubber. The forms must have dowel pins so that they line up accurately and do not slip as pressure is applied (Fig. 19-19). Pressure can be applied on small forms with hand-operated clamps or a vise. Production equipment uses air and hydraulic devices to apply pressure.

To make a wood mold, select the stock to be used. Lay out the curve to be formed. Cut a notch in the ends to provide relief when it is clamped. Drill the holes for the dowels. Cut the stock along the curved line with a bandsaw. Make an accurate cut so that little or no smoothing of the curved surface is necessary. If some smoothing must be done, make certain that the contours match. Line the mold with cork or rubber (Fig. 19-20).

To form the part, cut the laminates to size and apply adhesive to one side of each piece. Stack them together and wrap wax paper around the layers of laminate taping each end (Fig. 19-21). This contains the adhesive that is squeezed out as pressure is applied. Apply pressure with clamps or a vise.

After the adhesive has set the required time, remove the laminate from the mold and tape to a holding board. This is a flat wood piece which reinforces the laminate, to allow it to air cure. If this is not done, the laminate may warp. The length of time to keep it on the holding board must be found by experience. Once the laminate is cured, it can be

FIGURE 19-20
Steps to prepare a wood laminating mold.

1. DRILL THE DOWEL HOLES AND MARK THE CURVE.

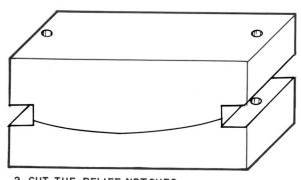

2. CUT THE RELIEF NOTCHES.

3. CUT TO THE LINE, APPLY PADS AND INSTALL DOWELS.

FIGURE 19-21
The laminated parts are placed in the mold.

sawed, filed, or otherwise worked like any piece of wood.

Another method is to use a single form cut to the desired curve and bend the laminate to it with a metal strap (Fig. 19-22). Both the wood form and metal strap methods require more pressure at the center of the curve than at the ends. The use of fluid

FIGURE 19-22
Metal straps provide firm clamping pressure on molded wood laminated parts.

CLAMP STRAP SECURELY

WOOD FORM

LAMINATIONS

METAL STRAP

FIGURE 19-23
Pressure can be applied to a laminated part in a mold using air or water pressure.

pressure (air or water) gives a more uniform pressure over the entire bend. This is accomplished by placing a flexible tube that will withstand the required pressure between one half of the form and the laminate. Firehose is a suitable material. After the laminations are bent and the form is securely clamped, introduce pressure into the hose (Fig. 19-23).

Making a Scarf Joint

When laminates are to be joined to form longer pieces, a scarf joint is used (Fig. 19-24). It is recommended that the pieces to be joined be placed in a shop-made miter box and cut at the same time. A fine-toothed backsaw is recommended. The pieces are placed side by side, blocked in place with scrap wood, and cut (Fig. 19-25). To do this, the scrap wood must also be cut. Use a fine cutting saw so that the surface is as smooth as possible.

After the cut is made, apply adhesive to the cut surfaces, and place the pieces together. Wrap the joint in wax paper. Put scrap stock on each side and clamp until dry (Fig. 19-26).

FIGURE 19-24
Wood laminates can be joined using a glued scarf joint.

FIGURE 19-25
The scarf joint can be cut using a specially made miter box.

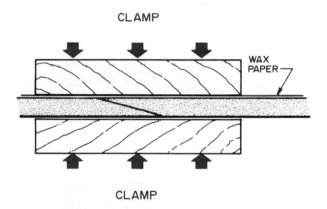

FIGURE 19-26
When the scarf joint is glued and clamped, wrap it in wax paper to keep it from sticking to the blocking.

Scarf joints can also be cut using the belt sander. Mask the angle of the joint on the wood. Clamp a wood fence onto the table at the same angle as the scarf joint (Fig. 19-27). Feed the stock against the belt until it reaches the line marked on the edge.

CURVED PLYWOOD

Curved plywood is produced by either bending and gluing the plies in one operation or bending previously glued flat plywood. The first method produces a product having a more stable curvature. A molded plywood chair is shown in Fig. 19-28.

CURVED PLYWOOD   **269**

FIGURE 19-27
Scarf joints can be cut on a belt sander.

FIGURE 19-28
This chair has a molded plywood seat and back. (Courtesy of Hardwood Plywood Manufacturers Association.)

Bend and Glue Process

In the bend and glue process, veneers are coated with adhesive, assembled, and pressed over as between curved forms. Sometimes heat is applied through steam or electrically heated forms until the adhesive sets. Some of the laminations are placed with their grain at 90° to others, as is done when making plywood. The grain of thicker pieces is placed parallel to the axis of the bend so that it is easier to form.

Usually, the two outer plies on each side are bonded together at 90°F and flat. Then the other veneers are coated with adhesive and assembled at any desired angle to each other. Then the entire assembly is hot pressed to form the desired curvature.

The bonding of the two outer plies before molding allows a higher degree of compound curvature without cracking the face plies. When a high degree of compound curvature is needed, use $\frac{1}{32}$-in. veneers with a moisture content of about 12%.

STUDY QUESTIONS

Answer each of the following questions. If you are not sure of an answer, review the chapter.

19-1. What are the common ways to produce curved parts?

19-2. When a wood member is bent, is the top under tension or compression?

19-3. What is the effect on the board when it is under compression?

19-4. When cutting curved parts, how should the grain run?

19-5. When is parallel kerfing used?

19-6. What qualities should exist in wood that is to be used for solid bending?

19-7. How is wood to be solid bent softened so that it will bend without breaking?

19-8. What chemicals are used to plasticize wood for chemical bending techniques?

19-9. What is laminated bending?

19-10. How are wood pieces joined together to make longer pieces?

19-11. When using the bend and glue process to form curved plywood, how are the plies arranged?

Following are technical terms that you should be able to use as part of your working vocabulary. Write a brief description of the meaning of each term.

Tension

Compression
Kerfing
Setting
Laminated bending
Chemical bending
Scarf joint

20

VENEERING AND INLAYING

Veneering is the process of bonding a thin layer of an expensive wood over a substrate (base) of less expensive but stable material such as plywood, particleboard, or hardboard. The veneer can be arranged so the surface appears as a series of boards joined at the edges or in a decorative pattern in which several species of wood are used (Fig. 20-1).

Veneers are cut from logs in several ways, including rotary cutting, plain slicing, quarter-slicing, semirotary cut, and rift cut (Fig. 20-2). The various cuts produce a variety of grain patterns. The grain pattern is also influenced by the part of the tree from which the veneer is cut. See Chapter 3 for more details.

Veneers can also be applied with the grain arranged in a variety of ways. Among these are slip, book, random, diamond, reverse diamond, four-way center and butt, V, and herringbone matches. Details for matching veneers are provided in Chapter 3.

BUYING VENEER

Large quantities of veneer are sold in a bundle called a flitch. A flitch contains pieces of veneer stacked in the order in which they were sliced from

FIGURE 20-1
This server makes extensive use of a variety of veneers on the top, doors, and drawers. (Courtesy of Drexel Heritage Furnishings Inc.)

the log. In this way the grain can be closely matched by using adjoining pieces.

Smaller quantities are sold in assortments containing 25 or 50 ft^2 of assorted species in various sizes. Sometimes they are sold in small bundles,

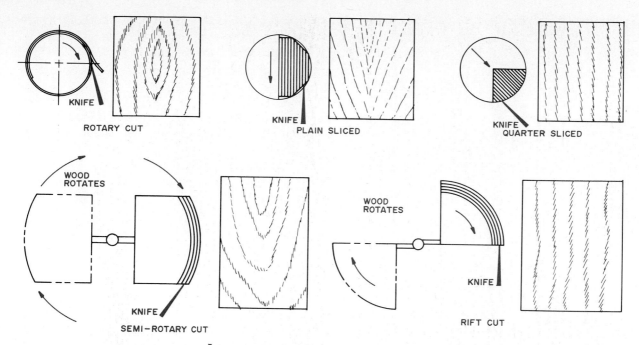

FIGURE 20-2
Veneers are cut several ways.

such as a 10-lb assortment or by the square foot. High-quality veneers are sold by the sheet. Although most veneers are sold in random widths and lengths, some are cut to size. Standard sizes include 24 × 96 in. and 36 × 96 in. These flexible-back veneers are laminated to a special polyester backing that makes them pliable, less likely to break, and more dimensionally stable.

Veneers are sold in precut strips for edge banding. Common sizes are ¾ in. × 8 ft, 1⅜ in. × 8 ft, and 1¾ in. × 8 ft. Some have a hot melt adhesive on the back and are applied by removing the protective strip from the back, placing the strip on the edge, and heating it with an electric iron. Pressure is applied while it is hot, to firm up the bond. A small roller works well for this operation.

TOOLS FOR VENEERING

Veneers are cut with a fine-toothed veneer saw, dovetail saw, a sharp knife, or a large sharp scissors (Fig. 20-3). The scissors are used for rough-cutting pieces to size. Sharp knives or razor blades are used for more accurate finished cuts. Veneer pins are often used to hold the material in place while the layout is checked before gluing. A brush or glue spreader is used for large surfaces and a small artist's brush is used to glue the edges of veneer sheets together. A block plane can be used to smooth or straighten the edges of veneers. When large pieces are being veneered, a veneer press is helpful.

FIGURE 20-3
Tools used to cut veneers: (A) scissors; (B) utility knife; (C) veneer saw; (D) dovetail saw.

CUTTING VENEERS

The pieces of veneer must be cut slightly larger than the surfaces they are to cover. A large, sharp scissors or shear is the easiest way to do this. It can be cut with a sharp knife that is run along a straightedge. A veneer saw can also be used (Fig. 20-4).

APPLYING VENEERS TO A FLAT PANEL

The first thing to do is to get the panel that is to receive the veneer smooth. Usually plywood, parti-

FIGURE 20-4
This piece of veneer is being cut with a utility knife.

cleboard, or hardboard is used. The surface must be smooth enough to prevent defects in the surface from showing through the veneer. If the surface is not smooth or if the plywood has a face species with a pronounced grain, it is necessary to glue a crossband over it. The crossband should be an inexpensive, tight-grained wood applied at right angles to the grain in the substrate.

Remember, the substrate must be of balanced construction. This means that it should have the same number of plies on each side of the core. Therefore, if a crossband is necessary on the top to be veneered, the bottom must also receive a crossband.

The finish veneer should be applied at right angles to the grain in the crossband. To apply a veneer:

1. After preparing the substrate, select the pieces of veneer and cut about 1 in. larger than needed. Use a sharp, large scissors (Fig. 20-5). There tends to be considerable waste as you attempt to match the grain and work around the splits in the ends of the veneer sheets.

FIGURE 20-5
Cut the veneer about 1 in. larger than the surface to be covered.

2. Lay out the veneers, noting where each joint will occur. Mark each joint with a light pencil line drawn along a straightedge.
3. Cut each joint with a veneer saw, dovetail saw, or sharp knife (Fig. 20-6). To cut the joint, place the adjoining pieces together, allowing them to overlap. Clamp a straightedge along the mark and cut both at the same time (Fig. 20-7).
4. If it is necessary to adjust the joint, clamp both pieces face side out in a wood clamp (Fig. 20-8). Lightly plane the edges smooth with a block plane.
5. Next lay the pieces *face side up* on a flat surface. Carefully place them so that the joint is

FIGURE 20-6
Use a cutting fixture and a veneering saw to cut a joint.

FIGURE 20-7
Overlap the veneers and cut through both at the same time.

FIGURE 20-8
A joint can be smoothed by clamping the adjoining pieces together and lightly planing them.

FIGURE 20-10
Apply adhesive to the edges of the joint.

FIGURE 20-11
Apply adhesive to the surface of the substrate.

perfectly closed and pin them to the surface with veneer pins. Then apply veneer tape or masking tape at right angles to the joint every 6 in. (152 mm). Then run a strip of tape the length of the joint (Fig. 20-9).

6. Lift the veneers and fold them back. Apply polyvinyl adhesive to the edges of the joint (Fig. 20-10).

7. Place the veneer flat on the table with the bottom side up. Apply tape to this side. Allow the adhesive to dry.

FIGURE 20-9
Place the joint together and hold with masking tape on the back side.

8. Remove the tape from the back of the veneer. Apply adhesive to the substrate. Use either polyvinyl or urea-formaldehyde (Fig. 20-11). Immediately position the veneer on the substrate and apply even pressure over the surface. A commercial veneer press is best (Fig. 20-12). It is necessary to place caul boards on each side of the veneered panel. Sheets of plywood, particleboard, or hardboard are gener-

ally used (Fig. 20-13). Place wax paper between the veneer and caul boards to prevent the panel from sticking to other pieces.

9. After the adhesive has dried, trim off the veneer extending over the edge of the panel. This is usually done by pulling a sharp knife along the edge of the panel using the panel as a guide. Turn the panel over with the veneer against a scrap board. Press down on the substrate as you cut. Do not try to make the cut in one pass. It is better to take several light passes.

If the veneer is bonded with contact cement, it will not be possible to reposition it even slightly after it touches the substrate. Follow the directions for bonding plastic laminate given in Chapter 21.

FIGURE 20-12
Apply pressure to the veneered panel with a veneer press. (Courtesy of Adjustable Clamp Co.)

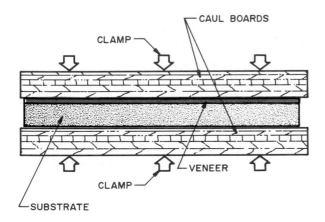

FIGURE 20-13
Use sheets of plywood, particleboard, or hardboard when clamping the veneered panel.

Veneering Small Surfaces

Veneers applied to small surfaces follow the procedures just discussed except when using polyvinyl adhesive. The veneer is bonded by applying heat with an electric iron set at 300°F, which is in the "rayon-synthetic" range. The veneer can be covered with aluminum wrap to protect it. Apply heat in one corner and work toward the center. Apply pressure on the veneer and iron with short, overlapping strokes. Work from one side of the panel to the other. Excessive adhesive should be worked out of the edge ahead of the iron (Fig. 20-14).

Veneering Edges

Edges may be veneered by applying veneer strips in the same manner as described for surfaces. Most

FIGURE 20-14
Small surfaces can be bonded using heat from an electric iron.

edge-bond veneers have a fabric backing. The edge must be smooth. Apply polyvinyl adhesive to the edge. Place the veneer on the edge and press in place. It can be heated with an electric iron followed by pressure, or clamped in place (Fig. 20-15). If contact cement is used, follow the directions for plastic laminates in Chapter 21.

If adhesive backed edge veneers are used, peel off the backing paper, press in position, iron on, and apply pressure. Trim as needed.

INLAYS

Inlays are thin wood strips or panels set into the wood surface used for decorative purposes (Fig. 20-16). While they can be made by the craftsman, there are many designs available from craft supply houses. Inlay bandings are narrow strips made of a variety of woods of various colors. The pieces are cut in various shapes and glued to form strips ranging from $\frac{1}{8}$ in. (3 mm) to about $\frac{5}{8}$ in. (16 mm) wide. They are usually $\frac{1}{20}$ in. (13 mm) thick (Fig. 20-17). Veneer marquetry panels are available in a variety of shapes and have a design, such as a flower or an animal, set in the center of the panel.

Cutting the Groove

When installing inlay bandings, first locate the position of the veneer on the surface. Using a very sharp pencil with a hard lead, mark a line on each side of the veneer. You can tape it to the top to keep it from moving.

Cut along these lines with a chisel. Then rout out the area between the chisel cuts. When routing,

APPLY ADHESIVE   PLACE VENEER   IRON VENEER   APPLY PRESSURE

FIGURE 20-15
Edge veneers can be bonded using an iron or pressure with a roller.

FIGURE 20-16
This console has extensive inlay work in the top, rails, and legs. (Courtesy of Drexel Heritage Furnishings Inc.)

FIGURE 20-17
Inlays are available in a wide range of sizes and designs. (Courtesy of The Woodworkers' Store.)

try to leave the line. This will make certain that the groove will not be cut too wide (Fig. 20-18). To cut with a router, use a cutter that leaves a flat-bottomed groove. After routing each edge of the groove, finish by routing out the center.

The router will leave round corners where two grooves meet. Cut these square with a sharp chisel (Fig. 20-19).

The depth of cut of the router should be slightly less than the thickness of the inlay. In this way, the inlay can be sanded flush with the top after it has been glued in place.

Now fit the inlay into the groove, adjusting the groove width or lightly sanding the edge of the inlay band. Once this is finished, the inlay strips must be cut to length.

Cutting the Inlay Bandings to Length

When the inlay bandings meet at a corner, they are mitered. Good-quality work requires that the pattern meet at the corners and continue the design (Fig. 20-20). This is done by marking the center of the length of the groove. Then cut a miter on the end of two inlay strips, making certain that the pattern

FIGURE 20-18
Steps to cut a groove for an inlay.

1. MARK THE LOCATION OF THE INLAY.

2. SCORE THE EDGES OF THE GROOVE WITH A CHISEL.

STRAIGHT EDGE TO GUIDE THE ROUTER

3. ROUT OUT THE GROOVE.

ROUTER WILL LEAVE ROUND CORNER.

CUT CORNER SQUARE WITH A CHISEL.

FIGURE 20-19
Square up the corners left round by the router.

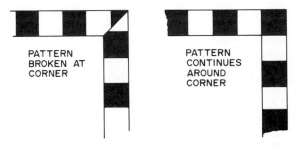

PATTERN BROKEN AT CORNER

PATTERN CONTINUES AROUND CORNER

FIGURE 20-20
It is best if the pattern continues around the corner.

FIGURE 20-21
Work the inlay strips from the mitered corner to the center.

UNION ON CENTER LINE COULD FALL MANY WAYS.

is the same. Lay the two strips in the groove, overlapping them at the center. Cut both strips on the centerline. Repeat this for each side of the top (Fig. 20-21). When the strips are cut, the design at the center will generally vary from the repetitive pattern. However, this will occur at the center of each side and will not be as noticeable as if each mitered corner were different.

Installing the Inlay Band

Apply glue very sparingly to the grooves. Remember, there is no place for excess glue to flow. If there is too much glue, it may not be possible to get the inlay down tight in the groove, or glue may be forced out of a loose-fitting edge onto the top of the inlay. Inlays are sold adhered to a paper backing. This helps hold them together as they are handled. Insert the inlay bands into the groove with the *paper side up*. Lay wax paper on top of the strip and place wood strips on top. Clamp these strips to the top to hold the inlay in place as the glue cures. If there is difficulty getting the inlay band to stay in the groove during gluing, tape it down with masking tape.

Finishing the Job

After the glue has cured, remove the clamps, wood strips, and wax paper. The wax paper and excess thickness of the inlay are removed by careful sanding. The inlay can be given a natural finish by applying a sealer to it. In this way it will not absorb stains used to finish the surrounding wood surfaces. Inlays can also be given a shaded appearance by applying color-fast fabric dyes to the edges of some of the pieces and letting them dry. Then sand lightly until you get the shaded appearance desired. Then apply a sealer.

STUDY QUESTIONS

Answer each of the following questions. If you are not sure of an answer, review the chapter.

20-1. What is veneering?

20-2. In what ways are veneers cut?

20-3. In what patterns are veneers applied to the substrate?

20-4. What are the standard sizes of veneer precut for edge banding?

20-5. Why are veneers laminated to a backing sheet?

20-6. How are veneers sold?

20-7. What tools are used to cut veneers?

20-8. What adhesives are often used to bond the veneer to the substrate?

20-9. Why are inlays set into a wood surface?

20-10. How is the groove that is to receive the inlay cut?

20-11. How are inlay strips joined at corners?

20-12. Why must the amount of glue used to install inlays be carefully controlled?

IMPORTANT TECHNICAL TERMS

Following are technical terms that you should be able to use as part of your working vocabulary. Write a brief description of the meaning of each term.

Veneering
Inlaying
Flitch
Veneer saw
Veneer press

21

APPLYING PLASTIC LAMINATES

Plastic laminates are used for countertops and facings on bulkheads, drawer fronts, doors, and face frames. They are manufactured in a wide range of colors, designs, and reproductions of natural wood grains and colors (Fig. 21-1).

A standard plastic laminate sheet is made from five to seven layers of paper that are treated with a phenolic resin. The top layer of paper has the color, design, or printed grain pattern. This layer is protected with a translucent coat of melamine plastic which is tough and resists heat and chemical attack. The layers are bonded together at a temperature of 265 to 305°F and under a pressure of 800 to 1200 psi. The sheet is held in this condition for 60 to 90 minutes. It is then trimmed to size.

Plastic laminates are made with shiny, suede, embossed, and wood grain finishes. The shiny finish is referred to as a furniture finish. Since it has a high gloss it shows wear and scratches easier than the others.

Plastic laminates used for furniture and cabinet construction are used on the top and back of panels. They are available in several types and thicknesses. These are:

1. *.050-in. (1.27-mm) general purpose.* This is used for both exposed vertical and horizontal

FIGURE 21-1
Plastic laminates are manufactured in a wide range of colors and patterns.

surfaces. It is the most widely used type. It is the thickest type and has greater impact resistance and is more dimensionally stable than the thinner type.

2. *.030-in. (0.76-mm) vertical surface.* It is used on exposed vertical surfaces only, such as cabinet interiors and exteriors and wall panels. It

is not as desirable as the general-purpose type, so is used where usage is light. It is not recommended for use on surfaces over 24 in. (600 mm) wide.

3. *.025-in. (0.63-mm) cabinet liner.* This is used on the interior surfaces of cabinets, where it will not be subjected to wear.

4. *.040-in. (1.00-mm) postforming.* This high-pressure laminate can be heated and bent around curved surfaces such as a countertop. It serves the same purposes as the general-purpose type.

It is often necessary to apply a backing sheet to a panel to balance the construction. This reduces moisture absorption. Following are the types of plastic laminates used for backing purposes:

1. *.050-in. (1.27-mm) and .060-in. (1.52-mm) balancing sheet.* This type is used for large unsupported surfaces and wall paneling. It is the thickest and stablest of the backing sheets.

2. *.040-in. (1.00-mm) backing sheet.* This is made from sheets of .050-in. (1.27 mm) general-purpose sheets that are damaged in manufacturing. The melamine facing is removed.

3. *.020-in. (0.50-mm) and .030-in. (0.76-mm) backing sheet.* These are used on small unsupported panels which are attached to other structural members. They serve to inhibit penetration of moisture into the substrate and produce a balanced construction.

Another type of plastic laminate is available that has the color through the entire thickness. This means that when scratched a dark line will not appear as does on standard laminates. Also, the edge of the laminate does not appear as a dark line when it is exposed. These full-depth color laminates are more expensive than standard laminates.

TYPES OF CORES

Particleboard and plywood are the most commonly used substrate materials to which plastic laminates are bonded.

Particleboard is the type most commonly used in furniture and cabinet construction. It is stable and has a defect-free surface. It is low cost and available in a variety of sizes. Medium density (45 lb) is most often used. It can be used with rigid glue or contact adhesives.

Hard-faced fir-core plywood is also an excellent substrate. It usually has a Philippine mahogany face veneer upon which the plastic laminate is bonded. It costs more than particleboard but has high structural strength. It can be used with rigid glue or contact adhesives.

Fir plywood finds some use as a substrate. However, the grain pattern of the face veneer often shows through the laminate. When contact adhesive is used, this is less noticeable.

If the plastic laminate product is to be used where it is exposed to the weather or other high-moisture conditions, use a waterproof-type plywood.

GLUES AND ADHESIVES

Several glues and adhesives can be used to bond plastic laminates to the substrate.

Rigid glues such as urea-formaldehyde and resorcinol develop a rigid glue line and have maximum bonding effectiveness and heat resistance. They require that the bonding be done in a press. Since they form a rigid glue line, any dimensional change in the panel must be absorbed by the substrate. It is important that the balancing sheet have approximately the same characteristics as the face laminate. Rigid glues are used only on flat pieces that will fit in a press.

Contact adhesives adhere when two coated surfaces are brought together. Pressure can be applied by a hand roller or power roller. This glue line is less rigid and will absorb some of the stresses due to dimensional change. Contact adhesives are universally used for applications to curved surfaces and those that cannot be press glued.

Hot melt glues are used to apply laminate edges. They are applied at very high temperatures and require immediate pressure. Specialized application is recommended for most efficient application.

POSTFORM AND SELF-EDGE TOPS

The two types of plastic laminate tops are postform and self-edge (Fig. 21-2). The postform top has a curved back and front edge. It uses the postforming grade of laminate and requires special equipment to do the forming and lamination. The self-edge top has square corners and can easily be produced.

PREPARING THE TOP

The surface to receive the plastic laminate must be flat and smooth. If the top is to appear thicker than the usual ¾-in. (18-mm) substrate glue and staple additional material to the bottom. On kitchen cabinet tops the front edge is usually 1½ in. (38 mm) thick (Fig. 21-3).

FIGURE 21-2
Laminate tops are available in postform and self-edge types.

FIGURE 21-3
Apply adhesive to the ¾-in.-thick strip, place on the bottom of the cabinet top, and staple in place.

LAMINATING SELF-EDGE TOPS

1. Cut the substrate to form the top to size. This could be plywood, particleboard, or hardboard. For a kitchen cabinet this would normally be 25 in. (635 mm) wide by the length of the cabinet. Tabletops vary a great deal in size. Be certain to allow for the required overhang over the base cabinet or rails or carcass of furniture units. The substrate must be cut square and smooth.

2. Cut the sheet of plastic laminate for the top 1 in. (25 mm) wider and longer than the substrate. Cut the plastic laminate for the edges of the top ¼ in. (6 mm) wider and 1 in. (25 mm) longer than required. Cut on a table saw with a carbide-tipped blade. Cut with the good side up. Be careful that the laminate does not slide under the fence of the saw. If it does not have a tight fit, clamp a piece of wood to the fence that fits tightly to the saw table (Fig. 21-4). Laminate can be cut with a saber saw that has a fine-toothed blade, but the blade will get dull fast and it is difficult to cut a straight line.

FIGURE 21-4
Clamp a wood strip to the rip fence to keep the laminate from sliding under it.

Laminates can also be cut by scoring a line with a carbide-tipped scoring tool. It looks like a utility knife but has a special carbide-tipped blade. To do this, place the laminate with the good side up. Score along a straightedge. It will take several strokes to cut into the dark material below. Hold the laminate firmly beside the score mark and *lift the edge of the sheet up* to break it on the score mark. A slitter is a tool used to trim off excess laminate after the sheet has been bonded to the substrate. The location of the blade is adjustable. It can also bevel the edge (Fig. 21-5).

3. Be certain that the substrate is free of dust. Brush it off carefully or blow it clean with compressed air. The back of the laminate should also be clean.

4. Apply the laminate to the edges first. Do this by applying contact cement to the back of the laminate edge strips and the edge of the substrate. A disposable paintbrush works well (Fig. 21-6). Be certain that all surfaces are covered with contact cement. After the cement has dried, apply a second coat on the substrate.

5. Allow both surfaces to dry. To test this apply a

FIGURE 21-5
Excess laminate is being removed with a carbide-tipped scoring tool.

FIGURE 21-7
Test the contact cement with paper to see if it is dry.

FIGURE 21-6
Apply contact cement to the edge of the substrate and the plastic laminate.

FIGURE 21-8
Let the plastic laminate extend a little above the top surface.

FIGURE 21-9
Firmly press the laminate against the edge.

piece of kraft paper to each. If the surface is dry, the paper will not stick to it. If it feels sticky, wait 5 minutes and check again (Fig. 21-7).

6. Now apply the edge band. Remember, once the laminate touches the edge it will stick and cannot be moved. It requires two people to handle longer pieces. Line up the laminate with the edge and allow it to extend a little above the top. The excess will be trimmed off later. Place one end of the laminate against the edge and applying light pressure work toward the other end (Fig. 21-8). After it is in place, apply pressure with a "J" roller (Fig. 21-9).

7. Using a router with a special cutter that cuts the plastic flush with the top of the substrate, trim the edge to size (Fig. 21-10). A laminate router designed for this operation can also be utilized. It has a special base which controls the depth of cut.

8. To give the edge a final trim, run over it with a belt sander, being careful not to slant it and cut down into the edge of the laminate. Position the sander so that the belt rotation is inward toward the top. Keep it moving from side to side so that you do not cut too deeply into the top at any one place. This should be a very

FIGURE 21-10
Remove the excess laminate with a router and a special laminate cutter.

light cut and should not be overdone (Fig. 21-11).

9. Clean the face of the substrate again and apply contact cement to it and the large sheet of plastic laminate. Let it dry as described above. Large surfaces can be coated with a small paint roller with a disposable sleeve (Fig. 21-12).

10. When the cement is dry place $\frac{3}{8}$-in.-diameter wood dowels across the top about 12 in. apart (Fig. 21-13). Place the plastic laminate on these with the cemented side down. The dowels keep the laminate from touching the substrate.

FIGURE 21-11
Lightly sand the edge laminate flush with the top.

11. Line up the laminate so that it overlaps the substrate on each side. Start sticking the laminate to the substrate at one end by removing a dowel. Carefully remove each dowel as you press the laminate against the substrate. Press them together with hand pressure (Fig. 21-14).

12. Using a laminate roller apply pressure to the laminate starting in the center of the top and working toward the edges (Fig. 21-15).

13. The edges are trimmed using a router with a

FIGURE 21-12
Apply contact cement to the top surface and the bottom of the sheet of laminate.

FIGURE 21-13
Place dowels across the dry contact cement on the top and lay the laminate on top of them with the glued side down.

FIGURE 21-14
Position the laminate over the top. Then start removing the dowels. This permits the laminate to stick to the top.

bevel-cut bit (Fig. 21-16). This top edge of the laminate is cut on a bevel, so it does not present a sharp edge. Be careful not to cut too deeply (Fig. 21-17).

14. The mill marks left by the router bit can be

FIGURE 21-15
Press the laminate firmly against the top with a large roller.

FIGURE 21-16
Trim the top laminate using a special bevel cutter.

TOP VIEW

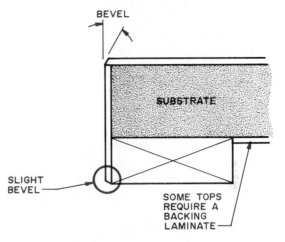

FIGURE 21-17
The top laminate is cut on a slight bevel.

FIGURE 21-18
The beveled edge can be smoothed with a very fine file if needed.

removed with a single-cut mill bastard file (very fine), but a plastic-cut file works the best. Work the file downward so that you do not pull the laminate loose (Fig. 21-18).

15. If contact cement has gotten on the laminate, clean it with a cloth dampened with lacquer thinner. Be careful not to soak the joints and loosen the laminate.

LAMINATE EDGE DESIGNS

In Fig. 21-19 is shown a typical application of standard laminates to countertops. They are applied as just described and the edge is cut on an angle. The edge shows as a dark line.

A top can be edged with a hardwood to give a rich look. One way to do this is to apply the plastic laminate to the edge and top as described earlier. Then using a rabbet router bit, take a very light cut along the edge, removing a little of the top laminate. A cut $\frac{3}{8}$ in. (9 mm) wide is adequate. Take the first light cut by feeding the router *with the bit rotation.* This will produce a very light cut out of the lami-

FIGURE 21-19
This edge design bevels both the edge and top laminates.

nate. Then take additional cuts against the rotation of the bit until the desired depth is reached. Usually, $\frac{1}{8}$ in. (3 mm) deep is enough. Cut and glue hardwood strips in this rabbet. Miter them at the corners (Fig. 21-20). Since the edges of the laminate are covered, standard laminate can be used.

Another way is to glue a strip of hardwood to the edge of the substrate. Trim it flush with the substrate. Apply the edge banding and top laminate as described earlier. Then using a router and bit that has the shape you desire, route the edge exposing the hardwood (Fig. 21-21). Apply a finish to the hardwood. Since the edge of the laminate is exposed, some prefer to use the color-through type.

The following procedures relate to the use of color-core laminates and take advantage of the full-depth color. When bonding these, it is important to use a transparent contact cement applied in a thin,

FIGURE 21-20
A hardwood edge is an attractive feature of this laminate top.

FIGURE 21-21
This hardwood edge is shaped to produce a decorative edge.

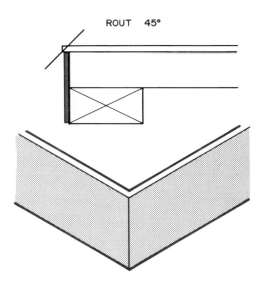

FIGURE 21-22
Beveling the edge that has two different color laminates produces two color corners.

even layer so that the glue line is not noticeable. In all cases apply uniform pressure on the glued laminate so that the glue line does not open up.

One procedure is to produce a two-color top. The edge is bonded in one color and the top in another. The edge can be shaped on an angle (Fig. 21-22). Another uses the same laminate on the edge and top, but the edge is rounded. Since the color is through the laminate, a single-color rounded edge is produced. The router bit should produce a $\frac{1}{8}$-in. (3-

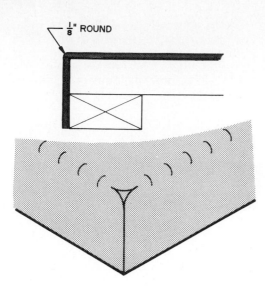

FIGURE 21-23
A slight rounding of the laminate will produce a solid-color corner.

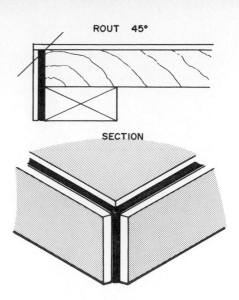

FIGURE 21-24
Bonding a single layer of laminate of a different color under the edge laminate will produce a striking edge.

FIGURE 21-25
Multiple layers of different color laminates will produce a multistriped edge.

mm)-radius curve. If it is much larger, it will cut through to the substrate (Fig. 21-23). Polish any routed edge with 600-grit wet or dry abrasive paper.

Attractive striped edge designs can be obtained by combining laminates in layers. One technique is to bond one color to the edge. Than sand it to roughen the surface and bond a laminate of a second color to it. Then bond the laminate to the top. When the edge is cut on a 45° chamfer, the inner layer will appear as a strip (Fig. 21-24). Another approach is to apply the top laminate first. Then apply several layers of contrasting colors on the edge. Then trim on a 45° chamfer to produce a multistriped edge (Fig. 21-25).

STUDY QUESTIONS

Answer each of the following questions. If you are not sure of an answer, review the chapter.

21-1. How are plastic laminate sheets made?
21-2. What finishes are available on plastic laminates?
21-3. What are the four types of plastic laminates used on exposed surfaces?
21-4. Which type of plastic laminate would be used on a countertop?
21-5. Which type of plastic laminate is the thickest?
21-6. What are the three types of plastic laminates used for backing purposes?
21-7. Why should panels have plastic laminate backing sheets applied?
21-8. What are the most commonly used substrate materials?

21-9. What glues and adhesives are used to bond plastic laminates to the substrate?

21-10. What are the two types of plastic laminate tops?

21-11. If you were going to apply plastic laminate to a top 24 × 48 in., how big would you cut the laminate?

21-12. How do you cut plastic laminates?

IMPORTANT TECHNICAL TERMS

Following are technical terms that you should be able to use as part of your working vocabulary. Write a brief description of the meaning of each term.

Plastic laminate

Substrates
Postform
Self-edge
Scoring tool
Slitter

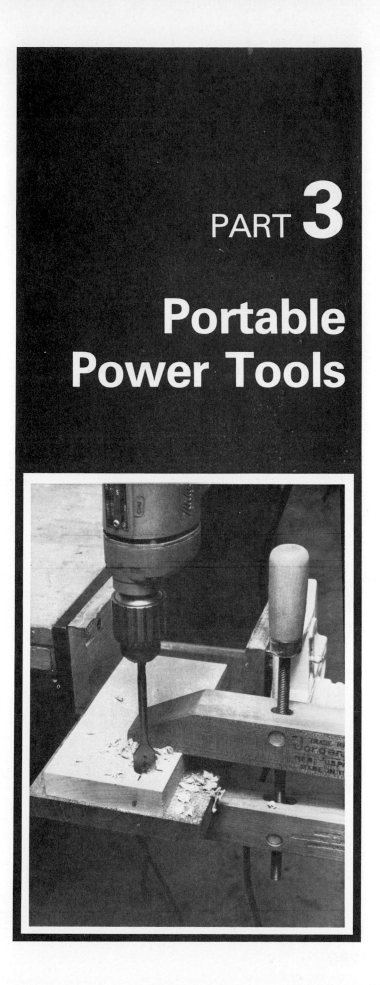

PART **3**

Portable Power Tools

22

PORTABLE ELECTRIC SAWS

Portable electric saws are utilized both in the woodworking laboratory and on the job site. Because of their portability these saws can easily be moved to the project. There are two portable saws from which to select: the portable circular saw and the saber saw. The *portable circular saw* is used primarily for carpentry-type jobs such as cutting dimensional lumber to length (Fig. 22-1). A *saber saw* is designed to saw curves and to make internal cuts (Fig. 22-15).

PORTABLE CIRCULAR SAWS

Portable circular saws are used almost exclusively for cutting stock to width and length (Fig. 22-1). Because this type of saw can easily be moved, carpenters often prefer this machine to cut material. It also has the advantage of cutting boards that have already been installed. A carpenter, for example, may cut a sheet of plywood sheathing after it has been nailed in place.

A portable circular saw is used by industry that is much like that used in schools. Industrial saws may have larger-horsepower motors. They allow heavier cuts and continuous cutting. A *worm-drive portable saw* is specifically designed for this type of sawing (Fig. 22-2).

Parts of the Portable Circular Saw

The major parts of the portable circular saw are the handle, motor, base plate, and retractable guard (Fig. 22-1). The saw is controlled by the operator gripping the *handle*. Located on the inside edge of the handle is the *on-off switch*. It is spring loaded and will provide power to the motor when the switch is depressed.

To adjust the depth of the saw blade, the *motor* is moved up and down. The *depth-adjustment knob* is loosened to raise and lower the *base plate*. Moving the base plate will expose more or less of the blade. The base plate can also be angled up to 45° for bevel-type cuts. Loosen the *bevel-adjustment knob* to tilt the base plate.

To protect the blade, the *upper blade housing* covers the majority of the saw blade. The portion of the blade below the base plate is covered with the *retractable guard*. It is spring loaded and automatically moves out of the way as the saw blade is fed into the stock. After the cut is finished and the base-plate lifted from the board, the retractable guard must snap shut. A *retractable guard handle* can be used to pull the retractable guard out of the way for specialized cuts.

Selecting the Saw Blades

As with other circular saws, there are many different types of blades that can be used with the portable saw. Refer to Chapter 28 for all the tooling that can be utilized.

For rough construction work a rough-cut combination blade is recommended. Finish cuts can be made with a four-tooth combination blade. If you need to make a fine cut on plywood and other panel products, install a plywood blade. Carbide-tipped blades are ideal for cutting abrasive materials such as particleboard. These blades will also stay sharper longer.

FIGURE 22-1
Major parts of the portable circular saw. (Courtesy of Black & Decker.)

Purchasing a Portable Saw

The first consideration when buying a portable saw is the size. The size of this machine is determined by the largest diameter of saw blade that can safely be mounted on the saw. General-purpose portable saws are typically $7\frac{1}{4}$ in. (181 mm) diameter in size. Saws as small as 4 in. (102 mm) are available for cutting wall paneling. Bridge timbers can be cut with the largest size, a $16\frac{5}{16}$-in. (414-mm) saw.

Portable saws are made with either direct-drive or worm gear design. *Direct drive* is the most common and may contain a friction clutch (Fig. 22-1). This allows the saw blade to slow to a stop when it becomes pinched or stuck in the stock. Having this feature prevents the saw motor from overheating. The *worm gear* drive provides a more positive drive that can make heavy cuts (Fig. 22-2).

FIGURE 22-2
Worm-drive portable saw. (Courtesy of Black & Decker.)

Installing the Saw Blade

To change the saw blade on a portable saw, you need to first unplug the power cord. Pull the retractable guard out of the way and secure the saw blade. Some models of saws have a blade lock for holding the

FIGURE 22-3
To change the blade, pull the wrench the same direction as the saw teeth are pointing.

FIGURE 22-4
Adjust the blade to ⅛ in. (3 mm) below the bottom surface of the stock.

blade. Other saws will have a shaft wrench to keep the blade from turning.

With the blade wrench, loosen the blade bolt by pulling the wrench the same direction as the saw teeth are pointing (Fig. 22-3). Remove the existing blade and install the new blade. Be certain that the teeth are pointing in the same direction as the rotation of the motor. Most saws will have a directional arrow to indicate the rotation.

Tighten the blade bolt and allow the guard to go shut. Turn the blade by hand to be certain that it will not rub against the guard. Plug in the power cord and make a trial cut. Check the accuracy of the cut by placing a square from face to face.

Setting Up the Portable Saw

To use the portable circular saw, first adjust the depth of cut. Loosen the depth-adjustment knob and place the base plate on the stock. Lower the blade until it is ⅛ in. (3 mm) below the bottom face of the board (Fig. 22-4). Tighten the depth-adjustment knob. Lift the saw from the stock and check that the retractable guard is working properly.

Next, set the saw blade to the desired angle. Although there is an angle gauge on the saw for establishing the approximate angle, cut a scrap piece to measure the angle (Fig. 22-1). Using a protractor to check this cut will assure an accurate cut.

Position the stock on a pair of sawhorses. Never hold the board with just your hands. For superior results the best face should be placed down against the sawhorses. Since the blade cuts on an upward swing most of the splinters will develop on the top surface.

Crosscutting

The most common operation with a portable saw is crosscutting stock to length. First position the material solidly on two sawhorses (Fig. 22-5). Clamp small boards to a sawhorse to keep them from moving. The point where the stock is to be cut should be approximately 12 in. (305 mm) from the edge of the horse.

Measure the stock to length and square a line at the point the board is to be cut. Place the base plate of the saw on the stock and align the *cutting notch* with the layout line (Fig. 22-6). This will position the saw blade in the same path as the layout line.

Make certain that the blade is not touching the stock, then turn on the power. Slowly push the saw forward checking that the blade is on the waste side of the layout line. After the cut is started, support the waste side of the stock with one hand (Fig. 22-7).

FIGURE 22-5
Positioning the stock on two sawhorses.

FIGURE 22-6
Place the cutting notch just to the side of the layout line to position the saw.

FIGURE 22-7
Use your free hand to support the waste side of the stock. Hands must come no closer than 4 in. (102 mm) to the blade.

Do not allow your hand to come closer than 4 in. (102 mm) to the blade. Keep the waste from pinching the blade or a kickback will occur. After the cut is completed, remove the saw from the stock and release the on-off switch. Do not lay the saw down until the blade has stopped turning.

Ripping

Ripping stock to width can be completed using either an adjustable fence or with freehand techniques. An *adjustable fence* is attached to the base plate, which can be moved in or out. *Freehand techniques* require the operator to guide the saw skillfully along a layout line.

To rip a board using the adjustable fence, move the fence the same distance from the saw tooth set to the right as the width of the board. Position the fence along the edge of the stock and turn on the power. Use your right hand to keep the fence against the board and your left hand to push the saw for-

FIGURE 22-8
Ripping a board using an adjustable fence.

FIGURE 22-9
Clamping a board to a sawhorse for ripping.

ward (Fig. 22-8). Your hand, however, must remain 4 in. (102 mm) from the blade.

To rip a board using freehand techniques, first scribe a line along the face of the board. Clamp the board to a sawhorse with one-half its length extending from the sawhorse (Fig. 22-9). Align the blade with the layout line and cut the board using the techniques discussed in the section "Crosscutting."

Stop the cut when the blade comes close to the sawhorse. Reposition the stock with the remaining end extending from the horse (Fig. 22-10). Place the saw blade back in the kerf. After making certain that the blade turns freely in the kerf, turn on the power and cut the remaining portion of the board.

Cutting Panel Material

Panel material can be cut using a portable saw. Most operators may have difficulty, however, in freehand sawing pieces that are straight and square. For beginners a straightedge can be used to guide the saw.

FIGURE 22-10
Ripping the second half of the board.

FIGURE 22-11
Measure the distance between the saw tooth set to the left and the base plate.

To cut a panel, first make a layout line where the cut is needed. Next measure the distance between the saw tooth set to the left and the outside edge of the base plate (Fig. 22-11). Measure and mark this same distance on the waste side of the layout line. Clamp a straight edge at this point and parallel to the layout line.

Position the base plate of the saw against the straightedge. Check that the blade is aligned with the layout mark (Fig. 22-12). By sliding the saw along the straightedge, a straight cut is made.

Pocket Cutting

Pocket cuts are internal cuts that do not touch an outside edge of the board. These may be utilized to cut windows in doors, make openings for utility boxes, or cut other inside holes.

To make a pocket cut, first lay out the desired pattern on the stock. With the retracting handle, pull the retractable guard up into the upper blade housing. Keeping the guard in this position, align the blade with the first layout line.

Place the nose of the base plate against the stock by tilting the saw forward (Fig. 22-13). Turn on the power and carefully pivot the blade down into the stock. The nose of the base plate must remain against the stock. Once the base plate is flat against the stock, release the retracting handle and continue the cut until the blade reaches the intersecting layout line. Repeat the process until all other cuts are made. Because the saw blade makes a circular arc as it enters the wood, use a handsaw to complete the cut at each corner.

Panel Saws

A useful attachment for the portable circular saw is the panel saw (Fig. 22-14). The saw is clamped into a frame that is mounted on a movable carriage. To use the panel saw, plywood and other panel material are placed on the incline table. Stock can be crosscut by

FIGURE 22-12
Cutting a panel using a straight edge.

FIGURE 22-13
Positioning the saw for a pocket cut. The nose of the base plate must be against the stock.

FIGURE 22-14
A panel saw uses a portable circular saw to cut plywood and particleboard. (Courtesy of Safety Speed Cut Manufacturing Co., Inc.)

pulling the carriage downward. By positioning and locking the carriage in place, the panel can be ripped by feeding it past the saw.

SABER SAWS

The saber saw is a portable power tool designed primarily to make curved cuts (Fig. 22-15). It has a blade that reciprocates or moves up and down much like the scroll saw. This saw is particularly suited for cutting irregular patterns that are too large to be placed on the table of a stationary power tool.

Parts of the Saber Saw

The major parts of the saber saw include the handle, motor, gearbox, and base plate (Fig. 22-15). The saw

FIGURE 22-15
Major parts of the saber saw. (Courtesy of Black & Decker.)

is controlled by the operator gripping the *handle*. Located on the underneath side of the handle is the *on-off switch*. Power is provided to the saw whenever the switch is depressed. A *switch lock* may also be located in the handle. It will hold the switch in the "on" position when lengthy cuts are required. Be careful, however, not to lock the power on when the saw may need to be quickly stopped.

The blade is driven by the *motor* located under the handle. A *gearbox* bolted to the front of the motor changes the rotary motion of the motor to the up-and-down movement of the blade. The blade located at the end of the *blade shaft* is held in place with the *blade chuck*. To operate the saber saw the *base plate* is positioned against the stock. Although the base plate is normally kept 90° to the blade, it can be angled for bevel cuts.

Purchasing a Saber Saw

There are not a great many features that can be selected with a saber saw. Although the size is not generally specified, it can best be found by checking the motor ampere rating. It varies from 2.5 to over 4.5 A. A general-purpose saber saw will have a motor of at least 3.5 A.

Some models of a saber saw have a *variable-speed on-off switch* (Fig. 22-15). This allows the blade speed to be regulated for different materials and types of cuts. The farther the switch is pulled, the faster the blade reciprocates. Fast speeds are used for softwoods and other easy-to-cut materials. Medium speeds work well for hardwoods. Slow speeds are selected for metal and plastics.

A few saws have an *orbital cutting action* feature. The blade not only moves up and down but also pivots forward and backward (Fig. 22-16). This cutting action produces a more aggressive cut which will saw the material at a much faster rate.

TABLE 22-1
Recommended Saber Saw Blades

	Blade type	Length (in.)	Teeth (per in.)	Applications
Carbide Coated Blades				
	Coarse— Tungston Carbide Grit	$2\frac{7}{8}$		Fiber Glass (Polyesters, Epoxies, Melamines, Silicones), Asbestos, Cement, Nail Embedded Wood, Plaster With Nails
	Medium—Tungston Carbide Grit	$2\frac{7}{8}$		Chalkboard, Carbon, Clay Pipe, Brick, Plywood, Hardwood Veneer Plywood.
	Fine— Tungston Carbide Grit	$2\frac{7}{8}$		Ceramic Tile, Slate, Cast Stone, Stainless Steel Trim, Sheet Metal to 18 ga., Ducting, Counter Top Materials, Tempered Hardboard.
Carbide-Tipped Blades				
	Carbide-Tipped	3	6	For cutting fiberglass and similar materials and all types of wood. Tooth configuration provides rapid cutting for production use.
High-Speed Metal Cutting Blades				
	Coarse-Set Tooth, Metal Cutting	3	14	Cuts steel—16 gauge (.059) to 10 gauge (.134). Cuts $\frac{3}{32}$" to $\frac{3}{16}$" aluminum, copper, brass. Cuts plastics, asbestos, Fiberglas, etc. $\frac{1}{2}$" to $\frac{3}{4}$" rigid conduit, 1/0 stranded cable and $\frac{3}{16}$" buss bar.
	Coarse-Set Tooth, Metal Cutting	3	18	Cuts ferrous metals from $\frac{1}{8}$" (.125) to $\frac{1}{4}$" (.250) thick; Non-ferrous (aluminum, copper, brass, etc.) from $\frac{1}{16}$" to $\frac{1}{8}$"; will cut pipe and tubing from $\frac{3}{64}$" to $\frac{1}{8}$" wall thickness.
	Medium-Set Tooth, Metal Cutting	3	24	Cuts ferrous metals from $\frac{1}{16}$" (.059) to $\frac{3}{16}$" (.187) thick; Non-ferrous metals under $\frac{1}{16}$" thick. Suitable for pipe and tubing under $\frac{3}{64}$" wall thickness.
	Fine-Set Tooth, Metal Cutting	3	32	Cuts steel—22 gauge (.023) to 13 gauge (.089). For cuts under $\frac{3}{32}$" in aluminum, copper, brass. Cuts plastics, slate, formica, Fiberglas. Also $\frac{1}{2}$" to $\frac{3}{4}$" thin-wall conduit.
All-Purpose Wood and Composition Cutting Blades				
	Hollow-Ground, Fine-Tooth, Wood-Cutting	3	10	Deluxe series for faster, smooth scroll cuts in wood up to $\frac{3}{4}$" thick. Precision-hollow-ground. Excellent for pocket cutting.
	Hollow-Ground, Medium-Tooth, Wood-Cutting	3	7	Deluxe series for faster, smooth scroll cuts in wood up to $\frac{3}{4}$" thick. Precision-hollow-ground. Excellent for pocket cutting.
	Hollow-Ground, Coarse-Tooth, Wood-Cutting	3	5	Deluxe series for faster, smooth scroll cuts in wood up to $\frac{3}{4}$" thick. Precision-hollow-ground. Excellent for pocket cutting.
	Knife Punch Blade	1		Especially useful to signmakers for scroll cutting all types of paperboard materials. Excellent for making intricate pocket cuts in vinyl floor tiles for inlay work.

Blade type	Length (in.)	Teeth (per in.)	Applications
Knife Edge Blade	$2\frac{1}{2}$		For smooth, fast cuts in leather, rubber, cork and other composition materials.
Fine-Tooth, M2 Steel, Hollow-Ground, Wood-Cutting	4	10	For fine finish scroll cutting in wood, plywood, Masonite, plastics, etc. Also for $\frac{1}{8}$" to $\frac{1}{2}$" soft aluminum, brass. Maximum cut in wood—3" thick.
Coarse-Tooth (Narrow) Hi-Speed Steel, Hollow-Ground, Wood-Cutting	4	6	For faster scroll cutting in wood, plywood, Masonite, etc. Maximum cut—3" thick.
Coarse-Tooth (Wide), M2 Steel, Hollow-Ground, Wood-Cutting	4	6	For fast "production" cutting. Handles wood and plywood up to 3" thick. Also cuts Masonite. Stays sharp longer. Saws through a 2 × 4 at 45°.
Fine-Set Tooth, Hi-Speed Steel, Wood-Cutting	4	10	For scroll cutting in wood, plywood, Masonite, plastics, etc. Maximum cut in wood—2". Set tooth designed for excellent sidecutting action.
Coarse-Set Tooth, M2 Steel, Wood-Cutting	4	6	Set tooth designed for excellent side-cutting action.
Coarse-Tooth, Plaster-Cutting	$3\frac{5}{8}$	9	For coarse, fast cuts in plasterboard and other highly abrasive materials.
Coarse-Tooth, Wood-Cutting	3	7	Makes fast cuts in wood, plywood, composition boards, etc.
Fine-Tooth, Wood-Cutting	3	10	For smoother cuts in wood, plywood, composition boards, etc.
Coarse-Tooth Hollow-Ground	3	7	For fast, very smooth cuts in wood, plywood, composition boards, etc.
Flush Coarse, Wood-Cutting	3	7	Very accurate flush cuts in corners and other tight spots permitted by projecting cutting area. Cannot be used with No. 3155.
Double-Edge Coarse, Wood-Cutting	3	7	Makes fast pocket cuts up to $\frac{3}{4}$" thick in wood, composition boards, etc. Exclusive: cuts forward and backward. Cannot be used with No. 3155, 3153-10, 3157-10, and 3159-10.
Double-Edge Fine, Wood-Cutting	3	10	
Scroll Fine, Wood-Cutting	$2\frac{1}{2}$	10	Makes intricate cuts, as small as $\frac{1}{8}$" radius, up to $\frac{1}{2}$" in wood, plastics, etc.
Skip-Tooth, Wood-Cutting	3	5	More efficiently cuts up to $\frac{3}{4}$" thick plywood, plastics, etc. due to extra space for chip clearance.
Coarse-Tooth, Wood-Cutting	6	4	For coarse cuts in wood over 2" thick. Also suitable for plastics and composition boards.
Medium-Tooth, Wood-Cutting	6	7	For smoother cuts in wood over 2" thick.

Source: Black & Decker.

FIGURE 22-16
An orbital cutting action moves the blade up and down
and forward and backwards.

Selecting the Saber Saw Blade

The primary reason the saber saw can cut a wide
variety of materials is the large selection of available blades. Although there are general-purpose
blades, there are also specialized blades for specific
materials and types of cuts. Refer to a blade selection chart such as that in Table 22-1 to match the
proper blade for your cutting. The blade package
will also contain valuable information on recommended applications (Fig. 22-17).

FIGURE 22-17
Information contained on a saber saw package will include length, number of teeth, type of recommended
cutting, and application.

It is important that the shank end of the blade
fit the blade chuck. Although most of the saber saw
blades will fit the majority of saws, there are some
machines which require a specially designed blade
shank. Always refer to the information on the blade
package for the brands and models the blade will fit.

Installing the Saber Saw Blade

To install a saber saw blade, first be certain that the
power cord is unplugged. Use a screwdriver or Allen
wrench to loosen the chuck screws (Fig. 22.18). After
removing the old blade, replace it with a new one.
The teeth should be pointing forward and down. Replace the chuck screws and tighten them securely.
Plug in the power cord and make a trail cut. You
will need to use a square to check the squareness of
the cut.

FIGURE 22-18
Loosening the chuck screws to remove the blade.

Setting Up the Saber Saw

Once the blade has been properly installed, a cut can
be made. Start the setup by laying out the desired
cut. Since the blade cuts on the upper stroke, place
the best face down. The majority of the splintering
will take place on the top face.

Use clamps or a bench vise to secure the stock
(Fig. 22-19). Plan your cut so that the first portion of
the cut is extended out away from the workbench or
sawhorse. In many cases it will be necessary to saw
up to the table and then reposition the stock for the
remaining portion of the cut. Arrange the power
cord so that it will not interfere with the cut.

Crosscutting and Ripping

Use a square to lay out the cut. Place the base plate
against the stock and align the blade with the layout
line. Turn on the power and apply light forward
pressure. Allow the blade to do the cutting and do
not force the saw. Too much forward or side pressure
and the blade will break.

FIGURE 22-19
Secure the stock with either a bench vise or clamps before starting the cut.

Crosscutting is done with freehand techniques (Fig. 22-20). Ripping can be completed either using freehand techniques or with a rip guide (Fig. 22-21). The rip guide rides along the edge of the board to control the saw.

Cutting Curves

Curves can be easily cut with a saber saw using freehand techniques. After the pattern has been laid out, plan the best path for the saw to take. If there are any sharp or small curves, use a series of *relief cuts* to enable the blade to cut the curve (Fig. 22-22). Relief cuts are shortcuts made in the waste portion of the board, allowing the blade to saw sharp curves. Keep the cut as close to the layout line as possible without crossing over the line. If you do accidentally come too close to the layout line, back the saw up and restart the cut.

FIGURE 22-20
Crosscutting a board using freehand techniques.

FIGURE 22-22
Relief cuts allow small curves to be cut.

Internal Cuts

FIGURE 22-21
Ripping a board with a rip guide.

Internal cuts are openings made on the interior face of a board and do not extend to an outside edge. To introduce the blade into the stock, a hole is bored or the moving blade is plunged into the wood. If the material is thicker than $\frac{1}{4}$ in. (6 mm), bore a hole in each corner of the layout lines (Fig. 22-23). The blade can then be lowered through the hole. The hole should be larger than the width of the blade so that the saw can be turned once the blade reaches the corner.

To make a plunge cut, make certain that the material is $\frac{1}{4}$ in. (6 mm) or thinner. Pivot the saw up on the nose of the base plate and turn on the power (Fig. 22-24). Slowly lower the saw, introducing the blade into the stock. The saw blade will make its own hole.

FIGURE 22-23
Introducing the blade through a hole for an internal cut.

STARTING POSITION

SLOWLY LOWER   FEED FORWARD

FIGURE 22-24
Plunging the blade into the stock for an internal cut.

STUDY QUESTIONS

Answer each of the following questions. If you are not sure of an answer, review the chapter.

22-1. Never allow your hands to come any closer than _____ in. (_____ mm) to the portable circular saw blade.

22-2. When using a saber saw, it is recommended to make a plunge cut only _____ in. (_____ mm) on thinner material.

22-3. What part of the guard covers that portion of the blade that is below the base plate?

22-4. A general-purpose portable table circular saw most generally has a blade diameter of _____ in. (_____ mm).

22-5. What direction is the blade wrench pulled when loosening the blade bolt?

22-6. To minimize splinters on the best face of the stock, position the board with the face up or down?

22-7. The _____ of the base plate must be positioned against the stock when starting a pocket cut.

22-8. Use a series of _____ cuts when using the saber saw to cut any sharp or small curves.

22-9. Internal cuts are openings made on the _____ face of a board and do not extend to an outside edge.

22-10. The blade of a saber saw is held in place with the _____ located at the end of the blade shaft.

Following are technical terms that you should be able to use as part of your working vocabulary. Write a brief description of the meaning of each term.

Portable circular saw
Saber saw
Worm-drive portable saw

Depth-adjustment knob
Bevel-adjustment knob
Direct drive
Cutting notch
Pocket cuts
Orbital cutting action
Relief cuts
Internal cuts

23

PORTABLE POWER PLANES

A portable power plane is utilized primarily for planing the edges of boards (Fig. 23-1). This portable power tool is often used when it is not convenient to use a jointer, such as planing a door on a construction site. It is also useful for jointing the edges of long or extra large pieces that cannot be safely surfaced on a jointer. A carpenter, for example, may select this machine for planing the edge of a door.

PARTS OF THE POWER PLANE

The major parts of the power plane are the bed, motor, and handle (Fig. 23-1). There are two parts to the bed of the plane. A *rear* or *fixed bed* is set at the same level as the bottom of the cutting circle of the cutter. In front of the cutter is the *front* or *adjustable bed*. It is moved up and down and set at a level equal to the depth of cut. Mounted to the side of the two beds is the fence. The *fence* is set at the angle of the cut. Although the fence is normally adjusted to the 90° position, it can be tilted up to 45°.

The *motor* provides power to the cutter. To the top of the motor is the *handle*. The handle is gripped firmly to control the plane. On the underneath side of the handle is the *on-off switch*. Pulling in on the

FIGURE 23-1
Major parts of a portable power plane. (Courtesy of Porter-Cable Corporation.)

switch turns on the plane. Releasing the switch automatically turns off the machine.

PURCHASING A POWER PLANE

The primary consideration when purchasing a power plane is the size. It is determined by the motor ampere rating and the size of the bed. Motors vary in size from 2.5 A to over 10 A. The larger the ampere number, the more powerful the motor. The size of

PORTABLE PLANE SAFETY RULES

1. When changing the cutter, always unplug the cord.
2. Before cutting any boards, clamp them to saw-horses or a workbench.
3. Use both hands to hold the plane securely.
4. Keep the power cord clear of cutter and cutting area.
5. Keep from reaching under the stock while cutting.
6. The maximum depth of cut is $\frac{1}{16}$ in. (2 mm).
7. Hands should come no closer than 4 in. (102 mm) to the cutter.
8. Keep the fence and rear bed against the stock until the cutter has stopped turning.

FIGURE 23-3
To change the cutter pull the wrench counterclockwise.

the bed varies from $1\frac{13}{16}$ to over $3\frac{1}{4}$ in. (45 to 82 mm) wide. The length of the bed also varies from $7\frac{1}{2}$ to over 18 in. (191 to 457 mm).

SELECTING AND INSTALLING THE CUTTER

The first consideration in the selection of the cutter is the number of cutting edges. The number of cutting edges varies from two to three or more. The more cutting edges, the smoother the cut will be. Some models of plane also have available carbide cutters. Carbide cutters will plane particleboard, high-pressure plastic laminates, and other abrasive materials (Fig. 23-2).

FIGURE 23-2
Planes with carbide cutters can be used to joint high-pressure plastic laminates.

To change the cutter, unplug the power cord. Use the correct size of wrench to fit the cutter nut. Wedge a piece of wood between the cutter and the bed and remove the cutter nut (Fig. 23-3). Replace the existing cutter with a newly sharpened cutter. Wedge a piece of wood against the cutter and tighten the cutter nut. Remove the wedge and check that the cutter turns freely.

SETTING UP THE PLANE

To set up the plane, unplug the power cord. Set the depth of cut by using the *depth-adjustment knob*. Refer to the owners' manuals for recommended maximum depth of cuts. Depending on the particular machine, recommended depth of cut varies from $\frac{1}{64}$ to $\frac{1}{16}$ in. (0.5 to 2 mm).

Next check the angle of the fence. Most planes contain an *angle gauge* to indicate the tilt of the fence (Fig. 23-4). For cuts requiring great accuracy, plane a scrap piece and check the cut with a square or protractor.

FIGURE 23-4
Setting the angle of the fence by using the angle gauge.

PLANING AN EDGE

To plane the edge of a board, secure it in a bench vise or clamp it to a sawhorse. Position the stock so that the clamps will not interfere with the travel of the plane. No matter how large or small the part, never hold the stock with your hands.

Adjust the depth of cut and check that the fence is at the desired angle. Plug in the power cord. Position the front bed on the edge of the board and the fence against the face of the stock (Fig. 23-5). If a bevel or chamfer is to be cut, the plane will be held at an angle (Fig. 23-6). It is important that the plane be held in a steady position if an accurate cut is to be made.

Grip the handle with your right hand and pull in on the power switch. Your hands must be kept up above the bed and away from the cutter. After the motor has gained full speed, push the plane forward.

FIGURE 23-6
The plane is positioned at an angle when jointing a bevel or chamfer.

FIGURE 23-5
The front bed and fence must be kept against the stock.

Feed the plane at a steady rate. Too fast a feed rate will cause the cut to be rough and the motor will be overloaded. If you use too slow a feed speed, however, the wood will be burned and the cutter prematurely dull.

Once the cutter has cleared the far end of the stock, release the on-off switch. Keep the plane in this position until the cutter has stopped turning. Remove the plane from the stock and repeat the planing process if additional passes are required. With each pass, be certain that the front and rear beds are kept against the stock. If the beds raise up off the stock, a bowed edge will be produced.

STUDY QUESTIONS

Answer each of the following questions. If you are not sure of an answer, review the chapter.

23-1. The maximum depth of cut for a portable power plane is _____ .

23-2. The primary purpose of a portable power plane is planning the _____ of boards.

23-3. Another name for the front bed is the _____ bed.

23-4. How is the power to the plane turned on?

23-5. What two items determine the size of the plane?

23-6. The more cutting edges, the _____ the cut will be.

23-7. What can be wedged in between the beds when changing the cutter?

23-8. The depth of cut is set by using the _____ knob.

23-9. Too fast a feed rate will cause the cut to be _____ and the motor will be _____ .

23-10. If the front and rear beds are not kept against the stock, what kind of edge will be produced?

Following are technical terms that you should be able to use as part of your working vocabulary. Write a brief description of the meaning of each term.

Rear bed
Front/adjustable bed
Fence
Depth-adjustment knob
Angle gauge

24

PORTABLE
ELECTRIC DRILLS

The most versatile portable power tool is the electric drill (Fig. 24-1). It is available in many sizes and can be used with numerous attachments. Although it is most commonly used with drill bits, many other accessories are available. A few of these attachments include drill press stand, grinding wheel, sanding disk, and others shown in Fig. 24-2.

Industry utilizes many of the same electric drills as those used in schools and homes. They will, however, generally have continuous-duty motors. Some manufacturers prefer *pneumatic* or air-driven

drills (Fig. 24-3). These drills are cooler running and more compact.

PARTS OF THE ELECTRIC DRILL

The major parts of the electric drill are the handle, motor, and chuck (Fig. 24-1). Most drills will have either a pistol grip or a T-handle, The *pistol-grip* handle is the most common for small to medium-sized drills. Larger drills will typically have *T-han-*

FIGURE 24-1
Major parts of a pistol grip portable electric drill. (Courtesy of Black & Decker.)

FIGURE 24-4
A T-handle design is used for larger drills. (Courtesy of Porter-Cable Corporation.)

FIGURE 24-2
Accessories for a portable drill.

FIGURE 24-3
Pneumatic drills are driven by compressed air.

dles for better control (Fig. 24-4). More pressure can also be applied for large holes or for drilling in very hard materials.

The motor and gearbox make up the majority of the drill. The motor provides power to the gearbox. The *gearbox* reduces the speed of the motor and increases the *torque* or turning power to the *chuck*.

At the end of the gearbox is the chuck. It holds the drill bit and can be adjusted to fit different shank diameters.

PURCHASING AN ELECTRIC DRILL

The first consideration in purchasing a drill is the size. The size is determined by the largest shank diameter than can be secured in the chuck. Drill chuck sizes include $\frac{1}{4}$, $\frac{3}{8}$, $\frac{1}{2}$, and $\frac{3}{4}$ in. (6, 10, 13, and 19 mm). A $\frac{3}{8}$-in. (10-mm) drill is recommended for general-purpose boring. Select a $\frac{1}{2}$-in. (13-mm) chuck size for large-diameter holes or for heavy boring.

Another consideration in buying a drill is the selection of an on-off switch. Simpler drills have switches that only turn the power on and off. A switch that provides more versatility is the *variable-speed switch*. The farther the switch is pulled, the faster the chuck will rotate. When boring in softer materials such as wood, a fast speed is selected. Use a slower speed for drilling in harder materials such as metal and plastic. A variable-speed switch is also convenient when slower turning speeds are required for installing screws (Fig. 24-14).

Drills may also contain a reversing switch. This feature allows the chuck to rotate either clockwise or counterclockwise. Although the clockwise rotation is generally selected, the counterclockwise direction is used when a bit becomes stuck or when removing wood screws. Do not move the reversing switch unless the chuck is not turning.

Portable drills are also available with rechargeable batteries (Fig. 24-5). This makes the drill highly portable and does not require a power cord to provide electricity. The battery is recharged in the charger once the power becomes weak.

SELECTING THE DRILL BIT

The portable electric drill can be used with most of the drill bits described in Chapter 35. Refer to this chapter for detailed information. Twist bits are the most common, however, and are utilized to bore holes ½ in. (13 mm) and smaller in diameter (Fig. 24-6). Spade bits can be used to bore larger-diameter holes (Fig. 24-7).

FIGURE 24-5
A rechargeable drill requires batteries with a charger. (Courtesy of Black & Decker.)

FIGURE 24-6
Twist bits are generally used with a portable drill.

FIGURE 24-7
Spade bits work well for large-diameter holes.

INSTALLING THE DRILL BIT

To install a drill bit, insert the shank of the bit a minimum of 1 in. (25 mm) into the jaws of the chuck. Any less than this and the chuck will easily be worn. Hand-tighten the outside chuck sleeve until the jaws hold the bit. Make certain that the bit is centered in the opening of the chuck.

Next use the chuck key by first inserting it in one of the chuck key holes (Fig. 24-8). By turning it clockwise the bit will be secured in the chuck. For large-diameter bits, use the chuck key in all three holes. This will prevent the bit from spinning in the chuck.

FIGURE 24-8
Securing the drill bit in the chuck with a chuck key.

BORING THROUGH HOLES

Holes that extend completely through the stock can be bored by first marking the center of each hole. Use an awl and make an indentation at these centers. This will provide a starting point for each hole and keep the bit from drifting away from the center.

Place the tip of the bit in the starting point and establish the desired angle to the surface of the stock. If an exact angle is required, use a square or a sliding T-bevel as a guide (Fig. 24-9). Commercial

FIGURE 24-9
Using a sliding T-bevel as a guide for boring an angular hole.

fixtures can also be utilized to give exact angles (Fig. 24-10).

Turn on the drill and apply light forward pressure. Drills having variable-speed switches should initially use a slow speed. Once the bit has fully engaged the material, additional forward pressure and rotation speed can be used. When boring deep holes, pull the bit back out of the hole to allow the chips to fall free from the bit.

As the bit approaches the far side of the stock, slow the feed rate and lighten the feed pressure. If no splinters are allowed on the back side of the stock, clamp a *backup board* to the stock before starting the hole (Fig. 24-11).

FIGURE 24-10
A commercial fixture guides the drill bit to the exact desired angle.

FIGURE 24-11
A backup board prevents splintering on the back of the board.

BORING STOPPED HOLES

Use the same techniques for boring stopped holes as recommended for through holes. Since the holes do not extend all the way through the stock, however, the bit must be marked in some fashion. The simplest method is to use a piece of tape at the desired length on the drill bit (Fig. 24-12). Commercial stops are also available which can be clamped on the bit (Fig. 24-13). They will keep the bit from going any deeper once the stop meets the surface of the board.

FIGURE 24-12
A piece of tape marks the desired depth of the hole.

FIGURE 24-13
A commercial stop keeps the bit from going too deep for a stopped hole.

INSTALLING WOOD SCREWS

A portable drill with a variable-speed switch can be utilized for installing screws. Start the process by boring the appropriate shank and pilot holes. A countersunk hole may also be necessary for flat-head and oval-head screws.

After lubricating the threads of the screw with paraffin wax, insert a screw into each hole. Place the

FIGURE 24-14
Installing a wood screw. Note the position of the hands of the operator.

FIGURE 24-15
A pneumatic screwdriver installs screws.

screwdriver bit squarely in the slot of the screw and slightly pull in on the switch (Fig. 24-14). Keep your fingers away from the end of the screwdriver bit and the stock surrounding the screw. Your hands will then be clear in case the bit should slip.

Once the screw has been started, the rotational speed can be increased. If the screw becomes stuck, reverse the rotation and remove the screw. Check that the shank and pilot holes are of the correct depth and diameter. Start the screw again and apply more downward pressure.

Specialized power screwdrivers can also be utilized to install screws (Fig. 24-15). They are designed only to drive screws and do not bore holes. Both pneumatic and electric models are manufactured.

STUDY QUESTIONS

Answer each of the following questions. If you are not sure of an answer, review the chapter.

24-1. Always remove the _____ after the chuck has been tightened.

24-2. Drills that are air driven or _____ run cooler and are more compact.

24-3. The size of a portable drill is determined by the _____ shank diameter that can be secured in the chuck.

24-4. A _____ switch varies the speed of the chuck.

24-5. _____ bits are the most common and are utilized to bore small holes.

24-6. Insert the shank of the drill bit a minimum of _____ in. (_____ mm) into the jaws of the chuck.

24-7. To prevent large-diameter bits from spinning in the chuck, use the chuck ken in all _____ holes.

24-8. If an exact angle for a hole is required, use a _____ or a sliding _____ as a guide.

24-9. Use a _____ board to prevent splintering on the back side of the stock.

24-10. If the screw has become stuck, _____ the rotation and remove the screw.

IMPORTANT TECHNICAL TERMS

Following are technical terms that you should be able to use as part of your working vocabulary. Write a brief description of the meaning of each term.

Pneumatic
Pistol grip

T-handle
Gearbox
Torque
Chuck
Variable-speed switch
Backup board

25

PORTABLE ROUTERS

The portable router is a multifunctional machine that can be utilized for both joinery and decorative-type cuts (Fig. 25-1). Most shops have several routers because of this versatility. Shapes produced by the router are usually clean, splinter free, and require little sanding.

Industry uses many of the same routers as schools. They do, however, sometimes contain larger continuous-duty motors. The heavier motors can be utilized for long periods without overheating. Occasionally, industrial routers will be driven by air. This allows heavy cuts and cooler-running motors.

PARTS OF THE ROUTER

There are only two major parts to the portable router (Fig. 25-1). They are the motor and base. The motor powers the router bit. At the end of the threaded motor shaft is the collet and collet nut (Fig. 25-2). The *collet* is a tapered split sleeve that secures the router bit to the motor shaft. Most heavy-duty routers have ¼-, ⅜-, and ½-in. (6-, 5-, and 13-mm) collets. This allows any common bit shank size to be used with the router.

The base slides up and down on the outside of the motor unit. Once positioned, a *depth lock* secures

FIGURE 25-1
Major parts of a portable router. (Courtesy of Robert Bosch Power Tool Corporation.)

the base to the motor. Along the sides of the base are the handles. The handles are gripped by the operator to control the machine. Attached to the bottom of the base is the plastic base plate. This provides a smooth surface to slide along the stock.

PURCHASING A PORTABLE ROUTER

There is a wide range of costs for portable routers. The primary difference is the size and construction

FIGURE 25-3
A laminate trimmer is a specialized router used for cutting high-pressure plastic laminates.

FIGURE 25-2
The motor unit contains a threaded shaft and collect.

FIGURE 25-4
A plunge router allows the router bit to be lowered into the stock.

FIGURE 25-5
A D-shaped handle provides ready access to the on-off switch.

of the motor unit. Horsepower ratings vary from $\frac{1}{4}$ to over 3 hp. Lower-horsepower routers are designed for light shortcuts. This may be ideal for a home handyman who does not utilize a router on a regular bases. A *laminate trimmer* is used to trim high-pressure plastic laminates (Fig. 25-3). It has a small motor because of the thin material.

Routers with motors larger than 1 hp can generally make most cuts. Heavy-duty motors are designed to be used continuously with little danger of overheating. Very deep cuts require a router of 2 hp and larger.

Some routers are available with a plunge base (Fig. 25-4). This allows the depth of cut to be locked at a specific level or for the rotating bit to be lowered into the stock. Once the bit reaches the desired depth, the downward travel is stopped. Blind grooves and other stopped cuts can be made without the base being lifted from the work.

Always purchase a router that feels balanced in your hands. You should be able to control it easily by gripping the handles. The on-off switch must also be readily accessible from the handles (Fig. 25-5). There should be no need to remove your hands from the machine to turn the router on or off.

A consideration when purchasing a router is the motor speed. The router spindle will generally turn at a constant speed between 15,000 to 30,000 rpm. Routers that turn at a fast speed will make a smoother cut and allow faster feed speeds. The horsepower of the motor, however, must be adequate to keep the bit turning at the desired speed.

SELECTING THE ROUTER BITS

There are hundreds of different router bits. Each style or pattern is available in several sizes. In addition, they are sold in a few different shank sizes and have cutting edges made from different materials.

The major parts of the router bit include the shank, cutting edge, and with some bits, a pilot (Fig. 25-6). The *shank* fits into the collet located in the threaded shaft of the motor. Shanks are made in $\frac{1}{4}$-, $\frac{3}{8}$-, or $\frac{1}{2}$-in. (6-, 10-, and 13-mm) diameters. Although the $\frac{1}{4}$-in. (6-mm) shank size is the most common for smaller routers, a $\frac{1}{2}$-in. (13-mm) size is recommended. The $\frac{1}{2}$-in. (13-mm) diameter will flex less and be less likely to break. The *cutting edge* contains the ground pattern to produce the router edge. Most router bits have two cutting edges. Bits designed to shape edges contain a pilot. The *pilot* controls the horizontal depth of cut. Pilots can be made either from solid steel or with a ball bearing. A solid pilot turns at the same speed as the rest of the bit and may burn the wood. A ball-bearing pilot will ride easily over the edge and turns only as fast as the feed speed. Bits that do not contain a pilot are designed primarily for interior cuts.

Cutting edges are either made of carbon steel or are carbide tipped. Although steel cutters are initially less expensive, carbide tipped will last much longer. Carbide will also shape hard abrasive materials such as plastic laminates and particle board.

FIGURE 25-6
The major parts of the router include the shank, cutting edge, and pivot. (Courtesy of Porter-Cable Corporation.)

This type of bit, however, does require a diamond grinding wheel to sharpen the hard cutting edge.

Router bits will be used primarily to make decorative or joinery-type cuts. Decorative bits will enhance the appearance of a project (Fig. 25-7). The major styles are as follows:

1. *Rounding-over bits* round a corner, providing a smooth appearance. The diameter of the pilot will be the same size as the adjoining cutting edge.
2. *Beading bits* are often confused with the rounding-over bit. The pilot is, however, smaller in diameter than the adjoining cutting edge. This creates a step at the bottom of the radius.
3. *Cove bits* make a concave-shaped cut on the corner of the board. The pilot controls the depth of cut.
4. *Core box bits,* like the cove bits, make a concave cut. They do not, however, contain a pilot and can shape a rounded-bottom groove.
5. *Chamfer bits* make a 45° chamfer on a corner. Because of the pilot they are designed to run along the edge.
6. *V-grooving bits* make a vee-shaped groove generally on the face of a board. The sides of the bit are ground at a 45° angle.
7. *V-groover and scorer bits,* like the V-grooving bits, also shape a vee-bottomed groove. It does, however, have a longer cutting edge along the sides and is available only in narrow widths.
8. *Roman ogee bits* make a highly decorative cut along the edge. It is often used in traditional-styled furniture to add detail to the edge of a top or shelves. The pilot controls the horizontal depth.

There are also router bits, which are designed primarily for joinery-type cuts (Fig. 25-8). They are as follows:

1. *Straight bits* are used mostly for making grooves. They are available in several diameters from $\frac{1}{16}$ to over 2 in. Straight bits are made in two styles, single flute and double flute. The *single flute* has only one cutting edge and contains the most metal to support the cutting edge. It is therefore the strongest of the two styles and less likely to break. The *double flute* has two cutting edges and produces the smoothest cut.
2. *Rabbeting bits* shape rabbets along the edges of boards. The pilot controls the horizontal depth of cut.
3. *Plunge bits* are similar to straight bits except that a vee-shaped starting tip is grounded into

ROUNDING OVER BIT

BEADING BIT

COVE BIT

ROUND NOSE (CORE BOX)

CHAMFER BIT

"V" GROOVING BIT

"V" GROOVER & SCORER BIT

ROMAN OGEE BIT

STRAIGHT BIT
(SINGLE FLUTE)

STRAIGHT BIT
(DOUBLE FLUTE)

RABBETING BIT

PLUNGE BIT

FLUSH TRIM

SLOTTING CUTTER

DOVETAIL BIT

FIGURE 25-8
Major router bits for joinery cuts. (Courtesy of Onsrud Cutter.)

FIGURE 25-7
Major router bits which produce a decorative cut. (Courtesy of Robert Bosch Power Tool Corporation.)

the end. This allows the rotating bit to be lowered into the stock. The bit makes its own starting hole and does not need an opening to being a cut. A smooth portion immediately above the starting tip is round and serves as a pilot. Once the cut begins the rounded portion keeps the cutting edge from cutting beyond the edge of the stock. Plunge bits are used frequently to cut away material from an opening such as plywood sheathing from a roughed-in window opening.

4. *Flush-trim bits* are used to cut away material that is overhanging the edge. It is an ideal cutter to trim high-pressure laminates and veneer.

5. *Slotting bits* are utilized to make narrow grooves along the edge of the stock. The pilot controls the depth of cut. This cutter works well for installing tee molding and splines.

6. *Dovetail bits* are used to shape dovetail joints and often used in association with a dovetail fixture. Both are discussed in detail later in this chapter.

INSTALLING THE ROUTER BIT

To install a router bit, unplug the power cord. To have easier access to the collet, remove the motor unit from the base. After selecting the desired cutter, insert the shank of the cutter into the collet. If the collet size does not match the diameter of the shank, change the collet.

The shank of the router bit must fit into the collet a minimum of $\frac{1}{2}$ in. (13 mm). Any less than this and the opening in the collet will be enlarged (Fig. 25-9). This process is called *bellmouthing*. After a collet becomes damaged, it should be replaced with a new part.

FIGURE 25-9
Bellmouthing occurs when the opening in the collect becomes enlarged.

Using the collet nut wrench and the collet wrench, tighten the collet nut. Reassemble the motor unit and base. With most models the bit can be raised and lowered in the base by turning the motor unit. Once the desired bit height has been set, tighten the depth lock. Be certain that the power switch is in the off position before plugging in the cord. It is also a good idea to make a trail cut on a scrap board before routing the finished stock.

SETTING UP THE ROUTER

Operating the portable router is relatively easy, but there are a few procedures that must be followed. First, solidly position the base against the stock. Arrange the power cord away from the path of the cutter. Holding the handles with both hands, check that the router bit is completely clear of the stock before turning on the power.

Turn on the power and move the router into the stock. Once the pilot or router guide reaches the material, immediately start moving it along the edge. If you are shaping the outside edge, move the router from left to right (Fig. 25-10). For inside edges move the machine from right to left. Always

FIGURE 25-10
Proper feed directions for routing the outside and inside edges of stock.

keep the router bit moving. Allowing the router to stop will cause the cutter to overhead and severely burn the stock.

Use a consistent moderate feed speed. Too slow a feed speed and the bit and stock will burn. Too fast a feed speed and a rough cut will be produced.

If a large amount of material is to be removed, make the cut with several light passes. You can determine when the appropriate depth of cut and feed speed are being used by listening to the motor. If the motor pulls down considerably, reduce the depth of cut. When the sound level is not lowered, increase the feed speed or take a deeper cut.

Once the cut is complete, pull the router bit away from the edge, but the base must remain against the stock. Keep the router resting on the material until the bit has stopped turning. Never rest the router against your body.

ROUTING AN EDGE

As with any routed surface, first decide which method to be utilized to guide the router. In most cases, either a piloted router bit or a commercial fence are selected to shape the edge.

Piloted Router Bits

The most common method of routing an edge is with a router bit that contains a *pilot*. This smooth bearing surface rides along the edge of the stock (Fig. 25-11). It controls the horizontal depth of the bit. Some router bits have changeable pilots which can be unscrewed from the bit. This allows the depth to be varied by using a smaller- or larger-diameter pilot.

FIGURE 25-11
A pilot of a piloted router bit rides on the edge to control the depth of cut.

With all piloted router bits, it is important that the edge be smooth and true. Any irregularities in the stock will be transferred to the routed shape. A ball-bearing pilot is less likely to burn the stock than a solid pilot.

Commercial Straight Guide

For router bits without pilot, a commercial straight guide can be used (Fig. 25-12). It contains two rods which are attached to the base of the router. The guide can be moved in and out on the rods to adjust the horizontal depth of cut. A wooden fence can be added to the front of the guide. This will increase the contact area with the stock and make it easier to guide the router.

FIGURE 25-12
A commercial straight guide contains an adjustable fence to control the router.

ROUTING A CIRCULAR EDGE

Outside curves and circular disks can be shaped easily using a router. Piloted router bits are most frequently used for routing the edges. Utilize the same procedure with the piloted bits as given in the preceding section. For router bits not containing a pilot, a modified commercial guide can be used (Fig. 25-13). It is referred to as the *commercial circular guide*. In addition, large-diameter circular grooves can be made using a *pivot point* attached to the commercial guide (Fig. 25-14).

FIGURE 25-13
The commercial circular guide controls the router when routing a circular shape.

FIGURE 25-14
Attaching a pivot point to a commercial guide allows routing a circular groove.

Commercial Circular Guide

After the circular guide has been installed, adjust the guide the desired distance from the router bit. If the edge is to be shaped, adjust the guide so that the bit is on the outside of the stock. For interior circular grooves, the guide can be set farther from the bit. Be careful to keep the vee-shaped guide against the stock (Fig. 25-13).

Pivot Point

When several circular grooves are required, install a pivot point on the commercial guide. The guide can then be moved in or out to adjust the diameter of the groove (Fig. 25-14).

ROUTING DADOS AND RABBETS

The router produces splinter-free smooth bottom dados and rabbets. In certain cases, it is one of the few ways to dado hardwood plywood smoothly and cut arc-shaped grooves. Dados and rabbets can be routed with either a commercial guide or a wooden fence. For further information on the commercial guide, refer to the section "Routing an Edge."

Wooden Fence

The wooden fence provides a surface against which the router can be guided (Fig. 25-4). The distance the fence is from the dado layout line should be equal to the space between the outside edge of the router base and the cutting circle of the bit. Clamp the fence to the stock.

When several dados of the same width are to be cut, make a custom fence that can be used repeatedly. Glue to the bottom of a wooden fence a piece of high-pressure plastic laminate. Install the same

FIGURE 25-15
The plastic laminate on the custom wooden fence will automatically gauge the location of the fence.

FIGURE 25-16
A secondary fence will keep the router from drifting away from the fence.

router bit as is to be used to make the dado. Carefully guide the router along the fence, trimming the laminate to width. To make a dado, align the edge of the laminate along the layout line for the dado (Fig. 25-15). The plastic laminate will automatically gauge the location of the fence. Any time a different-diameter bit is required, a new fence will need to be made.

To make certain that the router will not move away from the fence, use a secondary fence. A track is formed in which the router base just fits (Fig. 25-16). The double fence can be reused for other dados and rabbets.

ROUTING RABBETS

A rabbet can be routed with either a piloted rabbeting bit or with a straight bit and a commercial straight guide. Rabbeting bits will make either a $\frac{1}{4}$- or $\frac{3}{8}$-in. (6- or 10-mm)-wide rabbet. To make other sizes or rabbets, install a straight router bit larger in diameter than the width of the rabbet. Use a commercial straight guide to guide the router. A wooden fence attached to the guide will make it easier to keep the guide against the edge of the board.

ROUTING A MORTISE

Mortises can be accurately cut using a router. A spiral flute straight bit should first be installed. Use a bit that is one-fourth to one-third the thickness of the stock. Either $\frac{1}{4}$- or $\frac{3}{8}$-in. (6- to 10-mm)-diameter bits can be selected for $\frac{3}{4}$-in. (19-mm)-thick material. If a $\frac{1}{4}$-in. (6-mm)-wide mortise is required, however, make several shallow passes to achieve the desired depth. A $\frac{1}{4}$-inch bit breaks easily and should not be forced to make a deep cut. To guide the router a commercial straight guide can be utilized. Layout each mortise on the edge and best face of the stock. In addition, place an "X" on the best-face side of the boards.

Commercial Straight Guide

When the commercial guide is to be used to clamp to the faces of the stock two thick boards (Fig. 25-17). This will increase the width of the material on which to run the router

Attach a long board to the fence of the guide for better control of the router. Always run the fence along the face that contains the "X" mark. Use the same procedure to route the mortises as described in the section "Routing an Edge."

FIGURE 25-17
Routing a mortise using a commercial straight guide. Note the extra boards clamp to the sides of the stock.

ROUTING HALF-BLIND DOVETAILS

Half-blind dovetails are frequently utilized in high-quality drawer construction. Wedge-shaped tenons are cut to fit into socket shaped mortises.

Industry uses a machine called a dovetailer to shape the dovetails (Fig. 25-18). It contains many dovetail bits and produces all the tenons and mortises with one pass of the machine. Schools and small shops usually cut dovetails with a portable router, dovetail router bit, and a dovetail fixture.

To produce dovetails with a router first square all material to finish dimensions. In addition, make two more pieces from scrap material which will be the exact same thickness as the finished stock. Next, attach the template collar to the router base and install the dovetail bit. It is very important that the depth of cut for the bit be adjusted exactly $\frac{19}{32}$ inch (15 mm). Because it is difficult to measure the amount the bit extends below the base use a dovetail depth gauge (Fig. 25-19). The set screw of the gauge should just touch the end of the dovetail bit.

Clamp the dovetail fixture in a bench vise. Slip the scrap drawer side under the front bar of the fixture and let it extend beyond the top surface of the fixture by approximately $\frac{1}{2}$ inch (13 mm). Next slide the scrap drawer front under the top rail. Position the board against the front drawer side and against the indexing pin (Fig. 25-20). Tighten the top bar knobs. Loosen the front bar knobs and reposition the drawer side. Use a straight edge to flush the top end of the front piece with the face of the top piece (Fig. 25-21). The drawer side should be pushed against the front indexing pin and then tighten the knobs. Finish the set-up by placing the dovetail template over the two pieces of wood. Push the template tight against the top of the stock and tighten the template knobs.

Place the base of the router solidly on top of the template. Carefully check that the router bit will not cut into fixture base. Do not for any reason raise the router up off the template. This will cause the rotating router bit to cut through the template. Turn on the power and slowly trace around the fingers of the template (Fig. 25-22).

After the cut has been completed, turn off the power and allow the router to remain on the template until the bit has stopped turning. Remove the router and the boards from the fixture.

Check the fit of the two pieces. If the tenons do not fully engage the mortises, adjustments must be made. When there is too much play between the tenons and mortises, lower the dovetail bit $\frac{1}{64}$ in. (0.5 mm). When the mortise and tenons fit but the drawer side is not flush with the end of the drawer front, change the position of the template nuts located on the front of the template. Turn the nuts clockwise when the side extends too far into the front. Turn them counterclockwise when the side extends beyond the drawer fronts. Continue to make trial cuts until the joint fits perfectly. Make only one adjustment with each cut.

FIGURE 25-18
A dovetailer contains many dovetail bits.

FIGURE 25-19
Adjusting the depth of cut using a dovetail depth gauge.

FIGURE 25-20
Locating the drawer front in a dovetail fixture.

FIGURE 25-21
Locating the drawer side in a dovetail fixture.

FIGURE 25-22
By tracing around the dovetail template the dovetails are produced.

After the settings have been made, make the dovetail joints. Cut the right front and left rear on the left side of the fixture. Make the left front and right rear on the right side. The inside surfaces of the drawer front and drawer side must always be facing out.

Rabbeted Drawer Fronts

Because of the $\frac{3}{8}$- × $\frac{3}{8}$-in. (10- × 10 mm) rabbet on a rabbeted-style drawer, a different procedure is necessary (Fig. 25-23). A *positioning block* is required to locate the drawer front. Without a positioning block the lip of the rabbet prevents the inner part of the drawer from being dovetailed. To make a positioning block select a $\frac{3}{4}$-in. (19-mm)-thick scrap the same width as the drawer front. Approximately $\frac{1}{2}$ in. (13 mm) from the end of the block, cut a $\frac{1}{2}$ × $\frac{1}{2}$ in. (13 × 13 mm) dado.

After the drawer front has been rabbeted, slide

FIGURE 25-23
A rabbeted door front and positioning block.

FIGURE 25-24
Positioning the rabbeted drawer front in a dovetail fixture.

it under the top bar of the dovetail fixture. The outside face of the drawer must be against the fixture. Place the positioning block under the front bar and slide the rabbet of the drawer front into the dado of the positioning block (Fig. 25-24). Tighten the front bar knobs. Push the drawer front against the indexing pin and tighten the top bar knobs. After removing the positioning block and installing the dovetail template, route the dovetails.

To dovetail the mating drawer side, use a squared spacer of the same thickness as the drawer front. Place the spacer on top of the fixture and clamp the side on the front of the fixture. The end of the drawer side must be flush with the face of the spacer. Use the procedure to cut the dovetails recommended in the preceding section.

ROUTING A DESIGN OR RECESS

A decorative design or recess can be routed using a template and template collar. A template can be made from $\frac{1}{4}$-in. (6-mm) hardboard. Make the opening in the template the same size as the design plus twice the space between the cutting circle of the bit and the outside edge of the collar (Fig. 25-25). The template can either be held in place with small brads or by constructing a frame into which the stock can fit.

Once the template has been constructed, the routing can begin. Start the cut by positioning the template collar in the corner of the template. Ideally, use a plunge router to lower the bit into the stock. If a plunge router is not available, pivot the router bit into the stock. Keep the collar against the edge of the template or the desired pattern will not be produced (Fig. 25-26). For recesses, route around the perimeter of the template. Remove the interior area by making multiple passes.

FIGURE 25-25
Make the opening in the template the size of the design plus twice the space between the bit and the collar.

ROUTING INLAYS

Veneer inlays add a great deal to the appearance of projects. Commercial inlays come in a wide variety of colors and patterns (Fig. 25-27). They are made

FIGURE 25-26
Routing a design with a template.

FIGURE 25-27
Inlays are available in many colors and patterns.

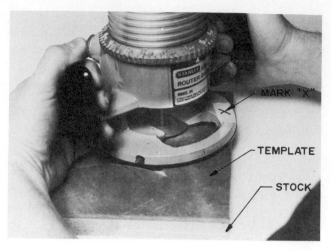

FIGURE 25-28
Routing an inlay to size using a template. Note the "X" on the base.

from pieces of veneer or dyed wood and are glued to a piece of paper to form a picture.

Once the inlay has been selected, lay out the desired outer circle, ellipse, or rectangle for the inlay on a piece of ¼-in. (6-mm) hardboard. This will serve as a template. Cut the template accurately and file the edges smooth.

With a few pieces of double-faced carpet tape, secure the inlay to a scrap piece of plywood. Center the opening in the template over the inlay and clamp it to the plywood. Using a template collar, trace carefully around the edge of the template (Fig. 25-28). To make the most accurate cut, place an "X" on the edge of the router base. As the router traces the template, always keep this "X" mark to the outside of the plywood. A plunge router with an ⅛-in. (3-mm) straight bit will work best to lower the bit easily into the inlay. The depth of cut should be set with the router bit just below the inlay.

Remove the template and carefully slip a putty knife under the inlay to remove it from the plywood. Clamp the template on the finish-sanded stock and place the guide bushing on the template collar (Fig. 25-29). This guide bushing will automatically provide the proper spacing for the recess for the inlay. Set the depth of cut to be slightly less than the thickness of the veneer. Route all the material within the template opening. As with the first cut, keep the "X" on the router base to the outside of the work. Make certain that the bottom of the router area is smooth.

Remove the template and apply a thin coat of adhesive in the recess for the inlay. Glue the inlay in place with the paper side of the veneer facing up. After the adhesive has dried, carefully sand the face of the veneer even with the face of the stock.

FIGURE 25-29
Mounting the guide bushing on the template collar.

ROUTING A DESIGN OR SIGNS

Because there are many decorative router bits, a broad variety of designs and signs can be produced. Either a duplicator or freehand techniques can be used to shape the desired pattern.

Duplicator

A commercial duplicator attachment has many stencils with cutouts of the alphabet and numbers. Custom stencils containing unique letter styles or patterns can be made out of hardboard. These stencils serve as a template that is clamped to the stylus table. After the stock is clamped to the machining table, a stylus is used to trace around the stencils. The letters, numbers, or patterns are then transferred to the board by the rotating bit (Fig. 25-30).

FIGURE 25-30
Using a duplicator to produce a sign.

Freehand Techniques

The freehand technique requires first that the design be drawn on the stock. A router bit is installed and the depth adjusted. To keep the router from following the grain of the board, set the depth of cut to less than $\frac{1}{4}$ inch (6 mm). Start in the center of the pattern and route to the outside edge. It is best to introduce the bit into the stock at a corner of the design. If words are to be routed, start at beginning of the word and trace each letter (Fig. 25-31). Practice will be required to make smooth, even designs.

ROUTING A TAPER

Occasionally, a tapered shape is required such as for the recessed area in the bottom of a gun cabinet for the butts of the gun stocks. A template collar and

FIGURE 25-31
Routing a sign using freehand techniques.

template are required as described in the section "Routing a Design or Recess." In addition, a rabbeted stop strip is attached to one side of the template to index the fixture on the stock (Fig. 25-32). The stop strip also elevates one side of the template. As the router is moved down the slope of the fixture, a recessed shape will be created.

To use the template, align the centerline drawn on the template with the centerline on the stock. Use two handscrews to secure the fixture to the stock. Using a spiral straight router bit, remove the material around the edge of the opening in the template. Make multiple passes to remove the rest of the material.

FIGURE 25-32
A slanted template will produce a routed taper.

PANEL ROUTERS

Although there are many accessories for the portable router, few are as important as the panel router. It is utilized primarily for making high-quality dados and other grooves. A high-horsepower portable router motor unit is attached to the movable car-

FIGURE 25-33
Making a dado on a panel router. (Courtesy of Her-Saf Products.)

riage. After the stock has been clamped to the incline table, the router is pulled down along the stock (Fig. 25-33). A straight groove will be produced.

By constructing a diagonal fixture, wooden grills can also be produced. The fixture holds the stock on an angle (Fig. 25-34). By making regularly spaced decorative grooves on both sides of the panel, the bit will cut through the stock wherever the grooves intersect. This creates an interesting geometric pattern.

FIGURE 25-34
A diagonal fixture produces a wooden grill on the panel router.

ROUTER TABLES

The router table holds the router in a stationary vertical position. Stock can then be fed past the bit much like a shaper. The table can be either shop built or commercial in style (Fig. 25-35). Both require the router to be bolted to the underside of the table. Cover the shop-built router table with high-pressure plastic laminate to provide a smooth, durable surface on which to guide the stock (Fig. 25-36). A tall fence should be constructed to support the stock.

FIGURE 25-35
Commercial router table. (Courtesy of Porter-Cable Corporation.)

After the bit has been installed, clamp the fence at the desired position on top of the table. Use featherboards and a push shoe to hold the stock against the table and fence (Fig. 25-37).

For stopped grooves or cuts that do not extend from end to end, make a layout mark at the beginning and ending of the cut. Draw an "X" on the best face of the board.

Place a pencil mark on the table at the beginning and ending of the cutting circle. Align the first layout on the stock with the far pencil mark on the table. Clamp a stop block against the leading end of the stock. Finish the setup by adjusting the bit to the proper height.

Turn on the router and place the stock against the first stop block (Fig. 25-38). The "X" mark should be facing out away from the table. Slowly lower the board onto the rotating cutter. After the face is against the table, feed the board forward. Once the leading end has reached the second stop block, pivot the stock off the bit. Run all identical pieces before removing the setup.

FIGURE 25-36
Shop-built router table.

FIGURE 25-37
Routing a through groove on a router table.

FIGURE 25-38
Routing a stopped groove with two stop blocks.

ROUTING RAISED PANEL DOORS

One of the newest router techniques is making raised panel doors. Refer to the section "Stuck Joinery" in Chapter 36 for details on how a shaper is used to make this style of doors. Many of the same concepts can be used with the router. With the availability of the specialized panel raiser, stile bit and cope bit doors can easily be constructed using the portable router (Fig. 25-39). These bits have $\frac{1}{2}$-in. (13-mm) shanks and usually are carbide tipped and contain ball-bearing pilots.

To make raised panel doors safely, you will need to use a $2\frac{1}{2}$-hp or larger router mounted to a router table. In addition, the router should have several rotational speeds available. Run the large bits on the slowest speed. Although the bits contain pilots, you will also need to install a fence on the router table. This fence will not only aid in guiding the stock, but also guard the cutter. Use a push stick and featherboards with each operation.

FIGURE 25-39
Router bits for making raised panel doors. (Courtesy of Freud Inc.)

To make a raised panel door, work the stock to finish size. Check that the edges are jointed and the pieces are cut to accurate length. No single part should be narrower than 2 in. (51 mm) or shorter than 10 in. (254 mm). It may be necessary to combine individual parts into one wide, long piece. For example, if two 1¾-in. (44-mm)-wide rails are required, combine them into one 3¾-in. (95-mm)-wide board. Once routed, the stock can then be cut to finish size.

Mount the cope bit on the router first. Using the router table fence and a miter gauge, cope the two ends of each rail (Fig. 25-40). A backup board held against the trailing edge of the stock will greatly minimize grain tearout.

Next use the stile bit to route the inside edge of all pieces (Fig. 25-41). Check that the tongue of the coped end matches the groove in the edge. Once the stiles and rails are assembled, the faces of jointing pieces must be even.

The raised panel is produced with the panel raiser. Set the depth of the router bit so that the face of the raised panel is even with the faces of the stiles and rails. On dense woods or lower-horsepower routers, set the depth to one-half this amount. Route the ends first and then the edges (Fig. 25-42). The tongue of the raised panel should easily slide into the grooves of the stiles and rails.

FIGURE 25-41
Routing the inside edge of the stiles and rails.

FIGURE 25-40
Coping the ends of the rails using a miter gauge.

FIGURE 25-42
Producing the raised panel.

STUDY QUESTIONS

Answer each of the following questions. If you are not sure of an answer, review the chapter.

25-1. Move the router in a _____ direction when routing an outside edge.

25-2. Your hands should come no closer than _____ in. (_____ mm) to the router bit.

25-3. The _____ is tapered split sleeve that secures the router bit in the motor shaft.

25-4. A laminate trimmer is used to trim _____.

25-5. A _____ allows the depth of cut to be locked at a specific level or for the rotating bit to be lowered into the stock.

25-6. Why is a ½-in. diameter shank size recommended?

25-7. A _____ can be used to control the horizontal depth of cut on a router bit.

25-8. A _____ router bit makes a 45° chamfer on a corner.

25-9. A straight bit with two cutting edges is called a _____.

25-10. Insert the router bit a minimum of _____ in. (_____ mm) into the collet of the router.

25-11. If you allow the router bit to stop while in contact with the stock, it will _____ the wood.

25-12. When utilizing a piloted router bit, it is important that the edges be _____ and _____ before any routing takes place.

25-13. A wooden _____ added to a commercial straight guide will make the router easier to guide.

25-14. The distance the wooden fence is from the dado layout line is equal to the space between the outside edge of the router _____ and the cutting _____ of the bit.

25-15. Industry often uses what machine to shape dovetails?

25-16. The dovetail router bit should be set at exactly _____ in. (_____ mm) depth of cut.

25-17. To dovetail rabbet drawer fronts, a _____ is required to position the front in the dovetail fixture.

25-18. When routing a design, make the opening in the template the same size as the design plus the space between the cutting circle of the bit and the outside edge of the collar.

25-19. To route inlays, the depth of cut should be set with the router bit just _____ the thickness of the inlay.

25-20. A commercial _____ can be utilized to route sighs.

25-21. When using a router table, install _____ on the tall fence and use a _____ to hold the stock against the table and fence.

25-22. To make raised panel doors, it is necessary to use a _____ raiser, _____ bit, and _____ bit.

IMPORTANT TECHNICAL TERMS

Following are technical terms that you should be able to use as part of your working vocabulary. Write a brief description of the meaning of each term.

Collet
Depth lock
Laminate trimmer
Shank
Cutting edge
Pilot
Rounding over bits
Beading bits
Cove bits
Core box bits
Chamfer bit
V-grooving
V-groover and scorer bit
Roman ogee

Straight bits
Single flute
Double flute
Rabbeting bits
Plunge bits
Flush trim bits
Slotting bits
Dovetail bits
Bellmouthing
Piloted router bits
Commercial straight guide
Commercial circular guide
Pivot point
Wooden fence
Rabbetted drawer fronts
Positioning block
Duplicator
Freehand techniques

26

PORTABLE SANDERS

Most furniture, cabinets, and other wood products are sanded with portable sanders. These machines can easily be moved over the surface of a project and will rapidly remove any millmarks.

There are two major types of portable sanders. They include the portable belt sander and the portable pad sander. Both electric and pneumatic models are available. The *portable belt sander* is used primarily for sanding major millmarks and removing large amounts of material (Fig. 26-1). Woodworkers use the *portable pad sander* for finish sanding and sanding minor millmarks (Fig. 26-7).

PORTABLE BELT SANDERS

Portable belt sanders can be utilized to sand face-frames, flat panels, and other solid lumber parts. This sander can have either narrow or wide belts for sanding minor millmarks (Fig. 26-7).

Parts of the Belt Sander

The major parts of the belt sander are the motor, handles, pullies, and platen (Fig. 26-1). The *motor* provides power to turn the sanding belt. In the front and to the rear of the motor are the handles. The

FIGURE 26-1
Major parts of the portable belt sander. (Courtesy of Porter-Cable Corporation.)

rear handle contains the *on-off* switch. Pulling in on the switch turns on the sander. The *front handle* is used to control the movement of the machine.

The belt is suspended between the power pulley and the front pulley. The belt is turned with the *power pulley* and is kept stretched tight with the pressure applied from the *front pulley*. To pull the front pulley back, use the *tension-release lever*. This will enable you to replace the belt. Between the two pullies is the *platen*. It provides a flat surface that the belt can run against.

FIGURE 26-3
Refer to the inside of the belt for the belt size, grit size, type of abrasive, and direction of rotation.

The *tracking knob* keeps the belt centered on the platen. By turning the knob, the belt can be moved from side to side.

Purchasing a Belt Sander

When purchasing a portable belt sander, the first consideration is the size. The size of the sander is determined by the length and width of the sanding belt. Sizes can range from 3 × 21 to 4 × 24 in. (76 × 533 to 102 × 610 mm). The larger the belt, the faster the belt will sand. Larger belts, however, cost more and require more strength to control.

A feature to consider when buying a sander is the dust bag attachment (Fig. 26-2). This accessory picks up any surplus sanding dust that is produced.

FIGURE 26-2
A dust bag attachment minimizes the sanding dust. (Courtesy of Porter-Cable Corporation.)

The dust bag is desirable when sanding large surfaces. It may, however, interfere with sanding small areas or inside projects.

Selecting the Sanding Belts

It is recommended that you have a wide selection of sanding belts from which to select. Be certain that the size of the belts fits the sander. You will be able to find this along with other information printed on the inside of the belt (Fig. 26-3). Aluminum oxide is

TABLE 26-1
Abrasives for Portable Belt Sanders

Application	Grit size	Abrasive
Removing paint, varnishes	60	Aluminum oxide
Rough glued-up panels, face frames, general rough sanding	80–100	Aluminum oxide
Removing minor defects, sanding planer marks, general smooth sanding	120	Aluminum oxide

generally used as the abrasive because of its ability to withstand the heat generated during sanding. Refer to Table 26-1 for specific grit sizes for each of your sanding operations.

Installing the Sanding Belt

To install the sanding belt, unplug the power cord. Pull back on the tension-release lever or with some models, manually push in on the front pulley. Remove the old belt and replace it with a new one. Be certain that the belt will rotate in the same direction as the printed arrow indicates on the back of the belt (Fig. 26-3).

After centering the belt on the platen, release the front pulley. Turn the sander over and hold it with the belt on top. Quickly turn the power on and off. The belt should remain centered on the platen. If it does not, turn the *tracking knob* a small amount (Fig. 26-4). Keep turning on the power and moving the tracking knob until the sanding belt stays centered.

FIGURE 26-4
Tracking a sanding belt by turning the tracking knob.

Operating the Belt Sander

A great deal of damage can be done with the belt sander if it is not properly operated. Applying uneven pressure or using improper feeding techniques will cause the sander to dig rapidly into the wood. These sanding marks are very difficult to remove and will become apparent when the finish is applied.

To use the sander, select the proper grit size for your sanding job. Refer to Table 26-1 for the recommended grit size. Course belts will sand faster but will leave deep scratches. Finer grit belts will produce smaller scratches but may burnish the wood.

Clamp the stock securely to the benchtop. Because the sander is difficult to control, do not attempt to sand a vertical surface. Lay the piece flat on the workbench or sawhorses for best results. Position the sander flat on the stock and arrange the cord away from the path of the machine. Grip the handles firmly and turn on the sander. Start moving the sander immediately and use a sanding pattern as shown in Fig. 26-5. The strokes of the sander should be short, straight, and slightly overlapped. Always keep the sander moving with the grain and

FIGURE 26-5
Recommended pattern for guiding the belt sander.

STRAIGHT, OVERLAPPING, STROKES

DIRECTION OF GRAIN

do not concentrate in one spot. This will produce a noticeable low area.

If the surface is large, divide the face into 24-in. (610-mm) squares. Sand each of these sections before moving onto the next. Because the sander cuts rapidly, be careful when sanding plywood and other veneered products. It is very easy to sand through the face and completely remove the face veneer.

Sanding Small Pieces

A portable belt sander can be clamped in a bench vise (Fig. 26-6). This allows small and irregular-shaped pieces to be sanded that are difficult to sand using conventional techniques. Cut wooden blocks to fit around the housing of the sander to prevent it from moving. Be careful not to get your hands close to the sanding belt.

CUSTOM MADE WOOD BLOCKS

FIGURE 26-6
Sanding small pieces by holding the sander in a bench vise.

MOTOR   REAR HANDLE

FRONT HANDLE

PAPER CLIPS   SANDING PAD

FIGURE 26-7
Major parts of the portable pad sander. (Courtesy of Porter-Cable Corporation.)

PORTABLE PAD SANDERS

Portable pad sanders come in a variety of styles and sizes (Fig. 26-7). They are utilized primarily to finish sand projects before the finish is applied. Because of this some woodworkers call these machines *finish sanders*.

There are three different styles of pad sanders: vibrating, orbital, and straight-line (Fig. 26-8). The *vibrating sander* is the least expensive of the sanders, but places scratches across the grain. An *orbital sander* is the most popular and has the fastest sanding action. It does, however, produce small elliptical sanding scratches. The *straight-line sander* moves back and forth only, producing straight scratches. Although it is the slowest cutting of all sanders, it does produce the superior results of hand sanding.

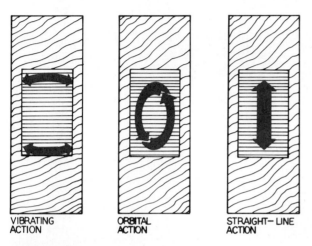

VIBRATING ACTION   ORBITAL ACTION   STRAIGHT–LINE ACTION

FIGURE 26-8
Pad sanders are either a vibrating, orbital, or straight-line style.

Parts of the Pad Sander

The major parts of a pad sander are the handles, motor, and sanding pad (Fig. 26-7). To use the sander, the *handles* are gripped by the operator. Some compact machines have the handle built into the motor housing (Fig. 26-9). This allows them to be used in small enclosed areas.

The *motor* frequently makes up the majority of the sander. It provides power to the sanding pad. Located under the motor is the *sanding pad*. It is generally covered with a soft rubber or felt. On each end of the pad are the *abrasive paper clips*. They are spring loaded and used to hold the abrasive paper on the pad.

Purchasing a Pad Sander

The major considerations when purchasing a pad sander are the sanding action of the pad and the size of the sander. As discussed earlier in this section, sanders are manufactured as either vibrating, orbital, or straight-line (Fig. 26-8). Each has its ad-

FIGURE 26-9
Small sanders can be utilized to sand inside projects.

vantages. Select the one that is the most important to your woodworking.

The size of the pad sander is determined by the width and length of the pad. The most common sizes use either one-fourth, one-third, or one-half a sheet of abrasive paper. Select a large pad for sanding big surfaces. A smaller pad is desirable for sanding inside projects or vertical surfaces.

Another consideration when purchasing a sander is the number of strokes or *oscillations per minute*. They will range from 10,000 to over 20,000 oscillations per minute. The more strokes per minute, the faster the wood will be sanded.

Pad sanders are either powered by electricity or compressed air. The *electric* sanders operate on 110-V power. This is readily available and generally the most common form of power. A *pneumatic sander* runs with 60 to 76 lb of air pressure. These sanders are lighter in weight and do not overheat (Fig. 26-10). Although pneumatic sanders are more expensive, they generally last longer. Industry frequently utilizes this type of sander.

FIGURE 26-10
Pneumatic sanders are compact in size and run on compressed air.

Operating the Pad Sander

For most sanding operations, start with 100-grit abrasive paper. Follow this with 120- and then 150-grit paper. Do not skip a grit number or sanding scratches will remain in the wood. Most projects that are to receive a transparent finish can be finish sanded with 180-grit paper.

To sand a surface with a pad sander, place the stock on a workbench. If the piece will be exposed on both faces, lay the board on a blanket or another protective pad. Place the sander flat on surface and move the machine over the entire area. A vibrating and orbital sander can be moved in any direction. The straight-line sander must be moved only with the grain.

Allow the weight of the sander to do the sanding. Pressing down on the machine will produce a low spot and rapidly wear out the sander. If you concentrate the sanding on a dent or other defect, a noticeable low spot will also be sanded. Be certain to cover the entire surface equally.

STUDY QUESTIONS

Answer each of the following questions. If you are not sure of an answer, review the chapter.

26-1. The two major types of portable sanders are _____ and _____.

26-2. The sanding belt is turned with the _____ pulley.

26-3. To keep the sanding belt centered on the platen, turn the _____ knob.

26-4. The size of a belt sander is determined by the _____ and _____ of the sanding belt.

26-5. The most common abrasive used on sanding belts is _____ _____.

26-6. Applying _____ pressure will cause the sander to dig rapidly into the wood.

26-7. Always keep the sander moving with the _____ to prevent cross scratches.

26-8. The primary purpose of a portable pad sander is to _____ sand projects before the finish is applied.

26-9. The three different styles of portable pad sanders are _____, _____, and _____.

26-10. Abrasive _____ at each end of the sanding pad hold on the abrasive paper.

26-11. The size of the pad sander is determined by the _____ and _____ of the pad.

26-12. Pressing down on a pad sander will produce _____ spots and rapidly wear out the sander.

IMPORTANT TECHNICAL TERMS

Following are technical terms that you should be able to use as part of your working vocabulary. Write a brief description of the meaning of each term.

Portable belt sander
Portable pad sander
Front handle
Power pulley
Front pulley
Tension-release lever

Platen
Tracking knob
Finish sanders
Vibrating sander
Orbital sander
Straight-line sander
Sanding pad
Abrasive sanding clips
Oscillations per minute
Electric sanders
Pneumatic sanders

27

LEMON SPLINERS

One of the newest forms of joinery requires the use of a lemon spliner (Fig. 27-1). This machine uses a sawblade type cutter to cut a short, circular kerf. In this groove is placed an elliptical spline which is used to reinforce miters, butt joints, and other assemblies (Fig. 27-2). Entire cabinets and pieces of furniture can be put together with this machine. It can take the place of dowels, mortise and tenons, and dados.

The lemon spliner is considered to be a very fast and accurate machine. It has the advantage over other forms of jointery because the parts can slide into alignment. The adjustment is made by cutting the kerfs slightly longer and deeper than the spline. This extra space allows the pieces to slide up to $\frac{1}{8}$ in. (3 mm).

PARTS OF THE LEMON SPLINER

The major parts of the lemon spliner are the motor, handle, and base (Fig. 27-1). The high-speed *motor* provides power to the 4-in. (102-mm)-diameter carbide-tipped cutter. Located below the motor is the *sliding base*. It allows the cutter to be moved into the stock. On the front of the base is the *indexing mark*. This mark indicates the center of the cutter. When

FIGURE 27-1
Major parts of the lemon spliner. (Courtesy of Colonial Saw.)

not being plunged into the work, the base is spring loaded and held in the forward position to keep from exposing the cutter. Attached to the base is the *adjustable fence*. It is tilted to the desired angle to establish the angle at which the cutter enters the stock. Located to the side of the base is the *depth control*. The depth control has three settings, one for

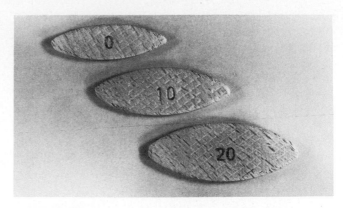

FIGURE 27-3
There are three sizes of compressed beech splines.

FIGURE 27-2
The lemon spline is inserted into the kerfs to reinforce the joint.

each size of splines. The *handle* is utilized to locate and control the spliner.

SPLINES

The splines, biscuits, or plates as they are sometimes called are made from die-cut compressed beech. The grain runs diagonally to the length of the spline. Once glue comes in contact with this compressed beech, it swells and locks it in the small circular kerf. This action occurs rapidly, so you must be ready to assemble your project quickly.

There are three sizes of splines from which to select (Fig. 27-3). They are numbered from smallest to largest: 1, 10, and 20. All of the plates are of the same thickness, but do vary in width and length. The dimensions of number 0 splines are $\frac{5}{8}$ in. wide by $1\frac{3}{4}$ in. long. A number 10 spline is $\frac{3}{4}$ in. wide by $2\frac{1}{8}$ in. long. Number 20 splines are 1 in. wide and $2\frac{1}{2}$ inches long. Use as large a spline as the stock will allow without the kerf breaking through the opposite side. Turn the depth stop to the same number as the number of the spline. If you are using a number 20 spline, for example, set the depth stop to 20.

The proper spacing between the splines depends on the application. In most cases the closer the

splines, the stronger the joint. As a general rule, however, place 5 in. (127 mm) between the centerlines of each spline.

SPLINING AN EDGE-TO-EDGE JOINT

To operate the lemon spliner, first cut the stock to exact size. Be certain that the cuts are made square and true. Any gaps between the mating pieces will be obvious when the parts are assembled.

Next dry assemble the parts and mark the center of each spline on the face of each piece (Fig. 27-2). In most applications, 5-in. (127-mm) centers provide adequate reinforcement. The layout line should extend onto each mating piece.

Place the stock flat against a true surface. A large piece of plywood or particleboard can be used for a work surface. Position the fence against the stock and center the cutter index mark on the first layout line (Fig. 27-4). Turn on the motor and

FIGURE 27-4
Cutting a groove by aligning the index mark on the layout mark.

plunge the cutter into stock. Continue pushing the motor forward until the motor has reached the end of the travel for the base. Allow the motor to return to its original position. Continue cutting all the kerfs by following the same procedure. One-half of the elliptical groove is cut in each mating part.

After all the kerfs have been cut, apply glue in each of the kerfs. A special designed glue bottle will spread an even coat of adhesive along the length of the kerf (Fig. 27-5). Since the compressed splines expand rapidly, you must work fast. Slide a spline into one side of each joint and utilize standard assembly techniques. Because the compressed beech in the spline expands rapidly, however, it is only necessary to apply clamp pressure for 10 minutes.

FIGURE 27-5
The special glue bottle will apply the adhesive evenly in the kerfs.

SPLINING A BUTT JOINT

Installing splines in a butt joint requires the pieces to be cut to exact size. Align the parts in their final position. Draw a line along one edge to lay out the position of the parts (Fig. 27-6). After determining the size of the splines, mark the desired centers of each spline. Either measure each center or use a template to locate the position of the splines (Fig. 27-7).

To make the kerfs for the splines, place the second piece along the layout line to serve as a guide for the lemon spliner (Fig. 27-8). Be careful that this guide board does not move or the kerfs will not be cut correctly. Cut each of the kerfs by placing the base of the spliner against the stock (Fig. 27-8). Next, position the fence in the 180° setting and cut the kerfs in the second piece (Fig. 27-9). The fence is kept flat against the face of the board. After all the kerfs have been made, the parts can be assembled.

FIGURE 27-6
Laying out the position of the partition for a butt joint.

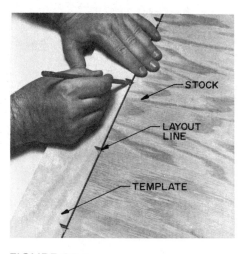

FIGURE 27-7
Drawing the centerlines for the splines.

SPLINING MITERS

The lemon spliner is an excellent machine for reinforcing miters. To make the grooves for the lemon splines, cut the miters to the desired angle. Select the largest spline size that will not break through the outside surface. If the contact area between the

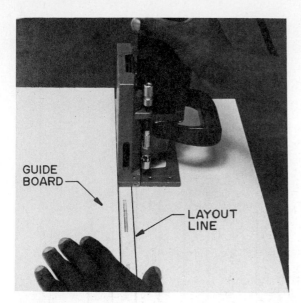

FIGURE 27-8
Splining the face of a board using the second piece as a guide.

FIGURE 27-9
Splining the end of a board with the fence in a 180° setting. (Courtesy of Colonial Saw.)

adjoining boards is large, use two or more splines. Thick material can be reinforced by stacking splines on top of one another (Fig. 27-10).

If a bevel has been cut along one edge, the adjustable fence needs to be set to the correct angle (Fig. 27-11). Adjust the fence to position the cutter 90° to the beveled surface. Place the fence against the stock. Make certain that the fence is kept tight against the face of the stock before turning on the machine. Cut all kerfs and assemble the miters.

FIGURE 27-10
Use two splines on thick material for maximum support. (Courtesy of Colonial Saw.)

FIGURE 27-11
Splining a miter by adjusting the fence. (Courtesy of Colonial Saw.)

STUDY QUESTIONS

Answer each of the following questions. If you are not sure of an answer, review the chapter.

27-1. Use _____ hands to hold the spliner securely.

27-2. The lemon spliner uses a sawblade to cut a short circular-shaped _____.

27-3. The _____ mark on the sliding base indicates the center of the cutter.

27-4. What is another name for a lemon spline?

27-5. The closer the splines are together, the _____ the joint.

27-6. Dry assemble the parts and mark the _____ of each spline on the face of each piece.

27-7. Because of the compressed _____ in the spline it is only necessary to apply clamp pressure for _____ minutes.

27-8. When splining miters, select the _____ spline size that will not break through the outside surface.

27-9. Thick material can be reinforced by _____ splines on top of one another.

IMPORTANT TECHNICAL TERMS

Following are technical terms that you should be able to use as part of your working vocabulary. Write a brief description of the meaning of each term.

Sliding base
Indexing mark
Adjustable fence
Depth control

PART 4

Stationary Power Tools

28

TABLE SAWS

In the opinion of most woodworkers, the table saw is the most basic and essential stationary power tool (Fig. 28-1). Most shops, both large and small, do have at least one of these machines. It is very versatile and capable of performing a broad variety of cuts. Although it is one of the best machines for ripping boards, the table saw can precisely crosscut, dado and make specialty cuts.

Industry frequently selects a sliding table saw (Fig. 28-2). This model of saw has a moving table that travels with the stock. The cut can be made more easily and with greater accuracy.

PARTS OF THE TABLE SAW

The major parts of the table saw include the table, miter gauge, rip fence, saw guard, and base (Fig. 28-1). Stock is placed against the *table*. It is usually a heavy casting which contains two *miter gauge grooves,* an opening for the saw blade, and the rip *fence guide rails*. Mounted on the table is the miter gauge, rip fence, throat plate, and saw guard. The *miter gauge* is used for crosscutting operations by sliding in one of the miter gauge grooves. The *rip fence* is used for ripping operations and is secured to

the table by locking on the rip fence guide rails. In the middle of the table is the *throat plate*. It is usually made of metal and contains a slot through which the blade extends.

The *saw guard* consists of the blade guard, splitter, and antikickback pawls (Fig. 28-3). The blade guard covers the raised blade and rides on top of the stock. To keep the saw kerf open the splitter is positioned in line with the blade. The antikickback pawls ride on top of the stock and dig into the board if there is a kickback.

Located in the base are the ways and trunnions. The *ways* raise the blade when the *height adjustment handwheel* is turned (Fig. 28-4). To lock the blade at a specific height, tighten the *locking knob*. The *trunnion* tilts the blade when the *tilting handwheel* is turned. A *tilting gauge* on the front of the base indicates the approximate angle at which the blade is tilted. To lock the angle of the blade into position, tighten its *locking knob*.

The treaded shaft located inside the throat plate area is the *saw arbor* (Fig. 28-4). The saw blade is mounted on this arbor along with the stabilizing washer and arbor nut. Arbors range in diameter from $\frac{5}{8}$ to over 1 in. (16 to 25 mm). The arbor size must be included when ordering table saw tooling.

PURCHASING A TABLE SAW

In purchasing a table saw, first consider the size. The size is determined by the largest-diameter saw blade that can safely be mounted on the arbor. Although sizes as large as 18 in. (457 mm) are manufactured, the 10-in. (254-mm) table saw is the most

FIGURE 28-2
A sliding tablesaw has a moving table that travels with the stock.

common. It will use a 10-in. (254-mm) and smaller saw blade. The larger the saw blade, the thicker the board can be cut. A 10-in. (254-mm) saw can typically saw a $3\frac{1}{8}$-in. (79-mm)-thick board in the 90° position.

Since it may be necessary to make heavy cuts, the motor size is also important. Most medium-size cuts can be made with a $1\frac{1}{2}$-hp motor. If thicker material is to be machined or if the saw is to be used on a continuous basis, specify at least a 3-hp or larger motor.

A good-quality saw will also have a slotted miter gauge and micro-adjustment for the rip fence. The *slotted miter gauge* can be pulled beyond the edge of the table without it falling to the floor (Fig. 28-5). This also allows wider material to be crosscut. A *micro-adjustment* knob moves the fence in small amounts. This is particularly important when positioning the fence for a precise cut.

FIGURE 28-1
Major parts to the table saw. (Courtesy of Oliver Machinery Company.)

FIGURE 28-3
The saw guard contains the blade guard, splitter, and antikickback pawls.

A sliding table allows large panels to be easily cut (Fig. 28-2). By placing the stock on the sliding table, the material is carried across the blade. Wide panels can also be cut with a table extension. With the table extensions, the rip fence can be positioned as much as 49 in. (1244 mm) to the right of the blade.

SELECTING THE TABLE SAW TOOLING

There are many different types of tooling which can be selected for use on the table saw. Some of them include saw blades, dado heads, and molding heads. Each of these types of tooling is available in a wide variety of styles.

FIGURE 28-4
The ways raise the blade while the trunnion allows the blade to be angled. (Courtesy of Delta International Machinery Corp.)

FIGURE 28-5
A slotted miter gauge allows wide material to be crosscut without the miter gauge falling to the floor.

Saw blades are made of carbon steel, high-speed steel, or have steel bodies with tungsten carbide tips. The carbon steel blades are the least expensive but dull rapidly. High-speed steel blades are better than carbon steel and stay sharp longer. Carbide-tipped blades, however, have become the most popular style of blade today. This is because they stay sharp at least five times longer and can easily cut abrasive materials such as tempered hardboard, particleboard, and even high-pressure plastic laminates. Because the carbide material is so hard, a diamond grinding wheel is required to sharpen the blade.

Both *carbon and high-speed steel blades* are available in five tooth styles (Fig. 28-6). They are as follows:

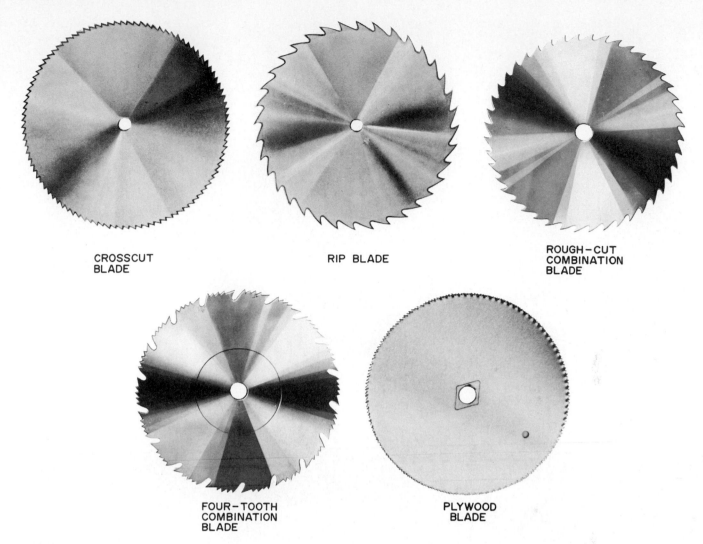

CROSSCUT
BLADE

RIP BLADE

ROUGH–CUT
COMBINATION
BLADE

FOUR–TOOTH
COMBINATION
BLADE

PLYWOOD
BLADE

FIGURE 28-6
Common carbon and high-speed steel blades. (Courtesy of Delta International
Machinery Corp.)

Crosscut blades have the smallest teeth and are designed to cut across the wood fibers. They will give the cleanest cut but require the slowest feed rate.

Rip blades have the largest teeth that are designed to cut with the grain. Rip teeth are filed at a right angle to the face. These blunt chisel-shaped teeth, along with the large gullets, allow a fast feed speed. A rough cut, however, is produced.

Rough-cut combination blades have teeth with the shape of a rip blade but have the top edges sharpened at an angle. This gives a smoother cut but with a fast feed speed.

Four-tooth combination blades are best for general-purpose cabinet and furniture work. Each of the sets of four crosscut teeth cleanly sever the wood fibers, while the one raker tooth digs the sawdust out of the saw kerf.

Specialty blades are designed to cut a specific type of material. A plywood blade, for example, has very small teeth designed to cut plywood. It provides a splinter-free cut in hardwood plywood.

Carbide-tipped blades are sold in four major blade styles (Fig. 28-7). Although blade manufacturers commonly use their own brand names, they are as follows:

Alternate top bevel (ATB) blades are made with crosscut teeth. They give one of the smoothest cuts across the grain. As with all carbide-tipped blades, an ATB can be purchased with a varying number of teeth. The more teeth a blade has, the smoother the cut.

Flat top grind blades have rip teeth and are designed for cutting with the grain. When only this style of tooth is used, it will generally be

ALTERNATE TOP BEVEL

FLAT TOP GRIND

COMBINATION RIP & CROSSCUT

TRIPLE CHIP GRIND

FIGURE 28-7
Common carbide-tipped blades. (Courtesy of DML, Inc.)

used on an industrial ripping machine. A flat top grind tooth style however may be utilized with other teeth to assist with cleaning out the saw kerf.

Combination rip and crosscut blades have both alternate top and flat top grind teeth. The wood fibers are first sheared with the alternate top bevel teeth and then the kerf is cleaned out with the flat top grind tooth. It is the ideal blade for table saws that are required to perform general-purpose cutting.

Triple chip grind blades are specialty carbide-tipped blades designed for cutting aluminum and certain plastics. The triple chip grind teeth remove the majority of the material in the kerf.

The flat top grind then cuts chips on both sides of the saw kerf.

To provide clearance for the saw blade, there must be some type of *blade set* (Fig. 28-8). As the blade turns, the teeth overhanging the body of the blade create a groove or *saw kerf*. The saw kerf needs to be wider than the thickness of the blade. If the proper amount of set is not present, the sides of the blade will rub the wood, creating friction, and the blade will overheat. This will burn the wood and cause a kickback. It could also warp the blade, which must then be discarded.

With steel blades, there are three forms of set: spring, swaged, and hollow ground (Fig. 28-8). *Spring set* has every other tooth bent to the left. The

FIGURE 28-8
Body clearance is developed by spring set, swaged set, or having a hollow-ground body.

remaining teeth are bent to the right. *Swaged set* is rarely used. It has the tip of each tooth flared on both sides. Swaged set is utilized on the inside chippers of a dado head. *Hollow-ground* blades develop body clearance by having a small amount of spring set and a tapered body. The thin, tapered body provides a narrow saw kerf which reduces waste. The hub, however, limits the depth of cut; a four-tooth combination tooth style with a hollow-ground body is called a *planer blade*.

Carbide-tipped blades develop body clearance through the *carbide inserts* overhanging the body. The carbide is usually wider than the body. Even though there is body clearance on this type of blade, pitch and resin will still accumulate on the sides of

FIGURE 28-9
Adjustable dado. Note the width markings on the side of the cutting tool. (Courtesy of Delta International Machinery Corp.)

the body. Keep the blade clean with oven cleaner or a solvent to prevent burning of the stock.

Dado heads are another major cutting tool utilized by the table saw. An 8-in. (203-mm) head will make most cuts. The larger the diameter, the deeper the cut it can make. There are two major styles: adjustable and standard. An *adjustable dado head* is a one-piece unit with graduated measurements spaced around the perimeter (Fig. 28-9). The outside sheaves are turned until the desired width of dado is aligned with the indicator mark. This method of width adjustment makes it easy to set the head to the exact dimension.

The *standard dado head* is more common and contains several parts (Fig. 28-10). The outside of the dado is made by the two *outside cutters*. Each is $\frac{1}{8}$ in. (3 mm) wide. To make wider dados, a variety of *inside chippers* are provided with the head. Most sets will contain one $\frac{1}{16}$-in. (2-mm) and four $\frac{1}{8}$-in. (3-

FIGURE 28-10
A standard dado head contains outside cutters and inside clippers. (Courtesy of Delta International Machinery Corp.)

OUTSIDE CUTTERS

INSIDE CHIPPERS

mm) chippers. Larger dado heads may also have $\frac{1}{4}$-in. (6-mm) and $\frac{1}{2}$-in. (13-mm) wide inside chippers. The outside cutters are usually used in combination with the inside chippers to produce the desired dado. The standard dado head is sold in both high-speed and carbide-tipped varieties.

To make shaper-type cuts, a *molding head* can be used (Fig. 28-11). It contains a solid body and a set of three replaceable cutters. Allen setscrews hold the knives into the head. As many as 40 different patterns of knives are available.

FIGURE 28-12
To remove a blade, pull the arbor wrench in the direction the teeth are pointing.

FIGURE 28-11
A molding head contains a body and set of three identical knives. There are many knife patterns available. (Courtesy of Delta International Machinery Corp.)

INSTALLING THE SAW BLADE

After you have selected the desired blade, disconnect the power. Remove the throat plate and raise the blade. Holding a piece of scrap material against the front edge of the blade, place the arbor wrench on the arbor nut (Fig. 28-12). Pull the wrench forward in the same direction the teeth are pointing. Finish removing the arbor nut by placing your finger on the end of the arbor. Unscrew the nut onto your finger. Holding your finger on the end of the arbor will prevent the nut from dropping to the floor. Remove the stablizing washer and blade. Do not place the blade on the saw table. Make certain that the blade is

stored in a safe place where it will not come in contact with other metal objects.

Install the new blade with the teeth pointing forward and in the same direction as the rotation. The brand name of the manufacturer should be facing out and up. This will assure that the blade will rotate in a true circle. Replace the stablizing washer and hand tighten the arbor nut. Placing the scrap piece back against the blade, tighten the nut with the arbor wrench. Reposition the throat plate and rotate the blade by hand. Check that the splitter of the guard is immediately behind the blade with a straightedge. Reconnect the power.

SETTING UP THE TABLE SAW

After the saw blade has been installed and the guard checked for proper operation, the stock can be cut. Start the setup by placing the thickest board on the table next to the blade. Adjust the height of the blade so that it is approximately $\frac{1}{4}$ in. (6 mm) above the top surface of the board.

Next decide whether the miter gauge or the rip fence is to be used to guide the stock past the blade. Never cut freehand on the saw. In most cases, when cutting solid wood across the grain, use the miter gauge. This is called a *crosscutting operation*. When cutting solid wood with the grain and when cutting panel materials, use the rip fence. This is called a *ripping operation*. Be certain that the board is larger than the minimum dimensions given for either crosscutting or ripping.

After turning on the power, slowly feed the board forward. Your hands must never come any closer to the blade than 4 in. (102 mm). Do not stand directly in line with the blade because sometimes the wood is kicked back toward the operator. Posi-

FIGURE 28-13
Proper body position for operating the saw.

tion your body either to the left or right of the blade (Fig. 28-13). Use a push stick, push block, and featherboards whenever the operation allows.

CROSSCUTTING

Crosscutting on the table saw usually requires the use of a miter gauge to saw across the grain. The board must be at least 10 in. (254 mm) long with a minimum of 6 in. (152 mm) in contact with the miter gauge. The face against the table and the edge against the gauge must be straight. To keep the stock from slipping, screw an abrasive-covered board to the front of the miter gauge (Fig. 28-14).

To cut a board to length, move the rip fence to the far right of the saw. Next, check that the miter

gauge is 90° to the blade. The fastest method to check the gauge setting is to turn over the miter gauge (Fig. 28-15). Place it back in the miter gauge slot and slide it against the rip fence rail. There should be no space between the rail and the miter gauge. With a square, also check that the blade is 90° to the table. Mark the point at which the stock is to be cut with a sharply drawn vee mark.

After adjusting the height of the blade, lower the guard. Although the miter gauge can be used on either side of the blade, most operators will prefer to place it in the slot to the left. Position the stock against the abrasive-covered board. Align the vee-shaped layout mark with the saw tooth set to the left. Turn on the power. Hold the stock with the left hand and push the miter gauge forward with the right hand (Fig. 28-16). Feed the stock forward until it completely clears the saw blade. Use a slow but smooth feed rate.

FIGURE 28-15
Squaring the miter gauge off of the front of the saw.

FIGURE 28-14
Screw a board to the front of the miter gauge. A piece of abrasive paper has been laminated to the face of the board.

FIGURE 28-16
Crosscutting a board with the miter gauge.

WOOD
FACE

ABRASIVE
CLOTH

Once the stock reaches the far side of the blade, slide the board away from the blade. Pull the gauge back to the beginning position. Turn off the power and allow the blade to stop before removing any scrap material.

CROSSCUTTING IDENTICAL LENGTHS

When several parts of the same length are required, use a clearance block, stop rod, or stop block.

Clearance Block

A clearance block is a short planed board clamped against the fence. Measure the desired length between the face of this board and the saw tooth set to the right (Fig. 28-17). Lock the rip fence to the table. Move the clearance blocks back to the front of the fence and clamp it into position. The front end of the clearance block must be well in front of the blade.

Placing the miter gauge in the slot to the left, square the first end of each board. Position the squared end of the stock against the clearance block. Be careful not to bump the block (Fig. 28-18). Crosscut the stock. Move the board completely past the blade and remove it from the table. Pull the miter gauge back and cut the next piece. For short pieces, keep the miter gauge in the left miter gauge slot. Turn off the power and frequently remove the parts left between the blade and rip fence.

Stop Rod

The stop rod is an accessory that is sold with the saw (Fig. 28-19). It is attached to the miter gauge. To use

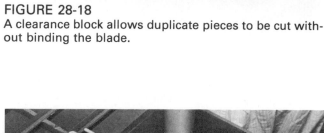

FIGURE 28-18
A clearance block allows duplicate pieces to be cut without binding the blade.

FIGURE 28-19
Cutting stock to length using a stop rod.

FIGURE 28-17
Measuring the desired length between the blade and clearance block.

the stop rod, square the first end of all the stock. Mark the first board to length. Align the mark with the path of the saw blade. Adjust the end of the stop rod against the squared end of the stock. This will gauge the length of the remaining pieces. Cut the pieces to length.

Stop Block

The stop block method requires an auxiliary fence to be screwed to the miter gauge (Fig. 28-20). Square the first end of each piece. Measure the length on the first board and align this mark with the saw blade. Clamp a stock block against the squared end. Cut the first piece and check the length. The remaining stock can then be cut to length.

FIGURE 28-20
Using a stop block to crosscut stock to length.

MITERING

Miters are used to make picture frames and other joints where end grain cannot be exposed. These joints are usually cut using crosscutting techniques.

Plain Miters

The first step in cutting a plain miter is determining the angle of the cut. Use the formula $90° - (180° ÷$ number of sides in the piece). For example, the angle of a five-sided project would be calculated as follows:

$$180° ÷ 5 \text{ sides} = 36°$$
$$90° - 36° = 54°$$

The angle would be set at 54°.

Plain miters can be cut by using either the miter gauge or a mitering fixture. To use a miter gauge, set the desired angle on the angle gauge. If two miter gauges are available, angle one gauge to the left and the other to the right.

Miter one end of each piece. After cutting the first part, check the angle for accuracy with a protractor. To cut the remaining ends, attach to this gauge a long abrasive-covered auxiliary fence. Use the second miter gauge or angle the first gauge in the opposite direction.

Measure the desired length on one of the pieces of stock. Align the layout line with the tooth set closest to the miter gauge. Clamp a stop block against the mitered end and cut the first piece (Fig. 28-21). Check that the part is to the desired length. After making any necessary adjustments, cut the remaining pieces.

Plain miters can also be cut with a sliding table mitering fixture (Fig. 28-22). The angle of the two fences has already been established on the auxiliary table. This makes the setup very fast and accurate. Most mitering fixtures are designed to make 45° miters. The guide rails on the bottom of the aux-

FIGURE 28-21
Mitering stock with a stop block attached to the auxiliary fence.

FIGURE 28-22
Construction of a sliding table mitering fixture.

iliary table slide in the miter gauge grooves. Each piece is first cut using the left fence. The stock is then switched to the right fence and the second miter cut.

Compound Miters

Compound miters require that both the miter gauge and the blade be angled. Use Table 28-1 to establish the angles. Cut two mating pieces to check the accuracy of the joint. To provide a more finished appearance, bevel the top and bottom edges. The bevel will be the complementary angle of the angle of the sides.

Slip Feather Miters

A *slip feather* is a triangular piece that is used for reinforcement of the outside corner of a plain miter

TABLE 28-1
Recommended Angles for Cutting Compound Miters

Tilt of work	Equivalent taper per inch	Four-sided butt		Four-sided miter		Six-sided miter		Eight-sided miter	
		Bevel (deg)	Miter (deg)	Bevel (deg)	Miter (deg)	Bevel (deg)	Miter (deg)	Bevel (deg)	Miter (deg)
5	0.087	$\frac{1}{2}$	85	$44\frac{3}{4}$	85	$29\frac{3}{4}$	$87\frac{1}{2}$	$22\frac{1}{4}$	88
10	0.176	$1\frac{1}{2}$	$80\frac{1}{4}$	$44\frac{1}{4}$	$80\frac{1}{4}$	$29\frac{1}{2}$	$84\frac{1}{2}$	22	86
15	0.268	$3\frac{3}{4}$	$75\frac{1}{2}$	$43\frac{1}{4}$	$75\frac{1}{2}$	29	$81\frac{3}{4}$	$21\frac{1}{2}$	84
20	0.364	$6\frac{1}{4}$	$71\frac{1}{4}$	$41\frac{3}{4}$	$71\frac{1}{4}$	$28\frac{1}{4}$	79	21	82
25	0.466	10	67	40	67	$27\frac{1}{4}$	$76\frac{1}{2}$	$20\frac{1}{4}$	80
30	0.577	$14\frac{1}{2}$	$63\frac{1}{2}$	$37\frac{3}{4}$	$63\frac{1}{2}$	26	74	$19\frac{1}{2}$	$78\frac{1}{4}$
35	0.700	$19\frac{1}{2}$	$60\frac{1}{4}$	$35\frac{1}{4}$	$60\frac{1}{4}$	$24\frac{1}{2}$	$71\frac{3}{4}$	$18\frac{1}{4}$	$76\frac{3}{4}$
40	0.839	$24\frac{1}{2}$	$57\frac{1}{4}$	$32\frac{1}{2}$	$57\frac{1}{4}$	$22\frac{3}{4}$	$69\frac{3}{4}$	17	75
45	1.000	30	$54\frac{3}{4}$	30	$54\frac{3}{4}$	21	$67\frac{3}{4}$	$15\frac{3}{4}$	$73\frac{3}{4}$
50	1.19	36	$52\frac{1}{2}$	27	$52\frac{1}{2}$	19	$66\frac{1}{4}$	$14\frac{1}{2}$	$72\frac{1}{2}$
55	1.43	42	$50\frac{3}{4}$	24	$50\frac{3}{4}$	$16\frac{3}{4}$	$64\frac{3}{4}$	$12\frac{1}{2}$	$71\frac{1}{4}$
60	1.73	48	49	21	49	$14\frac{1}{2}$	$63\frac{1}{2}$	11	$70\frac{1}{4}$

(Fig. 28-23). It exposes the face grain of the mitered frame to the face grain of the slip feather. This produces a very strong glue joint. The grain of the slip feather must run at a right angle to the miter joint. Ideally, it should be made from the same species of wood as the frame.

To make a slip feather miter, cut the frame pieces to size and assemble the frame using only adhesive. After the adhesive has dried, use a slip feather fixture to cut a groove across the corner of each miter.

The fixture can be constructed from a piece of hardwood plywood (Fig. 28-24). To the back of this plywood, attach a cradle that will fit over the top of the rip fence. Attach two angled fences to the face of the plywood. They should each form a 45° angle with the saw table. A 90° angle is formed by the two fences on the plywood.

FIGURE 28-23
A slip feather or spline can be utilized to reinforce a miter.

FIGURE 28-24
Fixture for cutting a slip feather.

Carefully place the frame against the plywood back and on top of the fences. Secure the frame to the fixture with clamps. Adjust the blade height to cut into the frame equal to the width of the feather. Turn on the power and slide the fixture past the blade (Fig. 28-25). The groove will be made in the frame. If a wider groove is needed, the two outside cutters from the dado head can be used instead of a blade.

Cut rectangular pieces to fit into the grooves. This will serve as the slip feather. Wait until the adhesive dries and then trim the feathers flush with the sides of the frame. Finish by sanding the entire frame. The grain of the feathers should run parallel with the bottom of the triangle.

FIGURE 28-26
Cutting the groove for a spline. The guard has been removed for demonstration purposes only.

FIGURE 28-25
Cutting the groove for a slip feather using a fixture. The guard has been removed for demonstration purposes only.

Spline Miters

Spline miters use rectangular pieces to reinforce a plain miter joint (Fig. 28-26). Unlike the slip feather, the spline extends along the entire edge or end of the miter. One-eighth-inch (3-mm) plywood will make excellent spline material.

Lay out the location of the spline on one piece. For spline miters that are cut along the edge of the stock, position the groove toward the heel of the miter. This will allow a wider spline and a stronger joint. Cut the groove for the spline by angling the blade so that it forms a 90° angle with the face of the miter (Fig. 28-26). Guide the toe of the miter along the rip fence.

For splines that are placed along the end of the stock, a fixture will be needed (Fig. 28-27). Cut each piece individually. The end of the miter should be positioned flat against the saw table. Keep the face of each part facing out away from the fixture. The spline should have its grain perpendicular to its long edge.

FIGURE 28-27
Universal fixture for cutting a spline on the end of a plain miter.

Rabbeted Miters

A *rabbeted miter* contains a rabbet and a miter. It is an easy way to assemble the joint that is utilized in cedar chests, jewelry boxes, and other box construction. The shoulders on the rabbet keep the frame members from slipping as clamp pressure is applied.

Start by laying out the rabbeted miter on the edges of one joint. The recommended dimensions for ¾-in. (19-mm) stock are given in Fig. 28-28. Cut the rabbets using the same techniques as given in the section "Rabbeting." You will note that the rabbets are cut differently on the mating pieces. Be careful that all cuts are made very precisely.

FIGURE 28-28
Recommended layout for cutting a rabbeted miter.

X = THICKNESS OF MATERIAL

Next, cut the miters by standing the stock on end. You will need to use a *support strip* clamped to the back to keep the pieces from dropping into the throat plate (Fig. 28-29). Follow the techniques given in the section "Beveling and Chamfering." After cutting the first two pieces of a joint, check the fit. Make any necessary adjustments before proceeding.

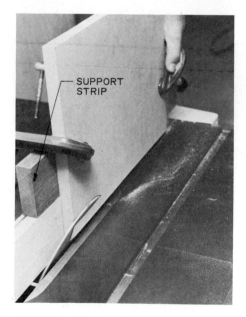

SUPPORT STRIP

FIGURE 28-29
Cutting a large bevel using a support strip clamped to the back of the stock. The guard has been removed for demonstration purposes only.

BEVELING AND CHAMFERING

An angle cut on an edge or end produces a bevel or chamfer. To make these cuts, the blade is tilted to the desired angle. The miter gauge can be used to make the cuts across the end grain. Most beveling and chamfering along the edge, however, is performed with a rip fence.

The blade can be set to the desired angle by one of two methods. The fastest method is to use the tilting gauge located on the front of the base. If an accurate cut is needed, however, use a combination square for a 45° angle or sliding T-bevel for any other angle (Fig. 28-30). Place the measuring device on the table and align the blade with it. Cut a scrap piece and check the angle with a protractor.

For angles greater than 45°, stand the board on end and set the blade to the complementary angle. For example, a 65° angle is needed, subtract 65° from 90°. Set the saw at a 25° angle. Clamp a *support strip* to the back surface of the stock (Fig. 28-29). It rides on top of the rip fence to keep the board from falling over and dropping down into the throat plate.

FIGURE 28-30
Accurately setting the blade to the desired angle with a sliding T-bevel.

CUTTING TENONS

A tenon is the peg portion that is inserted into the mortise (a rectangular opening) forming a mortise and tenon joint. Tenons are cut on the table saw using either a dado head or a single saw blade. Always make the mortise first using a mortising machine. It cannot be cut with a table saw.

To make a tenon, lay it out on a piece of stock cut to the finished size. Use a square to mark the *shoulder and cheek cuts* (Fig. 28-31). The tenon is then cut to fit the mortise. The tenon should slide into the mortise with a slight amount of hand pressure. If the joint must be driven together with a mallet, the tenon is too large.

FIGURE 28-31
Lay out the shoulder and check cuts on a tenon.

Dado Method

To cut a tenon with a dado head, raise the cutter to the same height as the cheek layout line (Fig. 28-32). Adjust the rip fence so that the left outside cutter is in line with the shoulder layout line. Using the rip fence as a stop, feed the material across the dado head with the miter gauge. If the tenon is longer than the cutter can cut in one pass, make multiple cuts. Finish removing all the material from one side and then turn the board over and complete the tenon.

FIGURE 28-32
Making a tenon using a dado head. The guard has been removed for demonstration purposes only.

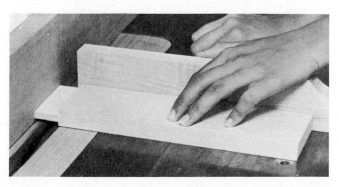

Single Saw Blade Method

To cut a tenon with a single saw blade, make the shoulder cuts first (Fig. 28-33). Raise the blade until it is the same height as the cheek layout line. Move the rip fence over until the saw tooth set to the left is in line with the shoulder layout mark. Keeping the stock against the rip fence, use the miter gauge to guide the material across the blade. Make all shoulder cuts on every tenon before going on to the next step.

The next step is to make the cheek cuts. Either a shop made or commercial *tenoning fixture* is required. The fixture safely holds the stock in a vertical position. Never attempt to hold the stock with only your hands. A kickback will occur. The commercial tenoning fixture slides in the miter gauge groove (Fig. 28-34). A shop-made fixture slides along the top and face of the rip fence (Fig. 28-35). It can be

FIGURE 28-33
Cutting the shoulder out using a single saw blade. The guard has been removed for demonstration purposes only.

FIGURE 28-34
Commercial tenoning fixture. (Courtesy of Delta International Machinery Corp.)

FIXTURE CLAMP
OR C-CLAMP

3/4" HARDWOOD
PLYWOOD

CLAMP STOCK
TO BE MITERED
HERE

3/4" X 2"

OPENING TO EXACTLY
FIT RIP FENCE

FIGURE 28-35
Shop-made tenoning fixture.

made with a backing board of hardwood plywood. A wooden fence is attached to the backing board, which is 90° to the saw table. The stock is secured to the fixture with clamps.

Raise the blade until it is even with the shoulder cut. Adjust the fixture until the saw tooth set to the right is in line with the outside layout cheek cut. The waste must fall to the outside of the blade. Make the first cheek cut (Fig. 28-36). Turn the board around and make the second cheek cut. Try the fit in the mortise before cutting any more tenons. Make any necessary adjustment and cut the remaining tenons.

FIGURE 28-36
Cutting the cheek cut with a tenoning fixture. The guard has been removed for demonstration purposes only.

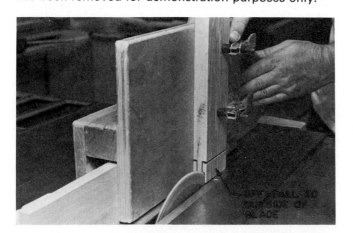

RIPPING STOCK TO WIDTH

Ripping material to width requires the use of the rip fence. Before ripping, check that the board will have a minimum of 10 in. (254 mm) in contact with the rip fence. To keep the stock from rocking, it must have a flat surface against the table and a straight edge to slide along the rip fence. Always adjust the blade height to no more than $\frac{1}{4}$ in. (6 mm) above the board. Position your body either to the left or right of the blade. Never stand in the path of the blade in case of a kickback.

Ripping Wide Boards

To rip boards 6 in. (152 mm) and wider, raise the blade guard. Measure the desired distance between the saw tooth set to the right and the face of the rip fence. If the stock is to be jointed later, add $\frac{1}{8}$ in. (3 mm) to this distance. For minor adjustments, use the micro-adjustment knob to move the fence. Lock the rip fence to the rip fence guide rails.

Lower the guard and turn on the power. Position the stock against the rip fence. Use a slow, steady feed rate to push the board forward (Fig. 28-37). Feed it in a straight line with your right hand and use your left hand to keep it against the fence. Do not use your left hand once the trailing end comes close to the blade. Applying pressure on the outside of the blade will pinch the saw blade and cause a kickback.

As the stock clears the blade, continue to push it forward. Allow rough pieces to fall to the floor or be fed onto a cart. Have a tail-off person catch material that needs special handling. Never reach over the top of the blade to retrieve the stock.

FIGURE 28-37
Ripping a wide board.

Ripping Narrow Boards

To rip boards less than 6 in. (152 mm) wide, use the same setup procedure as given in the section "Ripping Wide Boards." After the material has been started forward into the blade, pause and pick up a push stick with your right hand. Place it on the trailing end and against the rip fence (Fig. 28-38). Use the push stick to feed the material past the blade. In most cases, a ¾-in. (19-mm)-thick push stick will be used. For thin rippings, use a ¼-in. (6-mm)-thick push stick.

Use a second push stick in your left hand to keep the stock against the fence. Do not advance this second push stick past the front of the blade. It could cause the blade to be pinched and a kickback will occur.

FIGURE 28-38
Ripping a narrow board using push sticks.

CUTTING LARGE PANELS

The table saw is an ideal machine for cutting plywood, particleboard, and other panel materials. In most cases, the rip fence is used with ripping techniques. Because the pieces are usually quite large, you should have a tail-off person assist you with cutting the material.

Push the panels past the blade primarily with your right hand. Only use your left hand to start the piece and keep it against the rip fence. Once the training end of the stock comes close to the saw blade, push only between the blade and the rip fence. Pushing to the left of the blade will pinch the saw blade and cause a kickback.

After the panels have been ripped to width, a shop-built sliding table can be utilized to crosscut it to lengths (Fig. 28-39). The two rails located on the bottom of the auxiliary hardwood plywood table slide in the miter gauge slot. The stock is positioned against the miter gauge slot. The stock is positioned against the auxiliary fence. To cut the stock, the entire sliding table is pushed forward. A stop block can be clamped to the auxiliary fence or a clearance block mounted on the rip fence can be used to cut duplicate pieces to length. Keep the guide rails and the bottom of the table waxed to minimize the amount of drag.

FIGURE 28-39
A shop-built sliding table can be used to cut ripped panels to length.

Industrial-rated table saws may come equipped with a *scoring saw blade* (Fig. 28-40). This is a second small-diameter blade that is positioned in front of the main saw blade. The purpose of the scoring saw blade is to precut a shallow groove in the panel. It is frequently utilized to cut fine veneers, melamine board, and other easy-to-chip panels. This accessory will produce a chip-free cut. Most scoring saws are made from two blades, with spacing

FIGURE 28-40
A scoring saw blade precuts the material to eliminate chip-out. (Courtesy of Delta International Machinery Corp.)

shims mounted in between the cutters. It turns in the same direction as the direction of feed.

If a scoring saw unit is not available, a smooth cut can be achieved by using a tight throat plate. This is done by making a throat plate out of wood. Clamp the plate in the throat plate opening in the table. Slowly raise the saw blade up through the wooden plate (Fig. 28-41). The blade will make a groove exactly the same width as the saw blade. This will keep slivers from developing on the bottom surface of the stock.

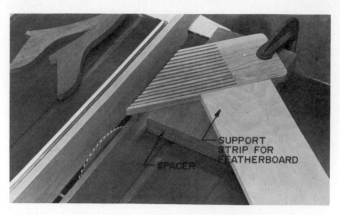

FIGURE 28-42
Proper setup for resawing stock. The guard has been removed for demonstration purposes only.

FIGURE 28-41
Raising the blade to produce a tight throat plate. Note that the throat plate is securely clamped into the table.

RESAWING

Resawing is the process of ripping stock on edge to produce two thinner boards. This process saves material and allows the grain in a panel to be book-matched.

Since the stock will not be completely sawed in half, the standard saw guard cannot be used. Set the distance between the rip fence and the blade equal to one-half the thickness of the board. To assist in holding the stock against the fence, install a featherboard. Place the featherboard on a thick piece of material to elevate the contact area on the stock (Fig. 28-42). The first finger on the featherboard must be in front of the blade. Positioning it any farther forward will cause a kickback.

Adjust the height of the blade to $\frac{1}{2}$ in. (13 mm). Mark an "X" on one of the faces of the stock and always keep this surface against the fence. With a push stick, feed the material forward. Use a second push stick to assist the featherboard with keeping the material against the fence (Fig. 28-43). End for end the board and cut the other edge. Raise the blade an additional $\frac{1}{2}$ in. (13 mm) and repeat the process. Continue these steps until the stock is cut in

FIGURE 28-43
Resawing a board with a featherboard and push stick. The guard has been removed for demonstration purposes only.

half or until the blade is raised to its highest point. If the stock is not cut in half, finish separating the pieces with a bandsaw or handsaw.

TAPER CUTTING

Cutting a taper produces a slanted side with one end wider than the other. A fixture is needed to feed the stock at an angle. If only one side is tapered, an *adjustable tapering fixture* can be used. Small one-sided tapers can be cut with a *wedge fixture*. Tapers having two or more slanted sides require a *two-stepped taper fixture*.

One-Sided Tapers

If an adjustable tapering fixture is not available, start by constructing this device (Fig. 28-44). It consists of two hardwood arms with a small butt hinge at one end. To provide a step to position the stock against, dowel a small block to the outside of one of the rails. The step should be the same distance from the hinged end as the length of the taper. A circular brace secures the two arms once they have been adjusted. To aid in the setting of the angle, a mark is scribed 12 in. (305 mm) from the hinged end.

FIGURE 28-45
Adjusting the angle of an adjustable tapering fixture using the sighting method.

FIGURE 28-44
Adjustable tapering fixture.

FIGURE 28-46
Adjusting the angle of an adjustable tapering fixture using the amount of taper per foot.

There are two methods of adjusting this fixture. The fastest is the sighting method (Fig. 28-45). A line is drawn on the stock indicating the path of the taper. The stock is placed against the tapering fixture and the fixture against the rip fence. Move the arm in or out while sighting down the layout line. When the line aligns with the saw blade, tighten the wing nut on the circle brace. A scrap piece may need to be cut to check the setting.

The most accurate method of adjusting the fixture is to establish the amount of taper per foot of the finish part. Adjust the hinged arms the same distance apart as the amount of taper per foot (Fig. 28-46). Measure this dimension at the 12-in. (305-mm) mark previously drawn on the fixture. If a part, for example, has a taper of ½ in. (13 mm) per foot, adjust the fixture with ½ in. (13 mm) between the arms.

Once the fixture has been adjusted, lower the guard and place the stock against the fixture. Position the rip fence so that the beginning of the layout line is aligned with the saw tooth set to the right. Turn on the power and feed the fixture forward (Fig. 28-47). Keep the fixture against the rip fence and the stock on the step of the fixture.

Wedges

A custom-made wedge fixture can be made if many wedges or one-sided tapered pieces are needed (Fig. 28-48). The outline of the tapered piece is first drawn on the face of a piece of ¾-in. (19-mm)-thick plywood. After the pattern has been bandsawed, glue a piece of ¼-in. (6-mm) plywood on top of the fixture. This

FIGURE 28-47
Cutting a one-sided taper.

will hold the stock against the table as it is being cut. To control the fixture, two handles are mounted on top.

Position the fixture against the fence and place the stock in the pocket of the fixture (Fig. 28-48). Cut the first piece by guiding the fixture against the rip fence. Do not pull the fixture back to you until an assistant has removed the tapered part. Turn the stock over with each cut. This will allow the grain to remain parallel with the edge and more parts to be cut from one piece of stock.

Four-Sided Tapers

A four-sided taper requires a custom two stepped taper fixture (Fig. 28-49). The arm is the same length as the length of the taper. A two-position step

FIGURE 28-48
Using a custom-made wedge fixture for cutting wedges.

T = AMOUNT OF TAPER

FIGURE 28-49
Two-stepped taper fixture.

is attached to the trailing end of the arm. The first position is equal to the amount to be removed from one side of the stock. Make the second position twice this amount.

To use this fixture, cut the first two adjoining edges by placing the stock on the first position. The other two sides are cut on the second position (Fig. 28-50). Since part of the stock has already been cut

FIGURE 28-50
Cutting a four-sided taper with the stock on the second step.

away, it is necessary to move the leg over farther into the path of the blade. The second position automatically moves the board into the path of the saw.

SAWING TO A PATTERN

To make triangles, hexagons, and other multisided pieces, you can use a sawing to a pattern technique. First, make a pattern out of ¾-in. (19-mm) hardwood plywood the exact size and shape of the desired part. Drive at least three 1-in. (25-mm) screws through the plywood. The protruding tips should be filed to a sharp wedge. The wedge should point in the same direction as the grain of the stock. Install two 1-in. (25-mm) dowel handles to control the pattern.

Clamp to the rip fence an auxiliary L-shaped fence (Fig. 28-51). The horizontal piece of the fence must be wider than the widest piece of waste to be cut from the stock. Place the stock to be cut on the table with a piece of ¼-in. (6-mm) plywood on top to form a clearance spacer. Position the auxiliary fence on top of this. Using two clamps, secure the auxiliary fence to the rip fence. Remove the stock and spacer.

FIGURE 28-52
Sawing after a pattern. The guard has been removed for demonstration purposes only.

FIGURE 28-51
Setting up to saw after a pattern.

Adjust the fence so that the saw tooth set to the left is aligned with the edge of the auxiliary fence. Place the stock with the back facing up. After centering the pattern on the stock, drive the screws into the stock with a mallet. Turn on the power and slide the pattern along the auxiliary fence (Fig. 28-52). The waste extends under the fence. As the pattern is guided past the blade, the shape is cut. Stop the blade frequently and clean out any scraps left under the fence.

COVING

A *cove cut* produces a concave decorative shape. It is used most often to produce wide moldings such as used for bases on furniture. To make this cut, first

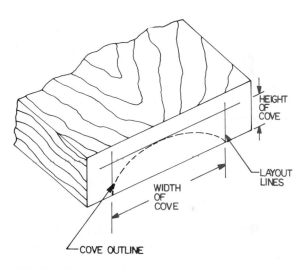

FIGURE 28-53
Layout of a cove cut.

layout the width and height of the cove (Fig. 28-53). Place the marks on the end of the board that will come in contact with the blade first. To make the cove, use either a rigid four-tooth combination blade or the outside cutter from a dado head. Raise the blade until it is even with the height layout line.

If an adjustable *parallel rule* is not available, construct one from hardwood lumber (Fig. 28-54). The legs are tied together with two diagonal pieces. As the rule is opened, the two legs will remain parallel. The legs can be secured by tightening the four wing nuts.

Set the legs of the parallel rule the same distance apart as the width of the cove. Place the rule over the raised blade and angle it until the rule

USE $\frac{3}{4}$" BY 2"
HARDWOOD

6"

$\frac{1}{4}$" WING NUTS

$\frac{1}{4}$" WASHERS

30"

COUNTERSINK HOLES ON BOTTOM

$\frac{1}{4}$"X2" F.H. MACHINE SCREWS

FIGURE 28-54
Construction for a parallel rule.

comes in contact with the saw teeth (Fig. 28-55). The angle the rule makes on the table is the angle for the auxiliary fence.

With a pencil, draw a line on the table along the inside of the parallel rule leg closest to you. Measure back from this leg the same distance as the cove is from the edge of the board. Clamp the auxiliary fence along this line on the front side of the blade.

Lower the blade to $\frac{1}{8}$ in. (3 mm) above the table. Place the stock against the edge of the fence and turn on the power (Fig. 28-56). Using a push shoe, feed the board forward. Never place your hands on top of the board directly over or behind the blade.

FIGURE 28-55
Establishing the angle of an auxiliary fence using the parallel rule.

FIGURE 28-56
Cutting a cove cut using a push shoe.

After each pass, raise the blade an additional $\frac{1}{16}$ in. (2 mm). The cove will be completely shaped once the blade has been raised to the height layout line. Remove the saw marks with abrasive paper and hand scrapers.

GROOVING

There are different types of grooves that can be cut on the table saw: dado, plough and rabbet (Fig. 28-57). The dado is a rectangular groove that runs across the grain. A *plough* is also a rectangular groove, but it is cut with the grain. *Rabbets,* however, can be either with or across the grain but are cut along a face and edge or face and end. All can be made using a dado head as discussed in the section "Selecting the Table Saw Tooling."

FIGURE 28-57
A groove can be either a through dado, plough, rabbet, or blind dado.

THROUGH DADO

BLIND DADO

RABBET

PLOUGH

Mounting a Dado Head

To mount a standard dado head, first determine the desired width of the dado. Next, select the outside cutters and inside chippers that will produce this cut. The two outside cutters, when mounted together, will make a $\frac{1}{4}$-in. (6-mm)-wide groove. Mount the cutters so that the teeth of one cutter fit into the gullets of the next (Fig. 28-58).

For grooves wider than $\frac{1}{4}$ in. (6 mm), add the appropriate size and number of chippers. Most dado sets include $\frac{1}{16}$ and $\frac{1}{8}$-in. (2- and 3-mm) chippers. To make a $\frac{1}{2}$-in. (13-mm)-wide dado, use the two outside cutters and two $\frac{1}{8}$-in. (3-mm) chippers. A $\frac{3}{4}$-in. (919-mm)-wide dado could be made with the two outside cutters and four $\frac{1}{8}$-in. (3-mm) chippers.

FIGURE 28-58
Mounting two outside cutters with the teeth of one cutter in the gullets of the second.

FIGURE 28-59
Spacing the chippers evenly around the arbor.

To mount the dado head, place the first outside cutter on the saw arbor. The teeth of this cutter and all others must point in the same direction as the rotation. Place the first inside chipper so that the tip is positioned in the gullet of the outside cutter. Balance the remaining inside cutters so that they are equally spaced around the arbor (Fig. 28-59). There should be equal space between each chipper. Bunching the cutters together will cause vibrations and wear on the bearings. The second outside cutter is mounted last on the arbor. The swaged teeth of the last chipper must fit into the gullets of the cutter.

Use the dado head throat plate with the extra-wide opening. A custom throat place can be made, however, by first making a blank the size of the opening in the table. Clamp it into the saw table and slowly raise the rotating head through the wooden insert (Fig. 28-41). This will leave no clearance between the dado head and the throat plate. The tight opening will eliminate most chipping that occurs on plywood and other veneered products.

Through Grooving

A through groove extends across the entire width or length of the piece. After the dado head has been mounted on the saw, raise it to the desired height. Install a guard to protect the area immediately surrounding the head. Some guards can be adjusted so they are wide enough to cover a dado head in the same manner as they cover a blade.

Cut a dado in a scrap piece of material. Check the fit and make any necessary adjustments. Paper washers can be placed between the chippers to make small increases in the width of the groove (Fig. 28-60). Do not place all the washers in one spot. They should be evenly distributed between all the chippers to prevent a ridge of wood from being left in the dado.

Grooves can be cut using either crosscutting techniques with the miter gauge or with ripping techniques on the rip fence. Use both the miter gauge and rip fence for wide material. The miter gauge helps guide the stock past the dado head. The

FIGURE 28-60
Using paper washers to make small increases in the width of the dado head.

rip fence also guides the stock but in addition serves as a stop (Fig. 28-61). This is helpful when cutting a pair of grooves. The rip fence assures that both dados will be the same distance from the ends.

Feed the stock over the dado head at a slow, steady rate. The larger the groove, the slower the feed rate. Never draw the stock back toward the direction of the operator. This will cause a kickback. Do not use your hand to hold the stock down directly over or behind the dado head. It is best to use a push stick or featherboard to keep the material against the table.

FIGURE 28-61
Making a through dado with the miter gauge and using the rip fence for a stop. The guard has been removed for demonstration purposes only.

Blind Dadoing

A *blind* or *stopped groove* conceals a dado once the project is assembled. It requires that the dado be stopped and not extended across the entire surface (Fig. 28-57). When laying out the dado on a pair of sides, it is important to determine the left and right side. With a square, transfer the stopping points of the dados on the top surface of each part.

Mount the dado head on the saw and raise it to the desired height. Move the rip fence against the cutter and with a square mark where the cut begins and ends (Fig. 28-62). This will be the point where the teeth first come up and go down into the table.

Adjust the rip fence the same distance from the dado head as the groove is from the end of the board. Lower the dado head below the table. Place the bottom surface of the board on the table with the end against the rip fence and align the front stopping point on the stock with the rear mark on the rip fence (Fig. 28-63). Clamp a stock block on the rip fence which is against the back edge of the stock. Slide a miter gauge up to the stock and clamp a second stop block against the end of the miter gauge rail.

FIGURE 28-62
Marking the beginning and ending points on the rip fence.

FIGURE 28-63
Setting up the saw to cut a blind dado for the right side. The guard has been removed for demonstration purposes only.

Reset the dado head to the same height. Place the board on its edge and against the stop block on the rip fence and miter gauge. Turn on the power and lower the stock carefully down on to the rotating cutter. Once the board meets the table, feed it forward.

To dado the left sides of your project, lower the cutter and align the rear stopping point on the stock with the front layout line on the rip fence (Fig. 28-64). Clamp a stock block against the leading edge of the board on the rip fence. Clamp a stock block against the leading edge of the board on the rip fence. Clamp a second stop block against the front of the miter gauge bar. Raise the dado head back to the original height.

Position the stock against the rip fence and miter gauge. Turn on the power and push the miter gauge forward feeding the board into the cutter. Once the stock meets the stop blocks, turn off the power. If you cannot reach the switch while holding

FIGURE 28-64
Setting up the saw for a blind dado on the left side. The guard has been removed for demonstration purposes only.

down the board, have an assistant turn off the power. The board must not be moved until the dado head has stopped turning.

Rabbeting

Rabbets can be cut with either a dado head or a single saw blade. With both cutters, be certain that the rip fence is covered with a piece of wood. This will protect the cutter if it comes in contact with the fence.

When several rabbets are needed, set up the dado head (Fig. 28-65). Adjust the rip fence just to the right of the cutter. Use a miter gauge to guide the stock past the dado head.

When just a few rabbets are needed, use a single saw blade. Layout the rabbet on the leading end of one of the boards. Place the face of the stock against the table and the marked end against the blade. Adjust the height so that it will be even with the horizontal layout line. Position the stock against

FIGURE 28-65
Cutting the rabbet with a dado head and using a featherboard.

the rip fence and move the fence over until the vertical layout line is aligned with the saw tooth set to the left. Feed each board over the blade using a push stock (Fig. 28-66). Do not place your hands directly over the blade or behind the blade.

Make the second cut by standing the stock on edge. Readjust the height of the blade and the position of the rip fence to be aligned with the layout lines. The waste from the rabbet must fall to the outside of the blade. If the waste is left between the blade and rip fence, a serious kickback will result.

Install a featherboard to keep the stock against the fence. Position it on top of a block so that the contact area of the featherboard is above the rabbet. Feed the stock across the rotating blade using a push stick (Fig. 28-67). Have a tail-off person catch the boards as they leave the saw table.

FIGURE 28-66
Make the first cut for a rabbet with the face against the table. The guard has been removed for demonstration purposes only.

FIGURE 28-67
Use a featherboard and push stick to make the second cut for a rabbet. The waste must fall to the outside of the blade.

MAKING A RAISED PANEL

Raised panels are usually made from solid wood and are utilized in a door. They will have a decorative chamfer cut on the face of the panel. Although a shaper is used most commonly to mold the edges, a table saw can produce a pleasing appearance on a raised panel.

First, compute the size of the panel. It will be based on the overall width and length dimensions of the stile and rail frame. Refer to the section "Raised Panel Doors" in Chapter 36 for further information on how the frame is fabricated. A groove for the raised panel is cut on the inside edges of the frame. It will usually be ½ in. (13 mm) deep. Calculate the inside dimensions of the frame and add 1 in. (25 mm) for the two grooves. This will give you the distance from the bottom of one groove to the opposite groove. Subtract from this amount ¼ in. (6 mm) for expansion and contraction of the panel.

Depending on the design of the door, the stock for the panel will be between ½ to ¾ in. (13 to 19 mm) thick. Raised panels for ¾-in. (19-mm)-thick doors are generally ½ to 9/16 in. (13 to 15 mm) thick. Design your door so that the face of the panel and the face of the frame are even with each other.

To provide a shoulder and a straight line for the chamfer, make a ⅛-in. (3-mm)-deep groove (Fig. 28-68). It should be 1½ in. (38 mm) from each of the four edges. If a wider chamfer is needed, make the groove farther from the edge.

Next, angle the blade to approximately 6°. Adjust the rip fence so that it is ¼ in. (6 mm) from the blade. Stand the stock on edge and clamp a support strip along the back (Fig. 28-69). The support strip will ride on top of the rip fence and keep the stock from dropping through the throat plate. Chamfer all four edges using the support board.

FIGURE 28-68
Cutting a groove for a raised door panel.

FIGURE 28-69
Making a chamfer cut for a raised panel. Note the support strip on the back of the door. The guard has been removed for demonstration purposes only.

Finish the raised panel by sanding the saw marks. If the door is to be stained, stain the chamfer before the door is assembled. This will keep a white line from developing when the panel later shrinks because of the natural movement of wood.

USING THE MOLDING HEAD

A molding head can be used to make many different types of decorative cuts. The parts of this cutter are discussed in the section "Selecting the Table Saw Tooling." There are several different patterns of shaper-like knives from which to pick.

After the three matching knives are selected, mount them in the molding head body. It is very important that each knife be mounted in the body so that the sharp edge is leading as the cutter rotates. Each Allen head bolt must be firmly tightened. Recheck each one several times before using. You will need to stop periodically during the cutting and retighten each bolt.

The miter gauge, rip fence, or combination of both can be used to guide the stock. Use the miter gauge when molding end grain and shaping small pieces (Fig. 28-70). A backup board screwed to the gauge will eliminate any tear out when shaping end grain. The rip fence works well for making long pieces of molding (Fig. 28-71). Cover the fence with a thick piece of wood. This allows only part of the cutter to be used while the remaining portion remains in the wooden fence. To cut a recess for the cutter to turn in, lower the head. Adjust and lock the rip fence in the desired location and bring the rotating cutter

FIGURE 28-70
Shaping the end grain using a miter gauge. The guard has been removed for demonstration purposes only.

FIGURE 28-71
Shaping molding using the rip fence. The guard has been removed for demonstration purposes only.

FIGURE 28-72
A tall fence allows the stock to be run on the edge.

up into the wooden fence. Be careful not to hit the metal rip fence. Attach a tall piece of plywood to the rip fence when molding the edge of large stock (Fig. 28-72).

To set up the molding head, mount it on the arbor. Use a throat plate with a wide opening. Raise the cutter until it meets the layout drawn on the end of the board. If a heavy cut is necessary to shape the pattern, make the molding in several light passes. Use a push stick and featherboards whenever possible. Never place your hands on top of the stock when it is over the molding head.

BOX JOINERY

The box joint is a highly decorative joint that has a similar appearance to a dovetail (Fig. 28-73). It can be cut entirely on the table saw and when assembled is very strong. With the many fingers cut on each of the two sides, the gluing surface is more than twice the length of the joint.

To make a box joint, first lay out the fingers on one pair of sides. Each finger and slot are to be the same size. Ideally, a full-width finger will begin and end the joint. The layout should be made with the finger width $\frac{1}{8}$ to $\frac{1}{2}$ in. (3 to 13 mm) less than the thickness of the stock. Usually, the smaller the fingers, the more decorative is the appearance. Also,

FIGURE 28-73
Layout of the box joint.

place an "X" on the outside surface of each piece. This mark will later be used to orient the stock when placed against the miter gauge.

Mount a dado head on the saw arbor. It should be the same width as the fingers. Raise the dado head to just slightly more than the height of the slot. Cutting the slots slightly deeper will assure a flush box joint. After assembly, the overhang on the fingers can be sanded flush with the outside surface. Place an auxiliary fence against the miter gauge and cut a dado through the board. Glue into this dado a wooden guide pin which is the exact width and height as the finger (Fig. 28-74). It should extend beyond the face of the fence at least the thickness of the stock.

To position the auxiliary fence on the miter gauge, place a spacer to the right of the dado head (Fig. 28-74). The spacer should be the exact same thickness as the width of the fingers. Slide the fence snuggly against the spacer. Attach the fence to the miter gauge with wood screws.

Place the inside surface of the first piece against the miter gauge (Fig. 28-75). Butt the edge of the board against the guide pin and firmly hold it against the fence. Turn on the power and cut the

FIGURE 28-75
Cutting the first slot on the first side. The guard has been removed for demonstration purposes only.

FIGURE 28-74
Setup for making a box joint.

first slot. Guide the stock past the dado head with the miter gauge. Once the stock has cleared the head, have an assistant remove it from the fence. Do not draw it back over the dado head.

Cut the remaining fingers by slipping the newly cut slot over the guide pin (Fig. 28-76). It will automatically position the board for the next finger. Use the same procedure as used for the first slot to feed the stock.

To cut the second mating piece, place the first board now with the outside surface against the fence (Fig. 28-77). The first slot that was cut should be over the guide pin. Position the second piece against

FIGURE 28-76
Use the guide pin to position the stock for the next cut. The guard has been removed for demonstration purposes only.

FIGURE 28-77
Making the first cut on the second side. The guard has been removed for demonstration purposes only.

the edge of the first piece of material. The inside surface should be against the fence. Remove the first piece being careful not to move the second. Feed the miter gauge past the dado head cutting the slot. Using the same procedure as for the first piece, make the remaining fingers.

After the first joint has been cut, check the fit. If the fingers do not easily slide into the slots, adjust the distance the guide pin is from the dado head or the width of the cut. You may also want to check that the dado head or miter gauge is perpendicular to the table.

STUDY QUESTIONS

Answer each of the following questions. If you are not sure of an answer, review the chapter.

28-1. Adjust the saw blade to project no more than _____ in. (_____ mm) above the stock to be cut.

28-2. Use a push stick when ripping stock that has less than _____ in. (_____ mm) between the rip fence and the blade.

28-3. The _____ is located in the middle of the table and contains a slot through which the blade extends.

28-4. The saw guard consists of the _____ guard, _____, and _____ pawls.

28-5. The size of a table saw is determined by the largest _____ of saw _____ that can be safely mounted on the arbor.

28-6. List the five tooth styles of high-speed steel blades.

28-7. As the blade turns, the teeth create a groove or saw _____.

28-8. When installing a new saw blade, make certain that the teeth are pointing _____.

28-9. Never stand directly in line with the _____ because of a possible kickback.

28-10. The fastest method of checking the accuracy of a miter gauge set at 90° is to turn it over and place it in the _____.

28-11. When crosscutting identical lengths, a _____ block is clamped to the rip fence.

28-12. Using the formula given to calculate the angle of a plain miter, what should be the setting of the miter gauge if a twelve-sided frame is needed?

28-13. A _____ is a triangular piece that reinforces a plain miter.

28-14. For miters greater than 45°, clamp a _____ to the back surface of the stock.

28-15. When cutting the cheek cuts for a tenon, use a _____ to hold the stock safely in a vertical position.

28-16. When ripping stock never reach _____ the top of the blade to retrieve the stock.

28-17. _____ is the process of ripping stock on edge to produce two thinner boards.

28-18. The most accurate method of adjusting an adjustable tapering fixture is to establish the _____.

28-19. To cut a triangle using sawing to a pattern techniques, adjust the fence so that the saw tooth to the _____ is aligned with the auxiliary fence.

28-20. Use a _____ rule to establish the angle of the auxiliary fence when cutting a core.

28-21. When mounting a dado head, place the _____ cutters to the outside and the _____ to the inside.

28-22. Never draw the stock _____ toward the operator when cutting a dado.

28-23. If a raised panel door is to be stained, stain the chamfer _____ the door is assembled.

28-24. Each knife of a molder head must be mounted so that the sharp edge is _____ as the cutter rotates.

IMPORTANT TECHNICAL TERMS

Following are technical terms that you should be able to use as part of your working vocabulary. Write a brief description of the meaning of each term.

Miter gauge grooves
Fence guide rails
Miter gauge
Rip fence
Throat plate
Saw guard
Ways
Height-adjustment handwheel
Locking knob
Trunion
Tilting handwheel
Tilting gauge
Saw arbor
Slotted miter gauge
Micro-adjustment knob
Carbon and high-speed steel blades
Crosscut blades
Rip blades
Rough-cut combination blades
Four-tooth combination blades
Specialty blades
Carbide-tipped blades
Alternate top bevel (ATB) blades
Flat top grind blades
Combination rip and crosscut
   blades
Triple chip grind
Blade set

Saw kerf
Spring set
Swaged set
Hollow ground
Planer blade
Carbide inserts
Dado heads
Adjustable dado head
Standard dado head
Outside cutters
Inside chippers
Molding head
Plain miters
Slip feather miters
Spline miters
Rabbeted miters
Support strip
Shoulder and cheek cuts
Tenoning fixture
Scoring saw blade
Resawing
Adjustable tapering fixture
Wedge fixture
Two-stepped taper fixture
One-sided tapers
Four-sided tapers
Cove cut
Parallel rule
Dado
Plough
Rabbets
Blind stopped groove
Raised panels

29

RADIAL ARM SAWS

The radial arm saw is one of the most suitable pieces of woodworking equipment for cutting stock to length (Fig. 29-1). When crosscutting with this saw, the board is kept in a stationary position and the blade is drawn across the material. This allows accurate cutting and easier aligning of the layout line with the blade. Many woodworkers also utilize the radial arm saw for other purposes. It can dado, rip, miter, cut saucers, and perform many other specialized cuts.

Industry uses another type of crosscut saw called a *chop saw* (Fig. 29-2). It is a highly specialized saw which can only cut material to length. After the guard hood drops down over the stock, the saw raises up rapidly out of the table. Since the saw blade is raised with air pressure, the cutting operation is very fast.

PARTS OF THE RADIAL ARM SAW

The major parts of a radial arm saw are the arm, column, table, fence, and motor unit (Fig. 29-1). All of these components can be adjusted in several positions.

There are two styles of arms utilized with radial arm saws. The original style uses a single piece that is suspended over the table by the column. This is the simplest style and called the *single arm* (Fig. 29-1). A newer style has two arms and is called a *turret arm* (Fig. 29-3). The top arm remains stationary while the bottom one pivots. This allows for a larger mitering capacity. With either style the *miter clamp handle* and *miter positive lock* secures the arm into either the crosscutting or mitering position.

Towards the rear of the saw is the *column*. It is a steel tube which is anchored to the base. An *elevation crank* raises or lowers the column to adjust the depth of cut.

Stock is positioned on top of the *table* against the *fence*. The blade should be adjusted so that it is $\frac{1}{16}$ in. (2 mm) below the top surface of the table. Occasionally, the blade may be lowered too far and the top weakened from too deep of a cut. Since the *table* is constructed from particleboard or plywood, it can be replaced with a new piece. The *fence* can also be replaced when it is cut away.

With most saws the fence can be positioned in several locations to the rear of the table. Although there must be space for the rotating blade next to the column, the farther back the fence is positioned, the wider the cutting capacity (Fig. 29-4). By moving it forward, a thicker board can be positioned against the fence (Fig. 29-4).

369

FIGURE 29-1
Major parts of the single-arm radial arm saw. (Courtesy of Black & Decker.)

FIGURE 29-2
A chop saw crosscuts material to length in industry. (Courtesy of Whirlwind, Inc.)

The motor unit is suspended from the arm by the *yoke*. Attached to the yoke is the motor. The blade is mounted directly to the shaft of the motor. On the front of the *yoke* is the *handle*. It is very important to always control the movement of the blade by grasping this handle. There are two adjustments for the motor unit (Fig. 29-5). The *yoke swivel clamp* and *rip positive lock* allow the blade to be swung into the ripping position. The *bevel clamp handle* and *bevel positive stop* are used primarily to set the saw in the bevel mode (Fig. 29-6).

An important part to this saw is the *blade guard* (Fig. 29-7, page 372). The guard is made of three major parts. An *upper blade housing* covers the top of the blade. It also contains the *sawdust spout*, which directs the sawdust away from the operator. The *ring guards* protect the operator from the bottom section of the blade when it is in the rearmost position. These ring guards may need to be removed in such operations as coving, resawing, and saucer cutting. The *antikickback assembly* covers

FIGURE 29-3
Major parts of the turret-arm radial arm saw. (Courtesy of Delta International Machinery Corp.)

FIGURE 29-4
The position of the fence will determine the maximum width of the board that can be cut.

FIGURE 29-5
Releasing the yoke swivel clamp and the rip positive lock allows the saw to be placed in the ripping position.

FIGURE 29-6
Releasing the bevel clamp handle and the bevel positive stop allow the saw to be placed in the ripping position.

the leading edge of the blade. It also keeps the boards from being thrown out of control when the saw is in the rip position.

PURCHASING A RADIAL ARM SAW

There are several items to consider when purchasing a radial arm saw. First select the size of the machine. Radial arm saws are sized by the diameter of the blade and the length of the arm. Diameters of saw blades range from 8 to over 20 in. (203 to 508

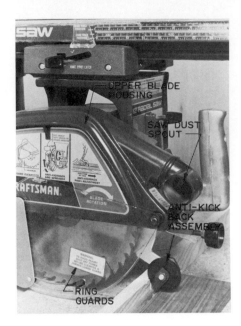

FIGURE 29-7
Major parts to a radial arm saw guard.

mm). Larger blades allow thicker boards to be cut. A good general-purpose size is 10 in. (254 mm). This will cut most boards 2 in. (51 mm) and thinner. The length of the arm is generally between 20 and 48 in. (508 and (1219 mm). Longer arms allow wider boards to be cut.

The horsepower of the motor is another aspect to consider when purchasing this machine. Generally, the larger the blade diameter, the bigger the H.P. of the motor. To make most cuts at least a 2-hp motor should be specified.

A good-quality radial arm saw will have adjustments that are easy to reach and solidly lock the movable parts in place. When pressure is applied to the end of the locked arm or other parts, they should not move.

SELECTING THE RADIAL ARM SAW TOOLING

Tooling for a radial arm saw includes saw blades, a dado head, a molding head, sanding disk, and many others. If the saw is used only for crosscutting, a carbide-tipped alternating top bevel blade will work the best. For crosscutting and occasional ripping, a carbide-tipped combination blade can make most cuts efficiently. Refer to the section "Selecting the Table Saw Tooling" in Chapter 28 for further details on tooling. These saw blades can also be used on the radial arm saw. In other sections of that chapter additional tooling is explained that can be utilized.

INSTALLING THE RADIAL ARM SAW BLADE

Always disconnect the power before changing any tooling. Next raise the column so that the blade is clear of the table and fence. Because the blade guard assembly surrounds the blade, it must be removed. Once the guard is taken off, both the blade and the *arbor* will be exposed. The *arbor* is the threaded shaft upon which the tooling is mounted.

Use either an Allen wrench or special arbor wrench to keep the arbor from turning (Fig. 29-8). You should never substitute a piece of wood wedged under the blade for a wrench. This will push the saw out of alignment when pressure is applied.

With the arbor nut wrench, loosen the arbor nut. The handle of the wrench should be pulled in the same direction as the saw blade teeth are pointing (Fig. 29-8). After the arbor nut has been unscrewed, remove the stabilizing washer and blade.

Select the new blade and slide it on the arbor. The teeth must point in the direction the arbor rotates. Place the stabilizing washer back on the arbor and tighten the arbor nut with the arbor nut

FIGURE 29-8
Removing the arbor nut.

wrench. Hold the arbor secure with the arbor wrench. Reassemble the guard and be certain the bottom on the upper blade housing is parallel with the table. The ring guards must cover the bottom cutting circle of the blade. For crosscutting operations, adjust the antikick fingers so that they are just above the top of your stock. Push the blade all the way back to the column and connect the power.

The blade should be adjusted to cut $\frac{1}{16}$ in. (2 mm) below the table. Occasionally, a groove will not be present in the table and fence at the desired location. If a new groove is needed, raise the blade up above the fence and turn on the power. Holding the motor unit securely in the rear most position have an assistant lower the rotating blade. Once it has cut $\frac{1}{16}$ in. (2 mm) into the rear table, stop lowering the blade. Pull the blade out until it reaches the end of the arm. Push the blade back to complete the groove.

To check the accuracy of the saw, select a scrap piece with a straight edge and a flat face. After cutting the board, check for squareness from edge to edge and face to face.

SETTING UP THE RADIAL ARM SAW

There are three basic adjustments for the radial arm saw. A few special cuts may require a combination of these. The power must always be turned off and the blade not turning any time an adjustment is made. With each setup make certain that no parts of the saw are forced into position and that all movable parts are locked after the adjustments are made.

The most common adjustment is the blade height. Make this adjustment when changing the depth of cut for regular cuts, making dados or other types of cuts. Use the *elevating crank* to raise or lower the column (Fig. 29-1). Turning the crank will then change the height of the blade.

Another common setup is the mitering adjustment. Miters are made with this setup by moving the arm either to the left or right. The arm can be moved by pulling up on the *miter latch,* loosening the *miter clamp handle* (Fig. 29-9). Saws will have a *miter scale and pointer* to indicate the angle of the blade to the fence. For fast adjustments a positive lock for the miter latch is provided at 90 and 45° to

FIGURE 29-9
Releasing the miter latch and the miter clamp handle allows the saw to be placed in the miter position.

right and left. Tighten both the handle and latch before turning on the power.

To produce bevel cuts, use the *bevel clamp handle* and *bevel locating pin* (Fig. 29-6). Start by raising the blade well above the fence. Loosen the clamp handle and locating pin. The motor should then rotate in the yoke. Move the motor until it is at the desired angle indicated by the bevel scale. Most saws have a positive stop at 90, 45, and 180°.

The third adjustment involves placing the saw in the ripping mode. This allows the saw to be used for ripping operations. To pivot the *yoke* to the right or left, first raise the blade. Next release the *yoke swivel clamp* and lift up on the *rip positive lock* (Fig. 29-5). Turning the yoke clockwise places the blade in the *in-rip position.* Turning the yoke counterclockwise places it in the *out-rip position.* With either position the rip positive lock will automatically lock the yoke into position. Tighten the yoke swivel clamp to secure the yoke.

No matter which setup is selected, always cut a scrap piece and check it for the desired angle of cut. Minor changes may be needed in the adjustments to produce an accurate cut. Cut off a piece at least 1 in. (25 mm) long and then use a framing square or protractor on the remaining board. Check for accuracy not only from edge to edge but also from face to face.

CROSSCUTTING

The radial arm saw is ideal for crosscutting boards to length. There must be at least 6 in. (152 mm) of material to the left of the blade for the operator to hold. Any less than this and your hands come dangerously close to the blade. Before making this cut, make certain that the saw is setup correctly. The blade should be $\frac{1}{16}$ in. (2 mm) below the table and the guard properly adjusted. Cut a scrap piece of material and check the cut for squareness.

When cutting a board to length, crosscut the first 1 in. (25 mm) off the end. End-for-end the board, and measuring from the fresh cut, end-mark the piece to length. Use a vee-shaped mark to indicate the position of the cut (Fig. 29-10). Align this mark immediately to the left of the path of the saw blade. Hold the board firmly against the table and fence with the left hand. Grasp the handle of the radial arm saw with the right hand and push the saw all the way to the column. Turn on the power and slowly pull the motor unit forward (Fig. 29-11). Since the blade may have a tendency to grab the stock, be certain to control the movement of the saw. Once the saw blade has cleared the front edge of the board, push the motor back to the column. Make the next cut or turn off the power.

FIGURE 29-10
Vee-shaped mark to indicate the location of the cut.

FIGURE 29-12
Use a rabbeted stop block to cut boards of identical length.

FIGURE 29-11
Crosscutting a board. Note position of hands.

FIGURE 29-13
Commercial stops provide more than one length setting when cutting boards to length.

(Fig. 29-13). These have a built-in tape measure for easy setup. Often, spring-loaded stops allow several lengths to be set up at one time.

CUTTING BOARDS TO IDENTICAL LENGTHS

When only a few boards are needed, it is usually best to mark each piece individually. Cut each board separately. For several pieces of the same length a stop block can be utilized. Each part will be of exactly the same length and much time will be saved.

When cutting several pieces, square the first end of one piece. Mark it to length. Align the mark with the path of the blade. Clamp a rabbeted stop block to the fence which has been placed against the end of the stock (Fig. 29-12). The rabbeted area will prevent sawdust from accumulating in front of the stop block. Cut the first piece to length and check the length with a tape measure. If the cut is not accurate, make any necessary adjustments. Industry frequently uses commercial stops and fences

PLAIN MITERING

There are three major methods of cutting plain miters. Although they can be cut at various angles, most generally a 45° angle is utilized. This angle setting will produce a four-sided frame. To calculate the angle for any given frame, use the following formula:

$$\text{angle setting on saw} = 90° - \frac{180}{\text{number of sides}}$$

A hexagon or six-sided frame would require the miter scale pointer to be set at 60°. The formula above would be worked as follows:

$$\text{angle setting on saw} = 90 \text{ degrees} - 30 = 60$$

After setting the saw to the desired angle, always cut a piece of scrap to check the accuracy of the angle. Use a protractor or sliding T-bevel to measure the miter. Make any needed adjustments. If the angle is off by only a small amount, the miter will not fit properly.

Once the angle of the miter has been calculated it may be necessary to figure the length of the picture frame members. To find the length, measure the size of one side of the picture. Add to this twice the width of the frame material. Subtract from this amount twice the width of the rabbet.

An example of calculating a piece of molding as shown in Fig. 29-14 for a 10-in. (254-mm)-wide picture would be as follows:

picture width	= 10 in.	10 in.	width of picture
molding width	= 2 in.	+ 4 in.	twice width of molding
		14 in.	
width of rabbet	= ½ in.		
		14 in.	
		− 1 in.	twice width of rabbet
		13 in.	finish length of molding

FIGURE 29-14
Picture frame molding.

PICTURE FRAME MOULDING

½"

2"

?

10"
PICTURE

PICTURE FRAME

METHOD 1. The first method requires the stock to be cut to rough length. Next, swing the arm to the right to the desired angle. If a 45° angle is desired, engage the miter latch. Always lock the miter clamp handle to secure the arm.

Miter all boards on the first end. Swing the arm to the left and set the miter scale pointer to the desired angle. Measure the length of the first piece and align the mark with the path of the blade. Clamp a stop block on the opposite end. Miter the second end of all pieces (Fig. 29-15).

FIGURE 29-15
Mitering stock with the arm set at the desired angle

METHOD 2. The second method of cutting plain miters requires the arm to be left at 90° angle. All pieces need to be cut to finish length. Install a mitering fixture on top of the table (Fig. 29-16). This requires the blade to be raised so that it will cut $\frac{1}{16}$ in. (2 mm) into the auxiliary table. Cut the first end by positioning the board against the left side of the vee. After cutting the first miter, end-for-end the board and cut the second end by placing the part against the right side of the vee. Be careful that the small piece that is cut away is not caught by the blade.

METHOD 3. The third method does not require stock to be precut to length. It will, however, work only for 45° angles. A large piece of squared plywood is clamped to the table (Fig. 29-17). This will serve as an auxiliary fence. Use a framing square placed against the saw fence to locate the auxiliary plywood fence. There should be just enough space left between the back edge of the plywood and the saw fence for the stock to slide.

Place the arm in the 45° position. Clamp a stop block to the right of the blade the same distance from the blade as the length of the finished board. Slide the stock against the stop block and miter the first end. Remove the piece and place it against the edge of the plywood. The second end can then be mitered.

BLADE AT 90°

NO. 7X1¼" F.H. WOOD SCREWS

45°

12"

20"

ALL STOCK ¾" PLYWOOD

PATH OF SAW BLADE

VEE FIXTURE

FIGURE 29-16
Mitering with a vee mitering fixture.

FIRST MITER POSITION

FENCE

STOP BLOCK

BLADE SET AT 45°

90°

PATH OF SAW BLADE

LARGE PIECE OF PLYWOOD

SECOND MITER POSITION

FIGURE 29-17
Mitering stock using an auxiliary fence.

TABLE 29-1
Angles for Cutting Compound Miters

| Work angle (deg) | Four sides | | Six sides | | Eight sides | |
	Blade tilt (deg)	Arm setting (deg)	Blade tilt (deg)	Arm setting (deg)	Arm setting (deg)	Blade tilt (deg)
5	$44\frac{3}{4}$	5	$29\frac{3}{4}$	$2\frac{1}{2}$	$22\frac{1}{4}$	2
10	$44\frac{1}{4}$	$9\frac{3}{4}$	$29\frac{1}{2}$	$5\frac{1}{2}$	22	4
15	$43\frac{1}{4}$	$14\frac{1}{2}$	29	$8\frac{1}{4}$	$21\frac{1}{2}$	6
20	$41\frac{3}{4}$	$18\frac{3}{4}$	$28\frac{1}{4}$	11	21	8
25	40	23	$27\frac{1}{4}$	$13\frac{1}{2}$	$20\frac{1}{4}$	10
30	$37\frac{3}{4}$	$26\frac{1}{2}$	26	16	$19\frac{1}{2}$	$11\frac{3}{4}$
35	$35\frac{1}{4}$	$29\frac{3}{4}$	$24\frac{1}{2}$	$18\frac{1}{4}$	$18\frac{1}{4}$	$13\frac{1}{4}$
40	$32\frac{1}{2}$	$32\frac{3}{4}$	$22\frac{3}{4}$	$20\frac{1}{4}$	17	15
45	30	$35\frac{1}{4}$	21	$22\frac{1}{4}$	$15\frac{3}{4}$	$16\frac{1}{4}$
50	27	$37\frac{1}{2}$	19	$23\frac{3}{4}$	$14\frac{1}{4}$	$17\frac{1}{2}$
55	24	$39\frac{1}{4}$	$16\frac{3}{4}$	$25\frac{1}{4}$	$12\frac{1}{2}$	$18\frac{3}{4}$
60	21	41	$14\frac{1}{2}$	$26\frac{1}{2}$	11	$19\frac{3}{4}$

COMPOUND MITERING

A compound miter is also called a hopper joint or bevel miter. The cut will produce a miter with sloping or angled sides. Use Table 29-1 to establish the angle settings for the arm and the motor unit. Both the arm and motor unit must be adjusted for this cut. After setting each to the desired angle, produce the compound miter using crosscutting techniques (Fig. 29-18).

FIGURE 29-18
Making a compound miter.

RIPPING

Ripping should be done on the table saw if one is available. It is generally easier, faster, and safer than using a radial arm saw. If there is not one to use, however, ripping can be done on the radial arm saw by following a specific procedure.

To rip a board, raise the motor unit well above the fence. Check that the arm is in the 90° setting. By loosening the yoke swivel clamp and lifting up on the rip positive lock, the motor yoke can be pivoted one-fourth of a turn into the rip position. The positive rip lock will automatically drop in a positioning hole once the blade is parallel to the fence.

By turning the motor to the left, the blade is placed in the *in-rip position* (Fig. 29-19). Use this position for ripping narrow-to-wide stock. Rotating the motor unit to the right places the blade in the *out-rip position* (Fig. 29-20). Use this position when ripping extra-wide material such as wide plywood. The saw should always rotate toward the stock as it is fed into it.

Pull the motor unit out on the arm until the space between the fence and the saw tooth close to the fence is equal to the desired width of out. Tighten the rip lock to secure the motor unit to the arm.

Turn on the power and slowly lower the blade toward the table. Once the blade has cut $\frac{1}{16}$ in. (2

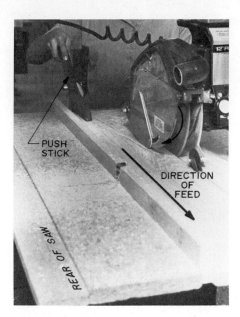

FIGURE 29-19
Ripping a board in the in-rip position

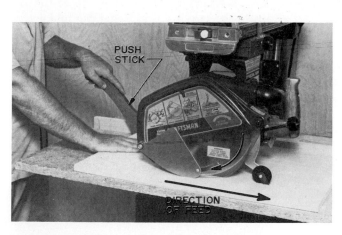

FIGURE 29-20
Ripping a board in the out-rip position.

mm) into the table, stop turning the elevation crank. Next adjust the nose or front of the upper blade housing so that it is no more than $\frac{1}{4}$ in. (6 mm) above the stock (Fig. 29-21). The antikickback fingers are set $\frac{1}{16}$ in. (2 mm) below the face of the stock. To finish the guard adjustment, aim the sawdust spout toward the rear of the saw.

Determine in which direction the stock is to be fed. The board must be directed against the rotation of the blade. When the saw is in the in-rip position, feed the material from right to left. The out-rip position requires the stock to be fed from left to right. Feeding a board from the wrong direction will lead to a serious kickback.

Turn on the power and feed the stock forward. Guide the stock along the fence and keep it flat

FIGURE 29-21
Proper setting for the blade guard when performing ripping operations.

FIGURE 29-22
Cutting a bevel cut.

against the table. Use a push stick to apply forward pressure between the fence and blade. Never place your hands in the path of the blade or closer than 4 in. (102 mm) to the cutting arc. Reaching under the arm can also lead to an accident.

CHAMFERING AND BEVELING

The saw is set up to make chamfers and bevels by raising the blade well above the fence. Next, swivel the motor unit. Use the bevel scale to determine when the blade has reached the desired angle.

On most saws there is a locating hole at the 30 and 45° settings. The bevel positive stop will automatically lock into these holes as the motor is swiveled. For angles other than these, use the bevel scale to set the angle.

With the blade in the rearmost position and the rip lock tightened, turn on the power. Slowly lower the blade until it is $\frac{1}{16}$ in. (2 mm) below the table. Securely holding the handle, loosen the rip lock and pull the motor unit out to the frontmost position. This will make a groove in the table.

When an accurate cut is required, cut a piece of scrap to check the angle (Fig. 29-22). Use a protractor to measure the angle cut on the board. Make any necessary adjustments. All cuts can then be made.

DADOING

The radial arm saw is ideal for cutting dados. Dados are grooves that run across the grain of the board and made use of crosscutting techniques. Layout lines are made on the top surface of the board. This makes them easy to see and for you to align the marks with the path of the dado head.

To dado a board, you will need to mount the dado head on the saw arbor. The procedure for attaching the dado head on the radial arm saw is the same as on the table saw. Refer to Chapter 28 for further details on this operation. Make certain that the inside chippers are equally spaced around the outside cutter and the teeth are pointed in the same direction as the direction of rotation. The guard assembly must be mounted and properly adjusted.

Lay out the lines on one board for each dado. Make the lines on the same side of the material as the dados are to be cut. Frequently, *blind dados* or *stopped dados* that do not extend across the entire face are made. Be careful that the two sides are laid out in pairs (Fig. 29-23). If the dados are not stopped at the correct edge, the two sides will not match up.

To make dados, adjust the depth of cut. Place the stock on the table and directly under the cutter. Lower the dado head until it just touches the top face. Pull the board back out of the way and lower the dado head the same amount as the depth of the dado. With most saws, each complete turn of the elevating crank will lower the dado head $\frac{1}{8}$ in. (3 mm). If the dado is to be $\frac{1}{4}$ in. (6 mm) deep, turn the crank two complete turns.

Next push the board against the fence and align the layout marks with the path of the dado head. If more than one dado is to be made in the same location, install a stop block against one end of the stock (Fig. 29-24). Turn on the power and firmly grasp the handle of the saw. Slowly bring the rotating head across the stock. Once the dado has reached the end of cut, push the motor unit back to the column. Check the cut for the proper depth and location. Make any necessary adjustments and proceed with the other dados.

FIGURE 29-23
Lay the blind dados out in pairs to make a right and left side.

FIGURE 29-24
Cutting a through dado with a stop block.

Specialized Dados

Dados can take several forms, including blind dados, corner dados, and ploughs. Although the basic procedure for each of these cuts is similar to that described in the preceding section, there are additional setup steps.

To make a blind dado, the forward movement of the dado head is stopped before it reaches the far edge of the stock. One method of making this dado is to mark the stopping point of each dado. You then carefully bring the rotating head up to these points as each dado is made. If several blind dados of the same length are to be cut, a stop clamp can be in-

stalled on the arm (Fig. 29-25). Once the yoke reaches the clamp, return it to the column.

Corner dados require that the stock be cradled in a 45° vee block (Fig. 29-26). Be certain that the vee block is large enough to support the stock and that the block is securely clamped to the fence.

Ploughing produces a cut running parallel with the grain. The saw is placed in the ripping mode for this operation. Refer to the section "Ripping" for the proper setup procedure. Be certain that the guard is adjusted and stock is fed from the correct side. Always use a push stick when the trailing end comes close to the cutter. If a stopped groove is needed install a stop block.

FIGURE 29-25
Cutting a stopped dado.

FIGURE 29-26
Cutting a corner dado.

RABBETING

Cutting rabbets is very similar to making dados and grooves. For making rabbets along an edge or face, the saw is set up in the ripping position. The rip lock secures the motor unit to the arm. Remove the existing fence and replace it with a straight scrap piece. This will allow the rotating dado head to be lowered into the fence, exposing the desired amount of the dado head. Guide the stock past the dado head (Fig. 29-27). Always use a push stick. Utilize standard crosscutting techniques for producing rabbets across the end of the board.

FIGURE 29-27
Cutting a rabbet.

COMBINATION RABBETING AND SAWING

By installing both a saw blade and a dado head, two operations can be accomplished with one pass of the saw. It is recommended that you use an 8-in. (202-mm) dado head with a 10-in. (254-mm) saw blade. Substitute one of the outside cutters on the dado head with the saw blade. This will allow the dado to make a groove while the stock is cut into.

When the stock is crosscut using this setup a rabbet will be made across the end and the stock cut to length (Fig. 29-28). By placing the saw in the rip mode, a rabbet is cut along the edge and the board is

FIGURE 29-28
Making a combination rabbet and saw cut.

ripped to width. To prevent the blade from cutting into the table, an auxiliary table and fence can be installed.

COVING

Cove cutting produces a recess or concave cut. Coves are sometimes used for decorative cuts on molding and trim. Either the outside cutter from a dado head or a molding head can be used to make this cut. You will need to start by laying out the desired depth and width of the cove (Fig. 29-29). Use a square to mark it on the end of the stock that will come in contact with the blade first.

FIGURE 29-29
Layout the width and depth of the cove to make the concave out.

Set up the saw by placing it in the bevel position. Raise the blade until the bottom of the cutting arc is equal to the depth of the cove. Pull the saw out on the arm until the blade is centered on the layout lines. Since only a light cut can be made with each pass of the board, raise the blade until only an $\frac{1}{8}$-in. (3-mm)-deep cut is made. Using ripping techniques, feed the stock past the angled rotating blade (Fig. 29-30). After each cut, lower the blade $\frac{1}{8}$ in. (3 mm). Continue this procedure until the cut has reached the width layout lines.

By varying the angle of the yoke and the diam-

FIGURE 29-30
Cutting a cove.

eter of the blade, different shapes of coves can be made. Using a smaller-diameter blade, for example, will produce a deeper recess for a fixed width of a cove. Angling the yoke at a larger angle will also make a deeper recess.

SAUCER CUTTING

Saucer cutting is a form of cove cutting where the board is kept in a stationary position (Fig. 29-31). The cutting action will produce a dish-shaped recess.

Since the side ring guards will interfere with the cut, they must be removed. Select a board long enough to be securely clamped to the saw table. Next, raise the motor unit. Place the saw in a 45° bevel position. While holding out on the bevel positive lock, use your left hand to grasp the antikickback rod or upper blade housing and pivot the motor unit back and forth. Note where the bottom of the arc is made. Center the stock under this arc or move the board wherever the saucer is to be made. Pull the motor unit out on the arm if the cut needs to be

FIGURE 29-31
Making a saucer cut. (Courtesy of Black & Decker.)

farther out on the board. Tighten the rip lock to keep the motor unit from moving. Be certain to clamp the stock securely to the table.

Setting the blade to take a very light cut, turn on the power. Make the first cut by pivoting the motor unit back and forth. Lower the blade $\frac{1}{16}$ in. (2 mm) and repeat the process. Continue this until the desired depth is reached. The last pass should be an extra light cut to achieve the best-quality surface.

HORIZONTAL CUTTING AND TENONING

To place the saw in the horizontal position, first raise the motor unit to approximately 4 in. (102 mm) above the table. Remove the standard blade guard assembly and install the special guard designed for this purpose. The motor unit is pivoted into the horizontal position. Once the blade is parallel to the table, the bevel positive stop will automatically slide into a positioning hole.

To make the cut the stock must be raised above the table and an auxiliary table must be constructed as shown in Fig. 29-32. It should be clamped securely to the radial arm saw table.

To make a tenon on the end of a board, use crosscutting techniques. Raise or lower the motor unit until the blade is in line with the layout lines on the sample stock. The depth of cut depends on how close the end of the board is to the blade. Keep your hands at least 4 in. (102 mm) from the path of the blade and make the cut.

To make a horizontal cut along the edge of a board, swing the yoke into the ripping position. A

FIGURE 29-32
Setting up to make a horizontal crosscut.

FIGURE 29-33
Making a groove in the horizontal cutting position. (Courtesy of Black & Decker.)

Crosscut molding cuts are done much like a dado cut. Remove the standard blade guard assembly and install the special guard. To prevent the edge of the stock closest to the fence from tearing out, a new fence which is taller than the top face of the stock should be installed (Fig. 29-35).

Sometimes horizontal-type cutting is used to shape the edges of the boards. An auxiliary molding table is used to raise the stock. Because the molding head is thick, a two-piece fence is required. Remove the standard fence and replace it with a shop-made two-piece fence. It must be tall enough to support the entire edge of the stock but allow the cutter to extend through the face of the fence. The molding head can also be utilized to make specialized cuts. By building a vee-shaped fence the edges of a circu-

MOULDING HEAD BODY

CUTTER SETS

FIGURE 29-34
Available cutters for a moulding head. (Courtesy of Delta International Machinery Corp.)

groove along an edge is shown in Fig. 29-33. Use an auxiliary table that extends across the entire length of the standard table. A push stick is required for narrow pieces. Use standard safe ripping techniques.

USING THE MOLDING HEAD

The molding head allows the radial arm saw to be used for shaper cuts. Because there are many different styles of changeable cutters for the molding head, the possible shapes you can produce are almost unlimited (Fig. 29-34). Trace around the cutter on the end of the stock to check the possible profile it can make. By adjusting the molding head from crosscutting to ripping to horizontal cutting positions, the same set of cutters will produce different-shaped patterns.

FIGURE 29-35
Crosscutting with the moulding head.

FIGURE 29-36
Shaping the edge of a circular disk.

FIGURE 29-37
Attach the pattern to the bottom of the stock.

lar disk can be shaped (Fig. 29-36). The larger the diameter of the disk, the wider the vee will need to be.

Decorative molding strips can be produced by running the edge on a wide board. The shaped strip is then ripped from the board to make the molding.

SAWING TO A PATTERN

When several pieces are needed of the same shape, pattern sawing can be used. Each side of the piece must be no smaller than 10 in. (254 mm) long.

Make a pattern exactly the same shape and size as the desired pieces (Fig. 29-37). Drive three or more sharpened screws through the pattern. The points should extend through the pattern by ⅛ in. (3 mm). Install a guide fence in place of the standard saw fence (Fig. 29-38). The height of the clamp guide fence should be the same as the thickness of the pattern. Clamp the guide fence to the standard fence. Set the saw in the out-rip position and align the saw blade exactly flush with the outside edge of the guide fence.

Cut the stock to rough size. Attach the piece to the pattern by tapping it lightly with a mallet. The

FIGURE 29-38
Set-up for sawing to a pattern.

tips of the screws must penetrate into the stock. Guide the pattern along the edge of the guide body. Any stock extending over the edge of the pattern will be cut away. Remove the pattern and attach the next piece.

STUDY QUESTIONS

Answer each of the following questions. If you are not sure of an answer, review the chapter.

29-1. The _____ should be properly adjusted for each different type of cut.

29-2. What type of crosscut saw is used in industry?

29-3. Name the two styles of arms utilized with the radial arm saw.

29-4. Name the major parts to the blade guard found on the radial arm saw.

29-5. How is the size of the radial arm saw determined?

29-6. When installing the saw blade, in which direction should the saw teeth point?

29-7. There must be at least _____ in. (_____ mm) of material to the left of the blade for the operator to hold for crosscut cuts.

29-8. When crosscutting several pieces to length, use a _____ to control the length of each board.

29-9. Using the formula given in the plain mitering section, how long would a piece of picture frame molding be if the picture is 12 in. long, the molding $1\frac{1}{2}$ in. wide, and the rabbet $\frac{1}{4}$ in. wide?

29-10. Another name for a compound miter is a _____ joint or _____ miter.

29-11. When cutting a six-sided compound miter with the sides angled to 10°, the blade should be tilted to _____°.

29-12. _____ dados or _____ dados do not extend across the entire face of the board.

29-13. _____ dados require the stock to be cradled in a 45° vee block.

29-14. For making rabbets along an edge or face, the saw is set up in the _____ position.

29-15. By installing a saw blade and a dado head, stock can be cut to _____ and _____ in one operation.

29-16. Saucer cutting is a form of _____ cutting.

29-17. When performing horizontal cutting an auxiliary _____ is clamped to the radial arm saw table to raise the stock.

29-18. The molding head allows the saw to be used for _____ cuts.

29-19. Pattern sawing can make several pieces the same _____.

IMPORTANT TECHNICAL TERMS

Following are technical terms that you should be able to use as part of your working vocabulary. Write a brief description of the meaning of each term.

Single arm
Turret arm
Miter clamp handle
Miter positive lock
Column
Elevation crank
Yoke
Yoke swivel clamp
Rip positive lock

Bevel clamp handle
Bevel positive stop
Blade guard
Upper blade housing
Sawdust spout
Ring guards
Antikickback assembly
Arbor
Elevating crank
In-rip position
Out-rip position
Blind dado/stop dado
Corner dado
Ploughing

30

BANDSAWS

The bandsaw is typically used to produce curves (Fig. 30-1). It is, however, well known for its large depth-of-cut capacity. This allows the machine to resaw thick stock into thinner boards. The bandsaw is unusual because the blade consists of a closed flexible band of steel with saw teeth cut on one edge.

Industry may use an automatic bandsaw (Fig. 30-2). Stock is first stacked on top of each other and clamped on the moving table. This table is then guided past the blade using a computer numerical control program. It is a very fast operation and will produce identical parts.

PARTS OF THE BANDSAW

A bandsaw has two blade wheels which are supported by a heavy framework. There is an *upper blade wheel* mounted above the table (Fig. 30-1). It keeps the blade tight and centered in the bandsaw guides. It is not directly connected to the motor and serves as an idler wheel. There is also a wheel located below the table. This wheel is connected to the motor usually by V-belts and drives the blade. Both the upper and lower wheels are protected by a door guard.

The outer edge of the wheels is covered with a *rubber tire*. The tire protects the blade so that it will not come in contact with the metal wheels. Smaller bandsaws have tires made of a strip of rubber cemented to the wheel. Larger models have steel-reinforced tires, which will last longer.

The *table* provides a work surface to position the stock. It is most generally located at a 90° angle to the blade. For cutting chamfers and bevels the table can be tilted to the right up to 45° and 5° to the left by loosening the tilt knob. By tightening the *tilt knob*, the table is secured to the desired angle. The angle scale will give the angle at which the table is positioned. A slot is cut into the table to slide the blade though. A *throat plate* is also inserted in the middle of the table to fill in the hole.

To the rear of the upper blade wheel are the controls for tightening and tracking the blade (Fig. 30-3). The *tension handwheel* raises and lowers the upper wheel. The higher the wheel is raised, the tighter the blade will become. In addition, the raising and lowering of this wheel allows for slightly different lengths of blades and for the blade to be removed. The *tracking knob* tilts the wheel in or out. This will angle the blade forward or backward in order that the blade can be centered on the wheel.

FIGURE 30-2
An automatic bandsaw cuts material using a numerical control program. (Courtesy of Tannewitz & Max Manufacturing Company.)

FIGURE 30-3
The tension handwheel and tracking knob keep the blade tight and centered between the two wheels.

FIGURE 30-1
Major parts of the bandsaw. (Courtesy of Delta International Machinery Corp.)

The two *bandsaw blade guides* keep the blade from twisting and being pushed off the wheels (Fig. 30-4). One guide is attached to the movable arm above the table. The bottom guide is permanently mounted on the bottom side of the table. Both the upper and bottom guides contain guide pins and a thrust wheel. The *guide pins* are adjusted in or out to the side of the blade and keep the blade from being twisted. The *thrust wheel* is located directly

FIGURE 30-4
A good-quality blade guide contains two guide pins and a thrust wheel.

behind the blade and supports the back edge of the blade. Without the thrust wheel the blade would be pushed off the wheels.

Some bandsaws contain a *footbrake* for rapidly stopping the blade. To use the brake the power is first turned off at the on-off switch. You can then step on the brake footpad which will stop the blade.

PURCHASING A BANDSAW

Always specify the size when purchasing a bandsaw. There are two considerations when determining size. The first is the distance or opening between the inside of the blade to the inside of the column. Most bandsaws have a throat size of 12 to 36 in. (305 to 914 mm). A good general-purpose bandsaw generally will have either a 14-or 20-in. (356- or 508-mm) throat size. The larger the opening, the wider a board can be cut between the blade and column. The second item in determining size is the maximum distance from the tabletop to the bottom of the raised upper blade guide. These heights range from $6\frac{1}{2}$ to 24 in. (165 to 610 mm). The larger size allows thicker or taller pieces to be cut.

A major consideration in the buying of a bandsaw is the blade guides (Fig. 30-4). The better the quality of the guides, the smoother the cut. They should have a large contact area to the sides of the blade and have a stable mounting. All parts should be replaceable to allow new components to be installed when they become worn.

The motor size for most general-purpose bandsaws should be at least $\frac{3}{4}$ HP. A larger motor size will

allow thicker boards to be cut. Smaller bandsaws will have a 120-V motor which can be plugged into a conventional outlet. Larger bandsaws will have 220- or 440-V motors which are typically wired permanently to a junction box. The blade should travel at a rate between 1500 and 6000 feet per minute (fpm). For most general-purpose cutting the blade should travel at 4500 fpm.

Another item to consider in buying a bandsaw is the blade capacity. Although narrow blades are most often used, being able to utilize a wide blade is desirable for straight cutting. A long blade length is also beneficial. A longer blade will run cooler and stay sharper longer.

Purchase a miter gauge and rip fence with the bandsaw. They will increase the versatility and safety of the machine. Many straight cuts and some fixtures require the use of these accessories.

Table size can be a factor if larger pieces are to be cut. The larger the surface, the more support will be provided. Some commercial bandsaws have a secondary table which bridges the space between the column and the edge of the main table (Fig. 30-5).

FIGURE 30-5
The secondary table provides support for extra wide material. (Courtesy of Oliver Machinery Company.)

SELECTING THE BLADE

Bandsaw blades are made from 100-ft-long coils of blade stock. The blade should be cut to proper length to fit around the bandsaw wheels according to the instructions of the machine manufacturer. The ends of the piece are welded with a band saw blade welder to form a finished blade (Fig. 30-6).

Blades can vary greatly in tooth styles and teeth per inch (Fig. 30-7). The most common tooth styles are the *skip, hook, buttress,* and *standard.* The set of the teeth provide clearance for the blade. Thick blades require more set than thin ones and are used primarily for making straight cuts. The additional set will produce a wide saw kerf and use up more material.

FIGURE 30-6
A bandsaw blade welder joins the two ends of the blade together.

The number of teeth should also be specified. More *teeth per inch* will provide a smoother cut. It is important, however, to have large enough gullets to remove the sawdust. In specifying the number of teeth, the term *points per inch* is used. There will be one more point than the number of teeth per inch (Fig. 30-7). A five-tooth blade will have six points.

The width of the blade also can be varied. Blade widths start at ⅛ in. (3 mm) and can reach over 1 in. (25 mm). The narrower the blade, the smaller the curve can be cut. Blades wider than ½ in. (13 mm) work best for straight cuts. The most common bandsaw blade for general-purpose sawing is ⅜ in. wide with five points per inch and having a hook set.

Most bandsaw blades are designed to be disposable. They are not resharpened or reset. Once the blade becomes dull, it is thrown away and a new one installed.

SKIP TOOTH

HOOK TOOTH

BUTTRESS OR SKIP TOOTH

STANDARD

MAJOR TOOTH STYLES

NARROW KERF — THIN BLADE LIGHT SET

WIDE KERF — THICK BLADE HEAVY SET

AMOUNT OF SET

6 POINTS   5 TEETH

POINTS PER INCH AND TEETH PER INCH

FIGURE 30-7
Styles of blade teeth and set.

REMOVING AND COILING THE BLADE

To remove a bandsaw blade, disconnect the power, remove the throat plate and open the door guards, then turn the tension handwheel counterclockwise. This will lower the upper wheel and loosen the tension on the blade. It can then be slipped from both wheels and passed through the slot in the table.

If the blade is to be stored, it should be coiled. This reduces the diameter of the blade. Start by holding the blade with the bottom of the loop just touching the floor (Fig. 30-8A). Place a foot on top the blade. The teeth should be pointing away from the operator. Bend the top of the loop downward by pushing the thumbs down (Fig. 30-8B). The teeth should point away from your body. Roll the hands outward until they face forward. Bend over and bring the hands together. The three smaller loops should form automatically (Fig. 30-8C).

If at any time the blade should start to knick or make a sharp bend, stop the procedure. Let the blade go back to the beginning step. Start the procedure over attempting to correct the mistake.

INSTALLING THE BLADE

Pull the bandsaw blade guides away from the sides of the blade and remove the throat plate. This will keep the guides from interfering with mounting the new blade. After uncoiling the new blade, hold it up in front of the bandsaw wheels. Make certain that the teeth next to the bandsaw guides are pointing forward and down.

Place the blade over the top of the upper bandsaw wheel. Slide the bottom of the loop over the bottom wheel. Center the blade in the middle of both wheels. Tighten the tension handwheel. This moves the upper bandsaw wheel upward and will tighten against the blade. Some bandsaws have a tension gauge (Fig. 30-9). This device indicates when the upper wheel has been raised the correct amount.

If a bandsaw does not have a tension gauge, tighten the blade until the blade deflects or moves to the side when pushed not more than $\frac{1}{8}$ in. (3 mm). Too little tension will cause the blade to move or lead to one side while cutting. A blade with too much tension will break. Narrow thin blades require more tension than do wider thicker blades.

(A)

(B)

FIGURE 30-8
Steps in coiling a bandsaw blade: (A) starting position; (B) second step; (C) third step.

(C)

FIGURE 30-9
The tension gauge indicates when the upper wheel has been raised to the proper height.

FIGURE 30-10
Paper spacers provide the proper side distance between the blade and guide pin.

Next, check the tracking of the bandsaw blade. Proper tracking requires the blade to ride in the middle of the bandsaw wheels (Fig. 30-3). Rotate the upper wheel by hand. If the blade does not center itself on the wheel, turn the tracking knob a small amount. Turn the bandsaw wheel again. Continue moving the tracking knob and turning the bandsaw wheel each time until the blade is centered.

Move the upper thrust wheel of the bandsaw guide in until it almost touches the back of the blade. Lock the guides into position. Do the same with the bottom thrust wheel. Turn the bandsaw wheels by hand. The thrust wheel should turn only when the blade is making a cut.

The side guides should be moved forward until the front edge of the guides are just behind the gullets of the blade. If the guides are too far forward, they will knock the set off of the blade. Place a piece of typing paper on each side of the blade (Fig. 30-10). Slide the side guides in until they just touch the paper. Lock into position. Remove the paper to provide the proper clearance. Repeat the procedure for the bottom set of guides.

Replace the guards and throat plate. Turn on the power by quickly switching the power on and off. This will cause the blade to coast. Check that the blade is properly tracking and make adjustments accordingly. Cut a scrap and check for squareness of cut with a square. If the cut is not square, adjust the table until it is perpendicular to the blade.

LAYING OUT THE PATTERN

Before laying out the pattern, plane the material to the desired finish thickness. Make certain that any surfaces which are not to be bandsawed are smooth and true. If the part requires straight edges and faces, it is better to use a tablesaw or jointer to produce these surfaces. It is much easier to do this initially when the board has square corners than after curves have been cut.

A major concern with laying out the material is achieving the maximum *yield* or usage from the material. If only one part is to be cut, select a piece of material that is slightly larger than the finished size. It is important always to have a small amount of waste on the outside edge of any curve (Fig. 30-11). This will prevent the blade from leaving the material and making it difficult to restart the cut. A great deal of waste material outside the cut, however, will only increase the cost of the project.

When more than one part is needed, layout becomes even more important. Study the shapes carefully and see how they can best fit on the stock to get

FIGURE 30-11
Lay out the pattern so that the blade will always be in contact with the material.

the best yield. It works best to cut patterns out of paper and then try different arrangements on the board. Sometimes the patterns can be angled to get a closer fit. Be careful, however, that there is sufficient room for the blade to pass between the pieces. Some pieces also require that the grain run in a certain direction. If this is the case, parts may need to lie in a particular direction.

When parallel curves are required, another form of stock utilization can be used. The size of the original board can be reduced considerably if the waste from the first cut is glued to the opposite straight edge (Fig. 30-12). After the adhesive dries, the second cut can be made. This is called *nesting of parts*.

Another consideration in layout is the face on which the pattern is drawn. This is particularly important with long boards. Marking it out on the wrong side will cause the board to strike the column as the cut is being made (Fig. 30-13).

SETTING UP THE BANDSAW

Before turning on the power, first determine if the proper blade is mounted on the machine. Next estab-

FIGURE 30-12
Nesting of parts saves a great deal of material.

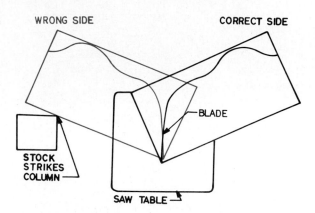

FIGURE 30-13
Laying the pattern on the right side of the board will prevent the stock from striking the column

lish what is the smallest radius on the pattern. Refer to Fig. 30-14 to see the maximum width of blade that can be used. The narrower the blade, the sharper the curve can be made. Wide blades will produce straighter cuts. Although relief cuts can allow smaller curves to be made, it is desirable to make the cut in one pass.

After the stock has been planed to thickness, place it on the table next to the blade. The material must have a flat surface to place against the table or be held in a fixture to keep it from rocking. Adjust the upper blade guide assembly to $\frac{1}{4}$ in. (6 mm) above the stock (Fig. 30-15).

OPERATING THE BANDSAW

After the pattern has been laid out, plan the order of cuts. There should be as little backing out of cuts as possible. Usually, it is best to cut the shortest distance first (Fig. 30-16). Also make straight cuts before cutting curves. It is easier to back out of a straight cut. If it is necessary to cut up to a line, turn off the power, allow the blade to stop turning and then back out of the cut. It may be easier to cut through the waste and start the cut from the opposite end.

To feed the material forward, use a firm pressure. Feed the material as fast as the blade will efficiently cut. Too fast a rate will break the blade. Too slow a feed will overheat the blade and dull it. It is very important to keep the hands out of the direct path of the blade. If the board should accidentally split or the hands should slip, the hands should be on either side of the blade.

CUTTING CURVES

The major secret to cutting accurate curves is to achieve a high degree of skill. This comes through a

FIGURE 30-16
Make the shortest cuts first.

WIDTH OF BLADE IN INCHES	SMALLEST RADIUS THAT CAN BE CUT
$\frac{1}{8}$"	$\frac{3}{8}$"
$\frac{3}{16}$"	$\frac{1}{2}$"
$\frac{1}{4}$"	$\frac{3}{4}$"
$\frac{3}{8}$"	$1\frac{1}{4}$"
$\frac{1}{2}$"	$1\frac{3}{4}$"
$\frac{3}{4}$"	2"

FIGURE 30-14
Smallest radius that can be cut with each width of blade.

great deal of practice. Since most are cut using free-hand techniques, the operator must be able to guide the stock successfully. With practice, the pattern can consistently be cut on the layout line in a minimal amount of time.

After the proper blade is selected, the machine adjusted and the best path for the blade selected, the cutting can begin. Although the blade must be kept in the waste area, stay immediately next to the layout line. This will reduce the amount of material that must be later sanded or filed away. If the blade wanders across the layout line, back the board up and recut.

If the pattern contains curves which are too small to cut with one pass, *relief cuts* are required (Fig. 30-17). These are short cuts through the waste within $\frac{1}{32}$ in. (1 mm) of the layout line. As the pattern

FIGURE 30-15
There should be no more than $\frac{1}{4}$ in. (6 mm) between the guide and stock.

FIGURE 30-17
Relief cuts allow small curves to be cut with a wide blade.

FIGURE 30-18
First boring holes will save a great deal of time.

is cut, the small pieces will fall free. This keeps the back of the blade from rubbing against the saw kerf. If internal circles or parts of circles are required, first bore them on the drill press using a drill bit of the same diameter as the layout (Fig. 30-18). This saves time and gives superior results.

MULTIPLE CUTTING

Several pieces of the same pattern can be cut at one time. Use a large bandsaw capable of making heavy cuts. Be careful not to cut more pieces than what can be easily cut. First layout the pattern on one piece. Stack two or more pieces on top of each other with the pattern piece on top. Drive nails through the waste portion. Cut the boards to pattern (Fig. 30-19). All pieces will be the exact same shape.

FIGURE 30-19
Cutting more than one piece at a time will speed production. Be careful not to saw into the nails.

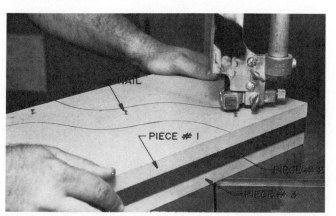

CUTTING TO A PATTERN

In some cases it is desirable to use a pattern to cut multiple parts. Cutting after a pattern has the advantages of producing identical parts and requiring a lower operator skill level. It does require time to set up and the curves must be moderate in size.

A modified *pivot block* is clamped to the table (Fig. 30-20). A step is made on the bottom side of the pivot block to allow the waste to pass under it. It has a curved end whose radius will match the smallest radius on the pattern. The center of the pivot block should be in the same line as the front edge of the blade. A notch is cut into the edge of the pivot block for the blade to fit into (Fig. 30-20). It is very important that the teeth set to the left are exactly on a line even with the edge of the pivot block.

Make a pattern out of ¾-in. (19-mm) hardwood the exact same size as the finished piece. Place screws through the pattern which will extend into the stock ¼ in. (6 mm). Center the pattern over the stock and drive the screw into the back of the board. Guide the pattern past the pivot block (Fig. 30-21). Keep the pattern at right angles to each curve. Remove the screws after the cut is made.

FIGURE 30-20
Proper set-up for cutting after a pattern.

FIGURE 30-21
Cutting a piece using a pattern and pivot block.

COMPOUND SAWING

Compound sawing requires that two adjoining surfaces be bandsawed to a curved pattern. The process produces a *compound curve*. Although there are many examples of compound sawing, the cabriole leg is the most popular.

To make a cabriole leg, square the stock to size and make any required mortises or dowel joints. Lay out and cut a full-size cardboard template (Fig. 30-22). This is the most important step when making a cabriole leg. Designing a leg that is both beautiful and strong can be a challenge.

If the cabriole leg is 15 in. (381 mm) or less in height, make the template no wider than $2\frac{1}{4}$ in. (64 mm). Legs that are longer than 15 in. (381 mm) can be made from a template up to 3 in. (76 mm) wide. It is of prime importance that the center line at the top of the leg pass through the foot. Ideally, the center line should pass through the center of the foot. After the cabriole leg has been cut, it should stand by itself.

Trace around the template on one of the sides. After installing a narrow blade, cut out the pattern on this side of the leg. Bandsaw each line with one smooth pass (Fig. 30-23). Do not make any relief cuts unless necessary.

Tape the waste or off-fall back on the leg. This will provide a flat surface for drawing the pattern and positioning against the bandsaw table. Roll the leg 90° and mark the second adjacent side.

Cut the second side using the same techniques as for the first (Fig. 30-24). After making the last cut, use rasps, files, and abrasive paper to smooth

FIGURE 30-22
Design a cabriole leg with the foot centered.

PARTS OF A
CABRIOLE LEG

CORNER POST
EAR
ANKLE
FOOT
PAD

11" STOOL LEG

29" TABLE LEG   17$\frac{1}{2}$" CHAIR LEG

FIGURE 30-23
Cutting the first side of a cabriole leg. The waste or off-fall is to the left of the blade.

FIGURE 30-24
Cutting the second side of a cabriole leg with the waste taped to the sides.

the surfaces (Fig. 30-25). The foot of the leg can be made round by also using hand techniques.

To give the cabriole leg a more flowing appearance, *wings* or *ears* can be added as a secondary operation (Fig. 30-22). These are small extensions doweled to the side of each leg. Use a file to blend the wings into the curved top of the cabriole leg.

Some compound curves are not symmetrical and require two templates. Examples of unsymmetrical compound curves include a boat hull and shoe blanks. They can be cut using the same techniques as discussed before except a different template is used for each cut.

FIGURE 30-26
Parts of a circle cutting fixture.

FIGURE 30-25
Work the cabriole leg smooth and to the final shape with files and abrasive paper.

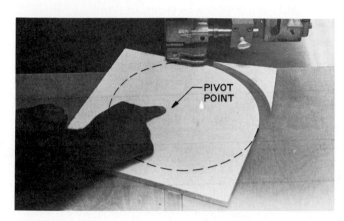

FIGURE 30-27
Making a circle with a circle cutting fixture.

CUTTING CIRCLES

Cutting a circle can be done in one of two ways. If only a few pieces are needed, first scribe the circle with a compass. The circles can then be freehanded on the bandsaw. This method requires a great deal of operator skill to produce a smooth true circle. A circle cutting fixture is recommended if a perfect circle or segment of a circle is required. Very little skill is needed to produce large quantities of circles with this technique. It does call for a sharp blade with even set.

To make a circle-cutting fixture, select a piece of plywood slightly larger than the right half of the bandsaw table (Fig. 30-26). Center a dovetail dado on the face of the plywood immediately to the right of the bandsaw blade. Insert a dovetail-shaped hardwood strip into the dado. Wax the strip so that it will slide in and out freely. Clamp the plywood to the tabletop. Scribe a mark from the leading edge of the blade across the *pivot strip*.

Remove the strip and from the bottom side drive a small flathead wood screw 1 in. (25 mm) from

the end. The tip of the screw should extend through the face approximately $\frac{1}{4}$ in. (6 mm). File this tip to a sharply tapered point to serve as a pivot point. Slide the strip in the dado positioning it so that the pivot point is the same distance away from the saw tooth set to the right as the radius of the circle. Clamp the pivot strip in the dado with a C-clamp. Square the stock to rough width and length on the tablesaw. Center the board over the screw point and push down. If the wood is hard, use a mallet to tap the center of the board. One edge must be against the blade. Turn on the power and slowly turn the stock (Fig. 30-27).

CUTTING ROUNDED CORNERS

A corner can easily be rounded on the bandsaw using a pivoting fixture (Fig. 30-28). Mount a piece of $\frac{3}{4}$-in. (19-mm) plywood over the right side of the

FIGURE 30-28
Rounding corners using a pivoting fixture.

bandsaw table. Draw a line perpendicular to the front edge of the blade. Place a short ½-in. (13-mm) dowel pin along this line (Fig. 30-29). The center of the dowel should be the same distance from the blade as the radius of the rounded corner. Construct a pivoting table to cradle the stock. It has a hole in it to fit over the dowel pin. Place a stop on the plywood to keep the stock from turning too far. Position the stock in the pivoting table and turn the table to cut the corner.

CROSSCUTTING A BOARD

To cut a board squarely across the end requires the use of a miter gauge. Place the gauge in the miter gauge groove to the right of the blade. The front of

FIGURE 30-29
Parts of a pivoting fixture.

the gauge should be covered with a piece of wood (Fig. 30-30). Glue a piece of coarse abrasive paper to the face of the board. This abrasive-covered board will prevent the stock from slipping to the side.

Mount the widest available blade on the saw. The wider blade will prevent the cut from drifting when cutting a straight line. Square a line where the cut is to be made. Align the layout line with the saw tooth set to the right. Hold the board against the miter gauge as it passes the blade.

FIGURE 30-30
Crosscutting a board using a miter gauge. Note the abrasive covered board on the gauge.

RIPPING STOCK

There are three methods of ripping stock on the bandsaw. Regardless of the method, use at least a ½-in. (13-mm)-wide blade. The freehand method requires that a line be scribed where the cut is to be made. Place the left hand flat on the table and use the edge of the thumb as a guide. Slide the stock along the thumb (Fig. 30-31). Move the trailing end to the left or right to keep the blade centered on the layout line.

The second method requires the use of a rip fence. Place it to the right of the blade (Fig. 30-32). Clamp the fence down so that the distance from the saw tooth set to the right is equal to the width of the board. Use a push stick to feed the board.

The third method requires that a pivot block first be made (Fig. 30-33). Round one end and sand it smooth. The height of the pivot block should be slightly less than the stock to be ripped. Clamp the pivot block to the right of the blade. The rounded end should be in line with the leading edge of the blade. Feed the stock past the blade. If the blade

FIGURE 30-31
Ripping a board using the freehand technique.

FIGURE 30-33
Ripping a board using a pivot block.

FIGURE 30-32
Ripping a board using a rip fence.

FIGURE 30-34
Resawing a board with a rip fence and featherboard.

starts to drift one direction or the other, move the trailing end of the board in the direction the cut is heading.

RESAWING A BOARD

Resawing lumber on the bandsaw allows two or more thin boards to be made from one thicker piece. Unlike the tablesaw, the bandsaw makes the cut in one pass. Because the bandsaw kerf is only $\frac{1}{16}$ in. (2 mm) wide much less waste is also generated. If book match grain is required for raised panel doors or in an attractive glue joint, resawing is an easy method of producing this material.

To achieve the straightest cut, install the widest blade available. A $\frac{3}{4}$-inch (19-mm) blade works well. A wide blade will run cooler and not drift away from a straight line. Use a slow feed rate because of the heavy cut.

Resawing can be accomplished with either a rip fence or a pivot block. With the rip fence method, first clamp it to the table (Fig. 30-34). Stock is fed

past the blade using a push stick. An elevated featherboard on the outside surface of the board will help keep the stock against the fence. Position the featherboard in front of the blade.

Resawing with a pivot block requires that a shop-made pivot block be constructed (Fig. 30-35). The device should be slightly less in height than the width of the board to be resawed. Bandsaw a curve on the front end of the pivot block. Sand this radius smooth.

Position the pivot block the same distance away from the blade as the desired thickness of the stock plus $\frac{1}{8}$ in. (3 mm). Since the bandsaw will not produce a finished surface, the extra $\frac{1}{8}$ in. (3 mm) will provide material to be planed. The front curve of the pivot block should be in line with the leading edge of the blade.

FIGURE 30-35
Resawing with a pivot block.

Turn on the power and push the stock forward. If the cut is not parallel to the face of the board direct the trailing end of the board to the right or left. Once the saw kerf returns to a straight line, move the trailing end back parallel to the blade.

CUTTING SQUARE INSIDE CORNERS

Square corners can be cut by a variety of methods. When several pieces are to be cut bore a large round turning hole in each corner (Fig. 30-36). This allows the blade to be turned without binding. A mortiser can also be used. It will give a square hole which needs no further attention.

A square corner can also be cut using only the bandsaw. Start by making a straight cut on each

FIGURE 30-36
A turning hole allows the board to be turned at the corner.

FIGURE 30-37
Cutting an inside corner using only the bandsaw.

side of the board along the layout line (Fig. 30-37). On the second straight cut, saw up to the intersecting line and back out partway. Next cut a large-diameter curve over to the first cut. Remove the waste and cut away the remaining portion.

Method B of cutting a square corner requires sawing up to the intersecting line and backing up the blade a couple of inches (Fig. 30-37). Saw forward again but to the side of the first cut. Repeat the process until a large notch is made in the waste portion. Turn the blade in the notch and cut in the next direction.

CUTTING CYLINDRICAL STOCK

Because round stock such as dowel pins have a tendency to roll, they must be cradled in a vee block. Never freehand-cut round stock. Use the miter gauge and vee block to crosscut cylindrical stock.

To rip a round piece requires the use of a rip fence (Fig 30-38). Position the rip fence so that when the vee block is positioned against the face of the rip fence, the blade is centered at the bottom of the vee. Cut into the vee block so that the blade is positioned halfway along the length of the block. Scribe a line along the length of the cylindrical stock. Rip the stock by using a push stick.

FIGURE 30-38
Ripping a cylinder using a vee block.

STUDY QUESTIONS

Answer each of the following questions. If you are not sure of an answer, review the chapter.

30-1. Before turning on the power, adjust the saw guard and guide _____ in. (_____ mm) above the stock to be cut.

30-2. The outer edge of the bandsaw wheels are covered with a _____ .

30-3. Which knob on the bandsaw will tilt the upper blade wheel in or out?

30-4. Name the two major parts of a bandsaw blade guide.

30-5. How is the size of a bandsaw determined?

30-6. The more _____ per inch on the blade, the smoother the cut will be.

30-7. When the blade is to be stored, it should be _____ to reduce the diameter of the blade.

30-8. When installing a blade, make certain that the teeth next to the bandsaw guides are pointing _____ .

30-9. A major concern with laying out the material is achieving the maximum _____ or usage from the material.

30-10. When the blade mistakenly wanders across the layout line, _____ the board up and recut.

30-11. If a pattern contains curves that are too small to cut with one pass, _____ cuts are required.

30-12. Cutting after a pattern requires a _____ block to guide the stock against.

30-13. A product produced in compound sawing is a _____ leg.

30-14. A _____ fixture is recommended if a perfect circle or segment of a circle is required.

30-15. To crosscut a board, install the _____ available blade.

30-16. Resawing can be accomplished with either a _____ fence or a _____ block.

30-17. When cutting several square inside corners, bore a large round turning hole in each _____ .

30-18. Use a _____ block to prevent cylindrical stock from rolling.

Following are technical terms that you should be able to use as part of your working vocabulary. Write a brief description of the meaning of each term.

Upper blade wheel
Rubber tire
Tilt knob
Angle scale
Throat plate
Tension handwheel
Tracking knob
Bandsaw blade guides
Guide pins

Thrust wheel
Tooth Styles:
    Skip
    Hook
    Buttress
    Standard
Teeth per inch
Points per inch
Nesting of parts
Relief cuts
Pivot block
Compound curve
Pivot strip
Resawing

31

SCROLL SAWS

The scroll saw is best known for its ability to produce small intricately curved shapes in thin material (Fig. 31-1). Many woodworkers also call this machine a *jig saw*. The scroll saw has an unusual cutting action when compared to other equipment. It has a *reciprocating blade* or a cutting tooling that is moved up and down to saw the material. This cutting action can be compared to a hand coping saw.

A scroll saw is used in industry for many of the same operations as it is used for in schools. Pattern-makers, for example, may use this saw for cutting small, detailed parts. To make heavier cuts, a larger model is sometimes selected (Fig. 31-2).

PARTS OF THE SCROLL SAW

The major parts of the scroll saw are the overarm, blade chucks, table, and crank shaft drive (Fig. 31-1). To the rear of the saw is the *overarm*. It is a structural part that connects the base to the *tension sleeve* and *upper blade chuck*. The base holds the *table, motor,* and the *crank shaft drive*. The crank shaft drive is responsible for changing the circular motion of the motor to the reciprocating movement for the blade.

To keep the blade running in a straight line, the scroll saw has two *blade chucks* and one *blade*

guide (Fig. 31-3). The upper blade chuck is attached to the end of the tension sleeve at the end of the overarm. Located below the table is the lower blade chuck, which is attached to the crank shaft drive.

The upper guide assembly is located on the end of the guide post (Fig. 31-3). Both are adjusted up or down by loosening the guide post thumb screw. At the end of the guide assembly is the support disk and guide roller. They keep the blade from twisting and being pushed backwards.

Stock is positioned against the table in order to be machined. To cut a bevel, the table can be tilted to the left or right up to 45° (Fig. 31-4). Loosen the *tilt knob* to allow the table to move. An *angle scale* located below the table indicates the set angle. In the center of the table is a hole that holds the *table insert*. Removing the table insert allows a new blade to be passed through the opening in the table.

PURCHASING A SCROLL SAW

There are not a great many items to consider when purchasing a scroll saw. This is because there are few options from which to select. Most manufacturers offer only one size. The size of the scroll saw is determined by measuring the distance to the nearest inch from the front of the blade to the front of the

FIGURE 31-2
Commercial-duty scroll saw. (Courtesy of Oliver Machinery Company.)

FIGURE 31-1
Major parts of a scroll saw. (Courtesy of Delta International Machinery Corp.)

FIGURE 31-3
The blade is controlled by the blade chucks and blade guide. (Courtesy of Delta International Machinery Corp.)

FIGURE 31-4
By loosening the tilt knob the table can be angled.

overarm. This is called the *throat opening*. The most common size is 24 in. (610 mm). With a 24-in. (610-mm) scroll saw, the operator can saw to the middle of a 48-in. (1219-mm)-diameter circle.

Another feature to specify is the speed control. The speed of the reciprocating blade is controlled by one of three ways. The simplest and least expensive is a *cone pulley* (Fig. 31-5). A V-belt is moved from one step on the pulley to another to regulate the speed. Available speeds include 610, 910, 1255, and 1725 *cutting strokes per minute* (CS/M). The largest diameter pulley on the motor will give the *slowest*

FIGURE 31-5
A cone pulley allows the V-belt to be moved to change cutting speeds.

FIGURE 31-6
A variable-speed pulley changes the cutting speed by turning the speed adjustment crank.

FIGURE 31-7
The electronic system changes speeds by turning a control knob. (Courtesy of Delta International Machinery Corp.)

speed. A more convenient method of adjusting the speed is with the variable speed pulley (Fig. 31-6). By turning the *speed-adjustment crank* the speed is changed. An infinite number of CS/M is available from 650 to 1700. Turning the crank to the clockwise will increase the CS/M rate. Only move the crank when the power is on. The newest method of varying the speed is with an *electronic system* (Fig. 31-7). By

TABLE 31-1
Recommended Operating Speeds

Material or operation	General features of blade	Operating speed (rpm)
Hardwood		
$\frac{3}{4}$-in. stock	Medium temper; set teeth; not over 15 teeth per inch	1000–1750
$\frac{1}{4}$-in. stock	Medium temper; teeth need not be set	1750
Softwood		
$\frac{3}{4}$-in. stock	Medium temper; set or wide-spaced teeth; not over 10 teeth per inch	1750
$\frac{1}{4}$-in. stock	Teeth need not be tempered or set	1300–1750
Puzzles, inlays, marquetry	Not tempered; not set; blade must be thin	1300–1750
Soft metals		
Over $\frac{1}{8}$ in.	Medium-hard temper; set teeth	650
Under $\frac{1}{8}$ in.	Medium-hard temper; set or not set	650–1000
Iron and steel	Hard temper; set teeth	650
Plastic, bone, ivory		
Rough cut	Medium temper; set teeth	1000–1300
Finish cut	Medium temper; with or without set	1000–1750

simply turning a control knob, the up-and-down blade movement is changed. Any speed between 40 and 2000 CS/M can be selected. A lighted gauge indicates the cutting speed. For hard materials such as metals and plastics, select a very slow speed. Hardwood with large to medium-sized curves can be cut at a medium speed. Softwoods are cut at a fast speed. Other recommended speeds are given in Table 31-1.

Most scroll saws have available a steel stand. It provides a stable table that is relatively easy to move around. If a stand is not purchased, make certain that the saw is securely bolted to a sturdy tabletop.

SELECTING THE SCROLL SAW BLADES

Because there are numerous available blades, the scroll saw can cut many different materials. Blades can vary by length, width, thickness, and teeth per inch. Table 31-2 gives the recommended blades for various materials.

Select a thin narrow blade with many teeth for sharp curves or for cutting thin material. For thicker stock and larger curves, use a wider thicker blade with fewer teeth. The more teeth per inch, the slower the cut will be, but the smoother the surface. There should be at least three teeth in contact with the stock at all times. Blades are specifically designed to saw wood, plastic, metals, and many other materials. By referring to the information on the blade package, match the blade with the type of stock being cut.

Most blades are rectangular in shape and designed to be gripped by both the upper and lower blade chucks. They are called *jeweler's blades* (Fig. 31-8). Specialty blades can also be used. The *saber blade* is a *specialty blade* which is tapered and designed to be held only by the bottom blade guide. It is used for making internal cuts which do not contain many sharp curves. A *circular blade* is another specialty blade that can cut from any direction without turning the stock.

When not on the scroll saw, keep all blades in some type of storage rack or in a protective cover. This will keep them from touching each other and becoming dull.

FIGURE 31-8
Styles of scroll saw blade.

INSTALLING THE BLADE

After selecting the best blade for the job, install it on the scroll saw. Start by unplugging the power cord. Remove the table insert in the middle of the table. With the teeth pointing downward and forward lower it through the hole in the table. Use a *guide*

404

TABLE 31-2
Recommended Blade Styles

Material cut	Width in.	Teeth per inch	Blade full size
Steel ■ Iron Lead ■ Copper Aluminum	.070	32	
Pewter Asbestos Paper ■ Felt	.070	20	
Steel ■ Iron Lead ■ Copper Brass	.070	15	
Aluminum Pewter Asbestos	.085	15	
Wood	.110	20	
Asbestos ■ Brake Lining ■ Mica Steel ■ Iron Lead ■ Copper Brass Aluminum Pewter	.250	20	
Wood Veneer Plus Plastics Celluloid Hard Rubber Bakelite Ivory Extremely Thin Materials	.035	20	
Plastics Celluloid	.050	15	
Bakelite	.070	7	
Ivory ■ Wood	.110	7	
Wall Board Pressed Wood Wood ■ Lead Bone ■ Felt Paper ■ Copper Ivory Aluminum	.110	15	
Hard and Soft Wood	.110	10	
	.187	10	
	.250	7	
Pearl ■ Pewter Mica	.054	30	
Pressed Wood Sea Shells	.054	20	
Hard Leather	.085	12	

As a general rule, always select the narrowest blades recommended for intricate curve cutting and widest blades for straight and large curve cutting operations.

Source: Delta Internation Machinery Corp.

board to make certain that the blade is perpendicular to the table (Fig. 31-9).

Insert the blade at least $\frac{1}{2}$ in. (13 mm) into the lower blade chuck. The blade must be placed between the chuck blocks before hand tightening the thumbscrew (Fig. 31-10).

Turn the motor shaft by hand until the blade chuck is at the bottom-most position. By loosening

the tension sleeve knob, adjust the tension sleeve until the top blade chuck is approximately 1 in. (25 mm) above the top of the blade. This will provide the proper tension on the blade and keep it from flexing. Pull the chuck down over the blade. It, too, should cover the blade by $\frac{1}{2}$ in. (13 mm). Tighten the chuck thumbscrew.

The thinner and narrower the blade, the more tension is required. If the blade does have a tendency to bend, raise the tension sleeve an additional $\frac{1}{2}$ in. (13 mm). Occasionally, the blade will also *drift*. This creates a sideways convex type of cut along the edge (Fig. 31-11). To straighten the cut, increase the tension, use a wider blade, or select a blade with more teeth per inch.

FIGURE 31-9
A guide board assures that the blade is at a right angle to the table.

FIGURE 31-10
Position the blade between the chuck blocks.

INSERT BLADE HERE

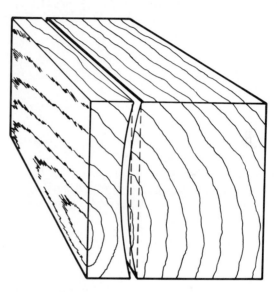

FIGURE 31-11
Drift produces a convex shape cut.

Spaced around the *support disk* are several slots for supporting the blade (Fig. 31-12). Select the slot that allows the blade to move freely up and down. It should prevent the blade from twisting as curves are being cut. The disk should support the blade but not touch the saw teeth. Check that the front of the disk is located immediately behind the blade gullets. Always check the fit of the slot when installing a different blade. The support disk may need to be rotated to position a better-fitting slot to support the blade.

Move the *guide roller* out to keep the blade from bending backward (Fig. 31-3). Replace the table insert and position the stock to be cut next to the blade. By loosening the guide post thumbscrew, lower the upper guide. The spring hold-down must rest lightly on top of the stock. If the table is tilted, it is also necessary to angle the holddown to the same angle.

FIGURE 31-12
The support disk keeps the blade from twisting.

Turn the motor shaft by hand to check for proper adjustments. See that the table is set at the desired angle by checking the angle gauge. Plug in the power cord.

To install a saber saw blade, install a *lower blade guide* below the table (Fig. 31-13). Since the upper blade guide is not used, this device will keep the saber saw blade from twisting. Rotate the lower blade chuck one-fourth of a turn. Insert the blade between the chuck thumbscrew. If much cutting is to be done with this type of blade, remove the overarm.

LOWER BLADE
GUIDE

LOWER BLADE
CHUCK

CHUCK THUMB
SCREW

FIGURE 31-13
Installing a saber saw blade. (Courtesy of Delta International Machinery Corp.)

MAKING A LAYOUT

Before any cutting can be done, the pattern needs to be drawn or laid out on the stock. The simplest but slowest method is to draw the pattern on each piece. If only one or two parts are needed, this may be acceptable. A slightly faster method is to use a piece

of carbon tracing over the drawing; the pattern will be transferred onto the material.

When several parts of the same shape are needed, the *template method* can be used (Fig. 31-14). First make a template out of cardboard, hardboard, sheet metal, or other long-wearing material. Place the template over the material and trace around it using a pencil. Keep the template from slipping as the pattern is being drawn. Using this piece will allow the original template to last longer.

Sometimes it is necessary to reduce or enlarge

TEMPLATE

STOCK

FIGURE 31-14
Laying out a part using the template method.

FIGURE 31-15
The graph method allows patterns to be reduced or enlarged in size. This illustration shows a part being enlarged.

$\frac{1}{2}$ INCH SQUARES
ORIGINAL
DRAWING

I INCH SQUARES
ENLARGED
DRAWING

a pattern. The *graph method* allows the size of pattern to be changed easily (Fig. 31-15). Decide how many times smaller or larger the pattern should be than the original. If the pattern is to be made twice the size of the original drawing, draw $\frac{1}{2}$-in. graph squares over the top of the drawing. Next draw 1-in. graph square on the stock. Wherever the object line of the pattern crosses a graph line on the drawing, place a corresponding mark on the same squire located on the stock. After all points are transferred, use a French curve to connect the points. By changing the ratio of the size of the square, the size can be enlarged or made smaller.

If many patterns are to be enlarged an opaque or overhead projector can be used (Fig. 31-16). The master used in the projector can be an actual drawing, picture from a magazine, or photograph. By moving the projector in and out or by adjusting the focal length of the picture, the projected image can be adjusted in size. The image can be traced around onto the stock or onto a piece of cardboard. The piece of cardboard then becomes a template after it is cut to shape.

FIGURE 31-17
Proper cutting procedure for making an external cut. Make the shortest cut first.

FIGURE 31-16
Making a pattern with an overhead projector.

MAKING EXTERNAL CUTS

The most common operation with the scroll saw is cutting irregular shapes. This requires the outline of the shape to be drawn on the stock. Use one of the methods discussed in the section "Making a Layout."

Install the recommended blade and set the cutting speed to the proper cutting strokes per minute. Adjust the upper blade guide assembly. The spring hold-down must be positioned against the top surface of the stock.

Study the layout and determine the most efficient path to guide the blade (Fig. 31-17). Ideally,

the entire shape can be cut with one pass of the blade. Very detailed complicated layouts, however, may need to be divided into sections and certain parts removed a section at a time. When small curves are required, *relief cuts* are necessary (Fig. 31-18). These short straight cuts are made in the waste portion of the stock. Relief cuts keep the blade from binding on sharp curves and eliminate having to back out of cuts. They divide the curve into sections and extend to within $\frac{1}{32}$ in. (1 mm) from the

FIGURE 31-18
Relief cuts allow small curves to be cut.

RELIEF CUTS

layout line. As the layout is then cut, small portions of the waste fall away, keeping the blade from binding.

Because the scroll saw is a very slow cutting machine, use a slow feed rate. The thicker the stock, the slower the feed rate should be. Keep the fingers and hands away from the path of the blade. Stay to the waste side of the layout line. If the blade drifts across the line, back the board up and recut the stock.

A scroll blade is fragile and breaks easily. Applying too much forward pressure will bend the blade backward and it will snap. Turn the stock slowly when cutting curves. Forcing the blade around corners will cause the blade to twist and break. Never push the board sideways because this action will also damage the blade.

MAKING IDENTICAL PIECES

Many projects require more than one part of the same shape. Although pieces can be cut one at a time, the job can go much faster if several parts are cut at the same time. One method of producing several parts is called *stack cutting* (Fig. 31-19). Several pieces are first placed one on top of the other. A few small brads are driven through the waste area to hold the pieces together. As the top piece is cut, so will the stock below it.

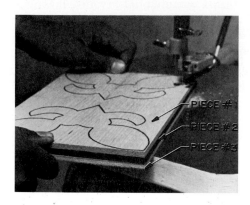

FIGURE 31-19
Stack cutting allows several pieces to be cut at one time.

MAKING IDENTICAL CURVED CUTS

If many identical curved cuts are required, a shop-built curved fence and template can be constructed (Fig. 31-20). The template is made from dense hardwood and is the exact size and shape of the finished product. The curved fence contains the opposite shape of the template. A notch is cut in the edge of this fence to position the blade. Spacers are attached

FIGURE 31-20
Identical curved parts can be made with a shop-made fence and template.

to the bottom of the fence to raise it off the table. The distance from the bottom of the fence to the table should be slightly more than the thickness of the stock to be cut.

Clamp the curved fence to the table. Position the blade in the notch of the fence. The saw tooth set to the right must be exactly in line with the curved edge of the fence. Cut the stock to the finish size. Attach the stock to the template with nails or screws. Turn on the power and guide the template along the fence. As the stock passes the blade, the curve will be reproduced in the wood mounted on the bottom. Once the stock has cleared the blade, remove the template and cut the next piece.

MAKING INTERNAL CUTS

An *internal cut* is required when a cutout is to be made that does not extend to an outside edge. Since this cut cannot be started on an edge, a hole is bored in the waste portion next to the layout line. If possible, make the hole part of the pattern. Use the same-diameter drill bit that will match a curve in the layout. Bore a hole in each corner to allow the board to be turned easily.

Remove the blade from the upper blade chuck. Raise the upper guide assembly to its topmost position. Feed the blade through the hole in the board (Fig. 31-21). Insert the blade into the upper chuck and tighten the thumbscrew.

Cut the pattern out staying on the waste side of the line (Fig. 31-22). If a piece is cut loose and lodges against the blade, stop the saw and remove it. Once the pattern has been completely cut out, remove the

FIGURE 31-21
The blade is fed through the hole bored in the waste area.

FIGURE 31-22
Making an internal cut. (Courtesy of Delta International Machinery Corp.)

blade and take the finished piece from the table. If no other internal cuts are to be made properly, install the blade.

SABER SAWS

Saber sawing utilizes a specialty blade that is held only by the bottom blade chuck. Saber saw blades are usually wide and have coarse teeth which have heavy sets (Fig. 31-10). This allows them to make heavier straighter cuts than that of the smaller jeweler blades. Most generally this cutting technique is utilized for internal cuts which contain large curves. Because the top end of the blade is free, stock can easily be lowered over the blade (Fig. 31-23). To al-

FIGURE 31-23
The saber saw technique is an ideal method of making internal cuts.

low the blade to enter the stock, a hole is first bored through the board for insertion of the blade.

Since only the bottom blade chuck secures the blade, an additional lower blade guide is installed (Fig. 31-13). The upper guide assembly should be moved out of the way. If much saber sawing is to be done, the entire overarm may be removed. This allows larger pieces to be cut and makes the blade more accessible for internal cutting.

MAKING STRAIGHT CUTS

There are other saws which are better suited than the scroll saw for making straight cuts. Because of the slow cutting and the narrow blade, it can be difficult to control the cut.

If the scroll saw should be selected, use the widest blade available that has coarse teeth. Clamp a wooden fence the same distance away from the blade as the desired width of the board. Use a slow feed speed and keep your hands out of the path of the blade.

MAKING BEVEL CUTS

A bevel cut on the scroll saw can be made simply by tilting the table (Fig. 31-24). Loosen the tilt knob and move the table to the desired angle. The angle scale will indicate the angle. Tighten the tilt knob to secure the table. To hold the stock against the table, also tilt the spring hold-down located on the end of the upper guide assembly. It should be the same angle as the table.

Since a different angle will be cut on each side of the blade, do all the cutting on only one side.

FIGURE 31-24
A bevel cut is made by tilting the table and the spring hold-down. (Courtesy of Delta International Machinery Corp.)

Sawing material on the opposite side will produce a reverse angle. In most cases it is easier to have the waste fall to the uphill side of the blade.

A tapered cone or bowl can be made by cutting concentric circles from one piece of stock (Fig. 31-25). Although trial and error can be used, 5° is a good starting point to tilt the table. The final shape of the bowl depends on the thickness of the stock, wall thickness of the rings, and angle of the sides of the ring. Lay out the number of circles desired. Bore a small hole on each layout line. Use a very thin

FIGURE 31-25
Producing a bowl using a bevel cut.

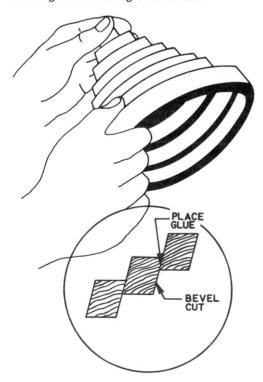

jewelry blade. Insert the blade through each bored hole and accurately cut the circles. The beveled sides of the rings are glued and then pushed outwards. The disks will tighten on each other.

SANDING AND FILING

Since the scroll saw uses an up-and-down cutting action, it can be converted for sanding and filing. Small square, triangular, round, and other shaped files can be utilized (Fig. 31-26). These files should have either an $\frac{1}{8}$-in. or $\frac{1}{4}$-in.-diameter shank. A special sanding attachment is also available (Fig. 31-27). One side of this attachment is flat for sanding straight edges. The other side is semicircular for sanding curves.

To either sand or file, the tool is held only by the lower blade chuck. The shank of these tools is held between the vee slots in the chuck blocks. It is best to use the slowest available machine speed. Too fast a CSM will only damage the file or sanding attachment.

Since the sanding and filing tools are much larger in diameter than the regular blades, a custom-made table insert should be made. The opening in the insert should match the shape of the tool. If much work is to be done, remove the overarm to make the tool more accessible. Do not apply excessive pressure against these accessories. This will shorten their life considerably.

FIGURE 31-26
Filing on a scroll saw.

FIGURE 31-27
Using a sanding attachment.

Answer each of the following questions. If you are not sure of an answer, review the chapter.

31-1. Make certain that the _____ is pressing lightly on the workpiece.

31-2. Another name for a scroll saw is a _____ saw.

31-3. To keep the blade running in a straight line, the scroll saw has two _____ and one _____.

31-4. How is the size of a scroll saw determined?

31-5. The more teeth per inch on a blade the _____ the cut will be but the _____ the surface.

31-6. Use a _____ board to make certain that the blade is perpendicular to the table.

31-7. How can drift be prevented?

31-8. When it is necessary to reduce or enlarge a pattern use the _____ method?

31-9. Applying too much pressure when cutting will bend the blade backward and it will _____.

31-10. Cutting several pieces by placing them on top of each other is called _____.

31-11. When cutting out a pattern, always cut on the _____ side of the line.

31-12. An internal cut first requires a _____ to be _____ in the waste portion.

31-13. _____ sawing utilizes a specialty blade that is held only by the bottom.

31-14. A tapered cone or bowl can be made by cutting _____ circles from one piece of stock.

31-15. If much sanding and filing is to be done, remove the _____ to make the tool more accessible.

Following are technical terms that you should be able to use as part of your working vocabulary. Write a brief description of the meaning of each term.

Jig saw
Reciprocating blade
Overarm
Tension sleeve
Upper blade chuck
Crank shaft drive
Blade chucks

Blade guide
Tilt knob
Angle scale
Table insert
Throat opening
Cone pulley
Cutting strokes per minute (CS/M)
Speed adjustment crank
Electronic system
Jeweler's blades
Saber blade

32

JOINTERS

The jointer is used primarily for straightening edges and flattening faces (Fig. 32-1). It can, however, make tapers and a few joints. The surfaces produced are usually smooth and require less sanding than with saw-cut surfaces.

Very few woodworking companies utilize a jointer. Most industries use precision saws and other specialized machines to perform jointer-type work. Those companies that do use a jointer generally have very large models (Fig. 32-2). This allows more accurate cuts on long boards.

PARTS OF THE JOINTER

The major parts of the jointer are the cutterhead, infeed table, outfeed table, fence, and guard. The *cutterhead* is a steel cylinder with slots cut across the surface (Fig. 32-3). In the slots are placed flat knives and gibs. Each knife is held into the cutterhead with the *gib*. Most jointers have three knives. Some commercial models may have up to six knives. The more knives contained in the cutterhead, the smoother the cut will be. As the cutterhead is turned by the motor, the tips of the knives produce a circle. This circle is called the *cutting circle*.

JOINTER SAFETY RULES

1. Keep your fingers and hands at least 4 in. (102 mm) away from the cutterhead.
2. A cutterhead guard should be used at all times.
3. The maximum depth of cut in one pass is $\frac{1}{16}$ in. (2 mm).
4. Stock must be at least 10 in. (254 mm) long before it can be face or edge jointed.
5. Stock that is less than 1 in. (25 mm) wide should not be edge jointed.
6. Stock that is less than $\frac{1}{2}$ in. (13 mm) thick should not be face jointed.
7. Use a push shoe or push stick whenever possible.
8. Stock must be held flat on the table and firmly against the fence.
9. The outfeed table should never be adjusted unless you are a skilled operator.
10. Disconnect the power before getting your hands close to the cutterhead.

The *infeed* and *outfeed tables* are positioned to each side of the cutterhead. Each is mounted on a set of *incline ways*. These are angled castings that allow the tables to be raised or lowered with a handwheel. The infeed table often contains the *rabbeting arm*. This supports the stock during rabbeting operations.

Mounted on the top surface of the tables is the *fence*. The fence can be moved anywhere across the table by loosening the fence handle. It can also be

FIGURE 32-1
Major parts of the jointer. (Courtesy of Delta International Machinery Corp.)

GUARD
FENCE TILTING LOCK
FENCE ADJUSTMENT LEVER
FENCE HANDLE
OUTFEED TABLE
FENCE
INFEED TABLE
OUTFEED DEPTH HANDWHEEL
RABBETING
TABLE LOCKS
DEPTH GAUGE
INFEED DEPTH HANDWHEEL
INCLINE WAYS
BASE
ON-OFF SWITCH

FIGURE 32-2
Large industrial model jointer. (Courtesy of Oliver Machinery Company.)

FIGURE 32-3
Parts of the cutterhead.

CUTTERHEAD
KNIFE
GIB
CUTTING CIRCLE

tilted for bevel cuts by loosening the *fence-tilting lock* (Fig. 32-4).

A *guard* must cover the cutterhead anytime a board is being jointed. It is retractable and kept under spring pressure. This allows the board to fit between the guard and fence but cover the remaining portion of the cutterhead. Never operate the jointer without the guard properly positioned.

PURCHASING A JOINTER

One of the few items to specify when purchasing a jointer is the size. The size of this machine is determined by the length of the knives. Smaller jointers are from 4 to 6 in. (102 to 152 mm). Commercial jointers may be as large as 12 to 24 in. (305 to 610 mm).

FIGURE 32-4
The fence can be tilted for the bevel cuts. (Courtesy of Delta International Machinery Corp.)

A general-purpose 6-in. (152-mm) jointer should be equipped with a $\frac{3}{4}$-hp or larger motor. Heavy cuts or continuous service may require a larger motor.

SELECTING THE JOINTER TOOLING

Although it is desirable to have an extra set of knives, there is not a great deal of selection. Most jointer knives are constructed from high-speed steel. Carbide knives may be needed if a large amount of abrasive material such as particleboard is to be jointed. Refer to the owner's manual for the proper size to fit each machine.

SETTING UP THE JOINTER

The first step in setting up the jointer is to adjust the depth of cut. In most instances no more than $\frac{1}{16}$ inch (2 mm) should be removed with one pass. Certain cuts may require a shallower depth of cut. Consider using lighter cuts for face jointing, jointing a dense wood such as hard maple, working with irregular grain such as knotty pine, or when making a finish cut on an exposed edge. By turning the *infeed-depth handwheel,* the infeed table can be raised or lowered. The distance from the top of the cutting circle for the cutterhead to the top of the infeed table is equal to the depth of cut (Fig. 32-5). For most cuts, the depth gauge will be sufficient for indicating the depth of cut. When a high degree of accuracy is required, make a trial cut partway across a scrap board. The difference between the freshly machined edge and the original surfaces will equal the exact depth.

FIGURE 32-5
Setting of the infeed table.

Although it is not necessary to check the setting of the outfeed table every time, you do need to know when it is out of adjustment. It should be set exactly in the same plane as the top of the cutting circle. Use a straightedge placed on top of the outfeed table to test for proper alignment. As the cutter head is turned by hand, the knives should just pass under the straight edge (Fig. 32-6).

The best clue for establishing when the outfeed table is not in adjustment is to evaluate a freshly made jointer cut (Fig. 32-6). If a taper is produced, the outfeed table is too high. Often with this condition, the leading end of the board will bump into the lip of the outfeed table. When the outfeed table is too low, a clipped end or *snipe* is produced on the trailing end of the board. This is caused when the board drops down over the cutterhead. Once both tables are adjusted to the correct height, they should be secured with the *table locks.*

There are also two adjustments to make on the fence. First see that the fence is at a 90° angle to the

FIGURE 32-6
Correct and incorrect settings of the outfeed table.

FIGURE 32-7
Checking the squareness of the fence with the table. The guard has been removed for demonstration purposes only.

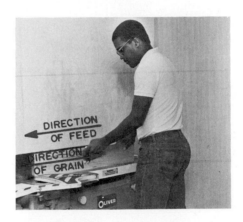

FIGURE 32-8
Proper position of the operator to feed the stock.

table. Use a square to check this setting (Fig. 32-7). If any adjustments are necessary, loosen the *fence tilting lock* and pivot the fence in or out (Fig. 32-4). Many jointers have a positive stop at 90 and 45°. The fence automatically stops at these settings as it is being pivoted. Move the fence across the table to expose a minimum amount of the cutterhead. Use the *fence-adjustment lever* to allow the lateral movement or in and out position of the fence.

Be certain that the retractable guard is working properly. It should spring shut covering the cutterhead any time a board is not between it and the fence.

Once the adjustments are made, the cut can be made. Position yourself to the left of the infeed table. Your hands must not be placed within 4 in. (102 mm) of the cutterhead anytime it is turning. Place the board on the infeed table with the grain pointing away from the cutterhead (Fig. 32-8). If a square cut is to be produced, the stock must also be kept against the fence.

Feed the board forward into the cutterhead. Keep it tight against the fence and table. Use a slow, steady feeding rate. To keep your hands away from the cutter, use a push shoe or push stick (Fig. 32-9). Once the leading end of the board has cleared the cutterhead by at least 6 in. (152 mm), transfer the left hand over to the outfeed table (Fig. 32-10). As the hands are moved, be careful not to rock the board. If you hear a tearing or chipping sound, slow the feed rate. Finish feeding the board forward by pushing with the right hand and holding it against the fence and outfeed table with the left hand. Never hook your thumb over the end of the board. It may slip into the cutterhead as the board clears the jointer.

JOINTING THE FACE

When squaring a rough board, the first surface to be jointed is the face. Inspect both faces and select the one that is the flattest. If it is cupped, place the

PUSH STICK

PUSH SHOE

FIGURE 32-9
Push stick for edge jointing and push shoe for face jointing.

FIGURE 32-10
Move the left hand to the outfeed fence to support the board.

FIGURE 32-11
Face jointing a short board with a push shoe.

FIGURE 32-12
Face jointing a long board with a push shoe and a foam-covered pusher.

concave side down. Set the depth of cut to no more than $\frac{1}{16}$ in. (2 mm). For dense woods or extra-wide boards, reduce this amount. Position this surface on the outfeed table. Place a push shoe over the trailing end and push forward with the right end (Fig. 32-11). Grasp the knob on the front of the push shoe with the left hand. If the board is long, use a foam-covered pusher to keep it against the table (Fig. 32-12). Keep pushing the board forward until it has cleared the guard.

Even if it is covered by the board, never place your hands directly over the cutterhead. After the first pass, inspect the jointed surface. If the face is chipped from the jointer cut, end-for-end the board and joint from the opposite direction.

JOINTING THE EDGE

The second surface to be jointed on a rough board is the edge. Sight down both edges and select the straightest edge. If both are very crooked, scribe a straight line on the face and bandsaw to the line.

Position the board on the infeed table with the jointed flat face against the fence. The grain should point toward the front end of the infeed table. If the edge is bowed with the length shorter than the infeed table, place the concave side down. When the stock is narrower than the jointer fence is high, a push stick is required (Fig. 32-10). Use it in the right hand to feed the stock forward. With the left hand, hold the board firmly against the fence. Allowing the board to lean away from the fence will cause a bevel to be jointed.

Never place your hands within 4 in. (102 mm) of the cutterhead. It is important to keep the stock against the outfeed table. If the board should raise up off of the table, a straightedge will not be produced.

JOINTING THE END GRAIN AND PLYWOOD

It is best to cut the board to the correct length with a fine-cutting saw blade than to joint to finish length. Accuracy is difficult to maintain when jointing across the ends of wood fibers. If the correct procedure is not used, the edge will be chipped off as the end clears the cutterhead.

When jointing end grain select one of two available methods. The first method requires that the first 1 in. (25 mm) be jointed and then pivoted off the cutterhead (Fig. 32-13). Turn the board around and joint from the opposite direction. Due to the material being jointed away from the trailing end, the last 1 in. (25 mm) will clear the cutterhead.

The second method of jointing end grain is to support the trailing end with a backup block (Fig. 32-14). As the stock is fed forward, the backup block is pushed immediately behind the stock. The backup block keeps the fibers from being chipped out.

JOINTING THROUGH BEVELS AND CHAMFERS

To produce a bevel or chamfer on the jointer, the fence is tilted to the desired angle. It can be angled either in or out. In most cases placing the fence in

FIGURE 32-13
Pivoting the stock off of the cutterhead after the first 1 inch has been jointed.

FIGURE 32-14
Supporting the trailing of the stock with a back-up block while jointing end grain.

the in-position is safer and easier to control the stock (Fig. 32-15). Angling the fence out may allow the board to slide down as it is jointed. Mark on the leading end of the stock the desired bevel or chamfer.

The angle of the fence can be determined in one of two ways. For most bevels and chamfers using the angle gauge is a precise enough of a method (Fig. 32-16). When the angle needs to be very accurate, use a T-bevel set to the desired angle (Fig. 32-17). To verify the setting, joint an edge and check its accuracy with a protractor.

Most bevels and chamfers should not be made with one pass. The maximum depth of cut should be $\frac{1}{16}$ in. (2 mm) deep. Multiple passes can then be made to produce the necessary width. Since the chamfer is

FIGURE 32-15
Beveling with the jointer fence in the in-position.

FIGURE 32-16
Setting the fence using an angle gauge.

FIGURE 32-17
Setting the fence using a sliding T-bevel. The guard has been removed for demonstration purposes only.

a narrower cut, fewer passes are needed. In either case continue to make cuts until the jointed edge meets the layout line.

JOINTING A STOPPED CHAMFER

A *stopped chamfer* is a decorative type of cut that does not extend along the entire length of the board. Making a stopped chamfer on the jointer will give a gentle curve at the beginning and ending of the chamfer. Start by marking the starting and ending points on the stock. Angle the fence to the desired angle. Most stopped chamfers are made at a 45° angle.

Since the chamfer is stopped, both the infeed and outfeed tables must be lowered to the same depth (Fig. 32-18). First lower the infeed table to the correct depth. Place wooden blocks of equal thicknesses on each table and bridge the two tables with a level. Lower the outfeed table until the level indicates both tables are in the same plane. Move the fence over to expose a minimum amount of cutterhead.

Place the stock on the infeed table with the first layout line on the lip of the outfeed table (Fig. 32-19). Clamp a stop block against the trailing end of the stock. Slide the stock forward until the second layout line is on the lip of the infeed table. Clamp a stop block against the leading end.

Make certain that the guard is operating properly and place the trailing end of the board against the first stop block. Have an assistant turn on the power and then draw the guard back only enough to lower the board into the revolving cutterhead. Release the guard once the board touches the tables. Feed the board forward with a push stick and foam-covered pusher. Once the stock reaches the second stop block, have the assistant turn off the power. Do not move the board until the cutterhead has completely stopped turning.

FIGURE 32-18
Setting up the jointer tables for making a stopped chamfer. The guard has been removed for demonstration purposes only.

FIGURE 32-19
Making a stopped chamfer.

JOINTING A RECESS

A recess can be made much the same way as a stopped chamfer is cut. The major difference is that the fence is kept at a 90° angle. Once the infeed and outfeed tables have been brought to the same level, install the stop blocks. Pivot the stock onto the rotating cutter (Fig. 32-20). Because of the stock having a tendency to chip out, feed the board forward only a short distance. Have an assistant turn off the power while the stock is held completely still. Do not move the board until the cutterhead stops turning.

Reverse the board and pivot it again onto the rotating cutterhead. Feed the stock forward until the leading end comes in contact with the stop block. Stop the jointer and allow the cutterhead to stop turning before removing the board.

FIGURE 32-20
Jointing a recess in a square to produce a decorative leg.

JOINTING AN OCTAGON

Clamp a long vee block over the cutterhead and against the fence (Fig. 32-21). A dado has been cut on the bottom of the vee block to allow the cutterhead to extend up through the vee groove. Lower the infeed and outfeed table to the desired level. Enough of the cutterhead should be exposed in the opening of the vee block to remove the desired amount of material.

A wood square is fed over the vee block to joint the bottom corner. The sides of the vee block form a trough for the square to slide along. The width of each flat of the octagon should be the same size. If they are not equal, adjust the depth of cut for the infeed and outfeed table. Always use a push shoe and keep your hands at least 4 in. (102 mm) from the cutterhead. This is particularly important because the guard cannot be utilized. After each corner has been jointed, an octagon is formed.

FIGURE 32-21
Setup for jointing an octagon.

JOINTING A RABBET

The major advantage of jointing a rabbet is that it produces a smooth surface. This may be important when making an exposed rabbet such as for a lipped door. On dense woods and plywood, make a shoulder cut with the table saw. This will eliminate any grain tearout on the face produced by the jointer (Fig. 32-22). The jointer must have a rabbeting arm and with the knives extending the same distance from the edge of the cutterhead.

To set-up the jointer for rabbeting, remove the guard. For maximum protection, an auxiliary guard can be clamped to the fence. Move the fence over until the exposed knives are equal to the width of the rabbet. Set the depth of cut to $\frac{1}{16}$ in. (2 mm). Since most rabbets are deeper than this, multiple passes will need to be made. After each cut the infeed table will need to be lowered an additional $\frac{1}{16}$ in. (2 mm).

FIGURE 32-22
Jointing a rabbet. Note the rabbeting arm supporting the stock.

Stabilize the board on the front of the rabbeting arm and turn on the power. Feed the board across the cutterhead. Never place your hands within 4 in. (102 mm) of the cutterhead. Always use a push stick and do not reach under the stock or auxiliary guard.

JOINTING A SHORT TAPER

For tapers shorter than the length of the infeed table, lay out a line around the stock at the beginning of the taper. Lower the infeed table the same amount as that to be jointed from one surface. Move the fence over exposing only the necessary cutterhead.

A stop block must be clamped to the fence on the infeed table (Fig. 32-23). The layout line should be located immediately over the top of the lip of the outfeed table. Place the stop block against the trailing end of the stock.

FIGURE 32-23
Making a short taper.

Remove the stock and turn on the power. Have an assistant pull back the guard only enough to lower the stock onto the cutterhead. Keeping the end of the stock against the stop block, carefully lower the board into the cutterhead. The assistant should release the guard once the board touches the outfeed table. With a push shoe feed the material forward until it clears the guard.

JOINTING A LONG TAPER

Long tapers are longer than the length of the infeed table, and require a two-step process. The key to producing a long taper is using the correct layout method (Fig. 32-24). Place the first layout line around the stock at the beginning of the taper. Mark a second layout line halfway between the first line and the end of the square. This distance must be less than the length of the infeed table.

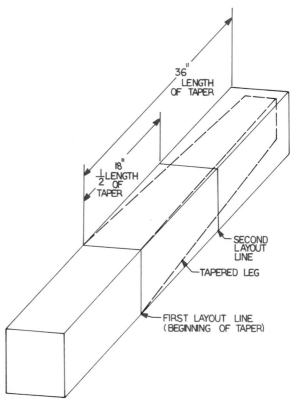

FIGURE 32-24
Layout for a long taper.

To cut the first part of the taper adjust the depth of cut to one-half the total amount to be taken off one side at the deepest point. Use the same procedure for jointing the first section as previously given for jointing a short taper (Fig. 32-25). The cut starts at the halfway point.

Leaving the depth of cut the same, remove the

FIGURE 32-25
Making the first series of cuts for a long taper.

FIGURE 32-27
Typical layout for a spade foot.

stop block. Turn on the power. Have an assistant pull the guard back enough to allow the stock to once again be lowered onto the rotating cutterhead. As the material is being slowly lowered, sight the first layout line so that it will be placed on the lip of the outfeed table (Fig. 32-26). Since the stock may have a tendency to kickback, grip the material firmly and stay at least 4 in. (102 mm) from the cutterhead. Feed the stock forward with a push shoe.

FIGURE 32-26
Making the second series of cuts for a long taper.

JOINTING A STOPPED TAPER

Although a stopped taper can be utilized for other items, it is generally used to make a *spade foot leg* (Fig. 32-27). This is a leg having a long stopped taper with a short taper at its base. A layout line is required at both the beginning and ending of the taper. Adjust the depth of cut to the same amount as to be removed from one side at the deepest point.

Set up the jointer as recommended in the section on jointing a short taper. A stop block must be positioned against the trailing end of the stock. Move the stock forward until the second layout line is even with the lip of the infeed table. Install a second stop block at the leading end of the board.

Remove the stock and turn on the power. Using a push stick feed the board forward (Fig. 32-28). Once the leading end meets the front stop block, have an assistant turn off the power. Do not move the board until the cutterhead has come to a stop. If the part requires tapering on the remaining sides, rotate the board and repeat the process. When a spade foot is to be made, the short taper can be cut with the bandsaw. It is then sanded to smooth the saw cut.

FIGURE 32-28
Making a stopped taper.

Answer each of the following questions. If you are not sure of an answer, review the chapter.

32-1. The maximum depth of cut in one pass is _____ in. (_____ mm).

32-2. The knives are installed in a steel cylinder called _____.

32-3. A _____ must cover the cutterhead anytime a board is being jointed.

32-4. How is the size of a jointer determined?

32-5. When the outfeed table is too low, a clipped end or _____ is produced.

32-6. If a taper is produced, the outfeed table is too _____.

32-7. When squaring a rough board, the first surface to be jointed is the _____.

32-8. Even if the cutterhead is covered by the board, never place your _____ directly over the cutterhead.

32-9. When edge-jointing stock that is narrower than the jointer fence is high, a _____ is required.

32-10. If is safer to place the fence in the _____ when jointing a bevel.

32-11. Since a stopped chamfer is stopped at both the infeed and outfeed tables, they must both be _____ to the same depth.

32-12. When jointing an octagon, the sides of the _____ block form a trough for the square.

32-13. A _____ is required before rabbeting can be done on a jointer.

32-14. When jointing a short taper, lower the _____ table the same amount as that to be jointed from one surface.

32-15. To joint a long taper place the first layout line around the stock at the _____ of the taper.

32-16. Jointing a stopped taper produces a _____ leg.

Following are technical terms that you should be able to use as part of your working vocabulary. Write a brief description of the meaning of each term.

Cutterhead
Gib
Cutting circle
Infeed table
Outfeed table
Incline ways

Rabbeting arm
Fence
Fence tilting lock
Guard
Infeed-depth handwheel
Snipe
Table locks
Fence tilting lock
Fence adjustment lever
Stopped chamfer
Spade foot leg

33

PLANERS

The *planer*, or as it is sometimes called the *surfacer*, is primarily a single-purpose machine (Fig. 33-1). It is used almost entirely for surfacing boards to a desired thickness. Occasionally, it may be utilized for planing boards on their edges and a few other operations. Many school laboratories and industrial firms, however, may use the planer only for face planing.

Although most woodworking companies will use a single planer, it is usually built much heavier than those purchased by schools. The heavier machine allows for continuous operation and heavier cuts. When a large number of boards need to be surfaced, a facer/ planer may be utilized (Fig. 33-2). It has a bottom-and-top cutterhead, which first joints the bottom face and then surfaces the top face to thickness. A newer method of surfacing boards is with an abrasive planer (Fig. 33-3). This machine sands the wood away with a coarse abrasive belt.

PARTS OF THE PLANER

The major parts to a planer include the feed system, chipbreaker, cutterhead, and pressure bar (Fig. 33-4). Those machine components located on the front of the cutterhead are on the *infeed side* of the machine. The remaining parts located to the rear of the cutterhead are on the *outfeed side*.

A very important part to the planer is the *feed system* (Fig. 33-4). It is made up of several rollers and drive components. There are two rollers located in the bed. They are called the *bottom smooth infeed roller* and *bottom smooth outfeed roller*. The tops of these rollers are slightly above the *platen* and help the board move over the top of the bed. Many planers have adjustable rollers which can be raised and lowered with the *adjustable bed roller handle* (Fig. 33-1). The rougher the board, the higher they should be raised. Those planers with fixed rollers and set for general-purpose planing are set at a height of 0.005 in. above the bed.

Another roller located above the bottom infeed roller is the *corrugated infeed roller*. The corrugations in the outer surface help to grip and feed the stock forward.

The fourth roller is located immediately above the *bottom outfeed roller*. It is called the *top smooth outfeed roller,* and like the corrugated infeed roller, is power driven. Once the board leaves the cutterhead, it is pulled out of the planer by this roller.

The drive system powers the corrugated and top outfeed rollers. On some planers the bed rollers

423

will also be driven. The *feed handwheel* regulates how fast the rollers rotate.

Located immediately in front of the cutterhead is the *chipbreaker*. It is responsible for holding the stock down and preventing the knives from tearing out the grain (Fig. 33-5). The chipbreaker is set at the same level as the bottom of the cutting arc.

To remove the material a circular *cutterhead* is utilized. It is a steel cylinder that holds the knives. Most planers have a conventional cutterhead with three or more straight knives. To reduce noise and provide a more efficient cut, several new cutterhead designs have been developed. The knives on these planers are either made in short segments or mounted in a spiral pattern (Fig. 33-6).

Located immediately behind the cutterhead is the *pressure bar*. It rides on top of the surfaced material and keeps it from vibrating. If not properly adjusted, the planer will produce *chatter marks*. This produces a washboard affect.

To regulate the depth of cut, the bed is raised and lowered. The level of the bed is adjusted by turning the *height-adjustment handwheel* (Fig. 33-1). The *depth gauge* indicates the current depth setting that the planer will surface material.

FIGURE 33-1
Major parts to a single planer. (Courtesy of Oliver Machinery Company.)

UPPER
CUTTERHEAD

BOTTOM
CUTTERHEAD

FEEDING
MECHANISM

FIGURE 33-2
A facer/planer combines a jointer and planer into one machine. It dresses both sides of the board with one pass through the machine. (Courtesy of Oliver Machinery Company.)

FIGURE 33-3
An abrasive planer uses a sanding belt to surface the stock. (Courtesy of Abrasive Engineering & Manufacturing.)

CHIP BREAKER
CORRUGATED INFEED ROLLER
KNIFE
CUTTERHEAD
GIB
PRESSURE BAR
TOP SMOOTH OUTFEED ROLLER
DIRECTION OF FEED
INFEED BED
PLATEN
BOTTOM SMOOTH INFEED ROLLER
OUTFEED BED
BOTTOM SMOOTH OUTFEED ROLLER

FIGURE 33-4
Internal parts of a planer.

PURCHASING A PLANER

The planer is generally one of the more expensive pieces of woodworking equipment for many wood shops. This is because it must be heavy to absorb the vibration and contains a feed system to feed the stock through the machine. It is wise, therefore, to make a very careful decision as to which model to purchase.

One of the first considerations is the size of the planer. The size is determined by the widest board that can be surfaced which is measured to the nearest inch. You can find the size by measuring the width of the bed. Sizes of planers range from 12 to over 60 in. (305 to 1524 mm). A good general-purpose size is 24 in. (610 mm).

Several features are available. The first you may like to consider is a *sectional* corrugated infeed roller and sectional chipbreaker (Fig. 33-5). These spring-loaded sectional parts enable several pieces of slightly different thicknesses to be fed into the planer at the same time. Each section will give as much as $\frac{5}{16}$ in. (8 mm).

ALLOWS FOR VARYING THICKNESSES

DO **NOT** USE WITH VARYING THICKNESSES

FIGURE 33-5
A sectional corrugated infeed roller is made of separate sections that move independently. A solid chipbreaker moves as one unit.

FIGURE 33-6
The knife sharpener is used to grind the knives in the cutterhead. (Courtesy of Oliver Machinery Company.)

Another optional feature is the variable feed system. An adjustable feed rate allows the operator to select how fast the stock is fed through the machine. The feed handwheel regulates the speed the material is fed through the machine (Fig. 33-1). Slow feed rates should be utilized for woods that are difficult to machine. Fast feed speeds are needed for roughing cuts.

You may also want to specify *adjustable bed rollers* (Fig. 33-1). They can be raised and lowered to reduce the drag on the bed. A rough board that has not been face jointed requires the rollers to be raised. For best results a finish cut or the final pass on a board needs to have the bed rollers lowered.

Other optional features include a *grinding attachment, brake,* and *dust collection hood.* The grinding attachment allows the knives to be sharpened in the cutterhead (Fig. 33-6). This is faster and usually more accurate than having the knives sharpened outside the machine. A brake will stop the machine in a matter of seconds if an emergency should arise. The dust collection hood directs the planer shavings to a pipe. The planer shavings can then be sucked away by the dust collector.

SELECTING THE PLANER CUTTERHEADS

The tooling used in a planer is not frequently changed as it is with many woodworking machines. This makes it very important to select the best cutterhead design at the time the machine is purchased.

Most planers have a solid steel cutterhead with rectangular slots which house the knives and gibs (Fig. 33-4). The *gib* and *locking nuts* hold the knife in the cutterhead. If the planer has a traditional cutterhead, it will contain three flat knives which reach across the entire cutterhead. Industrial models may have as many as six of these knives. This style of knife is the most inexpensive to purchase.

The newer planer cutterhead designs will have a knife configuration which provides a more efficient cut at a lower noise level. Some planer manufacturers mount their knives in a spiral pattern around the perimeter of the cutterhead (Fig. 33-6). The spiral pattern provides a quiet slicing pattern rather than the loud hammering which occurs with the traditional flat tooling. Rather than having a knife which extends across the cutterhead, these are made from many individual short knives. This allows only one or two small pieces of tooling to be sharpened if a nick is developed in the cutting edge. The many separate knives are often of carbide, which allows them to stay sharp much longer.

PLANING STOCK TO THICKNESS

To plane stock to thickness, determine which face is the straightest and flattest. With most planers it is desirable to flatten this face on a jointer to make a smooth true surface. This is particularly important when dealing with warped material. A planer will not flatten warped material that does not have one true surface to place against the planer bed.

Measure the stock at the thickest point and set the depth gauge to $\frac{1}{16}$ inch (2 mm) less this amount. For example, if the board measures 1 in. (25 mm) at the thickest point, the pointer for the depth gauge should be set at $\frac{15}{16}$ in. (24 mm). To set the height of the bed or depth of cut, turn the height-adjustment handwheel (Fig. 33-7).

For planers with adjustable bed rollers, set their height by using the bed roller handle. Use a setting of 0.9 to 0.6 in. (0.035 to 0.024 mm) for boards which are rough and relatively flat. A setting of 0.6 to 0.3 in. (0.024 to 0.012 mm) is selected for boards that have previously been surfaced or for the final pass.

FIGURE 33-7
Adjusting the depth of cut with the height adjustment handwheel.

If your planer has an adjustable feed rate, you will need to set the feed speed. Feed rates can be varied from 15 to 130 feet per minute (fpm). The faster the feed rate, the quicker the board will be planed but the rougher the cut. A slow feed speed will produce a smooth cut but reduces the production rate. For the first few passes through the machine or for a part that is not exposed, use a feed rate of 38 fpm. Use a 20-fpm feed rate for a high-quality cut or stock that has irregular highly figured grain.

Check that the stock to be planed is at least 2 in. (51 mm) longer than the distance between the bed rollers. The boards must be free of excess glue, metal fasteners, dirt, and any other foreign material. Any of this will dull and possibly nick the knives.

FIGURE 33-8
Proper position for the operator when surfacing a board to thickness.

Turn on the power and stand to the left of the bed (Fig. 33-8). Position the stock on the infeed side of the bed with the grain pointing toward the operator. Planing material with the grain pointing in the opposite direction will cause wood fibers to tear out. Placing the flattest, smoothest face down, slowly feed the material forward. Keep your hands from the underneath side of the boards and away from the throat of the machine. After the infeed roller starts to feed the board forward, continue to support the trailing end. If the board starts to be pulled at a slant, use a quick jerk to straighten it.

Have a tail-off person support the leading end of the board once it clears the bed. You should not allow long boards to hang from the outfeed bed.

When a board becomes stuck in the planer, apply forward pressure to the board. Keep hands clear of the throat of the machine and never look into the machine. If the board does not feed forward immediately, turn off the machine. After you are certain that the cutterhead has stopped turning, lower the bed and remove the board. Reset the depth of cut to one-half of the material being removed. Attempt to feed the board again. If it does not feed itself through the machine, check the machine adjustments.

When a great deal of material is to be removed, attempt to take equal amounts off of each side of the board. Once the face has been mostly cleaned up, turn the board over with each pass through the machine. Planing the board on only one side may release the internal stress or *casehardening,* which will cause the board to warp.

If several boards are to be planed to the same thickness, begin by planing the thickest piece first and measure the thickness after each pass. As the depth setting comes within $\frac{1}{16}$ in. (2 mm) of the remaining boards, start planing them. Working the boards down as a group will save a great deal of time and produce stock all of the same thickness.

PLANING BOARDS ON EDGE

If a planer comes equipped with a sectional corrugated infeed roller, boards can be planed on edge (Fig. 33-5). The advantage of using the planer over the jointer for this operation is that the two edges will be perfectly parallel. Do not attempt to plane boards on edge that are wider than 3 in. (76 mm) or shorter than 24 in. (610 mm).

It is recommended to joint the straightest edge of each board on a jointer. Rip the stock to $\frac{1}{8}$ in. (3 mm) oversize by positioning the jointed edge against the rip fence.

Set the planer to $\frac{1}{16}$ in. (2 mm) over the desired final width. Use the slowest available feed speed. Hold at least three of the boards together face to face with the saw cut edge facing up (Fig. 33-9). The grain must point toward the operator. There must also be a minimum of $2\frac{1}{4}$ in. (57 mm) of stock in contact with the table. Standing to the left of the planer, feed the boards through the machine.

FIGURE 33-9
Holding the boards to be edge planed.

As the material moves forward, continue tightly holding the boards together. Once the leading end has cleared the machine, have a helper on the outfeed side of the planer also squeeze the boards together. If the pieces are allowed to spread apart, they may tend to lean over.

To remove the remaining $\frac{1}{16}$ in. (2 mm), adjust the depth of cut to the desired finish width of the board. Inspect both edges of each board and place the poorest edge facing up. Plane the stock as previously stated.

FACE PLANING THIN BOARDS

Planing stock less than $\frac{3}{8}$ in. (10 mm) thick can be dangerous unless a *backup board* is utilized. The backup board raises the stock up off the planer bed

FIGURE 33-10
Using a backup board to plane thin boards.

(Fig. 33-10). If this board is not used, the cutterhead may come dangerously close to the planer platen. Material as thin as $\frac{1}{16}$ in. (2 mm) can be surfaced with this technique.

To surface thin boards, select a piece of $\frac{3}{4}$-in. (19-mm)-thick hardwood plywood 1 in. (25 mm) wider and longer than the material to be planed. Place the stock on top of the backup board and measure the total thickness of the two pieces. Set the depth of cut to $\frac{1}{16}$ in. (2 mm) less than this amount. Center the stock on the backup board and feed the material through the machine. Continue adjusting the depth of the cut with each pass through the machine and feed the stock and backup board forward.

PLANING SHORT STOCK

Short boards which are at least as long as the distance between the bed rollers can be planed. Feed them one at a time through the machine. Butt each piece against the trailing end of the preceding piece (Fig. 33-11). This part will then push the board in the planer clear of the planer.

After the last short piece has started through the planer, place a board at least 2 in. (51 mm) longer than the distance between the bed rollers against its trailing end. This longer board will push the last short piece through the planer.

FIGURE 33-11
Planing short boards by butting one against the other.

PLANING SQUARES

A planer can produce squares that are very accurate and contain surfaces that require minimal sanding. Start by ripping stock to rough thickness and width. It should be ⅛ in. (3 mm) larger than the finished dimensions.

Joint the flattest face using a jointer. Next place this freshly jointed surface against the jointer fence and joint the straightest edge. Place an "X" on the end of the stock next to the jointed surfaces (Fig. 33-12). This will allow you more easily to identify these surfaces at a later time. Using a square, check that the jointed surface forms a 90° angle. Move to the planer and set the depth of cut equal to the final dimensions. Placing one of the jointed surfaces indicated with an "X" against the planer bed, feed the material forward (Fig. 33-12). Rotate the stock 90° so that the second jointed edge is now against the bed. Feed the last surface past the cutterhead at the same depth of cut.

FIGURE 33-12
Planing a square. Note the "X" is against the planer bed.

PLANING OCTAGONS

Small octagons or eight-sided pieces can be produced with the planer. First prepare the stock by planing a square of the desired size. Make certain that the

FIGURE 33-13
A vee-fixture allows octagons to be planed.

square is 12 in. (305 mm) longer than the length of the bed. Mark out on one end the shape of the octagon. Make a vee fixture to fit against the planer bed (Fig. 33-13). The end of the fixture on the infeed side of the planer must have a flat piece to hook over the end of the table. This keeps the fixture from feeding through the planer with the square. Keeping the fixture stationary allows unlimited lengths of stock to be fed through the machine.

Because the bottom feed rollers are not used, the stock may not totally feed itself. The stock may be carefully pushed and pulled through the planer. Do not stand behind the stock. A tail-off person is needed on the outfeed side to pull the stock out.

If the planer has a bed roller adjustment, lower the rollers below the table. Position the vee fixture to one side of the bed. Pass the stock through the planer with the square cradled in the fixture. Rotate the board 90° and plane the remaining corners. If a larger octagon is being made, several passes are needed for each side.

STUDY QUESTIONS

Answer each of the following questions. If you are not sure of an answer, review the chapter.

33-1. Always stand to one side of the planer bed and never _____ behind it.

33-2. Another name for the planer is the _____ .

33-3. The _____ is responsible for holding the stock down and preventing the knivers from tearing out the grain.

33-4. How is the size of the planer determined?

33-5. Will a planer flatten warped material that does not have one true surface to be placed against the planer bed?

33-6. Position the stock on the infeed side of the bed with the grain pointing toward the _____ .

33-7. A slow feed speed will produce a _____ cut but _____ the production rate.

33-8. When a great deal of material is to be removed, attempt to take _____ amounts off each side of the board.

33-9. Boards can be planed on edge if a planer comes equipped with a _____ corrugated infeed roller.

33-10. Planing stock less than $\frac{3}{8}$ in. thick can be dangerous unless a _____ board is used.

33-11. When planing short stock, _____ each piece against the trailing end of the preceding piece.

33-12. When planing octagons, make certain that the square is _____ in. (_____ mm) longer than the length of the bed.

IMPORTANT TECHNICAL TERMS

Following are technical terms that you should be able to use as part of your working vocabulary. Write a brief description of the meaning of each term.

Planer
Surfacer
Infeed side
Outfeed side
Feed system
Bottom smooth infeed roller
Bottom smooth outfeed roller
Platen
Adjustable-bed roller handle
Corrugated infeed roller
Bottom outfeed roller

Top smooth outfeed roller
Feed handwheel
Chipbreaker
Cutterhead
Pressure bar
Chatter marks
Height-adjustment handwheel
Depth gauge
Adjustable bed rollers
Grinding attachment
Brake
Dust collection hood
Gib
Locking nuts
Backup board

34

LATHES

The spindle lathe is designed primarily for making spindle and faceplate turnings (Fig. 34-1). Parts produced on the lathe include chair and table legs, decorative spindles, and fruit bowls. Although the machine is relatively easy to operate, it does require more skill than most pieces of woodworking equipment.

Industry rarely uses a spindle lathe. Manufacturers are more likely to utilize an automatic lathe and the backknife lathe. An *automatic lathe* has a large custom-made rotating knife that turns at a high speed (Fig. 34-2). The stock is slowly rotated into this cutter. The spindle then takes on the pattern of the knives. If a very small or slender turning is needed, a *backknife lathe* can be used (Fig. 34-3). It has a single custom-shaped knife that is brought against a rotating spindle. This allows the turning to take shape without a great deal of pressure to be applied.

PARTS OF THE LATHE

The major parts of the lathe are the headstock, bed, tool rest, and tailstock (Fig. 34-1). To the left side of the lathe is located the *headstock*. It contains the *spindle,* which is a hollow, number 2 Morse tapered shaft with external threads. The inside of the spin-

FIGURE 34-2
An automatic lathe has a large rotating knife which
shapes spindles (Courtesy of Diehl Machines.)

FIGURE 34-3
A backnife lathe uses a custom-
shaped one-piece knife to shape
the spindle. (Courtesy of Seavey In-
corporated.)

dle holds the *live center* (Fig. 34-4). This center has
four spurs and a pointed center which dig into the
spindle. A *faceplate* can be screwed onto the headstock spindle. This attachment is available in several diameters. Large-diameter stock is attached to
the faceplate with wood screws. The face of the headstock closest to the bed is called the *inboard side*. All
spindle and most faceplate turnings are made on
this side of the lathe. The opposite surface is called
the *outboard side*. Very large diameter turnings are
made on the outboard side.

The headstock is mounted to the *bed* along
which the *tool post* and *tailstock slide*. If there is a
recessed area immediately adjacent to the headstock, it is called a *gap bed* (Fig. 34-5). This allows
larger-diameter faceplate turnings to be made.

The *tool post* is bolted to the bed but is adjustable anywhere along its length by loosening the *tool
post clamp* (Fig. 34-6). It holds the *tool rest,* which
provides a ledge to support the lathe chisels. Tool
rests come in various straight lengths ranging from
3 to 48 in. (76 to 1219 mm). For faceplate turning,
tool rests are also available in different shapes. The
"L" and "S" shapes allow turning on both the side
and face without adjusting the rest.

The *tailstock* is also bolted to the bed and can
be clamped anywhere along its length (Fig. 34-1). It
is moved close to the end of the stock and secured to
the bed with the *tailstock clamp*. By turning the *tailstock handwheel*, the *tailstock spindle* is brought forward. The *tailstock spindle clamp* secures the spindle and keeps it from moving. The tailstock holds
the *dead center* (Fig. 34-4). It is either a cup or cone

FIGURE 34-4
Accessories for the lathe include: live center, faceplate, ball-bearing cup dead center, solid dead center, ball-bearing cone dead center.

FIGURE 34-6
The tool post and tool rest are adjustable and can be positioned anywhere along the bed. (Courtesy of Delta International Machinery Corp.)

FIGURE 34-5
The gapped bed allows large-diameter stock to be turned. (Courtesy of Delta International Machinery Corp.)

FIGURE 34-7
The guard protects the operator during turning operations. (Courtesy of Delta International Machinery Corp.)

design which holds the end of the stock. Dead centers are either solid or ball bearing. Although not as costly, solid dead centers can easily burn the end of the rotating stock. The ball-bearing dead center turns with the stock and eliminates any burning.

An important part of the lathe is the *guard* (Fig. 34-7). It is either made of a plastic or a metal wire shield. The guard should fit over the top of the stock and will confine any flying chips or broken pieces of wood. Do not operate the lathe unless the guard is in the closed position.

PURCHASING A SPINDLE LATHE

To purchase a spindle lathe, first specify the size. There are two points to consider. The first item is the distance between live and dead centers. The longer the distance, the longer the stock that can be turned. The next item to specify is the *swing*. The swing is the maximum diameter of stock that can be mounted on the lathe. A general-purpose lathe will have a length of 38 in. (967 mm) and a swing of 12 in. (305 mm).

Another aspect to consider in purchasing a lathe is the speed control for the spindle. The simplest and least expensive is a step pulley. The step pulleys on the motor and headstock have several levels. To change speeds, the spindle is stopped and the belt is manually lifted to another level. Most operators prefer a *variable-speed control* (Fig. 34-1). This is a more expensive system, but allows the speed to be changed rapidly without stopping the lathe. The variable-speed control has a spring-loaded pulley that is mounted on the motor to change the speed. The *variable-speed control lever* is simply rotated to select the desired speed.

Buy a lathe with at least a ¾-hp motor. The larger the motor, the larger the stock can be turned. To do large-diameter and long spindles, at least a 1 HP is recommended.

SELECTING THE LATHE CHISELS

The basic lathe chisel styles are the gouge, skew, round nose, spear point, and parting tool (Fig. 34-8). They all have long handles and blades. This allows better leverage and control of the cut. The chisels come in a variety of styles, and each can make more than one type of cut. Operators develop their own

turning techniques and select which specific chisel to utilize for each type of cut.

The *gouge* is used initially to work a turning square into a cylinder. Some operators also utilize this chisel for shaping coves. It is the only one that has a rounded body and cutting edge. Gouges are sold in widths of ¼, ⅜, ½, ¾, 1 in. and wider (6, 10, 13, 19, and 25 mm).

The *skew* is used mainly to smooth a cylinder, turn beads, and shape vees. It can cut from either direction by placing either face of the chisel against the tool rest. It is available in ½, ¾, and 1 in. (13, 19, and 25 mm) and wider widths.

A *round nose* has a flat body and a rounded cutting edge. This makes it ideal for forming coves and other concave cuts. Widths of this chisel include ½, ¾, and 1 in. (13, 19, and 25 mm).

The *spear point,* or as it is sometimes called the *diamond point,* has a very sharp tip and flat body. It has a cutting edge on each side of the chisel. This allows cutting from either direction in small areas. Spear points are usually sold only in one width.

A *parting tool* is a multisided chisel used to layout depths of cuts and mark lengths of parts. It is rarely used to make a finish cut. The parting tool is only available in one size.

Lathe chisels are made from either steel or are carbide tipped. Most are made from a high grade of steel. The advantage of the steel tool is that it can easily be ground and honed to a keen edge. Carbide-tipped chisels are very hard and will hold a sharp edge longer. However, they will be severely damaged if dropped.

Both types of chisels should be properly stored when not in use. A holder such as that shown in Fig. 34-9 provides an individual space to place the chisels both on a temporary and a long-term basis. The block on the bottom of the fixture is placed between the lathe bed. This keeps the holder from being

FIGURE 34-8
Basic lathe chisel styles.

FIGURE 34-9
A lathe chisel holder protects the tools when not in use.

knocked off accidentally during use. When the lathe is not being used, the holder can be hung on the wall.

MEASURING TURNINGS

There are several general-purpose and specialized measuring tools used to measure turnings. Never use any of these tools while the stock is rotating. The rotating stock may grab them and throw them from the lathe.

An *outside caliper* can be utilized for checking the outside diameters of turnings in progress and when they are finished (Fig. 34-10). *Inside calipers* check inside dimensions such as on the inner spaces of a bowl (Fig. 34-11). Both of these calipers are adjusted to the desired dimension using a ruler. They can then be tried on the lathe turning to check

FIGURE 34-12
A rule can be used to transfer measurements.

FIGURE 34-13
Dividers mark off distance.

FIGURE 34-10
Outside calipers measure outside diameters of turnings.

FIGURE 34-11
Inside calipers measure inside diameters of turnings.

the fit. The workpiece is at the desired dimension when the caliper just slips over the stock.

A *wooden or steel rule* is a convenient measuring instrument for transferring key dimensions to a turning (Fig. 34-12). It can be laid on the tool rest and a pencil placed at the desired point. As the spindle is slowly turned by hand, a line will be scribed around the stock. The *dividers* can also be used to transfer measurements (Fig. 34-13). After setting them to the desired distance, the point can scribe a mark on the board.

When several identical turnings are required, time can be saved by making a layout board and template. The *layout board* has the profile drawn on its face (Fig. 34-14). Major dimensions are then drawn from the profile to the edge of the board. By laying it on the tool rest and rotating the spindle, a pencil mark can be scribed around the cylinder. The *template* has the reverse shape cut along one edge (Fig. 34-15). As the turning takes shape, the template is used to check the accuracy of the pattern.

Occasionally, the center must be found on a square or turned cylinder. To locate the center on a square, drawn a diagonal line connecting opposite

FIGURE 34-14
Layout boards can be used to quickly transfer measurements.

FIGURE 34-15
A template checks the progress of the turning. The edge of the spindle should match the profile on the template.

FIGURE 34-16
Use a centering jig to locate the center of a turning.

corners. Where the two lines intersect indicates the center. For cylinders use a *centering jig* to make several arcs around the edge of the stock (Fig. 34-16). Where the lines cross will mark the center.

MOUNTING THE STOCK

The first step in mounting the stock is preparing the material. Ideally, the turning square should be a solid piece without any glue joints. In most cases this is not practical, and the turning is made of several pieces. When glue joints are made, they must be of the highest quality. None of the wood should have knots, splits, or other defects.

Cut the stock to 1 in. (25 mm) longer and at least $\frac{1}{4}$ in. (6 mm) larger than the largest diameter of the turning. The ends should be square. If any of the original edge will remain in the finished spindle, it should be planed to the final dimensions. When the diameter is larger than $2\frac{1}{2}$ in. (64 mm), use a jointer or table saw to remove the four corners of the square. This will produce an octagon. An octagon will be safer and faster to turn into a cylinder.

Find the center of both ends (Fig. 34-17A). On the end that will hold the live center, cut $\frac{1}{8}$-in. (3-mm)-deep grooves on the diagonal center lines (Fig. 34-17B). This can be done with a backsaw or by placing the square in a vee block and cutting it on the bandsaw. The grooves will allow the spurs of the live center to be driven into the stock. On the end next to the dead center, bore an $\frac{1}{8}$-in. (3-mm)-diameter hole that is $\frac{1}{4}$ in. (6 mm) deep (Fig. 34-17C). The hole will hold the center of the dead center.

Slide the dead center into the tailstock spindle and raise the tool rest to $\frac{1}{8}$ in. (3 mm) above the tip of this center. Slide the tool rest out of the way and with a mallet, drive the live center into the stock with the diagonal cuts (Fig. 34-17D). In case the stock will need to be removed from the lathe and remounted, place an "X" on the end of the stock next to the groove which has been filed into the live center. This will assure that the stock will turn true between centers.

Slide the live center and square into the headstock spindle. Bring the tailstock up to within 1 in. (25 mm) of the stock. Secure the tailstock to the bed with the tailstock clamp. If a solid dead center is used, place a small amount of beeswax in the previously bored hole to serve as a lubricant. Bring the dead center forward until it penetrates the wood. Back off the tailstock handwheel one-quarter of a turn to release some of the tension on the center. Tighten the tailstock spindle clamp.

Bring the tool rest forward and adjust it to

FIGURE 34-17
Sequence of mounting a turning square: (A) locating the center; (B) cutting the diagonal center lines; (C) boring for the dead center; (D) driving in the live center.

(A)

(B)

(C)

(D)

FIGURE 34-18
Proper location of the tool rest should be $\frac{1}{8}$ in. above the center of the stock and $\frac{1}{8}$ in. away from the outside corner.

within $\frac{1}{8}$ in. (3 mm) of the corner of the stock (Fig. 34-18). Rotate the square at least one complete turn by hand to see that it turns freely and does not hit the tool rest. There should be no side-to-side movement. Adjust the guard to complete the setup.

REMOVING THE STOCK

There are two methods of removing material on the lathe. A skilled lathe operator will use both the *cutting method* and *scraping method* (Fig. 34-19). Each has its own advantages.

The *cutting method* is performed with the gouge, skew, and parting tool. As the stock is turned, thin shavings are formed. It produces the cleanest cut with the least amount of grain tear-out. The cutting method is performed by lowering the lathe chisel handle to approximately a 50° angle. Move the handle up and down until the best angle is achieved. Shavings should be removed in long, thin ribbons.

The *scraping method* can be done with any of the lathe chisels. The material is removed in the form of sawdust or fine particles. This is the simplest method and the best for beginning operators. It is considered to be the most accurate. To use the scraping method, the hand of the chisel is held at a 90° angle to the stock.

TURNING A STRAIGHT CYLINDER

After the stock has been properly mounted on the lathe, the first step is to turn a straight cylinder.

FIGURE 34-19
Material is removed on the lathe using either the cutting or scraping method.

Position the tool rest to the far left of the square. Take a large skew and place it on its edge. Turn on the power and select the turning speed indicated in Table 34-1. This initial setting usually will not exceed 600 rpm. Place a nick in the material every 2 in. (51 mm) (Fig. 34-20). This will cut the wood fibers and prevent long pieces from flying off of the square.

FIGURE 34-20
Nicking the corners of the square with a skew. The guard has been removed for demonstration purposes only.

Select a wide gouge and grip it firmly with one hand at the end of the handle (Fig. 34-21). With the other hand, grasp the blade immediately next to the tool rest. Use the index finger to slide along the rest to control the depth of cut. Lower the handle and slowly bring the cutting edge into the turning stock. Lean the handle in the direction the gouge is to be

TABLE 34-1			
Straight Cylinder Turning Speed			
Wood diameter (in.)	Roughing cut (rpm)	Shaping cut (rpm)	Sanding (rpm)
Up to 2	910	2590	4250
2 to 4	810	2375	3380
4 to 6	600	1825	2375
6 to 8	600	1200	1825
8 to 10	600	910	1025
Over 10	600	600	650

moved. This will expose the proper point to the stock.

With the gouge to the left of the tool rest, slowly start the cut 1 in. (25 mm) from the end of the stock. Not starting the cut right on the end will prevent the chisel from catching the corner and being thrown from the lathe. Carefully push the chisel inward until the cut begins. Once the chisel reaches the end of the rest, move the handle to the left and make a pass toward the tailstock. Next make a cut all the way back to the headstock. After making a few passes, stop the lathe and inspect the work. Adjust the tool rest in when ½ in. (13 mm) space develops between the edge of the rest of the stock.

FIGURE 34-21
Roughing out a cylinder with a gouge. The guard has been removed for demonstration purposes only.

Continue roughing the square into a cylinder until all the flat areas have disappeared. Be careful not to remove too much stock and make the cylinder too small. Next, use a parting tool to turn several grooves to 1/16 in. (2 mm) over the finished diameter (Fig. 34-22). The grooves should be placed every 2 in. (51 mm). Use a pair of outside calipers to check this

FIGURE 34-22
Use the parting tool to make depth grooves along the length of the spindle. The guard has been removed for demonstration purposes only.

diameter. The skew can then easily connect the grooves to make a straight cylinder. Move the tool rest to the right and work the remaining sections of the cylinder.

After the cylinder has been roughed to size, select the widest skew. Place the face of the skew against the tool rest and make the finishing cuts (Fig. 34-23). Keep the leading edge away from the stock. Either a cutting or scraping action can be used.

Frequently, turn off the power and check the diameter with a pair of outside calipers. They should be set to $\frac{1}{16}$ in. (2 mm) larger than the finished diameter. This last $\frac{1}{16}$ in. (2 mm) is for sanding. Once the cylinder is smooth, increase to a medium speed. The faster speed will produce a smoother surface. Continue working the cylinder until it is to the desired diameter set on the calipers. A straightedge placed along the turning will indicate any low or high points.

Start sanding the cylinder using 100-grit abrasive cloth. Refer to the section "Sanding Turnings" for further details. Measure the length of the cylin-

FIGURE 34-23
Smoothing the cylinder with a skew. The guard has been removed for demonstration purposes only.

FIGURE 34-24
Use a parting tool to cut the stock to length. The guard has been removed for demonstration purposes only.

der and scribe a line around the two ending points. With the parting tool, cut along the waste side of the line (Fig. 34-24). Continue cutting until only $\frac{1}{2}$ in. (13 mm) of material remains. If the turning is large in diameter, make two cuts side by side. This will reduce friction and keep the tool from overheating. Remove the stock from the lathe and cut off the tails of the turning with a back saw.

TURNING A TAPER

To turn a taper, first draw a full-scale pattern (Fig. 34-25). It should show the slope of the sides and the smallest and largest diameters. Make a straight cylinder the same size as the largest diameter of the pattern. Measure the length of the taper on the spindle and scribe a line at each ending point. With a parting tool, make a groove equal to the smallest diameter along the last layout line.

Scribe additional lines around the cylinder 1 in. (25 mm) apart. Taking the measurements from the drawing, cut a groove to the depths equal to the slope of the taper. Use a gouge to connect the bottoms of the grooves (Fig. 34-26). Smooth the taper with a skew and sand the taper to the finished diameters.

TURNING A VEE

Start making a vee by drawing a full-sized pattern (Fig. 34-27). Measure the largest diameter. Turn a cylinder to $\frac{1}{16}$ in. (2 mm) larger than this dimension. Using the pattern, scribe on the spindle the center and ending points of each vee.

With a spear point, cut down on the centerline to the smallest diameter of the pattern. If the vee is relatively small, finish the vee with this chisel. Larger vees can be made at a faster rate with the toe of the skew (Fig. 34-28). Only one-half of the vee is

FIRST:
TURN STRAIGHT CYLINDER AND LAYOUT

FIRST:
TURN STRAIGHT CYLINDER AND LAYOUT

SECOND:
TURN DEPTH GROOVES

SECOND:
TURN DEPTH GROOVES

THIRD:
CONNECT DEPTH GROOVES

THIRD:
CONNECT LAYOUT LINES AND BOTTOM OF GROOVE

FIGURE 34-25
Steps in turning a taper.

FIGURE 34-27
Steps in turning a vee.

FIGURE 34-26
Turning a taper. The guard has been removed for demonstration purposes only.

FIGURE 34-28
Turning a large vee with a skew. The guard has been removed for demonstration purposes only.

made at a time. Pivot the chisel from side to side to connect the ending points with the center groove.

TURNING A COVE

To turn a cove, first draw a layout pattern (Fig. 34-29). Measure the largest diameter and make a cylinder $\frac{1}{16}$ in. (2 mm) larger than this dimension. Using the pattern, scribe a line around the cylinder at the ending points and center of each cove.

FIRST:
TURN STRAIGHT CYLINDER AND LAYOUT

SECOND:
TURN DEPTH GROOVES

THIRD:
CONNECT LAYOUT LINES AND BOTTOM OF GROOVES

FIGURE 34-29
Steps in turning a cove.

Take a parting tool and cut down to the depth of the smallest diameter along the centerline. Check the diameter with a caliper set to $\frac{1}{16}$ in. (2 mm) larger than that indicated on the pattern. With a round-nose chisel, connect the ending points and the bottom of the groove (Fig. 34-30). Use a small round nose for small coves. A larger round nose should be selected for coves that have more space between the ending points.

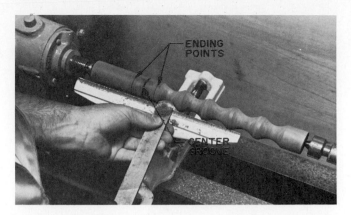

FIGURE 34-30
Turning a cove with a round nose. The guard has been removed for demonstration purposes only.

Using a scraping action, place the chisel at an ending point. Pivot it toward the centerline making a smooth concave cut. Be careful not to remove the pencil marks at the ending points or turn deeper than the groove in the center. Match the two halves of the cove so that the cut will appear uniform.

TURNING A BEAD

To turn a series of beads, make a full-sized pattern of the layout (Fig. 34-31). Measure the outside diameter of the largest bead. Turn a cylinder to $\frac{1}{16}$ in. (2 mm) larger than this diameter. From the pattern, transfer to the cylinder the ending points and the center of each bead. With a pencil, scribe a line around the turning at each of these marks.

Set a pair of outside calipers to $\frac{1}{16}$ in. (2 mm) larger than the small diameter of the bead. If the beads are at least $\frac{1}{4}$ in. (6 mm) apart, use a parting tool to cut down to the measurement of the caliper. When the beads are closer than $\frac{1}{4}$ in. (6 mm), select a small skew or spear point to make a vee-shaped groove (Fig. 34-32). Cut into the cylinder equal to the depth set on the caliper.

To shape the bead, use either the skew or spear point (Fig. 34-33). A skew works well for larger beads. Using a cutting action, start at the center point penciled on the bead. Roll the skew over with a smooth motion. For small or closely spaced beads, use a spear point with a scraping action. Be careful not to remove the pencil mark at the centerline.

If many small beads are required, you may like to use a specialty tool (Fig. 34-8). It is named the *beading chisel*. They come in various radiuses from $\frac{1}{8}$ to $\frac{5}{8}$ in. (3 to 16 mm). To use a beading chisel, simply hold the tool against the rotating stock (Fig. 34-34). The preshaped cutter automatically makes the bead.

FIGURE 34-31
Steps in turning a bend.

FIGURE 34-32
Making the shoulder cuts for a bead. The guard has been removed for demonstration purposes only.

FIGURE 34-33
Turning a series of beads with a spear point. The guard has been removed for demonstration purposes only.

FIGURE 34-34
A beading chisel automatically shapes beads by holding it against the turning spindle. The guard has been removed for demonstration purposes only.

TURNING A SQUARE SECTION

When a square section is required, make certain that the turning square is first planed on all four sides. Since part of this surface will be left, it should be free of chips and other defects. Lay out the location of the corner with a square.

Using a skew placed on its edge, nick the corners of the square. Next, turn a groove with a parting tool immediately next to the nick. Increase the width of the groove to $\frac{1}{4}$ in. (6 mm) by making another cut with the parting tool. If you desire, round the corners over with a gouge (Fig. 34-35).

TURNING OFF CENTER

Off-center turning produces a very attractive leg with a *clubfoot*. A clubfoot leg has tapered sides except for the back surface. The bottom part or *foot* extends toward the front much like a cabiole leg.

FIGURE 34-35
A gouge rounds the corners on a square section. The guard has been removed for demonstration purposes only.

FIGURE 34-37
A clubfoot will have a true center and offset center. The guard has been removed for demonstration purposes only.

FIGURE 34-36
Layout for a clubfoot.

Cut the material to exact size and make a layout as shown in Fig. 34-36. A line is extended through the first *true center* to locate the *offset center*. This second center should be ¼ to ⅜ in. (6 to 10 mm) from the true center (Fig. 34-37). The farther the distance between the two points, the larger the foot will be.

Mount the stock on the lathe with the end containing the layout marks against the tailstock. Turn a straight cylinder and make a small radius where the squared portions join the cylinder. Sand the spindle smooth and true.

Remove only the end of the stock next to the tailstock. Remount the material but with the dead center located in the offset center hole. Check that stock will not strike the tool rest. With the lathe set at no more than 600 rpm, carefully turn the bottom portion of the leg (Fig. 34-37). The leg will initially turn in a jump-rope fashion and the chisel may be difficult to control. Hold it firmly and take light cuts. Blend the sides of the two turnings together by sanding it on the lathe. Any additional blending can be accomplished by hand sanding.

DUPLICATING TURNINGS

In most cases, it is necessary to make more than one spindle of the same shape and size. As a result, identical turnings are required. This can be difficult if the proper procedure is not used.

To make duplicate turnings, draw a full-sized pattern on lightweight cardboard. Cut the pattern in half along the centerline of the spindle. Extend major measuring points from the drawn profile to the edge of the first half of the pattern. This portion of

FIGURE 34-38
A duplicator is used to produce multiple spindles. The stylus is used to trace the pattern spindle. (Courtesy of Toolmark Company.)

FIGURE 34-39
Shop-made steady rest supports slender turnings.

the pattern can be used as a layout board and to transfer these layout lines onto the turning (Fig. 34-14). The second half of the pattern is used as a template to check the development of the spindle (Fig. 34-15). Since the outline of the spindle has been cut out, the turning should match the pattern exactly.

Another method of producing multiple spindles is with a commercial *duplicator* (Fig. 34-38). It is an attachment which is mounted on the bed of the lathe. A hardboard template or pattern spindle is made of the profile of the finished spindle. The template or pattern spindle is then clamped to the duplicator. A movable arm containing a stylus is traced along the edge of the pattern spindle. As the stylus follows the spindle, the arm moves with it. The chisel mounted at the end of the arm then shapes the turning spindle.

FIGURE 34-40
A metal steady rest uses ball bearings to eliminate any burning.

TURNING SLENDER STOCK

Turning slender or long small-diameter stock can be difficult. These turnings are often used for decorative spindles on chairs, beds, and other furniture. When this type of work is machined, it has a tendency to "jump-rope" or vibrate. Unsupported, the spindle will often chatter and then break.

A support called a *steady rest* can be utilized to back up the slender spindle and keep it turning true. Although there are commercial models available, a shop-made steady rest can be utilized. The version shown in Fig. 34-39 is constructed of hardwood and is adjustable to various diameters of work. A metal model can also be made which will be sturdy and contain three rollers having ball bearings (Fig. 34-40). The rollers turn with the stock and reduce friction.

To use a steady rest, turn the cylinder down to $\frac{1}{8}$ in. (3 mm) oversize approximately in the middle of its length. Bring the rest up to the turned area and adjust the supporting arm to just touch the stock. Too much pressure will cause friction and burning. Using beeswax as a lubricant or wrapping the spindle with heavy cloth tape will eliminate any friction.

After the rest has been properly adjusted, turn the stock located between the steady rest and tailstock. Make light cuts and do not force the chisel inward. Next, turn the material between the headstock and rest. To finish the turning, remove the steady rest and finish the cut where the arms were touching the stock. Use even lighter cuts and on a very delicate turning, support the backside of the spindle with your left hand.

SPLIT TURNINGS

Split turnings are fabricated with standard spindle turning practices but later separated into halves, quarters, or other pieces (Fig. 34-41). It can be used to make furniture overlays, corner post, and other moldings.

To prepare the stock, determine what shape is desired and the location of the finished flat sides. A layout such as shown in Fig. 34-41 will aid in determining the size of the stock and the location of the flat sides. All parts should be 3 in. (76 mm) longer than the finished length. This will provide an area to later install wood screws. Glue the pieces together but with a glossy magazine cover in the glue joints that are later to be separated. Adhesive is applied to both sides of the joint. To prevent the spindle from splitting during turning, place a screw in each piece

FIGURE 34-42
Dividing a split turning with a wide chisel.

at each end of the square. Be careful not to hit these screws, however, with the lathe chisel.

After the square has been turned, remove the screws. Place a wide chisel on the glue line and drive the tip into the glue joint (Fig. 34-42). Slowly work the chisel down into the joint. Once the parts have been separated, remove the paper and glue.

MANDREL TURNING

Mandrel turning is utilized when a hole is first bored in the stock and then the outside is turned. Napkin rings are often made with this technique.

First, bore a hole through the stock of the desired finished diameter. Next, turn a mandrel on the lathe which has a slight taper to match the diameter of the bored hole. The stock should start to slip over the mandrel but must wedge against the spindle.

The mandrel can be mounted on the lathe and the material turned to the desired shape (Fig. 34-43). After it has been sanded and finished, tap the turning from the mandrel. It should slide off the small end.

FIGURE 34-41
Split turnings are made in three-quarters, halves, and quarters for decorative pieces on furniture.

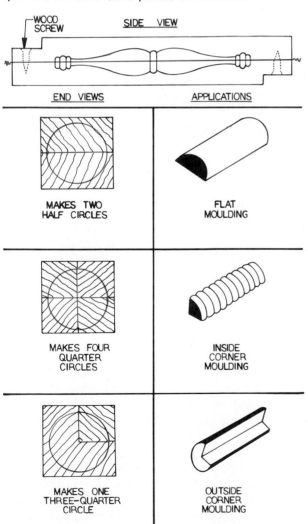

FIGURE 34-43
A mandrel allows the outside of a hollow cylinder to be turned.

FACEPLATE TURNING

Faceplate turning is used to machine work that cannot be accomplished between centers. This major division of turning primarily applies to large-diameter stock and turnings which are shaped on their faces. Products will include fruit bowls, trays, goblets, and circular picture frames.

Preparing the Stock

It is difficult and expensive to find stock thick and wide enough to use for most faceplate turnings. Because of this, most projects require glued-up stock. Use a thermoset adhesive such as *urea-formaldehyde* to prevent the adhesive from melting out of the joint during sanding.

The first method of gluing up material calls for the boards to be edge glued to the rough width. After the adhesive has cured and the stock surfaced to thickness, face-laminate the pieces. Match the layers for color and grain. To minimize warping, the end grain of every other layer should be reversed. Allow the adhesive to cure for at least 24 hours and bandsaw the blank to the rough diameter.

FIGURE 34-44
Gluing up rings for a faceplate turning. The rings are placed against a flat board for better clamping force.

The second method requires more time to assemble, but it does save a great deal of material. Rings are first cut from three to four boards. Each ring is smaller than the previous one. Depending on the shape and size of the turning, the waste from the inside of each ring can then be used for smaller rings or to make the bottom solid piece. Stack the rings in ascending order of size (Fig. 34-44). After matching them for grain and color, glue them together. Because the blank is already to rough shape, much time will be reduced in turning.

Faceplates, Screw Centers, and Chucks

The work is held on the machine with either a faceplate, a screw center, or a chuck (Fig. 34-45). *Faceplates* are sold in a variety of diameters from 3 to 12 in. (76 to 305 mm). They are screwed onto the headstock spindle. Mount the faceplate on the stock with flat-head wood screws. A *screw center* is a small faceplate with a permanently mounted screw. Because there is not space for wood screws, one screw holds the stock in place. *Chucks* are custom or commercially made fixtures which hold the turning after one of the surfaces has been shaped.

SCREW CENTERS

FACEPLATES

FIGURE 34-45
Stock can be mounted on the lathe spindle using a faceplate or screw center.

Mounting the Stock

Once the stock has been glued and cured, locate the center on the end to be positioned against the faceplate. Scribe a circle for the outside of the turning and also a circle the same diameter as the faceplate. Use a bandsaw to cut the outside circle. It should be $\frac{1}{4}$ in. (6 mm) larger than the largest diameter in your piece. Center the faceplate over the faceplate circle and install the wood screws (Fig. 34-46). These screws should be of the proper shank size that just fits the holes in the faceplate. To hold the faceplate and stock together securely, several screws should enter the wood a minimum of 1 in. (25 mm). Be careful, however, that the lathe chisels will not touch these screws as the stock is turned.

If the bottom is to be thin, the wood screw will break through exposing the screw holes from the faceplate. To eliminate this problem, use a *backing block* (Fig. 34-47). This is a scrap piece of material which is glued to the bottom of the lathe stock. A magazine cover is placed in the glue joint. This allows the scrap piece to be removed once the turning is complete. Upon removing the glue, the bottom is left clean and hole free.

FIGURE 34-46
Install large wood screws to attach the scrap to the faceplate.

FIGURE 34-47
A backing block allows the bottom of a faceplate turning to remain free of holes.

FIGURE 34-48
Use scraping techniques to turn the outside of a bowl. The guard has been removed for demonstration purposes only.

FIGURE 34-49
Boring a hole on the face of a bowl to gauge the inside depth. The guard has been removed for demonstration purposes only.

Place a thick leather washer on the lathe spindle (Fig. 34-47). This acts as a shock absorber to keep the faceplate from becoming locked on the spindle. Screw the faceplate all the way onto the spindle. Use the spindle lock to secure the spindle and the faceplate wrench to tighten the faceplate.

Turning the Stock

After positioning the tool rest along the side of the material, rotate the spindle at least one complete turn. This will assure that the wood does not strike the tool rest. Bring the tailstock against the stock to support the work. Turn on the power using the slow-est rpm and use scraping techniques with a round nose chisel to turn the stock to a cylinder (Fig. 34-48). Use calipers and a template to establish depth grooves at key points. Connect the points using the chisels that will match the shape of the pattern. They can include the round nose, skew, or spear point. Completely turn and sand the outside before moving onto the inside.

Move the tailstock back and install a drill chuck. Bore a hole into the material equal to the depth of the turning (Fig. 34-49). Use a 1-in. (25-mm) Forstner bit. Position the tool rest across the face and use the round nose chisel only on the front half of the rest. Placing the chisel on the back half will cause the chisel to be thrown from the lathe.

FIGURE 34-50
Extend the tool rest inside the turning to support the chisel. The guard has been removed for demonstration purposes only.

Turn on the power and turn the inside. Keep the tool rest within $\frac{1}{8}$ in. (3 mm) of the stock. As the inside area takes shape, it will be necessary to extend the rest inside of the turning (Fig. 34-50). Check the development of the shape often with inside calipers and a template. Sand the inside surface until it is free of defects.

CHUCKING

Chucking can be used to shape the bottom of surfaces which have been previously turned with a faceplate. Unless a commercial, universal chuck is available, a custom wooden chuck will need to be constructed (Fig. 34-51). The commercial chuck can be adjusted to many sizes. The custom chuck should be made from a medium-density hardwood such as poplar. Each different-diameter turning will require a new chuck to be constructed. There are two different forms of chucking, inside and outside. *Inside chucking* holds the turning from the inside. *Outside chucking* secures the turning from the outside edge.

The stock to be used for the recessed block of the chuck is bandsawed to a rough size. A 1-in. (25-mm)-diameter hole is bored through the center. This will be used later to remove the finished piece from the chuck. Attach the recessed block to the faceplate with wood screws. For outside chucking, turn a recess in the chuck which is slightly larger than the outside diameter of the lip of the turning. In most cases, a $\frac{1}{2}$-in. (13-mm)-deep cavity is sufficient. For inside chucking, turn a plug that will fill the inside cavity of the turning.

Press the turned piece into the chuck. There must be a tight fit between the chuck and the turning. With the chuck rotating at a slow speed, use

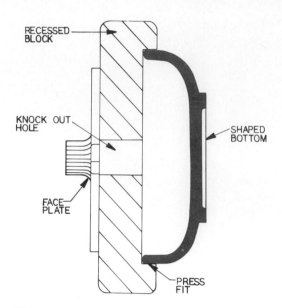

FIGURE 34-51
A chuck holds the turning so that the bottom surface can be shaped.

FIGURE 34-52
Turning the bottom of a bowl using an outside chuck. The guard has been removed for demonstration purposes only.

light scaping techniques to remove the material (Fig. 34-52). After sanding the bottom, the turning can be removed from the chuck. Use a large dowel rod to push the turning gently out of the recessed block.

BORING HOLES

Occasionally, it is helpful to bore holes using the lathe. This is particularly true when the stock is already mounted on the lathe.

A drill chuck containing a tapered shaft is inserted into the tailstock. For small holes, use a brad point drill bit. Larger holes can be made with either Forstner or multispur bits.

Make certain that the stock is securely attached to the headstock. Turn on the power and slowly turn the tailstock handwheel to bring the bit into the stock (Fig. 34-49). Use a slow turning speed. Back the bit out often to clean the sawdust.

TURNING LARGE-DIAMETER STOCK

Most projects can be turned on the in-board or live center side of the lathe. There are, however, some turnings which are very large in diameter and will not fit between the spindle and the bed. In this case, stock can be turned on the *outboard side* of the lathe or to the left of the headstock (Fig. 34-1).

Use a heavy-duty lathe and bolt the machine to the floor. Large turnings will create vibrations, and this will stop the lathe from moving. To hold the chisels, a *floor stand* is used (Fig. 34-53). It is separate from the lathe and can be positioned next to the stock.

Because the stock is large, select the slowest available speed. Use scraping techniques and take light cuts.

FIGURE 34-53
A floor stand supports the tool rest on the outboard side of the lathe. (Courtesy of Delta International Machinery Corp.)

SANDING TURNINGS

Before sanding spindles or faceplate turnings, make certain that they are turned to the desired size and shape. Sanding should not be relied on to substitute for removing stock with a lathe chisel. To minimize the amount of sanding, carefully shape the stock with a sharp chisel with proper turning techniques.

Before turning on the power, be certain to remove the tool post. If there are no major defects or torn grain, start sanding with a 100-grit abrasive cloth. Old sanding belts work well for this abrasive. Serious defects can be removed with 80 grit.

With the lathe turning at the speed recommended in Table 34-1, bring the abrasive cloth against the rotating stock (Fig. 34-54). Use medium pressure and keep the abrasive moving from side to side. Do not hold it in one spot. This will create friction and a low area. Be careful not to round over any shoulders or other sharp details.

FIGURE 34-54
Sanding a spindle with a piece of abrasive cloth. The guard has been removed for demonstration purposes only.

FIGURE 34-55
Sanding a small recess with a folded piece of abrasive paper. The guard has been removed for demonstration purposes only.

For small recesses, fold the abrasive and use your fingers to hold it against the stock (Fig. 34-55). For general sanding, hold the abrasive cloth between your hands and bring it in contact with the turning on the top surface. Do not wrap the abrasive around your hands. It is very easy to remove more than the excess $\frac{1}{16}$ in. (2 mm) left from turning. If the dimensions are critical, stop the lathe often and check your measurements with calipers.

Finish sanding the turnings with 120-grit and then 150-grit abrasive cloth. If any sanding scratches remain, stop the lathe and sand them by hand with the grain. Do not use the lathe chisels after sanding. The abrasive worked into the wood will rapidly dull the tools. Be certain that the turnings are completely sanded before removed from the lathe.

Answer each of the following questions. If you are not sure of an answer, review the chapter.

34-1. Be certain that stock to be turned is free of _____, _____, or improper _____ joints.

34-2. What type of lathe has a large custom-made rotating knife that turns at a high speed?

34-3. Which lathe center has four spurs and a pointed center that digs into the turning?

34-4. How is the size of the lathe determined?

34-5. List the five basic lathe chisel styles.

34-6. What can be used to check the inside dimensions of inner spaces on turnings?

34-7. In preparing stock for the lathe, cut the material _____ in. (_____ mm) longer and at least _____ in. (_____ mm) than the largest diameter.

34-8. Name the two methods of removing material on the lathe.

34-9. Which lathe chisel is usually used first to rough out a straight cylinder?

34-10. In turning a taper, a _____ pattern must be drawn.

34-11. When turning a cove, check the smallest diameter with a _____ set to _____ in. (_____ mm) larger than that indicated on the pattern.

34-12. To shape a bead, use either the _____ or _____.

34-13. Off-center turning produces a very attractive leg with a _____ foot.

34-14. Duplicate turnings can be made with a commercial attachment called a _____.

34-15. A support called a _____ _____ can be utilized to back up the slender spindle and keep it turning true.

34-16. Split turning can be used to make furniture _____, corner _____, and other _____.

34-17. What is a good thermoset adhesive to be used on faceplate turnings?

34-18. A _____ is a small faceplate with a permanently mounted screw.

34-19. A thick _____ can be mounted on the lathe center to act as a shock absorber to keep the faceplate from locking on the spindle.

34-20. _____ can be used to shape the bottom of surfaces that have previously been turned with a faceplate.

34-21. When boring holes, use a _____ turning speed.

34-22. Very large diameter stock can be turned on the _____ side of the lathe.

34-23. When sanding turnings, be certain to remove the _____.

Following are technical terms that you should be able to use as part of your working vocabulary. Write a brief description of the meaning of each term.

Automatic lathe
Backknife lathe
Headstock
Spindle
Live center
Faceplate
Inboard side
Outboard side
Bed
Tool post
Tailstock slide
Gap bed
Tool post clamp
Tool rest
Tailstock
Tailstock clamp
Tailstock handwheel
Tailstock spindle
Tailstock spindle clamp
Dead center
Swing
Variable-speed control
Gouge
Skew

Round nose
Spear point
Diamond point
Parting tool
Outside caliper
Inside caliper
Wooden or steel rule
Dividers
Layout board
Template
Centering jig
Cutting method
Scraping method
Beading chisel
Clubfoot
Offset center
Duplicator
Steady rest
Split turnings
Mandrel turning
Urea formaldehyde
Screw center
Chucks
Backing block
Inside chucking
Outside chucking
Outboard side
Floor stand

35

DRILL PRESSES

Although the drill press is a multifunction machine, it is designed primarily for boring holes (Fig. 35-1). It can, however, perform many other jobs. With the proper setup the drill press can make circular disks, produce plugs, route shapes, and even sand curves.

The woods industry frequently utilizes a drill press. Woods companies also utilize commercial boring machines. This specialized equipment is much faster than the standard drill press. A multispindle boring machine, for example, can bore more than one hole at a time (Fig. 35-2).

PARTS OF THE DRILL PRESS

There are two types of drill presses, a floor model and a table model. Most woodworkers prefer a floor model because it can bore holes in the ends of long pieces (Fig. 35-1). A table model is fastened to a bench. It is generally not as expensive as the floor model.

The main parts of a drill press are the *base, table,* and *head* (Fig. 35-1). The *column* is anchored in the base and supports the head and table. The table can be moved up and down the column by loosening the *table locking clamp.*

The head of the drill press consists of several

parts. The hollow shaft that contains the rotating *spindle* is called the *quill* (Fig. 35-3). The quill raises and lowers the *spindle.* Attached to the end of the spindle is the chuck. Chucks are sized according to the largest diameter bit shank it can hold. Most woodworking drill presses have a $\frac{1}{2}$-in. (13-mm) chuck. This allows the operator to use a drill bit of shank diameter of $\frac{1}{2}$ in. (13 mm) or less.

At the top of the spindle is a drill pulley (Fig. 35-3). A V-belt is used to connect this pulley to the motor pulley at the top of the motor. The motor at the rear of the head provides power to drive the chuck. It is generally a 110-V motor which is plugged into a wall outlet. A pulley guard surrounds the pulleys and belt to protect the operator. Never turn on the power unless the guard is in place. Most drill presses will contain an on-off switch conveniently located on the front of the head.

The *feed level* is manually turned to lower the quill and the drill chuck (Fig. 35-4). A spring automatically returns the quill to the topmost position once the feed lever is released. To keep the quill and chuck at a particular height, the *quill lock* is tightened. The *depth stop* allows the chuck to be lowered to the same depth every time. It consists of two threaded nuts on a graduated shaft. The nuts can be turned toward each other to lock them into position.

FIGURE 35-2
This multispindle boring machine can bore up to eight holes. (Courtesy of B. M. Root Co.)

FIGURE 35-3
The spindle rotates inside the quill. (Courtesy of Delta International Machinery Corp.)

FIGURE 35-1
Major parts of a floor model drill press. (Courtesy of Delta International Machinery Corp.)

Some drill presses have an automatic feed feature. Once the machine is setup, the chuck is lowered by a power drive.

PURCHASING A DRILL PRESS

There are several items to consider when purchasing a drill press. The most important is the size. The

FIGURE 35-4
The feed lever lowers the quill while the depth stop controls the depth of the hole.

FIGURE 35-5
Changing the speed on a stepped pulley. Disconnect power before attempting this operation. (Courtesy of Delta International Machinery Corp.)

size of a drill press is first determined by measuring the distance from the center of the bit to the front of the column. This amount is then doubled. For example, if there is $7\frac{1}{2}$ in. (188 mm) from the center of the bit to the front of the column, the drill press would be rated at a 15-in. (381-mm) size. It would bore holes in the center of a 15-in. (381-mm)-wide piece of stock. Another indication of size is the stroke length. The *stroke length* is the amount the chuck can be lowered from its highest position. Most drill presses have a stroke length of 6 in. (152 mm). The longer the stroke length, the deeper a hole can be bored.

In purchasing a drill press, always consider the motor size. Purchase a motor that will have enough horsepower to perform the jobs required. For most wood boring operations, a $\frac{3}{4}$-hp motor is sufficient. If it is anticipated that routing, shaping, or other heavy-duty jobs are to be performed, buy a heavier motor.

The method of changing the chuck speed must also be selected. The speed can be varied by either a stepped pulley or variable-speed control. The *stepped pulley* is the least expensive and generally will have only three to five speed selections (Fig. 35-5). This many speeds are usually enough, but it does take time to move the pulley from one level to another. The *variable-speed control* is preferred but does cost more money (Fig. 35-4). Any speed between 200 and 4600 rpm can be selected. Only change speeds on a variable-speed pulley when the motor is running.

A drill press can also be purchased with a variety of table designs. A simple utility table has a hole in the center for the drill bit to pass through (Fig. 35-6A). Two other sets of slots are in the table to aid in clamping stock. A tilting table can be tilted for boring holes at an angle (Fig. 35-6B). Production tables provide larger surfaces for boring holes in big pieces (Fig. 35-6C). Many of this type will also include an *elevating crank* for raising and lowering the table.

SELECTING THE DRILL BIT

The secret to any boring operation is the proper selection of the drill bit. There are many to pick from but only one right bit for each job.

Twist Drill

The most common boring tool for a drill press is a *twist drill* (Fig. 35-7). It is used primarily for boring holes less than $\frac{1}{2}$ in. (13 mm) in diameter in wood, metal, or plastic. General-purpose twist drills have a spiral groove for removing waste from the hole and a tip ground at 118°. Twist drills designed for boring only in wood are ground at 60°. They are available in sizes from $\frac{1}{32}$ to $\frac{1}{2}$ in., varying in increments of 32nds. These bits are also sold in metric sizes of 1 to 13 mm.

Twist drills are kept in a metal storage box

FIGURE 35-6
(A) A utility table contains slots for clamping down work and a bit hole to allow the drill bit to pass through the table. (B) A tilting table can be angled to bore holes on an angle. (C) A production table has a large surface and an elevating crank to raise and lower the table. [(A) and (C) courtesy of Delta International Machinery Corp.]

(A)

(B)

(C)

FIGURE 35-7
Twist drills for woods are kept in a metal drill index.

TABLE 35-1
Twist Drill Speeds for Boring in Wood

Tool diameter (in.)	Spindle speed (rpm)
Up to $\frac{1}{4}$	3800
$\frac{1}{4}$ to $\frac{1}{2}$	3100
$\frac{1}{2}$ to $\frac{3}{4}$	2300
$\frac{3}{4}$ to 1	2000
Over 1	700

called a *drill index*. It can be kept close to the drill press by attaching it to the column with hose clamps. Although twist drills are available in different lengths, the most common length is specified as jobbers length.

Recommended speeds vary depending on the diameter of the bit. Table 35-1 gives speeds for boring in wood.

Spur Bit

A bit that looks similar to the twist drill but with a different point is the *spur bit* (Fig. 35-8). It is sometimes called a *brad point*. Two outside cutting lips produce a clean hole and the centering tip prevents it from following the grain of the wood. This is particularly desirable when boring dowel holes. The spur bit will also eliminate surface chip-out in material such as plywood. Use the same boring speeds as recommended for twist drills. Sizes range from $\frac{3}{16}$ to $1\frac{1}{4}$ in. (31 mm) by $\frac{1}{32}$ in. (1 mm). They are to be used on wood products only.

Machine Bit

A *machine bit* is sometimes used in a drill press (Fig. 35-9). More commonly, however, they are used in

FIGURE 35-8
A spur bit is recommended for dowel holes and boring in plywood.

FIGURE 35-9
A machine bit contains a lead screw which pulls the bit into the stock.

industrial boring machines. An auger bit with a tang or an enlarged end should not be used in a drill press. Machine bits are similar in appearance but have smooth, straight shanks. These bits have a self-feeding screw center that pulls the bit into the wood. Stock being bored with a machine bit must be clamped to the drill press table. The positive feed action of the screw may throw the stock from the table. The body style may be either fluted or solid center. The *fluted center machine bit* will provide the smoothest hole because it contains the most spirals. The *solid center* is the stiffest and will take the most abuse. Use boring speeds of less than 700 rpm. Sizes of machine bits range from $\frac{1}{4}$ to over 1 in. (6 to 25 mm) by increments of $\frac{1}{16}$ in. (2 mm). They are to be used on wood products only.

Forstner Bit

Large-diameter holes with a flat bottom can be bored with a *Forstner bit* (Fig. 35-10). The small

FIGURE 35-10
Forstner bits have a smooth cutting lip and make flat-bottomed holes.

centering tip is very short. It will not break through the bottom surface when boring a stopped hole until the hole gets very close to the bottom surface. It should be used at speeds given in Table 35-2 and at a slow constant feed speed. Forstner bits work well for boring a hole for a dowel pin or other round work. Sizes range from $\frac{1}{4}$ to 2 in. (96 to 51 mm) by $\frac{1}{16}$ in. (2 mm). They are to be used on wood products only.

TABLE 35-2 Recommended Speeds for Forstner and Multispur Bits			
Soft (low-density) wood		Hard (dense) wood	
Tool diameter (in.)	Spindle speed (rpm)	Tool diameter (in.)	Spindle speed (rpm)
$\frac{1}{4}$–$\frac{5}{8}$	2400	$\frac{1}{4}$–$\frac{5}{8}$	1800
$\frac{11}{16}$–1	1800	$\frac{11}{16}$–1	1400
$1\frac{1}{16}$–$1\frac{7}{16}$	1200	$1\frac{1}{16}$–$1\frac{7}{16}$	900
$1\frac{1}{2}$–over	600	$1\frac{1}{2}$–$2\frac{1}{8}$	450
		$2\frac{1}{4}$–over	250

Multispur Bits

Multispur bits look very similar to Forstner bits (Fig. 35-11). They do, however, have teeth ground into the outside cutting lip. This allows them to cut at a faster feed rate. Although it appears that they would make a very rough hole, the cut is actually smooth. Speeds should be as given in Table 35-2. Sizes range from $\frac{1}{2}$ to 4 in. (13 to 102 mm) by $\frac{1}{16}$ in. (2 mm). They are used in wood products only.

Spade Bit

A *spade bit* is used to make large-diameter holes with flat bottoms (Fig. 35-12). It is less expensive

FIGURE 35-11
The teeth in the outside lip make a multispur bit cut rapidly and cleanly.

than the multispur or Forstner. The spade bit gives good results if only a few holes are needed. Because it heats up rapidly, it should not be used for heavy boring. It has an extra-long tapered centering point which may break through the bottom surface of a stopped hole. Chuck speed should be less than 1000 rpm. Sizes range from $\frac{1}{4}$ to 2 in. (6 to 51 mm) by $\frac{1}{16}$ in (2 mm). They are used on wood products only.

FIGURE 35-12
Spade bits are recommended for boring small numbers of large-diameter holes.

Hole Saw

Hole saws produce large-diameter holes (Fig. 35-13). As they cut a hole, they also cut out a circular disk which is the inside of the hole. This is an ideal method of making wooden wheels for toys. The hole saw has a $\frac{1}{4}$-in. (6-mm) twist drill in the center which bores a lead hole in the wood. After boring each hole the drill press is turned off and the circular disk removed from inside the hole saw. The chuck speed should be less than 800 rpm. Sizes range from $\frac{9}{16}$ to 6 in. (15 to 152 mm). They can be used on wood or plastic.

FIGURE 35-13
Hole saws produce a large diameter hole and a circular plug.

Circle Cutter

The *circle cutter* makes the largest-diameter hole of all boring tools (Fig. 35-14). It consists of a $\frac{1}{4}$-in. (6-mm)-diameter guide bit and an adjustable arm with a cutter. The arm can be adjusted in or out to make various diameter holes. It is secured to the cutter body with a setscrew. Because the bit is aggressive in its cutting, the stock to be bored must be clamped to the drill press table to keep it from being thrown. Most generally, the hole must be bored from both sides of a thick board to produce a through hole. A circular plug is produced from the operation. Rotate the cutter less than 500 rpm. Holes can be made from $1\frac{1}{8}$ to $8\frac{3}{8}$ in. (28 to 213 mm). They are used on wood and plastics.

Counterbore

Counterbores are used to make two holes with one pass of the bit (Fig. 35-15). Normally, the counterbores are attached to a twist drill. The hole in the

FIGURE 35-14
Circle cutters are adjustable and make the largest of all holes.

FIGURE 35-15
Counterbores make two holes with one pass.

counterbore must match the outside diameter of the twist drill. The twist drill enters the wood first and produces the small-diameter hole. As the chuck is lowered further, the counterbore makes the larger hole at the top of the surface. They can either produce a flat bottom hole for a bolt or a tapered bottom hole to match a flat-head wood screw. Select a chuck speed recommended for the twist drill being used. Sizes range from $\frac{3}{8}$ to $1\frac{1}{2}$ in. (10 to 38 mm) by $\frac{1}{8}$ in. (3 mm). They are utilized only in wood products.

Screw Bit

Screw bits are specialized boring tools for making a combination of holes for a wood screw (Fig. 35-16). They will produce the countersink, shank hole, and pilot hole in one pass. Most are made from light-gauge material and are not meant for heavy use. Some have a positive stop which limits the depth of the hole to equal the length of the screw. Other styles allow the bit to go deeper, requiring a plug to cover the surface opening. Sizes of screw bits are

FIGURE 35-16
Screwbits make the countersink, shank hole, and pilot hole in one pass.

designated by flat-head wood screw sizes. Chuck speed should be less than 1000 rpm. They range from $\frac{3}{4}$ in. × 6 to 2 in. × 12. Use this bit only with wood products.

Taper Point Bit

Taper point bits are tapered bits specially designed for wood screws (Fig. 35-17). The angle on the sides of the bit closely matches the taper of the threads of a screw. The tapered hole will give the screw maximum holding power. An adjustable countersink head allows a combination hole to be bored. Boring speeds are the same as given in Table 35-1. Sizes range from $\frac{1}{8}$ to $\frac{3}{8}$ in. (3 to 10 mm).

FIGURE 35-17
Taper-point bits have the same taper as the threaded portion of a wood screw.

Countersink

Countersinks can produce the tapered hole for the head of an oval- or flat-head wood screw (Fig. 35-18). The shank hole is first made with a twist drill. The countersink then enlarges the top of the hole to an 82° angle. Chuck speed should be less than 1500 rpm. The diameter of these boring tools are $\frac{1}{2}$, $\frac{5}{8}$, and $\frac{3}{4}$ in. (13, 16, and 19 mm). Depending on the type of material from which the countersink is made, it can be used in wood, plastic, or metal.

Plug Cutter

A *plug cutter* is used to make wood plugs to cover the heads of flat-head wood screws (Fig. 35-19). Before the screw is inserted a counterbore hole is made the same diameter as the inside diameter of the plug cutter. A thick scrap of matching color and grain is selected and a plug is cut. The plug cutter is not used to bore all the way through the waste piece of stock. A chisel is used to break off the plug produced in the block of wood. Adhesive is applied to the hole to

FIGURE 35-18
Countersinks make the tapered holes to match the head of oval- or flat-head wood screws.

FIGURE 35-19
Plug cutters produce short wooden plugs for screw holes.

fasten the plug. Use a chuck speed of 500 rpm, or less. Plug cutters commonly come in $\frac{3}{8}$-, $\frac{1}{2}$-, $\frac{5}{8}$-, $\frac{3}{4}$-, and 1-in. (10-, 13-, 16-, 19-, and 25-mm) diameter. Sizes up to 2 in. (51 mm) are available. Use plug cutters only on wood products.

SETTING UP THE DRILL PRESS

The first step to setting up a drill press is to install the bit. After selecting the desired drill bit, unplug the drill press. Insert the shank of the bit into the drill chuck a minimum of 1 in (25 mm) and center the bit in the chuck. Hand tighten the chuck collar and then tighten the chuck using the chuck key. Insert the key into each of the three holes in the chuck and tighten. If the chuck is not tightened using each hole, the bit may slip in the jaws. This will damage the bit and may cause the bit to seize (stick) in the hole. Be certain to remove the key after tightening at each hole.

Next select the boring speed that the bit should turn. As a general rule, the larger the diameter of the bit, the slower it should turn. Use the recommended speeds given for each type of drill bit shown earlier in this unit as a starting point. Harder, denser materials require a slower speed than softer materials. If the chips are not smooth or if burning occurs, reduce the speed.

The speed can be changed on some drill presses by moving the position of the belt on a stepped pulley (Fig. 35-5). By changing the belt to pulleys of various diameters, the boring speed is changed. Consult the owner's manual for speeds and procedure of changing pulleys. When the belt is on the largest pulley on the motor and the smallest pulley on the arbor, the chuck will run at the fastest speed. When it is on the smallest motor pulley and the largest arbor pulley, it will be at the slowest revolutions per minute position.

Some drill presses have a variable-speed selector on the front of the head (Fig. 35-4). The boring speed is changed simply by turning the speed selection knob. Any speed is available between 200 and 4600 rpm. By turning the knob a spring-loaded pulley mounted on the quill will get smaller or larger. Move the selection knob only when the motor is running.

The height of the drill press table needs to be adjusted each time the bit or thickness of stock is changed. By loosening the table locking clamp, the table can be raised or lowered on the column (Fig. 35-1). Larger production tables have an elevating crank to move the table more easily (Fig. 35-6C). Since the table is a heavy casting, be careful not to allow it to drop to the floor. If not held up, it will fall as soon as the lock is loosened. A 6-in.-long board should be permanently attached at the bottom of the column. This will prevent the table from striking your foot if it is ever dropped accidently. The table should be adjusted until the distance between the bit and the work is $\frac{1}{2}$ in (13 mm). Secure the table to the column with the table lock clamp.

Always cover the drill press table with a flat scrap piece or *wood pad*. This will protect the metal table top and keep the stock from breaking out when the bit comes through the bottom surface (Fig. 35-20). Make certain that the hole in the table is centered under the bit so that if a bit does reach the table it will enter the hole.

SECURING THE STOCK

Unless the stock to be bored is large and can be safety held, it should be secured to the drill press table. A commercial hold-down clamp works well

FIGURE 35-20
A wood pad protects the tabletop.

(Fig. 35-21). C-clamps or hand screws are also used to secure stock to the table (Fig. 35-22). When boring into the end of a cylinder, a modified hand screw is used to hold the stock (Fig. 35-23).

FIGURE 35-21
Commercial hold-down clamps secure the work to the drill press table.

FIGURE 35-22
(A) C-clamps work well to keep the stock from moving. Note the protective block to keep the clamp from marring the panel.

FIGURE 35-22 (*Cont.*)
(B) A hand screw supports small pieces.

FIGURE 35-23
A V cut into a handscrew holds cylindrical shape stock.

BORING THROUGH HOLES

To bore a *through hole,* first install the correct drill bit in the chuck. Raise the table to the proper height and position the hole in the table immediately below the bit. Cover the table with a wood pad. Lower the bit until the tip is just below the top surface of the scrap. Set the depth stop to this level by turning down the depth stop nuts to the depth stop flange (Fig. 35-4).

Lay out the center of the hole on the stock by using two intersecting lines at right angles to one another. Mark the center with a awl to start the bit more accurately. Center the cross marks of the layout lines under the tip of the bit (Fig. 35-24). It may be helpful to lower the bit to bring the bit closer to the marks before turning on the power. Clamp the stock to the table if it is small or any piece that has a rounded surface. Always clamp metal or plastic pieces to be drilled to the table.

Turn on the power and with the right hand, lower the feed lever. Steady the stock with the left hand but keep the hand at least 4 in. (102 mm) from the bit. Continue lowering the bit into the stock at a slow constant speed. Too rapid a feed rate and the bit may grab and throw the stock. Too slow a feed rate and the bit will burn and become dull.

If the hole is deep, back the bit out occasionally to allow the bit to clean itself of chips. Keep feeding the bit downward until the depth stop meets the bottom flange. The bit should have cut through the stock and cut into the scrap piece. Remove the chips from the table with a brush or compressed air before boring the next hole.

FIGURE 35-24
The two intersecting lines show exactly where the tip of the bit should be located.

BORING STOPPED HOLES

Holes that do not extend completely through the stock are called *stopped holes*. First mark the desired depth of the hole on the side of the stock. Then place the stock on the drill press table. Lower the bit until the tip is level with the depth layout mark (Fig. 35-25). Secure the quill with the quill lock. Set the depth stop and release the quill lock.

Start the motor and bore the hole in the same manner as a through hole. Once the depth stop reaches the bottom flange, return the quill to the top position. Measure for the correct depth of the first hole before boring any others.

FIGURE 35-25
Lower the bit until it is level with the layout mark.

BORING DEEP HOLES

Most drill presses have a stroke length of 6 in (152 mm). A hole up to twice the distance of the stroke length can be bored by using a three-step method. Use a spur bit because it has less tendency to follow the grain.

Bore the desired hole in one end of the stock as deep as possible. Then bore another hole in a ¾-in. (19-mm)-thick scrap piece to serve as a base board. Clamp this base board to the table. To line up the hole with the drill, replace the drill bit with a straight dowel of the same diameter as the original bit (Fig. 35-26). The dowel must be as long as the total depth of the deep hole plus the length of the drill.

FIGURE 35-26
The dowel rod centers the scrap board on the drill press table.

Lower the chuck and center the hole in the base board on the end of the dowel. Lock the table in this position. Put a 1-in. (25-mm) length of dowel in the hole in the base board and place the first hole in the original piece over this dowel (Fig. 35-27). The third and last step is to bore the hole from the opposite end of the stock (Fig. 35-28).

FIGURE 35-27
Place the previously drilled hole over the short dowel.

FIGURE 35-28
Boring through the first hole to complete the deep hole.

BORING HOLES SPACED EQUALLY APART

Holes that are to be equally spaced can be made with a variety of methods. Laying out the holes each time takes time and leaves room for error. It may be justified, however, if only a few pieces are to be bored.

The centers of the holes can be located using a *template*. Carefully mark the centers of the holes on a cardboard, plastic, or sheet metal template. Arrange it so that two edges of the template line up with two adjoining edges of the stock. Place the template on the stock and mark through each hole to locate the center (Fig. 35-29).

The *auxiliary fence method* of spacing holes requires that a wooden fence be constructed. Holes $\frac{17}{32}$ in. (14 mm) in diameter are bored into a straight

FIGURE 35-29
A cardboard template is used with an awl to locate the center of the hole.

fence the same distance apart as the holes of the finished product (Fig. 35-30). Turn the fence on edge and position the edge of the first hole the desired distance away from the side of the bit. Clamp the fence in place with C-clamps. Insert a $\frac{1}{2}$-in (13-mm) dowel pin into the first hole. Butt the end of the board against the dowel and bore the first hole. By moving the dowel and the board, the series of holes can be bored.

A *stop pin technique* can also locate equally spaced holes. A bolt of the same diameter as the desired hole is clamped to a fence attached to the table (Fig. 35-31). The inside edge of the bolt is the same distance away from the side of the bit as the space between holes. After measuring and boring the first hole, slide the stock along the fence until the pin drops into the bored hole. As many holes as are necessary can be made by repeating the process. This is an excellent process for boring holes for adjustable shelving.

A *commercial boring head attachment* is the fastest method of boring multiple holes (Fig. 35-32). The head is simply brought down into the stock. Each of the several bits will make a hole.

FIGURE 35-30
The dowel is moved from hole to hole in the fence. The holes in the stock will be the same distance (2 in.) apart as those in the fence.

FIGURE 35-31
The distance from the center of the bolt to the center of the bit is equal to the space between the holes.

FIGURE 35-32
A commercial boring head makes several holes. (Courtesy of Reynolds Multi-Drill.)

BORING ANGULAR HOLES

Holes at an angle can be made by first tilting the table. This requires a drill press with a tiltable table (Fig. 35-6B). A sliding T-bevel set to the desired angle serves as the gauge (Fig. 35-33). Some tables have a positive stop at 45°.

FIGURE 35-33
Use a sliding T-level to set the drill press table to the desired angle.

Since the stock will have a tendency to slide off the table, clamp the material into position. Use a stiff shank bit such as a Forstner. If a small-diameter hole is to be bored or a sharp angle is necessary, cut a corresponding triangular wedge to be clamped on top of the stock and bore through it (Fig. 35-34). The level top surface of the triangular piece will keep the bit from bending when the hole is started.

For drill presses without tiltable tables construct a tilting fixture (Fig. 35-35). *Pocket holes* used for attaching tabletops to aprons can be made using a tilted drill press table or tilting fixture. The angled screw holes are an excellent method of securing most tops (Fig. 35-36).

FIGURE 35-34
The triangular wedge keeps the bit from slipping to the downhill side.

FIGURE 35-35
The tilting fixture allows angled holes to be bored on a drill press table that does not tilt.

POCKET HOLE

BULKHEAD

FIGURE 35-36
Pocket holes are angular screw holes used to attach tops.

COUNTERBORING AND PLUGGING HOLES

A *counterbore* is a large-diameter circular hole placed on top of a smaller hole. It is used primarily for sinking the heads of screws and bolts below the surface of the board. A wooden plug is often glued into the counterbored hole (Fig. 35-37). If the hole is to blend into the surrounding wood, select a piece of wood for the plug with the same color and grain characteristics as the piece it is to be glued. Contemporary furniture often used plugs with contrasting color and grain which is run at right angles to the surrounding wood. Use a plug cutter to produce the plugs.

To counterbore a hole, always make the larger-diameter hole first. This will leave a center point for

WOOD PLUG

COUNTERBORE

FIGURE 35-37
A wooden plug is glued into a counterbored hole.

the smaller bit to follow. A Forstner or multispur bit works the best for the largest hole. Counterboring bits can be attached to a twist or spur bit (Fig. 35-15). This will allow both the large and small hole to be bored at the same time.

If for some reason the smallest hole is bored first, it will be difficult to bore the largest hole. The material needed to locate the center of the bit has been removed. Insert a dowel pin of the same diameter as the drill bit into the hole and then bore the larger hole (Fig. 35-38). This method also works well when it is necessary to enlarge a hole.

DOWEL

FIGURE 35-38
A dowel glued into the small hole will provide a center for the counterboring bit.

BORING HOLES IN CYLINDRICAL STOCK

Because a cylinder or round does not have a flat bottom, it requires a vee block holding fixture (Fig. 35-39). The fixture can easily be made by making two 45° cuts in a block of wood.

FIGURE 35-39
The V-block cradles the cylinder and keeps it from turning.

Place the cylinder in the vee groove and bore the desired holes. Locate the centers of the holes with an awl mark to keep the bit from sliding to the side.

BORING HOLES
IN A CIRCULAR PATTERN

To bore a series of holes in a circular pattern, first attach an auxiliary table to the drill press (Fig. 34-40). A pivot point is established at a distance from the bit equal to the distance from the center of the circle to the center of the holes. The pivot point may be a dowel pin which extends completely through the board. If a through centering hole is not acceptable, use a wood screw with an exposed tip that has been filed to a sharp point. The screw is

FIGURE 35-40
An auxiliary table with a pivot point provides a method of producing holes in a disk.

driven through the auxiliary table from the bottom until the tip protrudes slightly above the top surface. Center the stock over the pivot point and drill the desired holes. The holes may have their centers marked on the surface or some form of stop can be made.

Use a vee block clamped to a vertical table for boring holes on the edge of a disk (Fig. 35-41). The face of a circular part can be bored with angular holes by tilting the table (Fig. 35-42). A fixture with a matching curve cradles the disk.

FIGURE 35-41
Holes in the edge of a disk can be made by using a vee block and tilting the table.

FIGURE 35-42
Boring holes on the inside of an arc requires a curved cradle board.

BORING HOLES
IN ODD-SHAPED STOCK

Stock that cannot be placed flat against the horizontal drill press table must be secured by some other means. A special fixture or holding device generally needs to be constructed. It is often helpful to be able to tilt the table to assist with the setup. Several possibilities are shown in Fig. 35-43.

(A)

(B)

HOLDING BOARD

FINISHED PIECE

STOCK

VERTICAL DRILL PRESS TABLE

(C)

FIGURE 35-43
(A) Two intersecting V-grooves can steady ball-shaped pieces. (B) Ends of long pieces can be bored by securing them in a hand screw. Make certain that the board is parallel with the top of the clamp. (C) Ends of curved pieces can be bored by using a holding board.

BORING SCREW HOLES

A shank and anchor hole are required for installing a wood screw. The flat head and oval head also require a countersink hole. Use a twist drill for making the shank and anchor holes. A countersink bit will make the countersink hole. A spur or Forstner bit can make the counterbore hole.

Screw bits and specialized boring bits can be used as a quick method of making all three screw holes with one pass of the boring tool (Fig. 35-16). The best method of selecting the correct size of standard twist drill bits for a screw is by using a screw chart (Table 35-3).

When a chart is not available, make the shank hole slightly larger than the shank of the wood screw. It should slip through the hole with little pressure. The anchor hole size can be determined by holding drill bits against the thread portion of the screw. Select the bit whose diameter is equal to the root or small diameter of the wood screw roughly one-third up the length of the threads. For dense hardwoods or with brass screws, make the anchor hole slightly larger.

If possible, position the two boards to be joined as they are to be assembled. Bore the anchor hole through the top piece and into the bottom board. Follow this by boring the shank hole by enlarging the anchor hole through the first piece.

When the two pieces cannot be placed together on the drill press, bore the shank hole first. Put the top board over the bottom piece and with a scratch awl mark the location of the anchor hole. Bore the anchor hole separately.

MORTISING ON THE DRILL PRESS

To cut mortises on the drill press, first install the yoke around the drill chuck (Fig. 35-44). Slip the mortising bit into the chisel. Place the shank of the chisel into the yoke and bit into the drill chuck. Position a dime between the top shoulder of the chisel and the bottom of the yoke (Fig. 35-45). Push the bit all the way up into the chisel. Tighten the chuck securing the bit. Position the slot in the side of the chisel facing toward the front of the drill press. Remove the dime and push the chisel up tight against the yoke. Tighten the yoke nut to secure the chisel. This procedure will provide the proper clearance between the flared end of the bit and the inside edge of the chisel. The slot in the side of the chisel is used to remove the chips.

Mark out each mortise on the edge of the board. Bolt the mortising fence to the drill press table. Place the stock against the fence. Raise the

TABLE 35-3
Recommended Hole Sizes for Wood Screws[a]

Screw no.	Pilot holes: twist drill (nearest size, in.)		Shank clearance holes: twist drill (nearest size, in.)	Countersink: twist drill to counterbore (in.)
	Hardwoods	Softwoods		
0	$\frac{1}{32}$	$\frac{1}{64}$	$\frac{1}{16}$	—
1	—	$\frac{1}{32}$	$\frac{5}{64}$	—
2	$\frac{3}{64}$	$\frac{1}{32}$	$\frac{3}{32}$	$\frac{3}{16}$
3	$\frac{1}{16}$	$\frac{3}{64}$	$\frac{7}{64}$	$\frac{1}{4}$
4	$\frac{1}{16}$	$\frac{3}{64}$	$\frac{7}{64}$	$\frac{1}{4}$
5	$\frac{5}{64}$	$\frac{1}{16}$	$\frac{1}{8}$	$\frac{1}{4}$
6	$\frac{5}{64}$	$\frac{1}{16}$	$\frac{9}{64}$	$\frac{5}{16}$
7	$\frac{3}{32}$	$\frac{1}{16}$	$\frac{5}{32}$	$\frac{5}{16}$
8	$\frac{3}{32}$	$\frac{5}{64}$	$\frac{11}{64}$	$\frac{3}{8}$
9	$\frac{7}{64}$	$\frac{5}{64}$	$\frac{3}{16}$	$\frac{3}{8}$
10	$\frac{7}{64}$	$\frac{3}{32}$	$\frac{3}{16}$	$\frac{3}{8}$
11	$\frac{1}{8}$	$\frac{3}{32}$	$\frac{13}{64}$	$\frac{7}{16}$
12	$\frac{1}{8}$	$\frac{7}{64}$	$\frac{7}{32}$	$\frac{7}{16}$
14	$\frac{9}{64}$	$\frac{7}{64}$	$\frac{1}{4}$	$\frac{1}{2}$
16	$\frac{5}{32}$	$\frac{9}{64}$	$\frac{17}{64}$	$\frac{9}{16}$
18	$\frac{13}{64}$	$\frac{9}{64}$	$\frac{19}{64}$	$\frac{5}{8}$
20	$\frac{7}{32}$	$\frac{11}{64}$	$\frac{21}{64}$	$\frac{11}{16}$
24	$\frac{1}{4}$	$\frac{3}{16}$	$\frac{3}{8}$	$\frac{3}{4}$

[a] Sizes of holes are recommended for average application. Slightly larger or smaller holes may be required.

FIGURE 35-44
Major parts to a mortising attachment for a drill press (Courtesy of Delta International Machinery Corp.)

CHUCK — YOKE — BIT — CHISEL — HOLD DOWN DOGS — FENCE — FENCE RODS

DIME — LAYOUT LINES

FIGURE 35-45
Use a dime as a spacer when installing the chisel.

table until the end of the chisel is $\frac{1}{2}$ in. (13 mm). from the top of the stock. Place a square against the chisel and fence to square each.

Position the stock against the fence with the face side out. Adjust the fence in or out so that the layout marks are centered under the bit. If the mortise is to be punched completely through the stock, place a scrap piece on the table. This will protect the chisel and minimize chip-out on the bottom side of the stock when the chisel breaks through.

Mark on one end of the stock the desired depth of the mortise. After placing the board against the fence, lower the chisel until the tip is level with the layout line. Secure the quill with the quill lock. Adjust the depth stop to this level. Release the quill lock. Position the hold-down dogs and fence rods against the stock. These two devices will hold the stock against the fence and table.

Adjust the chuck speed to 1500 rpm and turn on the power. Check that the clearance between the tip of the bit and chisel are maintained. They must not rub against each other. Make the first punch to the extreme right of the layout (Fig. 35-46). Move the board to the right and make the second punch to the extreme left. Remove the rest of the mortise using the steps shown in Fig. 35-46. This procedure will prevent the chisel from being bent to one side.

FIGURE 35-46
To prevent bending the chisel use this sequence in making the mortise.

ROUTING ON THE DRILL PRESS

Routing on the drill press should only be attempted on a heavy-duty machine. No less than a ¾-hp motor should be used. The chuck should rotate no slower than 15,000 rpm. Use the fastest speed available.

Make an auxiliary wood table from plywood and bolt it to the regular drill press table (Fig. 35-47). An adjustable wooden fence with a 1¼-in. (31-

FIGURE 35-47
An auxiliary table and sliding fence are used for routing.

mm) half circle at the cutter location is attached to the top surface and serves as a guard and an edge to guide the stock against.

Insert the router bit a minimum of ½ in. (13 mm) into the chuck. Tighten the chuck securely with the chuck key. Lower the bit to the desired depth and lock into position with the quill lock. Clamp the wooden fence to the plywood table.

Routing Straight Edges

Clamp the wooden fence the desired distance from the router bit. Start the drill press and shape any end grain first. Edge and face grain are shaped last. On all surfaces use a slow feed speed. Keep hands at least 4 in. (102 mm) from the router bit (Fig. 35-48). Use a push stick whenever possible.

Take only very light cuts. If a great deal of material is to be routed, make multiple passes setting each to cut deeper than the previous cut. Raise the chuck so that no more than ¼ in. (6 mm) material is removed in one pass. Lower the chuck to take a deeper cut after all edges have been routed with the first-depth setting.

FIGURE 35-48
Use a push stick and keep hands at least 4 in. (102 mm) from the router bit.

Pin Routing

A drill press can also be turned into a pin router. Refer to unit on the pin router for details of what this machine can do. Attach a short bolt to the auxiliary table to serve as a guide pin (Fig. 35-49). It is important that the center of the bolt and the center of the router bit be exactly in the same line (Fig. 35-49). Make a template from hardboard the same size and shape as the finish piece. Use small brads to attach the template to the bottom of the stock.

Position the stock and pattern over the pin. Use a router bit the same diameter as the pin in the table. Lower the turning bit into stock (Fig. 35-50). Use the quill lock to secure the quill. Move the stock keeping the template against the pin. This routes a groove in the stock the same shape as the template. Do not take any cut deeper than $\frac{1}{4}$ in. (6 mm). Keep the hands at least 4 in. (102 mm) away from the bit.

FIGURE 35-49
Auxiliary table with a guide pin centered under the bit.

FIGURE 35-50
Keep hands at least 4 in. (102 mm) from the router bit.

SPINDLE SANDING

The drill press makes an excellent spindle sander. This type of sander works best on inside curves. Commercially manufactured sanding drums with abrasive sleeves of many diameters can be purchased (Fig. 35-51). Shop-made drums can be made by first turning a hardwood cylinder on the lathe (Fig. 35-52). Cut a $\frac{1}{4}$ in. $\times$ $\frac{1}{4}$ in. groove the length of the cylinder. Insert a $\frac{1}{2}$-in. carriage bolt through the center for a shaft and wrap abrasive cloth around the outside. The cloth is held in place with a recessed

FIGURE 35-51
Commercial sanding drums come with abrasive sleeves.

FIGURE 35-52
A shop-made drum uses abrasive cloth wrapped around the outside.

strip of wood in the $\frac{1}{4} \times \frac{1}{4}$ in. groove. Several screws secures the wood strip. Set the strip and screws a little below the surface of the drum.

Select a sanding drum that is slightly smaller than the diameter of the curve to be sanded. Set the chuck speed between 1000 and 2000 rpm. If burning occurs, lower the chuck speed and use a new position on the abrasive. Install an auxiliary table with a hole in the center slightly larger than the drum (Fig. 35-53). Lower the sanding drum into the table and secure with the quill lock. Sand the curve. Raise or lower the drum once a section of the abrasive becomes clogged or burned.

There are several fixtures that increase the versatility of the sanding drums. Stock can be sanded to size by using a large-diameter drum (Fig. 35-54). Clamp a fence the same distance away from the surface of the abrasive as the desired size of stock. Cut the material to $\frac{1}{64}$ in. (0.5 mm) over the desired size on the table saw. Feed the stock only from the direction where the drum is turning into the board. Do not sand more than $\frac{1}{64}$ in. (0.5 mm) at a time.

Stock can be sanded to a pattern using the setup shown in Fig. 35-55). A wooden collar of exactly the same diameter as the drum is inserted into the table. Make a hardwood pattern of exactly the same shape and size as the desired product. Bandsaw the stock to shape, but do not cut into the layout line. Attach the stock to the pattern with wood screws. Push the pattern against the collar in the auxiliary table. Any stock extending over the pattern will be sanded away.

FIGURE 35-53
The auxiliary table allows the sanding drum to be raised and lowered.

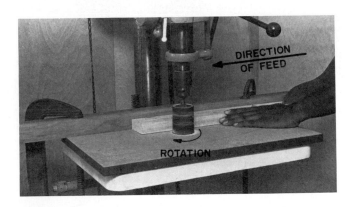

FIGURE 35-54
Stock can be sanded on the face using a drum. Take only light cuts feeding the board from the right direction.

FIGURE 35-55
Setup for sanding stock to a pattern.

470   CHAPTER 35   DRILL PRESSES

Answer each of the following questions. If you are not sure of an answer, review the chapter.

35-1. Remove the _____ key before turning on the power.

35-2. The hollow shaft that contains the rotating spindle is called the _____.

35-3. How is the size of the drill press determined?

35-4. What is the most common boring tool for a drill press?

35-5. The centering _____ of a spur bit prevents the bit from following the grain of the wood.

35-6. Forstner bits bore large-diameter holes with _____ bottoms.

35-7. _____-_____ bits have teeth ground into the outside cutting lip.

35-8. _____-_____ make the largest-diameter hole of all boring tools.

35-9. _____-_____ bits are tapered bits specially designed for wood screws.

35-10. Insert the shank of the bit into the drill chuck a minimum of _____ in. (_____ mm).

35-11. Always cover the drill press table with a flat scrap piece of _____ _____.

35-12. Holes that do not extend completely through the stock are called _____ holes.

35-13. A hole up to twice the distance of the _____ length can be bored by using a three-step method.

35-14. _____ holes are angular holes for attaching tabletops to aprons.

35-15. To counterbore a hole, always make the _____ diameter hole first.

35-16. A _____ and _____ hole are required for installing a wood screw.

35-17. When a screw chart is not available, make the shank hole slightly _____ than the shank of the wood screw.

35-18. If the mortise is to be punched completely through the stock, place a _____ on the table.

35-19. Routing on the drill press requires the chuck to rotate not slower than _____ rpm.

35-20. If burning occurs during spindle sanding, _____ the chuck speed and use a new _____ on the abrasive.

Following are technical terms that you should be able to use as part of your working vocabulary. Write a brief description of the meaning of each term.

Base
Table
Head
Column
Table locking clamp
Spindle
Quill
Feed level
Quill lock
Depth stop
Stroke length
Stepped pulley
Variable-speed control
Elevating crank
Twist drill
Drill index
Spur bit

Brad point
Machine bit
Fluted center machine bit
Solid center machine bit
Forstner bit
Multispur bits
Spade bits
Hole saws
Circle cutter
Counterbores
Screw bits
Taper point bits
Countersinks
Plug cutter
Wood pad
Through hole
Stopped holes
Auxiliary fence method
Stop pin technique
Commercial boring head
    attachment
Pocket holes

36

SINGLE-SPINDLE SHAPERS

A single-spindle shaper is typically utilized to make moldings and other decorative cuts (Fig. 36-1). Occasionally, it is also used for jointery-type cuts such as rabbets and stuck joints. Some woodworkers feel this machine is an unimportant accessory. Advanced furniture, cabinets, and architectural woodwork, however, often cannot be constructed without the shaper.

The single-spindle shaper is a common machine in industry. Industrial models are frequently larger and heavier built than those used by schools. This allows larger and more elaborate cuts. There are also specialized shapers utilized in industry. For example, an automatic shaper operates from a pattern to produce curved raised panels and other shaped parts. A drive spindle automatically guides the pattern past the cutter (Fig. 36-2).

PARTS OF THE SINGLE-SPINDLE SHAPER

The major parts of the single-spindle shaper consists of a fence, table, spindle, and base (Fig. 36-1). There are also a few other secondary parts which are necessary for safe operation: the motor, height-adjustment system, and power switch.

Although there are several fences that can be

SHAPER SAFETY RULES

1. Keep fingers and hands at least 6 in. (153 mm) away from the rotating cutter.
2. Stock to be shaped on an edge must be at least 2 in. (51 mm) wide and 10 in. (254 mm) long.
3. Use a holding device whenever shaping end grain that is less than 10 in. (254 mm) wide.
4. Whenever possible, use guards, hold-down devices, and featherboards.
5. Remove all wrenches and other tools from the table before turning on the power.
6. Have the instructor check all setups before turning on the power.
7. Whenever possible, shaping should be completed from the bottom side of the board to minimize cutter exposure.
8. Stock should always be cut by moving it forward into the cutter.
9. The cutter must always rotate into the stock.
10. Use a push stick whenever possible.
11. Disconnect the power before making any tooling changes or major adjustments.

installed on the shaper, the most common is the *commercial split fence* (Fig. 36-3). Stock is guided against the fence to control the depth of cut. The fence is bolted to the table with the *fence studs*.

473

FIGURE 36-1
Major parts of a single spindle shaper. (*Courtesy of Oliver Machinery Company.*)

FIGURE 36-2
An automatic shaper guides the pattern past the spindle. (*Courtesy of A & B Automated Woodworking Machinery.*)

FIGURE 36-3
A commercial split fence is bolted to the table with fence studs.

The table provides a surface to lay the material. It will be made from a piece of cast metal and contains a milled slot and several holes. The slot or *miter gauge groove* guides the miter gauge. In the center of the table is the large spindle hole where the threaded *spindle* is found. The other smaller holes are for the *fence studs* and *starting pin*.

The vertical spindle holds the *cutter, collars* and *spindle nut* (Fig. 36-4). It is either direct or belt driven by the motor. Most medium-size to large shapers will have changeable spindles. They can be

unscrewed from the shaper shaft and then a different-sized spindle is mounted (Fig. 36-4). Standard spindle sizes are $\frac{1}{2}$, $\frac{3}{4}$, 1, $1\frac{1}{8}$, and $1\frac{1}{4}$ in. (13, 19, 25, 28, and 31 mm).

The *base* is located below the top. It houses the height-adjustment system, shaper shaft, and *on-off switch*. The height-adjustment system raises and lowers the spindle with the *height-adjustment handwheel*. Heavy shapers may have a second handwheel for tilting the spindle. Once the desired spindle height has been reached, it can be secured into place

FIGURE 36-4
Shaper spindles can vary in size from $\frac{1}{2}$ to $1\frac{1}{4}$ in.

with the *height-adjustment lock*. The *on-off switch* turns the power on or off to the motor. Some machines will also have a *reversing switch* which changes the direction of spindle rotation from clockwise to counterclockwise.

PURCHASING A SHAPER

The first thing to consider when buying a shaper is the size. Shapers are sized by spindle diameter and motor horsepower rating. Smaller shapers come equipped only with a $\frac{1}{2}$-in. (13-mm) diameter spindle. This size of spindle will work well on most small cutters with relatively light cuts. Medium- to heavy-weight machines will have changeable spindles which range from $\frac{1}{2}$ to $1\frac{1}{4}$ in. (13 to 31 mm). This allows larger cutters to be used and deeper cuts to be made.

Motor sizes range from a $\frac{1}{2}$ to over 5 hp. The larger the horsepower rating, the heavier the cut can be made. Deep cuts should be made on shapers with a motor of at least 3 hp.

There are many other features available for this machine. A reversible power switch allows the spindle to be rotated in either direction. Some shapers come equipped with a router collet attachment. This allows router bits to be used with the shaper.

SELECTING THE SHAPER CUTTERS

There are literally hundreds of different cutters which are available for the shaper. A cutter can be used individually where the entire cutting edge is used or only a portion of the cutter is utilized to shape the whole pattern. When a more complex shape is required, several cutters can be selected to

develop the edge. Make a separate pass for each cutter that is required.

Shaper cutters are either of a multiwing style or loose-leaf style. Multiwing shaper cutters contain two, three, or more cutting edges or *wings* (Fig. 36-5). They are commercially made and are available in all standard patterns. The more wings a cutter contains, the smoother the cut will be and the faster the feed rate is required. Three wing cutters are the most common.

Loose-leaf shaper knives are made from several parts (Fig. 36-6). The assembled cutter consists of a top and bottom collar which holds the two custom-ground knives. Two bolts are used to hold the collars together and secure the knives in the assembly. Knife stock is either plain or notched. The notched style is considered to be safer because the small notches are locked in between the collars and the setscrew allows small adjustments on extending the knives.

Knife blanks are cut from a bar. Using special layout techniques, the desired shape is drawn on the back side of the piece of steel. Next, the shape is freehand ground on a pedestal grinder (Fig. 36-7). The two knives should weigh within 0.5 g of one another. If one is heavier than the other, the assembled cutter will run out of balance. This will create vibration which will lead to excessive wear on the spindle bearings and could produce an uneven cut.

After the two knives are installed between the notched collars, the assembly can be placed on the spindle. The knives should not extend beyond the edge of the collar more than three times the thickness of the knife. Any more than this amount and the knife may break. Always use a dial caliper to check that both knives extend the same amount past the collar (Fig. 36-8). The setscrew can be turned in or out to adjust the amount of extension.

All shaper tooling is either made totally of high-speed steel or contains carbide-tipped cutting edges. The steel cutters are the least expensive and can be easily sharpened. Use a flat oil stone to hone the back side of the knife. Never sharpen the beveled edge because the contour of the pattern will be altered. Carbide-tipped cutters stay sharper longer and work the best when machining abrasive materials such as particleboard.

INSTALLING THE SHAPER CUTTER

To install a shaper cutter, make certain that the power has been disconnected and the fence removed. If the spindle has a cutter on it, raise the cutter well above the table and lock the spindle so that it does not rotate. On some commercial machines there is a spindle lock for this purpose (Fig. 36-9A). By engag-

3-LIP SHAPER CUTTERS

1/2" Cove 5/16" Qr. Rd.	
5/16" Cove 1/8" Bead	
1/8" & 3/8" Qr. Rd. 1/4" Bead	
1/4" & 1/2" Qr. Rd.	
90° V-Groove	
1/4" Flute	
Drawer Joint	

Ogee — Female Sash — Cab. R.H. Male — Cab. L.H. Male — Cab. R.H. Female — Cab. L.H. Female — Male Sash

Glue Joint — Cove & Bead Mldg. L.H. — Cove & Bead Mldg. R.H. — Cove & Bead Cope. R.H. — Cove & Bead Cope L.H. — 3-Bead (3/16" Bead) — 5-Bead (1/8" Bead)

Wedge Tongue — Wedge Groove — Ogee & Bead Table Edge — 1" Convex Edge — 1/2" Flute — 1/2" Bead — 1/4" Bead

3/4" Flute — 1" Flute — 3/8" Bead — Panel Raising — 1" Bead — 9/16" Qr. Rd.

3/8" Flute — 3/4" Bead — Door Lip — 1/2" & 1/4" Radii R.H.

FIGURE 36-5
Commercial multiwing shaper cutters are available in a variety of sizes. (*Courtesy of Delta International Machinery Corp.*)

FIGURE 36-6
Parts to a loose-leaf shaper knife assembly.

FIGURE 36-7
Grinding a knife blank.

FIGURE 36-8
Use a dial indicator to set the loose-leaf shaper knife in the knotched collars.

(A)

(B)

(C)

FIGURE 36-9
Secure the spindle by the (A) spindle lock, (B) wrench at the base, or (C) wrench at the top of the spindle.

ing the lock, the spindle will not turn. On other machines a wrench is utilized to hold the spindle secure. In this case the wrench is placed either at the base of the spindle or on the flattened area at the very top of the spindle (Fig. 36-9B and C).

Use a second wrench and turn the nut in a counterclockwise motion to loosen the spindle nut. Finish unscrewing the nut and remove the collars and shaper cutter. Because the cutter can easily be damaged off the machine, store it in the original container or in a shaper cutter cabinet. It must not touch other cutters or any metal objects.

INSTALLING THE SHAPER CUTTER   477

Next select the shaper cutter that will produce the desired shape. Check that the bore hole in cutter is the same diameter as the spindle. If it is not, remove the existing spindle and replace it with the correct size following the instructions of the machine manufacturer. When the cutter is mounted on the spindle, determine which side of the cutter should be facing up. If at all possible, have the largest portion or biggest diameter of the tool on the bottom side (Fig. 36-10). This will expose the least amount of the cutter to the operator.

There are four pieces that are generally mounted on the spindle (Fig. 36-11). A *collar* is first placed on the spindle to provide the accurate machined surface to place the cutter against. Next posi-

tion the cutter next to the first collar. After inserting another collar on top of the cutter, tighten the spindle nut. While keeping the spindle from turning, use the spindle wrench to secure the nut. If the spindle has a keyway cut along its length, install a *keyed washer* before screwing on the spindle nut. This will keep the nut from loosening once the power is turned on. Be certain to remove all wrenches and other parts from the shaper table before starting the machine.

Unlock the spindle and install the proper fence and guards. Turn the cutter by hand to be certain that the knives will not strike anything. Connect the power.

SETTING UP THE SHAPER

After tracing around the cutter on the end of the board and installing the shaper cutter, the machine setup can be completed. Next determine which direction the cutter must rotate (Fig. 36-12). Most shapers have reversible spindle which allows them to rotate in either direction. The cutter must be turned so that the cutting edge is leading and the beveled edge is trailing. Quickly turn the power on and off to determine which direction the spindle is rotating. If the cutting edge is not leading, place the reversing switch in the opposite position.

FIGURE 36-10
Mount the cutter with the largest portion below the table.

FIGURE 36-11
Correct order of parts in the mounting of a cutter.

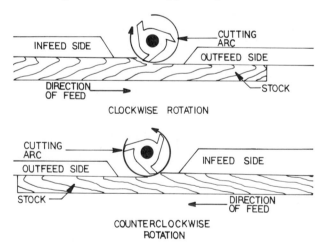

FIGURE 36-12
The rotation of the cutter will determine the direction of feed.

By using the height-adjustment handwheel, adjust the height of the spindle. Raise or lower the spindle until the outline of the cutter aligns with the layout lines on the end of the board (Fig. 36-13). Tighten the height-adjustment lock once the position is established. To serve as a guide, a fence is usually installed. There are several styles from

FIGURE 36-13
By raising the cutter, align the cutter with the layout lines.

which to select. Most fences are held in place on the table with either fence studs or clamps. The fence studs are threaded rods which are screwed into the table (Fig. 36-3). The fence is then mounted over the top of these studs. When clamps are utilized, they are used to secure the fence to the underneath side of the table.

SHAPER FENCES

Any time a straight edge is to be shaped, a fence should be installed. This forms a surface to guide the stock along and also protects the operator from the rotating cutter. In addition, it provides a surface to which hold-downs and featherboards are attached.

With all fences it is important that the fence halves are as close together as possible. The closer they are, the less likely the stock will dip into the opening and less chipping of grain. On some fences, the two halves can be adjusted inward so that the rotating cutter just clears the tips of the fence.

FIGURE 36-14
Pivoting the fence into the rotating cutter to provide a minimum amount of clearance.

To provide the least amount of clearance, first attach a piece of scrap material to the face of the fence (Fig. 36-14). Clamp one half of the fence to the table and turn on the power. Slowly pivot the free end of the fence into the rotating cutter. The knives will cut its pattern through the scrap piece. Stop moving the fence once the cutter is extending through the fence the desired amount.

There are several different styles of fences. They include the wooden fence, the commercial split fence, and specialized fences. Each has certain advantages. All of these are secured to the table with either two fence studs or by C-clamps.

Wooden Fence

Wooden fences are made in the shop and come in several versions (Fig. 36-15). This fence is the best style when only a portion of the edge is removed. The face of the fence shown in Fig. 36-15 is made from one piece of hardwood. This assures that both fence halves are even with each other. An extension is added to the back of the fence to provide an area to clamp the fence to the table. Covering the face of the fence with high-pressure plastic laminate will form a hard, smooth surface. This surface will allow the stock to be fed more easily across the machine.

FIGURE 36-15
A wooden fence can be attached to the table with fence studs.

Commercial Split Fence

Shapers are generally sold with a split fence (Fig. 36-3). Although it can be used as a guide to remove a portion of the edge, the split fence is ideally suited for shaped surfaces that cover the entire edge. The two fence halves can be adjusted independently. By turning the depth-adjustment knob, one-half of the fence can be moved in or out. This allows the outfeed portion of the fence to be moved forward to support the freshly shaped edge.

Specialized Fences

Specialized fences are designed for a specific purpose. The only limitations are the creativity of the operator and the safety requirements of the machine.

A few of the specialized fences include a high fence, long fence, miter fence, strip molding fence, and circular fence. With all of these fences, remember to have a minimal opening between the fence halves. To keep from making a new fence for each cutter, a replaceable insert can be used to fit into the specialized fences (Fig. 36-16). When a new cutter is to be used, install another insert and allow the cutter to cut through the insert.

FIGURE 36-17
A high fence provides additional support for large pieces. Note that the featherboard also adds more support.

FIGURE 36-18
A long fence provides support for extra long stock.

MITER FENCE. A miter fence will shape a bevel or chamfer on the edge or end of a board (Fig. 36-19). The incline base holds the board at the desired angle. If a different angle is required, a new fence is made.

FIGURE 36-19
A miter fence angles the board for a bevel or chamfer cut.

FIGURE 36-16
A replaceable insert provides a new throat opening without making a new fence.

HIGH FENCE. A high fence is utilized primarily for shaping wide pieces that are shaped on their faces (Fig. 36-17). The tall vertical fence provides support for the stock and also gives a large surface to clamp featherboards.

LONG FENCE. A long fence is used primarily on small shapers with short tables (Fig. 36-18). This fixture not only makes a long fence but also provides a base or table to feed the stock against. This makes it ideal for long boards or for attaching stop blocks.

STRIP MOLDING FENCE. Thin pieces of molding can be made by either of two methods. When a wide board is available, the edge can be first shaped and then the molding ripped to thickness on a table saw. The second method is to construct a strip molding fence (Fig. 36-20). This allows thin pieces to be fed safely past the cutter. The featherboard holds the stock against the fence while the top piece keeps it against the base. Make certain that the stock is long enough to be pushed and pulled past the fixture.

FIGURE 36-21
Construction details for a featherboard.

FIGURE 36-20
A strip molding fence allows the material to be shaped.

OPERATING THE SHAPER

After the cutter has been mounted and the fence adjusted, featherboards must be installed. Featherboards are shop-made wooden hold-downs which keep the board against the table and serves as a barrier against the rotating cutter. Figure 36-21 shows the recommended dimensions for featherboards that are used with the shaper.

Position a piece of stock of the same thickness as the material to be shaped against the fence. A featherboard is to be mounted on each side of the fence and as close to the rotating cutter as possible (Fig. 36-22). With a C-clamp, secure each one in place. Rotate the cutter by hand to be certain that the cutter does not come in contact with the featherboards.

Check to see that the stock is at least 2 in. (52 mm) wide and 10 in. (254 mm) long. Never shape a piece with less than 10 in. (254 mm) in contact with fence unless a special holding device is used. The sliding miter gauge with hold-downs works well when shaping the end grain on narrow boards (Fig. 36-23). Turn on the power and slowly feed a scrap piece forward into the cutter. After the piece has reached the outfeed fence, pivot the board away from the cutter. Check that the shaped surface matches the desired profile. If the cut is too heavy for the

FIGURE 36-22
Use two featherboards to hold the stock down and to guard the cutter.

FIGURE 36-23
A sliding miter gauge can be selected to hold small stock or when shaping end grain.

machine to make in one pass, adjust for a lighter cut. Make the shaped edge in two or more passes.

Use a push stick to guide the boards past the cutter. Your hands must not come within 6 in. (152 mm) of the cutting circle. Use a slow constant feed speed. To minimize the torn grain at the corners of the board, always shape the end grain first. Any chipping that occurs will usually be removed when the edges are shaped.

SHAPING PART OF AN EDGE

When only part of the edge is to be shaped, start by jointing the surface. Since part of the edge will not be removed and left exposed, make certain that this jointed edge is straight and free from chipped grain (Fig. 36-24).

Install either a commercial split fence or a wooden fence to guide the stock. If a split fence is utilized, use a long, straight edge to align the two fence halves. A wooden fence, as shown in Fig. 36-15, does not need to be aligned.

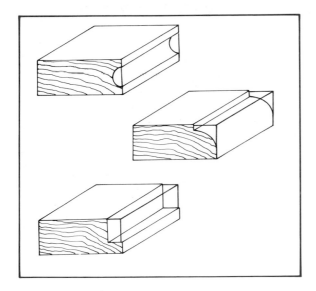

FIGURE 36-24
Part of the original edge may be left with some types of cuts. The colored lines indicate the original edge that has been shaped away.

Raise the cutter to the desired height and move the fence to expose the correct amount of the cutter. Fasten the fence to the table using the fence stud. Next, determine which direction the cutter must rotate (Fig. 36-12). If it does not rotate opposite the direction of feed, reverse rotation. Complete the remaining setup and follow the operating procedure as given in the section "Operating the Shaper."

SHAPING THE ENTIRE EDGE

Many profiles require that the whole edge be shaped (Fig. 36-25). To produce this type of a cut, mount the desired cutter and adjust it to the correct height. Determine which direction the cutter is to rotate and set the rotation switch to the proper position.

The split fence next needs to be mounted in the proper position. To do this, place the stock on the infeed side of the fence and slide the fence in or out until the desired amount of the cutter extends past the face of the fence. At least $\frac{1}{16}$ in. (2 mm) should be removed from all areas of the edge. Tighten the

FIGURE 36-25
Some shapes require that all of the original edge be machined. The colored lines indicate the original edge that has been shaped away.

fence stud nut on the infeed side of the fence and install a featherboard (Fig. 36-26).

Turn on the power and check that the cutter is rotating the opposite direction of the feed (Fig. 36-12). Slowly feed a large scrap piece forward until the leading end is approximately 3 in. (76 mm) past the cutter. Pivot the stock away from the cutter and turn off the power. Make any necessary adjustments to produce the desired shape.

By turning the depth-adjustment knob, move the outfeed side of the fence forward until it just touches the newly shaped edge (Fig. 36-27). If it is brought too far forward, the stock will hit the lip of the outfeed fence and a taper will be shaped. Not bringing it far enough forward will produce a snipe at the end of the board. Lock the fence with the depth-locking handle and then tighten the remaining fence stud nut.

FIGURE 36-26
Tighten the fence stud on the infeed side of the fence to secure that half of the fence.

FIGURE 36-27
Adjust the outfeed side of the fence up to support the freshly shaped edge.

Install a featherboard on the outfeed fence and feed a large scrap board across the rotating cutter. Check that the fence has been properly adjusted and the cut is correct. The stock can then be shaped. Remember each time the boards are passed over the shaper, it becomes smaller. If the stock is run more than once, it may become too small. Use the operating instructions as given in the section "Operating the Shaper."

COLLAR SHAPING

Curved or irregularly shaped stock can be shaped by using a contact collar (Fig. 36-28). The precut piece is simply fed against this special collar. Make certain that the piece is large enough to allow you to keep your hands a minimum of 6 in. (152 mm) from

FIGURE 36-28
Collar shaping utilizes a contact collar to control the depth of cut.

the cutter. In addition, with this method only part of the edge is shaped. Since a portion of the original edge will remain, it must be perfectly smooth and true. This edge also serves as a pattern to run the stock against. Any irregular surfaces will be transferred to the shaped edge.

To set up the machine, install the cutter in the normal manner with the largest diameter of the cutter on the bottom side. It is recommended to place a contact collar immediately on top of the cutter against which to run the stock. The collar can also be placed under the cutter or mounted between two cutters. These last two positions, however, leave more of the shaper knife exposed. Contact collars can be either a *highly polished solid collar* or a *ball-bearing collar*. The solid collar is the least expensive but does tend to burn the stock. The ball-bearing collar does not spin with the spindle once it comes in contact with the stock. This prevents burning from occurring. Keep both types of collars smooth and shiny.

The amount the cutter overhangs the contact collar determines the depth of cut (Fig. 36-28). The smaller the collar, the heavier the cut. If a great deal of material is to be removed, initially use a larger-diameter contact collar or lower the spindle.

To protect the operator and cutter, install either a *plastic shield* or a *ring guard* (Fig. 36-29). Both are suspended over the top of the cutter and should extend farther out than the cutting circle. These guards will protect you only from the top side of the cutter. Be careful that your hands do not slide into the cutter from the side.

Never attempt to perform collar shaping without a starting pin. A *starting pin* acts as a fulcrum point for the material to be pivoted into the cutter (Fig. 36-30). It generally fits into a tapered hole which is located on the infeed side of the shaper.

Once the shaper has been set up, raise the cut-

(A)

CUTTER

(B)

FIGURE 36-29
Use (A) a plastic shield or (B) a ring guard when a fence is not used.

ter to the desired height. Check that at least ¼ in. (6 mm) is against the contact collar. Any less, and the stock may plunge into the cutter.

Turn on the power and firmly grip the stock. Place the board against the starting pin and slowly pivot it into the rotating cutter. Plan the cut so that it will not start on the corner. The cutter should first come into contact with the stock immediately behind the corner. This will keep the cutter from grabbing the work.

FIGURE 36-30
Collar shaping with a starting pin.

PLASTIC SHIELD

STARTING PIN

CONTACT COLLAR

CUTTER

After the stock has come against the contact collar, feed it forward. Swing the board off the starting pin and use only the collar to guide the stock. Once a corner is reached, rotate the stock to the next edge and continue shaping until the entire board is shaped. As the board is being fed forward, keep working your hands back away from the cutter. After the shaped edge is complete, pivot the stock away from the cutter.

PATTERN SHAPING

Pattern shaping can be used when the entire edge is to be molded on a curved or irregular shaped piece. Industry often uses this method because it is one of the fastest methods of producing parts such as plaque backs, mirror frames, and other curved furniture parts. Pattern shaping does require a pattern or form to produce the part. This requires time and skill to produce.

To produce parts using the pattern-shaping technique, first make the pattern (Fig. 36-31). For a small number of parts, ¾-in. (19 mm) dense hardwood such as northern hard maple works well. If a large number of pieces are required, the pattern will wear much longer if it is made from tempered hardboard, plastic, or metal. After the outline of the part has been laid out, carefully use a scroll saw to cut out the form. With files and other hand tools, work the edge until it is smooth and true. The pattern will be complete when it is exactly the same size and shape as the finished part. Any remaining imperfections will be reflected in the shaped parts.

To secure the stock to the pattern, use at least three flat-head wood screws. The larger the part, the

FIGURE 36-31
Proper setup for pattern shaping.

PATTERN HANDLE

PLASTIC GUARD

COLLAR

F.H. SCREW

CONTACT COLLAR

PATTERN

CUTTER

STOCK

COLLAR

SHAPER TABLE

SHAFT

more screws should be utilized. File the first $\frac{1}{8}$ in. (3 mm) of each screw to a flat chisel shape. Drive the screws through the patterns until the $\frac{1}{8}$-in. tip is extending through the face of the pattern. To achieve maximum holding power, the flatten tip should be oriented parallel to the grain of the part.

Finish the pattern by attaching two handles to the back of the pattern and gluing 100-grit abrasive paper to the face. The handles provide a method of safely holding and controlling the pattern. The abrasive paper provides more gripping power and the stock is less likely to twist off the pattern.

After the pattern is finished, install the cutter and set up the shaper as described in the section "Collar Shaping." Ideally, the contact collar should be just slightly smaller in diameter than the deepest part of the cutter (Fig. 36-32). Always mount the contact collar on top of the cutter to provide maximum safety. A ball-bearing collar is less likely to burn a groove in the pattern.

FIGURE 36-32
Select a collar that is slightly smaller in diameter than the deepest part of the cutter.

The pattern and stock can be run much like a part as described in "Collar Shaping." The stock, however, is first roughly sawed to shape. After placing the pattern on top of the stock, draw around the outside edge. Cut each piece to within $\frac{1}{16}$ to $\frac{1}{8}$ in. (2 to 3 mm) of this layout line. Place the precut piece with the face against the shaper table and the back or poorest side facing up. After centering the pattern over the stock, use a mallet to drive the screw tips into the board. Check that the stock and pattern are firmly seated together.

Place the pattern against the starting pin and pivot the pattern into the rotating cutter. Begin the cut in the middle of one of the edges (Fig. 36-33). Pivot the pattern away from the starting pin keeping it against the rotating cutter. Keep the stock moving at all times, and your hands on the handles. Once the cut is complete, slide the pattern away from the cutter.

FIGURE 36-33
Shaping a circular edge with a pattern.

STUCK JOINERY

Stuck joinery is commonly found on good-quality traditional furniture and cabinets (Fig. 36-34). This joinery is frequently used on raised panel doors and frame plywood bulkheads. It requires a matched set of cutters that will cut the molding on the inside edges of stiles and rails and the shaped end on the mating ends of the rails. The shaped edges on the inside edge are called *sticking*. The shaped ends are referred to as *coped ends*. There are many different styles of cutters available which will provide different patterns.

FIGURE 36-34
Stuck joint sticking and coped ends.

Because grain tear-out is always a problem, the ends of the rails are shaped first. Cut the material to the finished length and $\frac{1}{4}$ inch (6 mm) wider than the finished widths. The length can be determined by establishing the inside dimension of the panel. This is called the *between the shoulder length*

(Fig. 36-35). To this amount, add the length of the two tenons. With most cutters, this is a total of 1 in. (25 mm). For example, if there is 10 in. (254 mm) between the stiles, add 1 in. (25 mm). The finished length of the rails will then be 11 in. (279 mm).

FIGURE 36-35
Check the between the shoulder length to determine the overall width of the frame.

Set the shaper up with a wooden fence (Fig. 36-36). Ideally, a ¼-in. (6-mm)-thick piece of plywood should be attached to the face of the fence. After the cutters have been adjusted to the proper height, the fence should then be pivoted into the rotating cutter (Fig. 36-14). This will provide a minimum of clearance between the cutting circle and the fence. Hav-

FIGURE 36-36
Shaping the coped ends of stuck joint.

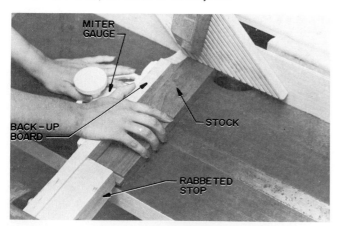

ing this small space will make coping much safer and reduce grain tear out.

As the fence is installed, it must be mounted parallel to the miter gauge groove. Check that the distance between the face of the fence and the edge of the miter gauge groove is the same at each end of the shaper table. Once the fence is secure to the table, attach featherboards to the face of the fence.

To the face of the miter gauge, screw a piece of squared stock to serve as a backup board (Fig. 36-36). It will extend to the fence. It should be at least 12 in. (305 mm) longer than the longest rail. This serves as an additional surface to hold the material but also prevents grain tear-out. After it has been attached to the gauge, turn on the power and run the miter gauge past the cutter. This will cut the shape into the end of the stock. Check that this profile is correct. If not, make any necessary adjustments.

Place the first piece of material with the edge against the miter gauge and the end against the fence. There must be a minimum of 10 in. (254 mm) in contact with the gauge. Clamp a rabbeted stop on the backup board and against the other end of the stock. Turn on the power and grip the board securely against the miter gauge. Feed the stock slowly past the cutters. End for end the piece and cope the remaining end. After this first piece has been run, check that between the shoulder dimension is correct. Run all the remaining pieces.

Tear the setup down and install the matching cutters for the sticking (Fig. 36-37). Place a rail on the table to determine the correct height of the cutters. Match the cutters up with the coped end of the rail. Place the split fence on the shaper and adjust it to remove $\frac{1}{16}$ in. (2 mm) from the original edge. Finish the set up by installing featherboards.

Stock for the stiles should be the same thickness as the rails and ¼ in. (6 mm) wider than the finished width. This extra width will allow the pieces to be run a second time if there is any chipped grain. Stiles will need to be cut to the finished length.

FIGURE 36-37
Match the sticking cutters with the coped end by raising the spindle.

For the sticking operation, feed the stock past the cutters with a push stick. Be careful not to push in on the stock immediately around the throat of the fence. A sniped end is very likely to occur.

After the first piece is run, check that the rails properly fit into the sticking. The faces of the two pieces should be even, and there should be a slight amount of drag as the tenon is inserted. If the fit is correct, run the remaining pieces. Any shaped edges that develop torn grain can be rerun. Feed the piece at a slower rate. After all parts have been shaped, rip them to rough width and joint the outside edge to finish width.

GLUE JOINERY

One method of adding quality to a solid wood panel is to make the edge glue joints on the shaper. A special glue joint cutter is used to make both mating surfaces. It provides a decorative tongue and groove appearance on the end grain while assuring the alignment of the boards. Because the stock does overlap on each joint, it requires an additional $\frac{1}{4}$ in. (6 mm) of material per joint.

To run this glue joint, first rip all material to width and surface it to thickness. In addition, plane a piece of scrap material to this exact thickness to be used for setup. Install the cutter and adjust the height where the top shoulder (surface A) and the bottom shoulder (surface B) will be *exactly* the same width (Fig. 36-38). Unless this is done, the face of the boards will not be even.

FIGURE 36-38
Setup for shaping a glue joint.

Place the split fence on the shaper and adjust the fence halves to remove $\frac{1}{16}$ in. (2 mm) with the smallest diameter of the cutter. The outfeed fence will need to be moved forward to support the newly shaped surface. By removing the entire edge, not only is the joint cut but also the boards will be straightened.

After installing featherboards, run the scrap stock. Crosscut the piece in half and fit the two halves together. Make any necessary adjustments so that the faces are even and a straight edge is produced. Shape the stock following the recommended procedure as given in the section "Operating the Shaper." Run one edge of each board with the face side up (Fig. 36-39). Then turn the boards over and shape the mating edges with the face side down. To glue the panel up, be certain a glue brush is used to work the adhesive into the grooves.

FIGURE 36-39
Run a shaped glue joint with the face up of the first edge. Turn the board over to shape the second edge.

SHAPING WITH SPECIALIZED FIXTURES

Using a fixture to hold and guide the material allows custom patterns to be made and undersized material to be run. They should be made so that the stock is held firmly and that the hands of the operator do not come within the 6-in. (152-mm) danger zone of the cutter.

A few of the possible specialized fixtures are as follows:

Circular Fixture

The circular fixture provides full support on stock that is a true circle or a segment of a true circle (Fig. 36-40). A fixture is made the reverse shape and same

FIGURE 36-40
A circular fixture provides a method of shaping circular parts.

An indexing pin of the same diameter as the template holes is installed in the table on the infeed side of the cutter. After the cutter and contact collar are mounted, screw the stock to the template. The part can then be run. The indexing pin determines the distance between the cuts. The contact collar sets the depth of cut. Move the template to the first hole and pivot the stock into the rotating cutter. Once the contact collar meets the template, swing the work back away from the cutter. Move the template to the next hole and repeat the process until all the notches are made. The cutter can be raised and another row of cuts can be made.

diameter as the piece to be shaped. Since featherboards are not used, install a ring guard or other form of protection.

Fretting Fixture

To make an ornamental piece of molding, a fretting fixture can be utilized (Fig. 36-41). Although there are many variations possible, one method of producing the required template is to bore a series of holes. The template is then ripped in half leaving one-half of each hole.

FIGURE 36-41
Making a piece of molding using a fretting fixture.

STUDY QUESTIONS

Answer each of the following questions. If you are not sure of an answer, review the chapter.

36-1. The shaper cutter must always rotate _____ into the stock.

36-2. Stock is guided against the _____ to control the depth of cut.

36-3. How is the size of a shaper determined?

36-4. Multiwing shaper cutters contain two, three, or more cutting edges or _____.

36-5. Loose-leaf knives should not extend beyond the edge of the collar more than _____ times the thickness of the knife.

36-6. When installing cutters, a _____ is first placed on the spindle to provide the accurate machined surface to place the cutter against.

36-7. The cutter must turn so that the cutting edge is _____ and the beveled edge is _____.

36-8. Any time a straight edge is to be shaped, a _____ should be installed.

36-9. A _____ fence is the best style when only a portion of the edge is removed.

36-10. The _____ fence is ideally suited for shaped surfaces that cover the entire edge.

36-11. A miter fence will shape a _____ or chamfer on the edge or end of a board.

36-12. After the cutter has been mounted and the fence adjusted, _____ must be installed.

36-13. Not bringing the outfeed fence far enough forward will produce a _____ at the end of the board when the entire edge is being shaped.

36-14. Contact collars for collar shaping can be either highly polished _____ collars or _____-_____ collars.

36-15. A _____ acts as a fulcrum point for the material to be pivoted into the cutter when performing collar shaping.

36-16. _____ shaping can be used when the entire edge is to be molded on a curved or irregular shaped piece.

36-17. To secure the stock to the pattern for pattern shaping, use at least _____ flat-head wood screws.

36-18. The shaped ends in stuck joinery are referred to as _____ ends.

36-19. The length of the rails of a raised panel door is determined by establishing the _____ dimension of the panel.

36-20. _____ joinery provides a decorative tongue-and-groove appearance on the end grain, while assuring the alignment of the boards.

IMPORTANT TECHNICAL TERMS

Following are technical terms that you should be able to use as part of your working vocabulary. Write a brief description of the meaning of each term.

Commercial split fence
Fence studs
Miter gauge groove
Spindle
Starting pin
Cutter
Collar
Spindle nut
Height-adjustment handwheel
Height-adjustment lock
Reversing switch
Wings
Keyed washer
Highly polished solid collar
Ball-bearing collar
Plastic shield
Ring guard
Sticking
Coped ends
Between the shoulder length

37

PIN ROUTERS

The pin router is one of the newer stationary power tools to be used in the woods industry (Fig. 37-1). It can make both joinery and decorative-type cuts. Because this machine utilizes router bits for cutters, there are many different available patterns. The pin router has the advantage over a portable router because the cutter is held in a fixed position. This allows both large and small stock to be shaped.

Schools and small shops will generally have a *shaper-router* (Fig. 37-2). This allows the motor unit to be suspended over the table or mounted below the table. To make heavier industrial cuts, a larger *pin router* is used (Fig. 37-1). It may have a floating head which moves up and down over the top of curved stock. A *numerically controlled router* is a computer-controlled machine which is not guided by an operator (Fig. 37-3, page 492). A computer program is developed which automatically moves the router bit up and down and the table from side to side. The information may be fed to the machine using a special coded tape (Fig. 37-4).

PARTS OF THE PIN ROUTER

There are relatively few major parts to the pin router (Fig. 37-1). It is made from a base, column,

FIGURE 37-1
Major parts of the pin router. (*Courtesy of Ekstrom, Carlson & Co.*)

490

There are two methods of introducing the router bits into the stock. The simplest technique employs a *foot-operated treadle* to raise and lower the table (Fig. 37-2). With the treadle, the operator manually steps down on the peddle to raise the table. This second technique uses a *pneumatic spindle height control* (Fig. 37-1). A foot control switch activates an air cylinder which raises and lowers the spindle. This is much faster and easier than with a foot treadle. With both methods a *height-adjustment handwheel* moves the table up and down to regulate the depth of cut. The *height-adjustment lock* secures the table once the desired depth of cut has been set.

PURCHASING A PIN ROUTER

An important consideration when purchasing a pin router is the size. It is determined by three items. The first is the *motor horsepower rating*. Larger motors allow deeper and heavier cuts. A good general-purpose size is 3 hp. The second item in establishing the size is the *throat dimension*. This is the distance from the center of the spindle to the front of the column. The larger this space, the wider the stock or pattern that can be run. The last item in determining size is the *collet size*. The collet holds the shank of the cutter. Sizes of collets include $\frac{1}{4}$, $\frac{3}{8}$, $\frac{1}{2}$, and $\frac{3}{4}$ in. (6, 10, 13, and 19 mm). (Fig. 37-5). Although some routers have only $\frac{1}{4}$-in. (6-mm) collets, they can still perform a great deal of work. Those having up to $\frac{1}{2}$-in. (13-mm) collets allow larger bits to be used. Only the very large pin routers have $\frac{3}{4}$-in. (19-mm) collets.

Another item to specify when purchasing a pin router is the *spindle speed*. Most pin routers will rotate at 20,000 (rpm) or faster. This is ideal for most router bits. Larger machines, however, may have a spindle speed selector which provides either 10,000 or 20,000 rpm's. The slower setting is for shaper cutters and other larger-diameter tooling.

The last item in purchasing a pin router to consider is the method the router bit is to be introduced into the work. As described in the section "Parts of A Pin Router," either a foot-operated treadle or the pneumatic spindle height control can be specified. The treadle has the advantage of the operator controlling the rate at which the table is raised toward the cutter. A pneumatic control is faster and less tiring for the operator to work.

SELECTING THE ROUTER BITS

Any router bit that can be used with a portable router can also be run on a pin router. Refer to the section "Selecting the Router Bits" in Chapter 25 for

MOTOR
ARM
SPINDLE
COLUMN
HEIGHT ADJUSTMENT CRANK
TABLE
PIN HOLE
HEIGHT ADJUSTMENT LOCK
BASE
FOOT OPERATED TREADLE

FIGURE 37-2
A shaper-router can have the cutter mounted either above or below the table. (*Courtesy of Delta International Machinery Corp.*)

and arm. An *arm* is suspended over the top of a table. Inside this arm is located the motor and drive system. At the end of the arm is the *spindle*. On most routers, the spindle moves the router bit up and down and rotates the cutter in a clockwise direction.

The *table* holds the stock while it is being machined. In the center of the table will be the *pinhole*. A *guide pin* is inserted through this hole against which the patterns can be run.

FIGURE 37-3
A numerically controlled router is controlled by a computer. (*Courtesy of Ekstrom, Carlson & Co.*)

FIGURE 37-4
Each row of holes gives the numerically controlled router a command on what task to perform. The guard has been removed for demonstration purposes only.

FIGURE 37-5
Collet sizes vary from $\frac{1}{4}$ to $\frac{3}{4}$ in.

$\frac{3}{8}$" COLLET

$\frac{1}{2}$" COLLET

$\frac{1}{4}$" COLLET

$\frac{1}{4}$" COLLET

detailed information. There are, however, a few additional important points to remember when working with a pin router.

For joinery cuts, such as rabbets and dados, use as large a straight bit that will produce the cut. With larger sizes, a higher-quality cut is made and there is less chance of chattering. *Chattering* is created when the tip of the bit turns in an untrue circle and the bit flexes as it cuts. This produces a rough cut and will eventually lead to the bit breaking.

Whenever possible, select a bit with a $\frac{1}{2}$-in. (13-mm) shank. This will provide a stronger bit which is less likely to break. For example, a $\frac{1}{4}$-in. (6-mm) straight bit with a $\frac{1}{2}$-in. (13-mm) shank will last six times longer than the same bit with a $\frac{1}{4}$-in. (6-mm) shank.

INSTALLING THE ROUTER BIT

To install a router bit, first secure the spindle. On some models, a spindle lock is provided (Fig. 37-6). Other spindles are secured with a spindle wrench. Check that the tapered internal hole inside the spindle is clean and free of corrosion. Select the desired router bit and the matching collet. Be very careful that you do not drop or abuse either of these precision made items.

Insert the collet into the spindle and screw on the collet nut. Next, place the shank of the router bit into the collet. It must extend into the collet a minimum of $\frac{1}{2}$ in (13 mm). If this is not done, the collet will become enlarged at the shank hole opening. This is called *bellmouthing* (Fig. 37-7).

Using a collet nut wrench, tighten the collet nut. Free the spindle and check that the bit is secure and turns freely. Lower the guard and make certain that the operator is protected from the rotating cutter.

FIGURE 37-6
Changing a router bit using the spindle lock.

FIGURE 37-7
Bellmouthing is created when the shank is not inserted in the collet at least $\frac{1}{2}$ in.

SETTING UP THE PIN ROUTER

To set up the pin router, install the router bit according to the directions given in the section "Installing the Router Bit." Next, lower the table to the lowest point with the depth-adjustment handwheel. This will prevent the bit from accidentally being driven into the table. Step down on the foot treadle or the pneumatic spindle height control. Depending on the drive system mounted on the machine, this will either raise the table or lower the spindle.

Mark on the end of the stock the desired depth of cut. Place this board on the table and raise the table until the tip of the bit is aligned with the layout mark (Fig. 37-8). If a fixture is being used, position the stock on top of it and then adjust the depth. Secure the depth of cut setting by tightening the height-adjustment lock.

Adjust the guard so that it provides full protection surrounding the cutting circle (Fig. 37-9). The height of the guard should be set so that the stock will just pass under the bottom edge. After the fence or guide pin is installed, release the treadle or pneumatic spindle height control. Rotate the spindle by hand to check that the cutter will not strike the guard or fence.

FIGURE 37-8
Aligning the end of the router bit with the layout mark.

FIGURE 37-9
Properly adjusted guard. Note the stock will just pass under the bottom edge.

ROUTING THROUGH STRAIGHT EDGES

A pin router is an ideal machine for making dadoes, gains, and rabbets. Because of the cutting action of the router bit, the groove will be free of torn grain and provide a smooth bottom. This is particularly important when machining plywood and other easily chipped materials.

To cut a groove, set up the pin router as described in the section "Setting Up the Pin Router." Prepare the stock to finish size. The edge against the fence must be straight and the flat face against the table. Mark the depth and width of cut on the leading end of a piece of the stock. Place this on the table and adjust the router for the proper depth of cut. For a deep cut, make the groove with multiple passes.

If part of the original edge is to remain, use either the commercial fence or a wooden fence for guiding the material. A wooden fence will assure you that both the left and right fence halves will be in a straight line (Fig. 37-10). When the commercial split fence is utilized, a straight edge can be used to align the two fence halves. Secure the wooden fence to the table with C-clamps. Fence studs work well for attaching the commercial fence.

When the entire edge is to be routed, a commercial split fence is needed (Fig. 37-11). Adjust the left side of the fence to remove the desired amount from the edge. After positioning the guard, feed the board past the cutter until it reaches the outfeed side of the fence. Pivot the stock away from the cutter and turn off the power. When the bit has stopped turning, move the right side of the fence to support the freshly cut edge. Make certain that both fence studs are tightened before running the material.

Once the fence is positioned, the stock can be run. Be certain to have a push stick within reach of the operator and that the guard has been properly adjusted. Stock must be at least 12 in. (305 mm) long

FIGURE 37-10
Routing a groove with a wooden fence.

FIGURE 37-11
An entire edge can be routed using a commercial split fence. (*Courtesy of Delta International Machinery Corp.*)

and 4 in. (102 mm) wide. To keep the stock from raising off of the table, install featherboards on both sides of the cutter (Fig. 37-9). Turn on the power and slowly feed the stock from left to right. When running a shape on the edge, cut only on the front side of the cutter. Keep your hands at least 4 in. (102 mm) from the cutting circle. Once the trailing end comes close to the cutter, use a push stick to guide the stock past the cutter. On long material, have a tail-off person assist with supporting the stock as it leaves the table.

ROUTING A STOPPED GROOVE

To route a stopped groove, set up the router as directed in the section "Routing through Straight Edges." The fence must be at least 12 in. (305 mm) longer than twice the length of the stock. This extra length allows stop blocks to be installed at either end of the fence. Lay out on the face of the stock the starting and stopping points of the cut. Position the piece against the fence and table. With the height-adjustment handwheel, bring the tip of the bit to the top surface of the board. Move the board to the starting point of the groove and align the edge of the cutting circle with this mark (Fig. 37-12). Clamp a stop block to the fence at the trailing end of the material. Move the board along the fence until the second stopping point of the cut is aligned with the cutting circle. Clamp a second stop block against the leading end of the board. Remove the stock and reset the depth of cut for the router bit. If the groove is

FIGURE 37-12
Setting up to route a stopped groove.

Hold it in a stationary position and withdraw the bit to its original position. Remove the stock from the table. With compressed air blow the router table free of chips before running the next piece.

PATTERN ROUTING

Pattern routing can be used to produce plaque backs, picture frames, highlight furniture parts, and make internal cuts. This method requires a fixture on which to mount the material and to be guided against a pin mounted in the center of the table. Because of the fixture, small parts and pieces having a great deal of detail can be run.

Making the Fixture

The first step in pattern routing is to develop the fixture. It is made of several parts as shown in Fig. 37-13. They are the *template, fixture body, hardwood rails, spacer, handles,* and *fixture clamps.* All should be made of high-quality materials and with high craftsmanship.

A template is cut out using a scroll saw or band saw. The template should be the exact size and shape of the path the router bit is to travel. Be care-

stopped at only one end, install only one stop block.

After the guard has been adjusted and featherboards installed, position the board against the stop block on the infeed side of the fence. Turn on the power and hold the stock securely against the fence and table. Using either the foot treadle or pneumatic height control, plunge the bit into the stock. Do not move the board until the bit has stopped moving downward. Push the stock forward along the fence until the leading end meets the second stop block.

FIGURE 37-13
Parts to a pin router fixture.

ful to follow the layout marks precisely so that little filing is required. Any irregularities left in the template will be duplicated in the routed part. Although several different materials can be used for this part of the fixture, tempered hardboard works and wears well.

The template is next glued to the bottom of a fixture body. This is usually a piece of ¾-in. high-quality hardwood plywood. It must be large enough to hold the stock, fixture handles, and fixture clamps. To raise the template up off the router table, hardwood rails are mounted around the outside edge of the body. This reduces drag as the fixture is moved over the table and eliminates the accumulation of sawdust around the template.

On the top surface of the fixture body is a spacer and handles. The ¼-in. (6-mm) spacer raises the stock up off of the body. This prevents the router bit from cutting into the plywood body. There should be at least two handles to control the movement of the fixture. They provide a place to keep your hands and to keep them from the cutter.

There are a variety of techniques utilized to secure the stock to the fixture. Study the path of the router bit and be certain that the holding devices will not interfere with the cutter. If the fixture clamps come too close to the bit, two fixtures may be needed. Part of the cut is made with the first fixture. The part is then moved to the second fixture, which has the clamps located in different positions than the first. This allows the cut to be completed.

The simplest method of holding the stock is to use wood screws placed through the fixture and into the stock (Fig. 37-14). If the shape of the part will

FIGURE 37-14
Using screws to hold the stock on the fixture.

allow, homemade cam clamps can apply pressure to the side (Fig. 37-15). Two sides of the stock are held with rabbeted fences. In addition, there are commercial fixture clamps that are sold in a variety of sizes (Fig. 37-16). They apply pressure either from the side or top.

FIGURE 37-15
Cam clamps apply side pressure towards the rabbeted fences.

FIGURE 37-16
Commercial fixture clamps apply pressure either from the side or top.

Routing the Pattern

After the fixture is completed, the stock can be routed. Install the router bit and guide pin on the router. If a straight edge on the stock is desired, an upward spiral straight router bit is recommended (Fig. 37-17). It will produce a high-quality cut and remove the chips from the routed groove. For most general-purpose straight routing, a ½-in. (13-mm) diameter router bit works well. Pattern bits can also be used if they do not contain a pilot.

The diameter of the guide pin can also be var-

FIGURE 37-17
A spiral straight router bit lifts the chips up and out of groove.

ied (Fig. 37-18). To make the stock the same size as the template, use the same-size diameter bit and pin. If the piece is too small, the outside dimensions can be increased by using a larger-diameter pin. For parts that are larger than the desired size, the dimensions can be decreased by a smaller pin. After the correct size of pin is selected, secure it in the table so that it comes in contact with the template by at least $\frac{1}{4}$ in. (6 mm).

Clamp the stock to the fixture, making certain that it will not move. Adjust the guard and, without turning on the power, trace around the template with the guide pin. This will give you an indication of how the pattern should be run and which direction it should be moved. Check that the handles and clamps do not interfere with the machine. Continue practicing until you are confident of how to move the fixture. It is best to start and end the pass on an inside corner. The starting and stopping point are therefore less likely to show.

Turn on the power and adjust the depth of cut. If the bit is to extend all the way through the stock, be certain that it does not cut into the fixture body. Firmly grasp the handles of the fixture and always keep your hands on these handles while the cutter is turning (Fig. 37-19, page 498). Plunge the bit into the work. Move the fixture slowly around the pin, going against the rotation of the cutter. Once the pass is complete, retract the cutter from the material. Inspect the first part for quality of cut and dimensions. Once any needed adjustments have been made, run the remaining pieces.

PIN ROUTING

Irregular shaped stock can be routed on its edges by using a pin installed in the table (Fig. 37-20). The

FIGURE 37-18
Varying the diameter of the guide pin changes the size of the finished piece.

material must first be bandsawed to shape and the edges worked smooth with files and abrasive paper. Select the desired router bit and install a pin with a diameter that is equal to the smallest diameter of the router bit.

After adjusting the guard, turn on the power and slowly pivot the stock into the cutter. Do not start the cut on the corner of the board. Your material must be large enough to keep your hands at least 4 in. (102 mm) from the cutter. Once the cut is complete, move the piece away from the cutter.

FIGURE 37-19
Routing with a pin router fixture. (*Courtesy of Delta International Machinery Corp.*)

FIGURE 37-20
Routing an irregular shape with a guide pin. (*Courtesy of Delta International Machinery Corp.*)

STUDY QUESTIONS

Answer each of the following questions. If you are not sure of an answer, review the chapter.

37-1. Always feed the material _____ the rotation of the router bit.

37-2. Which type of router is computer controlled and is not guided by an operator?

37-3. A _____ is inserted through the pinhole in the table to run patterns against.

37-4. How is the size of the pin router determined?

37-5. _____ is created when the tip of the bit turns in an untrue circle and the bit flexes as it cuts.

37-6. The shank of the router bit must be inserted into the collet a minimum of _____ in. (_____ mm).

37-7. The height of the guard should be set so that the _____ will just pass under the bottom edge.

37-8. When the entire edge is to be routed, a _____ fence is needed.

37-9. Name the major parts of a pattern fixture.

37-10. The template for a fixture can be cut out using a _____ saw.

37-11. A _____ prevents the router bit from cutting into the plywood body of the pattern fixture.

37-12. To make the stock the same size as the template, use the _____ size diameter bit and pin.

37-13. Irregular-shaped stock can be routed on its edges by using a _____ installed in the table.

IMPORTANT TECHNICAL TERMS

Following are technical terms that you should be able to use as part of your working vocabulary. Write a brief description of the meaning of each term.

Shaper-router
Pin router
Numerically controlled router
Spindle
Pinhole
Guide pin
Foot-operated treadle
Pneumatic spindle height control

Height-adjustment handwheel
Height-adjustment lock
Throat dimension
Collet size
Spindle speed
Chattering
Bellmouthing
Template
Fixture body
Hardwood rails
Spacer
Handles
Fixture clamps

38

MORTISERS
AND SINGLE-END TENONERS

The mortiser and single-end tenoner are highly specialized machines. They are specifically designed to produce mortise-and-tenon joints. This is a very strong joint commonly used to join edge and end grain.

The mortiser makes the rectangular hole into which the tenon fits. There are three different types of mortisers. The *chisel mortiser* is the oldest and most common style (Fig. 38-1). It contains a hollow chisel and an auger-type bit. The chisel punches a square hole, and the bit removes all the material inside the square. In place of a mortiser, many schools use a chisel mortising attachment on the drill press. This accessory is discussed in Chapter 35. A *chain mortiser* is the fastest-cutting mortiser (Fig. 38-2). It has a chain-saw-type cutting tool which is plunged into the stock. The newest style of machine is the *reciprocating chisel mortiser* (Fig. 38-3). This machine uses a saw-tooth-type cutting tool which moves rapidly back and forth (Fig. 38-4, page 502).

The single-end *tenoner* shapes the square peg which fits into the mortise (Fig. 38-17). With three cutting stations, it can cut a plain tenon, shape the shoulder of the tenon, and cut the stock to length. This machine is described at the end of this chapter.

Industry often uses mortisers and tenoners.

The mortisers are frequently power driven and contain more than one cutter. Wood companies will typically use a double-end tenoner instead of the single-end variety (Fig. 38-5). It shapes both ends of the stock with one pass through the machine. Double-end tenoners will have several other cutting stations besides the tenoning heads. They may include dadoing, boring, and even sanding. Newer machines are computer controlled and can be set up in a few minutes.

PARTS OF THE CHISEL MORTISER

Because the chisel mortiser is the most popular style of mortiser, it will be discussed in this chapter. The major parts include the column, ram, table, frame,

500

FIGURE 38-1
Major parts of a chisel mortiser. (*Courtesy of Oliver Machinery Company.*)

FIGURE 38-2
A chain mortiser uses a chain-saw-type cutter to form the mortise. (*Courtesy of Power-matic.*)

FIGURE 38-3
This reciprocating chisel mortiser can be used either in the vertical or horizontal position. (*Courtesy of Danckaert Wood-working Machinery Co.*)

and foot treadle (Fig. 38-1). The *column* is the framework of the machine. At the top of the column is mounted the *ram,* which provides power to the cutting tool. The ram also includes the *motor,* which turns the bit, and the *yoke,* which holds the chisel.

Below the ram is the *table.* It contains the *screw clamp hold down, feeding handwheel, transverse handwheel, fence,* and *stop rods.* All of these either secure or position the stock. Below the table is the *foot treadle;* it lowers the ram when pushed down with your foot.

SELECTING THE CHISEL AND BIT

The tooling used on a chisel mortiser includes the hollow chisel and auger-type bit (Fig. 38-6). Both are made from high-speed steel. The size of the tool is determined by the width of the chisel. Sizes range from $\frac{1}{4}$ to $2\frac{1}{2}$ in. (6 to 64 mm). Most $\frac{3}{4}$-in. (19-mm) thick stock will require a $\frac{1}{4}$-in. or $\frac{3}{8}$-in. (6- or 10-mm) chisel.

The inside of the chisel is hollow and holds the rotating bit. At the tip is a sharpened inside cutting

FIGURE 38-4
The cutter of a reciprocating chisel mortiser moves rapidly back and forth. (*Courtesy of Danckaert Woodworking Machinery Co.*)

FIGURE 38-5
A double-end tenoner shapes both ends with one pass through the machine. (*Courtesy of Jenkins Woodworking Machinery.*)

FIGURE 38-6
Mortising chisels and bits are available in a variety of sizes.

has a flared end that is larger in diameter than the hole in the chisel. The bit is mounted slightly below the end of the chisel. Always match the proper size of bit with the chisel.

PURCHASING A CHISEL MORTISER

There are very few items to specify when purchasing a chisel mortiser. They are not specified by any size. One consideration, however, is the weight of the machine. The heavier the machine, the more vibrations it can absorb and the heavier the cuts it can make. Occasionally, it is beneficial to have a mortiser with a tiltable table (Fig. 38-8). This allows mortises to be cut on an angle.

Although there is rarely more than one motor size available, a mortiser should have at least a 2-hp motor. This will provide sufficient power to turn small to large-diameter bits.

INSTALLING THE CHISEL AND BIT

To install the tooling for a chisel mortiser, first disconnect the power. Select the matching chisel and bit. Check that they are both sharp and in good condition. To mount the tooling on the machine, also choose the *bit bushing* and *chisel bushing* which will fit the bit and chisel.

Install in the mortiser the two bushings (Fig. 38-7). The *bit bushing* is inserted in the *bit spindle*. Place the opening of the bushing in the spindle facing the *bit bushing set screw*. Tighten the set screw only enough to catch the outside edge of the opening in the bushing. Use the same procedure for the *chisel bushing* located in the yoke. The flat side of the bushing should be facing the *chisel bushing bolt*.

To establish the necessary clearance between the tip of the chisel and the flared end of the bit, a spacer is utilized. For bits ¾ in. (19 mm) and smaller,

edge. The wood chips escape from inside the chisel through one or two openings cut into the sides of the chisel (Fig. 38-7). Because the chisel is fragile, you should handle it with care and not bend or drop this tool.

The bit rotates inside the chisel and augers the wood chips up and out of the mortise (Fig. 38-7). It

FIGURE 38-7
Proper installation of mortising chisel and bit.

FIGURE 38-8
A mortiser with a tiltable table can punch mortises on an angle. (*Courtesy of Oliver Machinery Company.*)

FIGURE 38-9
Use a dime as a spacer between the shoulder of the chisel and the bottom of the chisel bushing.

use a dime placed between the shoulder of the chisel and the bottom of the chisel bushing (Fig. 38-9). For larger bits, use a thicker spacer. If the bit is allowed to rub against the chisel, the tooling will overheat and dull.

Place a scrap piece on the table to protect the tooling if it is dropped. Slip the bit into the chisel and place your finger on the flared end of the bit. Push the bit and chisel up into the bushings. Hold the tooling up against the yoke with the dime on the shoulder of the chisel. First tighten the bit bushing setscrew to secure the bit. Remove the dime and push the chisel up against the bushing. Placing a square against the fence, square the chisel (Fig. 38-10). Tighten the chisel bushing setscrew to secure the chisel.

Turn the bit spindle by hand to check that there is no rubbing between the bit and chisel. If a high-pitched rubbing noise occurs, reset the clearance between the bit and chisel. Retighten all setscrews and tighten the knurled nut against the bit spindle.

FIGURE 38-10
Square the edge of the chisel with the fence.

SETTING UP THE CHISEL MORTISER

After the bit and chisel have been installed, square the material to finished size. Mark out each mortise on one piece that has a different arrangement or size of mortise. If there are several parts of the same pattern, it is necessary to only lay out one piece. You will need, however, to lay out one left and one right of a matching pair of stiles or rails (Fig. 38-11). Place a "X" on the face side of each piece. This will assure that the outside surfaces will be flush when the mortise and tenon joints are later assembled.

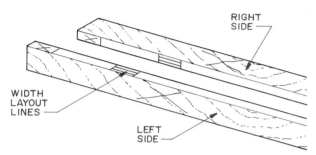

FIGURE 38-11
Layout of mortises for a left and right stiles.

On the end of one part, mark the depth of the mortise (Fig. 38-12). It should be $\frac{1}{8}$ in. (3 mm) deeper than the length of the tenon. The additional depth provides a space for excess adhesive and the rough bottom left by the mortise chisel.

Step down on the foot treadle and lower it to the floor. This should lower the chisel to the lowest position. Place the marked end against the chisel

FIGURE 38-12
Raising the table to adjust the depth of cut with the height-adjustment crank.

and adjust the table height with the height adjustment crank (Fig. 38-12). Raise the table until the layout line is even with the tip of the chisel. Occasionally, it is necessary to punch a mortise completely through the stock. To protect the chisel, place a plain piece of material under the stock before the depth of cut is set.

Lower the table by releasing the foot treadle. Move the board under the chisel and center the layout marks in front of the screw clamp hold-down. Place the end stop against the stock, and secure it to the stop rod. Turn the feeding handwheel until the left layout line is aligned with the left side of the chisel. Move the right table lock against the stop rod arm and tighten (Fig. 38-13). Move the table to the left and follow the same procedure for the right layout line. Use the left table lock to stop the travel of the table. The distance between the two stops should be equal to the length of the tenon.

FIGURE 38-13
Tightening the right table lock to locate the left side of the mortise.

Use the transverse handwheel to adjust the in-out adjustment of the table. Turn the wheel until the layout marks are aligned with the tip of the chisel. Adjust both hold-down dogs to just slightly above the top edge of the stock (Fig. 38-14). These dogs will prevent the stock from being lifted off the table when the chisel is withdrawn from the stock.

Be certain to cut all identical mortises before tearing down the set up. If any dimension or location of the mortise changes, the machine will need to be adjusted.

MAKING A MORTISE

After positioning the stock on the table check that the "X" mark is facing out (Fig. 38-14). Clamp the

FIGURE 38-14
Adjusting the hold-down dogs.

FIGURE 38-16
Correct procedure for punching a mortise.

piece to the table using the screw clamp hold-down. Move the table to the left and right to be certain the stops have been set correctly.

First introduce the chisel into the stock to the far right of the mortise (Fig. 38-15). Push the foot treadle to the floor using your foot. Use a slow steady feed rate. Give the bit time to remove the material but do not feed it so slow that the tooling overheats. After the treadle reaches the floor, let it return to the top position.

FIGURE 38-15
Lowering the chisel to the far right of the mortise.

By turning the feeding handwheel, move the table to the far-left position. Lower the chisel and make the cut. Finish the mortise by using the cutting pattern shown in Fig. 38-16. Initially, taking a full cut with the chisel will prevent it from bending.

After removing all the material in the mortise, release the stock with the screw clamp hold-down. Make all other mortises that are of the same size and location before tearing down the setup.

PARTS OF THE SINGLE-END TENONER

The major parts of a single-end tenoner include the tenoning units, cope unit, cutoff saw unit, and sliding table (Fig. 38-17). The two *tenoning units* contain a motor, arbor, and the tenoning heads (Fig. 38-18). They, like the cope motor, can be adjusted up and down and in and out with the adjustment handles.

The next cutting station is the *cope unit*. It is oriented vertically with a horizontal shaper-like cutter. At the far end of the machine is the *cutoff unit*. This station contains a vertical saw blade for cutting stock to length. Stock is placed on the *sliding table* and against the *fence*. Both are then fed through the machine. The table is mounted on rollers that run on two tracks. This assures the stock being fed in a straight line with little effort.

CUTTING TENONS

To cut a tenon, lay out the first piece of stock. All material should be to finished thickness and width. The boards can be left to rough length.

Position the marked out board against the fence. Secure the stock to the table by tightening the table clamp. Align the shoulder layout lines with the scoring fingers of the tenoning heads (Fig. 38-19). Adjust the heads to the proper height. Place a stop block against the opposite end and clamp it to the fence. Turn on the tenoning heads and cut the first tenon. After the stock has completely cleared the tenoning heads, remove it from the table before returning it to the starting position.

If the shoulders of the tenon are to be shaped or *coped*, adjust the coping heads. They should be

FIGURE 38-17
Major parts to a single-end tenoner. (*Courtesy of Oliver Machinery Company.*)

FIGURE 38-18
The tenoning, cope, and cutoff units shape the ends of the stock. (*Courtesy of Powermatic.*)

FIGURE 38-19
Align the shoulder layout lines with the scoring fingers of the tenoning heads.

FIGURE 38-20
Coping the shoulder of a tenon.

FIGURE 38-21
Trimming the tenon to length with the cutoff saw unit.

aligned with layout marks. Turn on the power to the cope motor and shape the shoulders (Fig. 38-20). For tenons that do not have molded shoulders, raise the cope unit out of the way.

Push the sliding table to the cutoff blade. Move the blade in or out to trim the end of the tenon to the desired length (Fig. 38-21). After the stock has cleared the blade, release the table clamp. Remove the board and pull the table back to the beginning position. End for end the stock and run the opposite end through the cutting stations.

Measure the length between the two shoulders.

It will determine the overall dimension of the assembled frame. The length of the frame is equal to the shoulder length plus the width of the two stiles. You will also need to check the fit of the tenon in the mortise. It should slip into the mortise with a slight amount of hand pressure. If a mallet is needed to drive the tenon into the mortise, adjust the tenoning heads. Also check that the faces of all the parts are flush. Most tenoners have an elevating crank which will move the tenoning units up or down as a pair.

Once the adjustments have been made, run all the remaining parts. Feed the stock through at a slow, steady pace. Do not stack the stock on the sliding table. It could vibrate into the cutters.

Answer each of the following questions. If you are not sure of an answer, review the chapter.

38-1. Stock to be tenoned must be at least _____ in. (_____ mm) long.

38-2. The _____ mortiser is the oldest and most common style of mortiser.

38-3. The _____ mortiser uses a saw-tooth type of cutting tool which moves rapidly back and forth.

38-4. The size of the mortising chisel is determined by the _____ of the chisel.

38-5. The mortise bit has a _____ end that is larger in diameter than the hole in the chisel.

38-6. What two items hold the chisel and bit when mounted in the mortiser?

38-7. What is the purpose of the "X" placed on the face side of each piece of stock to be mortised?

38-8. After positioning the stock on the mortiser table, secure the stock with a _____ hold-down.

38-9. What might happen if the punching pattern is not followed as shown in Figure 38-16?

38-10. Name the major parts to the single-end tenoner.

38-11. When cutting tenons all material should be to the _____ thickness and width.

38-12. If the shoulders of the tenon are to be shaped or _____, adjust the coping heads.

IMPORTANT TECHNICAL TERMS

Following are technical terms that you should be able to use as part of your working vocabulary. Write a brief description of the meaning of each term.

Chisel mortiser
Chain mortiser
Reciprocating chisel mortiser
Tenoner
Ram
Yoke
Screw clamp hold-down
Feeding handwheel
Transverse handwheel
Fence
Stop rods
Foot treadle
Bit bushing
Chisel bushing
Bit spindle
Bit bushing setscrew
Tenoning units
Cope unit
Cutoff unit
Sliding table
Coped

39

SANDING MACHINES

There are many different types of sanding machines utilized in the woodworking field. There are specialized machines which are designed to sand faces of flat panels, edges of boards, and even curves.

You should remember that this equipment is not designed to remove large amounts of material. Before using a sander, your wooden parts should be machined closely and accurately. Sanders are not meant to sand joints or substitute for a cleanly cut surface.

Industry utilizes most of the sanding machines shown in this chapter. They will also have sophisticated equipment which is power fed. The automatic turning sander, for example, sands chair legs and other spindles after they have been turned on the lathe (Fig. 39-1).

ABRASIVES FOR SANDING MACHINES

Most sanding machines require belts, disks, or sleeves which are ordered for each specific piece of equipment. Aluminum oxide is the most common abrasive. It is very hard and resists breaking down with high temperatures. This is important because of the friction developed while sanding hardwoods.

The backing materials used with machine

abrasives are usually either cloth or synthetic materials. Since most machines require a flexible backing, a J-weight cloth is commonly furnished.

Another item to specify is the grit size or coarseness of the abrasive. Refer to Table 39-1 for information concerning the sizing. The smaller the grit number, the larger the individual particles or abrasives. Smaller grit numbers will cut faster but leave deeper sanding scratches.

FIGURE 39-1
This specialized industrial automatic turning sander sands lathe spindles. (*Courtesy of The Nash Company, Division of Crouch Machinery, Inc.*)

TABLE 39-1
Recommended Abrasive Grit Sizes for Sanders

Sanding operations	Garnet and aluminum oxide grit sizes
Fine	180
	150
	120
Medium	100
	80
Coarse	60
	50
	40
	36

DISK SANDERS

Disk sanders are made with vertical metal disks which are covered with abrasive (Fig. 39-2). Because it sands with a circular action, sanding scratches will be developed across the grain. If these scratches are not removed or covered, they will become very obvious when the finish is applied. This sander is used primarily for rough sanding and sanding end grain. The size of the disk sander is determined by the diameter of the disk. Although the size can range from 12 to over 36 in. (305 to 914 mm), most general-purpose disk sanders are 12 in. (303 mm) in diameter.

FIGURE 39-2
Major parts to the disk sander. (*Courtesy of Delta International Machinery Corp.*)

The abrasive disks for the disk sander are usually purchased precut to the proper diameter. Because the disk sander is designed primarily for rough sanding, coarser grits are utilized. They cut faster and are less likely to load up and burn. Grits range from 36 to 60.

FIGURE 39-3
Sand the stock only on the downward side of the disk.

FIGURE 39-4
Sanding an angle with the assistance of a miter gauge. (*Courtesy of Delta International Machinery Corp.*)

To use a disk sander, first lay out the desired pattern on the board. Use a square to mark out straight lines. If more than $\frac{1}{8}$ in. (3 mm) is to be removed, bandsaw or otherwise cut the pattern close to the layout. Position the stock flat against the table on the downward side of the rotating disk (Fig. 39-3). Sanding on the opposite side of the disk will cause the stock to be thrown from the table. Hold the stock firmly against the rotating disk and move it from side to side. Because the disk cuts faster toward the outer rim than the center, apply slightly more pressure on the left side of the board. Be careful not to sand beyond the layout line.

Straight edges can be sanded with the aid of a miter gauge. The gauge fits into a *miter gauge groove* and can be adjusted to any angle from 90 to 45° (Fig. 39-4). Angle the table for sanding bevels and chamfers (Fig. 39-5). The *angle gauge* will indicate the tilt of the table.

If a disk sander is not available, a disk attachment can be purchased for a radial arm saw or table saw. It is mounted in place of the saw blade (Fig. 39-6). Use the same sanding procedure as with the disk sander.

As the abrasive disk is used, it becomes loaded with material. An abrasive cleaning stick can be utilized to remove resin and minor burn marks. Move the stock back and forth against the rotating disk (Fig. 39-7). When the abrasive paper becomes severely worn, however, it must be removed and replaced with a new disk. Abrasive paper that is not easily removed can be soaked. Remove the metal disk from the sander and place it in a container filled

FIGURE 39-5
Use the angle gauge to set the table for sanding bevels and chamfers. (*Courtesy of Delta International Machinery Corp.*)

FIGURE 39-6
Using a disk sanding attachment on a table saw.

FIGURE 39-7
An abrasive cleaning stick will extend the life of the abrasive paper.

FIGURE 39-8
Apply a new thin coat of stick cement while the disk is turning.

FIGURE 39-9
Clamping the metal plate and abrasive disk in a shop-made press.

FIGURE 39-10
The chamfer fixture allows corners to be sanded.

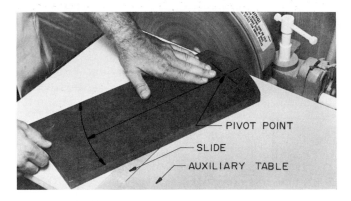

FIGURE 39-11
A radius can be sanded using a pivot fixture. Stock is swung from side to side.

with warm soapy water. After the paper has softened, scrape it clean with a putty knife.

The new abrasive paper can be applied with either stick cement or a polyvinyl adhesive. To use the stick cement, turn on the power (Fig. 39-8). Press the stick against the cleaned disk and apply a thin even coat of adhesive. Turn off the power and allow it to stop turning. Use your hands to press a new disk onto the metal plate. The polyvinyl method requires the use of a shop-made press (Fig. 39-9). Spread polyvinyl adhesive evenly over the entire face of the disk. Position the disk over the metal plate and clamp it in a press overnight.

A variety of fixtures can be utilized on the disk sander. A chamfer fixture aids in sanding chamfers on the corners of a post (Fig. 39-10). Each side of the stock is placed against the side of the fixture. A pivot fixture allows a smooth radius to be sanded (Fig. 39-11). Use a sharpened nail driven through a moveable slide as the pivot point. The distance from the disk to the nail should be equal to the radius of the

curve. Use a mallet to tap the stock onto the pivot point. Move the slide toward the revolving disk until the stock touches the abrasive. Hold the slide in a stationary position and pivot the stock back and forth.

FIGURE 39-12
Major parts of a spindle sander. [*Courtesy of Robert A. Martin Co. (RAMCO).*]

FIGURE 39-13
Abrasive sleeves are available in a variety of diameters.

SPINDLE SANDERS

The spindle sander contains a cylinder that has been covered with an abrasive sleeve (Fig. 39-12). These *abrasive sleeves* are professionally made tubes of a heavy backing material covered with either aluminum oxide or garnet abrasive (Fig. 39-13). Although grit sizes range from 60 to 220, for general-purpose sanding, use 100 grit.

Because of the shape of the spindle, this sander is ideal for sanding inside curves. Select the spindle that most closely matches the diameter of the curve. Most sanders will have spindles that range from $\frac{1}{2}$ to 3 in. (13 to 76 mm) in diameter (Fig. 39-13). Using too small of a spindle will create small dips. They will become quite obvious when the finish is applied.

After selecting the proper spindle, slide the abrasive sleeve over the rubber mandrel. To hold the sleeve in position, tighten the *mandrel nut*. Place the assembled spindle on the sander and turn on the power. Position the stock on the table and move the piece side to side against the rotating abrasive (Fig. 39-14). Use moderate inward pressure and keep the stock moving at all times. Sand along the entire edge of the curve. Concentrating in one area will create a low spot. Stop sanding once you have reached the layout line.

Some spindle sanders are *oscillating*. Their spindles not only rotate but also move up and down. This distributes the wear over a larger area making the life of the sleeve longer. Other sanders may have the tiltable tables. This enables bevels and chamfers to be sanded.

For those shops who may not have a spindle sander, inside curves may be sanded with a drill press or lathe. Refer to Chapters 34 and 35 for de-

FIGURE 39-14
Sanding an inside curve on a spindle sander.

tailed information concerning sanding. A wooden mandrel mounted between lathe centers can be used on the lathe (Fig. 39-15). Abrasive cloth is wrapped around the mandrel and tacked in place on each end.

FIGURE 39-15
Using a wooden mandrel to sand on the inside curve on the lathe.

FIGURE 39-16
Major parts of a small stationary belt sander. (*Courtesy of Delta International Machinery Corp.*)

SMALL STATIONARY BELT SANDER
SAFETY RULES

1. Follow general sander safety rules.
2. Disconnect the power before changing the belt or making other adjustments.

SMALL STATIONARY BELT SANDERS

The small stationary belt sander is one of the most versatile sanding machines (Fig. 39-16). Although belts are available from 60 to 220 grits, most sanding can be done with 100-grit belts.

Because the belt and table can be placed in three different positions, it is capable of sanding many different shapes. Most work is positioned against the table. A miter gauge can be used to aid in guiding the stock. Sanding outside curves, edges and ends can be accomplished with the belt in the vertical position (Fig. 39-16). Use a miter gauge as a guide when sanding straight lines (Fig. 39-17). The

FIGURE 39-17
Sanding end grain using a miter gauge with the belt in the vertical position.

belt can be angled for bevels and chamfers (Fig. 39-18). Faces and edges of stock can be sanded with the belt in horizontal position (Fig. 39-19). Inside curves can be sanded on the exposed pulley (Fig. 39-20). Remove the pulley guard to expose this pulley. Fixtures can also be used to hold the stock. The chamfer fixture forms a trough in which the stock is placed (Fig. 39-21). The far side of the trough serves as a stop to make the same width chamfers. The angle of the sides determines the angle of the chamfer.

Small, narrow-belt sanders are also used in woodworking shops (Fig. 39-22). They work well to sand small curves and sharpen tools.

FIGURE 39-18
The table is tilted by loosening the tilt handle. (*Courtesy of Delta International Machinery Corp.*)

FIGURE 39-19
Sanding the face with the belt in the horizontal position. (*Courtesy of Delta International Machinery Corp.*)

FIGURE 39-20
Sanding an inside curve using the exposed pulley. (*Courtesy of Delta International Machinery Corp.*)

FIGURE 39-21
The chamfering fixture positions stock for sanding chamfers.

FIGURE 39-22
A small belt sander can reach into small area. (*Courtesy of Delta International Machinery Corp.*)

WIDE-BELT SANDERS

A wide-belt sander is utilized to sand the faces of boards, faceframes, and other flat panels (Fig. 39-23). It will remove torn grain, millmarks, and other minor defects. Most wide-belt sanders have a single belt which is run on one head. Industrial firms, however, may have a sander with as many as four heads (Fig. 39-24). Each sanding head has a progressively finer grit sanding belt. This allows a board to be completely sanded and polished with one pass through the machine.

The major parts of a wide-belt sander include the contact drum, idler drum, platen, and endless

(A)

FIGURE 39-23
Major parts of a wide-belt sander. (*Courtesy of Timesavers, Inc.*)

(B)

FIGURE 39-24
A four-headed wide-belt sander will completely sand a flat panel. (*Courtesy of Timesavers, Inc.*)

FIGURE 39-25
The contact drum brings the abrasive belt against the stock.

feed belt (Fig. 39-25). The *contact drum* is a steel cylinder which is coated with rubber (Fig. 39-25). It is responsible for bringing the abrasive belt against the stock. Some sanders have in addition to the contact drum a *polishing platen* (Fig. 39-26). This platen produces a longer sanding scratch pattern and polishes the surface. Above the contact drum is the *idler drum*. It applies upward tension on the abrasive belt. Associated with this drum is the *tracking system*. The belt is tracked or kept centered on the drums by either a photoelectric cell or a pneumatic cylinder.

To feed the stock forward, the board is placed on the rubber *endless feed belt* (Fig. 39-25). Immediately under the belt is the steel *platen*. It provides a

FIGURE 39-26
A polishing platen is mounted immediately behind the contact drum. It increases the area where the belt comes in contact with the stock.

FIGURE 39-27
A storage rack properly holds the belts when not in use.

flat surface to feed the material over. Stock is held against the platen with *hold-down rollers*.

The size of the sander is determined by the width of the belt. Sanders can be purchased which have belts from 6 to 106 in. (152 to 2692 mm). Most shops need a sander that is 24 to 37 in. (620 to 939 mm) wide. Larger belts are more expensive but do allow wider pieces to be sanded.

For most freshly planed material, select a 100-grit belt for the initial passes. If a smoother sanding finish is desired, use progressive finer belts. Do not skip a grit number or the sanding scratches may not be removed. Most stock will be adequately sanded with the final passes made with a 120- or 150-grit belt. Hang new belts for a minimum of 48 hours from a rack as shown in Fig. 39-27. This will allow them to equalize and straighten.

Depending on the brand and model of wide-belt sander, the procedure for changing the belt varies. On most sanders, however, the tension is released on the belt by lowering the idler drum. After the safety bar is removed, the belt can be slid from the sander. Store the belt on a rack as shown in Fig. 39-27. Large cardboard tubes should be mounted on the top of the rack arms. This prevents the belts from developing a sharp bend. Replace the belt with another and check which way the directional arrow points on the back of the belt. Mount the belt on the sander with the directional arrow pointing the same direction as the rotation of the belt (Fig. 39-25).

To operate the wide-belt sander with a contact drum, measure the stock at the thickest point. Set the depth gauge to this dimension minus 0.010 to

0.015 in. Use less than this amount for 120-grit and finer belts. The sander is not designed to remove a great deal of material with one pass. Apply tension to the belt and turn on the power. Place the stock to the left of the feed belt with the grain pointing in the same direction as the direction of the feed. Start it through the machine. The material must be supported and not allowed to hang off the table on either the infeed or outfeed side (Fig. 39-28). If more than one pass is required, position the stock to the right of the first location. Continue moving the board to the right with each pass until the entire width of the belt has been utilized. This will provide more even wear and longer life to the belt. After the last pass, stop the machine and release the tension on the belt.

FIGURE 39-28
Sanding a faceframe.

FIGURE 39-29
Major parts of a stroke sander. (*Courtesy of Oliver Machinery Company.*)

STROKE SANDERS

A stroke sander uses a narrow belt to sand flat surfaces (Fig. 39-29). It is a sander that requires some skill to operate. The operator must move the *shuttle table* in and out while pushing down on the top of the belt with the *pressure block* (Fig. 39-30).

A *pressure block* is moved along the belt. Powdered graphite can be worked into the block to reduce the drag. Operators need to practice to keep their two hands working together. If the pressure block and shuttle table are not kept moving, a low spot will develop.

FIGURE 39-30
The shuttle table is moved in and out while the pressure block is moved side to side.

FIGURE 39-31
Shaped edges can be sanded with a custom pressure block.

Most stroke sanders utilize either 120- or 150-grit abrasive-cloth-backed belts. To sand the shaped edges, make a custom pressure block (Fig. 39-31). It should have the reverse pattern of the shaped edge. Use a flexible back belt and release some of the tension on the belt. If you sand the edge for too long a time, some of the sharp detail will be sanded away.

EDGE SANDERS

Edge sanders are utilized for sanding the edges and ends of flat panels (Fig. 39-32). Inside curves can also be sanded on the *exposed pulley* (Fig. 39-33). A cloth-back abrasive belt is mounted vertically between two pulleys. Stock is placed on the table and gently pushed against the moving belt (Fig. 39-34). A fence is attached to the table to keep the stock at an accurate angle. Although the fence is normally kept at the 90° position, it can be angled for miter.

Depending on the material being sanded, an

80- to 120-grit belt is used. Beginners should scribe a line along the edge to indicate the amount of material to be sanded. It is easy to sand away more stock than what is desired. Once the belt becomes worn, lower the table to another position to expose a new area of the belt.

FIGURE 39-32
Major parts of an edge sander. (*Courtesy of Crouch Machinery, Inc.*)

FIGURE 39-33
Sanding an inside curve on the exposed pulley.

FIGURE 39-34
Sanding the edge of a panel.

Answer each of the following questions. If you are not sure of an answer, review the chapter.

39-1. Applying excessive pressure when sanding will result in torn _____ material.

39-2. _____ is the most common abrasive used for sanding machines.

39-3. The backing materials used with machine abrasives are usually either _____ or _____ materials.

39-4. Sanders are not meant to sand _____ .

39-5. _____ sanders are used primarily for rough sanding and sanding end grain.

39-6. Sanding on the upward side of the rotating disk will cause the stock to be _____ from the table.

39-7. Spindle sanders utilize abrasive _____ to sand the stock.

39-8. An _____ spindle shaper has a spindle that moves up and down.

39-9. The belt and table can be placed in _____ different positions on a small belt sander.

39-10. The belt on a wide-belt sander is kept _____ or centered by either a photoelectric cell or a _____ cylinder.

39-11. For most freshly planned materials, select a _____ grit belt for the initial pass on a wide-belt sander.

39-12. Mount the belt on the wide-belt sander with the directional arrow pointing the _____ direction as the rotation of the belt.

39-13. On the stroke sander, the operator must move the _____ table in and out while pushing down on the top of the belt with the _____ block.

39-14. Edge sanders are utilized for sanding _____ and _____ of flat panels.

Following are technical terms that you should be able to use as part of your working vocabulary. Write a brief description of the meaning of each term.

Abrasive sleeves
Mandrel nut
Oscillating
Small, narrow-belt sanders
Contact drum

Polishing platen
Idler drum
Tracking system
Endless feed belt
Platen
Hold-down rollers
Shuttle table
Pressure block
Exposed pulley

40

INDUSTRIAL PRODUCTION TECHNIQUES

For furniture, cabinets, and architectural woodwork to be produced, many steps and processes are required. The equipment utilized by industry is organized in an efficient arrangement to best produce a product. Some of the machines are discussed in this book. A typical wood manufacturing company would be organized as shown in Fig. 40-1.

MANAGEMENT AND ADMINISTRATION

The key to any successful manufacturing firm is the *management and administration team*. This is a group of people who control and run the day-to-day operations of the company. The team consists of the president, vice presidents, personnel director, and other supervisors (Fig. 40-2). These managers make executive decisions on what new products are to be developed, purchases of new equipment, sales procedures, and other important matters that will determine the future of the company.

PRODUCT ENGINEERING DEPARTMENT

Product engineering is responsible for taking the design developed by the product designers and de-

FIGURE 40-1
A woods company has many departments which work together to produce a product.

521

FIGURE 40-2
The management team makes critical decisions which affect the future success of the company. (*Courtesy of Riverside Furniture Corp.*)

FIGURE 40-4
Craftsmen in the model shop use custom techniques to make a prototype. (*Courtesy of Riverside Furniture Corp.*)

velop the drawings from which the product is produced. They plan the product so that it can economically be manufactured in their plant (Fig. 40-3).

The drawings may be first utilized to produce a working model called a *prototype*. The prototype is hand made to the exact size of the finished product. Those doing this work are skilled craftsmen (Fig. 40-4). This permits any unforeseen problems in the design to be solved before the product goes into production.

FIGURE 40-5
A quality control inspector uses a gauge to check the accuracy of a piece of molding. (*Courtesy of Riverside Furniture Corp.*)

other critical points. Gauges and other measuring devices are utilized to check the parts at crucial points during production.

DRYING YARD AND DRY KILN DEPARTMENT

Wood manufacturing companies often purchase their wood green, so it contains a great deal of moisture. Moisture content is reduced by stacking the lumber in a *drying yard,* where it is allowed to air dry (Fig. 40-6). After it reaches approximately 30% moisture content, the material is loaded in a *dry kiln* (Fig. 40-7). The kiln is used to dry the boards to 6 to 8% moisture content.

ROUGH MILL DEPARTMENT

In the rough mill the lumber is cut and planed to rough thickness, width, and length. The pieces are then sorted to size and stacked for further machining (Fig. 40-8).

FIGURE 40-3
Product engineers frequently utilize computers to plan a product. (*Courtesy of Riverside Furniture Corp.*)

QUALITY CONTROL DEPARTMENT

Each part and assembly must be carefully produced at an acceptable quality level. The design, price range, and the customers' expectations require a certain level of quality. Each company, therefore, must establish and enforce a *quality control program* (Fig. 40-5). This program sets standards such as maximum gap between doors, sizes of parts, and

FIGURE 40-6
Lumber is stacked outside to allow it to air dry. (*Courtesy of La-Z-Boy Chair Co.*)

FIGURE 40-7
Lumber is loaded into the dry kiln to season the material to the final desired moisture content. (*Courtesy of La-Z-Boy Chair Co.*)

FIGURE 40-8
Parts cut at the rough mill are stacked until they are machined in the finished machining department. (*Courtesy of Riverside Furniture Corp.*)

VENEER AND PLYWOOD DEPARTMENT

There is a great deal of plywood utilized in wood products. A company may purchase plywood already manufactured into panels or make their own plywood to the required sizes. To manufacture the plywood, the veneer is first cut and spliced and taped to size (Fig. 40-9). After the adhesive has been applied to the veneer, it is stacked and placed in a veneer press (Fig. 40-10). Once the panel has cured, it is cut to finished size and sanded.

FIGURE 40-9
Veneer is spliced into large sheets before it is made into plywood. (*Courtesy of Riverside Furniture Corp.*)

FIGURE 40-10
A glue coater applies the adhesive to both faces of the veneer. (*Courtesy of Riverside Furniture Corp.*)

FINISH MACHINING DEPARTMENT

Upon receiving the lumber from the rough mill and panels from the plywood department, the material is machined to the final shape. Frequently, this is the largest area in a wood manufacturing company and contains the most sophisticated equipment. Parts will be cut to finished dimensions, holes bored, shaped, or molded and tenoned (Fig. 40-11). Equipment is first adjusted and setup to machine the

FIGURE 40-11
The computer-controlled router shapes parts automatically. (*Courtesy of Riverside Furniture Corp.*)

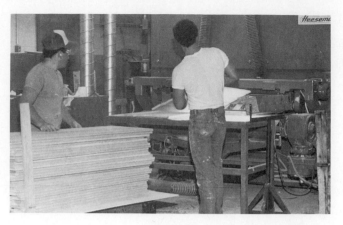

FIGURE 40-13
A wide-belt sander sands the face of panels. (*Courtesy of Riverside Furniture Corp.*)

FIGURE 40-12
The setup person installs the cutters and adjusts the machine to produce the parts. (*Courtesy of Riverside Furniture Corp.*)

FIGURE 40-14
A spindle sander sands these small parts to final shape. (*Courtesy of Riverside Furniture Corp.*)

FIGURE 40-15
Drawers are assembled using pneumatic staple guns. (*Courtesy of Riverside Furniture Corp.*)

needed parts accurately (Fig. 40-12). Most parts will have several operations performed on them before they are moved on to the next department.

SANDING DEPARTMENT

After the parts have been machined to the desired shape, the pieces are sanded. It is easier to sand the parts before assembly than after the pieces have been assembled into a finished product. The faces of the flat parts are sanded with wide-belt sanders (Fig. 40-13). Other specialized sanders are utilized to sand the part for finishing (Fig 40-14).

ASSEMBLY DEPARTMENT

In the assembly department individual parts are nailed, stapled, screwed, and glued together (Fig. 40-15). These fasteners are normally driven by compressed air such as with a pneumatic staple gun.

FIGURE 40-16
A frame clamp accurately positions the pieces during assembly. (*Courtesy of Riverside Furniture Corp.*)

Most wood products contain many parts and need to be assembled using clamping fixtures (Fig. 40-16).

FINISHING DEPARTMENT

One of the most important areas in a wood manufacturing plant is the finishing department. Many materials and different types of wood have been assembled to make a product. It is the finisher's job to take all of these different colors and textures and finish them into a high-quality wood product. The products are usually placed on a conveyor line and automatically moved past sprayers, who apply the various coats of finish (Fig. 40-17). After the products have past through an oven to dry, the wet finish is hand rubbed. This polishing produces a glasslike appearance.

FIGURE 40-17
The sprayer applies the lacquer as the product moves on a conveyor line. (*Courtesy of Riverside Furniture Corp.*)

UPHOLSTERY DEPARTMENT

The upholstery department produces the wooden frames, applies the springs and padding, and sews and attaches the fabric (Fig. 40-18). Some companies specialize in upholstery and have an entire plant for this process. Other manufacturers may have a limited line of upholstered furniture which only a section of the plant is devoted to cutting and applying the fabric.

(A)

(B)

FIGURE 40-18
(A) Upholstery fabric is cut to size on the cutting table; (B) An upholsterer attaches the fabric to cover a sofa. (*Courtesy of Riverside Furniture Corp.*)

PACKING AND WAREHOUSE

After the finish is completely polished, each product is usually carefully wrapped in soft foam or cardboard (Fig. 40-19). Most commercial products are then placed in a cardboard box for shipping. This packing protects the products until they are received by the customer. Because the sizes of furniture, cabinets, and other wooden articles vary considerably in size, many different boxes are required to pack the merchandise. For custom products such as architectural woodwork, the finished material may be wrapped in protective blankets instead of being protected by cardboard.

Many companies have a *warehouse* to store the finished goods. This is a large area where the products are stored until they are sold. The boxed merchandise is then shipped as sales are made. Specialized *squeeze lifts* may be used to move the boxes into trucks and train cars for shipment (Fig. 40-20). A squeeze lift is a specialized forklift that can lift the boxes from the sides for easy stacking.

FIGURE 40-19
Soft foam packing is wrapped around the product to protect it during shipping. (*Courtesy of Riverside Furniture Corp.*)

FIGURE 40-20
The squeeze life moves the boxed products for storage in a warehouse. (*Courtesy of Riverside Furniture Corp.*)

STUDY QUESTIONS

Answer each of the following questions. If you are not sure of an answer, review the chapter.

40-1. The key to any successful firm is the _____ and _____ team.

40-2. A _____ is a full-scale working model made from the help of drawings which are used to produce the product.

40-3. A _____ _____ program consists of checking parts at crucial points during production.

40-4. Moisture content is reduced by first letting the lumber _____ dry and then at 30% moisture content the material is put in a _____ kiln.

40-5. A _____ mill cuts and planes the lumber to rough thickness, width, and length.

40-6. To manufacture plywood the veneer is first cut and _____ and _____ to size.

40-7. The _____ machining department machines the parts to the final shape.

40-8. It is easier to sand parts _____ assembly than _____ the pieces have been assembled.

40-9. In the _____ department, individual parts are nailed, stapled, screwed, and glued together.

40-10. The products are usually placed on a conveyor line and automatically moved past _____, who apply the various coats of finish.

40-11. The _____ is a large area where the products are stored until they are sold.

Following are technical terms that you should be able to use as part of your working vocabulary. Write a brief description of the meaning of each term.

Management and administration team

Quality control program
Drying yard
Air dry
Dry kiln
Warehouse
Squeeze lifts

PART **5**

Finishing

41

PREPARATION FOR FINISHING

One of the most important steps in producing a project is the finishing process. Even the best constructed piece of furniture or cabinet can be ruined if a high-quality finish is not applied. To develop a superior finish, you must first repair or remove defects. This can be accomplished by utilizing a variety of techniques, including applying wood dough or simply steaming out a dent. Minor defects such as torn grain can often be removed by sanding with coarse abrasive paper. After the defects have been dealt with it is extremely important that you sand the project thoroughly. This requires you to have a complete knowledge of abrasives and sanding techniques.

REPAIRING DEFECTS

Open defects become very apparent when the finish is applied. Any opening, whether a dent or a nail hole, should be repaired. There are several methods from which to select.

A small dent or other defect where the wood fibers have not been removed or torn can be raised with steam (Fig. 41-1). Dampen a piece of cloth and fold it into several layers. Position the cloth immediately over the defect and place a heated soldering

FIGURE 41-1
Removing a dent using a soldering iron to produce steam.

iron on top. Keep the iron moving over the cloth. Occasionally, stop and check to see if the dent has disappeared.

Large open defects such as knotholes can be patched with *water putty* (Fig. 41-2). This is an unexpensive powder that is mixed with water. Powdered pigments may be mixed with the putty to match the color of the wood more closely. Mix only what you can use in a short period of time. It cannot be reused.

A filler that is more likely to match the surrounding wood is *putty filler* (Fig. 41-3). It is sold in a variety of colors to match the major species of wood.

FIGURE 41-2
Using water putty to repair a large open defect.

FIGURE 41-3
Putty filler dries rapidly and blends with the surrounding wood.

Most putty fillers become very obvious when stains and other finishing materials are applied. There are a few brands, however, that will absorb stain and more closely match the finished wood.

A shop-made filler can also be used to repair defects. This filler is composed of sanding dust and a mixture of adhesive and water. It is frequently called cabinetmaker's filler. To make *cabinetmaker's filler*, take sanding dust from your project and mix it with a small quantity of polyvinyl adhesive and water. Once mixed, the filler should form a thick paste. Carefully apply it to the defect, being careful not to wipe it on the surrounding area. When dry, sand all excess from the surface.

Small defects, nail holes, and open joints can be filled with a *putty stick* (Fig. 41-4). These contain a pigmented wax that will blend with the surrounding wood. However, the stick must be rubbed into the defect after the last coat of finish has been polished. Two or more colors can be combined to form an exact match.

FIGURE 41-4
Putty sticks are rubbed into open defects on a finished wood.

The best method of repairing an open defect is the *stick shellac* or *lacquer stick* (Fig. 41-5). It does require the most skill. Select the stick or sticks that best match the wood. Use stick shellac for varnish finishes and lacquer stick on lacquer. With a hot *burn-in tool*, melt the stick into the defect. Be careful not to smear it on the surrounding wood. Once cooled, the filler can be sanded level with the surface. With practice you will be able to match the finished wood exactly.

FIGURE 41-5
Lacquer sticks require burn-in tools and a knife oven to melt the lacquer into the defect.

SANDING TECHNIQUES

To further prepare a surface, start by working out any defects, such as small knots, checks, or raised surfaces. If a wide-belt sander or other power sanders are available, use them to remove the torn grain and other minor defects. Refer to Chapters 26 and 39 for proper safe operating procedures on power sanders. A hand scraper can also be used to work the stock. Be careful, however, that too much material is not sanded or scraped. This will affect the appearance and fit of adjoining pieces.

Apply the selected filler to repair any open defects. After it has dried, sand the surfaces with 100-grit abrasive paper. Use a sanding block or portable pad sander to keep the surface flat (Fig. 41-6). Never use just your hand because the softer spring wood will be sanded away faster than the denser summerwood. This will produce high and low spots on your boards. Sand only with the grain. Sanding across the grain will produce noticeable cross scratches. Because it is difficult to sand inside corners, sand inside surfaces before they are assembled. Be very careful to remove equal amounts over the entire surface. Sanding only the defects will produce low areas that will be very noticeable.

FIGURE 41-6
Sand flat surfaces using a sanding block.

After the millmarks have been removed with the 100-grit abrasive paper, you will need to sand all surfaces with 120 grit. Use the sanding techniques discussed in the preceding paragraph. Continue sanding until all the sanding scratches created by the 100 grit have been removed. Next sand the exposed surfaces with 150-grit, and finally, 180-grit abrasive paper. Do not skip a grit number in your sanding procedure. Sanding scratches will be left in the wood, which will be very difficult to sand away with the finer abrasive. Blow off the surface with compressed air to remove all sanding dust that is left in corners and in the pores of the wood.

Just before you apply the finish, use a damp sponge to wipe down your project (Fig. 41-7). This will raise loose fibers, which will cause problems when the finish is applied. After the surface has dried, use a sanding block and resand all areas with 180-grit abrasive paper.

FIGURE 41-7
Sponging the surface with water to raise the grain.

ABRASIVES

Abrasives are available in a broad variety of types and degrees of fineness. You will need to know the abrasive material, backing material, and grit size so that you can select the correct material for your job. This information will be printed on the back of the sheet of abrasive (Fig. 41-8). Information generally given includes the abrasive material used, type of backing, backing weight, density of coverage, and grit size.

FIGURE 41-8
Information on the back of abrasive paper.

Abrasive Materials

When selecting abrasive paper or sanding belts, first pick the type of abrasive mineral that will best suit your job. For sanding most wood projects either garnet or aluminum oxide is used. *Garnet* is usually reddish brown in color and ideal for hand sanding. *Aluminum oxide* is typically brown or black in color and withstands the heat generated during machine sanding. Because of this, it is the most commonly used abrasive in the woods industry. Another abrasive is *silicon carbide;* it is bluish black in color and utilized for sanding finishes on wet or dry abrasive paper.

Backing

The backing materials commonly used include paper, cloth, and synthetics. Paper is selected for most hand sanding and for pad sanders. It is specified by A, B, D, or E weights. A weight is very thin and is the most flexible. E weight, the heaviest, is similar to light cardboard and rarely used in woodwork. C weight, sometimes called *cabinet paper,* is well suited for hand sanding and for use with portable electric sanders.

Cloth backing is more durable than paper. It is, however, more expensive. Cloth backing is sold in either J or X weight. J weight is the most common and the more flexible of the two.

Synthetics are the newest backing materials. They are used exclusively for machine sanding. This material is very resistant to wear and is quite durable.

Grit Sizes

The *grit size* determines the relative diameter of each particle of abrasive. The larger the particles, the faster the abrasive will remove the material. It will, however, leave deep scratches in the stock. Smaller particles produce a smoother surface, but sand the wood at a slower rate.

You can determine the grit size by finding the *grit number* or *ough size* printed on the backing. The larger the grit or ough number, the finer or smaller the particle size. For example, 220 grit is finer than 100 grit. Refer to Table 41-1 for recommended grits.

An additional item to consider is the spacing between the particles (Fig. 41-9). When little space is found between particles, it is labeled closed coat. Closed coat is selected for sanding dense hardwoods.

TABLE 41-1 Available Grits for Abrasives			
	Garnet	Aluminum oxide	Silicon carbide
Very fine	—	600–12/0	600
(sanding	—	500–11/0	500
between	—	400–10/0	400
coats of	—	—	360
finishing	—	320–9/0	320
or polishing)	280–8/0	280–8/0	280
	240–7/0	240–7/0	240
	220–6/0	220–6/0	220
Fine	180–5/0	180–5/0	180
(final	150–4/0	150–4/0	150
sanding)	120–3/0	120–3/0	120
Medium	100–2/0	100–2/0	100
(rough	80–1/0	80–1/0	80
sanding	60–1/2	60–1/2	60
Coarse	50–1	50–1	50
(abrasive planing)	40–1½	40–1½	40
Very coarse	36–2	36–2	36
(grinding	30–2½	30–2½	30
or rough	24–3	24–3	24
shaping)	20–3½	20–3½	20
	—	16–4	16
	—	12–4½	12

Open-coat abrasives have additional space between the particles. Approximately 50 to 70% of the backing will be covered with open coat. It works best when sanding softwoods and other materials that are prone to load or fill in the abrasives.

FIGURE 41-9
Spacing between abrasive particles is labeled as either closed coat or open coat.

41-4. The larger the grit size or ough number, the _____ the particle size.

41-5. Use a dampened piece of cloth and a heated _____ to raise a dent.

41-6. _____ filler is made from a mixture of sanding dust, adhesive, and water.

41-7. The best method of repairing an open defect is with stick shellac or _____. stick.

41-8. Raise the loose fibers that cause finishing problems with a damp _____.

IMPORTANT TECHNICAL TERMS

Following are technical terms that you should be able to use as part of your working vocabulary. Write a brief description of the meaning of each term.

Water putty
Putty filler
Cabinetmaker's filler
Putty stick
Stick shellac
Lacquer stick

Burn-in-tool
Garnet
Aluminum oxide
Silicon carbide
Cabinet paper
Grit size
Grit number
Ough size
Closed coat
Open coat

42

FINISHING EQUIPMENT

There are two primary methods of applying finishing materials, brushing and spraying. Both require specialized equipment to work with the finishing material. There are several types of brushes and many different spray guns from which to select. In addition, you will need to consider related equipment that must be utilized to control the fumes and overspray produced in the finishing process. You should not proceed with your finishing until you have an understanding of finishing equipment.

FINISH BRUSHES

There are several items to consider when selecting a brush. If you purchase a high-quality brush, it will allow you to apply a superior finish with a minimum amount of effort.

The first consideration will be the kind of bristles used to make the brush. Pure bristles, nylon bristle, and polyester bristles are available. *Pure bristles* are made from the hair of an animal, the China boar. These bristles make a brush that is used almost exclusively for varnishes. *Nylon bristles* will wear longer and are designed primarily for water-base or latex finishes. *Polyester bristles* can be used for almost all finishes. They will outlast a pure-bris-

tle brush and apply a high-quality finish. Most recently, brushes have been developed with a *sponge pad*. The brushes are inexpensive and most are thrown away after one use.

All high-quality brushes should have bristles with *flagged ends* (Fig. 42-1). These split ends will hold more finish and produce fewer brush marks.

A good brush should also contain a *chisel-shaped edge* composed of many bristles. The best brush will develop the chisel shape by having the

FIGURE 42-1
Parts of a good-quality finish brush.

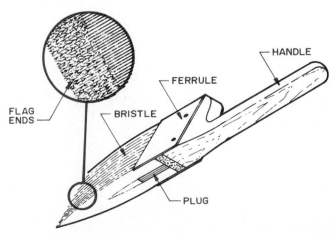

535

longest bristles in the center. Shorter bristles are utilized toward the outside of the brush. The more bristles a brush contains, the longer it will last and the more finish it will carry to the surface.

Another item to select is the width. Finish brushes range from ½ to 8 in. (13 to 203 mm). The wider the brush, the faster the surface can be covered. Wide brushes do become awkward, however, when finishing smaller projects. Most projects can be finished with a 2- or 2½-in. (51- or 64-mm) brush.

The handle is also important when selecting a brush (Fig. 42-2). The handle should fit your hand comfortably. Some finishers prefer an oval shape, while others prefer round shapes. To reach into corners use a *sash brush,* which has a long handle. *Trim brushes* have angled bristles for comfortably holding the handle at a slant.

FIGURE 42-3
Pour the finish material into a brush cup.

edge, work from the center out. Hold the brush at approximately a 45° angle and lightly draw the tips of the brush across the surface (Fig. 42-4).

For large areas first brush across the grain. Follow the cross brushing by brushing with the grain. As you are applying the finish it is best to flow the coating onto the surface. Overbrushing the finish will leave brush marks. Avoid putting too thick a coating on the surface. This might cause runs and drying problems. After you have completed an area, inspect the surface for holidays. *Holidays* are small areas that have not been coated with finish. They will usually appear as dry, nonglossy areas.

FIGURE 42-2
Brushes are available in various styles.

BRUSHING TECHNIQUES

To brush a project properly, start by slowly pouring a small amount of the finish material into the brush cup (Fig. 42-3). Only pour the amount of finish that is required to coat your project. Do not put the brush in the original can. The brush may deposit dirt and other foreign material in the can. This will contaminate the material remaining in the can. Any finish left in the brush cup should be disposed of properly, not poured back into the finish can. Never pour the remaining finish down a sink drain.

Dip the brush into the finish until approximately one-third of the length of the bristles extends into the finishing material. To remove the surplus finish from the brush, draw the bristles across the strike wire of the brush cup. Place the loaded brush in an uncoated area and brush toward the coated surface. To prevent runs from occurring near the

FIGURE 42-4
Hold the brush at a 45° angle.

Cleaning and Care of Finish Brushes

A high-quality brush will last only as long as it is properly cared for and cleaned. It is very important that you clean your brush immediately after each use.

Brushes used only for varnish can, however, be stored in a *brush keeper* (Fig. 42-5). This is a con-

FIGURE 42-5
A brush keeper can be used to store varnish brushes.

FIGURE 42-7
Comb and wrap the brush bristles for proper storage.

tainer in which the brush is suspended in a solution of one-half varnish and one-half turpentine. The bristles must remain submerged in the solution. After a period of time the solution becomes thick and must be replaced.

To clean a finishing brush for storage, use a three-container wash (Fig. 42-6). The first container has solvent which contains some finish from previous cleanups. The second container is filled with cleaner solvent. Your last container should have new solvent. When the solvent becomes dirty in containers 2 and 3, it can be used to replace the dirtier solvent in the next-lower-numbered container.

Work the bristles back and forth in container 1. Continue cleaning the brush in container 2 and finally, in container 3. Use your hands to work the finish from the bristles. The solvent in 3 should remain relatively clean if the brush has been cleaned properly in 1 and 2.

Use a stiff bristle brush or a brush comb to comb the bristle away from the handle (Fig. 42-7).

For long-term storage, work a small amount of turpentine into the bristle's brushes. All brushes must be wrapped in their original package or paper.

SPRAY GUNS AND RELATED EQUIPMENT

To spray a finish you will need a compressor, extractor, air hose, spray booth, and respirator. The *compressor* produces the pressurized air to spray the finish (Fig. 42-8). You need to select a compressor which is large enough to provide continuous dry air for your particular gun. The *extractor* adjusts the amount of air entering the spray gun and removes

FIGURE 42-8
A compressor provides pressurized air. (*Courtesy of Binks Manufacturing Co.*)

FIGURE 42-6
Use a three-container wash to clean brushes.

moisture from the compressed air (Fig. 42-9). An *air gauge* on the extractor indicates the pounds per square inch (PSI). To connect the extractor and spray gun, an *air hose* is utilized (Fig. 42-10). To prevent a serious loss in air pressure, the hose must be no longer than 96 in. (2400 mm) and contain no air leaks.

FIGURE 42-11
All spraying must take place inside of a spray booth. (*Courtesy of DeVilbiss Co.*)

FIGURE 42-9
The extractor regulates the amount of pressurized air entering the spray gun. (*Courtesy of Binks Manufacturing Co.*)

FIGURE 42-10
An air hose connects the extractor to the spray gun. (*Courtesy of DeVilbiss Co.*)

FIGURE 42-12
Use a respirator any time the spray gun is used. (*Courtesy of Binks Manufacturing Co.*)

Spray operators must protect themselves by using a spray booth and wear a respirator. The *spray booth* is a sheet metal enclosure in which the project is placed to be sprayed (Fig. 42-11). It will contain some type of filtering system to remove the excess finish from the exhausted air. The spray booth and filters must be kept clean. The walls of the booth can be protected with a stripable paint. This is a special paint that can be peeled off once it becomes covered with overspray. The *respirator* covers the face of the finisher and filters out harmful vapors (Fig. 42-12). You should frequently check that the filter cartridges are working properly.

There are several parts to a conventional spray gun. They are shown in Fig. 42-13. The *gun body*

contains all the working parts. Once the *trigger* is pulled, pressurized air enters the bottom of the handle and the finish enters through the opening under the nozzle. The air and finish are mixed either in or immediately outside the *fluid nozzle*. The stream of air and finish are directed by the *air nozzle*. Adjustments are made with the *pattern control* and *fluid control knobs*. The *pattern control knob* shapes the spray pattern. Patterns will vary from a round to an oval shape. The *fluid control knob* adjusts the amount of finish allowed to pass through the nozzle. Adjusting these two knobs will provide the proper

FIGURE 42-13
Major parts of a conventional spray gun.
(*Courtesy of Binks Manufacturing Co.*)

Labels on figure:
AIR VALVE
PATTERN CONTROL
FLUID PACKING NUT
AIR NOZZLE
FLUID NOZZLE
HORN
NEEDLE VALVE
TRIGGER
FLUID CONTROL KNOB
GUN BODY (OR HANDLE)

spray pattern. Refer to Fig. 42-14 for common spray pattern problems and their remedies.

A smaller spray system may use a *bleeder gun*. It allows the air to pass continually through the gun. Most systems, however, utilize a *nonbleeder gun*. Initially, pulling the trigger will release only the air. When the trigger is pulled all the way to the rear finish will also then come out of the nozzle.

Spray guns can also vary by the way the finish is fed into the gun. *Siphon feed guns* create a vacuum and the finish is sucked into the gun (Fig. 42-15). It is used primarily for thinned lacquers. The *pressure-feed gun* keeps the finish under pressure and forces the coating material up into the gun (Fig. 42-16). It can spray thicker materials such as paints.

One of the newest spray systems is the *air-assisted airless* concept. With this spray gun the finish is atomized for a full spray pattern at low pressures. This minimizes overspray and the amount of finish that stays on the project.

Spray Techniques

To spray a project, adjust the gun. Refer to the section "Spray Guns and Related Equipment" for the parts of the spray gun and their adjustments. Then practice on a piece of paper to learn how to control and trigger the gun. Make any necessary adjustments to achieve an even oval spray pattern.

The spray gun should be held 6 to 8 in. (152 to 203 mm) from the item to be finished (Fig. 42-17). Hold the gun at a right angle to the surface. Rotate the horns of the air nozzle horizontally when moving the gun from side to side. Move the horns vertically when you direct the gun up and down.

Plan the path that the spray gun will take. Start by coating each edge (Fig. 42-18). The trigger

should be squeezed and the finish material started through the nozzle before the spray pattern reaches the project. Next coat the part of the surface closest to you and work to the farthest side (Fig. 42-19). The overspray should fall on the uncoated area. Each pass of the gun should overlap the previous pass by one-half the width of the pattern.

The gun must be kept moving at all times. If you do not keep it moving for even a second, too heavy a buildup will occur and a run will develop. Keep your wrist stiff and move the gun in a straight line. Swinging the gun in a natural arc will produce light and heavy spots (Fig. 42-20, page 542).

Cleaning a Suction-Fed Gun

It is extremely important to keep your spray gun very clean. Any finish left in the gun will cause future problems. Allowing lacquer, stain, or other material to remain in the gun may require that the components be completely disassembled and several parts replaced.

Once you are through spraying, empty the fluid cup and allow it to drain completely. While it is draining, unscrew the air cap a few turns and place a folded rag over the air cap (Fig. 42-21, page 542). Pull the trigger to drive the finish back through the gun. Never attempt to hold anything in front of the air cap unless you are certain that it is a conventional gun.

Refill the fluid cup approximately one-half full of solvent and attach it to the gun. Screw the air cap back on the nozzle. Pull the trigger several times and allow the solvent to spray through the gun. Turn the horns of the air cap to several positions and pull the trigger each time.

Unscrew the air cap and fluid cup and place the

Faulty Patterns and How to Correct Them

CAUSE

Dried material in side port "A" restricts passage of air through port on one side. Results in full pressure of air from clean side of port in a fan pattern in direction of clogged side.

REMEDY

Dissolve material in side port with thinner. Do not use metal devices to probe into air nozzle openings.

CAUSE

Dried material around the outside of the fluid nozzle tip at position "B" restricts the passage of atomizing air at one point through the center ring opening of the air nozzle. This faulty pattern can also be caused by loose air nozzle, or a bent fluid nozzle or needle tip.

REMEDY

If dried material is causing the trouble remove air nozzle and wipe off fluid tip, using rag wet with thinner. Tighten air nozzle. Replace fluid nozzle or needle if bent.

CAUSE

A split spray pattern (heavy on each end of a fan pattern and weak in the middle) is usually caused by: (1) atomizing air pressure, too high (2) attempting to get too wide a spray with thin material, (3) not enough material available.

REMEDY

(1) Reduce air pressure. (2) Open material control "D" to full position by turning to left. At the same time turn spray width adjustment "C" to right. This reduces width of spray but will correct split spray pattern.

SPITTING

CAUSE

■ Air entering the fluid supply.

■ Dried packing or missing packing around the material needle valve which permits air to get into fluid passageway.

■ Dirt between the fluid nozzle seat and body or a loosely installed fluid nozzle.

■ A loose or defective swivel nut, siphon cup or material hose.

REMEDY

■ Be sure all fittings and connections are tight.

■ Back up knurled nut "E", place two drops of machine oil on packing, replace nut and finger tighten. In aggravated cases, replace packing.

■ Remove air and fluid nozzles "F" and clean back of fluid nozzle and nozzle seat in the gun body, using a rag wet with thinner. Replace and tighten fluid nozzle using wrench supplied with the gun. Replace air nozzle.

■ Tighten or replace swivel nut "G".

CAUSE

A fan spray pattern that is heavy in the middle, or a pattern that has an unatomized "salt-and-pepper" effect indicates that the atomizing air pressure is not sufficiently high, or there is too much material being fed to the gun.

REMEDY

Increase pressure from air supply. Correct air pressures as discussed elsewhere in this manual.

Jerky or fluttering pattern. Check for:

■ Air leaking into fluid line or passageway.

■ Lack of paint.

■ Loose or cracked fluid siphon tube.

■ Loose fluid nozzle.

■ Loose fluid packing nut or worn packing

FIGURE 42-14
Faulty patterns and how to correct them. (*Courtesy of Binks Manufacturing Co.*)

FIGURE 42-15
Atmospheric pressure is utilized with a siphon feed gun to create a vacuum. (*Courtesy of Binks Manufacturing Co.*)

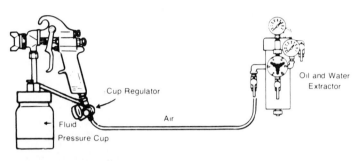

FIGURE 42-16
Pressure feed guns have an airline to the pressure cup. (*Courtesy of Binks Manufacturing Co.*)

FIGURE 42-17
Position the gun 6 to 8 in. (152 to 203 mm) from the project. (*Courtesy of Binks Manufacturing Co.*)

Banding edges

FIGURE 42-18
Coat each corner before spraying the larger flat areas. (*Courtesy of Binks Manufacturing Co.*)

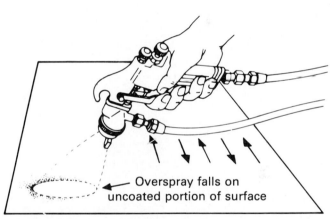

FIGURE 42-19
Allow the overspray to fall on the uncoated area. (*Courtesy of Binks Manufacturing Co.*)

cap in the cup. There should be at least 1 in. of solvent remaining in the cup. Wipe the outside of the gun clean with a solvent-soaked rag. In addition, check that the vent hole of a siphon feed gun is free of any finish. It may be necessary to unclog the hole with a wooden toothpick (Fig. 42-22, page 542); never use any metal object.

Leaving approximately 1 in. (25 mm) of solvent in the fluid cup, reassemble the gun. Occasionally, lubricate the points identified in Fig. 42-23 with light machine oil to prevent excessive wear. Hang the gun in a safety cabinet until you are ready for it again.

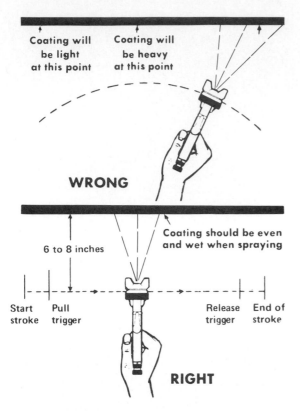

Coating will be light at this point
Coating will be heavy at this point

WRONG

6 to 8 inches
Coating should be even and wet when spraying

Start stroke | Pull trigger | Release trigger | End of stroke

RIGHT

FIGURE 42-20
Do *not* swing the gun in an arc but move it parallel to the surface. (*Courtesy of Binks Manufacturing Co.*)

FIGURE 42-21
Hold a rag over the air cap to force the finish material back through the gun.

FIGURE 42-22
Clean the vent hold with a wooden toothpick only.

Trigger pivot
Side port and control knob
Fluid needle spring
Fluid packing nut
Air valve packing

FIGURE 42-23
Lubrication points for a spray gun. (*Courtesy of Binks Manufacturing Co.*)

Answer each of the following questions. If you are not sure of an answer, review the chapter.

42-1. What are the two primary methods of applying finishing materials?

42-2. List the three types of bristles used to make a finish brush.

42-3. After applying the finish, should the left over finish in the brush cup be disposed of or poured back into the finish can to be used later?

42-4. When applying a finish, hold the finish brush at approximately a _____ degree angle.

42-5. Use a three _____ wash to clean a brush.

42-6. The moisture in the compressed air is removed with an _____ .

42-7. Always wear a _____ to cover the face and harmful vapors when spraying.

42-8. What two knobs on the spray gun can be adjusted to control the finish materials?

42-9. _____ feed guns create a vacuum and cause the finish to be sucked into the gun.

42-10. Hold the spray gun _____ to _____ inches from the item to be sprayed.

42-11. The overspray from the spray gun should fall on the _____ area.

42-12. The vent hole in a spray gun should be cleaned only with a _____ .

These technical terms are very important to have in a good working vocabulary. Write a short definition of each term.

Pure bristles
Nylon bristles
Polyester bristles
Flagged ends
Chisel shaped edge

Sash brush
Trim brush
Holidays
Brush keeper
Compressor
Extractor
Air hose
Spray booth

43

FINISHING SCHEDULES

There are hundreds of different types of finishing materials from which to select. As a finisher you will need to pick the various components that will produce the desired effect. The finishing materials chosen determine color, the degree of gloss, durability, and the depth of finish.

DEVELOPING A FINISHING SCHEDULE

Your first step in finishing a project is to develop a finishing schedule. A *finishing schedule* is a list of the steps and the materials necessary to produce the desired effect. Not only should the stains, lacquers, and other coatings be included but abrasive paper and rubbing steps as well.

It is very important to try the finishing schedule on a small piece of wood of the same species as your project. The finished piece is called a *finish sample* (Fig. 43-1). The sample will allow you to practice applying the finishing materials. It will also indicate how the final finish will appear. Be sure to place the finish schedule on the back of the finish sample. This will allow you to use the sample later and know how the finish was produced.

The selection of the finishing schedule will depend largely on several items. The first consider-

FIGURE 43-1
Finishing samples show the final results of each finish schedule.

ation is the species of wood used in the project. Ring porous or open-grain woods, for example, may require a contrasting stain and filler to emphasize the wood pores. Another item to consider is the durability of the finish. An exterior door will require a finish that will weather. Novelty items, however, may only require a simple wax finish. Always evaluate your available time and skill level. Some finishes dry rapidly and require a minimum effort to apply. The last item to consider is the available finishing equipment. Having a spray booth with a spray gun allows many more finishing materials than if the finish must be applied in a dusty environment.

Although there is no all-purpose finish schedule, there is a checklist that you can utilize to develop your own. Table 43-1 includes most of the items that may be used in your finish. Although items 1 through 3 should always be practiced, it is not necessary to select every step listed in the illustration.

TABLE 43-1
Steps for Complete Finishing Schedule

1. _____	Repair major open defects (knots, cracks)
2. _____	Scrape or machine sand millmarks
3. _____	Sand with 100, 120, 150, and 180 grit abrasive paper (some concealed areas may not require the finer grits)
4. _____	Bleach (optional)
5. _____	Stain—water, penetrating oil, pigmented oil, nongrain-raising
6. _____	Wash Coat
7. _____	Paste wood filler (primarily open grain woods)
8. _____	Sealer—shellac, lacquer sealers
9. _____	Glaze (optional)
10. _____	Topcoats—lacquer, varnish, oil, wax
11. _____	Rubbing—320 wet or dry abrasive paper
12. _____	Polishing—for high gloss finishes; pumice, rottenstone, rubbing compound
13. _____	Waxing (optional)

STEPS IN A FINISHING SCHEDULE

As indicated in Table 43-1, there are numerous steps that can occur in a very complete finishing schedule. In this section we describe briefly the major items that may or may not be included in your schedule. The remaining chapters in Section V will provide you with a more detailed description of the various finishing materials.

Bleaching

Bleaching is the process of chemically lightening the color of the wood. It is utilized to produce "blond" finishes and to remove the major differences in colors found in some wood. Bleach wood is often called harvest wheat, honey maple, or amber walnut.

A two-part commercial bleach is utilized to bleach wood (Fig. 43-2). Be extremely careful of these strong chemicals and wear protective clothing. Rubber gloves, safety goggles, and an apron must be worn.

FIGURE 43-2
Bleaching removes the color from wood.

Staining

Although many projects are left *natural* and not stained, staining does add color. Staining the surface will also bring out the grain, emphasizing the pores and latewood. Staining is discussed in Chapter 44.

Washcoating

A *washcoat* is utilized after staining and before filler and sealers are applied. This step in the finishing schedule prevents stains which are prone to bleeding from leaching into the finish (Fig. 43-3). In addition, the washcoat keeps the wood from turning gray after being filled.

FIGURE 43-3
Apply a washcoat to prevent the stain from eventually bleeding.

Filling

Woods with visible pores are usually filled with a paste wood filler. *Paste wood filler* levels the surface of the wood and adds color. Some coarse-grained woods are left unfilled to allow a more natural-appearing project. Filling is discussed in Chapter 45.

Sealing

Sealing is the step in which shellac or lacquer sealer is applied to keep the stain and filler from bleeding into the topcoat. Because it is easy to sand, some finishers utilize sealers to fill the pores of the wood. This gives the project a more natural appearance. Because this will require several coats, it is important that each be sanded until very little remains on the surface. Allowing the sealer to build up on the surface will cause the topcoat to chip easily. Sealing is described in Chapter 45.

Glazing

Glazing applies an additional coat of color to the surface which shades or darkens portions of the project (Fig. 43-4). Areas such as edges and flat surfaces are wiped more than others to produce an antique appearance. The glaze will add depth and interest to the finish.

FIGURE 43-4
Glazing gives a new piece of furniture an antique appearance.

Topcoating

Topcoats are most commonly varnish, lacquer, or some type of synthetic finish. Each has its own characteristic as described in Chapter 47. The more coats that are applied, the thicker the topcoat will be. In most cases it is better to apply several light to medium coats rather than a few thick layers. Remem-

ber, however, that the thicker the topcoat, the more likely it will crack and the more difficult it is to repair.

Rubbing

The finish must be rubbed between coats. Rubbing the finish levels the surface and removes any dust and other foreign material that may have become trapped in the wet finish.

For rubbing between the coats select 320 wet or dry abrasive paper (Fig. 43-5). To keep the abrasive paper from loading with finish, frequently dip the abrasive in water. Utilizing a felt pad or cork sanding block will produce a flatter surface than just using your hand to hold the abrasive paper. Be very careful about sanding through the finish along corners and edges.

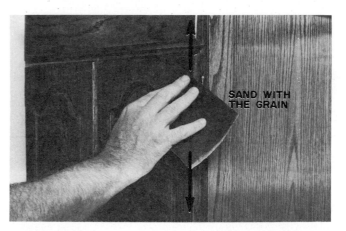

SAND WITH THE GRAIN

FIGURE 43-5
Rub the finish between top coats with 320-grit wet or dry abrasive paper.

Polishing

After the last coat of finish has cured it can be polished. Be certain, however, that the finish has totally cured or you will develop white areas. Polishing is used to remove any defects from brushing or spraying and produces a smooth, slick surface. Not polishing your project will leave it with an unfinished appearance that still needs additional attention.

The first step in polishing is to work the finish with pumice and water (Fig. 43-6). Sprinkle a small amount of pumice onto the surface and dip a felt pad into water. Rub the pad back and forth with the grain. A slurry of pumice and water should be developed to polish the finish.

After the finish has been thoroughly rubbed with the pumice, rottenstone can be used (Fig. 43-7). Rottenstone will produce an even higher polish. Se-

FIGURE 43-6
Polishing the surface with pumice and water.

FIGURE 43-8
Waxing the project to provide additional protection.

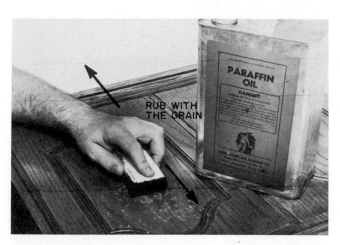

FIGURE 43-7
Rottenstone and rubbing oil will produce a deep shine.

lect the same procedure as recommended for pumice stone except use a lightweight rubbing oil as a lubricant. Clean the surface with mineral spirits once the job is completed.

For very high quality finishes, further polishing can be completed with rubbing compounds. These are very fine abrasive materials that are rubbed over the finish with a soft cloth. Use a clean cotton cloth to polish the surface and remove the excess compound.

Waxing

To protect the finish further, a coat of paste wax can be applied. Rub the wax on with a circular motion, but polish the finish by rubbing with the grain (Fig. 43-8). Waxing a surface will repel dirt and moisture, but it does make it very difficult to apply another coat or finish at a later time.

A FURNITURE FINISHING SCHEDULE

Now that you are more familiar with some of the items in a finishing schedule, one is listed below that you may like to use as a pattern. The final results should produce a deep-looking finish that will add greatly to a high-quality piece of furniture.

To apply a furniture finish:

1. Prepare the surface by thoroughly sanding all exposed areas with 100-, 120-, 150-, and 180-grit abrasive paper. No millmarks should remain. Inspect the various surfaces by reflecting a light at a slight angle to the exposed areas. Note any defects that need additional attention. After the last sanding, clean the entire project using compressed air and a soft brush.
2. Moisten the surfaces with a sponge that has been dipped in water. After the wood has dried, lightly sand the raised grain with 220-grit abrasive paper.
3. After mixing the stain thoroughly, apply it following the instructions given in Chapter 44. Before proceeding, allow the stained project to dry for the period recommended.
4. Apply a wash coat of shellac if there is danger that the stain may bleed.
5. If the project is constructed from one of the woods requiring a paste wood filler (Fig. 45-1), use the procedure given in Chapter 45.
6. Spray on a lacquer sealer to provide a proper base for the lacquer topcoat.
7. Lightly sand the project with 320-grit wet or dry abrasive paper. Do not sand the outside corners or areas where the stain may easily be removed. Blow off the project with compressed air. Clean the surface with a new tack rag (Fig.

43-9). A *tack rag* is a cloth that is sticky and easily picks up any remaining loose dirt.

8. Using a spray gun, apply the first topcoat of lacquer. First test the spray gun, however, on a piece of paper to be certain that the spray pattern is correct. Refer to Chapter 42 on how to adjust the gun. Spray a full wet coat in order that the lacquer will level itself. Be careful to prevent runs and sags.

9. Lightly sand the surface using water and 320-grit wet or dry abrasive paper. Always wet sand with the grain. Wipe the surface clean and dry with a lint-free cloth.

10. After allowing the last coat to cure for a minimum of 24 hours, rub the surfaces with pumice stone and then rottenstone. For an even deeper finish, polish the project further with extra-fine rubbing compound.

FIGURE 43-9
A clean tack rag will remove any remaining loose dirt.

STUDY QUESTIONS

Answer each of the following questions. If you are not sure of an answer, review the chapter.

43-1. Develop a _____ to list the steps and materials necessary to produce the desired effect.

43-2. Always wear _____ clothing when using bleach.

43-3. A _____ coat prevents stains from bleeding into the finish.

43-4. The visible wood pores can be filled with _____ to level the surface.

43-5. Rub between finishing coats with _____ abrasive to flatten the surface.

43-6. The first step in polishing the finish is to work the surface with _____ and water.

43-7. Apply wax using a _____ motion, but polish the finish by rubbing with the grain.

43-8. After blowing off the project, clean the surface with a _____ rag.

IMPORTANT TECHNICAL TERMS

Following are technical terms that you should be able to use as part of your working vocabulary. Write a brief description of the meaning of each term.

Finishing schedule
Finish sample

Bleaching
Natural
Wash coat
Paste wood filler
Sealing
Glazing
Tack rag

44

STAINING

Staining is the process of applying a dye or pigment that modifies the color of the wood. Finishers will use stain to bring out the grain in the wood, add color, or to imitate a more expensive species. On simple finishes it is often the first step in the finishing schedule.

Stains consist of either a *soluble dye* or *insoluble pigment* and a *vehicle*. The dye and pigment contains the color, while the vehicle keeps the colorants in liquid form. The *vehicle* allows the stain to be spread on the surface and to penetrate into the wood.

Always read and follow the directions given on the label of the stain container. The directions will provide specific information on application and cleanup procedures. It will be very important that you note the proper length of drying time. Thoroughly stir the stain to mix the dye or pigments into the liquid. Not stirring the stain will cause the wood to vary in color. It is also recommended that you pause periodically and restir the stain, to keep the colorants from settling to the bottom of the container.

The most common stains are water stains, penetrating oil stains, pigmented oil stains, and non-grain-raising stains. Each has certain advantages and disadvantages to be considered. General characteristics are given in Table 44-1.

It is a good practice to wear rubber gloves when working with stains. Eye protection is also recommended.

WATER STAINS

Water stain is sold as a powder that is mixed with water. It is known for a fade-resistant, clear permanent color. You should sponge the surface with warm water, allow it to dry, and sand before applying the stain. This stain streaks easily and also requires light sanding after the stain has dried to remove the raised grain. Do not attempt to wipe on the wet stain unless the project is quite small (Fig. 44-1). Always wipe with the grain and do not overlap any of the passes. Ideally, use a spray gun to apply water stain. Stain applied with a spray gun should have stainless steel passages to prevent corrosion.

PENETRATING OIL STAINS

Penetrating oil stains are sold premixed in a variety of colors. They are very likely to fade and bleed into other coats of finish. Penetrating stains are not recommended for most applications.

TABLE 44-1
Characteristics of Stains

Stain	Characteristics	Application methods	Drying time
Water stain	Produces one of the clearest color; nonbleeding; raises grain, which requires light sanding	Wiping Spraying	12 hours
Penetrating oil stains	Non-grain-raising; likely to bleed; fades	Wiping Brushing Spraying	24 hours
Pigmented oil stains	Easiest to apply; non-grain-raising; hides grain	Wiping Brushing Spraying	3 to 12 hours
Non-grain-raising stains	Dries rapidly; nonbleeding non-grain-raising; clear colors; streaks easily	Spraying	15 minutes to 3 hours

FIGURE 44-1
Only wipe one water stain when the project is quite small.

PIGMENTED OIL STAINS

Pigmented oil stains are ideal for finishers who need an easy-to-apply stain. This stain is available in a broad variety of colors and is sometimes called a *wiping stain* (Fig. 44-2).

Pigmented stains can be applied by wiping, dipping, brushing, or spraying. Brushing or wiping is often used for small to medium-sized projects. Use short overlapping strokes from the bottom of the surface to the top (Fig. 44-3). After five to ten minutes, use a lint-free cloth to remove any excess stain. Rub across the grain and be certain that all corners are free of surplus stain. The longer the unwiped stain is allowed to stay on the surface, the darker the wood will become. Once the stain is applied, wait at least 24 hours before applying any other finish. Because the end grain tends to darken rapidly, the penetrating process can be slowed by first rubbing linseed oil into the pores.

FIGURE 44-2
Pigmented oil stains are available in a broad variety of colors.

FIGURE 44-3
Brushing on a pigmented oil stain.

NON-GRAIN-RAISING STAINS

Non-grain-raising (NGR) stains are made from a dye base and a fast drying vehicle. This stain is best known for its rapid drying characteristics and clear transparent colors. It does not "muddy" the wood grain, giving the finish a clear appearance.

NGR stains are difficult to apply evenly except with a spray gun (Fig. 44-4). Any overlapping will cause dark streaks. Apply a light coat and be careful that the project does not become too dark. You can always apply additional coats to achieve a darker color.

FIGURE 44-4
Spraying NGR stains to develop an even color.

STUDY QUESTIONS

Answer each of the following questions. If you are not sure of an answer, review the chapter.

44-1. Stains consist of either a soluble _____ or insoluble _____ and a vehicle.

44-2. The four most common stains are _____, _____, _____, and _____.

44-3. List the drying times for water stains, pigmented oil stain, and non-grain-raising stain.

44-4. Water stain is mixed with _____ and requires light sanding to remove _____ grain.

44-5. Pigmented oil stains are sometimes called _____ stains.

44-6. Unless a _____ is used, NGR stains are difficult to apply evenly.

IMPORTANT TECHNICAL TERMS

Following are technical terms that you should be able to use as part of your working vocabulary. Write a brief description of the meaning of each term.

Soluble dye
Insoluble pigment
Vehicle
Wiping stain
NGR stain

45

FILLING AND SEALING

After a project has been stained, it can be filled and sealed. Each of these is an important step which is often found in a finishing schedule. Not all finishes, however, require filling and sealing. Paste wood filler will aid you in developing a flat surface on woods containing visible pores. Sealing the project will provide a good base on which to apply most top-coats.

PASTE WOOD FILLERS

Paste wood filler is utilized to fill the small recesses created by the pores in wood. Open-grained woods such as oaks, ash, and mahogany need a paste filler (Table 45-1). Birch, red gum, and cherry have smaller pores and require liquid filler, which is thinner than the paste filler. Poplar, willow, and pine have no visible pores and do not need any type of filling. Paste wood filler should not be confused with wood putty. Wood putty is designed to fill larger recesses and defects.

Most finishers purchase the paste wood filler already mixed in a neutral color. For darker-colored woods concentrated oil pigments should be thoroughly mixed with the filler (Fig. 45-1). A color of filler can be made that matches the surrounding

TABLE 45-1 Woods Requiring Filling		
No filler needed	Liquid filler	Paste filler
Basswood	Beech	Ash
Fir	Birch	Butternut
Hemlock	Cherry	Chestnut
Holly	Cottonwood	Elm
Larch	Gum, red	Hickory/pecan
Magnolia	Maple, hard	Locust
Pine, white	Maple, soft	Mahogany
Pine, yellow	Sycamore	Red and white oak
Poplar		Walnut
Willow		

wood. You may wish to use a contrasting color filler to highlight the pores.

Applying Paste Filler

To apply the paste filler, completely mix the required amount to a uniform creamy consistency. A *wash coat* should have been applied previously to seal in the stain. Not using a wash coat of thinned shellac or lacquer sealer will lighten the stain and make the color irregular.

FIGURE 45-1
Use concentrated oil pigments to color paste wood filler.

FIGURE 45-3
Remove the excess filler by rubbing across the grain.

Use a stiff-bristle varnish brush to work the filler into the grain. Brush across the grain to achieve the maximum penetration (Fig. 45-2). Some finishers prefer to rub the filler into the pores by using a circular motion with their hands. You may want to wear rubber gloves to prevent your hands from being stained. The more filler worked into the pores, the leveler the finish will be.

FIGURE 45-4
Use a sharpened dowel rod to remove filler from corners.

FIGURE 45-2
Brush filler across the grain.

After the filler has turned from a glossy wet appearance to a dull color, the excess can be removed from the wood. Rub the filler across the grain with a folded pad of burlap (Fig. 45-3). Frequently refold the pad to expose a clean area of the burlap to better remove the excess material. Use a sharpened dowel rod with a rag covering the point to dig out the filler in corners and other recesses (Fig. 45-4). Use a soft cotton cloth to clean the surface further by rubbing with the grain.

It is extremely important that all wood filler left on top of the surface be removed. Any remaining

material will turn gray and require a great deal of effort to remove. After waiting for 24 hours, inspect the surface. If the pores are still somewhat open, repeat the process using a liquid filler.

LIQUID FILLER

For woods with smaller pores, use a liquid filler. (Table 45-1) Being a thinner-bodied material, the liquid filler will penetrate smaller pores and fill them more easily than with the thicker paste wood filler. Use the application techniques recommended for paste wood filler.

SEALING THE SURFACE

A very important step in finishing a project properly is the application of sealer. Sealers are typically utilized as the last step before the application of the topcoat. This coating should be utilized to serve as a barrier between the filler, stain, and the remaining layers of finish. Sealers will keep stains from bleeding and fillers from eventually turning gray. A coat of sealer will also provide a good base for topcoats in order that they may have proper adhesion to the wood substrate. They will also cause loose wood fibers to stand up in order that they be later sanded away.

Select the type of sealer based on the kind of topcoat finish. Varnish finishes are generally sealed with shellac. A mixture of 7 parts of alcohol with 1 part of 4-lb-cut white shellac will seal a stained and or filled surface which is to be varnished. Lacquer sealers are utilized for lacquer finishes. They are usually thinned in a sufficient amount to be sprayed. Polyesters, polyurethanes, and other synthetic finishes often require specialized sealers. For any finish, always read and follow the instructions on the topcoat container for the exact recommended sealer and method of application.

To seal most surfaces properly, two coats of sealer are required. Apply the first coat of sealer across the grain. After the sealer has been allowed to dry thoroughly, sand the surface. Lightly sand with the grain using 180-grit abrasive paper. It will remove any raised wood fibers. Be very careful about sanding through the stain, exposing the raw wood. You may find that you should not sand on or near the corners. The sealer will be very thin at these locations and can easily be sanded through. Follow the same procedure for the second coat of sealer, but apply with the grain.

Be careful about applying an excessive amount of sealer. Being a soft coating, it will cause cold cracking and chipping of the topcoat. Ideally, the majority of the sealer should be left in the wood with very little remaining on the surface.

STUDY QUESTIONS

Answer each of the following questions. If you are not sure of an answer, review the chapter.

45-1. Paste wood filler is utilized to fill small recesses created by the _____ in wood.

45-2. Filler for darker-colored woods can be tinted with concentrated _____ pigments.

45-3. Brush _____ the grain to achieve the maximum penetration.

45-4. Use a sharpened _____ _____ with a rag covering the point to dig out the filler in corners and other recesses.

45-5. Woods containing smaller pores can be filled with a _____ filler.

45-6. Select the type of sealer based on the kind of _____ finish.

45-7. Applying excessive amounts of sealer will cause _____ cracking and _____ of the topcoat.

IMPORTANT TECHNICAL TERMS

Following are technical terms that you should be able to use as part of your working vocabulary. Write a brief description of the meaning of each term.

Paste wood filler
Wash coat
Sealer
Filling
Liquid filler

46

SPECIAL FINISHING EFFECTS

Some projects require additional attention in the finishing process. Special finishing effects are used to add depth and interest to the pieces. They are not used on every project but can add a unique appearance to the finish of those requiring them.

SHADING

Shading is the process of spraying tinted lacquer on the outside edges of tops, doors, and drawers (Fig. 46-1). The contrasting colored lacquer is feathered out from each of the corners before the topcoat is applied. Make the color darkest on the corners fading to a light tint toward the center. Avoid regular geometrical patterns. When done properly, shading produces an antique look. The project should appear as if the finish has lightened through wear. The areas that normally would be worn should appear light.

SURFACE DISTRESSING

Surface distressing is the process of artificially producing wear marks as would be produced naturally in an antique. There are two types of surface dis-

FIGURE 46-1
Shading applies colored lacquer along corners of doors and drawers.

tressing, chemical and mechanical. *Chemical distressing* is produced by spattering ground pigments mixed with Japan drier across the surface (Fig. 46-2). The brown or black color can be applied with a stiff toothbrush. Spray guns and distressing aerosol sprays can also be utilized if a great deal of distressing is required. An irregular dot pattern should be produced by rubbing your finger across the end of the brush bristles or spraying the dark color. Be careful about applying too much colorant.

555

FIGURE 46-2
Chemical distressing can be done by spattering ground pigment from the bristles of a brush.

Mechanical distressing can be done with a chain, chisel, and with other tools and hardware (Fig. 46-3). You will need to imitate the years of wear that would take place with a very old piece of furniture. Worm holes can be produced with an elec-

tric drill. Corners can also be rounded irregularly as if the wood has been worn away. Striking the project with a chain will make impressions in the surface.

SAP STAINING

Sap staining is the process of applying a non-grain-raising (NGR) stain only to the sapwood or light areas of the projects (Fig. 46-4). This process is also utilized when different woods are used in the same project. A tabletop, for example, may be made from walnut while the base could be constructed from poplar. The additional stain produces a more uniform color between the two woods. After the sap stain has dried, you will then need to apply a stain over the entire project. If done correctly, the various parts will appear to be all heartwood.

FIGURE 46-3
The surface can be distressed with chains, drills, and rounding the edges.

FIGURE 46-4
This piece of walnut furniture has been sap stained to produce a more uniform color.

STUDY QUESTIONS

Answer each of the following questions. If you are not sure of an answer, review the chapter.

46-1. _____ is the process of spraying tinted lacquer along the outside edges.

46-2. _____ distressing is produced by spattering ground pigments on the surface.

46-3. A stiff _____ can be used for chemical distressing.

46-4. _____ distressing imitates the wear of an old piece of furniture.

46-5. _____ staining applies NGR stain to sapwood and other light areas.

IMPORTANT TECHNICAL TERMS

Following are technical terms that you should be able to use as part of your working vocabulary. Write a brief description of the meaning of each term.

Shading
Surface distressing
Chemical distressing
Mechanical distressing
Sap staining

47

TOPCOATS

The most common topcoats include penetrating finishes, varnishes, and lacquers. Like the other finishing materials discussed in this section, there are advantages and disadvantages to each. Your selection will depend on the final desired appearance, amount of skill required, available time, and existing equipment and facilities.

SOLVENTS

Solvents are used to dissolve topcoat materials such as those needed for cleaning finishing equipment. Some solvents are also utilized as thinners to reduce the viscosity of the topcoat material. Thinning allows the finish to penetrate the wood better when applying the first layer of the topcoat, and can also be more easily sprayed. Be certain to select the proper solvent for each application. A solvent that will dissolve one material may not affect another. Refer to Table 47-1 for recommended solvents, or more important, use the exact solvent indicated on the printed instructions on the finish can. Some topcoats require a specific type and brand of solvent.

TABLE 47-1
Finishes and Their Solvents

Finish	Solvent[a]
Lacquer	Lacquer thinner
Latex paint	Water
Oil paint and enamel	Turpentine or mineral spirits
Oil stain	Turpentine or mineral spirits
Oil varnish	Turpentine or mineral spirits
Polyurethane varnish	Mineral spirits
Shellac	Alcohol

[a] Always read the directions on the finish container for the recommended solvent.

LACQUERS

Lacquers are one of the most common wood finishes. Many woodworkers select this finish because it dries rapidly, is widely available, and comes in a broad variety of colors and sheens. The *sheen* indicates the amount of gloss or the degree of shine. Lacquers are available in gloss, semigloss, dull, and flat sheens.

Lacquers do have some disadvantages that you should consider. This finish should never be applied over other coatings. It will soften paint and varnishes. Lacquer is likely to check and crack if the substrate or wood expands or contracts a great deal. Once cured the lacquer becomes quite hard and inflexible.

There are several varieties of lacquer-based materials from which to select. In addition, you will want to purchase the type and size of container that will best suit your application. Since it is possible to buy lacquer in containers ranging from small aerosol spray cans to rail tank cars, there is no need to purchase more than you can use in a reasonable period. Most woodworkers find 1- or 5-gallon containers to be the most convenient.

Lacquer Sealers

Lacquer sealers are applied to the raw wood surface and form a base for the other coats of lacquer. Because of its softness, it should never be used as a finish by itself. Many people prefer a *water-white lacquer sealer* because it darkens the wood less than do standard lacquer sealers (Fig. 47-1).

FIGURE 47-1
Water-white lacquer sealer darkens the wood very little.

Clear Lacquers

Although there are several different kinds of clear lacquer, finishes made from *nitrocellulose* remain the most popular. Clear lacquer is utilized as the topcoat and applied over the lacquer sealer. You will need to select the sheen that will provide the desired luster on your project.

Shading Lacquers

Shading lacquers are tinted with a dye and will change the color of the wood (Fig. 47-2). The more shading lacquer that is sprayed, the darker the wood will become. This lacquer can be utilized for making different colors of wood a more uniform color.

FIGURE 47-2
Shading lacquer tints the wood.

Opaque Lacquers

Opaque lacquers are utilized as fast-drying paints (Fig. 47-3). They will completely hide the grain. Most generally, opaque lacquer will be purchased in an aerosol container.

FIGURE 47-3
Opaque lacquers serve as a fast-drying paint.

Brushing Lacquer

Brushing lacquer is a slower-drying lacquer which is applied with a brush (Fig. 47-4). Because these lacquers dry at a slower rate, it is possible to brush the finish without developing brush marks.

FIGURE 47-4
Brushing lacquers are slower drying and can be brushed.

Water-Reducible Lacquers

One of the newest lacquers is acrylic based and thinned with water. Water-reducible lacquer has the advantage of being less polluting to the environment and less flammable. To prevent corrosion, you will need to use spray equipment with stainless steel passages.

Procedure for Spraying Lacquer

Before applying a lacquer finish, check that the stain, filler, and other preliminary steps in the finishing schedule are thoroughly cured. Use the spraying techniques discussed in Chapter 42. Spray on the lacquer sealer or sanding sealer. If you choose a natural appearance, select a water-white lacquer sealer. Sealers fill the pores and provide proper adhesion for the remaining coats of lacquer.

After the sealer has dried, select the lacquer to build up the desired depth of finish. Depending on the amount of lacquer sprayed with each coat, you may want to consider applying two to three coats of lacquer. The more coats applied, the deeper appearing the finish. Too much lacquer, however, will produce a finish that fractures easily. The last coat of lacquer should be the desired sheen. Remember, however, that the higher the gloss, the more the imperfections and defects will show. Be certain to sand lightly with 320-grit wet or dry abrasive paper between each coat of lacquer.

PENETRATING FINISHES

Penetrating finishes soak into the wood rather than building up a substantial layer on top of the surface of the wood. Examples of penetrating finishes are oils and waxes. They will produce a low sheen which gives a hand-rubbed appearance. Both can be applied with a soft cloth and do not necessarily require any other application equipment. Some woodworkers prefer waxes and oils because they do not require a dust-free finish room for their application. It is also easier to repair a penetrating-finished project than those finished with other topcoats.

Oil Finishes

Oil finishes are available as Danish oil, boiled linseed oil, and most recently, Food and Drug Administration (FDA)-approved wipe-on oil. Danish oil is the most common and frequently utilized for school mass-production projects and contemporary walnut furniture (Fig. 47-5). Boiled linseed oil is no longer popular because of its lengthy drying time and odor. The FDA-approved wipe-on oil is designed to be applied on fruit bowls and other wooden articles that will come in contact with food.

FIGURE 47-5
Danish oil produces a hand-rubbed appearance.

Procedure for Wiping Oil

To finish a project with Danish oil, soak a soft cloth in the finish and rub it into the pores of the wood. Use a circular motion (Fig. 47-6). The more oil worked into the surface, the better the project will be protected. After 30 minutes rub the surface dry with a clean cloth. Wipe with the grain. After 1 hour repeat the process to work more oil into the wood. Once the oil has cured completely, you may want to use a paste wax to develop a deeper-looking finish.

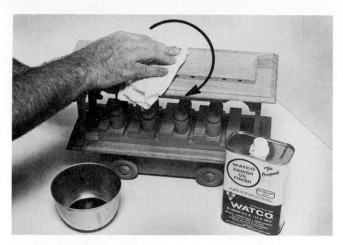

FIGURE 47-6
Rub the oil into the wood with a circular motion.

Wax Finishes

Wax finishes are sold either as pigmented or unpigmented rubbing waxes. Pigmented waxes contain a colorant and will tint the wood. Unpigmented waxes are an amber color and leave the surface a natural color. Although both varieties require a great deal of rubbing, they will produce a defect-free finish.

Procedure for Applying Wax

To apply wax, finish thoroughly and clean the project with pressurized air. Using a soft clean cloth, rub the wax into the pores of the wood with a circular motion. For maximum penetration, heat the wax in a double boiler and apply the wax hot (Fig. 47-7).

FIGURE 47-7
Heating the wax in a double boiler will increase the penetration.

Because the wax is highly flammable, apply only enough heat to melt the wax. After 5 minutes buff the surface thoroughly with a folded soft cotton cloth. Rub with the grain until the entire surface achieves a dull luster. Repeat the process if additional protection is needed.

VARNISHES

Varnishes are one of the oldest finishes utilized for wood surfaces. Over the years many different types have been developed for a variety of applications. Although this type of finish requires several hours and even days to dry, there are types which are water resistant and very durable. The four major categories of varnishes include spirit varnishes, linseed oil varnishes, tung oil varnishes, and synthetic varnishes.

Spirit Varnishes

The most common spirit varnish is *shellac*. (Fig. 47-8) Although at one time utilized as a complete finish, it is used primarily today as a barrier coat and sealer. When used as a finish, shellac yellows and tends to *water spot* if a wet dish is left standing on the surface. Water spotting leaves a white ring in the finish. Denatured alcohol should be used to thin the shellac and clean brushes.

FIGURE 47-8
Shellac is frequently utilized as a barrier coat.

Linseed Oil Varnishes

Linseed oil varnishes can be purchased in three varieties: short-oil, medium-oil, and long-oil. *Short-oil varnishes* are rarely used for furniture. *Medium-oil*

FIGURE 47-9
Medium oil varnishes can be used on kitchen cabinets.

FIGURE 47-10
Spar varnishes are recommended for exterior applications.

varnishes, however, are commonly used for interior furniture and cabinets. (Fig. 47-9). *Long-oil* varnishes are marketed as *spar varnishes* and ideal for wooden surfaces exposed to the exterior. (Fig. 47-10) Outside doors, lawn furniture and boats should be finished with this type of linseed oil varnish.

Tung Oil Varnishes

Tung oil varnishes, the third type of varnish, are designed for high demand areas such as children's

furniture and lawn furniture. They are, however, difficult to find.

Synthetic Varnishes

Synthetic varnishes are known for their toughness and durability. Although there are several types, polyurethane, alkyd and epoxy are the most common. (Fig. 47-11) Alkyds and epoxies are limited primarily to industrial production. They along with polyurethanes dry to such a hard film that unless recoated within 24 hours, additional coats may not adhere.

FIGURE 47-11
Polyurethane varnish produces a very hard, durable finish.

Procedure for Brushing Varnish

After the project has been stained, filled, and sealed, a varnish finish can be applied. Read the directions carefully on the varnish container and follow them exactly.

Slowly stir the varnish and after it is completely mixed, gently pour a small amount into a brush cup. You must be very careful not to develop any air bubbles in the finishing material. Thin the varnish for the first coat by 25 percent. The thinner varnish will more readily penetrate the wood. Stir the mixture to completely disperse the thinner.

Because varnish is very slow drying use a dust free environment to apply the finish. The room must be completely dust free before brushing on the finish and at least two hours after the varnish has been applied. Wipe the project with a clean tack rag and flow on the varnish. Use the brushing techniques as given in Chapter 42, Finishing Equipment.

Be certain the finish is dry before lightly sanding with 320 wet or dry abrasive paper. Three coats of varnish will most generally coat a project. If the initial layers of varnish are sanded flat the last coat should produce a glass-like appearance.

Answer each of the following questions. If you are not sure of an answer, review the chapter.

47-1. Thinning the finish allows better _____ in the wood.

47-2. The amount of gloss or degree of shine is indicated by the _____.

47-3. _____-_____ lacquer sealer darkens the wood less than other sealers.

47-4. Most clear lacquers are made from _____.

47-5. Opaque lacquers are generally sold in a _____ container.

47-6. Brushing lacquers dry at a _____ rate.

47-7. The most common oil finish is _____.

47-8. Use a _____ motion to work the Danish Oil into the pores of the wood.

47-9. Use a soft clean _____ to rub the wax into the pores of the wood.

47-10. Thin shellac with _____ _____.

47-11. _____ varnishes are recommended for exterior surfaces.

47-12. Unless polyurethane varnishes are recoated within _____ hours, additional coats may not adhere.

These technical terms are very important to have in a good working vocabulary. Write a short definition of each term.

Lacquers
Sheen
Water-white lacquer sealer
Nitrocellulose

Penetrating finishes
Oil finishes
Wax finishes
Shellac
Water spot
Short-Oil varnishes
Medium oil
Long oil
Spar Varnishes

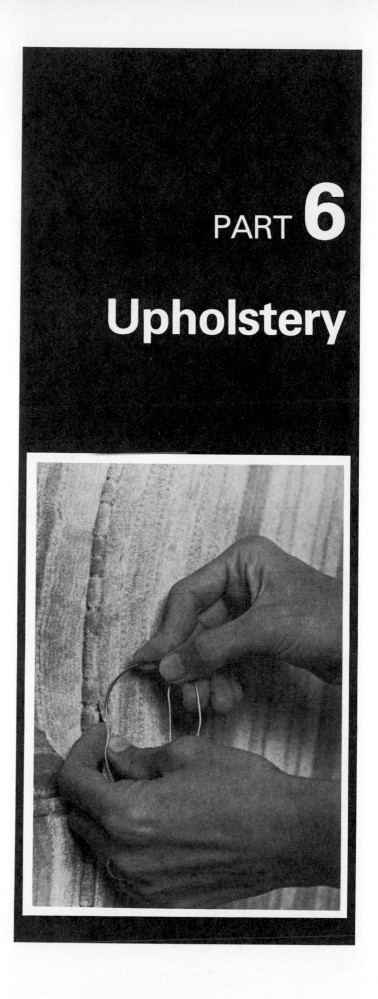

PART 6

Upholstery

48

UPHOLSTERY TOOLS
AND MATERIALS

Most upholstery work is done in factories that manufacture furniture. Factory upholstering is usually done with machines. A limited amount of skilled handwork may have to be done.

The upholsterer who repairs and reupholsters furniture does most of the work by hand. This person must have considerable skill and craftsmanship.

UPHOLSTERING TOOLS

The techniques described in this book are only a few of the simpler ones performed by a skilled upholsterer. To help the upholsterer do this skilled work, a number of specialized tools have been developed. The tools shown in this unit are the commonly used hand tools.

Upholsterers' Hammer

Upholsterers' hammers have 12-in. handles and heads $4\frac{1}{2}$ to $5\frac{1}{2}$ in. (114 to 140 mm) long (Fig. 48-1). They weigh from 5 to 10 oz (142 to 283 g). The head ends are used for driving tacks. One end is about $\frac{5}{16}$ in. (8 mm) in diameter and magnetized to help start tacks. The tack is magnetically held to the hammer face and driven into the wood frame with one blow.

FIGURE 48-1
Upholsterers' hammer.

The other face is about $\frac{1}{2}$ in. (13 mm) in diameter. It is not magnetized. It is used to finish driving tacks into the frame.

The hammer head is curved. This shape helps the upholsterer work corners. The smooth-edged face permits tacking gimp without marring exposed wood or cutting fabric. You use the side of the hammer head to knock out loose tacks that need to be removed.

Shears

Shears are used to cut fabric, webbing, burlap, twine, and foam rubber. Shears are important and should be of good quality. Ten- to 12- in. (254-to 305-mm) shears are preferred for most work (Fig. 48-2). Electric shears are used in mass production because they can cut through many layers of fabric at one time.

FIGURE 48-2
Upholsterers' shears.

Electric Foam Cutter

An electric foam cutter makes straight and curved cuts in foam rubber and polyurethane foam pads. Foam is often cut with a bandsaw.

Webbing Stretcher

A webbing stretcher stretches webbing across the openings in furniture frames (Fig. 48-3). Place the padded end of the stretcher against the furniture frame. The padding prevents marring of the wood surface. The other end has pins that penetrate the webbing. Push the stretcher down to tighten the webbing.

FIGURE 48-3
Typical webbing stretchers.

Ripping Tool

You use a ripping tool to remove tacks holding old upholstery material to the frame (Fig. 48-4). The ripping tool is driven with the side of the upholsterers' hammer to speed up the removal of tacks (Fig. 48-5).

FIGURE 48-4
Ripping tools.

FIGURE 48-5
Tacks are removed with a ripping tool.

Pins

You use upholsterers' pins and T-pins to hold cover fabrics in place temporarily before they are tacked. Use of the pins enables the upholsterer to make folds and straighten the cover before finally tacking it in place. Upholsterers' pins are usually 3 to $3\frac{1}{2}$ in. (76 mm to 89 mm) long. T-pins are $1\frac{1}{4}$ in. (32 mm) long (Fig. 48-6).

FIGURE 48-6
Upholsterers' pin and T-pin.

UPHOLSTERER'S PIN

T–PIN

Curved Needles

Curved needles are used to sew flat surfaces where a straight needle would be difficult to use (Fig. 48-7). Often it is impossible to reach behind the fabric to pull a straight needle through because of the wood frame. Because of its shape, you do not have to pull the curved needle all the way through the fabric before bringing it through from the other side (Fig. 48-8).

FIGURE 48-7
Curved needles.

FIGURE 48-8
Sewing a seam with a curved needle.

Curved needles are from 2 to 10 in. (51 to 254 mm) long. They are available with both round and triangular points. The larger needles are used to sew stuffing to burlap and stitched edges. Smaller needles are used for sewing the outside cover fabric.

Straight Needles

Straight needles for upholstery work are from 6 to 12 in. (152 to 305 mm) long. They are made with single and double points (Fig. 48-9). The double point permits sewing up and down without turning the needle around. They are used for the same jobs as the curved needles.

FIGURE 48-9
Straight needles.

Stuffing Regulator

Stuffing regulators are from 6 to 12 in. (152 to 305 mm) long (Fig. 48-10). They are used to redistribute stuffing before the cover fabric is installed. A stuffing regulator is inserted through the muslin cover. The end of the regulator is moved around to distribute stuffing easily. They are not used after the cover fabric has been put on because they may leave a hole in the fabric.

FIGURE 48-10
Stuffing regulator.

Stapling Gun

Staples are often used instead of upholsterers' tacks to hold fabric to wood frames (Fig. 48-11). Stapling guns hold a large supply of staples and can be oper-

FIGURE 48-11
Compressed-air-powered stapling machine. (*Courtesy of Bostitch Textron.*)

ated with one hand. They greatly speed production. They are available in hand, electric or compressed-air-powered models.

Hot Melt Adhesives

Hot melt adhesives are discussed in Chapter 18. Figure 48-12 shows the adhesive being used to bond gimp on a chair. The gimp hides tack heads and gives a finished appearance. Hot melts can be used to bond fabrics to wood.

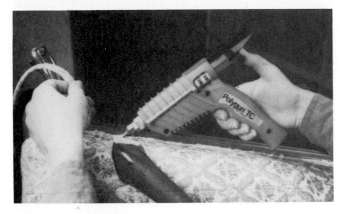

FIGURE 48-12
Upholstery materials can be bonded with a hot melt adhesive applied with a hot melt applicator. (*Courtesy of Adhesives, Coatings and Sealers Division/3M.*)

Spring End-Forming Tool

You use the spring end-forming tool to form the needed arc or angle in sagless springs. (Fig. 48-13). The curved spring fits into a slot in the end of the bender. Pressure is applied to the handles to bend the wire.

FIGURE 48-13
Spring end-forming tool used with sagless springs.

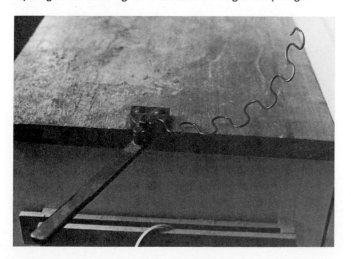

Hog Rings and Hog Ring Pliers

You use hog ring pliers to hold and force closed the metal rings and clips (Fig. 48-14). Hog rings are metal loops that are used to hold springs to burlap (Fig. 48-15).

FIGURE 48-14
Hog ring pliers being used to secure a hog ring through fabric and around a spring wire.

1. INSERT HOG RING THROUGH BURLAP AND AROUND A SPRING WIRE.

2. SQUEEZE THE HOG RING CLOSED OVER THE SPRING WIRE.

FIGURE 48-15
How hog rings hold fabric.

Benches and Trestles

Place furniture that is to be upholstered on padded benches or trestles (Figs. 48-16 and 48-17). The bench or trestle holds the work at normal working height. The typical bench height is 18 to 24 in. (457 to 610 mm). Benches and trestles should be strong enough to support large furniture units such as sofas. The top of these supporting units can be completely padded or a large padded roll edge can be applied around the top. The padding prevents damage to finished wood frames of furniture.

FIGURE 48-16
Padded upholsterers' table.

FIGURE 48-17
Upholsterers' trestles hold large furniture units.

Button Machine

A button machine covers buttons with material to match the finished cover material (Fig. 48-18). You can have buttons covered in shops that sell upholstery materials.

Sewing Machine

You will need an upholstery sewing machine for most jobs. Special heavy-duty machines are necessary to sew three or four layers of fabric together (Fig. 48-19).

Cushion-Filling Machine

A cushion-filling machine is shown in Fig. 48-20. The filler material for the cushion is put in the metal box and compressed. Then you slide the cushion

FIGURE 48-18
Button covering machine.

FIGURE 48-19
Heavy-duty power sewing machine.

FIGURE 48-20
Cushion-filling machine.

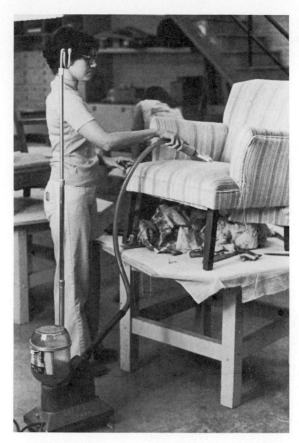

FIGURE 48-21
Steaming the fabric on a finished upholstered chair.

FIGURE 48-22
Upholstery tacks.

OUNCE	1	1½	2	2½	3
LENGTH	$\frac{3}{16}$"	$\frac{3.5}{16}$"	$\frac{4}{16}$"	$\frac{5}{16}$"	$\frac{6}{16}$"

OUNCE	4	6	8	10	12
LENGTH	$\frac{7}{16}$"	$\frac{8}{16}$"	$\frac{9}{16}$"	$\frac{10}{16}$"	$\frac{11}{16}$"

OUNCE	14	16	18	20
LENGTH	$\frac{12}{16}$"	$\frac{13}{16}$"	$\frac{14}{16}$"	$\frac{15}{16}$"

cover filler over the metal box. The box is removed leaving the filler inside the cover. These are not used for foam rubber cushions.

After a unit is upholstered the fabric can be steamed to remove indentations. A steamer is shown in Fig. 48-21.

UPHOLSTERING MATERIALS

Upholstering Tacks

Many sizes of upholstery tacks are available (Fig. 48-22). The tacks range in length from $\frac{3}{16}$ in. (No. 1) to $\frac{15}{16}$ in. (No. 20). Factors in choosing a tack size are thickness of the material, thickness of the frame, and the weight to be held. You are responsible for choosing the right size. Upholstery tacks have a blued finish and are sterilized.

Some upholsterers carry the tacks in their mouths because the tacks are small and hard to handle. They take the tacks from their mouths with the magnetic end of the hammer. This technique is not recommended.

Upholsterers' tacks are sold by weight. They come in quantities of 25 or 100 lb.

Webbing Tacks

Webbing tacks are similar to upholsterers' tacks. A tapered point with barbs gives these tacks greater holding power (Fig. 48-23). They are made in $\frac{11}{16}$- (No. 12) and $\frac{12}{16}$-in. (No. 14) lengths.

OUNCE	12	14
LENGTH	$\frac{11}{16}''$	$\frac{12}{16}''$

FIGURE 48-23
Webbing tacks.

Gimp Tacks

Gimp tacks have small round heads and a blued finish (Fig. 48-24). They are available in sizes from $\frac{5}{16}$ (No. 2) to $\frac{10}{16}$ in. (No. 8) long. Gimp tacks are used to attach cloth gimp to the furniture (see Fig. 48-29). They are sold in $\frac{1}{8}$-, $\frac{1}{4}$-, 1-, 10-, 25-, and 100-lb quantities.

OUNCE	2	$2\frac{1}{2}$	3	4	6	8
LENGTH	$\frac{5}{16}''$	$\frac{6}{16}''$	$\frac{7}{16}''$	$\frac{8}{16}''$	$\frac{9}{16}''$	$\frac{10}{16}''$

FIGURE 48-24
Gimp tacks.

Decorative-Head Tacks

A variety of tacks with decorative heads are available (Fig. 48-25) . These are used mainly when upholstering furniture patterned after antiques where the tacks are exposed and become part of the design. They are also used with leather and plastic coverings. Decorative-head tacks are available in brass-

FIGURE 48-25
Tacks with decorative heads.

plated, nickel, and lacquered styles with bright, dull, and antique finishes.

Buttons

Several kinds of buttons are available. Buttons add a decorative touch to large upholstered surfaces. They also provide a means of holding the fabric under slight tension to reduce sagging. The common types of buttons are tuft, loop, tack, and clinch (Fig. 48-26).

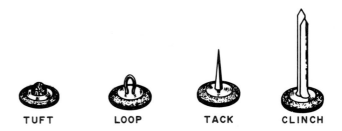

TUFT   LOOP   TACK   CLINCH

FIGURE 48-26
Types of buttons.

Welt Cord

Welt cord is sewed inside $1\frac{1}{2}$-in. (38-mm) strips of covering material. The finished product is called the welt (Fig. 48-27). Welt is sewed between the seams

FIGURE 48-27
Welt cord sewed in fabric forming a welt.

WELT CORD

FABRIC USED TO UPHOLSTER FURNITURE UNIT.

FIGURE 48-28
Welt is sewed between adjoining pieces of finished fabric.

in upholstery (Fig. 48-28). Welt cord is sold in diameters of $\frac{1}{8}$, $\frac{5}{32}$, and $\frac{1}{4}$ in.

Gimp

Gimp is a trimming material. It is woven with a decorative pattern. It is about $\frac{1}{2}$ in. (13 mm) wide and is available in a variety of colors. Gimp is applied over exposed upholstery tacks by gluing or with gimp tacks (Fig. 48-29).

FIGURE 48-29
One type of gimp.

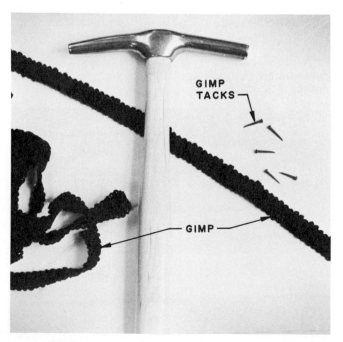

Thread

Upholstery thread must be strong. You can get upholstery thread in several materials, including cotton, linen, and nylon and other synthetics. Thread is available in a variety of colors. The color selected should match the predominant color of the upholstery fabric. You can use transparent monofilament thread for sewing fabrics of all colors.

Twine

Twine is a coarse strong cord. There are three kinds: spring, jute, and flax. Spring twine is sold in 1-lb balls. Spring twine is used for heavy work such as tying heavy coil springs in seats. Jute twine is lighter and softer than spring twine. It is used to tie the lighter coil springs that are in pillows for furniture backs. Flax twine is used for sewing coil springs to webbing, for sewing on buttons, and for other types of hand sewing.

Webbing

Webbing is a tape strip used as a base for coil springs and cushion materials. It carries the weight of the seat and back and must be very strong (Fig. 48-30). Common materials used for webbing are jute, steel, cotton, and plastic.

Jute webbing is made from coarser jute fibers. Jute is a plant that grows in India. The coarse, woody fibers from this plant are woven into webbing tapes and burlap.

The standard widths are 3, $3\frac{1}{2}$, and 4 in. (76, 89, and 102 mm). The $3\frac{1}{2}$-in. (89-mm) width is most commonly used. It is sold in rolls 72 yd (66 m) long.

Steel webbing is made in several types. The

FIGURE 48-30
Jute webbing.

FIGURE 48-31
Rubber webbing.

most commonly used width of steel webbing is ¾ in. (19 mm). It is made in either plain or perforated bands. Perforated bands help when nailing steel webbing to the frame. Another kind of steel webbing has a corrugated, punched surface. The ends of coil springs slide into the corrugations. Steel webbing has less give than jute webbing and provides less comfort.

Cotton webbing is a lightweight tape used for chairs that normally will not receive a lot of heavy use. It is available in widths of ½, ⅝, 1, 1¼, 1½, and 2 in. (13, 16, 25, 32, 38, and 51 mm). Cotton webbing is not strong enough to use as a substitute for jute webbing.

Plastic webbing is used mostly on yard furniture. It withstands exposure to the weather. Exposure to sunlight over a period of time will cause it to weaken and crack. Plastic webbing is available in a variety of colors and patterns. Common widths range from ¾ to 5 in. (19 to 127 mm).

Rubber webbing is used on furniture with loose seat and back cushions. It is strong and has enough give to be comfortable. It is sold in rolls 2 in. (51 mm) wide (Fig. 48-31).

Fabrics

Burlap is a cloth made from jute fibers. It is sold in a variety of weights, such as 7½, 10, 12, and 16 oz. (213 283, 340, and 454 g) and in a variety of widths, such as 36, 40, and 45 in. (914, 1016, and 1143 mm). The 10- and 12-oz weights are most commonly used. A major use is to cover springs.

Unbleached muslin is a cloth used as the first cover over cushion stuffing. It separates the stuffing from the finished fabric cover. Unbleached muslin is sold in 36- and 39-in. (914- and 991-mm) widths.

The finished fabric covering can be made from a variety of materials. Common fabrics are made from such materials as cotton, rayon, silk, wool, and nylon. Some fabrics are combinations of these. A variety of plastic and artificial leather materials are available as well as genuine leather.

When you select a fabric, consider how much wear it will have to stand. A fine silk cover will not withstand hard use. A nylon fabric will wash easily and is tough. The cheapest material is not always a good choice. More expensive materials often will last longer.

Stuffing

There are a variety of materials used for stuffing cushions, seats, backs, and arms. Foam rubber, rubberized hair, and polyurethane foam are most often used.

Foam rubber cushions are easy to handle and provide a satisfactory cushion. They are mounted over a wood base, webbing, or springs. You can cut material easily with a shears or knife. Foam rubber withstands moisture and hard use. It is sold in sheets and preformed cushions. Solid, flat sheets are available in thicknesses from ½ to 2 in. (13 to 51 mm) in medium and firm densities (Fig. 48-32). Cored sheets have molded openings on one side and are available in thicknesses from 1 to 4½ in. (25 to 114 mm). Full molded units are available. These are finished cushions with cavities inside. They are available in a wide range of sizes.

Rubberized hair is made by coating curled hog, horse, and cattle hair with pure rubber. You use rubberized hair in seats, backs, and arms of furniture. This padding is very light and self-ventilating. Sheets of rubberized hair 24 × 72 in. (610 × 1829 mm) and 25-yd (23-m) rolls are common sizes (Fig.

FIGURE 48-32
Foam rubber pads are available in a wide range of thicknesses.

FIGURE 48-33
Rubberized hair stuffing.

48-33). It comes in thicknesses from $\frac{3}{4}$ to 3 in. (19 to 76 mm). Several layers can be glued together to form thicker pads.

Polyurethane foam is formed into blocks of various sizes. It is used as a cushion filler as well as for seats and backs. It is made in three densities—soft, medium and hard—to provide the softness or firmness desired. This foam is light, tough, and difficult to tear, but it can be easily cut. You can use a special cement to glue blocks of it together. It can also be glued to wood, metal, and fabric. Polyurethane foam is sold in 24 × 72 in. (610 × 1829 mm) pieces in 1-, 2-, and 4-in. (25-, 51-, and 102-mm) thicknesses.

Cotton batting is padding used as the top layer of filler in parts of upholstered furniture. It is a blend of cotton fibers. Cotton batting is sold in 15-lb rolls and 100-lb bales (Fig. 48-34). The batting should not be cut to size with shears because a definite edge is formed that will not flow out smoothly under the fabric. You should pull the batt apart

FIGURE 48-34
Cotton batting.

by hand. This leaves an edge that gradually gets thinner.

Dacron fiber padding can be used in place of cotton. It is sold in rolls 27, 30, and 36 in. (686, 762, and 914 mm) wide. A polyester fiber pad is also available for padding cushions.

Springs

The two types of springs used are *upholstery* and *sagless. Upholstery springs* are coil springs (Fig. 48-35). Those used for seats are made from heavy wire. The spring is larger in diameter on each end than in the center. Each end of the coil is open. One end has the wire bent at a 90° angle to keep it from piercing the burlap. This end of the coil is placed up. The other end goes against the webbing.

FIGURE 48-35
Coil-type upholstery springs.

Seat springs are made from spring numbers 00 through 6. The following are typical sizes:

Spring number	00	0	1	2	3	4	5	6
Height (in.)	4	5	6	8	$9\frac{1}{2}$	$10\frac{1}{2}$	12	14
Wire gauge	11	11	11	$10\frac{1}{2}$	$9\frac{1}{2}$	$9\frac{1}{2}$	$8\frac{1}{2}$	8

The smaller the number of the wire gauge, the larger the diameter of the wire.

Seat springs are made in three degrees of compression: soft, medium, and hard. The degree of compression is determined by the size of the coil at its center.

The smaller the coil diameter, the harder the spring.

Pillow springs are made of lighter gauge wire than seat springs. Typical sizes are:

Height (in.)	4	6	8	10
Wire gauge	14	14	12	12

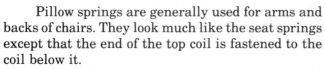

FIGURE 48-36
Sagless springs are available in coils and precut lengths.

FIGURE 48-37
Clips used to secure sagless springs to the furniture frame.

Pillow springs are generally used for arms and backs of chairs. They look much like the seat springs except that the end of the top coil is fastened to the coil below it.

Sagless springs are made of strong, resilient wire formed in a zigzag shape. They are sold in coils ranging in length from 50 to 140 ft (Fig. 48-36). Sagless springs are available in 7- to 12-gauge wire.

The 10- to 12-gauge wire springs are smaller and are used in chair backs. The 7- to 9-gauge wire springs are heavier and are used in seats. Sagless springs are also sold in precut lengths.

Sagless springs are held to furniture frames with a variety of clips (Fig. 48-37). Links connect the rows of springs. Helical springs connect the wood frame to the outside spring.

STUDY QUESTIONS

Answer each of the following questions. If you are not sure of an answer, review the chapter.

48-1. How does an upholsterer's hammer differ from the carpenter's claw hammer?

48-2. Why is the upholsterer's hammer magnetized?

48-3. What tools are used to cut materials used in upholstering?

48-4. What tool do you use to remove old upholstery material?

48-5. What are two ways to hold fabric to wooden frames?

48-6. For what purpose are hog ring pliers used?

48-7. What is the range of sizes of upholsterers' tacks?

48-8. What factors do you consider when selecting upholsterers' tacks?

48-9. Where are decorative-head tacks used?

48-10. What use is made of webbing?

48-11. What kinds of webbing are available?

48-12. What materials are used for stuffing?

48-13. What are the two types of springs used in upholstering work?

IMPORTANT TECHNICAL TERMS

Following are technical terms that you should be able to use as part of your working vocabulary. Write a brief description of the meaning of each term.

Upholsterers' hammer
Shears
Webbing
Pins

Needles
Hog rings
Welt cord
Gimp
Burlap
Muslin
Stuffing
Upholstery springs
Sagless springs

49

METHODS
OF UPHOLSTERING

There are many ways to combine the various springs, stuffings, and fabrics to achieve a satisfactory solution to an upholstery problem. Following are a few examples of common solutions.

WEBBING

A footstool design using a wood frame, rubber straps or jute webbing, and a foam rubber cushion stuffing is in Fig. 49-1. On this design the fabric cover is cut to size and welt is sewn in the edges. The welt could be omitted from the cushion.

FABRIC AND SPRINGS

A bench is shown in Fig. 49-2. The foam pad is held to the frame by the finished fabric. The pad can be supported by a heavy canvas which is suspended by metal helical springs. The canvas can be sewed around a wire edge. The hook in the end of the spring will loop around the wire edge. Grommets can also be used. A grommet is a round metal reinforcing ring set in the fabric. The hook of the spring will slip into the hole in the grommet.

The corners of the cushion are finished with welts, although they could be left off and the fabric pulled around the wood frame and tacked. Instead of canvas, webbing or plywood could be used to support the foam pad. Clinch-type buttons could be used since the foam pad will be $1\frac{1}{2}$ to 2 in thick.

WOOD BASE

A kitchen stool is shown in Fig. 49-3. The foam seat pad is placed over a wood base. To finish a plain seat the upholstery fabric or plastic can be finished with welts or pulled under the plywood and tacked. The channeled seat is formed by cutting the foam in sections the shape of each seat section. The fabric is pulled over each foam section and tacked to the plywood. Then the next foam section is placed on this and the fabric is pulled over it. The fabric is nailed around the edges to the bottom of the plywood base.

OTHER TECHNIQUES

Several techniques for upholstering straight chairs are shown in Fig. 49-4, page 580. The easiest to use

578

FIGURE 49-1
Simple foam cushion supported by webbing.

FIGURE 49-2
Upholstered bench with a foam cushion supported on a canvas base pulled tight with helical springs.

FABRIC

CARDBOARD
TACK STRIP

TACK

FOLD FABRIC
AND TACK

FOLD FABRIC
AND TACK

FOAM
SECTION

CHANNELLED SEAT

PLYWOOD

FOAM

WELT COULD
BE OMITTED

PLYWOOD

PLAIN SEAT

WELT

FIGURE 49-3
Stool with a plywood seat
base covered with a foam
pad.

is high-quality plastic webbing. The webbing is woven across the seat and nailed under the wood frame. A solid sheet of leather nailed to the frame forms a strong seat. A solid piece of plywood can be covered with a foam cushion. A fabric or plastic material can cover the foam and plywood. It is nailed on the bottom of the plywood. The finished seat is held to the chair with wood screws through the frame into the plywood. A softer seat can be made by using webbing and a fiber stuffing. The stuffing is pulled

around the front of the chair. The fabric is nailed to the wood frame under the seat.

An easy way to upholster an occasional chair is shown in Fig. 49-5. The seat frame is covered with webbing. It is sealed with burlap. A foam cushion is placed over the burlap. The finished fabric is placed over the foam cushion. The back of the chair can be upholstered in the same manner. Often, a padding material such as cotton is used instead of foam in the back.

WEBBING SEAT

WEBBING — —POLYESTER OR DACRON FIBER SEAT

AIR HOLES

—PLYWOOD   FOAM CUSHION

LEATHER OR PLASTIC SEAT—

WEBBING

SECTION THROUGH WEBBING SEAT

LEATHER —

SECTION THROUGH LEATHER SEAT

FOAM

PLYWOOD —

SECTION THROUGH PLYWOOD AND FOAM SEAT

FIBER

BURLAP

WEBBING

SECTION THROUGH POLYESTER OR DACRON FIBER SEAT

FIGURE 49-4
Straight chair with a variety of ways to upholster the seat.

WELT

WEBBING

FOAM RUBBER
SEAT CUSHION

BURLAP

FABRIC
COVER

WEBBING

COTTON OR POLYESTER
FIBER PADDING

FOAM RUBBER

WELT

WEBBING

BURLAP

CAMBRIC
DUST COVER

WELT

FIGURE 49-5
Occasional chair with padded back and seat.

SAGLESS SPRINGS

A chair using no-sag springs is shown in Fig. 49-6. The springs are used in the seat and back, and are covered with burlap. The seat has a layer of padding placed on the burlap. This is covered with another layer of burlap, forming a pad between the springs and the foam seat cushion. On this unit the foam seat cushion is a separate unit. It is a loose cushion.

A chair using coil springs in the seat is in Fig. 49-7. The springs are supported with jute webbing or metal strips. The coils are sewed to the webbing. They are then tied together forming a unit. A layer of burlap is placed over the tied springs. A foam pad rests on the burlap. A thin layer of padding is placed on the foam before the finished fabric cover is nailed in place.

FINISHED FABRIC

NO-SAG SPRINGS

BURLAP

FOAM CUSHION

SAGLESS SPRINGS

BURLAP

SAGLESS SPRINGS

PADDING

CAMBRIC

FIGURE 49-6
Upholstered chair with a removable foam cushion as the seat. Notice the use of sagless springs.

FIGURE 49-7
Occasional chair using coil springs on webbing as the seat.

Answer each of the following questions. If you are not sure of an answer, review the chapter.

49-1. Why is it important to fasten webbing tightly to the frame?

49-2. How is webbing installed?

49-3. How many tacks should you place in the ends of webbing strips?

49-4. How should you fasten sagless springs to a frame?

49-5. What gauge sagless springs should you use on chair seats? On chair backs?

49-6. How much space should you leave between sagless springs?

49-7. What is crown?

49-8. Where should you cut sagless springs?

49-9. How should you prepare the end of a sagless spring to enter a clip?

49-10. How much stuffing should you install over burlap and sagless or coil springs?

49-11. Why are springs covered with burlap before a foam cushion is placed on them?

49-12. How much extra fabric do you need to use a fabric stretcher?

49-13. How is a clinch button installed? A loop or tuft button? A tack button?

IMPORTANT TECHNICAL TERMS

Following are technical terms that you should be able to use as part of your working vocabulary. Write a brief description of the meaning of each term.

Crown
Spring end forming tool
Clips
Nap

50

UPHOLSTERY TECHNIQUES

The following techniques are some of the simpler, widely used approaches to upholstering a product.

APPLYING WEBBING

Webbing supports the upholstered seat and back in chairs. It must be installed properly because everything else depends upon it. It is the foundation on which the rest of the material is built.

To install webbing, support the chair frame on an upholsterers' bench. Find the center of the frame and mark it on the front and back rails (Fig. 50-1). Center a piece of webbing on the center mark. Fold over about 1 in. of webbing so that it is double thick. Tap it with a hammer so that it stays folded. Drive four 16-oz. upholstery tacks through the double thickness into the rail on the inside edge. Space the tacks evenly. Then drive three tacks between the others but put them on the outside edge of the rail (Fig. 50-2).

Stretch the webbing over to the back rail and center it over the center mark. Hook the teeth of the webbing stretcher into the webbing. Place the rubber end against the frame. Press down on the stretcher to pull it as tight as you can (Fig. 50-3). Drive three 16-oz tacks through the webbing while

it is stretched tight. Space evenly across the webbing. Remove the webbing stretcher and cut off the webbing about 1 in. beyond the frame. Fold this back over the three tacks. Drive four more tacks through the two layers of webbing. Space between the three driven earlier.

Apply other strips of webbing in the same manner. Space about 1 in. apart. Plan so the webbing fits evenly across the frame. The frame will appear as shown in Fig. 50-1.

Now run webbing from the side rails. The first strip can be placed about 2 in. from the front rail. It is woven between the other layers of webbing. Nail as just described. Space the other rows about 1 in. from the first. Repeat this until the seat is covered. A finished frame is in Fig. 50-4, page 587.

INSTALLING SAGLESS WIRE SPRINGS

Sagless springs are made from spring wire bent into a zigzag shape. The wire is rolled into coils. The needed lengths of springs are cut from the coil. The cut lengths are arched due to being formed into a coil. This arched shape provides the resilience needed because the spring tries to return to its coiled shape.

BLOCKING

SIDE RAIL

FRONT RAIL

BACK RAIL

THE FRAME

WEBBING

CENTER OF FRAME

CENTER WEBBING ON THE FRAME

THE WEBBING STRETCHED FROM FRONT TO BACK OF THE FRAME.

FIGURE 50-1
How to install the first rows of webbing.

WEBBING

UPHOLSTERER'S TACKS

FURNITURE FRAME

FIGURE 50-2
The tacking pattern for securing webbing to the wood frame.

FIGURE 50-3
The webbing is pulled tight with a webbing stretcher.

Sagless wire springs are fastened to the wood frame with special clips. The interior rows of springs are joined with metal links. The outside springs are attached to the wood frame with helical springs. Sometimes helical springs are used on the inside

FIGURE 50-4
Finished webbed unit.

springs as well (Fig. 50-5). The proper-gauge (wire diameter) spring must be selected. Seven- or 8-gauge springs are generally used in seats; 10- to 12-gauge springs, in backs. The smaller the gauge number, the larger the wire diameter.

The amount of crown wanted in the seat influences the length of the spring and its gauge. Crown is the amount the spring bows above a straight line (Fig. 50-6).

Recommended lengths and gauges for springs manufactured by the No-Sag Company are listed in Tables 50-1 to 50-3. They offer three types of springs, No-Sag, XL and Supr-Loop. The inside seat and back dimensions are taken inside the chair frame (Fig. 50-7).

FIGURE 50-6
The crown is the distance between the frame and to the top of the spring.

FIGURE 50-5
Finished sagless spring installation.

FIGURE 50-7
Inside measurements are taken to find lengths for sagless springs.

TABLE 50-1
Recommended Lengths and Gauges: Original No-Sag

A. Seats

Inside seat dimension (in.)	Standard crown (in.)	Gauge	Length (in.)
12	$1\frac{1}{4}$	11	$11\frac{3}{4}$
13	$1\frac{1}{4}$	$10\frac{1}{2}$	$12\frac{3}{4}$
14	$1\frac{3}{8}$	10	$13\frac{3}{4}$
15	$1\frac{1}{2}$	10	$14\frac{3}{4}$
16	$1\frac{5}{8}$	10	$15\frac{3}{4}$
17	$1\frac{5}{8}$	$9\frac{1}{2}$	$16\frac{3}{4}$
18	$1\frac{3}{4}$	9	$17\frac{3}{4}$
19	$1\frac{3}{4}$	9	$18\frac{3}{4}$
20	$1\frac{7}{8}$	9	20
21	$1\frac{7}{8}$	9	21
22	$1\frac{7}{8}$	$8\frac{1}{2}$	22
23	2	$8\frac{1}{2}$	23
24	2	$8\frac{1}{2}$	24
25	2	8	$24\frac{7}{8}$
26	2	8	$25\frac{3}{4}$
27	2	8	$26\frac{3}{4}$

B. Backs

Inside rail dimension (in.)	Standard crown (in.)	Gauge	Length (in.)
16	$1\frac{1}{2}$	12	16
17	$1\frac{5}{8}$	12	17
18	$1\frac{3}{4}$	12	$18\frac{1}{4}$
19	$1\frac{7}{8}$	12	$19\frac{1}{4}$
20	2	12	$20\frac{1}{4}$
21	2	12	$21\frac{1}{4}$
22	2	12	$22\frac{1}{4}$
23	$2\frac{1}{4}$	$11\frac{1}{2}$ or 12	$23\frac{1}{2}$
24	$2\frac{1}{4}$	$11\frac{1}{2}$	$24\frac{1}{2}$
25	$2\frac{1}{2}$	11	$25\frac{1}{2}$
26	$2\frac{1}{2}$	11	$26\frac{1}{2}$

Source: No-Sag.

TABLE 50-2
Recommended Lengths and Gauges: Supr-Loop

A. Seats

Inside seat dimension (in.)	Standard crown (in.)	Gauge	Length (in.)
12	$1\frac{1}{4}$	10	$11\frac{1}{2}$
13	$1\frac{1}{4}$	10	$12\frac{1}{2}$
14	$1\frac{1}{4}$	$9\frac{1}{2}$	$13\frac{1}{2}$
15	$1\frac{1}{2}$	$9\frac{1}{2}$	$14\frac{1}{2}$
16	$1\frac{3}{4}$	9	$15\frac{5}{8}$
17	$1\frac{3}{4}$	9	$16\frac{5}{8}$
18	$1\frac{3}{4}$	9	$17\frac{5}{8}$
19	$1\frac{7}{8}$	9	$18\frac{1}{2}$
20	$1\frac{7}{8}$	9	$19\frac{1}{2}$
21	$1\frac{7}{8}$	$8\frac{1}{2}$	$20\frac{1}{2}$
22	$1\frac{7}{8}$	$8\frac{1}{2}$	$21\frac{1}{2}$
23	$1\frac{7}{8}$	$8\frac{1}{2}$	$22\frac{1}{4}$
24	2	8	$23\frac{1}{2}$
25	$1\frac{3}{4}$	8	$24\frac{1}{2}$
26	$1\frac{3}{4}$	8	$25\frac{1}{4}$
27	$1\frac{3}{4}$	8	$26\frac{1}{4}$

B. Backs

Inside rail dimension (in.)	Standard crown (in.)	Gauge	Length (in.)
16	$1\frac{3}{8}$	$11\frac{1}{2}$	$15\frac{1}{2}$
17	$1\frac{1}{2}$	$11\frac{1}{2}$	$16\frac{1}{2}$
18	$1\frac{3}{4}$	$11\frac{1}{2}$	$17\frac{3}{4}$
19	2	$11\frac{1}{2}$	19
20	2	$11\frac{1}{2}$	20
21	2	11	$20\frac{7}{8}$
22	2	11	$21\frac{7}{8}$
23	$2\frac{1}{4}$	11	$22\frac{3}{4}$
24	$2\frac{1}{4}$	11	$23\frac{3}{4}$
25	$2\frac{1}{4}$	11	$24\frac{3}{4}$
26	$2\frac{1}{4}$	$10\frac{1}{2}$	$25\frac{7}{8}$

Source: No-Sag.

TABLE 50-3
Recommended Lengths and Gauges: XL

A. Seats					B. Backs			
Inside seat dimension (in.)	Standard crown (in.)	Gauge	Length (in.)		Inside rail dimension (in.)	Standard crown (in.)	Gauge	Length (in.)
12	$1\frac{7}{8}$	$11\frac{1}{2}$	$11\frac{1}{4}$		16	$1\frac{1}{8}$	12	$15\frac{1}{2}$
13	1	11	$12\frac{1}{4}$		17	$1\frac{3}{8}$	12	$16\frac{1}{2}$
14	$1\frac{1}{8}$	$10\frac{1}{2}$	$13\frac{1}{4}$		18	$1\frac{1}{2}$	12	$17\frac{3}{4}$
15	$1\frac{1}{8}$	$10\frac{1}{2}$	$14\frac{1}{4}$		19	$1\frac{5}{8}$	12	$18\frac{3}{4}$
16	$1\frac{3}{16}$	$10\frac{1}{2}$	$15\frac{1}{4}$		20	$1\frac{7}{8}$	12	$19\frac{3}{4}$
17	$1\frac{3}{8}$	10	$16\frac{1}{4}$		21	$1\frac{5}{8}$	12	$20\frac{3}{4}$
18	$1\frac{1}{4}$	$9\frac{1}{2}$	$17\frac{1}{4}$		22	$1\frac{5}{8}$	12	$21\frac{3}{4}$
19	$1\frac{1}{4}$	$9\frac{1}{2}$	$18\frac{1}{4}$		23	$1\frac{3}{4}$	12	23
20	$1\frac{1}{2}$	$9\frac{1}{2}$	$19\frac{1}{2}$		24	$1\frac{3}{4}$	12	24
21	$1\frac{9}{16}$	$9\frac{1}{2}$	$20\frac{1}{2}$		25	$1\frac{7}{8}$	$11\frac{1}{2}$	25
22	$1\frac{3}{4}$	9	$21\frac{1}{2}$		26	2	$11\frac{1}{2}$	26
23	$1\frac{13}{16}$	9	$22\frac{1}{2}$					
24	2	9	$23\frac{1}{2}$					
25	$1\frac{1}{2}$	$8\frac{1}{2}$	$24\frac{3}{8}$					
26	$1\frac{9}{16}$	$8\frac{1}{2}$	$25\frac{1}{4}$					
27	$1\frac{3}{4}$	$8\frac{1}{2}$	$26\frac{1}{4}$					

Source: No-Sag.

FIGURE 50-8
Seat clips used with No-Sag springs. (*Courtesy of No-Sag Company.*)

Sagless wire springs are joined to the frame with metal clips. Special clips are used to hold seat springs (Fig. 50-8) and back springs (Fig. 50-9).

The spacing of springs depends on the distance between the arms of the chair. Recommended spacing is listed in Table 50-4. For example, a 21-in. chair has five springs. They are spaced 2 in. in from each handle. The others are spaced $4\frac{1}{4}$ in. on center from the centers of the outside springs. The connecting links used between the springs are $2\frac{5}{8}$ in. long.

FIGURE 50-9
Back clips used with No-Sag springs. (*Courtesy of No-Sag Company.*)

TABLE 50-4
Recommended Spacing for Sagless Springs

Distance between arms along front seat rail	Number of springs	Center-to-center spacing of clips (in.)	Center spacing of two outside clips from inside arm posts (in.)
Chairs			
20-in.	5	$4\frac{1}{8}$	$1\frac{3}{4}$
22-in.	5	$4\frac{5}{8}$	$1\frac{3}{4}$
24-in.	5	$5\frac{1}{8}$	$1\frac{3}{4}$
Sofas			
48-in.	10	$5\frac{1}{2}$	$1\frac{3}{4}$
52-in.	11	$5\frac{1}{4}$	$1\frac{3}{4}$
72-in.	15	$5\frac{1}{4}$	$1\frac{3}{4}$
78-in.	17	$4\frac{7}{8}$	$1\frac{3}{4}$
86-in.	18	$5\frac{1}{8}$	$1\frac{3}{4}$

The springs are normally run from the front to the back seat rails and bottom to top back rails. They can be installed in the other direction if it is important to the design of the chair (Fig. 50-10). The frame should be strong enough to withstand the pull of the springs. If they are installed from front to back, the front and back rails should overlap the side rails. In this way the springs are pulling against the side rails (Fig. 50-11). Wide chairs or sofas should have one or two supports in the center (Fig. 50-12). Following are the steps to follow to prepare and install sagless springs.

FIGURE 50-10
Sagless springs are usually applied from top to bottom on the back and front to back on the seat.

SAGLESS SPRINGS

1. Determine the length of the spring. Measure the inside dimension for the seat and back. Select the proper spring gauge and length from Table 50-1, 50-2, or 50-3. If more crown than that provided in the table is wanted, cut the spring longer. The height of the crown is increased $\frac{1}{4}$ in. for each $\frac{1}{2}$ in. added to the length of the spring. The crown can be lowered by subtracting this from the length.

2. Determine the number of springs. Measure the length of the chair between the arms. Then refer to Table 50-4.

3. Cut the springs to length. Unroll a section of the spring from the coil. Lay it flat on the workbench. Hold it flat and measure the length (Fig. 50-13). Cut the wire by notching it with a file or hacksaw. The wire when bent will snap at the notch. Cut just at the end of the curve (Fig. 50-14).

4. File any rough edges off the cut end. Then bend each end as shown in Fig. 50-14. The best way to bend the end is to use a spring end forming tool. Place the end of the spring in the tool. Pull the handle to bend the end (Fig. 50-15).

5. Locate and nail the clips to the frame. Use $\frac{7}{8}$-in. serrated nails (Fig. 50-16).

6. Place the ends of the springs in the clip and nail the clip closed (Fig. 50-16). To pull the springs into the clips a spring stretcher is useful. One type is shown in Fig. 50-17.

7. Mark the locations of the clips to hold the helical springs. Nail the clips and install the springs. The exact location and number depend on the judgment of the upholsterer.

8. Install the metal connecting links between the inner springs. Again placement is a matter of judgment. Helical springs or specially made heavy rubber bands could be used instead of the links.

FIGURE 50-11
The front rails should overlap the side rails. Center braces are needed on long units.

FIGURE 50-12
Back of a sofa. Notice that the springs run vertically. A wood center brace helps the frame withstand the tension of the springs.

FIGURE 50-13
How to measure the length of a sagless spring.

FIGURE 50-14
How to cut a sagless spring.

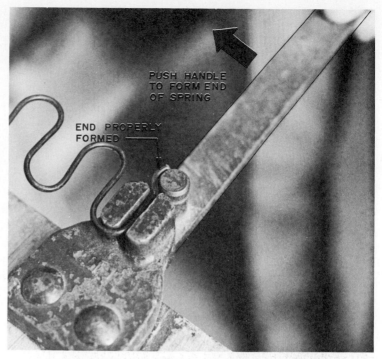

FIGURE 50-15
How to bend the end of the sagless spring so that it will not slip out of the clip.

FIGURE 50-16
Sagless springs are held to the frame with metal clips.

FIGURE 50-17
Device used to pull sagless springs across the frame into the clips.

1. NAIL THE CLIP TO THE FRAME.

2. INSTALL THE SPRING AND NAIL THE CLIP CLOSED.

ATTACHING BURLAP

Sagless springs are covered with a layer of burlap. It provides a foundation for the stuffing above it (Fig. 50-18).

1. First measure the width and length of the area to be covered (Fig. 50-19). Allow about $\frac{1}{2}$ in. extra on each side. This is used to turn under to form a hem for tacking. Cut the burlap to size.
2. Place the burlap over the springs. Center it so it hangs equally on all sides.
3. Fold under $\frac{1}{2}$ in. on the front side and tack it in the center to the rail (Fig. 50-20).

FIGURE 50-18
Sagless springs are covered with burlap.

4. Fold under ½ in. on the back side, pull the burlap tight, and tack it in the center to the rail. Do not pull so tight that the springs are depressed.
5. Cut and fit the burlap around the arm posts and back posts.
6. Fold under ½ in. on each side and tack the burlap in the center. Make certain that it is pulled tight but not under excess strain.
7. Now start at the center tack on either side and nail the burlap to the rail. Nail right and left from the center tack. Do this on all four rails. Remember to keep the ½-in. hem turned under.
8. Cut the burlap at each corner, make the fold, and tack it (Fig. 50-21).
9. Fold the burlap under at the arm and back posts and tack to the frame. (Fig. 50-22).

FIGURE 50-19
Measure the width and length of the area to be covered with burlap.

FIGURE 50-20
Tack the burlap to the frame beginning at the center of the front rail.

CUT

TACK

1. FOLD OVER THE CORNER AND CUT. TACK THE FLAP TO THE FRAME.
2. FOLD UNDER EXCESS FABRIC AND TACK TO THE FRAME.

FIGURE 50-21
Cut the burlap at the corner, fold under the excess, and nail the burlap to the rail.

FIGURE 50-22
Cut and tack the burlap around arm posts and rear posts.

TACK AT CENTER

FOLD AND TACK AT REAR POST

FOLD AND TACK AT ARM

Burlap is also applied over webbing. Following is a suggested procedure.

1. Measure the area to be covered. Allow about $\frac{1}{2}$ in. for a fold.

2. Place the burlap over the webbing. Make a fold and center tack it on one side.

3. Pull the burlap tight to the other side and center tack it. Repeat this by center tacking the other sides. Keep the burlap pulled tight. Instead of a fold, the edges could be tacked using a tacking strip. This is a thin piece of cardboard. It keeps the heads of the tacks from pulling through the burlap.

4. Finish tacking each side, starting at the center tack. Tack right and left of the center tack. Keep the burlap tight as it is being tacked (Fig. 50-23).

FIGURE 50-24
Sagless springs with a single layer of stuffing forming the seat.

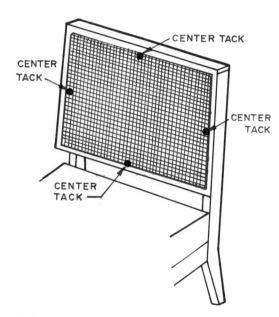

FIGURE 50-23
Cover webbing with burlap. In this example it is tacked to the face of the frame of the back.

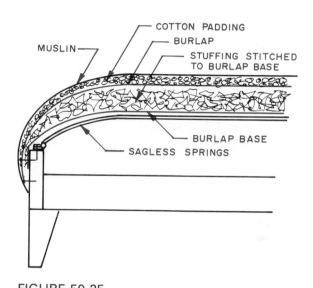

FIGURE 50-25
A seat over sagless springs which has a layer of padding over stuffing.

INSTALLING STUFFING AND PADDING

The purpose of stuffing and padding is to give the softness desired in the chair seat and back. The stuffing is the main, thickest layer. It rests on the burlap. There are several ways these layers are combined with the springs.

One way is to lay the stuffing on the burlap. It is joined to the burlap with random stitches (Fig. 50-24). This is then covered with a layer of burlap. This burlap layer is covered with a muslin cover.

A second system is to cover the stuffing with burlap. This is stitched to the burlap base. A thin layer of padding is placed over the stitches. A muslin cover holds the padding in place (Fig. 50-25).

Another procedure is to stitch the stuffing to the burlap base without covering it with a burlap layer. The padding is laid on top of the stuffing. The entire thing is covered with a muslin cover (Fig. 50-26).

Stuffing should be thick enough so that the springs cannot be felt when pressed down by hand. It should be free of lumps and evenly distributed. Stuffing, as rubberized hair pads or foam rubber, is in uniformly thick layers and removes these problems. Stuffing on sagless springs and webbed seats should be at least 1 in. thick.

FIGURE 50-26
The padding can be placed on top of the stuffing with no fabric layer in between.

USING FOAM STUFFING

Foam stuffing can be applied over many different bases, such as webbing, springs, and plywood. When applied over solid materials, such as plywood, holes must be drilled in the plywood to let the foam breath. Foam pads can be secured in place by cementing them to the base. They are also attached by sticking tacking tape to the foam and tacking the tape to the frame (Fig. 50-27).

FIGURE 50-27
Foam stuffing applied over a plywood base. This forms a square edge seat.

FIGURE 50-28
Foam stuffing applied over webbing.

FIGURE 50-29
A foam pad can be pulled over at the edge to form a curved edge cushion.

1. ATTACH TAPE TO PAD.

2. FOLD PAD UNDER AND NAIL TAPE TO WOOD BASE.

596

When foam pads are used over springs, a layer of cotton is placed below it next to the burlap. This helps keep it from sagging between the springs.

Foam pads can be used to form square or tapered edges. Typical square-edge installations are shown in Figs. 50-27 and 50-28. Curved-edge installations are shown in Figs. 50-29 and 50-30. Notice that tacking tape is cemented to the foam pad. It is pulled and tacked to the frame.

A seat with a crown is easily built with foam pads. A crown is where the seat is high in the center and tapers to the front and back. Select a foam cushion of the desired thickness. Mark the tapers wanted for the crown (Fig. 50-31). Use a large shears to cut away the foam, thus forming a taper.

FIGURE 50-31
A shears can be used to cut away the square edge of a foam pad to form a curved edge.

FIGURE 50-30
A foam pad can be cut on an angle on the front edge to help form a curved edge.

FIGURE 50-32
A crown can be formed by gluing small pads below the main foam pad.

Another way this is done is to place thin pieces of slab foam under the main pad (Fig. 50-32). When the proper crown is achieved, cement these layers together.

APPLYING FABRIC

Upholstery supply houses and upholstery shops have hundreds of fabric and plastic patterns and materials available. The choice depends on where the furniture will be used, the colors and patterns desired, and the amount of use. Cheap fabrics are usually a poor investment.

Following is a suggested plan for finding the sizes of each piece of fabric.

1. List each piece of fabric needed. Record the width and length of each piece and the number

Cover piece	No. of pieces	Width in inches	Length in inches
top back	1	33	6
lower back	1	33	18
seat top	1	26	26
seat boxing	1	78	5
frame boxing	1	78	6
back cover	1	26	34

FIGURE 50-34
How to measure the width and length for the finished fabric parts.

FIGURE 50-33
A fabric parts list should have each piece identified by name.

FIGURE 50-35
Each finished fabric part is carefully laid out on the fabric so that the pattern runs in the proper direction.

of pieces that size (Fig. 50-33). Give each piece a name so that it is clearly identified.

2. Measure each piece in the order in which they appear on your list. This will help prevent missing a piece. Add 4 in. extra for parts to be pulled around a frame and tacked. Allow 2 in. for parts that will be pulled tight with fabric stretchers. Allow ½ in. for each seam required or for tacking to a wood frame. Use a tape measure. Pull it tightly over the surface.

3. Measure the width first. Take these measurements to the widest part of the area. The width is measured first because fabric is made 54 in. wide. The pattern in the fabric must run across the width. (Fig. 50-34).

4. Lay out the measurements on paper. This forms a pattern for each part. Cut these to size.

5. Pin the patterns on the fabric. Be certain to observe the direction the design in the fabric will run. Place the patterns so that the design runs in the direction desired (Fig. 50-35). Observe the nap of the fabric. Nap is the raised,

fuzzy surface of the fabric made by the fibers from which the fabric is made. The nap should run down the back and arms and toward the front of the chair on the seat material.

The fastening of the actual fabric to the frame can be done in many ways. The following discussion includes some of the most useful techniques.

Fabric must be cut, folded, tacked, and sewed around legs. Figure 50-36 shows how to cut and tack fabric around a chair leg where the fabric covers the chair frame. The corner is cut, forming a wedge-shaped piece. The ends are folded back to the edge of the leg and tacked. The wedge is tucked up under the fabric at the corner. The remaining tacks are placed along the bottom of the frame.

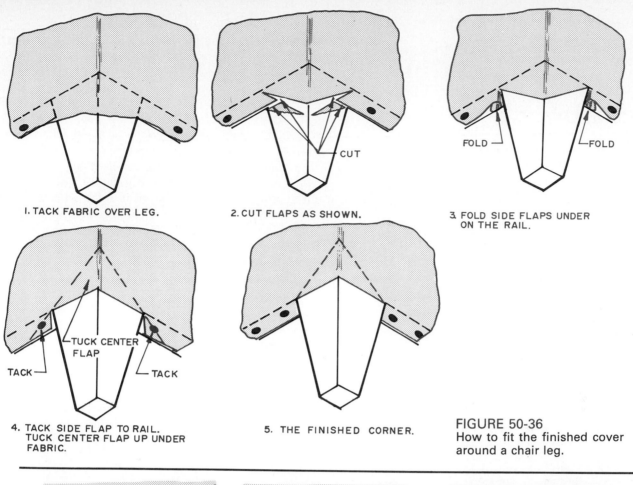

1. TACK FABRIC OVER LEG.

2. CUT FLAPS AS SHOWN.

CUT

3. FOLD SIDE FLAPS UNDER ON THE RAIL.

FOLD — FOLD

4. TACK SIDE FLAP TO RAIL. TUCK CENTER FLAP UP UNDER FABRIC.

TUCK CENTER FLAP

TACK — TACK

5. THE FINISHED CORNER.

FIGURE 50-36
How to fit the finished cover around a chair leg.

FINAL COVER —

FINISHED WOOD FRAME

LEG —

①

PULL THE FABRIC TO THE REAR AND TACK

②

CUT TO CORNER — 1"

③

PULL FABRIC FORWARD FORMING A FLAP

DRIVE A TACK

④

CUT FLAP ONE INCH LONG

1'

⑤

TUCK IN FLAP AND NAIL CORNER

⑥

FIGURE 50-37
The finished fabric on a seat can be tacked to the face of the chair rail.

Another approach is to tack the material into the face of the chair frame (Fig. 50-37). The frame can be left partially exposed or completely covered. The fabric is tacked to the frame. The corner is formed by pulling the excess material to the side and tacking the front. Then a cut is made on the side and

FIGURE 50-38
Exposed rows of upholstery tacks can be covered with gimp.

the fabric is pulled forward, forming a flap. All but one in. of the flap is cut away. The flap remaining is tucked behind the fabric on the front. The edge is tacked into the frame. The tacks could be decoration and left exposed. If upholstery tacks were used, they could be covered by gluing gimp over them (Fig. 50-38). Decorative nails could be used with gimp instead of gluing.

One way to form a corner at a leg when the frame is covered is shown in Fig. 50-39. The fabric is cut at the corner so that when it is folded down, the edge parallels the corner of the leg. A small flap is left for tacking. The flaps are folded and the fabric is tacked to the bottom of the rail. The fabric at the corner is sewed together.

Chairs with exposed wood arms present a special upholstery problem. One way to secure the fabric around the arm post is shown in Fig. 50-40. Cut the fabric to the center of the post. Cut from there to each corner on a 45° angle. Fold the flaps formed under the fabric and tack to the chair frame. The

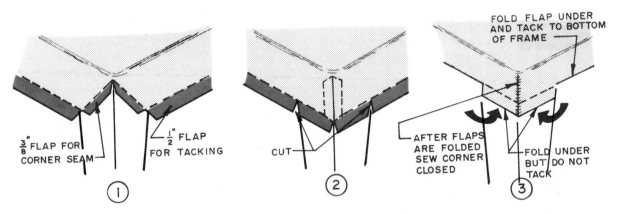

FIGURE 50-39
How to fit a finished cover of a chair seat so that it covers the chair rail and fits across the leg.

FIGURE 50-40
How to fit the finished cover around an exposed chair arm post.

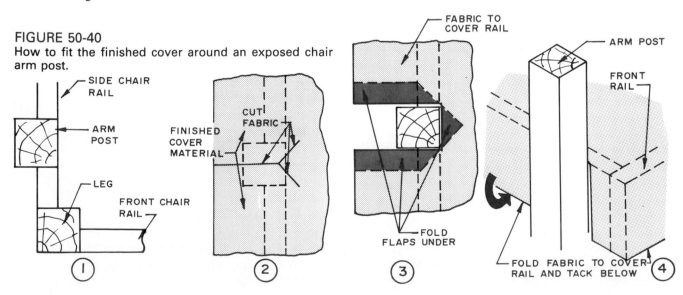

same technique can be used on rear corner posts (Fig. 50-41). Cut the fabric on a 45° angle through the diagonal of the post. Fold the flaps formed under until they are even with the faces of the post. Fold down and tack to the frame.

Welts help join fabric at corners (Fig. 50-42). They also add a finished appearance to the product. The welt cord is covered with the same fabric to be used to upholster the chair. Generally, this is sewed on an industrial sewing machine. If none is available, it can be done in a local upholstery shop. Welt cord can be hand sewn, but it is a slow difficult task (Fig. 50-43).

The covered welt can be power sewed or hand sewed to the fabric. This is shown in Fig. 50-44. The fabric to meet the welt has a ½-in. fold. The crease of

FIGURE 50-41
How to fit the finished cover around a rear chair leg.

FIGURE 50-42
Welt is used to join two pieces of finished cover material.

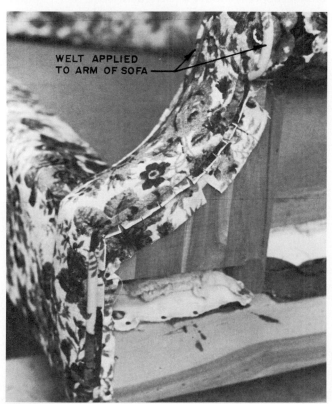

FIGURE 50-43
How welt is formed from welt cord and finished cover material.

1. PLACE CORD 1" FROM END OF FABRIC.

2. FOLD FLAP OVER END OF CORD.

3. FOLD FABRIC OVER CORD. SEW CORD IN FABRIC.

FIGURE 50-44
The welt is sewed in between the two pieces of finished cover forming a corner.

FIGURE 50-45
How to cover the open back of a chair back.

1" FLAPS

FOLD FLAP UNDER AND TACK TO BOTTOM RAIL.

INSIDE SURFACE OF FABRIC TO COVER BACK OF CHAIR BACK.

PUT TACKING STRIPS ON SIDE FLAPS

FIRST NAIL TOP EDGE USING A TACKING STRIP

COVER OF FRONT OF CHAIR BACK

the fold is sewed tightly to the welt just below the cord. Again, this is a difficult slow task if done by hand.

Often, it is necessary to cover the open back of a chair after the front is upholstered. One technique is shown in Fig. 50-45. The fabric for the back is cut the same size as the finished back plus a 1-in. flap on all sides. The top flap is nailed to the frame with a cardboard tacking strip. Tack from the center to each edge, to remove wrinkles. Notice that the inside of the fabric is the side against which the tack strip is placed.

Place a tacking strip on the bottom flap and push the tacks through the fabric. Lower the fabric over the opening. Pull it tight and blind-tack several of the tacks in the center of the bottom edge.

Next, place tacking strips on the two vertical sides. Tack one side to the frame starting in the center. Then pull the fabric tight across the opening and tack the other side. Finally, pull the fabric down tightly and finish blind tacking the bottom.

INSTALLING BUTTONS

Buttons are used to improve the appearance of an upholstered piece. They reduce large sections of fabric into smaller, tighter units.

To place buttons, mark their locations on the fabric with chalk. Measure carefully so that the seat or back is divided into a pleasing number of divisions. Insert the buttons at each location.

The clinch-type button is installed by pushing the long pointed legs through the finished cover, stuffing, burlap, and/or webbing. A cardboard washer with a rectangular hole is placed over the legs next to the burlap or webbing. The button is pushed into the stuffing the desired depth and the legs are bent over the washer. (Fig. 50-46).

Loop and tuft buttons are put in place using stitching twine. The twine is placed through the loop on the loop button. On the tuft button it is sewed through the fabric bulge on the back of the button.

The twine from the button is placed in a large upholsterers' needle. The needle is pushed through the final cover, stuffing, burlap, and/or webbing. The needle is removed. A ball of cotton, about 2 in. in diameter, is placed between the pieces of cord. A single knot is tied and the cord pulled tight against the cotton. This pulls the button into the stuffing. When the desired depth is reached, the knot is tied permanently (Fig. 50-47).

The tack button is nailed through the final cover and padding into the wood frame. Care must be exercised so that it is not damaged. Some people prefer to cover the button with a piece of cloth and use a soft-face mallet to drive it in place.

1. PULL CORD FROM BUTTON THROUGH THE BURLAP.

1. PUSH THE CLINCH BUTTON THROUGH THE STUFFING AND BURLAP.

2. PUSH BUTTON TIGHT, SLIDE WASHER OVER LEGS AND BEND LEGS OVER.

FIGURE 50-46
How to install a clinch-type button.

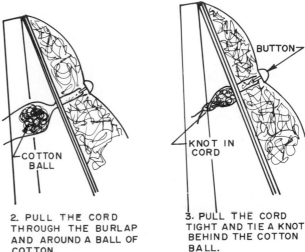

2. PULL THE CORD THROUGH THE BURLAP AND AROUND A BALL OF COTTON.

3. PULL THE CORD TIGHT AND TIE A KNOT BEHIND THE COTTON BALL.

FIGURE 50-47
How to install a loop or tuft button.

STUDY QUESTIONS

Answer each of the following questions. If you are not sure of an answer, review the chapter.

50-1. How do you tack webbing to a chair frame?

50-2. What tool do you use to pull the webbing tight?

50-3. How far apart are the strips of webbing spaced?

50-4. How are sagless springs fastened to a chair frame?

50-5. What size sagless springs are used for seats and backs?

50-6. How do you decide what spacing to use for sagless springs?

50-7. What is the crown of the seat?

50-8. After the sagless springs are installed, what is used to cover them?

50-9. Describe three ways to install stuffing over sagless springs.

50-10. Over what type of bases can foam stuffing be applied?

50-11. How is a crown built on a seat using foam stuffing?

50-12. How is the fabric fastened to the frame?

50-13. How is welt cord installed?

50-14. Why are buttons used on chair seats and backs?

50-15. What kinds of buttons are used?

IMPORTANT TECHNICAL TERMS

Following are technical terms that you should be able to use as part of your working vocabulary. Write a brief description of the meaning of each term.

Sagless spring clips
Crown

Burlap
Stuffing
Nap
Clinch button
Loop and tuft buttons

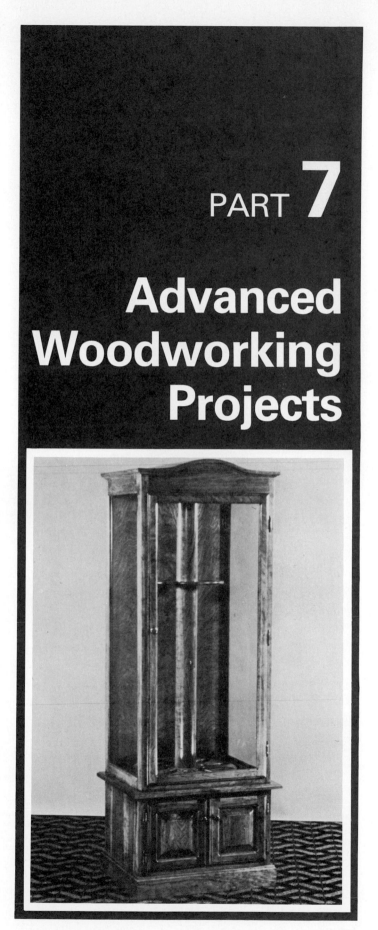

PART 7

Advanced Woodworking Projects

As you studied Chapter 2 you learned the fundamentals of design. Now is the time to apply these to the product you wish to build. After you decide what it is you want to make, begin to collect ideas. Visit furniture stores and examine the units to see how they are constructed. Critically analyze the design. Just because a piece of furniture is in a store does not mean it is well designed or constructed. Look at catalogs from furniture manufacturers and from retail outlets as Sears, J.C. Penney and Montgomery Ward. There are many ideas and good designs in magazines. Some magazines are designed especially for those who enjoy building furniture and cabinets. Some publishers have project books that have detailed drawings. Some companies sell plans for wood projects of all kinds. By exploring many sources you will find a variety of solutions to the project you have in mind. From these you can develop your plans.

Remember, it is always acceptable to carefully copy a product that was so well designed it has been popular over the years. There are many books explaining the historical development of furniture. These have excellent photographs of these classical pieces and are an excellent source.

Following are detail drawings for a variety of projects. Some are rather easy to build while others are very complex. Do not get into a project that is too difficult or expensive. Success with a smaller project is more rewarding than failure with one that is large and complex.

TURNINGS

THE FOLLOWING PROJECTS ARE BASED ON THE PURCHASE OF
GLASS AND PLASTIC PARTS. BEFORE FINALIZING THE SIZE OF
THE WOOD TURNING, BE CERTAIN THE PARTS ARE ON HAND SO
THE WOOD CAN BE CUT TO FIT THEM. THE FOLLOWING ARE
TYPICAL EXAMPLES OF UNITS AVAILABLE.

BUD VASE

GLASS BUD INSERT

CANDLE HOLDER

VOID FOR WEIGHT

HOLE TO FIT
CANDLE OR
CANDLE HOLDER

VOID FOR WEIGHT

BOXES

WOOD OR
CERAMIC LID

GLUE FELT
ON BOTTOM.

TYPICAL BOX PROFILE

CHEESE SERVER

DISPLAY DOMES

SHAPE TO SUIT.
GROOVE FOR GLASS

THICKNESS
AS DESIRED
BASES FOR LAMPS
AND DOMES

HURRICANE LAMP

CAP   BODY

SIZE TO SUIT
MECHANISM.

PEPPER GRINDER

ARMOIRE

COURTESY STANLEY TOOLS
AND RANDY BEGIN

NOTE: ALL SIDES
AND FRONT
$\frac{5}{8}$" STOCK.

19$\frac{3}{8}$"

28$\frac{1}{2}$"

10

10

6$\frac{3}{4}$"

60°

DRAWER – UPPER UNIT

$\frac{1}{8}$" MASONITE

34$\frac{3}{4}$"

NOTE: DRAWER SIDES
$\frac{5}{8}$" STOCK. DRAWER
FRONT $\frac{3}{4}$".

DOVETAIL

36

8$\frac{5}{8}$"

20"

$\frac{1}{8}$" MASONITE

7$\frac{3}{4}$"

DRAWER – LOWER UNIT

BOTTOM SHELF
OF UPPER UNIT.

$\frac{1}{2}$" X 1$\frac{1}{2}$"

TOP OF
LOWER
UNIT

BLOCKING

$\frac{1}{4}$" CARRIAGE BOLT

DETAILS FOR JOINING
THE TWO UNITS

15$\frac{1}{4}$"

2$\frac{1}{2}$"

2$\frac{3}{8}$"

10$\frac{3}{8}$"

40$\frac{1}{2}$"

35$\frac{1}{2}$"

$\frac{3}{8}$" X $\frac{3}{8}$" RABBET ON
THREE SIDES

2$\frac{1}{2}$" AND 2$\frac{3}{8}$"

1$\frac{1}{2}$"

SECTION E–E

DOOR
PANEL

E   E

2$\frac{1}{2}$"

DOOR

ARMOIRE—UPPER UNIT

SHELF FRAME

RABBET SIDE FOR INNER FRAMEFACE

NOTCH SHELF TO RECEIVE INNER FRAMEFACE

INNER FRAMEFACE

DETAIL 2

36"

3/4"

3/4"

3"

1/4" PLYWOOD

20

4"

1/8" HARDBOARD

4"

20 3/4"

INNER FRAMEFACE

3"

DRAWER OPENING 28 3/4"

DOOR OPENING 30"

SEE DETAIL 2

NOTE: INNER FRAMEFACE 3 1/4
OUTER FRAMEFACE 3.

C

OUTER FRAMEFACE

DADO DUST PANELS TO SIDE

INNER FRAMEFACE

DRAWER GUIDE

DOOR OPENING 42"

D

D

C

FRONT ELEVATION
WITH DOORS AND DRAWERS REMOVED

22"

3

3/4" TOP

INNER FACEFRAME

8 1/2

3/8" SOLID WOOD BACK

3/4

OUTER FACEFRAME

3/4" SOLID WOOD SHELF

7"

3/4

7"

3/4

DRAWER DUST PANEL

47"

7"

3/4

1/4" PLYWOOD BACK

7"

3/4

2 1/2

SECTION "C-C"

ARMOIRE – BASE UNIT

WALNUT EDGES JOINED TO
OAK INTERIOR PANEL.

42"

3"

3"

24"

3"

$\frac{3}{4}$" OAK CENTER PANEL

TOP VIEW OF BASE WITH TOP IN PLACE.

40"

2-"

22

$\frac{1}{4}$" PLYWOOD

$\frac{1}{8}$"HARDBOARD

DRAWER
GUIDE

PANEL

$\frac{3}{4}$" THICK
SIDE
PANELS

$2\frac{1}{2}$"

$2\frac{1}{2}$"

$2\frac{1}{2}$"

FACEFRAME

$\frac{3}{4}$"

DRAWER OPENING 35"

$2\frac{1}{2}$"

SECTION "A-A" SHOWING SHELF PANEL

1"

$\frac{7}{8}$"

$3\frac{5}{8}$"

DETAIL I

TOP

B

FACEFRAME – JOIN WITH DOWELS

A

A

DRAWER
GUIDE

B

FRONT ELEVATION WITHOUT DRAWERS

$\frac{3}{4}$"

1"

8"

1"

$23\frac{3}{4}$"

8"

$4\frac{1}{2}$"

$22\frac{3}{4}$"

FACE
FRAME

$\frac{3}{4}$"

DUST
PANEL

$\frac{3}{4}$"

$\frac{3}{4}$"

SEE DETAIL

SECTION "B-B"

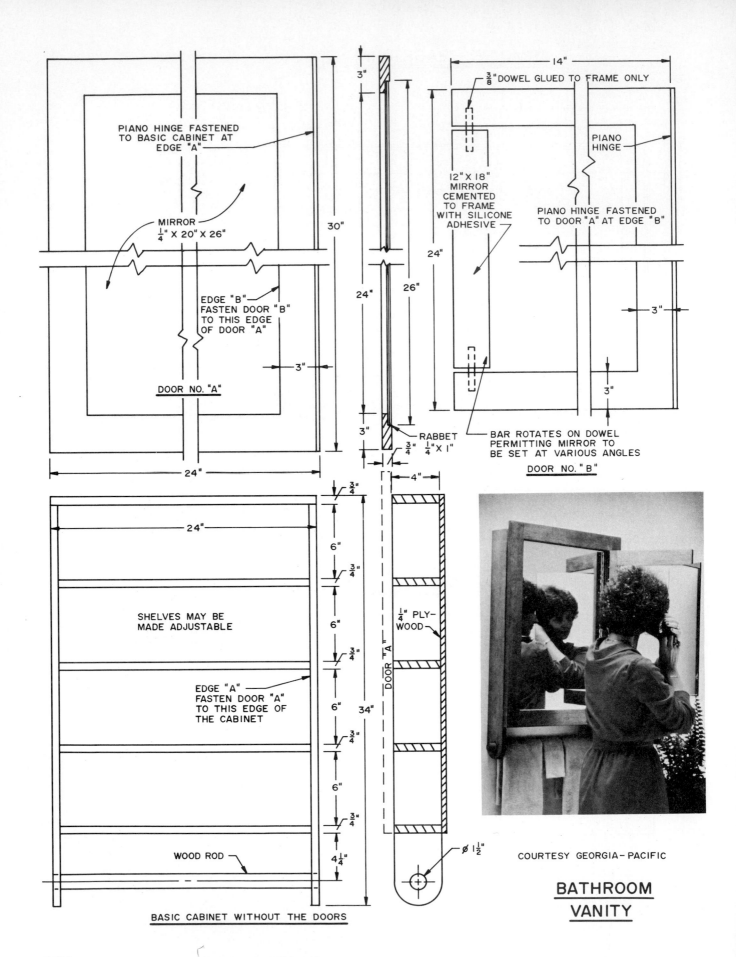

PIANO HINGE FASTENED
TO BASIC CABINET AT
EDGE "A"

MIRROR
$\frac{1}{4}$" X 20" X 26"

EDGE "B"
FASTEN DOOR "B"
TO THIS EDGE
OF DOOR "A"

DOOR NO. "A"

30"

24"

3"

24"

3"

3"

26"

RABBET
$\frac{3}{4}$" $\frac{1}{4}$" X 1"

$\frac{3}{8}$" DOWEL GLUED TO FRAME ONLY

14"

PIANO
HINGE

12" X 18"
MIRROR
CEMENTED
TO FRAME
WITH SILICONE
ADHESIVE

PIANO HINGE FASTENED
TO DOOR "A" AT EDGE "B"

24"

3"

3"

BAR ROTATES ON DOWEL
PERMITTING MIRROR TO
BE SET AT VARIOUS ANGLES

DOOR NO. "B"

24"

$\frac{3}{4}$"

6"

$\frac{3}{4}$"

6"

$\frac{3}{4}$"

SHELVES MAY BE
MADE ADJUSTABLE

EDGE "A"
FASTEN DOOR "A"
TO THIS EDGE OF
THE CABINET

6"

$\frac{3}{4}$"

34"

6"

$\frac{3}{4}$"

6"

$\frac{3}{4}$"

WOOD ROD

4$\frac{1}{4}$"

BASIC CABINET WITHOUT THE DOORS

4"

DOOR "A"

$\frac{1}{4}$" PLY-
WOOD

Ø 1$\frac{1}{2}$"

COURTESY GEORGIA-PACIFIC

BATHROOM VANITY

STUDENT'S DESK

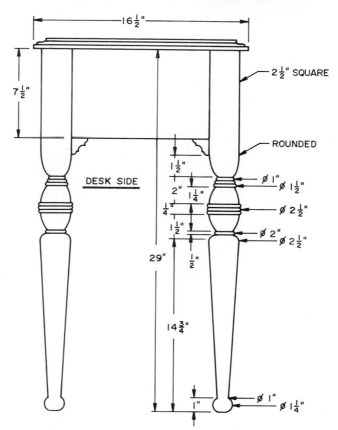

DESK SIDE

16½"

7½"

2½" SQUARE

ROUNDED

1½"

2"

1¼"

¼"

1½"

½"

Ø 1" Ø 1½"

Ø 2½"

Ø 2"
Ø 2½"

29"

14¾"

1"

Ø 1"
Ø 1¼"

CHANNEL FOR HINGED
TOP SUPPORT — SEE
DETAIL "A"

TOP VIEW OF
BOTTOM OF DESK

SLIDING LID SUPPORT
FOR HINGED TOP

DRAWER GUIDE

2½"

11½" 16½"

2½"

2½" ¾ 1½"   13"   ¾   13"   1½" ¾ 2½"

39½"

SLIDING LID
SUPPORT — SEE
DETAIL "B"

DRAWER GUIDE

1½"

4½"

1½"

FRONT VIEW
BOTTOM OF DESK

CHANNEL
DETAIL "A"

SLIDING LID SUPPORT
DETAIL "B"

6"

¾" 12½"

4½"

DIVIDER SEE DETAIL "C"

9¼"

9⅜"   3¾"   3¾"   3¾"   3¾"   9⅜"

¾"   ¾"   ¼"   ¼"   ¼"   ¼"   ¾"

37½"

SECTION THROUGH UPPER UNIT

DESK TOP

HINGE

FOLDING DESK TOP

3"

A

¾"

1"
2¼"
1"
12¼"   2¼"
1"
2¼"
1"

DRAWER

¾"

A

FRONT VIEW OF UPPER UNIT

SECTION A—A

5¼"

27½"

DRAWER — LOWER UNIT

¼" PLYWOOD

4¼"

¼"

12¼"

¼" PLYWOOD

2¼"

¼"

10⅛"

8½"

DRAWER — UPPER UNIT

6½"

11¾"

8"

¼"

DIVIDER
DETAIL "C"

STUDENT'S DESK

COURTESY STANLEY TOOLS AND
JEFFREY COUTURE

BUTLER SERVING
TRAY TABLE

COURTESY VERMONT AMERICAN CORPORATION, TUGGLE LUMBER DIVISION.

23¾"

19⁵⁄₁₆"R

9⅜"R

15½"

4"

1"R

NOTE: MAKE A FULL SIZE DRAWING OF THE TOP

LEG
DETAIL "A"

CUT ON 45°

LOWER SELF

LEAVES FOLDED UP

10⅜"

¾"

¾" X ¾" FASTEN TO TRAY TO

2½"

18¾"

2½"

RAILS DOWELED TO LEGS

LEGS 1⅝" SQUARE

POSITION IN THE FRAME.

SEE DETAIL "A"

24"

GLASS

¾"

5"

SECTION

APPLIANCE CENTER

ELECTRICAL OUT STRIP

19" OPEN

THIS SHELF 15½" ABOVE BOTTOM

OPEN

¾"

RIGHT SIDE

10¾"

HORIZONTAL SECTION A-A

COURTESY GEORGIA-PACIFIC

32½"

¾"

10"

¾"

20¼"

¾"

1½"

⅜" DOWELS AT 45°

15½"

¾"

⅜" DOWELS

34¼"

A   A

15½"

¾"

2" X 2" X 21¾"   CASTOR

2"

FRONT OF CABINET

22½"

1½ 1½ 1½ 1½ 1½ 1½ 1¾"

10"

5½"

RIGHT SIDE VIEW

SUN SEAT

$1\frac{1}{2}$" $\frac{1}{4}$" $\frac{3}{16}$ $\frac{1}{2}$" $\frac{3}{4}$"

SEAT AND BACK
FRAME - DETAIL "A"

SPLINE   CANE

SETTING CANE IN
SPLINE GROOVE
DETAIL "B"

COURTESY THE WOODWORKER'S JOURNAL.

NOTE: DOWEL ALL CORNERS

$15\frac{7}{8}$" $\frac{3}{4}$R

$1\frac{1}{2}$" $1\frac{1}{2}$"

$1\frac{1}{2}$"

SEE
DETAIL "B"

FRAME - SEE
DETAIL "A"

$16\frac{1}{2}$"
(WIDTH OF SEAT) $\frac{7}{8}$"

BRASS ROD $5\frac{5}{8}$" $\frac{3}{4}$"

DOWEL

$\frac{3}{4}$ $\frac{3}{4}$
$17\frac{1}{2}$"

BACK

SIDE

SEAT $\frac{1}{2}$" $\frac{7}{8}$"

WOOD
DOWEL

DETAIL OF
FOLDING BACK

BACK FOLDS
FORWARD

$17\frac{3}{4}$"

2"

CANE

$\frac{5}{16}$"X17"
BRASS
ROD

$2\frac{3}{4}$"

SEAT IN
STOPPED
DADO   CANE

FRAME - SEE
DETAIL "A"

$1\frac{1}{2}$"

$\frac{3}{4}$" DOWEL

1"

2" $14\frac{1}{4}$" $5\frac{3}{4}$"

18"

22"

ROOM DIVIDER

MULTIPLE UNITS JOINED WITH HINGES

10"

24"

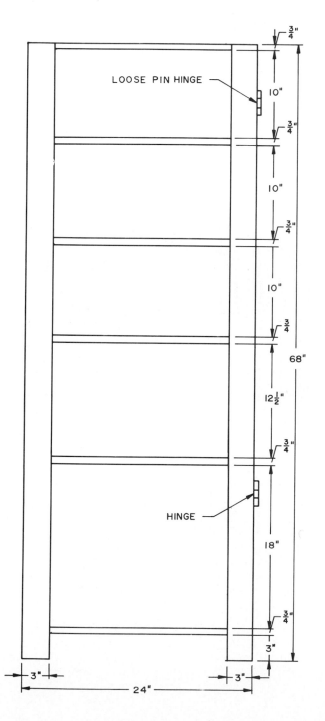

LOOSE PIN HINGE

HINGE

$\frac{3}{4}$"

10"

$\frac{3}{4}$"

10"

$\frac{3}{4}$"

10"

$\frac{3}{4}$"

68"

12$\frac{1}{2}$"

$\frac{3}{4}$"

18"

$\frac{3}{4}$"

3"

3"   3"

24"

SHELVES TO BE
DADOED TO VERTICAL
MEMBERS

$\frac{3}{8}$"

EDGE BAND
PLYWOOD
SHELVES

$\frac{3}{4}$" $\frac{3}{4}$"

3"   3"

11$\frac{1}{4}$"

STEREO UNITS

COURTESY GEORGIA – PACIFIC

27"

3/4

3/4

36"

3/4

3/4

3/4

3/4

24"

25½"

16"

12"

2"

3/4

SPACE AS NEEDED

SHELVES MAY BE
MADE ADJUSTABLE

3/4

3/4

3/8" DOWEL

45°

13"

3"

SMALL SIDE CABINETS
SMALL AS THIS SECTION

LENGTH 18" OR
AS DESIRED

COURTESY STANLEY TOOLS AND
DANIEL BOTTO.

BACK PANEL
DETAIL "B"

RAISED DOOR
PANEL
DETAIL "A"

SECTION

GUN CABINET

METRIC
ALL DIMENSIONS IN MILLIMETERS

22 R
100
45°
50 R
RADIUS 250
LOWER RACK – DETAIL "B"
ONE–FOURTH OF RACK

OPENING FOR GUN BUTT 10 mm DEEP

GUN BARREL HOLE
Ø 25
45°
125
178 R
TOP RACK – DETAIL "A"
ONE–FOURTH OF RACK

712
636
35 SQUARES
50
50
50
1445
1336
1584
2030
GLASS IN HINGED DOOR
18
50
358
536
190
712

140
Ø 100
SEE DETAIL "A"
Ø 50 DOWEL
1444
SEE DETAIL "B"
38
18
38
342
38
METAL LAZY SUSAN DIA. ABOUT 300
DOOR
100
18
565
SECTION

109
50
50
FIXED GLASS
SIDE VIEW

COURTESY STANLEY TOOLS AND RICHARD GAMBLE.

SERVING CART

COURTESY STANLEY TOOLS AND
DANIEL O'HARA

DRAWER SIDES ½"

DRAWER FRONT ¾" WITH ⅜"
LIPPED EDGES.

TOP VIEW

SECOND OUTSIDE SUPPORT
4½" 3¾" 3¾" 4½"   Ø 3"

CENTER SUPPORT
2⅝" 1⅞" 1⅞" 1⅞" 1⅞" 1⅞" 1⅞" 2⅝"   Ø 1"

FIRST OUTSIDE SUPPORT
2⅝" 3¾" 3¾" 3¾" 2⅝"   Ø 3"
16½"

WINE RACK DETAIL A

Ø 4"
1" DOWEL
28"
1½"
2"
DRAWER OPENING
¾" 3"
16"
4½"
LEG 2½" SQ.
13⅛" WINE RACK SEE DETAIL "A"
¾" DOWEL
Ø 10"
Ø 7"
2½"
SPOKED 1½" WIDE
CASTER
FRONT VIEW
6"
¾" 4"
¾" 4"
¾" 4"
6"
27"

NOTE: FRONT LEG LENGTH MAY BE
ADJUSTED DEPENDING UPON CASTOR
DIAMETER.

TOP ¾" LAMINATIONS
23¼"
2¾"
5"
2"
SHELF ¾"
1½"
¼" WOOD WASHER
WOOD PIN
SIDE VIEW

GAME TABLE

COURTESY STANLEY TOOLS AND
MATT WAGNER

GLASS HOLDER

16"

2" SQUARES INLAID WITH
LIGHT AND DARK WOOD.

16"

48"

16"

16"

GLUE BLOCK

Ø 3" - $\frac{1}{4}$" DEEP

3"

5"

1$\frac{1}{2}$"

35"

1$\frac{1}{2}$"

3"

48"

TOP

EDGE
BANDING

$\frac{1}{4}$"

SECTION THROUGH TOP
DETAIL "A"

SEE DETAIL "A"

JOIN WITH $\frac{3}{8}$" DOWELS

LEG DETAILS
SEE DETAILS "B"

1$\frac{1}{2}$"

3"

32"

3"

3$\frac{3}{4}$"

$\frac{3}{4}$"

$\frac{3}{4}$"

1"

1$\frac{1}{2}$" X 1$\frac{1}{2}$" LEG

Ø 1$\frac{1}{4}$"

LEG DETAILS
DETAILS "B"

PIECRUST TABLE

METRIC – ALL DIMENSIONS
IN MILLIMETERS.

SECTION "A"

TABLE TOP

914

COLLAR

∅ 25

SLOT FOR WEDGE

88

CROW'S NEST POST

110

20 10 4 46 6 6 6 12

12

∅ 20

WEDGE

HOLE FOR PIN IN
CROW'S NEST

∅ 20

38

786

BATTEN

114

20

CROW'S NEST

228

25 25

25

∅ 1.

204

102

25

114

20

WEDGE

6

25

12

88

CROW'S
NEST

∅ 25

WEDGE
THRU POST

110

25

COLLAR

200

470

114

44

25

∅ 200

EACH SQUARE = 20 m m.

79°

28

22

LEG DOVETAIL

COURTESY STANLEY TOOLS AND
BARRY KENT

12

18

TRADITIONAL COFFEE TABLE

LINE OF TOP

RAILS ¾" THICK

¾" THICK – FASTEN TO LEG AND TOP

12"

15"

125°

6"

35"

40"

3 ¼"

1 ¾"

20"

COURTESY STANLEY TOOLS AND
TIMOTHY LACKEY

LEG 1$\frac{1}{4}$" THICK

DETAIL "A"

$\frac{1}{4}$"

1$\frac{1}{2}$"

$\frac{1}{2}$"

DETAIL "A"

$\frac{3}{4}$R

7$\frac{1}{2}$"

3$\frac{1}{2}$"

7$\frac{1}{2}$"

LEG   1" SQUARES

DETAIL "B"

20"

$\frac{1}{4}$"GLASS

2$\frac{1}{4}$"

$\frac{3}{4}$" THICK

DETAIL "B"

Ø 4

2$\frac{1}{2}$"

1$\frac{1}{2}$"

2$\frac{1}{2}$"

12$\frac{1}{4}$"

1$\frac{1}{2}$"

3$\frac{1}{2}$"

INDEX